Guelph Public Library

Breaking Point

Mario Cardinal

Translated by Ferdinanda Van Gennip

With Mark Stout

BREAKING POINT
Quebec • Canada

The 1995 Referendum

CBCtelevision

Bayard
CANADA

971,404
CAR

Translation: Ferdinanda Van Gennip, with Mark Stout

Editorial Direction: Jean F. Bouchard
Revision: Greg Hunter and Claude Auger
Cover design: CBC
Layout: Mardigrafe

ISBN: 2-89579-068-X

Bayard Canada Books Inc.
4475 Frontenac Street
Montreal, Quebec H2H 2S2 – 514 844 2111
CANADA

We acknowledge the financial support of the Government of Canada through the Book Publishing Industry Development Program (BPIDP) for our publishing activity.

We acknowledge the financial support of the Canada Council for the Arts through the Block Grants Program for our publishing activity.

Printed in Canada

CONTENTS

Foreword

R eturning to Ottawa on the night following the October 1995 referendum, one politician, Brian Tobin, turned the page: "Nobody will remember, a few years from now, whether we won by 1% or by 20%."

The NO had won by 1.16%, a margin of 54,288 votes out of the 4,757,509 ballots cast.

Another politician, Lucien Bouchard, as he arrived back to the House of Commons after the summer recess, on September 13, 1995, warned, "It's a non-ending issue as long as it will not be resolved by a YES vote." He would stay on this same page.

As spring blossomed in 2005, sovereignty still found favour with approximately half the population of Quebec.

It appears that the October 30, 1995, referendum settled nothing and was destined to be just one of the striking events in Canada's history. However, ten years later, the promises it carried and the plans it nurtured are still with us, awaiting a replay of the suspense of 1995. At the mere mention of the event, the collective memory relives the hope and the despair evoked that night by the swing of the pendulum, which lasted two and a half hours until, finally, at the finish tape, it inclined towards the NO. It was a result that took away from the federalists any desire to celebrate, and from the sovereigntists any temptation to give up.

Ten years on, the referendum of October 30, 1995, remains a topical subject.

This book covers the pre-referendum period, from Jacques Parizeau's election as premier of Quebec, on September 12, 1994, to the official referendum campaign of the month of October 1995 and voting day itself. It seeks to serve as a reminder of what this great calling-into-question was all about—which should be remembered "the next time." It contains testimonies that shed new light on the fears, hopes, ambitions and strategies of those who were the principal players. Most of them gave interviews. My only regret is that Paul Martin, Lucien Bouchard and Bernard Landry declined to do so; while they had their reasons, their contribution, which would have been of significant import, will be missed in this story of the referendum.

The idea for this book was born in the offices of Société Radio-Canada. I am profoundly grateful to them for inviting me to write it and deeply indebted to them for the wealth of research they made available to me. That material includes the transcripts of the 64 interviews—some of which were several hours in length—that were used in producing the television documentary series *Breaking Point*. The numerous quotations contained in this book were drawn from those interviews. Several of them were conducted in both French and English, which explains why, often, certain quotations are adaptations of the remarks actually made in the other language, in which case the latter are reproduced in an endnote in the original language.

I extend thanks to Colette Forest, of the *Service de documentation et archives* (archives and research department) of Radio-Canada, who entrusted me with the writing of this book; Jean Pelletier, manager of the *Service documentaire de l'information* (news documentary department); the transcultural projects team for being available without fail; the team's director, Hubert Gendron, and the director of the television series, Jackie Corkery. I wish to thank in a particular way André Royer, whose care in revising the manuscript, chapter by chapter, spared me from making several factual errors. A very special thank you to Christiane Sauvé, an outstanding colleague whose contribution was invaluable in the organization of the research material. My thanks also go to the team at Bayard and editor Jean-François Bouchard, who eased the pressure through a relationship of constant understanding and respect. And a final thank you to Françoise Leroux, my wife, who remained a patient and indefatigable ally throughout the twelve months it took to complete this book.

Mario Cardinal

Translator's Note

I t has been a great privilege to translate this work, first, because of its importance for the future of Quebec and of Canada, and secondly, because Cardinal is master of his craft. As I received the manuscript, chapter by chapter, I became swept up in the suspense. At the same time, I recognized the challenge that the unbiased and nuanced treatment of the characters and events, the complexity of the facts and emotions involved in this tumultuous moment in Canada's history, represented for me as a translator. I only hope that my translation has reflected Cardinal's approach and done justice to his achievement. In other respects, the court rulings, speeches, reports, agreements and other documents quoted in this book are, in most cases, taken from the official English versions I was able to locate in my research, and not simply translations or re-translations. I have made very few grammatical or idiomatic changes to the words of personalities interviewed in English, as I felt it important to keep each individual's unique manner of expressing themselves.

My task could not have been completed in just six months without the contribution of talented literary translator Mark Stout, who came to the rescue when deadlines became otherwise impossible to meet, and translated chapters 6, 7, 12 and 13. Many thanks! I am particularly grateful to my husband, Bruce Burton, who gave so generously of his time to read over my work carefully, bringing to the task the benefit of his political science background and his experienced eagle eye!

Ferdinanda Van Gennip

CHAPTER I

Jacques Parizeau Returns

T hose were the longest two hours in the history of Canada. "I'll never forget it. The only comparable experience that I can think of is the birth of our first child and being there with my wife through that whole process. It's a strange analogy but it was absolutely intense. I found myself glued to this little bar graph, and a slave to this electronic measurement of how the campaign was going. And it was awful close, terribly close." Like millions of Canadians and Quebecers, Brian Tobin found the tension almost unbearable. Then, while half the population of Quebec struggled to stifle its disappointment, a deep sigh of relief could be heard from the Atlantic to the Pacific, around 8:20 p.m. that October 30, 1995. The victory of the NO side in the Quebec referendum on independence, confirmed almost simultaneously by all the electronic media in the country, marked the culmination of a merciless campaign, replete with angry words and low blows.

The first sentence uttered by the premier of Quebec the night of the defeat was testimony to the relentless battle that had just ended: "We have lost, but not by much!" said a bewildered Jacques Parizeau. Indeed, if half a percent of the voters, that is, a little over 27,000 out of 4,757,509, had chosen the other option, the history of Canada would have come to an end after 128 years of confederation. It would have taken a radically new direction with the secession of a major part of its geographical and political identity.

For the second time in 15 years, Canada had survived, but this time in a much more dramatic fashion, a referendum on the sovereignty of Quebec—the separatist's dream ever since the late 1950s. The 1995 referendum was a well-developed project that had benefited from reflection on the hesitations and mistakes of the 1980 referendum. This previous one had asked the people of Quebec for a mandate to negotiate an agreement with the rest of Canada: it was to be based on the equality of the founding nations and would involve an economic association built around a common currency.

René Lévesque could not imagine sovereignty without that insurance policy. There had to be an association with Canada so that Quebec would not come to be seen as a foreign country. Lévesque felt "the risk was too great," according to Jacques Parizeau who, at the time, was his Finance minister. The important thing for the organizers of that referendum was first of all to reassure certain members of the government. The idea of association was not new. It had been approved at the founding congress of the Parti Québécois. But what did it mean? A lot of things. So many, in fact, that the 1980 referendum question became, to paraphrase Parizeau's expression, "a veritable hodgepodge!" At first, it included a common currency, to which the Finance minister was opposed at the time. He had made his views public back in the spring of 1978, in an interview with *The Times* of London. The question of a common currency had not been pursued more than necessary, however. The important thing was association in the economic sphere. And maybe other areas as well... why not the postal system? René Lévesque's advisors had even suggested an army, and common negotiations within GATT. What mattered was to reassure as many people as possible. Jacques Parizeau was opposed to the idea of a question that made association an unavoidable condition of sovereignty. "But the economic argument was so important to me, so crucial," he recalls 24 years later, "that if 'Paris was well worth a mass,'[1] then I was prepared to be totally flexible on the meaning of the term association."[2]

One of the lessons Jacques Parizeau would draw from that first referendum was that he should start the process leading up to the second one as soon as he came to power. Between the time it was elected, on November 15, 1976, and the 1980 referendum, René

Lévesque's government did not undertake any kind of reflective process on the topic of sovereignty or how to achieve it. "In 1974, it was decided that this would be determined by a referendum," Jacques Parizeau recounts. "We will give you good government, but we won't take action on anything until there has been a referendum. That does not make the task of analyzing, building and developing the idea of sovereignty any easier."[3] The Lévesque government had in fact commissioned some studies to be carried out under the direction of economist Bernard Bonin, who was teaching at the *École nationale d'administration publique* (National school of public administration) at the time. "These were studies that had very little impact and remained fairly abstract," Parizeau says. "And they continued to promote sovereignty-association more and more passionately. They even put the hyphen in to show how inseparable the two concepts were."[4] That hyphen had been in René Lévesque's head ever since he left the Quebec Liberal Party to found the *Mouvement souveraineté-association* (sovereignty-association movement) in 1967. English Canada would respond that the best association, as far as it was concerned, was still Canadian federalism. The concept would gradually lose credibility and wind up as the object of Pierre Elliott Trudeau's famous "no thanks." If association was not possible, then neither was sovereignty. That was the thinking of Parizeau and of those who saw the inclusion of association in the question as leaving the government no way out if association was rejected.

In Jacques Parizeau's view, the sovereignty option would lose so much of its substance that, during the final days of the 1980 referendum campaign, it would be reduced to a kind of federal reform. "It was pathetic!" he says.

A quarter of a century has gone by since that first referendum and Jacques Parizeau is still critical of the question it posed. It stipulated a mandate to negotiate association, a common currency and, if the negotiations were successful, a second referendum to approve the results of those negotiations. At the time, Jacques Parizeau expressed his reservations about the question quite emphatically to the cabinet presided over by René Lévesque. He remembers the meeting of

December 19, 1979, which lasted all day and ended late at night. By wearing them down, as the ministers went back and forth—some of them feeling they had no say in the matter of a confrontation between René Lévesque and his Finance minister—Parizeau finally obtained, at the stroke of midnight, the compromise that brought the meeting to a close. "There were only four or five ministers left around the table," Parizeau recalls. "I was tired and went to bed. The next morning, at 10 a.m., René Lévesque got up in the National Assembly to announce the text of the question. It was not the one we had agreed on the night before. I was outraged! I saw Lévesque and said that it made no sense to do it this way. He said, 'Sorry, I forgot to tell you.'"[5] During the night, the premier's advisors had amended the question and they had got René Lévesque to accept the new formulation over breakfast.

René Lévesque's version of this episode is considerably different. "As for the idea of a second referendum, it literally brought Jacques Parizeau to a boil, since even the first wasn't easy for him to swallow!" he wrote. "By midnight we were approaching a fairly solid consensus. And so we continued until the small hours, when our jurists were called upon to weigh our words in the delicate balance-pans of legality. Then, next morning, a night's sleep unluckily having allowed time for second thoughts, I arranged with (Claude) Morin and (Louis) Bernard to change two words at a place where Parizeau had been especially upset, and more unluckily still, one thinking the other had done it, neither of us told him, which he almost took for a foul blow."[6]

From the moment the PQ came to power on November 15, 1976, both René Lévesque and Pierre Elliott Trudeau, prime minister of Canada at the time, waited for the other to make the first move. The premier of Quebec had no desire to cross swords with Pierre Elliott Trudeau in a referendum. And time was working in his favour: Trudeau had been voted back in on July 8, 1974 and the legislative mandate of five years would require that he call another election sometime before the summer of 1979. While Trudeau was eager to test Lévesque in a referendum, Lévesque waited, in the hope of confronting someone else, a new government leader, whether Liberal or Conservative. Pierre Elliott Trudeau was forced to hold an election and ceded power on May 22, 1979 to Conservative Joe Clark. But the new government was in a minority position.

Lévesque was encouraged and began to develop his referendum strategy. However, in the meantime, the Conservative government was defeated and fresh elections were called. Trudeau had already let his caucus know that he was bored as leader of the Opposition and intended to bow out. The defeat of the Clark government and the prospect of resuming power, however, made Trudeau change his mind. He launched his electoral campaign and regained power on February 18, 1980. Lévesque was now in a bind: the referendum machinery was already running and it was the fourth year of his term.

Furthermore, Lévesque had to deal with a disastrous economic situation. The United States was entering a recession, Canadians—Quebecers included—were seeing their purchasing power decline, and job creation was slowing, with the result that 1980 became Canada's worst year in a quarter of a century. Two months prior to the referendum, the Conference Board projected that the Canadian economy would experience zero growth and would not resume its pattern of stable prices and full employment for another five years. It predicted a growth of 0.1% for Quebec along with an unemployment rate of 10%.

Lévesque no longer had a choice: he would have to confront Trudeau. Trudeau though did not lose sight of the two projects closest to his heart: repatriation of the Constitution and the Charter of Rights. But he would first have to block the Quebec government's independence project. When the PQ came to power in November 1976, "Mr. Trudeau was somewhat dismissive of it," says Jean Chrétien, "and you'll probably dig up a tape where he'll say: well, it's just another provincial election. I think that people didn't take René Lévesque's intentions seriously." But once the Quebec government's project really started taking shape, Trudeau summoned Chrétien, who wanted to be appointed Foreign Affairs minister. "The house is on fire, but you want to be in Paris or in Washington?" he asked him. "I'm appointing you minister of Justice and putting you in charge of the federal forces in the upcoming referendum campaign!"[7] "So, I became Trudeau's firefighter," Jean Chrétien recalls, as he looks back on these events

24 years later. "I was out there, on the road every night. Michelle Tisseyre was our master of ceremonies and Camil Samson, whom I know well because we are from the same parish, represented the *Créditistes*. He was funny. He would say, 'Mr. Lévesque is asking us to jump from an 80-storey building and saying that if we don't like it when we get down to the 30th floor, they'll pass legislation to change the law of gravity...' Then he said, 'I should be on the YES side because my mother-in-law is from Ontario—she would need a passport to come and visit me in Rouyn-Noranda.'"[8]

It was a ferocious campaign. A few days before the referendum, René Lévesque made remarks that started a controversy. Jean Chrétien remembers the incident very well. It was May 14, and, that evening, Trudeau was to take part in a big rally for the NO side at the Paul-Sauvé Arena. "I was on my way to meet Trudeau for breakfast (to discuss his speech) when I heard the news. Mr. Lévesque had said, 'Trudeau is not a real francophone, not a real Quebecer, because his Scottish blood is thicker than his French blood.'[9] When I arrived at Trudeau's home, I said to him, 'Pierre, *you*'re not a pure one, but *I* am...' At that, our Trudeau, who could have chosen to be an anglophone, who could have gone with the people of Westmount instead of with Marchand and Pelletier, said, 'We are going to risk our seats in the House.' (I said,) 'Pierre, unlike me, you are nearing retirement age. It will be no laughing matter to risk our seats.' He said, 'We have no choice, so bring 'em on. Let's go!'"[10]

That night, at the Paul-Sauvé Arena, after telling the audience how far back his Quebec origins reached, Trudeau made a promise that would influence the course of events quite considerably: "And I make a solemn declaration to all Canadians in the other provinces: we, the Quebec MPs, are laying ourselves on the line, because we are telling Quebecers to vote NO and telling you in the other provinces that we will not agree to your interpreting this NO as an indication that everything is fine and can remain as it was before. We want change and we are willing to lay our seats in the House on the line to have change."[11]

"I was 25," Brian Tobin recalls. "I was walking on Parliament Hill with a friend from Newfoundland who was visiting me in Ottawa.

It was a beautiful, sunny day. We were walking along when a bus pulled up beside us. On board, there were Quebec MPs who called out, 'Get on Brian. We're going to Montreal to hear Trudeau.' We got on. And let's be honest, you could have a finger or two of cognac on board this bus. We went to Montreal and I think Trudeau's speech was a turning point in the referendum campaign." Tobin recalls that even though the Quebec question could fuel Liberal caucus discussions, it was clearly Trudeau's responsibility: "The strategy was defined by Mr. Trudeau and his closest advisors, people like Jean Chrétien and Marc Lalonde."

The rest of the referendum campaign revolved around Trudeau's remarks, without Trudeau ever developing them any further, and leaving Quebecers with the hope of constitutional changes that would take their aspirations seriously. "(Jean Chrétien) felt," says Eddie Goldenberg, who was his advisor at the time, "that Mr. Trudeau had created expectations in 1980. Whether they were expectations that were realistic, whether the expectations were what he actually intended to do, or how they were interpreted was irrelevant. But over a period of time there was a perception that he didn't deliver." In any event, what he would deliver was not what the majority of Quebecers had been hoping for. Four and a half months later, on October 2, Trudeau would announce that he intended, without the support of the provinces if necessary, to repatriate the British North America Act, the British law that served as the Constitution of Canada. All he would have to do was ask the British Parliament to amend it in accordance with his wishes and ask them to transfer responsibility for it to the Canadian government.

For René Lévesque and his government, the referendum results were hard to bear: almost 60% of Quebecers rejected the sovereigntist option and, even among the francophones, no majority of any kind emerged in favour of the YES option. The defeat would cause divisions within his own party. Nonetheless, even weakened by the referendum defeat, René Lévesque and his government were returned to power on April 13, 1981. Three days later, the premier joined ranks with seven other provinces to form a "common front" to bring down the project of the unilateral repatriation of the Constitution. These provinces deemed that the Canadian Charter of Rights and Freedoms, which would be entrenched in the Constitution, would reduce their powers. The Supreme Court got involved: it ruled that, with the support of only two provinces, Ontario and New Brunswick, the project, while being within the law, was not legitimate, that is, "not in conformity with the dominant constitutional values and principles of the time (…) or the wishes of the electorate." But the Court did not specify how many provinces would have to support Trudeau's plan for it to be in conformity with the principles and values of the Constitution. The prime minister was now in a real quandary.

Trudeau convened a federal-provincial conference, which took place on November 5, 1981. The conference would end in what has come to be known in the political literature as "the night of the long knives." That night, from November 4 to 5, while René Lévesque and his delegation took a break in Hull, the other provinces agreed on a proposal they would put to the federal government the next day. During the night, Jean Chrétien, Roy McMurtry, Ontario's minister of Justice, and Roy Romanow, Saskatchewan's minister of Intergovernmental Affairs, finalized the proposal. Four months later, Romanow acknowledged that it had not appeared profitable to the English-speaking provinces "to involve Quebec too soon in a negotiating session that we hoped would be constructive."[12] These remarks prompted René Lévesque, when Premier Lougheed of Alberta wrote him in an attempt to explain the attitude of the other provinces of the common front, to reply as follows: "The promises made to Quebec at the time of the referendum were ignored, the April 16 agreement (among the provinces) was violated and, during the night of November 4 to 5, taking advantage of Quebec's absence, the nine provinces concluded an agreement with Ottawa."[13]

For Jacques Parizeau, the constitutional defeat of November 1981 confirmed Quebec's vulnerable state. Ever since the referendum, Quebec had found itself trapped in a blind alley. In Parizeau's mind, the referendum question had been so "vague" that Quebec had come away from the whole experience significantly weaker, lacking the power it needed to negotiate with the federal government and, therefore, forced to consider all sorts of compromises. Claude Morin, minister of Intergovernmental Affairs at the time, acknowledged this implicitly when he said in 1991, "We had lost the referendum. We were not going to propose sovereignty-association (at the November 1981 conference). We were prepared to sign an agreement if acceptable proposals had been made to us."[14]

The Parti Québécois was enraged by the humiliation it had been made to suffer at the conference. The following month, at its general convention, its 2,500 delegates endorsed a radical change of direction that scrapped any notion of association with the rest of the country. René Lévesque, who had fanned the flames a bit during the convention, would write these words three years later: "While the Parti Québécois finished wiping itself out, it was the implacable face of the old RIN (*Rassemblement pour l'indépendence nationale*) that was reappearing, accompanied by pure, tough, inaccessible independence."[15]

The new Canadian Constitution, repatriated without Quebec's consent, was signed in Ottawa in a spirit of euphoria on April 17, 1982 and, for a few days, everyone forgot the unhappy state of the Canadian economy. Canada, particularly Ontario, was in a recession. As early as 1980, the C.D. Howe Institute had sounded the alarm with respect to the country's declining productivity, the Conference Board projected a zero growth rate and the Economic Council of Canada deplored the climate of indecision and uncertainty pervading several of the country's domestic policies. Unemployment exceeded 8%, the rate of inflation had reached 12% and interest rates were fluctuating between 15 and 20%. The U.S. situation did not help, but the main responsibility rested with the Canadian government, which accumulated deficits year after year.

Ahead to 1984. A new man had just appeared on the Canadian political scene. In the midst of his electoral campaign, in a fiery speech drafted by Lucien Bouchard and delivered on August 6 in Sept-Îles, Brian Mulroney promised to convince the National Assembly of Quebec to give its assent to the new Canadian Constitution "with honour and enthusiasm." He assumed power on September 4 with

211 members elected across Canada, including 58 of Quebec's 75 members. The departure of the Liberals, especial those loyal to Trudeau, and the arrival of a Conservative government in Ottawa, led by another Quebecer, rekindled in Lévesque the hope of a new association between Quebec and the rest of Canada. The Conservative leader inspired confidence. Jacques Parizeau explains Lévesque's determination to maintain an association with Canada, which was already an integral part of his plan when he founded the *Mouvement souveraineté-association* in 1967: "The only large market available to Quebec industry is English Canada. There are no others," says Parizeau. "Imagine that Quebec becomes independent and the Canadian government treats Quebec like a foreign country, that it applies, for example, the GATT tariff, which would be normal. Quebec would find itself caught between the U.S. tariff and the Canadian tariff. Our markets, for all our industrial production, would suddenly become almost non-existent. That was the scenario René Lévesque feared. That was the significance of association. If there was no association, the risk was too great. It was a risk that could not be taken." The Sept-Îles speech and the formal contacts Mulroney established with Quebec as soon as he was elected left no doubt as to his sincerity. "It was clear he wanted to get along with Quebec," says Parizeau. "He was deeply troubled, as were many other federalists like him, that Quebec had not ratified the 1982 Constitution and that it remained completely outside of the constitutional process. He sought a solution..."[16] Finding his confidence renewed, Lévesque used the occasion of his inaugural speech in the National Assembly on October 16, 1984, to say that the openness Mulroney had displayed towards Quebec's aspirations offered the opportunity for a *beau risque* (literally noble risk, or good bet) to be taken.

The rift between the "associationists" and the "unconditional sovereigntists" in the government grew even wider. On November 10, 12 ministers signed a declaration reaffirming that Quebec's sovereignty remained a necessary objective. A week later, Lévesque addressed a letter to the militants in his party advising them that sovereignty would be "neither the whole issue nor part of it" in the next electoral campaign. The next day, Pierre de Bellefeuille became the first member of the National Assembly to resign. Then, Louise Harel. At the cabinet meeting of November 21, disagreement was so strong and the debate had become so violent that reconciliation between the two camps was no longer possible. A split occurred. The very next day, several ministers resigned: Gilbert Paquette, Jérôme Proulx, Jacques Léonard, Denise Leblanc-Bantey, Camille Laurin and others. Seven in all. Jacques Parizeau quit his post the same day. In mid-January, at a special meeting, the delegates amended Article 1 of the Parti Québécois' program to reflect what René Lévesque wanted, thus provoking 500 participants and several ministers to leave the meeting.

René Lévesque lasted another six months. He resigned on June 20, 1985. His departure did not end the crisis tearing his party apart. His successor, Pierre Marc Johnson, elected party president on September 29 by almost 60% of the members, shared Lévesque's views. The *beau risque* became "national affirmation" within Canada. "It was over how the *beau risque* was expressed that I finally resigned," says Parizeau, who freely admits he is not interested in being in politics for its own sake. "I didn't see any future in that. The only reason I was in politics was to achieve autonomy for Quebec. But I didn't see this happening at all. Pierre-Marc Johnson would draw his own conclusions from that same impasse: national affirmation was a position to take while waiting. We really didn't know what was going to happen. National affirmation arose from the 1980 failure, just like 'the night of the long knives,' and the acceptance of the *beau risque*. In each case, we said to ourselves, 'what else can we do?'"[17]

Pierre-Marc Johnson managed in spite of everything to rally a good number of party members around the principle of national affirmation and to prolong the agony of the Parti Québécois into December. But the government had aged considerably in four and a half years. It was tired, both from a difficult governing period and from internal conflicts that were due as much to the principles at issue as to the individuals who inspired them. On December 2, 1985, they were defeated by a reinvigorated Robert Bourassa, back from a long period of reflection and hailed as the saviour of Quebec's economy. It was Bourassa, rather than René Lévesque, who would put to the test the seriousness of Brian Mulroney's intentions.

On October 29, 1987, a PQ member who was respected by his party, poet Gérald Godin, launched an unprecedented attack on its leader: "This party is going nowhere under its present leader and that has got me very worried,"[18] he said. The next day he added, "The Parti Québécois must resume its sovereigntist discourse and emerge from its sleepwalking."[19] Then he invited the members to put on their glasses and look around to identify the most suitable candidate to re-place Johnson. He himself had made his choice: Jacques Parizeau. "He's my man," he said. When Pierre-Marc Johnson learned of the mutiny, which now included long-standing ministers like Camille Laurin, he was in London, en route to Paris, where he was to meet with President François Mitterrand. His advisers encouraged him to return home. He decided instead to continue his travels. When he ar-rived in the French capital, another, more serious piece of news awaited him: René Lévesque was dead. Despite the affection he had for Lévesque, Johnson did not cancel his meetings, except for the one with Mitterrand. He could have returned to Quebec the same day, but he would not reappear there until November 3.

In this party, traditionally identified with its leader, there was no one on that November 1, to guide them in analyzing what was happen-ing to them. Their founding father had just died, their official leader was travelling abroad, and Jacques Parizeau, who was no longer any-thing in the party, found himself keeping a close watch, with an ear to the ground and open heart. What followed was a matter of pressure and criticism: five days after laying René Lévesque's body to rest, Pierre-Marc Johnson resigned.[20]

It was the end of national affirmation. The hyphen that had per-sisted against all odds for 20 years, between sovereignty and associa-tion, was thrown out, and the Parti Québécois turned resolutely towards the single objective of independence. Jacques Parizeau had left politics three years earlier. He had divided his time between teach-ing, lecturing, writing academic articles, and all kinds of interesting projects. He had become an independent man. The Conservative government was contemplating the idea of an economic free trade agreement with the United States. Trudeau's successor, John Turner, was not unaware that Parizeau had defended a doctoral thesis on international trade. He therefore sought out his expertise on the subject. Brian Mulroney, not wanting to be outdone, offered him a place in the Senate. "He did this in a very proper manner," Parizeau says. "I am grateful to him for it, even today. It did not correspond in any way to the direction I wanted to pursue personally, but nevertheless, that was OK."[21]

The Parti Québécois no longer had a leader and many people turned to Parizeau. "I was not convinced that everyone in the party had been won over to my vision of sovereignty, which was far from being a half-measure," he says. "And that was why I would go out looking for 10,000 new members. Show me that you agree, that a good number of people agree, with my idea of Quebec sovereignty, and then I will get on board." And he did get on board. Was it to become premier of Quebec? "No, no, no, no!" he replies. "But I had to be premier of Quebec in order to have a referendum. For me, politics is an instrument."[22]

On December 21, 1987, Jacques Parizeau presented himself as a candidate for the presidency of the Parti Québécois and on March 18, 1988, he was crowned, unopposed, at a special national council of the party in Montreal. "My first act, when I was elected party president," says Parizeau, "was to phone Michel Bélanger, the president of the National Bank (which had been created in 1979), who was threatening to pull the plug on us. I said to him, 'Please give me a few months.' The party owed the National Bank half a million dollars. I didn't know where I was going to get it. That was my first act!"[23]

Jacques Parizeau was now president of the Parti Québécois but he did not have a seat in the National Assembly. The party's parliamentary leader was Guy Chevrette and the two men would henceforth have to get along. "(We were) two men with diametrically opposed temperaments and characters," Chevrette recalls. "He was an intellectual while I was a populist. I was the great pragmatist while he was a conceptual thinker with a very structured mind. (But) there was no petty quarrelling between us. He left me the reins in the House and he looked after the party."[24]

Parizeau the intellectual had not always been sovereigntist. He had come to that position, as with all the major decisions he had taken in his political life, through reflection and reason. "We were headed for an absurd situation," he says, recalling his years spent as advisor to three premiers of Quebec. "Ottawa had been sufficiently stripped of power to prevent it from really operating like a true government and we, on the other hand, had not received enough power to be a real government. We were going nowhere fast. Since things were like that, since there was no true government in Ottawa, I felt we should establish a true government in Quebec. And I came to sovereignty as the solution, not emotionally, not because I felt particularly sovereigntist, but simply because it seemed to me a logical conclusion."[25] Parizeau had joined the Parti Québécois in 1969 and, during political rallies, met with people at the opposite end of the social spectrum from those he was accustomed to socializing with, having grown up in bourgeois Outremont and graduating from the London School of Economics. "Those first public gatherings, at which I became aware of a very deep wave of Quebec nationalism, made an enormous impression on me," he likes to recount. "For me, never having been in contact with the real people of Quebec, this was beautiful!"[26]

Jacques Parizeau returned to the National Assembly in November 1989, this time as leader of the Opposition. He came back because he still wanted to see a true government in Quebec. All the more so now that globalization of the economy had changed everything. "The future belongs to sovereign states, not provinces," he says. "To be premier of a province interested me 30 years ago when I was younger. Free trade, for sovereigntists, is major, very, very important."[27] He recalls that in the 80s, the U.S. Congress was becoming increasingly protectionist but, by proposing the Free Trade Agreement to the Canadian government, the White House acted first. Ontario, under David Peterson's Liberals, did not want free trade; the West did. Robert Bourassa saw the advantages of such an agreement, but he feared the unions, who were the natural allies of the Parti Québécois. Opposition leader Parizeau would then, to a certain extent, turn his back on the unions and pay more attention to the Chambers of Commerce and the small and medium-sized businesses, as they would see enormous advantages to free trade. He proposed to Premier Robert Bourassa that they put partisanship aside and support Mulroney. "When they say it was Quebecers who enabled Canada to sign the Free Trade Agreement with the United States, it is perfectly true. We provided Mr. Mulroney with the political weight he needed." For Parizeau, the agreement freed Quebec from necessary economic association with Canada and from blackmail by the premiers of the other provinces, who were saying, "If you decide to become independent, we won't buy your textiles, we won't buy your shoes, we'll stop selling you our beef!"[28]

The free trade question would become the central theme of the 1988 federal election campaign. On November 21, Brian Mulroney was returned to power thanks to the massive support of Quebecers: of 169 Conservative seats, 63 were in Quebec, where the Liberals only managed to retain 12. At the same time, Ontario sent 46 Conservatives to Ottawa, along with 43 Liberals and 10 New Democrats. The Canada-United States Free Trade Agreement (CUSFTA) came into effect on January 1, 1989.

Mulroney had promised in his Sept-Îles speech in 1984 to draw Quebec back into the constitutional family. Robert Bourassa established the conditions for this in March 1985: later that year, less than two weeks after being elected head of the Quebec government, he reaffirmed them to the prime minister of Canada at a meeting with him on December 13. Quebec's five conditions were now public. Bourassa would sign the Constitution only if Quebec was recognized as a distinct society, if its powers with respect to immigration were increased, if it had a right to participate in appointments to the Senate and the Supreme Court, if it had the right to withdraw from federal programs with full financial compensation and if it had the right to veto any change the rest of Canada wanted to make to Canadian institutions, in short, a right to veto any change to the Constitution. Mulroney believed he could get the other provincial premiers to adopt the substance of these five conditions and he called a meeting at the federal government's chalet on Meech Lake on April 30, 1987. Mulroney was an astute negotiator. He gathered all the premiers in a small room, without their political advisors. The five conditions put forward by Bourassa were accepted in principle. Another meeting was set for June 2 and 3 in the Langevin building in Ottawa. The premiers then signed the final version of the agreement.

No sooner had the ink dried at the bottom of the page than the rumbling began. On May 27, Pierre Elliott Trudeau came out of the shadows to denounce the agreement in a text published simultaneously in English Canada and in Quebec. "What a magician this Mr. (Brian) Mulroney is, and what a sly fox! He has not quite succeeded in achieving sovereignty-association, but has put Canada on the fast track for getting there."[29] The opponents of the Meech Lake Accord acted fast to influence public opinion: in the summer of 1987, 70% of Canadians outside Quebec were against it and this percentage would hold till the winter of 1990.

The agreement carried within it the promise of its failure: the ten provincial governments were given three years in which to have it successfully passed in their respective legislatures. To allow this was to ignore the importance that premiers give to the moods of Canadians and to disregard the changes in government that would inevitably take place in a three-year period. Indeed, in New Brunswick, while Conservative Richard Hatfield had signed the agreement, it was Liberal Frank McKenna who assumed power four months later, winning every seat in the province. Today he denies the fact that he campaigned on the back of the Meech Lake Accord and says he subscribes to the principles underlying it. "Richard Hatfield had a chance to put it through the House," he says. "And, in my view, we probably would have supported that if such a vote had been held." But the election campaign would convince McKenna that the Accord had to be, if not scrapped, at least amended. "The approach that we took was not to rip Meech," he adds, "but to try to introduce new reforms, protection of the Charter of Rights, sacred to Canadians, protection of francophones outside of Quebec and, very important, Aboriginal community recognitions, Senate reform." McKenna was not unaware that by transforming the Meech agreement into a constitutional hodgepodge, he was diverting it from its primary objective, which was to induce Quebec to sign the new Constitution of 1982.

But he was not the only new player in the forthcoming tight match. In the spring of 1988, the people of Manitoba elected Conservative Gary Filmon, chasing from power and from politics the New Democrat signatory of the Meech Lake Accord, Howard Pawley. Filmon wanted ratification of the agreement, while Sharon Carstairs, a close associate of Jean Chrétien and head of the Liberal party, opposed it. The only aboriginal member of the Manitoba legislature, New Democrat Elijah Harper, would systematically block any vote on the Accord between June 12 and 22, 1990. His fight to have aboriginal rights recognized in the document would allow the West to stand in the way of an agreement concerning Quebec, to which they had been opposed from the start. "There's nobody in Western Canada who does not recognize Quebec as a distinct society," says Deborah Grey, an Alberta teacher who became the first elected member of the Reform Party in 1989. "The frustration that we felt was that this would be something enshrined in the constitution." Reform leader Preston Manning explains the frustration further: "The West had been talking about Senate Reform, which can require a constitutional change. It never got anywhere on the Mulroney agenda," he says. "But Quebec's desire for recognition as a distinct society went from zero to the top of the pile in a short period of time. This is what people would say: the constitutional concerns of one part of the country that's got 75 seats go sky-high. The constitutional concerns of another part of the country that has more than 75 seats don't even get on the radar screen." In Manning's view, the Western provinces had already been alienated by the Liberal party, and they were soon disillusioned with the Mulroney government too. "When reform started," he adds, "there was the ingredients for a full-blown secession crisis in the West in the '80s."

It was not only in the West that the Meech Lake Accord was sowing discontent. The grumbling could be heard all across the country, except in Quebec. Newfoundland did a spectacular about-face: in July 1989, Clyde Wells, who had been elected premier in April, cancelled the motion of support for the agreement that had been adopted in July 1988 by the Parliament led by Conservative Brian Peckford. In a letter to Prime Minister Mulroney, he gave the reason for the reversal: the Accord would destroy the country in a very short time. Finally, in Ontario, Premier Peterson, a signatory of the Accord, paid the price in the provincial elections of September 1990. His successor, New Democrat Bob Rae, believes, however, that the Meech Lake Accord should have been adopted by the whole country: "I thought that what was being proposed was modest and was rational and was fair and reasonable. And I still believe that."

On March 16, 1990, Frank McKenna wrote Mulroney and suggested that he include in the document of the Meech Lake Accord "provisions reflecting the diverse concerns raised not only in New Brunswick, but everywhere else in Canada." Six days later, three months from the deadline of June 23, Mulroney despatched his young minister Jean Charest across the country to try to elicit a consensus that would enable him to save the Accord. At the end of two months, the Charest commission had heard 190 witnesses and read 800 reports. Its report, submitted on May 17, proposed about 20 amendments to the Meech Lake Accord and a new premiers' conference to discuss it. This was devastating for Quebec, especially because the distinct society clause would become an interpretative clause, which would be applied jointly with the Charter and could not compromise the rights and freedoms guaranteed by it. "The committee recommends," the report reads, "that the premiers declare in an accompanying resolution that the application of the distinct society clause will not diminish in any way the efficacy of the Charter (...). This accompanying resolution should also stipulate that the clauses recognizing that the provincial legislatures and parliaments have roles shall not have the effect of conferring legislative powers on them." In summary, the clause no longer had any real effect.

The Charest report had an initial dramatic consequence for the Mulroney government. Lucien Bouchard had been in the cabinet since March 1988. He had given his approval to the creation of the Charest committee, but "with the proviso that the Meech Lake accord be accepted as is, without any modifications, at the time or subsequently."[30] He says that he learned of the report only when he was in Norway, where he was to participate in a meeting of Environment ministers. He took the decision to resign and to announce it publicly. On May 19 and 20, the Parti Québécois would hold its national council at Alma, in Lucien Bouchard's constituency, and celebrate the 10th anniversary of the 1980 referendum. This was the moment Mulroney's minister chose. He sent a telegram of welcome to Jacques Parizeau and the 200 delegates. "The first evening of the national council, one of his messengers handed me the letter, the famous letter, which would have such great importance afterwards," Parizeau recalls. "I had difficulty believing that it was authentic. This was so big, I thought, that I said to the messenger, 'Listen, go and talk to your boss. If this letter I have received is official, I am going to make it public.' He came back after an hour or so and said to me, 'He has no objection to your making the letter public tomorrow.' Well, in that case, if he has thought it all out, all right then, very well. I took the letter and I read it before the national council."[31] Bouchard's telegram read as follows: "Your meeting will also celebrate the tenth anniversary of one of the high points of Quebec's history. (…) Its commemoration offers another opportunity to recall the sincerity, the pride, and the generosity of the YES we defended at the time, around René Lévesque and his team. René Lévesque's memory will unite us all this weekend. He was the one who led Quebecois to realize they had the inalienable right to decide their own destiny."[32] The next day, there was upheaval in Ottawa: Bouchard submitted his resignation to Prime Minister Mulroney, both as minister and as Conservative member for the electoral riding of Lac-Saint-Jean in the House of Commons. Already, the Friday prior, the member for Mégantic-Compton-Stanstead, François Gérin, had left the ranks of the Conservative party. Others would follow, six in all, four Conservatives and two Liberals, including Jean Lapierre, then member for Shefford.[33] Lapierre, who had fought against the YES camp alongside Pierre Elliott Trudeau in 1980, now blamed Jean Chrétien for the failure of the Meech Lake Accord. "You have succeeded once again in denying Quebec her rightful identity," he wrote. "I know you have betrayed us!"

Despite one final premiers' conference, which went on for six days at the beginning of June, the Meech Lake Accord died, having run out of breath, on Friday, June 22. Robert Bourassa had really believed that the agreement was possible. Back in February, he had created within the Liberal party a constitutional committee, presided over by Jean Allaire, whose mandate was to define the political content of a second round of negotiations once the Meech Lake Accord was ratified. He had not given up hope until three days before the end. "He believed until the Tuesday that it was possible," John Parisella, his chief of staff, recalls. "Starting that day, he began to feel it would not happen. I think it was a great disappointment for him, especially thinking of the verdict of History..."[34] Bourassa had just seen his constitutional option rejected by the rest of the country. So, he turned to rallying the people. That same day, before the National Assembly, he delivered a speech, which became famous, that would make you think for a moment that he had become a sovereigntist. He said, "Whatever they say, whatever they do, Quebec is today and always will be a distinct society, free and capable of assuming her destiny and her economic development." "For Mr. Bourassa, this was a terrible and frightening defeat," says Parizeau. "Politically Quebec was on her knees, now completely empty-handed. It was that evening that I extended a hand to 'my Prime Minister,' as I called him."[35]

Was Bourassa tempted at that moment to join the sovereigntist troops? John Parisella thinks not. "No, no one could send him in a direction he did not want to go. He appreciated Mr. Parizeau's gesture, which was one of magnanimity. But this helped Mr. Bourassa in his efforts to rally the people. If his speech had managed to win over the head of the Parti Québécois, that very day, then he could get through Saint-Jean-Baptiste Day firmly in the saddle."[36] Nor does Parizeau believe that Bourassa could become sovereigntist: "He was too cautious. Should sovereignty have become very popular, he might have had to manoeuver in that direction for a while. But he was really too prudent to commit himself to such a path. However, he was deeply impressed by the kind of wave that unfurled after the failure of Meech Lake."[37]

The wave was very strong indeed. From June through to the fall, the surveys steadily showed, to within a few percentage points, that between 55 and 60% of Quebecers were in favour of sovereignty. And Bourassa would adapt. First of all, he announced that he was no longer willing to negotiate anything whatsoever with the rest of Canada, with 11 people around the table. From now on, negotiations would have to be on a bilateral basis between Canada and Quebec. On September 5, he created the Bélanger-Campeau Commission, whose mandate was to present to the government recommendations on the constitutional future of Quebec. Because Parizeau had extended his hand to him the day after the failure of Meech, and had proposed they work together to build Quebec's future, Bourassa agreed for the two co-chairs and most of the members of the Commission to be chosen jointly.[38] "Not only were there Liberals and Parti Québécois members around the table," Parizeau recalls. "There had to be federalists. And that was where Bouchard would prove to be invaluable. As a former Conservative minister, very much appreciated in Quebec by the *vieux bleus* of the Union Nationale, he sought out people who were really fed up with the Péquiste movement!"[39] The Commission received 600 reports, heard 235 groups and associations and consulted more than 50 experts. It submitted its report on March 27 of the following year. Here is how Jean Campeau summarizes the conclusions of the Commission: "There were two choices. Either we repatriate our powers and tell the federal government, 'Stop encroaching on our territory, the fence is up. Stop coming over and taking our money to spend it however you like in our jurisdictions.' Or, if that doesn't work, we hold a referendum on sovereignty."[40] The Commission even specified when the referendum would take place; in the absence of a renewed federalism, it would be held no later than October 16, 1992.

The conclusions of the Bélanger-Campeau Commission forced Bourassa to introduce a bill creating two parliamentary committees. One would examine any proposal that might be received from Ottawa.

Even while playing its own game, Quebec felt that, following the failure of Meech, the ball was in the court of the federal government. The other committee's mandate would be to prepare the steps towards sovereignty should Ottawa's proposals prove unsatisfactory. But already, Bourassa and his Minister of Intergovernmental Affairs Gil Rémillard were softening the impact of the report's conclusions by affirming that the Quebec government would retain its initiative and its ability to assess the measures that would be in the best interest of Quebec. The wording of the preamble to the bill made Parizeau so suspicious that the Parti Québécois voted against its adoption on June 20.

The failure of Meech had dampened Prime Minister Mulroney's enthusiasm on the subject of integrating Quebec into the constitutional family. However, he was obliged to respond in one way or another to Bourassa's initiatives. He did not make any new proposals to Quebec. He responded to the conclusions of the Bélanger-Campeau Commission by convening another first ministers conference in Charlottetown. "He used to say, 'We've got to put something in the window. We've got to put a Cadillac in the window. We've got to show them that there's something there,'" recalls Bob Rae, then premier of Ontario.[41]

Despite his promise, made two years earlier, to engage only in bilateral negotiations with the federal government, and despite the Allaire Committee report, which proposed reclaiming 22 areas of provincial jurisdiction that were federally held, Robert Bourassa went to Charlottetown.[42] On August 28, 1992, the first ministers of the provinces and the territories signed an agreement, which gave Quebec, among other things, the distinct society clause, but limited it to language, culture and civil law. Put to a pan-Canadian referendum, the agreement was rejected by Quebecers as well as by Canadians in five provinces. Bob Rae admits that the Charlottetown Accord "was not a beautiful Cadillac. It was not perfect. It was sort of half a camel and half a horse, but it was there. It was better than the alternative of breaking up the country."

Ever since resigning from the federal government, Lucien Bouchard had been seeking a way into provincial politics. His aim was to found a party that would attract some of the sovereignty vote from the Parti Québécois. "We need a new party," he said. "I will never join your ranks in order to become a Parti Québécois member. That party is too militant."[43]

It was, however, alongside the Parti Québécois that he would fight the sovereignty battle. Not two months after having walked out on the Mulroney government, the Conservative MPs who had resigned gathered at Longueuil and appointed Bouchard as leader of their parliamentary group. On July 25, they chose their official name, the Bloc Québécois, and stated the basic principles of a platform that would be drafted by Jean Lapierre during the interval leading up to the party's founding congress, which they held on June 15 of the following year. The idea of a sovereigntist party in Ottawa initiated by former minister Marcel Léger, who had even founded one himself much earlier, did not bring unanimous support from the Parti Québécois. "To me, it seemed important that there be one," says Jacques Parizeau, who continues to be amazed at how Quebecers could have voted for Lévesque in Quebec and Trudeau in Ottawa. He felt that the idea of a new sovereigntist party in Ottawa dated back to the strategy meetings that used to take place every Monday at his office in Place Ville-Marie, meetings attended by Bernard Landry, parliamentary leader Guy Chevrette, Jean Royer, Hubert Thibault and a few others. "That's where the creation of the Bloc started," he says. "It didn't come about all by itself. They had to be called, one by one, those former Conservatives in Ottawa. They wanted to sit as independents. We had to organize a framework, and then, have long discussions with Bouchard. Because Bouchard was not at all convinced that he should be party leader. It took quite some time before he accepted the idea. It was Mr. Landry who was appointed, by us, to help establish what has become the Bloc Québécois. He was the one who ensured that the Jell-O would set and that Mr. Bouchard would accept the leadership!"[44]

Condemned to work together, Parizeau and Bouchard were however very different. "You wouldn't exactly say they hit it off," says Pierre-Paul Roy, who, in June 1992, was chief of staff to the leader of the Bloc for a time before becoming his political advisor. "Maybe it was just the difference in their personalities, but there was no love lost between them. Their conversations were polite, and limited to their respective responsibilities. They stuck to politics. There was no other relationship or connection between these two."[45] The differences between the two men would become even more apparent during the 1995 referendum campaign and the months leading up to it.

On October 25, 1993, Jean Chrétien came to power in Ottawa. But he faced Lucien Bouchard as leader of the official Opposition.[46] "We had made the constitutional status quo an element of our election program," Eddie Goldenberg recalls. Goldenberg would be one of the most influential figures in the Prime Minister's Office for the duration of Chrétien's regime. "Mr. Chrétien had made it clear that the Constitution, on a priority list of 100 priorities, was 101. One of the planks of the platform was no constitutional change. But the Bloc was more of a problem because we had to deal with the prospect of another referendum in Quebec. The Bloc would not have been satisfied with constitutional change. I don't know that there was ever such a bizarre occurrence in Canadian history, as to have a bunch of separatists serving as Her Majesty's Loyal Opposition. They're not keen on Her Majesty and they're not very loyal because they wanted to leave the country."

To have to relinquish their status as official opposition was a bitter experience for the Reform Party who had lost three seats by a total of just 329 votes, in the Edmonton region. "If anybody ever gets up in an audience and says to me, 'well, my vote doesn't count,'" says Preston Manning, who was head of the Reformists during the 1993 election, "I say, 'Look, if the country had cracked up in 1995, one of the reasons would have been that the separatists have been given for two years a national platform by being the official Opposition. If 150 or 160 people in Edmonton had voted differently, they could have made that difference.'"

In Quebec, Robert Bourassa, now overcome by illness as well as by two bitter failures in the matter of the Constitution, handed over the reins of power. He had known for over a year that his skin cancer was spreading, and he was tired. The chairman of the Treasury Board,

Daniel Johnson, encountered no opposition in his bid for the Liberal leadership. He was declared leader of the party on December 15, 1993 and became premier on January 11, when Bourassa permanently relinquished his responsibilities. "Mr. Johnson had a past, at least his father had a past, that could be identified as 'Tory,'" says John Parisella, who was chief of staff to both Bourassa and Johnson. "But he had roots in the Liberal party dating back to 1977 or 1978. He had joined in the days of Claude Ryan. Those who knew Mr. Johnson well knew that he was a very pragmatic man. And then, Mr. Bourassa saw the choice of Mr. Johnson as a way to maintain continuity."[47]

"After the Charlottetown referendum, everyone had more or less turned the page on the great constitutional debates," Daniel Johnson recalls. "That is why in 1993 and 1994, we chose to put the emphasis on Quebec's economy, creating employment, reducing government, and providing services to our citizens. Essentially, I have always reiterated the Meech conditions as being, I would say, the foundation of our political program in constitutional matters. There was no point in reinventing a constitutional program. At the provincial premiers' conference in Toronto in the summer of 1994, we agreed on a text whose purpose was to ensure improved cooperation towards further decentralizing the Canadian federation while seeking consensus among the provinces regarding the exercise of their jurisdictions within the Canadian context."[48] In fact, the failure of Charlottetown had made more evident than ever the impossibility of envisaging a Canadian Constitution based on the recognition of the country's two founding peoples.

When Daniel Johnson became premier, the Liberal party had been in power for three years and three months. He had to prepare for a general election during his first year in office, against an adversary who was not only gearing up to fight an election battle, but also to promote his sovereignty option.

CHAPTER II

Power

It was the evening of September 12, 1994, and the Parti Québécois should have been celebrating. They had just regained power after nine long years in opposition. Yet, they were disappointed. Armed with lessons learned from the 1980 referendum, Jacques Parizeau had wanted to hold *his* referendum as soon as possible following the election, but the election results would force him to delay. While they had won 76 seats compared to only 47 for the Liberal party, the percentage of voters who had supported the PQ left him with no hope of winning a referendum: 44.7% versus 44.3% for the Liberals. In a two-way match between the YES side and the NO side, it looked like a tie. In the words of Parizeau's chief of staff, Jean Royer, "We were not satisfied with the result. We had expected to do better."[1] "I arrived at the National Assembly and there I saw Bernard Landry, Jacques Parizeau, Jean Royer, Guy Chevrette, all with long faces, and certainly no air of victory about them," recalls Jean-François Lisée,[2] who that very day would become Parizeau's political advisor. The party leaders had hoped to score better, 48 or 49%. "Some had even allowed themselves to hope for 50% on election day, to build momentum for the referendum," Lisée adds: "Now, the *post-mortem* of the campaign was already under way: What had gone wrong...?"[3] The night of the election, Pierre-Paul Roy, Lucien Bouchard's chief of staff, ran into Jean Royer, who asked him, "Pierre-Paul Roy, what did we fail to do? Where did we go wrong?"[4]

Today, Jacques Parizeau gives his explanation of what went wrong: "People want to know what we are going to do with sovereignty," he says,

37

as he recalls the economic disparity between certain regions or certain districts of Montreal. "There are seven kilometres between the south-west and the east parts of Montreal, but the difference between the two districts in the number of years of life expectancy is greater than seven! It was important not just to go for sovereignty. Sovereignty doesn't get you anywhere. People want to know what you're going to do with it."[5] He believes he had not sufficiently "rattled the cage" with respect to what he called "Quebec broken in two," or perhaps there weren't enough of them to rattle it.

Jean-François Lisée adds another explanation. He refers back to a public analysis he had done in the spring of 1994 when he was still a journalist. "Back in the spring," he recalls, "I had said in a public analysis that, if the Parti Québécois wanted to win the referendum, they should, at the start of the electoral campaign, arrive at an under-standing with the Alliance démocratique du Québec (ADQ), who would bring them additional votes. The reaction of the people I knew in the party was, 'You're not serious? What sense does that make? It's too complicated and, anyway, we don't need it!' The electoral situation was poorly read at the outset."[6] The ADQ got only one member elected, but it took 6.3% of the vote.

"That wasn't huge at the time," party leader Mario Dumont ac-knowledges, "but in the context of the election results, it was a per-centage that became significant, in fact, crucial, and obliged the Parti Quebecois to take more of a listening stance. I think it might also ex-plain (what started the idea of) the commissions on the future of Quebec. It was to try and build for the PQ some of the momentum that the election results had failed to provide."[7]

The Bloc Quebecois was every bit as disillusioned as the Parti Quebecois. Moreover, they were quite surprised. The election results fell short of their expectations. "Mr. Bouchard was very disillu-sioned," says Pierre-Paul Roy, recalling that the PQ's margin of vic-tory would serve as a gauge for the referendum. The election outcome was all the more disappointing given that there were factors other than the Parti Quebecois' own program which favoured a change of govern-ment. "The Liberal party was seeking a third term and Daniel Johnson was not particularly charismatic. This was on the heels of the Bloc's victory, and a post-Meech atmosphere still hung in the air, hinting that Quebecers might be presented with a major choice."[8] Bob Dufour was the electoral campaign manager for the Bloc Quebecois in 1993 and continued working for them in the years that followed. He identified another event, which he believes did not help: "The end of the campaign had been a little erratic," he recalls. "On the Friday, (three days prior to the election), Mr. Parizeau was congratulating everyone; he was practically saying that it was over, that they had won. This kind of triumphalism does not help you in an electoral campaign. You are triumphalist the night you get the results—and, even then, you still wait until 11 o'clock to be sure you've got the real figures. You never say things like that before (the end of) the election campaign. On the contrary, you get people fired up... No, with the results they obtained, they could not hope, in the short space of time of eight or ten months or a year, to be in a position to hold a referendum and be sure of winning it."[9]

While the PQ's exaggerated optimism and lack of openness towards moderate nationalists, refugees from the ADQ, may have made for a bumpy campaign, the Liberal campaign was not totally smooth either. Their leader lacked charisma. They had to defend their two terms of office, which had certainly not been crisis-free. They also had to deal with the moods of Liberal big brother in Ottawa. The Canadian government under Jean Chrétien followed with keen interest what was going on in Quebec. "Our role was not to do anything in a positive sense but it was to avoid making mistakes that could be used against the federalist forces, against Mr. Johnson," recalls Eddy Goldenberg. "There were weekly meetings for months before the election between myself and Jean Pelletier and John Parisella and Pierre Anctil in Mr. Johnson's office. To keep each other informed of our plans..."

On election night, Daniel Johnson learned of the results in his office, surrounded by some ten people: friends, family members, Pierre Anctil, his chief of staff, and his advisor John Parisella. He was bitter. "Despite his defeat, it was very important," says Parisella, "that

Mr. Johnson conduct himself like a future premier, not a defeated premier. We told him that this was the beginning of the next campaign. First there would be a referendum campaign, and then, eventually, there would be another election campaign. It would be a mistake to think that Mr. Parizeau would hesitate…"[10] But Johnson's immediate concern was to analyze the reasons for his defeat. He was not unaware that he could have done better if the federal Liberals had supported him. "As soon as Mr. Chrétien was elected, we expressed our objective of exercising more control over workforce training and other areas of that nature," says Daniel Johnson. "What I soon understood (insofar as it is possible to intimate anything from the actions of others) was that the Liberal Party of Canada was steadily developing over time the habit of trying to prove to Quebecers—while the Parti Quebecois was in power—that the federal government had something to offer, that it could deliver the goods. This was meant to counter the discourse on sovereignty… You would almost say the federal government felt more comfortable dealing with Quebec when the federalists were not in power. I was not catching on to the strategy of Mr. Chrétien's government: they were refusing to take action on workforce training, perhaps waiting to see if the PQ might get into power, and actively hurting us by closing the military college in Saint-Jean, which had been there for 40 years. It was inexplicable."[11]

The closing of the Saint-Jean military college, which fuelled the electoral debate, fell under the budget restrictions announced by Paul Martin in his 1994 budget. Martin was committed to reducing expenditures by more than four billion dollars over five years. In May, the federal Minister of Intergovernmental Affairs, Marcel Massé, announced that an agreement had been reached between Ottawa and Quebec to have the college converted to a French-language learning centre for the military and for federal civil servants. This news was immediately denied by Daniel Johnson. "I think it's somewhat premature; it takes two to negotiate," was his reply to Massé's remarks. In fact, the negotiations lasted all summer and continued with the PQ government for part of the fall, until Jean Chrétien closed the file in December, with a federal proposal to strip the college of its military designation and convert it to a post-secondary institution. Needless to say, the Bloc Québécois scored a few points in the House of Commons over what Lucien Bouchard called "this iniquitous decision." "The military college was founded in 1952 to put an end to the scandal of an army that was hostile to the French fact," he proclaimed. "The military school in Kingston, which will now become officially bilingual, was one of the bastions of that hostile attitude. We are now back to square one and the francophones in the army will have to live as anglophones."[12] The saga of the military college lasted a year and Daniel Johnson has no doubt as to its impact: "Was it a case of gross negligence (on the part of the federal government) or was it part of a grand master plan? Whichever way you describe it, it didn't help us!"[13]

In a book published one year after his defeat as premier of Ontario, Bob Rae maintained that Jean Chrétien was ambivalent with respect to Daniel Johnson's re-election. "I saw Jean Chrétien for another long meeting in the summer of 1994," he wrote. "He was preoccupied with Quebec, but was curiously ambivalent about Johnson's election. 'From one point of view,' (he said,) it would be better to deal with an unpopular Parizeau now than a popular Bouchard later on. We can beat Parizeau in a referendum. But of course, I want Johnson to win.'"[14] Looking back today on this passage in his book, Rae is somewhat amused as he tries to explain it: "Well, if I wrote it down, it would have been something that he said. There's a side of Mr. Chrétien that says: If there's going to be a fight, let's have a fight. I certainly think he believed very strongly that he could beat Mr. Parizeau and that Mr. Bouchard was a much more clever, ambiguous kind of person, who had an ability to appeal to a whole sort of middle ground of Quebecers. In that sense, it's better to face it with a guy like Parizeau than to face it with Bouchard." Daniel Johnson states it less categorically, but he does wonder about Bob Rae's hypothesis: "I would not be surprised, in the sense that the federal government at that time may have wanted to do battle with the sovereigntists, wanted the fight, wanted the referendum to take place, so they could close the matter once and for all," he says. He remembers one or two meetings with Chrétien where he expressed his dissatisfaction concerning the federal budget: "It had clearly embarrassed us, certain decisions were not appropriate. But it didn't change a thing! We were asking the Liberal Party of Canada, the federal government, not to hurt our cause, not to take actions that were harmful to the federalist cause. We asked, but they didn't listen."[15]

For Jacques Parizeau, the task of forming the Cabinet—which would total only 19 members—became a delicate operation. The key post to be filled was in the Department of Finance. Quebec's public finances were in bad shape and the federal government had already announced that transfers to the provinces would be severely cut back. "No one knows the financial milieu like Jean Campeau," Jacques Parizeau says today. "No one has the same experience in international loans. For a province wanting to become an independent country, he is an indispensable man, indisputably."[16] Campeau had served under Parizeau as deputy minister; he had managed the government's loans and presided over the fortunes of the *Caisse de dépôt et placement*. These responsibilities had allowed him to create a considerable network of contacts throughout the world. Parizeau did not yet know the amount of Quebec's deficit when he was forming his cabinet, but he did know it would be high, so he sought out "the best borrower Quebec ever had."

Establishing the first link in the chain did not mean the others would fall into place automatically. The choice of Campeau deeply disappointed Bernard Landry, who had coveted Finance more than any other portfolio. Having turned down Education, he would have to be content with International Affairs, Cultural Communities and Immigration, and, as a consolation prize, the post of deputy premier.

There was another problem facing the new premier, also of a financial nature. All the collective agreements of the provincial public service unions would expire in 1995 and it was absolutely crucial that their renewal, during a referendum year, be carried out without too much damage to either the public or the employees. "Madame Marois would be on the Treasury Board specifically to see to that," says Parizeau. "And she was a superb negotiator: the new agreements were not very costly and remained firmly in place for three years without a single day's strike."[17] Industry and Commerce went not to

Richard Le Hir, who had been eyeing it, but to one of Parizeau's old right hands in the riding of Crémazie and the new member for Prévost, Daniel Paillé. This move would elicit from Landry the comment that "Parizeau the premier appointed himself minister of Finance, chair of the Treasury Board and minister of Industry and Commerce. He wanted to have his own people and be the only economic decision-maker, so he could control everything."[18]

The delicate task of forming the cabinet was also distressing for Parizeau. He wanted to bring in young blood, but that meant he had to sacrifice some of the earliest collaborators and finest members. "My youngest minister, Daniel Paillé, was 44. It was becoming the oldest cabinet in Quebec's history and people were beginning to notice," he says. "The two psychiatrists, (Denis) Lazure and (Camille) Laurin, were over 70. It was getting difficult. Maybe I was wrong. I know I hurt (Laurin). It was a dreadful thing to do. He was such a close friend…"[19] After resisting for a few hours, Laurin agreed to be just the regional delegate for Montreal, and Lazure, simply a member of the National Assembly.

Parizeau appointed 14 of these regional delegates, one for each administrative region of Quebec. Their role consisted of representing their region on a Board of regional delegates, chaired by the premier himself. While, in certain cases, such an appointment might seem to be a consolation prize, most of the delegates were actually keen to assume this role, one which Parizeau considered important: to allow the government to gain a better understanding of the dynamics and problems of the regions. Furthermore, as the delegates were firmly rooted in their respective territories, "their primary role would be to act as a mainspring in the forthcoming referendum campaign."

On September 26, Parizeau unveiled his Cabinet, one that "had the look and feel of Quebec"; he entrusted to each minister specific objectives and mandates of governance. He set forth, at the same time, the principles on which this governance was founded. They would act and govern with the tools they had now, "even while waiting to acquire them all," and, with the help of the regional delegates, they would clearly identify the diverse needs and projects relevant to the different regions of Quebec. He was already looking ahead to the referendum—which could not be put off too long—and to the new sources of support he would need to win it. "Sovereignty, like freedom," he said on this occasion, "will not let itself be imprisoned by a single party or a single concept. It will flow out beyond partisan boundaries."

With that vision in mind, he appointed a journalist whose career had included, among other places, Washington and Paris, and who had witnessed first-hand the campaign for the referendum on the Charlottetown Accord. Jean-François Lisée recalls, "In (Parizeau's) office, I said to him, 'Be prepared to hear from me every day that you have to broaden your coalition, that you cannot win this alone?' Then, Mr. Parizeau looked at me and said, 'Mr. Lisée, you are going to realize that I am not in the habit of surrounding myself with idiots!'"[20]

His chief of staff, Jean Royer, had known Parizeau for a long time and was in some ways the extension of the Premier's authority. "We understood each other," Parizeau says. "He was the only one who knew exactly what I wanted, where I was going, what I was trying to do. I took for granted that he knew everything that happened in my office. The chief of staff is a kind of advisor of the possible."[21] "As I had known Mr. Parizeau for many years," Royer confirms, "I did not have to go and ask him for instructions every 15 minutes. I could move things forward. Advisor of the possible? I reminded him that Cardinal Richelieu told Louis XIII 'the possible has been done and the impossible will be done!'"[22] Lisée and Royer got on like a house on fire. "Jean-François is incredibly talented at coming up with ideas and most of them are good ideas," Royer says.[23] Lisée, for his part, realized that his ideas received more attention from the premier when they were endorsed by Royer: "Jean Royer's support of several of my strategies was fundamental," he says, "because Mr. Parizeau had enormous confidence in him, in Michel Carpentier. (...) Often, we consulted one another, he could see we all agreed and that gave a lot more weight."[24] Michel Carpentier was the strategy and logistics man. He became increasingly important in Parizeau's entourage as the referendum date approached. Finally, he was made assistant to the general secretary of the Executive Council.

More than most ministers, these "Premier's men" would play a major role in preparing for the October referendum alongside Louis Bernard, Parizeau's deputy minister. Bernard was a man with vast experience: With the exception of one or two brief interruptions, he had been part of the government apparatus since the 1960s, in various roles. He had been assistant to lawyer Yves Pratte, Jean Lesage's legal advisor; chief of staff to Camille Laurin, during the time when Bourassa was premier and Laurin was leader of the Opposition; and general secretary of the Executive Council from 1976 to 1985, for the duration of the first Parti Québécois régime. When Parizeau sought him out for the post of deputy premier, it took some persuading: he said he was happy in the private sector. He agreed, however, in Parizeau's words, "to give him a year of his life."

Another important person, more self-effacing, without any specific duties in Parizeau's cabinet but very effective, would accompany him very closely throughout this entire period. Parizeau met him for the first time in rather unusual circumstances, on the night of October 17 to 18, 1970. "The night of Pierre Laporte's death," he likes to recall, "René Lévesque called a meeting of a few people, at two in the morning, at the party's office on Christophe-Colomb Street. I was one of them. I showed up. There was a young man pacing up and down in front of the building. He stopped me and said, 'Good evening, Mr. Parizeau.' I said, 'Good evening. May I go in? Mr. Lévesque asked me to be here.' He replied, 'I don't have your name on the list, so you're not going in.' I said, 'Oh? What do you mean, I can't go in?' He said, 'Listen, I may be a lot younger than you, but I'm a lot stronger too. If you want to fight with me, you can, but you're not going in.' (I said to him,) 'Go in and see Mr. Lévesque and ask if there has been a mistake.' He said, 'OK, but stand back,' which I did. He returned and said, 'Yes, it's a mistake. You may go in.' I asked him his name and he told me 'Serge Guérin.' (I said to him,) 'Good, as of tomorrow morning, you're working for me!'"[25] Serge Guérin was 18 and drawn to politics. He had just dropped out of CEGEP, but would later earn a Bachelor's and then a Master's degree in administration. Of all the premier's colleagues, he was the one who, on a personal level, with the exception of Lisette Lapointe, would be the closest to him, his friend and his confidant.[26]

However, there was one person in Parizeau's entourage whose appointment gave rise to a fair amount of questioning and commentary: Lisette Lapointe, his wife.[27] Mother of two, Lisette Lapointe was an active woman, a former teacher, who had carried out various duties in the party since the 1976 election. "In other countries, you could do that; a prime minister could give his wife some very specific dossiers," Parizeau says. "But here, it had never been done, so that made it impossible. They accepted it with respect to Hillary Clinton (who was responsible for the health insurance dossier in the United States when her husband was president), so I did the same in the case of my wife."[28] Lisette Lapointe had a lot of influence on her husband. She became his advisor. Her office was located in the apartments formerly occupied by Robert Bourassa, right next door to the office of the premier, who mandated her to carry out various political duties. She took part in all the meetings of Parizeau's entourage. "After all, she was an employee of the cabinet," he says. "There was no reason for her not sit on a whole series of strategy committees within the cabinet."[29]

Nevertheless, Lisette Lapointe's presence at his side did manage to create a certain "uproar," as the former premier put it. Integrating her into the Parizeau team was extremely difficult and her relations with certain ministers were not always pleasant, far from it. "At meetings," she says, "they sometimes say things that are not really very kind about the boss. But when his wife is there, they might be afraid that in the evening, some of their remarks might slip out. It takes a while before trust is established."[30] Parizeau did not deny it. "As she is my wife, I was not going to deny that in the evening, when we had dinner together, we certainly talked about these matters. She gave me advice, which I appreciated very much. After all, I was not, in order to appease jealous parties, going to divorce my wife on the grounds that I was the premier." In order to silence the critics, Lisette Lapointe received no remuneration whatsoever. Parizeau divided his salary in half. "Every two weeks, I received my cheque. I would keep one, and the next one, I would sign over to my wife's name," he says.[31]

Lisette Lapointe had a double role to play. As the Premier's wife, she was called upon to represent him from time to time. As an advisor, she managed numerous dossiers that had been merged under the catch-all label "community action" as part of Parizeau's initiative to prune the bureaucracy, to humanize it, and generally to make things easier for volunteer organizations. The largest of these files was, without a doubt, the *Réseau des Carrefours jeunesse-emploi* (youth employment forums network), a program through which the government granted financial assistance for a project, wherever the local business community, the municipality, the school board, the *caisse populaire* (credit union) or the parish, had contributed to its establishment.[32]

When Jacques Parizeau came to power, he did not see Quebec City as a real capital. During the 1994 election campaign, he had discussed with mayor Jean-Paul L'Allier and the city's business people the possibility of creating a National Capital Commission. Saturday mornings, they visited various neighbourhoods to determine what financial or other contribution the government could make to certain major renovation projects when the PQ would take over. To Parizeau, it was important that official meetings take place in Quebec City and that major decisions be made in the capital. He therefore felt it was essential that the premier live there. This inspired the idea of an official residence, which materialized after the election, in November 1994. In popular parlance, it came to be called the "Élysette": Lisette Lapointe became its hostess, its "first lady."[33] "You know," she says, "it was nothing like an 'Élysée,' not even a small one: there was a laneway at the back with clotheslines! But it was a good place to live, very lovely…" The house had been offered to the premier by the Quebec Chamber of Commerce and, as Parizeau paid the rent, there was no cost to the taxpayers. There was a reception every Thursday evening. In the short period during which Parizeau was in office, Lisette Lapointe estimates that some 5,000 guests were received at the official residence: "For many citizens, it was the first time they had been able to spend two hours socializing with their premier," she says.[34]

With his cabinet and his staff firmly established, Parizeau's next step was to ensure that all heads of large public institutions, especially the head of the *Caisse de dépôt et placement*, were sovereigntists. Established in 1965 to administer the funds of Quebec's pension plans, insurance plans and public institutions, the *Caisse's* total assets, as of December 31, 1994, came to 45.9 billion dollars. "The mission of the *Caisse* is to be profitable," Jean Campeau says, "to make money for the citizens of Quebec and to support Quebec's economy. Consequently, the president of the *Caisse*, in the case of a sovereign Quebec, would have paid attention to Quebec's portfolio of government bonds, its portfolios of stocks and bonds. So, did it help to have a sovereigntist? Maybe, but first of all, the individual had to be competent."[35] The *Caisse* had a bond portfolio of 24 billion dollars and held 14 billion in shares in Canadian and Quebec corporations. The *Caisse* was Canada's largest shareholder. The government amended the *Loi de la Caisse* such that one and the same person would be chairman of the board and chief executive officer, and on April 1, 1995, Jean-Claude Scraire, who had been recruited to the *Caisse* by Campeau 14 years earlier, became its chairman and CEO.

Jacques Parizeau had great plans for Hydro-Québec. He envisioned it would play an important role, not just in the energy sector, but also in the cable distribution and telephone communication industries. "Hydro-Québec is the admiral ship of crown corporations," he says. "Its financial statements are almost as important as those of the Quebec government. In that respect, it's better to have someone whose fundamental outlook is the same as the government."[36] By the end of March 1995, 10 of the 17 positions on Hydro-Québec's board of directors were filled, mostly by individuals close to the Parti Québécois, and Yvon Martineau, Parizeau's legal advisor, assumed the presidency. A month and a half later, Richard Drouin, appointed by the former government, relinquished his duties as president and CEO.

As new posts opened up in other public institutions, Parizeau ensured the appointment of officers whose general vision was in tune with that of the government. This applied especially to the police, who, in an independent Quebec, would have to absorb some Royal Canadian Mounted Police members and create new divisions for investigation and border control.

At that time, the premier was already considering creating an army. "Quebec would not be totally without an army," he says. "Even if it was limited to a minimum, even if this army was for ensuring peace-keeping missions, even if it was only in order to have a number of people who would not strike when everyone else was on strike, a minimum was necessary." Parizeau obviously realized that some of the equipment for this army already existed, in the Canadian Armed Forces, but that it would need to be adapted. "Our share of the 12 Canadian frigates was three," he says. "What were we supposed to do with three frigates? When you see the kind of port facilities you need for three frigates, it would be better to sell them and buy small Swedish patrol boats... All we need is a coast guard!" But Parizeau did want to keep the Bagotville airport operational: "The Americans would never tolerate leaving a huge geographic territory like Quebec unpatrolled. If we didn't patrol it ourselves, they would do it for us, that's clear." In the premier's thinking, there was no doubt that when it came time to share assets with the Canadian government, a certain number of airplanes should remain in Quebec. "It is an accounting transaction, first and foremost," he says.[37]

Parizeau was not wrong with respect to American interest: they were following very closely what was going on in Quebec. The morning after the election, the U.S. Consul in Quebec, Marie T. Huhtala, reported to the secretary of state in Washington, to the embassy in Ottawa and to the other U.S. consuls in Canada: "The Parti Québécois will form the next government in Quebec, but its majority is less impressive than expected," the report reads, "(...) four-tenths of a percent separating the two major parties. (...) The Equality Party, which ran 17 candidates, failed to take a single riding and will probably disappear. (...) In his victory speech, Jacques Parizeau began with a conciliatory tone (...) but he quickly moved on to the upcoming struggle; recalling his hockey metaphor, he told voters that the 'second period' is over and it is time to move on to the 'third period,' the sovereignty referendum."[38] From that day onward, the U.S. government's interest in the unfolding of events in Quebec would grow, and develop into increasingly clear support for the NO forces.

In Ottawa, the federal cabinet did not perceive the election of a sovereigntist government as just another provincial election. In the words of Brian Tobin: "We recognized that Mr. Parizeau, given his grudges, would put the country through yet another gut-wrenching trial of its future. We were very mindful of the probability of a referendum campaign. And much was being done. You saw a lot more flags, you saw a lot more signage of federal government programs and expenditures; the so-called sponsorship program... That was all about enhancing the federal government presence in the province of Quebec."[39] The Canadian Unity Council, already active in a certain number of programs aimed at helping the cause of Canadian unity, quickened its pace with the Option Canada program.[40] In conjunction with other organizations committed to the same objectives, such as the *Conseil Québec*, the Coalition of Partners and Impact 95, the Council became a kind of forum for drawing together various militant groups motivated by the desire to block Jacques Parizeau's plans. The Council gathered around one table representatives from different fields, all fighting for federalism: business people, former politicians, members of political parties. The leader of the Conservative party, Jean Charest, asked Senator Pierre-Claude Nolin to represent him personally on the Council: "Starting in the late fall of 1994," Nolin recalls, "Mr. Parizeau spoke publicly of the famous regional tours. It was at that point that the Canadian Unity Council called its first meeting. We began to work together. The objective was to follow these regional meetings, which were, in fact, meetings staged by the pro-independence forces."[41] The Canadian Unity Council would be very present during the entire pre-referendum campaign, still issuing news briefs on October 1, 1995. As they were not part of the committee for the NO side, they would be very discreet during the official referendum campaign.

The Reform Party did not want to be outdone and asked to be part of the Canadian Unity Council. "We explained to them that this was an issue for Quebecers," Nolin says, "and that if they really wanted us to succeed in our objective, it would be better for everyone that they not get involved."[42] The federal government would spend

35 million dollars in the months leading up to the referendum, increasing the number of advertising billboards and media messages. A month before the referendum, Quebec's Chief Electoral Officer, Pierre F. Côté, would admit he was powerless to enforce Quebec's Referendum Act, since other governments are not subject to it.[43]

There was no longer any doubt a referendum would take place, but when? Support for sovereignty had dropped dramatically to the 40% level. At one cabinet meeting, as early as October 26, 1994, certain members expressed their fear that consulting the people prematurely would lead to failure. There was so much uncertainty in the government and in Parizeau's entourage that they decided to launch an appeal to mobilize the PQ supporters, and especially to revive the large coalition that had managed to bring down the Charlottetown Accord in the 1992 referendum.

The first opportunity presented itself when the Parti Québécois held a national council meeting on November 5. Jean-François Lisée tells us that Parizeau understood the importance of recreating the coalition but was still reticent deep down. A speech had been prepared for Parizeau by his close associates to be delivered at the national council meeting. It contained a sentence that stated, in essence, that there were former federalists in the room, Jacques Parizeau being the first, and that the last to enter must leave the door open to all who wished to enter. Lisée recalls today the doubt that assailed Parizeau at that moment: "Everyone had been in agreement, but at the last minute, Mr. Parizeau hesitated: 'I'm going to do this *ad lib* after all,' (he said). I saw Jean Royer, Marie-José Gagnon and Eric Bédard: they were shattered. They succeeded, especially Royer, in convincing the premier to carry on with the text as planned."[44] In his speech to the 350 delegates gathered at the meeting, Parizeau dealt first with the pessimistic attitude of the militants concerning a successful referendum, and then added, "Pessimism is not our only enemy. We have others: radicalism, cliquishness and partisanship. Many people think that when sovereignty is achieved, we will enter a kind of cloister, adhere to certain dogmas and practise familiar rites. But it is the opposite. Sovereignty will mean opening the door. We will be on the threshold of a whole range of possibilities for the future."[45]. Lisée recalls that the speech was very well received by the national council: "It brought the house down. This was the first time Mr. Parizeau had tested the idea of inclusion, and he came away reassured he could count on his party's support."[46] It seemed the premier was espousing the "open door" principle. Three weeks later, during the inaugural speech for the next session of parliament, he extended his hand to the leader of the Opposition and said, "I do not expect to convince him, personally, to join me in seeking to build a sovereign Quebec. But, through my offer to him, I invite every federalist or undecided Quebecer to do so," he suggested. Needless to say, Daniel Johnson did not shake his hand.

To those who reproached him for giving too much importance to his independence project and not enough to administering the province, Parizeau replied: "We have learned how to walk and chew gum at the same time." And he intended to prove this by taking measures to "shake things up," as he put it. Stabilizing Quebec's public finances and reducing the deficit were at the top of his list. He estimated the deficit to be "around six billion" when he took office. "As soon as the ministers were sworn in," Jean Campeau recalls, "he gave to the president of the Treasury Board, Pauline Marois, and myself, as minister of Finance, the task of reducing the deficit to zero, of bringing some order to the revenues and expenditures."[47] Parizeau wanted to ensure his government could not be accused of mismanagement. "A six-billion dollar deficit was very dangerous," he says. "If we wanted to hold the referendum and we were constantly threatened by credit ratings or by mini-crises on the financial markets, six billion was too high." To achieve this, the government would limit expenditures by implementing a new technique for administering departmental budgets. Each deputy minister received a limited budget, which maintained expenses at the same level as the preceding year. It was then up to the deputy minister to manage the funds as he or she saw fit, subject to the approval of the minister. "The deficit dropped from six to four billion the year of the referendum," Parizeau says, with a hint of pride, both at having reduced the deficit and at having given back to the deputy ministers, who are managers, a sense of initiative and involvement.[48]

Parizeau's objective was to reassure everyone in the high finance world. Prior to the elections, to the extent that the polls predicted a PQ victory, investors gradually modified their portfolios. Foreign investors were selling more of their Canadian stocks than usual, and more investors were buying bonds than securities in U.S. dollars. Some analysts attributed these trends to the lowering of short-term interest rates in Canada, but others interpreted them as an indication of a nervous market. In fact, investors were split as to what attitude to adopt. A few days before the election, Bernard Landry met with analysts from the large holding company Solomon Brothers, to reassure them with respect to the Parti Québécois' economic policy. At the time, one of the company's analysts, Peter Plaut, considered the policy "financially conservative." The narrow victory of the PQ would do the rest: Solomon Brothers predicted that Canadian and Quebec bonds would outperform U.S. bonds.[49] Investors scaled back their apprehensions and optimism returned to the financial markets. The day after the election, the Canadian dollar rose by 1.05 to 74.15 cents U.S., and the banks lowered their prime rate.

However, the euphoria was short-lived: rates climbed back up as early as December and the dollar, after a series of consecutive dives, despite intervention by the Bank of Canada on the foreign exchange market, hit 72.35 cents U.S., its lowest level since mid-August, closing the 1994 year at 71.05 cents U.S., a low not seen in eight years. Analysts did not agree on how to interpret these fluctuations. "Nothing to do with Jacques Parizeau's sovereignty project," said Royal Bank economist Benoît Durocher.[50] "The political situation in Quebec has come to the fore and is simply an addition to the fact that interest rates in the U.S. are rising," was the response from Marc Desmeules, chief foreign exchange broker for Toronto-Dominion Bank.[51]

Whatever the case, on November 15, Jacques Parizeau began his campaign of persuasion. Before the members of the Metropolitan Montreal Chamber of Commerce, whose founders included his great-grandfather Damase, he announced that the referendum campaign was under way and that the time had come to stop stalling. The applause was polite but sustained. A week later, he took his message to Toronto, where he spoke to guests at the Canadian Club. His message was broadcast all across English-speaking Canada by the Newsworld network.

Before arriving at the Club, he paid a visit to the premier of Ontario. Bob Rae's entourage maintained that they had not issued an invitation, but that "Mr. Parizeau had invited himself." The meeting lasted 45 minutes. "It was a very blunt meeting. Before the meeting, I'd spoken to Mr. Chrétien and also to Mr. Trudeau, because I wanted to get their advice (...). I told them what I was going to say to him, and they said: that's fine with us. It was a very unfriendly meeting. There was nothing protocol about it." Rae recalls that whenever he met with Johnson, Bourassa, Chrétien or Trudeau, they would use the two languages interchangeably. This time, it was different. "When Mr. Parizeau came in, I started speaking to him in French," says Rae. "He stopped the conversation and he said, as only he can say, 'My dear boy, I think we'd be much more comfortable if we both spoke in English.' And he said this in this very English-English accent. I was quite taken aback. I made it clear to him that I thought the referendum should be held as soon as possible but the government of Ontario is not bound by a referendum in Quebec. He just said, 'Well, I'll have the referendum when the government of Quebec thinks it's the appropriate time. And we'll have it with the appropriate question.' Normally, when you go outside after one of these one-on-one meetings, you both stand before the cameras and the flags are behind you, you do your Mutt-and-Jeff Show, he says something, you laugh and you smile, and you pat each other on the back, and then go off. He said, 'We'll both go outside and meet the media.' I said, 'No. I'm not meeting the media with you. I'm not going to be part of your show, of a game at all.' He was quite taken aback."

The premier of Ontario declined to accompany his Quebec counterpart to the Canadian Club. However, this did not prevent Parizeau from launching an appeal to his listeners at the Club for mutual respect, whatever should happen. "If Ontario politicians want to come (and) make the case for (Canadian) unity in Quebec in the next campaign, if Mr. Preston Manning, Mr. Rae and Mr. Harris want to come, we will be friendly and polite."[52] But that was not the essence of his remarks. He presented a picture of Quebec society as being traditionally tolerant and open toward its minorities, anglophones and native peoples in particular. He emphasized that Quebec intended to keep the Canadian dollar: "Quebecers have 110 billion of them." He said Quebec would assume its share of the national debt: "Quebecers have a share of responsibility for that debt."

Two months later, Parizeau travelled to Paris—as he often did. Immediately upon being elected leader of the Parti Québécois in 1988, he had gone there to meet Michel Rocard, prime minister of France at the time. He had predicted two things to him: The Meech Lake Accord would fail and the PQ would not take more than 40 percent of the vote in the next provincial election, in September 1989. He was right, on both counts. According to Parizeau, since the time of the failed referendum of 1980, the French had not taken the sovereigntists very seriously. However, once his predictions proved to be correct, he began to gain credibility with them. Parizeau returned to France every year thereafter. Each time, he was welcomed by President Mitterand who, while he was a great friend of Trudeau's and an opponent of any form of separatism, saw in Parizeau a kind of insurance policy, should Quebec ever became independent. Thus, Parizeau was very well received in Paris when he returned there as premier of Quebec, staying from January 25 to 27, 1995. He met not only with political figures but also with French business owners. He reassured them, particularly the president of the *Patronat* (national employers' association), Jean Gandois, whose company had invested a billion dollars in the Bécancour aluminum plant. In essence, what he told business management was that an independent Quebec would not cut its ties with Canada or the rest of North America. He added that the people of Quebec were in favour of international trade agreements. It was what they wanted to hear.

What made investors nervous, more than the election of a sovereigntist party in Quebec, was the federal deficit. The federal government's debt was 550 billion dollars. The governor of the Bank of

Canada, Gordon Thiessen, could not be any clearer. He said, "If Canada did not have such a large debt, the uncertainty in Quebec would still be a social concern but it would not be financially worrisome for investors. It is only because of the high levels of the debt and the deficit that political uncertainty is another cause for concern. It is almost impossible to separate them."[53] As if to confirm Thiessen's remarks, Parizeau announced on November 2, 1994, that Quebec was heading for a deficit of 5.5 billion. This immediately sent out the signal that Quebec and Hydro-Québec faced the threat of having their credit ratings downgraded by the large credit agencies. At the time, they both had a rating of A+, but their combined debt was 106 billion dollars, one of the largest in the country in relation to the size of the Quebec economy. A month later, Quebec's minister of Finance gave the following update on public finances: the deficit would climb to 5.7 billion dollars, exceeding by 1.3 billion the budget projections of the preceding Liberal government.

Campeau, who was fond of likening Canada to a Titanic from which one should disembark in a hurry before it sank, accompanied Parizeau to New York on December 12. Their purpose was to meet with brokerage houses that sold Quebec bonds on the U.S. and international markets and to convince the credit rating agencies that they should not lower Quebec's rating, given that "the former government's projections were deliberately underestimated." The next day, CBRS[54] placed Quebec's rating under surveillance and, two days later, downgraded it from A+ to A, with negative prospects. On the other hand, another equally important agency, Standard and Poor's, announced that it would not modify Quebec's rating before Campeau's next budget. It deemed that the government was serious about its intent to regain control over public finances and pointed out that "the sovereigntist project (did) not appear to be weakening the PQ government's resolve to reduce its deficit."[55]

The financial community feared that the federal government would opt for too mild a reduction of its deficit. On February 16, Moody's, a major credit rating agency, placed Canada's rating under surveillance. The Canadian dollar dropped to 70.80 cents U.S. and the

Bank of Canada increased its interest rate on day-to-day loans by half a point. Paul Martin was very unhappy with Moody's evaluation, but two weeks later, in his February 27 budget, he promised a deficit reduction and a decrease of 2.8 billion dollars in federal transfers to the provinces, which Quebec would naturally have to take into account.

Parizeau, who had never made a secret of the fact that his approach to politics was essentially economic, was intent above all on demonstrating that Quebec was viable. There were three economic motors that drove the action for him. They were public finance, Canadian currency and free trade. Since the beginning of Confederation, trade had moved along an east-west axis, but this was gradually shifting to a north-south axis, increasingly so with the Free Trade Agreement. Quebec now had more trade relations with the United States than Brazil, Argentina and Chile combined. Parizeau knew very well that an independent Quebec would not automatically be admitted to NAFTA,[56] if only for the simple reason that an agreement among three partners must be modified in order to admit a fourth. But he was convinced that when the moment came to start considering the possibility of expanding free trade to include all three Americas, it would be ridiculous to imagine Quebec being excluded from it. He recalled the conference held in Miami in December 1994, at which the heads of state of 34 countries had gathered to discuss that possibility. "Americans could not imagine for an instant that there would be a Free Trade Area of the Americas (FTAA) stretching from the North Pole to Tierra del Fuego without Quebec or Cuba," he says. "The amount of trade between Quebec and the United States is too significant for Quebec to be excluded from such a project. It wouldn't make any sense, either legally or politically."[57] This conviction also rested on remarks he had heard made by Peter Murphy, the American senior official who had, on behalf of the United States, negotiated the first Free Trade Agreement with Canada. This was during a visit to Washington in November 1991. Parizeau was having a meal in a restaurant of the State Department, in the company of an Under-Secretary. Enter Peter Murphy. Some Quebec reporters who were present headed directly over to him and asked whether an independent

Quebec would remain in the Free Trade Area. "Then Murphy looked at them and said, 'Why not?'" Parizeau recalls. "This took place thirty feet from where I was sitting! The journalists were taken aback. They made big headlines the next day..."[58]

Parizeau knew very well that if the international community had been sympathetic, he would have had an easier time of it. He also knew that among the dossiers that could make other countries view him unfavourably was the one on Aboriginal Peoples. A week after the election of September 12, the grand chief of the Crees, Matthew Coon Come,[59] was in Washington for nothing less than to ask the United States to protect the First Nations people against the possible violence to which they might be subjected in an independent Quebec. In a speech at the Center for Strategic and International Studies, which gathers influential intellectuals, such as State Department civil servants, he declared, "If the Crees want to remain in Canada, we will have to face the police forces and army of a State that is itself acting in defiance of Canadian and international law."[60] "I knew that would really hit hard. I was bracing for reaction from Canada and from Quebec," Matthew Coon Come admits today.

Quebec wasted no time in reacting. After his speech, Coon Come flew to Ottawa. There was a stopover in Philadelphia and the Native leader asked the flight attendant if he could get out to make a phone call. "She says, 'You've only got fifteen minutes.' I made a call to Bill Namagoose, who was executive director of the Grand Council of the Crees," recounts Coon Come. "And I said, 'How are things?' And then he said, 'Did you hear? There's just an announcement made by Parizeau, the cancellation of the Great Whale.' And I asked what were his exact words? I think he said something (like) 'We'll put it on hold, it's on ice now.' On the plane, from Philadelphia to Ottawa, I had to reflect a lot... We did say we want to stop this project and, now, it appears that the government has made a decision. I had to respond to that."

As he got off the plane, Coon Come praised Parizeau's courage but was cautious at the same time. "My father is a hunter, never went to school, lived off the land. He used to tell me, 'Son, when you go out on the land, make sure you know the animals, you know them well, know the land. If you know the land, the layout of the land, and you know the behaviour of the animals, then you'll know how to get them.' And I always thought about that. I realized I have to apply the same thing: I have to think as if I'm after an animal and my survival depends on this. I had to try to think like the animal. And I said: what is he thinking? It's just not the, well, we had enough of this Coon Come in the States. There's always other under layers. Maybe to pull the rug from us, because that was the platform which gave us great publicity."

Parizeau makes no effort to hide his opinion that the Crees were travelling all over the world making life miserable for Quebecers. The financing they got from Ottawa enabled them, "on one and the same weekend," to hold meetings "in Oslo, Paris and Rome." Thus, he abandoned the project, which, in any event, was not a project of the government, but of Hydro-Québec. In 1994, the public corporation faced a noteworthy slowdown in domestic consumption and was not selling a lot of electricity to the Americans. This led Parizeau to conclude that Quebec simply did not need the Great Whale project.[61] But if, this time, he literally pulled the rug out from under their feet, he had not seen the last of Matthew Coon Come and the Crees: he would meet them again standing in the way of his vision in October 1995.

CHAPTER III

Building Support
for Sovereignty

O n December 6, 1994, not three months after forming his government, Jacques Parizeau unveiled his political vision in the
National Assembly of Quebec. It would "resolve, once and for all, the
constitutional problem Quebec (had) been struggling with for generations." The project consisted of a draft bill, which proposed that
"Quebec become, by democratic means, a sovereign country, capable
of creating its own legislation, levying taxes within its borders and
acting on the international level (…)."

The tabling of this document marked the first step on the road to
the referendum. "From the moment Meech Lake collapsed," explains
Parizeau's chief of staff, Jean Royer, "we started developing a strategy,
a 'corridor' which would allow us, based on free trade, a strong economy, and a clear 'no,' from the rest of Canada in response to a mini-
malist position, to come up with a plan that was modern and would
involve everybody."[1] Relying on regional commissions that would
consult the people was the brainchild conceived by Parizeau's strategists so they could avoid having the National Assembly adopt a
solemn declaration on sovereignty. However, it would boil down to the
same thing in the end, a referendum that Parizeau called "a referendum of execution." The draft bill provided for a period of discussion
with Canada "on the interim measures to be taken, in particular, with
respect to the sharing of assets and liabilities," but, for the premier, it
was the referendum on sovereignty that mattered. He was open to

making compromises to the extent that the fundamental question was not altered. The process leading to sovereignty was clearly outlined in the draft bill.

First, commissions would be formed. They would be made up of people from various backgrounds and meet in every region of Quebec, with the aim of collecting as many suggestions as possible that might improve the draft legislation. This information-gathering period of participation by the people would facilitate the writing of the preamble to the Act, which would state "the fundamental values and principal objectives that the Quebec nation wishes to uphold," once sovereignty had been achieved. To this end, the document left blank a page entitled, *Preamble: Declaration of Sovereignty*, the title being followed by the words, "to be completed." The text to be inserted would provide the necessary foundation for drafting the future Constitution of Quebec. The bill would then have to be adopted by the National Assembly. Finally, there would be a referendum. If it confirmed the will of the government, it would be followed by negotiations with the federal government prior to Quebec's accession—irrespective of the outcome of these negotiations—to full sovereignty.

The tabling of the draft bill provoked an immediate negative reaction from the leader of the Opposition: "A sad day indeed for democracy in Quebec," said Daniel Johnson. In the National Assembly, he challenged the legitimacy of the draft bill: "How can the premier think it is legitimate for him, as head of the government, or legitimate for the majority, here, in the National Assembly, to ask people across Quebec, who, until we learn differently, do not, for the most part, share his project or his political gamble, how is he going to ask them to complete, on his behalf, the declaration of sovereignty? It seems to me that when you are a sovereigntist party, it is up to you to draft a declaration of sovereignty."[2] The Liberal party would not participate in the process of consulting the people. Furthermore, the day after the draft bill was tabled, the Liberals tried to prevent the government from mandating the *Commission des institutions de l'Assemblée nationale* to prepare the consultation, and they left the National Assembly when the time came to vote on the draft bill.

Mario Dumont, leader of the *Action démocratique du Québec* (ADQ) and its sole member in the National Assembly, made his position clear right away: no sovereignty without a partnership with the rest of Canada. He needed to be coaxed: "I don't want to be just a fifth wheel on the sovereignty wagon,"[3] he confided to a reporter. This was precisely what the government feared: that the consultations with the people would look like a government-financed PQ wagon, where the dice were loaded and the conclusions pre-determined.

In the federal camp, reaction to the draft bill was initially somewhat confused, and then quickly straightened out. In an interview with *The Globe and Mail,* the president of the Canadian Unity Council, Michel Vennat, indicated his support for all federalists who wanted to participate in the process of consulting with the people. The error was immediately corrected by the federal minister of Intergovernmental Affairs. "We must not participate in this process," Marcel Massé declared. "Why would we join in Mr. Parizeau's game? He is asking questions about an Act that is undemocratic, and it is not the right question."[4] Despite the Bloc Québécois' efforts in the House of Commons to get the government to recognize the legitimacy of the process being followed by Quebec, the Liberal Party of Canada denounced the "antidemocratic shrewdness" of the PQ government and called the process fraudulent. Prime Minister Chrétien, who, in the early seventies, had declared that the federal government would respect the wishes of the people of Quebec and accept separation,[5] now maintained that the draft bill was illegal and that there was no clause in the Canadian Constitution permitting a province to leave Confederation.

No sooner had the draft bill been mailed out to the four million households in Quebec, in mid-December 1994, than the referendum campaign began to show signs of deep confrontation ahead, not only on the question to be posed, but on the interpretation of the results. What is a democratic majority? Jacques Parizeau's position on this was very clear and he took advantage of every opportunity to confirm it. In the days following the tabling of the draft bill, Parizeau went to New York, where he met with journalists from several media, including

The New York Times, Forbes magazine, *Business Week* and the PBS network. During one of the interviews, arranged on PBS[6] by his entourage
and broadcast on the prestigious public affairs program *The McNeil-
Lehrer NewsHour*, he did not dismiss the possibility of a referendum in
the spring, but he did use the opportunity to establish clearly that, following the example of the European countries, where a simple majority was sufficient for membership in the European Union, Quebec
would consider a simple majority of 50 plus one to be sufficient for it
to become independent.

Daniel Johnson reacted instantly: to take this "leap in the dark,"
he said, "this opinion must be massively, significantly and substantially that of a great number of Quebecers."[7] The Liberal party's own
strategy, with respect to the referendum campaign, was still vague and
its leader could feel that time was running out. Therefore, he announced on December 20, that his party planned to provide content
for the NO side, that a committee to study the matter and articulate
this content would be established, and that it would be the subject of
discussions at its national council meeting at the end of January 1995.
The Liberal leader would need to overturn the sustained popularity
being enjoyed by the Parti Québécois. At the end of November, the
PQ would have obtained more than 50% of the vote if there had been
an election then. Johnson would also have to reverse the growing popularity of the ADQ. Support for the *Action démocratique* was approaching the same level as support for the Liberal party and was on a
par with it by the end of January 1995.

Ever since its election in September, there were ongoing discussions within the Parti Québécois about the date of the referendum and
the question that would be put to the people. But Parizeau was unable
to achieve unanimity. In mid-November, he said, "When the Société
Saint-Jean-Baptiste prizes are given out, next year, we shall already
have decided to become a country." Bob Dufour, campaign manager
for the Bloc Québécois in 1993, reacted to this by commenting that
"he had just about set it to be June 25; all that was missing was the
hour (…). You know, the 25th at noon! A direct strategy like that is not
always the best." Parizeau's precipitous approach did not sit at all well

with Lucien Bouchard, who did not want, at any price, to venture into a referendum without some assurance of winning. "That was his great fear," says Dufour. "Rushing headlong into a challenge like that before matters (particularly, the deficit Quebec faced) had been analysed from all angles was very dangerous. Mr. Bouchard is someone who takes the time to consider things calmly and quietly. Mr. Parizeau would say that when you have a program, you have to carry it out and, if you see that you're about to slam into a wall, then you remove the wall!"[8]

The sovereigntists were being torn apart by a major split over the referendum date. According to his advisor, Jean-François Lisée, "Mr. Parizeau said, 'It is certain that Quebecers would rather not have to settle this painful question. If you do not give them a deadline, they will not make their decision. We will not be able to mobilize without a deadline.' Mr. Parizeau did not want to say publicly: we won't go ahead if we can't be sure of winning, because that would run counter to mobilizing the people. (But) Mr. Bouchard and others, like Mr. Landry, wanted to get him to say it. There was a 'dance' between Mr. Bouchard and Mr. Parizeau for several months, which put us somewhat at odds with the people from the Bloc."[9] The fear of choosing a referendum date hastily, with no certainty as to the outcome, would haunt Lucien Bouchard all winter long. In February, in an interview with Michel Vastel, he stated, "I do not want to see sovereignty defeated yet again. Because if they say NO, we will be done for."[10]

The Bloc was not the only source of resistance. Parizeau had established a time frame for holding the referendum long ago and he had reaffirmed it during the months leading up to the September election: eight to ten months after the Parti Québécois took office. "We were to do everything possible so that the premier would be able to call a referendum during the first year of his mandate," says Jean Royer. "We didn't know right down to the week, but we knew it would have to be held in 1995. We structured the government in such a way that it would function, that it would operate, with the awareness that it had a deadline to meet." Some of his ministers, Jean Garon in particular, wished "they would hold the referendum right away and move on to other things," but other ministers, important ones at that (Bernard Landry, Jacques Brassard and Louise Beaudoin), urged their leader to be cautious. The atmosphere in the Cabinet and in the party as a whole was tense. Royer does not deny it: "There were people who said to us, 'Do we have what it takes to hold a referendum and win it?' It was normal. People had doubts: should we head into it now, postpone it, wait?"[11]

The vacillation around the referendum date would go on all winter and spring, and for a good part of the summer. The pressures on Parizeau regarding the choice of a date were as insistent as they were discordant. Lisette Lapointe says that Royer himself doubted briefly whether the premier really wanted to hold the referendum in the fall of 1995. "In a brief conversation, a few weeks before the referendum campaign was launched," she recalls, "Jean said to me, 'Do you think he could still decide not to do it now?' Well, more or less those words... The sentence took me completely by surprise. I thought for a moment he was trying to be funny, but that didn't seem to be the case. Probably, among those he had consulted, there were some who were too fearful of losing."[12]

"In the spring, it was tempting," says Jacques Parizeau, "but I did not feel we were ready. We were not doing spectacularly well in the polls and, very importantly, we needed not to rush the commissions on the future of Quebec. There are limits to hurrying! We had to give them time to present their conclusions, to absorb them, and to treat the process with the attention it deserved."[13] With spring ruled out, it was narrowed down to the fall, "but the last thing we wanted to do was give the impression we were just ignoring the spring," says Royer, "in a way that would allow those who had timetables to follow, to say to themselves: we have an extra season to work with. No, the pressure never let up, but I personally always had the impression it would be the fall."[14] After the summer, however, the window was narrowing: there were just two months left. Beyond November 1, there was too much chance that a good part of Quebec, Abitibi, Saguenay, the Côte-Nord, and even the Gaspé Peninsula, would be snowed in.

It was just the actual date of the referendum that people were waiting for now. And the question. Everyone knew that the question

Parizeau would like to present would be as simple and direct as: Do you want Quebec to become sovereign as of such and such a date? But, as he had partners to deal with, he prevaricated, which led to suggestions pouring in from all sides. The party's younger members were getting impatient. On January 12, 1995, in an open letter to *La Presse*, their president, Éric Bédard, proposed a question that would present an alternative: "Do you want the government to declare the sovereignty of Quebec, in accordance with the Act declaring Sovereignty, or to declare its membership in the Federation of Canada in accordance with the Constitution Act of 1982?" This question went against what Jean-François Lisée had in mind. For him, a simplistic alternative, a clear choice between two options, was to be avoided: "Political life in Quebec has been flooded with surveys for 40 years," he says, "and we know there is no majority for independence in Quebec and no majority for the current federalism. Only two majorities are possible: renewed federalism or the sovereignty of Quebec with an association, in one form or another, with the rest of Canada. To try to reduce Quebecers to either the current federalism or secession without any desire for an agreement (with the rest of Canada) is to reject their political reality and their political will."[15]

Those drafting the referendum question had another reality to think about: Lucien Bouchard's reaction. He didn't want to hear anything about a question with a choice. He didn't like the one presented in the draft bill tabled before the National Assembly, which read as follows: "Are you in favour of the Act adopted by the National Assembly declaring the sovereignty of Quebec? YES or NO?" If the question were simply to present a choice between two options, secession or federalism, Bouchard might withdraw from the referendum campaign. "That's part of the political game," Parizeau comments. He does not deny that there were serious confrontations. "When you want to bring people round to your position, you threaten, from time to time, to pull out. I had done that enough times myself, during my 30 years in politics, that I couldn't very well reproach others for doing it. The closer you get to a deadline, the more determined you are to see a thing succeed. In that sense, there are times when you will use a threat to get what you want. Politics is not for the faint-hearted."[16] As had been the case with the referendum date, disagreements around the referendum question would continue right up until it was finally made public, at the beginning of September 1995.

The date and the question were of vital importance, but certain ministers were plagued by concerns of another nature, as they faced what promised to be a merciless campaign. The important thing, according to Jean-Pierre Carbonneau, was to tell people the truth: "Let's talk about the consequences they fear, like the loss of their old-age pensions and everything else," he said to Le Devoir journalist Pierre O'Neill. "Because there is still a lot of fear out there. You need to recognize the legitimacy of those anxieties and help Quebecers overcome them."[17] As pragmatic as ever, Guy Chevrette resolved matters by saying, "Let us stop this speculation on our chances of winning in ten months. We have a timetable. Let's get to work!"[18]

Barely two months after forming his cabinet, Parizeau faced a situation potentially affecting his government's credibility and requiring him to do a ministerial shuffle. Marie Malavoy,[19] minister of Culture and Communications, was forced to resign for having voted in an election while not a Canadian citizen. To replace her, he appointed Rita Dionne-Marsolais, who was already in the cabinet as minister of Tourism as well as minister responsible for the Régie des installations olympiques (Olympic facilities board). Bad luck would catch up with Parizeau again when he was in France in January and was told that his new minister had appointed, as head of Télé-Québec, someone who was in conflict with the law. Typically, although he had chosen not to assume any portfolio when he was forming his Cabinet, so he could dedicate more time to dossiers of special interest to him, like Aboriginal issues and the "information highway," Parizeau now decided to appoint himself minister of Culture and "borrow" Roland Arpin, of the Musée de la civilisation in Quebec City, "for six months" to be his deputy minister. Today he likes to recall how together they shook up the department and brought to a successful conclusion projects that had dragged on for over a year.

On Thursday, December 1, 1994, the U.S. ambassador to Canada, James Blanchard, an adamant opponent of Quebec separation, visited Jacques Parizeau. "I met with Parizeau that very day. And I said, 'How is Lucien doing? We were supposed to have dinner last week and they called and said he had the flu.' And Parizeau said, 'Oh, I think he's doing fine.' And as I left, people came running down the hall and said to me, 'We have not yet told Mr. Parizeau.'" The premier was still unaware at that moment that Lucien Bouchard, the man on whom the referendum's success might well depend, who had been hospitalized two days earlier for what was believed to be simply phlebitis, was now desperately fighting for his life.

The weekend prior, members of the Bloc and party leaders had gathered at Mont Sainte-Anne east of Quebec city to hold a general council meeting and, at the same time, mark the first anniversary of their arrival in the House of Commons. The atmosphere was one of celebration. Lucien Bouchard had spent the Saturday evening in a hall with his MPs and had danced—not typical of his leisure pursuits—with Suzanne Tremblay, the member for Rimouski-Témiscouata. "On Sunday, when he got into the limousine, he was experiencing pain in one leg," recalls Pierre-Paul Roy, his chief of staff. "On Monday, we didn't see him. Then, Gaston Clermont, who sort of looked after him and chauffeured him around, told us he was in hospital with phlebitis."[20] In fact, it was on Sunday night, on returning from Mont Sainte-Anne, that Bouchard had gone to Saint-Luc Hospital in Montreal, where doctors diagnosed him with phlebitis. After giving him the appropriate care and advice for the circumstances, the doctors suggested he return home and rest.

But the symptoms persisted and, during the night from Tuesday to Wednesday, the leader of the Bloc returned to hospital. More thorough tests then showed that he was suffering from the illness caused by flesh-eating bacteria, necrotizing fasciitis,[21] which left doctors very little time to react, as it can cause death in less than 24 hours. "Madame Bouchard had kept this private," says Pierre-Paul Roy. "She did not want it made public at that time. To my knowledge, it was not until Wednesday that we learned of it."[22] Lucien Bouchard's doctors made the decision, that same day, to amputate his left leg, hoping the operation would halt the spread of this terrible illness. The surgery was done during the night.

On Thursday morning, the Premier's Office in Quebec was still unaware of the seriousness of the Bloc leader's illness. After the U.S. ambassador's visit, Parizeau met with some of his assistants, including Serge Guérin, to prepare for a meeting to be held a few hours later with Noranda representatives. Suddenly Jean Royer came in, right in the middle of the meeting, announcing that Bouchard was in danger of losing his life. Jacques Parizeau was shaken. He decided nevertheless to meet with the Noranda representatives, but the exchange lasted only a few minutes. Guérin handled the rest of the discussion.

In the afternoon, Dr. Patrick D'Amico issued a terse health bulletin announcing that during the night, the doctors had had to amputate Lucien Bouchard's left leg. It made no mention of the patient's chances of survival. The news was on radio broadcasts throughout Quebec. It was 5 p.m. Quebec was plunged into a state of anxiety and held its breath. "That evening," recalls Pierre-Paul Roy, "the doctors had told us that the chances of his not pulling through were about 75 to 80%. If he made it through the night, we would know more in the morning."[23] The rumours that spread among the people of Quebec were most alarming, and they were justified: the state of Lucien Bouchard's health was worse than could be imagined, the bacteria were threatening to spread to the abdomen and the thorax. The fact that, at the family's request, the doctors had stopped issuing health bulletins only deepened their fears and fed the profusion of wild suppositions.

"The normal times for press briefings or press conferences were over," recalls Parizeau. "I was in the parliamentary gallery building. I had gathered any reporters I could find at that moment. It was early evening, around 7 p.m., something like that. That's when I offered my best wishes to Bouchard. I was totally distraught. All I could say was, 'Hang in, old fellow.' It had been a kind of psychological shock for me, a deep, deep shock... You cannot imagine such an abominable thing as that. I had never heard of this kind of illness, and I tried to imagine what it might be like. It was terrible!"[24]

In front of the Saint-Luc Hospital, a crowd gathered for a vigil. In the House of Commons, the Reform member for Calgary Southwest, Jan Brown, placed a yellow rose, as a symbol of hope, on Lucien Bouchard's empty desk. "I was going home west to Edmonton on a flight that night, and everything was quiet when I left Ottawa," recalls Deborah Grey, another Reform MP. "When I got off the plane, four-and-a-half, five hours later, my husband picked me up at the airport and he said, 'Have you heard the news? Lucien Bouchard has had this flesh-eating disease in his leg and they don't know whether he'll live through till morning or not.' I remember feeling very sad because we were cordial. And I remember praying for him that night on the way home and wondering what this would do to the whole cause of separatism. Because he was the magnetism (…)."

It was not only Deborah Grey and the federalists who wondered what would become of the independence project if Bouchard were gone. Jean-François Lisée feared that the death of Bouchard could have a considerable impact on the psyche of the people of Quebec. "My initial sentiment was to tell myself that his death would confirm, in the minds of many Quebecers, that the sovereigntist project was under a curse," he said, "that it was doomed to failure. The moment we wanted to try it, we would lose it. It just felt like a malediction. It would have been very serious because it would have nourished an almost superstitious feeling Quebecers have about our deepest political desires never being fulfilled. (…) We know that in our big political decisions on the national question, the history of Quebec is a story of a series of failures, so it would have deepened a groove that was already well-worn."[25]

The same afternoon, Lisette Lapointe was giving a talk in Quebec when she learned of the turn of events. "That evening, we had a reception, as we did every Thursday, at the residence," she says. "As we learned the news at the last minute, it was impossible to cancel." The guests, Rosaire Bertrand, member for Charlevoix and president of the PQ caucus, and his wife Line, shared the consternation of Jacques Parizeau and Lisette Lapointe: "It was a sad gathering, everyone was in shock," Lapointe says.[26]

Among those present at the official residence that evening was the head of protocol, Jacques Joli-Coeur. He knew that, should Lucien Bouchard die, Quebec would have the necessary latitude to organize a state funeral, even though, in principle, the funeral of a leader of the Opposition in the House of Commons fell under the jurisdiction of federal protocol. He therefore asked the premier what his instructions were. Parizeau answered, "It would first of all be a decision for his family and for his political group."[27] Meanwhile, Lisette Lapointe and Rosaire Bertrand's wife were wondering what they should do in these circumstances. "Line and I were fairly close to Audrey,[28] Line more so than I," Lapointe says. "We tried to reach her at home. The nanny, who was simply beside herself, told us repeatedly that she was in the shower and was not coming out. So, Line and I decided to go to Montreal to see if Audrey might need our help."[29]

Jacques Parizeau wrote a letter to Lucien Bouchard's wife and asked Jean-François Lisée to deliver it in person. On the way to Montreal, Lisée was haunted by a feeling he could not shake: if we lose Bouchard, we will probably lose everything. A barrage of reporters awaited him as he entered the hospital. Lisée simply said, "I am the bearer of a letter. I am just here as a messenger."[30] He gave the letter to Gilbert Charland, Bouchard's chief of staff.

Lisette Lapointe and Line Bertrand arranged to be driven to the hospital and entered by a back door, to avoid the reporters who stood cooling their heels in the hallway. Lucien Bouchard's wife, his brother Gérard, and members of his immediate entourage, Gilbert Charland and François Leblanc, were taking turns staying at his bedside. The visit from Lisette Lapointe and Line Bertrand was over quickly. As they left, Lisette Lapointe exchanged a few words with the media. This, at such a difficult time, provoked the anger of Audrey Best. "When Audrey saw Madame Lapointe on television the next day, boasting about her gesture, she was shocked," says Lucien Bouchard. "There was a total parting of the ways between the two after that. Audrey will no longer accompany me when she knows Madame Lapointe will be there."[31] "Audrey was very upset," says Lisette Lapointe. "And at that moment, there was a terrible misunderstanding that has lasted all this time. I don't know if she thought I was trying to represent the premier so that I could go and see what was happening. It was nothing like that at all." The coolness between the two women would cause enormous tension between them throughout the entire referendum campaign. "We spoke to one another politely and very formally, but we were never able to talk about it again," says Lisette Lapointe. She claims that the incident did not, however, affect relations between Parizeau and Bouchard: "It was an incident between women," she concluded.[32]

It was not only Lisette Lapointe's actions that aroused the indignation of Bouchard's entourage that Friday morning. The head of protocol, who had interpreted Parizeau's remarks as authorizing him to make arrangements, phoned Charland to talk to him about a state funeral, in the case of the death of the leader of the Bloc. Charland was furious; he had just learned that the patient was out of danger.

At about the same time, at 8 a.m., the referendum committee, led by Louis Bernard, was holding a meeting. "Mr. Bernard asked for a minute or two of silence," says Pierre-Paul Roy. "We were waiting for news. I had my cell phone. I said to Louis Bernard that Gilbert (Charland) might already have learned from the doctors what the situation was and that he would call me. Indeed, around 8:15 or 8:30 a.m., Gilbert did call me to let us know, 'The doctors say his life has been saved; he is going to pull through.'"[33]

A little later, as proceedings began in the National Assembly, the premier got up and stated in a solemn tone, "Mr. Bouchard is hovering between life and death. I am sure I express the sentiments of both sides of this House when I say that we send him our wishes and prayers that he will survive the terrible trial he is undergoing." Then Daniel Johnson evoked the terrible illness. "I was saddened," he says today, "to see a man of such vigor, and such keen intellect, struck by illness." Mario Dumont made similar remarks, expressing the hope that encouraging news would be received as soon as possible.

Around noon, Dr. D'Amico agreed to meet the media. The patient had been saved, he announced: "It is a miracle that he is alive!" Surgeon Pierre Ghosm then made public a note handwritten by Bouchard, given to the medical team. It read, "Carry on. Thank you."

Sovereigntist sympathizers would quickly exploit the note: the same day, a banner reproducing it would be put up on the building across from the hospital. The federalists were put out. In the words of Allan Rock, minister of Justice in Ottawa at the time: "And he passed that famous note when he was semi-conscious: *'Que l'on continue,'* 'Carry on.' He had the persona of a mystic to the people around him, as someone who'd come back from that near-fatal experience."

Saturday afternoon, Jacques Parizeau went to the hospital alone to see the patient, but he had to be satisfied with seeing him through a window as no visitors were allowed. He visited with Audrey Best and Dr. D'Amico. It was not until the next day that he was able to talk to Bouchard on the phone, specifically, about the draft bill that he would have to table two days later in the National Assembly.

It had been a tough week for Parizeau. He and Bouchard did not get on all that well, and it was hard for him to know how to manage their relationship. Nevertheless, he was personally very affected by Bouchard's illness. "For reasons that were not political," explains Jean-François Lisée, "but for personal reasons. One could feel that beyond their character differences and their inability to really communicate, there was a new bond, a complicity, that had formed between them."[34]

Bob Dufour, who had organized the campaign for the Bloc in 1993 and was very close to Bouchard, says he felt there was a real sympathy for him among Canadians in general. "For them, Mr. Bouchard was someone they could talk to," he says. "Those were the remarks you would get from the premiers or people in politics in the other provinces, though not necessarily in Ottawa. People had a lot of respect for Mr. Bouchard. They found him more approachable than Mr. Parizeau, whom they felt was more rigid and a lot less open to discussion."[35]

It was not just outside Quebec that Mr. Bouchard projected the image of a more flexible leader, but in Quebec too. Parizeau knew full well that, without Bouchard, there was at least a whole segment of the population that could turn its back on his sovereignty project. Even members of his own party were convinced of that. A month earlier, at the beginning of November, André Boisclair, the young member from Gouin, whose idea of spreading sovereignty beyond the Parti Québécois had already earned him a serious reprimand from Parizeau, stated that "it was not just the Parti Québécois who could lead the referendum campaign. We must remobilize our partners from the campaign against the Charlottetown agreement. It's not just a question of talking about openness, we must show it in our behaviour, in our attitudes, in the decisions the government takes."[36] Parizeau was not against broadening the membership base: he likes to recall that he played a major role between Gilles Grégoire and René Lévesque when, at the founding congress of the Parti Québécois, in 1968, the *Ralliement national*, with its roughly 5,000 *Créditistes*, amalgamated with the sovereigntists that had come from the sovereignty-association movement. However, it was much more difficult for him to imagine having to deal with duly constituted groups who would keep their own identity and political orientation when it came to specific and jointly planned action.

The cause being more important than all else, Parizeau declared, at the party's national council held at the beginning of November, that the "open door," the "overhaul" of the "flagship" of sovereignty was not enough. A whole "fleet" was needed in order to win," he said.[37] At the same time, Monique Simard, who had just been elected vice-president and manager of the party, announced that she was committed to "the formidable task of political leadership that lay before them."[38] Finally, on November 29, in a gesture judged by some as purely theatrical, Parizeau offered to shake hands with the leader of the Opposition in the National Assembly.

Today, he apologizes a bit, on his own behalf as well as his party's, for appropriating the sovereignty project: "The Parti Québécois has always had sort of a weakness for considering the sovereignty project its own," he says. "Quebec's independence is not the affair of just one party. The Parti Québécois can spearhead it, ensure the necessary resources, but does not own the project." That is why, from the time the regional commissions were created, Parizeau offered to shake hands with Daniel Johnson. "It's too bad the Liberals didn't want to get involved in this operation," he adds, "because just about everybody else in our society did."[39] He believed Johnson's position was so peremptory that any efforts to attract the Liberals were cut short.

On December 16, in Lucien Bouchard's absence, Gilles Duceppe led a Bloc Québécois team in a strategic meeting with representatives of the Parti Québécois. At the end of it, the two groups announced that they would merge their operations and act, up until the referendum, as if they were one single party.

"This is our version of Team Quebec," quipped Duceppe. "It will be neither the campaign of the PQ or the Bloc," Bernard Landry declared. "It will be the campaign of the sovereigntists. We are setting an example for the abolition of boundaries between parties."

Despite Landry's remarks, it was becoming increasingly evident, to Parizeau and his entourage, that the campaign could not be just sovereigntist. They had to present people with a more inclusive process, referred to as the "rainbow operation." On the referendum committee, there were the big unions, the *Société Saint-Jean-Baptiste* and the *Mouvement national des Québécois*. Organizations had to be created for the YES side, groups of young people, of economists, of women, and so forth.

And then there was Mario Dumont. On December 13, the government started an all-out offensive campaign to persuade the man whom they believed best represented that fringe of nationalists who rejected federalism as it was but who, all the same, were not sovereigntists. Jean Royer and Jean-François Lisée met with Dumont and tried by every means to convince him to participate in the work of the commissions. But the leader of the ADQ remained lukewarm toward the government's project and he said so: "They were more interested in the photo op (...) than in the contribution of the *Action démocratique*," he declared at the end of the meeting. He added, "I did not expect to conduct the train, but, at least, that I would be on it in a position from which I could influence the process."[40]

Negotiations between the government and the ADQ went on for a good week. Dumont wanted to keep his party outside the PQ dynamic. He planned to keep control of his troops, which represented only 6.3% of the Quebec electorate and which could rapidly be absorbed into the big PQ machine. Parizeau understood this and, moreover, did not hide his respect for Dumont, whom he found a "refreshing element" in the National Assembly. "He asked intelligent questions," he recalls today. "(He spoke) in a language that was a bit novel, without waffling, often making a lot of sense. It was pleasant to be able to say to him, 'Listen, yes, we are going to look into that...' I had a very good rapport with him in the National Assembly."[41]

It was not an easy struggle. Dumont placed a number of conditions on his participation in the regional commissions. He wanted the people to be able to give their opinion, not just on the details of accession to sovereignty, but also on its timeliness. He wanted discussions to be open to the point where participants would be able to debate the constitutional options of each of the parties, and these options would be outlined in a brochure to be distributed to every household, before the commissions began their work. He finally asked that the parties should have a say, in the National Assembly, in choosing the commission presidents.

There was a lot of pressure on Dumont and his team: 55% of Quebecers were in favour of the government's approach and wanted the federalists to participate in it.[42] But there was just as much pressure on the sovereigntists, who needed the support of the ADQ. On December 16, Premier Parizeau let it be known by means of a communiqué that he agreed to the conditions set by the ADQ. The reaction of the leader of the Opposition was swift: "An episode arranged with the poster boy," said Daniel Johnson. "Dumont has already indicated he is for Quebec independence. The Siamese twins have made a deal."[43] In the English-language press, Johnson's expression became the "Tweedledum and Tweedledee of separatism."[44]

Did the Liberal party, then, miss a perfect opportunity to go with the nationalist trend in the population? "I would be surprised if people (in the party) would have made that effort," John Parisella, Daniel Johnson's chief of staff at the time, says today. "They had established that Mario Dumont had made his bed and that in his mind there was no question of partnering with the Quebec Liberal Party to defend federalism."[45] Besides, there was a fair amount of bitterness among the Liberal MNAs towards Dumont, as some considered his walking out on the party barely two years earlier to be one of the main factors in the electoral defeat of September 1994.

There was no shortage of signs of openness that fall in 1994. But while all political parties were represented on the Bélanger-Campeau commission, there were only sovereigntists in the movement towards the referendum, with the exception of the ADQ. Consequently, Bouchard's participation was indispensable. In Parizeau's estimation, the former Conservative was very much appreciated by those he called the *vieux bleus*, the people from the former *Union Nationale*, and he could go and seek out "people who found the PQ crowd getting on their nerves." It was after all Bouchard who would convince two of his former colleagues in the Mulroney government, Monique Vézina, who had been minister of External Relations, and Marcel Masse, who had been minister of Communications, to assume the presidency of the commissions of consultation on the future of Quebec. "I am not for pure independence," said Vézina, "but you cannot take two steps backward during the referendum. Better to take one step forward."[46] "If the federal government cannot offer anything other than the status quo," said Masse, "and there is no other route possible with them, I think we have no choice but to vote for sovereignty."[47]

Far from being disappointed by these lukewarm professions of faith, Parizeau found them to fit exactly into his rainbow objective. In fact, in the last week of December, his government appointed three anglophones to important positions: Kevin Drummond, former Liberal minister, to the general delegation from Quebec to New York, Peter Dunn to the Quebec office in Toronto and Francis Rae Whyte was made Rector of the University of Quebec in Hull. The coalition was taking shape. Former Conservatives like Monique Vézina and Marcel Masse, former Liberals, like the mayor of Quebec, agreed to be associated with the great process of the regional commissions on the future of Quebec. Even Pierre Bourgault, who, since the founding of the Parti Québécois, had always had differences with the party's leadership, walked into

Jean-François Lisée's office one day to say, "It has never been better than now!" Slowly they were climbing in the polls, "but, despite everything, people were constantly talking to us about the danger of another failure," says Lisée. "The spectre of failure was there and we were in the process of emerging from it. And we were certain that the presence of Lucien Bouchard and his charisma were part of that combination."[48]

When Parizeau defined the role he had in mind, at that point, for Bouchard to play in the referendum campaign, that of a harvester of soft supporters, he underestimated the importance Quebec people attached to the involvement of the Bloc leader, not only in the campaign, but especially after a victory for the YES. Yet this concern had cropped up as soon as the Parti Québécois came to power, in September. One day Jean-François Lisée was giving a talk in the Saguenay on referendum strategy. "One of the first questions following the talk was, 'What will Mr. Bouchard do after the referendum if the YES side wins?' he recalls. "The only response I could think of was, 'That is an excellent question. We need to reflect on that!'" Lisée returned to Quebec and asked his team the same question. The answer was, "We had not thought about it." "It was a very delicate issue, given Parizeau-Bouchard relations," Lisée adds. "So, I wrote Mr. Parizeau, saying that as soon as possible, before the referendum, we needed to establish the role to be played by Mr. Bouchard, who was already the most loved and most respected politician in the history of Quebec. (...) If we did not say, during the referendum campaign, what he would do after the YES, then our adversaries would say, voting YES is losing Bouchard and being left with only Parizeau to deal with."[49]

Lisée repeatedly raised the thorny question. Even though they saw its importance, no one in his entourage seemed to appreciate the urgency of settling it, especially since there was this feeling that Bouchard was "not the type to take that sort of decision far in advance of when it has to be taken." The problem would remain unresolved until half way into the referendum campaign, in October the following year. Pierre-Paul Roy, the Bloc leader's political advisor, does not deny that in Parizeau's entourage, nothing was settled in this regard. "No one really knew just how to situate Mr. Bouchard in the referendum campaign," he says. "But Bouchard's approach at that time, and right up till October 7, was to say, 'I will play whatever role is assigned to me during the campaign.' He was quite aware that Mr. Parizeau was the architect here. I never heard Mr. Bouchard say, 'It's got to be a certain way, or else I won't be part of it.'"[50]

Lucien Bouchard was making a speedy recovery. His close associates marvelled at his courage and determination. He showed no desire to abandon politics. On the contrary. His popularity with the people continued to rise: the week following his hospitalization, it reached a peak rarely attained by a political personality in Quebec, 72% of the population saying they had a favourable opinion of him.[51] He applied himself to his rehabilitation program with uncommon energy, with the result that, according to Bob Dufour, he was ahead of the schedule doctors had set for him. In an interview with the daily Le Soleil, in mid-February, Bouchard confirmed: "Politics seems more important than ever to me now. I've come a long way, I've been at death's door," he said. "When you have come through that, you have a profound sense of the fragility of human life, how time is meted out to us. On the other hand, you say to yourself, 'the time that I am given, I will utilize it to the maximum for the things that really matter.'" The "things that really mattered" for Lucien Bouchard consisted primarily of his private life, "but," he added, "I missed politics."[52] "After his illness," Pierre-Paul Roy recalls, "he said to me, 'There's more to life than politics. Remember that: the other things are more important.' For Mr. Bouchard, being in politics was not something that came naturally. He did not see himself as a career politician. He was a lawyer; that was the work he loved. He had his family late in life. One of his most fundamental values was his family. One can be sure he experienced inner conflict over his commitment to politics."[53]

However, it was Lucien Bouchard's political commitment that won out and his return to public life was carried off most brilliantly. The media were ready to make any kind of deal to be able to report a small exclusive slice of the hell he had lived through in the course of the last three months. The parliamentary press in Ottawa was all worked up. The Chrétien government was so aware of what was going on that, in order not to disappear from the screens altogether, it planned to announce, that same week, the date of the next budget, a new pension plan for MPs and a possible cabinet shuffle, a shuffle that would give Lucienne Robillard the halo she needed—in the form of a Cabinet seat—to establish her credibility during the referendum campaign. All to no avail. Every journalist's notebook, every camera and microphone on Parliament Hill was trained on the leader of the Bloc.

The party negotiated the interviews as if at a bazaar, their entire strategy geared to one climax: President Bill Clinton's visit, set for February 22. "He (Lucien Bouchard) had not quite recovered, in terms of his prosthesis and so forth," says Bob Dufour, "but he had decided to go and meet Mr. Clinton. For, obviously, as leader of the Opposition, he was entitled to a visit with him."[54]

Even before resuming contact with the House of Commons, Lucien Bouchard welcomed interviews with the media. The first one he granted was to Jean-François Lépine, broadcast Sunday, February 19 on *Radio-Canada* on the program *Le Point*. Why such a precipitous return? "What is going on in Quebec is very current, very intense," he replied. "We are living through defining moments for our future. (…) I have no illusions about what one individual can do in politics, but I am making a public commitment." He reaffirmed his conviction that Quebec could not continue with the *status quo*, "with this stagnant situation," and that sovereignty was the only solution. He had in mind a question that would be able to draw "a clear and final response" and he reiterated his position with respect to a referendum date: "I cannot consider the scenario where we would deliberately agree to expose Quebec to a NO vote on sovereignty, knowing what would happen afterwards…" He then said that the note "Carry on," communicated to the press by the doctors while he was in hospital, was indeed intended as a political message. The following day and Tuesday, all the stops were pulled out: *Le Soleil* in Quebec, *Le Droit* in Ottawa, *Le Quotidien* in Chicoutimi, *Radio-Canada*'s English-language network, CBC, and several English-language newspapers focused their attention only on Bouchard's return. Finally, on the Wednesday, he returned to his seat in the House of Commons.

The next day, a glorious sun rose on a federal capital under siege: bridges closed, traffic diverted, buses rerouted, police everywhere, and black cars moving at great speed. Jean and Aline Chrétien were receiving the president of the United States and Lucien Bouchard was there as official leader of Her Majesty's Loyal Opposition. The House of Commons was packed to the rafters: MPs, senators, dignitaries, ambassadors and special guests. In his welcome address, Prime Minister Chrétien did not allude in any way to the Quebec situation. He stuck to evoking the close economic ties that existed between the two countries and expressed his wish that the United States play an increasingly important role in the world. But Clinton, for whom this was his first official visit to Canada, had done his homework: "The United States, as many of my predecessors have said, has enjoyed its excellent relationships with a strong and united Canada," he said. Then, interpreting the remarks made by Chrétien, for whom friendship between the two countries was a friendship between equals, he added, "but we recognize, just as the prime minister said with regard to your relationship to us a moment ago, that your political future is of course entirely for you to decide. That is what a democracy is all about."[55]

Clinton's speech had been carefully prepared by James Blanchard, the United States ambassador to Ottawa, and the Prime Minister's Office. "Mr. Clinton went out of his way to make it clear that it was not in the interest of the United States to have Canada break up," says Eddie Goldenberg, who had worked with Blanchard to prepare for the president's visit. "I don't think Mr. Chrétien had to speak to the president about it because the president was more than happy to do that." According to journalist Douglas Jehl of *The New York Times*, the president had submitted his speech to Jean Chrétien on the Tuesday evening.[56]

While the American president had officially adopted a position of non-interference, his ambassador to Canada had never had any scruples about considering the fight against separatism a personal cause. Back in December 1993—Jean Chrétien had only just assumed power—he broached the subject with the Canadian minister of External Affairs, André Ouellet: "It was at that point, speaking for myself during a freewheeling private conversation in front of the fire, that I first raised the idea that the United States should perhaps reassess its traditional position regarding the independence of Quebec. (...) I wondered whether we shouldn't move at least a little farther (...). And once I had raised the thought, I couldn't shake the desire to do something about it."[57] He would keep his word, in a singular way, during Clinton's visit: "The fact was, whenever a president of the United States had been pressed, his answer was always, 'Yes, sure, we want Canada to stay united,'" recounts the former ambassador. "Then, the State Department would jump in and say that wasn't our official position. So I wanted to go farther in order to dispel anyone's belief that we were indifferent or that the break-up of Canada was somehow in our political interests. And I was confident that Warren Christopher (the Secretary of State) shared that view."[58] During the private conversation of about 90 minutes between the president and the prime minister, the Quebec question was not raised again. The two heads of state dedicated their visit, rather, to topics of bilateral interest.

The precedents found in the history of presidential visits to Ottawa allowed quite naturally for Lucien Bouchard to meet with Clinton, if the president's schedule allowed it. But the leader of the Bloc feared the federal government would manipulate things in such a way as to ensure such a meeting would not take place. Therefore, on February 3, he took the unusual step of presenting to the government a formal request to arrange an official visit with the president for him. He wanted to convince Clinton to adopt an official attitude of benevolent neutrality. "I wanted to remind him, insofar as this was possible, that sovereigntists are democrats, that their project is fundamentally democratic, that it was not an anti-American project. On the contrary. And that Quebecers are not protectionist, that we were responsible for imposing free trade on English Canada," he told journalist Michel Vastel of Le Soleil. And Bouchard knew he could count on understanding from Canada's ambassador to the United States, Raymond Chrétien.[59] The two had known each other since their student days at Laval University. Their paths had often crossed since. They both loved reading and would on occasion exchange books. They had also met in Washington, when Bouchard was there on an official visit as leader of the Opposition, during the weeks following Raymond Chrétien's appointment in the American capital.

At noon, on the day Governor General Roméo Leblanc received the U.S. president for lunch, nothing had been settled with respect to the meeting between Bouchard and the president. All of Ottawa's political elite were there, 50 people or so. "Until two in the afternoon," recounts Raymond Chrétien, "the meeting could have not taken place. But if it had not taken place, we would have had a different kind of problem, a media problem that might have been hard to resolve." Chrétien acknowledges that he himself had reservations about the idea of giving that much visibility to the sovereigntist leader. But he was called upon to play a key role in these negotiations because he enjoyed the confidence of both the prime minister and Lucien Bouchard. "I had spoken to James Blanchard, to André Ouellet and to the prime minister," he recounts. "Now I had to talk to Lucien Bouchard. We could be frank with one another, and say, 'Lucien, this won't work, we can't do this,' or 'Raymond, now you're going too far!' Who was in favour? Who was against? There were seven or eight of us in the small group that made these decisions."[60]

The prime minister and his minister of External Affairs were inflexible on one point: if the meeting were to take place, a representative of the Canadian government would attend. The ambassador finally submitted the conditions established by the federal government to the sovereigntist leader. Bouchard did not see them in any way as a constraint: the presence of a representative of the Canadian government, namely Raymond Chrétien, the absence of any photographers or reporters, and a meeting with the president to be scheduled for the leader of the Reform Party, Preston Manning. 'Obviously, he had to agree," Chrétien continues. "'Perfect, Raymond!' he said. It was settled over dessert, at the Governor General's home. And we finished our coffee in good spirits, because the meeting would take place."[61] And it would be at the residence of James Blanchard.

Lunch ended around 3 p.m. and everyone returned home. The ambassador suggested he come round for Bouchard with his car at the arranged time and that they drive together. It was about a 20-minute ride to the American ambassador's residence. "I'll never forget it," says Raymond Chrétien. "It was cold. It was awful weather. It was raining and hailing and I had no umbrella. For me, this was a chance to chat in a more leisurely and relaxed way than at the lunch. So, he shared with me something of how he intended to proceed. I replied that I felt that what he had in mind was indeed the best approach... We got there. I'll always remember it. The car slid—that's how dangerous the ice was. I was really afraid we would fall flat on our faces. We walked, both of us, I don't know anymore if it was arm in arm or hand in hand, but trying not to fall, to get to the top of the porch steps, it was that slippery. All the bodyguards, instead of looking at us, were looking up at the hills, out at the trees, as if the heavens were about to deliver an omen. So, we were all alone, climbing those steps... It really was an incredible scene!"[62]

Meanwhile, Blanchard was putting the president in the picture: "Now, here's the situation, I said. No matter what you tell this guy, he'll interpret it as support for separation. If you tell him it's a nice day, he'll go out and tell the press you're in favor of an independent Quebec. So you're going to have to watch it. I would say as little as possible. Ask a few questions, be real nice. He's a decent guy, he's beloved in his province, but he wants to be king of Quebec."[63] And when Blanchard saw the White House photographer approach, he fired at him, "No, no photos, none. I want you to disappear. I don't want him to even see there's a photographer around."[64]

The meeting, scheduled to take 20 minutes, took place in a small room adjacent to the large parlour. There were six people: Clinton, Anthony Lake, the president's advisor on security matters, Blanchard, Bouchard, Gilbert Charland, Bouchard's chief of staff, and Raymond Chrétien. The conversation opened with small talk: the terrible weather; Bouchard knew the United States well, a country which fascinated his children; his wife was American. "Bouchard chose to sit right next to Clinton,' Blanchard said. 'I wanted you to see in flesh and blood, first hand, a separatist,' he began. 'For most Quebecers, Quebec is first, not Canada. (...) We're a different nation.' He talked for a while about the background to the founding of the Bloc Québécois. 'We're democratic. We're peaceful. (…) Nothing is going to change when we separate. We're going to have good relations with you. We're still going to be one of your major trading partners. We're going to be part of all the alliances and treaties. (…) We love Americans. We share the same values as the rest of Canada, but we want to end the duplications and the antagonisms."[65] "He did it in a very structured, very organized way," recalls Raymond Chrétien. "Everyone listened to him. He did it calmly, not passionately, very appropriately and, of course, in English."[66]

Then, according to Blanchard, "There was a long pause. Bouchard seemed surprised that Clinton didn't say anything in response. Finally Clinton said, 'How many people are there in Quebec?' It was (…) exactly the right thing to do. 'Seven million,' we all answered at once. Then more silence. Raymond didn't say anything. Lake didn't say anything. So I chimed in and said, 'I want to remind you that we met you because you're the leader of the Opposition, not because you're a leading separatist.' (…) Then Clinton asked, 'How is your illness?' 'Oh, I'm doing okay,' Bouchard answered. 'Thank you.' Then, he got up and left."[67] Preston Manning was waiting his turn in the anteroom.

When he was asked the next day to comment on his meeting with Lucien Bouchard, President Clinton told reporters, "I met Mr. Bouchard because he was the leader of the Opposition. He happens to be a separatist and he stated his case clearly and articulately. I think the people who agreed with him would have been pleased with the clarity with which he expressed his position." In the American newspapers on Friday, Clinton's trip to Ottawa was crowded out by an item considered more newsworthy: Secretary of State Warren Christopher was suffering from an ulcer.

CHAPTER IV

The Road to Sovereignty

T he first arena Jean Chrétien chose for battle was the constitutionality of the Quebec project. "It's not in the Constitution," he said
on December 20, in an end-of-year interview broadcast on CTV. "It's
one of the questions they will have to answer: Who will they negotiate
with?"[1] "They" obviously referred to the sovereigntists. Chrétien was
relying on a statement made by his minister of Justice, Allan Rock,
during a dinner hosted by *Cité libre* magazine in Ottawa the week
before. "Clearly, there exists no provision in Canada's constitution for
one province to leave the federation," he had stated. "To my mind, it's
not constitutional. But that's a technical question. The real question is
for Quebecers, in a referendum. That may be the answer of a politician, not a lawyer."[2] The topic of Allan Rock's speech was *The Just
Society, 25 Years Later*, but the topic of the referendum quickly resur-
faced during the question period. "There is a bill before the Quebec
National Assembly at this time which may be unconstitutional. What
are you going to do about it?" they asked him. The former minister remembers that moment today. "My answer was in essence: if a referendum is to come and if the issue is to be put, then we're going to win or
we're going to lose based on our ability to persuade Quebecers that
Canada is the better option. We're not going to win this with a barrage
of constitutional arguments or a team of constitutional lawyers."

Quebec's deputy premier, Bernard Landry, did not miss this
opportunity to embarrass Chrétien with respect to his minister and
the position he himself had taken in his autobiography.[3] "The prime

minister is fighting a rearguard action by casting doubt on the constitutionality of a declaration of sovereignty by Quebec after a YES in the referendum," he said. "The minister of Justice, Allan Rock, was much wiser!"[4]

Wise as it may have been, Rock's position raised controversy in English Canada. "It was startling to have the minister of Justice dismiss the constitutionality of secession," William Johnson wrote in *The Gazette*, "as of mere technical interest. (...) But he merely confirmed what Jean Chrétien and his ministers have conveyed... I think they are profoundly wrong."[5] *The Ottawa Citizen*, on the other hand, was sympathetic to the Justice minister's position. "Objecting to the constitutionality of the Quebec legislation," the editorial said, "is, at best, irrelevant, and at worst, a dangerous distraction."[6]

It was, however, not just a theoretical question. If there was no provision in the Canadian Constitution allowing for the secession of Quebec, it was feared by Ottawa that independence supporters might resort to violence to obtain constitutional changes. In such a case, the Canadian Security Intelligence Service would have been justified, by virtue of its mandate, in infiltrating movements favouring independence. "CSIS could be interested in one or more persons, from any political party, who might be advocating constitutional change by violent means," lawyer Michel Robert declared before a House of Commons sub-committee. He was a member of the Security Intelligence Review Committee[7] at the time. Sovereigntists had too vivid a memory of the police tactics used by the RCMP in the 1970s to not pay close attention to this aspect of the approaching battle.

Jacques Parizeau felt that the question of legality should not even be asked. In his opinion, it was all very well for Chrétien to say that nowhere does the Constitution allow for a province to secede: In British law, what is not forbidden is authorized. He recalled the fact that in 1992, Robert Bourassa had demanded, and obtained, for Quebec—since it was not forbidden by the Constitution —, the right to hold its own referendum on the Charlottetown Accord. Taking that referendum as a model, Parizeau maintained that if the principle of 50 plus one was valid then, it should be respected in 1995.

What preoccupied federal strategists was the haste with which Parizeau might declare the sovereignty of Quebec if the YES side won, regardless of the size of the majority. "Mr. Parizeau was not going to compromise on his formula of 50 plus one," says Jean Pelletier, who was Prime Minister Chrétien's chief of staff at the time. "He would have gone ahead. We would have been in a terrible state of political chaos in Canada, if it had turned out to be 50 plus one, but for the YES side." What Pelletier then adds explains why, in the minds of the federalists, the significance of the 1995 referendum was different from that of the 1980 referendum. "I always sensed that Mr. Lévesque did not want to break up Canada," he says. "What he wanted was a better deal. He wasn't necessarily looking for hard-line separation."[8] Daniel Johnson agrees. "The 1995 referendum was not just a consultation," he says, "insofar as the government of Quebec, once it had presented its offer of partnership, and without specifying how long the other party had to reply, could declare the sovereignty of Quebec in the National Assembly. So, a unilateral declaration of independence, really, after an offer of partnership, whether it was discussed or not, that was it, that was Parizeau's approach, and he would have let no one deprive him of it!"[9]

Nevertheless, Jacques Parizeau was somewhat bound by the draft bill he had introduced at the beginning of December 1994. Article 2 of the bill stipulated that "the government (was) authorized to conclude with the Government of Canada an agreement establishing the maintenance of an economic association between Quebec and Canada." "In order," one reads in the explanatory notes, "to maintain the free movement of goods and services, capital and persons, already existing and to be developed." Parizeau would therefore negotiate.

But he was preparing these negotiations. "You don't do that all in one day," he says. "That was why the one-year timeframe we were talking about was necessary. We had to have, as early on as possible, a fairly clear set of ideas as to what we intended to do."[10] Responsibility for preparing for negotiations fell to a senior civil servant, Carl Grenier. Grenier was assistant deputy minister for the department of Governmental Affairs, Immigration and Cultural Communities.

Seconded for this task to the Executive Council, he led a team of some twenty people whose mandate was to articulate the position of the government of Quebec. In the case of a victory for the YES side, it was he and his team who would, on the technical level, assist the chief negotiator in presenting his arguments to the representatives of the federal government.

No one had any illusions as to the climate that would prevail at these negotiations. But Mario Dumont believed that English Canada would have no choice. "You resist for a while and, then, eventually, there are a couple of subjects that force you to come to the table," he says, recalling his own negotiating experience. "At first, you don't agree, but then, when you hear the clock ticking, time, events and pressure from the people, all conspire, at a certain point, to let common sense win out."[11]

Among the "couple of subjects" that could force the two parties to come to the table the very next day after a YES vote, there was the isolation of the Atlantic provinces. According to Parizeau, an agreement that would allow "the free movement of vehicles, aircraft, boats and trains between Ontario and New Brunswick" would have to be signed immediately. Even if just because of the need to deal with this, he could not imagine the federal government saying: We are not prepared to sign, we do not want to talk with you... "That would have to be a joke," he says. As far as other matters were concerned, for Parizeau, the inveterate economist, this was first and foremost an accounting transaction. "We are entitled to a quarter, a little less than a quarter, of the assets of the federal government," he says. "It depends on the criteria you use. Do you go by the population or the gross national product? Obviously the percentage in question would also be applied to the federal debt."[12] He estimated that debt to be around 400 billion dollars. The Quebec government relied, in its approach to the sharing of assets and liabilities, on the Bélanger-Campeau commission report of 1991, and particularly on a study it had commissioned from two actuaries, Claude Lamonde and Jacques Bolduc, according to which, Quebec would inherit a lot more debts than assets.[13] But Parizeau knew full well that "some adjustments would be necessary," for example, with respect to the federal fixed assets, or for the portion of the debt relating to the Canada Pension Plan, which Quebec would not have to assume because it has its own plan. He considered, however, that the sharing principle itself was simple enough.[14]

While the Parizeau government found ways to improve the credibility of its project among Quebecers, it was, however, up against another type of difficulty about which it could do nothing: English Canada was not ready to negotiate an economic association with Quebec, either politically or technically. On January 15, 1995, 200 intellectuals from all over the country gathered at McGill University to debate the possibilities and the consequences of economic association. One of them, Professor Alan Cairns of the University of British Columbia, was categorical: "Even if it wanted to," he said in a lecture broadcast by the two continuous news channels of *Radio-Canada*/CBC, "Canada would be incapable of negotiating the separation of Quebec within a twelve-month period. It would not be like in Czechoslovakia, where the two camps were organized. English Canada would go through a period of great instability, marked by the use of extreme language." And he added: "There is no guarantee that the rest of Canada would emerge as a single entity."[15]

Few people in the federal government really believed that, one day, a new Parti Québécois government would put Canada through another 1980. Therefore, everyone was taken by surprise when the Parizeau government set the referendum process in motion immediately after it was elected. It should not be forgotten that the Chrétien government had been in government for only a year and that the preceding government, of Brian Mulroney, had staked everything on the Meech Lake and Charlottetown Accords rather than on a strategy to fight a sovereigntist offensive. "There was no game plan. We had to draw one up fast," admits Jean Pelletier, Jean Chrétien's chief of staff at the time. "In Ottawa, a certain segment of the civil service, who claimed to have a monopoly on truth, said we didn't need to do anything, that it was not going to happen... When the referendum was launched, the federal apparatus realized that it was rather ill-prepared, and so, was forced to react quickly: it set up a team to create an office that would be responsible for referendum strategy. The job was entrusted to senior government official Howard Balloch, who joined the Privy Council Office as Cabinet Deputy Secretary for Operation Unity.[16] This team worked at lightning speed to make up for lost time. We weren't ready because we hadn't envisaged that the final answer could be a YES vote. We had always been convinced that the NO side would prevail."[17] As the referendum season got under way, the federal government did not have a campaign plan and had not achieved unanimity in the federalist camp, which explains, in part, the confusion that would characterize the strategy of the NO side for several months.

There was another reason why the federal government had not been preparing for a referendum fight and, especially not, for negotiations: By making such preparations, it could give the impression that it was not dismissing the possibility of a YES victory. Its strategy was and, until the beginning of the referendum campaign, would be, to assume that the NO side would win the day, handily. "The sense in Ottawa was," says Allan Rock, "that we should not formally organize contingency plans. I don't recall there having been an express instruction from the Prime Minister's Office or anywhere else. But I think it was understood that we were not going to be engaging in contingency planning because to do so would signal weakness. And the fact would certainly leak out and we would be seen to be afraid, we would be giving credence to the YES side, acknowledging that they might win, and then people would ask us what we were planning to do. So, there was a certain unspoken understanding that no departments were going to formally engage in what if, or what might happen if the YES vote was to succeed." The Chrétien government's minister of Industry, John Manley, also recalls that it was not possible to establish a strategy. "The thinking was that, if there were a strategy, this could, if it became known, create the idea that it was clear, it was over. That could even help the YES cause." The tension experienced by Cabinet members at the time threatened to disrupt their family life. Some, like John Manley, chose not to bring their anxieties home with them. "I wanted to avoid a situation where, at school, if they asked my children what did their Dad think, they would be saying, 'He thinks we're going to lose' or 'We might lose' or 'He is very worried.'"

While the federal government was not ready to enter the referendum campaign, it was even less disposed to comment on the appropriateness of agreeing to negotiate with Quebec. Not a single member of the government could be found who would suggest it should be a willing player in the case of a YES win, who would suggest openness to discussion, even if it meant demanding an extension of the one-year timeframe, should one year be too short. In any event, such an attitude would run counter to the strategy that had gradually been developing since the Parti Québécois' return to power. Several figures, who were influential with the political class, suggested the federal government adopt a resolutely hostile position, likely to instill fear in the people of Quebec. Stanley Hartt and Stéphane Dion are two examples among others. Stanley Hartt, a former advisor to Brian Mulroney, used the occasion of a C.D. Howe Institute symposium to invite Chrétien to promise to make Quebec suffer so much that secession would become impossible. Stéphane Dion, an academic and advisor to the Privy Council at the time, stated, on that same occasion, "The more it hurts, the more support for sovereignty will decline!"[18]

As the pre-referendum campaign got under way, the situation in Ottawa remained confused on at least three fronts. How ought they to deal with the strategy of the Quebec government? Should they, as of now, start giving the impression that the federal government would recognize the victory of independence supporters in the case of a YES side win? With that scenario, what attitude should the government adopt with respect to negotiation? The situation was all the more confusing as there were other players who claimed they should have a say in the matter. The provinces wanted a chance to voice their opinion, especially in negotiations, if they were to take place. Ontario, in any case, was getting ready, now that a YES victory could not be absolutely ruled out. Two teams were set up, one under the minister of Finance and the other under the minister of Intergovernmental Affairs. "I learned very quickly that New York and London and the major financial centres around the world don't like any kind of uncertainty," Mike Harris recalls today. At the time of the referendum, he was premier of Ontario. "And so, we were working on a strategy to assure them that this vote meant nothing other than business as usual. And then, of course, beginning to gear up for what we saw would be very difficult discussions with Quebec. And at no point did we feel that the federal government would speak for us. We would speak for Ontario, we would speak for Ontarians. The premiers, I think, would have declared unanimously that they understood and expected and demanded to be part of those discussions and negotiations." One premier however did not share that view. Frank McKenna of New Brunswick was categorical: neither he nor Chrétien could sit down opposite Quebec's negotiator. "I have no authority to negotiate on behalf of Canada," he said. "The prime minister of Canada does not have the mandate to negotiate the separation of Quebec from Canada."[19]

In 1995, Preston Manning sat in the House of Commons as leader of the Reform Party.[20] Seeking a solution to the Quebec question, he took the more serious step of consulting the British North America Act. He points out that when the Confederation of Canada was created in 1867, Quebec and Ontario made up one united province, the province of Canada. When this province was split up, its assets had to be distributed between the two new provinces. "There were some assets that they'd had in common, some buildings that they'd paid for, some land that they'd acquired, to be divided between Ontario and Quebec," he says with a laugh. "I think they set up a commission to do that, with a commissioner from each province. It took them 35 years to come to some agreement over this relatively small pile of assets and a little bit of debt and they never were able to agree on it. If you couldn't divide assets and debt when you were in a context of confederating, can you imagine the problem that would have been created if you'd tried to do that because Quebec had separated?"

Caught off guard and bombarded by so many contradictory opinions about how to deal with the possibility of negotiation, Jean Chrétien and his advisors chose the confrontation option, the only option capable of creating consensus in English Canada: Rather than speak about the possibilities for negotiation, they decided instead to block the secession project itself.

Whether to be open to negotiations or to reject them outright was not the only dilemma the federal government faced. Could it or should it prevent an independent Quebec from continuing to use its dollar? Ever since Parizeau's position on this question was known, the debate around it never stopped and the arguments employed by the specialists, in both camps, did nothing to help clarify the issue in the eyes of the people.

In the spring of 1995, there was a confidential document circulating in the corridors on Parliament Hill. It had been prepared by the Privy Council. Entitled *The Canadian Dollar and the Separation of Quebec*, it had been prepared as a resource for Prime Minister Chrétien to use in his speeches during the referendum campaign. This document stated that Parizeau was not telling Quebecers the truth when he claimed that an independent Quebec could continue to use the Canadian dollar. The study maintained that Quebec could use Canadian currency for a period of time, but would, in all likelihood, have to create its own money. Why? The financial world would lose confidence, capital would flee from Quebec, and the Parizeau government would have no choice but to create its own unique currency in order to resolve liquidity problems. The same study pointed out that the monetary union of the Czech Republic and Slovakia was short-lived, when Czechoslovakia broke up in 1991, because the Slovak banks could not withstand the assault made on them. The document then touched on the possibility that one day "the beaver" could replace "the loon" or that the currency of Quebec might be the U.S. dollar.[21]

In mid-March, in a study published by the C.D. Howe Institute, political analyst William R. Robson claimed that it would be not only possible, but desirable, for Canada and an independent Quebec to have the same currency. He believed that Quebec, however, would have no other option than creating a new currency of its own, if the large institutions in the rest of Canada, including the Bank of Canada, refused to cooperate with the institutions in Quebec, in order to, for example, prevent the flight of capital and the massive withdrawal of deposits. Robson went back to the example of Czechoslovakia to show that Quebec, like Slovakia, would find it more advantageous to create its own currency. Robson's study received serious support the following week when, at a press conference with the governor of the Bank of Canada, who was presenting his annual report, the senior deputy governor, Bernard Bonin, made this reply to a reporter who questioned him on Quebec's use of the Canadian dollar: "All I have to say to you on this subject is to refer you to the study Bill Robson has just published at the C.D. Howe Institute. Bill Robson is one of the best analysts in Canada on monetary issues."[22] Bonin clarified his views in an interview with *Le Soleil* a few weeks later. He felt that in a Free Trade area, Canada, the U.S. and even an independent Quebec should have a common currency. "Economically, it is feasible," he said. "It is politically that we run into obstacles!" He had not changed his mind since he had studied the matter for the Lévesque government.

Jacques Parizeau held stubbornly to a common currency because he wanted to protect Quebec from Canada's mood swings. "As long as we belong to the area using the Canadian dollar, we are safe,"[23] he said. He was convinced that, in 1995, he would not have to go through the experience of René Lévesque who, in 1980, endured the sarcasm of people talking about the "Lévesque *piastre*[24] at 65 cents"! In his view, just the fact that Quebecers held one quarter of the Canadian monetary supply would be reason enough for the Canadian government to give up the idea of preventing an independent Quebec from using its currency. Finally, Parizeau had difficulty imagining Canada would refuse a common currency just when Europe was going in the opposite direction with the treaty of Maastricht, signed three years earlier, and adopting the Euro as the single currency the very same year as the Quebec referendum. Parizeau was so convinced that Canada could not prevent Quebec from using its currency that he included in the draft bill on Quebec sovereignty the provision that "the money that is legal tender in Quebec shall remain the Canadian dollar." He believed that the very short-term movement of capital, brought about by derivatives,[25] was responsible for money coming into Canada which far exceeded the amounts from trade or export transactions. In that kind of environment, which can turn hostile very quickly, which can even cause the collapse of a currency in the space of a few days, Parizeau could not imagine Quebec having its own currency.

The question of borders would assuredly occupy an important place in any potential negotiation. The Quebec government would have to find solutions to two major problems: the situation of the communities in northern Quebec, and the situation of the anglophones living on Montreal's West Island. Each of these cases raised the question of the territory's integrity in a glaring way. During the 1994 election campaign, the Parti Québécois had repeatedly affirmed its stand on the territorial question: There would be only one legal system in Quebec, and every means would be taken to protect the integrity of the territory. Its recognition would become fundamental in any negotiation with the Aboriginal peoples. But no sooner had the government been elected than it faced an outcry from Native leaders. In a meeting at Lac Delage, these leaders reaffirmed the right of their peoples to govern themselves, and their ancestral rights over their territory. The government responded by inserting in the draft bill on the sovereignty of Quebec, tabled on December 6 in the National Assembly, the following provision: "(The new Constitution of Quebec) must recognize the right of First Nations to govern themselves on the lands they possess in their own right. This guarantee and this recognition shall be applied within the context of respect for the integrity of the territory of Quebec." Three days later, through their spokesperson, Zebedee Nungak, the Inuit appealed to the federal government to come to their aid.[26] Nungak was the same Inuit spokesperson who in Toronto, at the February 1992 constitutional conference on Canadian identity, rights and values, presented a map severing two-thirds of Quebec's territory. This map thumbed its nose at the laws of Canada and Quebec, which, in 1898 and 1912, incorporated into Quebec all of what is today Northern Quebec and Abitibi, which had been Crown lands prior to that time.[27]

A week after the draft bill was tabled, the First Nations of Canada, represented by their leaders, reminded the federal government of its historical obligations toward them. At the end of December, the Quebec government, in a gesture intended as concrete testimony to the seriousness of its policy with respect to Aboriginal claims, proposed to the Attikamek and Montagnais peoples the creation of territories having a surface area of 4,000 square kilometres for their traditional activities, resource areas of 40,000 square kilometres, to be managed jointly, and conservation areas of 10,000 square kilometres.[28] Jacques Parizeau's position was supported by the fact that when they signed the James Bay and Northern Quebec Agreement, the Crees and the Inuit had relinquished all territorial rights, principally in article 2.1 of the agreement. The article said: "In consideration of the rights and benefits herein set forth in favour to the James Bay Crees and the Inuit of Québec, the James Bay Crees and the Inuit of Québec hereby cede, release, surrender and convey all their Native claims, rights, titles and interests, whatever they may be, in and to land in the Territory and in Québec, and Québec and Canada accept such surrender."[29] Parizeau comments: "For us, there is a principle on which we have never wavered. We recognize eleven Aboriginal nations in Quebec, we recognize their right to self-determination, we recognize their right to participate actively in their development, while maintaining the integrity of the territory of Quebec. Until all parties are ready for discussion within that kind of framework, I can live with the *status quo*."[30]

The Crees did not see things the same way. Matthew Coon Come resumed his crusade against the Quebec government's position. He was well aware that if the YES side carried the day, Quebec would have to seek recognition internationally, including from the U.S. "And certainly our next door neighbour would have a great say should that happen," he says. In mid-November, on a trip to the U.S., he made this attack on the premier of Quebec: "In another attempt to deny our status and rights, Mr. Parizeau asserts again and again that our aboriginal rights have been extinguished. First, we don't agree. But this is an assertion that Mr. Parizeau should be ashamed to make." He added that such a claim should be condemned as colonialist and racist and belonged "in the garbage can of the history of apartheid."

In fact, Matthew Coon Come proved himself to be remarkably shrewd: it was a perfect opportunity and he did not let it slip. He acknowledges today that the election of a government advocating the secession of Quebec allowed him to publicly reopen the cause of Aboriginal rights everywhere. "Why not take that opportunity?" he says. "I wanted to make it very clear that we weren't denying Quebec their right to determine their own future or to exercise their right of self-determination. What we were saying was: if you claim that right of self-determination, do not deny that same right to apply to First Nations, in this case, to the Crees of Quebec. That's the language we use in the international community." During the week following the election of the Parti Québécois, Coon Come obtained the mandate to hold his own referendum among his people. "Yes, there would be some kind of international human rights watchdog saying: what about the referendum that the Crees had?" he says. Coon Come admits that the circumstances also allowed him to put considerable pressure on the federal government. "We created a situation where we were putting Canada in a very difficult position. We wanted to paint the picture that they could not just transfer the fiduciary responsibilities of the federal government over Indians and land to Quebec, without our consent." With a certain candour, he adds, "If there was no PQ government, we wouldn't probably have this discussion. But because it was inevitable that there was going to be a referendum, then, we decided that we will assert our right."

The campaign led by the chief of the Grand Council of the Crees was deeply irritating to the government of Quebec. "It's all a big farce," said David Cliche, who was handling the Aboriginal file for the PQ, and who chose not to respond to the Cree leader's attack.[31] Farce or not, Matthew Coon Come had an impact on the big decision-makers in Washington. "This statement didn't go unnoticed, believe me," says Raymond Chrétien, Canada's ambassador in the American capital at the time. "Probably no effect on the U.S. as a whole, but on the people who counted in Washington, yes, definitely." The former diplomat recalls that in the House of Commons at that time, one member had asked whether the Canadian Ambassador had seen Coon Come's speech before it was delivered. "No. Who was I to tell the leader of the Cree nation what to say or not to say?" Raymond Chrétien answers today.[32]

The territorial problem involved more than just the claims of the Crees. Even if the Quebec government acknowledged the right of

Aboriginal peoples to self-determination, for the Assembly of First Nations, governmental autonomy could not be disassociated from land. In Quebec, four Aboriginal nations were claiming territories that extended beyond the province's borders: the Inuit of the Côte-Nord, the Micmacs of the Gaspésie, and the Algonquins in the western part of the province and the Mohawks of the Saint-Régis area. Their basic stand was backed up by a threat. The president of the Congress of Aboriginal Peoples, Jim Sinclair, represented over half a million Indians, Inuit and Metis people living off-reserve in Canada. Sinclair promised a crisis like the one at Oka if the Quebec government did not change its position on the territorial question.

While the Aboriginals were demanding their share of Quebec, Jacques Parizeau faced the threat of having to deal with another demand for border revisions to his new country, this time from Montreal's West Island. The seed had been planted at least fifteen years earlier. During the first referendum, some anglophones from that part of Quebec had raised the possibility of becoming part of Ontario. In a book published in 1980,[33] William F. Shaw and Lionel Albert listed portions of Quebec that might no longer remain part of it, should it become independent. One of these portions was western Quebec, from Montreal to the Ontario border. After a good part of northern Quebec is severed,[34] and all of southern Quebec, along the St. Lawrence as well,[35] the authors add, "Among the territories thus affected would be the western half of the Montreal archipelago, the Ottawa Valley, including its tributary valleys, the Temiscaming region and the lower part of the North Shore of the Gulf of St. Lawrence."[36] The map accompanying this passage, in the book by Shaw and Albert, reduces Quebec to a strip along the North Shore of the St. Lawrence River, ending in the vicinity of Anticosti Island.

Parizeau responded to these claims by invoking the Constitution. To his way of thinking, ever since 1871 and in the new Constitution of 1982, there had been the same underlying principle: The borders within Canada cannot be changed without the consent of the province concerned.[37] Shaw and Albert had foreseen this line of reasoning fifteen years before the 1995 referendum: "If Quebec decided to cease being a province, then the Constitution would no longer apply." But Parizeau takes their logic one step further: "While Quebec was in Confederation," he says, "the federal government could not change Quebec's borders. And when Quebec is no longer in Confederation, if Canada wants to change Quebec's borders, it's a violation of international law. Before, it can't, and after, it's too late!"[38]

As for the anglophones living in the Montreal West Island, they would enjoy, in an independent Quebec, the same protections they have in Canada now, and the government made a commitment to this effect in its draft bill: "(The new Constitution) must include a charter of human rights and freedoms. It must guarantee to the anglophone community the preservation of its identity and its institutions."

Jacques Parizeau, on the other hand, did not contest the legality of the Labrador border. Labrador had been taken from Quebec in 1927 by a decision of the Privy Council in London and annexed to Newfoundland, a British colony at the time. He considered that the government of Quebec had shown in a number of ways, since 1927, that it was in full agreement with that decision and that the matter had been closed long ago. But defining maritime borders would be more complex. From the Atlantic to Anticosti Island, the Gulf of St. Lawrence is certainly not an inland sea. It is what Jacques Parizeau calls "an open sea." With a coastline on an open sea, an independent Quebec would be entitled, according to the rules for sharing waterways, to twelve miles and to half the water separating it from its neighbours, Newfoundland and New Brunswick. Hudson Bay presented a different challenge in that it was an inland sea. Consequently, Quebec, as a province, had no jurisdiction over a twelve-mile stretch or even one mile off that coastline. According to old documents, its jurisdiction ended "at the point where a horse would be breast-deep" in the water if it ventured in at low tide. The Quebec government would not rule out the possibility of having to plead its case before the International Court at The Hague.

In any event, before having to face this type of conundrum, the Parizeau government would first have to get over the hurdle of the referendum itself, and win it. Thus, on February 6, 1995, seventeen regional consultative commissions on the future of Quebec swung into action. They counted no fewer than 288 commissioners who, in one month, would receive 4,591 reports and hear as many as 55,000 people. The president of the Montreal commission, Marcel Masse, gives this summary of the spirit that dominated the entire process: "The people wanted to know in what respect and how this new tool of sovereignty would change their lives. In 1995, they wanted to know, 'sovereignty to do what?' and no longer just 'why sovereignty?' as in 1980. Sovereignty was a tool for changing society."[39] Journalist Gilles Lesage was not mistaken about the mood of Quebecers when he said, "There is an enormous thirst for change. The *status quo* is scorned and the grievances against Ottawa are numerous. But confidence in its own government is limited."[40]

The Quebec Liberal Party remained absent from the whole operation, but the American Consulate in Quebec made sure it had an observer at the commissions' sittings. Periodic reports were sent to the Secretary of State. They give a good idea of the atmosphere at these gatherings. Here is one example, taken from the February 28 consular report, on the sixth meeting of the national capital regional commission, held on the 24th. The report is entitled *An Evening with a Commission on the Future of Quebec.* "Like an American town meeting, conducted with dignity and good humor, such was (the consulate officer's) impression of the sixth sitting of the capital commission on the future of Quebec, on 24 February. Held in a school auditorium in the small town of Saint-Marc-des-Carrières, some 45 miles southwest of Quebec City, the session was well attended. In spite of the evening's high winds and driving snow, roughly 150-200 people filled perhaps two-thirds of the chairs for the three-hour meeting. The atmosphere was expectant and attentive, tinged with a dash of excitement. Sixteen commission members, presided over by Jean-Paul Lallier (sic), Mayor of Quebec, sat at two ranks of tables facing the audience. Among the commissioners was Richard Le Hir, minister (and occasional loose cannon) for restructuring, responsible for crafting the eventual transition from a provincial to a national government. To the commission's right was a raised table for those making prepared presentations, while at their left, behind a small mountain of recording and amplifying equipment, sat those responsible for maintaining a record of events for later consultation and posterity. The scene was dressed in Quebec blue (indistinguishable from PQ blue) and a Quebec provincial flag flanked the commission (...). The great majority of the audience, clearly of sovereigntist sympathy, warmly applauded pro-sovereignty presentations. Nevertheless, dissenting and questioning voices received a respectful hearing."[41]

There was sustained interest in the commissions throughout the whole month during which they sat. Jacques Parizeau likes to recall how, one evening, André Chagnon, the president of Videotron, whose community television network in Quebec was re-broadcasting the sessions, phoned him: "He asked, 'Do you know how many viewers you had yesterday?' I said, 'no.' He said, '400,000! For a commission on the future of Quebec!'"[42]

From March 22-28, following the work of the regional commissions, the national commission met at Manoir Montmorency, in Beauport, near Quebec City. As a first step, the commission received some 50 reports submitted by the regional bodies. Then, presided over by Monique Vézina, it prepared the conclusions to be submitted to the government. On April 9, several commissioners met to make a final revision of the report, which would also have an English version. It was already known that it would recommend political sovereignty as an essential tool for Quebec's cultural and economic development, and the conclusion of an association of an economic nature with the rest of Canada. On April 19, in a formal ceremony in parliament's *Salon rouge* (Red room), Jacques Parizeau received the report. He refrained, however, from commenting on it, not yet having read it carefully, thus leaving the president of the national commission and its two vice-presidents, Marcel Masse and Jean-Paul L'Allier, the time and opportunity needed to present it to reporters.

According to Mario Dumont, whose party took part in the work of the commissions, it is difficult to assess how much influence they may or may not have had on the course followed by Premier Parizeau. "I would have a hard time saying that the commissions are what made Mr. Parizeau go in the direction he did," he says. "I think that, rather, what determined the direction he took was something very simple, which you could call political reality. He knew what the polls said; he had heard public opinion. After the commissions were over, the fundamental reality remained unchanged: Putting a question to Quebecers proposing the idea of Quebec independence, without partnership, without anything. People were not prepared to go for that."[43]

Even before the national commission had submitted its report, that "fundamental reality" led the premier to defer the date of the referendum. At a PQ Youth convention, on March 27, he declared, "Quebecers are not ready to vote for sovereignty." The next day, his deputy premier invoked that same reality by using an analogy that deeply offended Parizeau. "I do not wish," said Bernard Landry, "to be the second-in-command of the Light Brigade, that was exterminated in twenty minutes in the Crimea, because of irresponsibility on the part of its leaders."[44] In Ottawa, this declaration was perceived as evidence that the Parizeau project was starting to founder. "What had happened at the time," recalls Eddy Goldenberg, "was that separation was not going to work. There was that reality. Mr. Landry said he didn't want to be the general in charge of the Light Brigade. So, what they were trying to do was find a way to get a YES vote, which they would use to separate, to ask an unclear question."

Jean-François Lisée, for his part, plays down the significance of Landry's statement, pointing out that Parizeau had just announced the day before, that the referendum would not be held in the spring. "Certainly the decision would have been made much earlier, maybe in March, not to have a referendum in the spring," he says. "It was just a question of waiting for the right time to announce it. And we thought, we'll announce it before the Bloc Québécois convention, to lighten their load and give them more space. It was the next day that Landry made his statement to the press that he didn't want to be like the Light Brigade and get needlessly decimated. But, the day before, the order to attack had been suspended. In fact, Landry more or less walked through a wide-open door. Obviously, he wanted to position himself publicly between Mr. Parizeau and Mr. Bouchard. (…) He wanted to appear as a moderate in this debate."

Discussions about the referendum date took up a lot of time at the strategy committee meetings held every Tuesday. "The nature of the exchanges between Mr. Landry and Mr. Parizeau was much like that between Mr. Bouchard and Mr. Parizeau," Lisée continues. "Mr. Landry wanted assurance no referendum would be held without a certain probability of victory and Mr. Parizeau refused to agree to this publicly, because of the effect it would have on the voters. So, there was some tension."[45] Even ten years later, Landry's words still leave Parizeau feeling bitter: "I had better not comment," he says, "because I could say something rude. And I don't like to be rude. But episodes like this are part of life."[46]

The polls confirmed Landry's flair. In the final week of March, despite all the exposure the referendum had gained from the regional commissions, public opinion had not budged one iota since mid-December. To the question, "If a referendum were held today, would you vote for or against Quebec becoming an independent country?," 41% answered for and 59% answered against, after distribution of the undecided vote of 17%. Among francophones, fewer than 50% were for. There wasn't even a majority in favour of sovereignty in the event of failed negotiations with Canada (44% vs. 56%).[47] What is more, the PQ had lost points over the previous three months. During that period, in a survey organized by the *Conseil du patronat du Québec* (Quebec Employers Council), the heads of large corporations indicated they were not very impressed by the new government's performance; and it was Jean Chrétien, in power only just over a year, who got the best rating.[48]

Parizeau faced up to the evidence. On April 5, before the Chamber of Commerce of the South Shore of Quebec, he officially announced the postponement of the referendum. He reminded his listeners that he had never fixed a date or season and he maintained that he needed time to analyze thoroughly the information gathered by the regional commissions, whose conclusions had been made public, but whose report had not yet been submitted.

Although they were ready for action, the YES campaign organizers were also aware that the spring was not a favourable time for a victorious campaign. "We would have liked a more impressive sweep (in the September 1994 general election), so we would have been better positioned for an earlier referendum," says Alain Lupien, coordinator of the referendum financing campaign.[49] "But, as the results were below our expectations, we knew very well, as organizers, that it might mean we would have to delay the referendum in order to rebuild the momentum." He was not the only one to think this way, but, as long as the premier had not clearly indicated his intentions, the organizers, according to Lupien, worked to "recognize windows of opportunity, perhaps for the spring, if worse came to worst, for the fall after that. As far as organization was concerned, the spring window had to be left open, because there could have been a magic moment and they would have had to be ready. But the window of opportunity, from the organizers' perspective, looked more promising in the fall, for two reasons. First, the question of political momentum and, secondly, as there had been restructuring within the party, it left more time to hold a series of training workshops that we wanted to do. To prepare the troops, four rounds of training were planned with respect to content and organization. We had to take the time to do that."[50]

The timing of Parizeau's announcement that the referendum would be postponed was not fortuitous. In two days, the Bloc Québécois would hold its annual convention, and the remarks Lucien Bouchard had been making since his return to health, created anxiety in the premier's entourage. Back in February, Bouchard had told a *Radio-Canada* reporter, "I cannot entertain a scenario where we would deliberately subject Quebec to a NO vote…" and to another, from *Le Soleil*, "I do not want to see sovereignty beaten yet again." Therefore, it was with a certain apprehension that Parizeau's strategists viewed the upcoming Bloc convention. "We were unpleasantly surprised," Jean-François Lisée recalls today. "For, when (Bouchard) came back, we were no longer climbing (in the polls). We had suffered a small setback." And, alluding to the work of the regional commissions, he adds, "the way we saw things, there would be a listening phase, then a phase for making proposals again. We knew we would not be going back up in the polls during the listening phase. Our strategy at the time was, let's return to proposal-mode now, with the improvements to be made and taking into account what we have heard. In other words, 'we have heard what you said, we have amended our project, here is our new proposal.' And then, we would shift back into marketing gear. But when Mr. Bouchard spoke, he said he didn't agree with that and that we had to change our strategy. And that was the beginning of the *virage*[51]. What he said was not something that could really be implemented. While he said we needed to change our strategy, he did not tell us what to replace it with. It was more a sign of ill humour, a criticism. And our reaction was, 'what does he propose, then?' That would be revealed in the weeks ahead, but not right away."[52] Bouchard's assertions created a real malaise, which would prevail from mid-February until the Bloc's convention and beyond, while the strategy of common action threatened to fall apart.

On Friday evening, April 7, 1995, the Great Hall of Montreal's *Palais des congrès* (Convention centre) was packed to the rafters. Jacques Parizeau and his wife were seated in the front row. Lucien Bouchard, leader of the Bloc Québécois, was to open his party's convention with what his assistants termed a "major" speech. During the week his entourage and that of the premier had met, as they did every week, and the matter of this speech had arisen. Everyone knew that Bouchard would read a speech and, on Thursday, Parizeau's group learned of its content. Until then, everything had gone on normally despite a certain atmosphere of mistrust that prevailed in the premier's camp, towards the other camp. The memory still lingered of a Lucien Bouchard who, as a Conservative minister in Brian Mulroney's cabinet, had helped orchestrate the *beau risque*, a venture that had prompted Jacques Parizeau to walk out in disagreement on René Lévesque and the Parti Québécois. "There was a suspicion, always lurking there, that Mr. Bouchard was not a true sovereigntist," says Pierre-Paul Roy, his political advisor, who does not try to hide the fact that his leader's vision of sovereignty was much closer to that of René Lévesque than that of Parizeau. Since his meeting with Parizeau on

March 12, when Bouchard had clearly explained his perception of events to the premier, and even gone so far as to raise the idea of a second referendum, his vision had not changed. And so, "there was a suspicion of betrayal more or less hanging in the air," Roy adds.[53]

All day Friday, Bouchard, his chief of staff, Gilbert Charland,[54] and Pierre-Paul Roy kept coming back to the text of the speech to be delivered that evening. Roy remembers: "One of the big questions Bouchard had was, 'do I use the term *virage* or not?' He was aware that the impression people would get from it might be a bit stronger than what he wanted. He was looking for just the right word, but at the same time, he wanted the message to be understood, to be clear. He asked us to find him a synonym for the word *virage*. We got out the dictionaries..." All day, Bouchard's advisors searched, to no avail. "We made headway with the (rest of) the text," Roy continues, "but that sentence still refused to be nailed down, so to speak. And, by the end of the afternoon, someone said to Mr. Bouchard, 'Look, we have analyzed this from every angle and it's called a *virage*.' Mr. Bouchard still hesitated, then he said, 'OK, let's just go with it then!'"[55] Bouchard's secretary, Lise Pelletier, who had come from Ottawa especially, then gave the text its finishing touches.

In the late afternoon, around 5:30, Jean Royer, the premier's chief of staff, arrived at the *Palais des congrès*. "Mr. Bouchard wanted to see me," he recalls. "He had me read the changes that had been made to the text. They included the word *virage*. And the illustrations of the *virage*, which appeared in the text, were examples taken directly from the Parti Québécois' program. I didn't see any problem with it. But even so, it wasn't up to me. I talked to Mr. Parizeau about it."[56] Royer read the text to his leader, who did not express any objection either.

"The work of the regional commissions," Bouchard proclaimed before the delegates, "has shown that our citizens were not ready to respond immediately to the referendum question. Even were it only in this respect, the commissions will have rendered to Quebec an inestimable service, namely that of sparing it a referendum that would have been premature, by virtue of being held under insufficiently favourable conditions. But the commissions proved themselves to be more useful still in that they have identified the questions that the referendum process continues to raise. These commissions have therefore opened up avenues of reflection that we cannot reject." And he added, "(Quebecers) are ready to say YES to a unifying project. The sovereignty project must quickly embrace a change of direction *(virage)* that will draw Quebecers closer to one another and to the project itself, and will open up a credible future path for new Quebec-Canada relations, responding to the legitimate concerns of the men and women of Quebec." He went on to explain, "Sovereigntists have always insisted on the need to maintain a common economic space, both for Quebec and for Canada. (...) We must reflect further on concrete ways to strengthen that space. There is a need to seriously examine whether it might be appropriate to frame it by common institutions, even political ones. The establishment of a new economic partnership between a sovereign Quebec and Canada could flow from a comprehensive agreement." The two key terms had been used: "change of direction" *(virage)* and "partnership." He had used the first only once, the second three times, one of which was in reference to the European Union.

Parizeau listened without moving a muscle. "He closed his eyes," recalls the Bloc Québécois' director general, Bob Dufour, who had found himself a seat in the hall from which he could observe the premier's reactions during Bouchard's speech. "He listened to it like someone listening to music or listening carefully to what is being said; he showed no reaction. Sometimes, you can feel that something is being met with approval or disapproval, that it stirs an emotion. That night, no. I did not feel that."[57] In fact, Parizeau seemed satisfied. "The proof," Royer says, "was that he was seated in the very first row and applauded."[58]

In Dufour's view, Parizeau's attitude during and after Lucien Bouchard's speech was not so much a sign that he approved in principle of Bouchard's remarks as a sign that he did not wish to let anything of his disagreement show in front of the delegates at the convention. "Mr. Parizeau was familiar with Mr. Bouchard's position," he says, "but if I told you Mr. Parizeau agreed with it, I think I would be telling you a big lie. When one of the major partners, like Mr. Bouchard, comes up with a strategy that may be different, it is bound to offend Mr. Parizeau a little bit. But Mr. Bouchard's position was shared by important ministers in Parizeau's cabinet."[59] Lisette Lapointe, who was seated at her husband's side during the speech, does not deny it was a painful experience for him: "Those are the more difficult moments," she says, "because Jacques Parizeau had a certain way of looking at things. But, on the other hand, he wanted so much for things to succeed..."[60] In Parizeau's entourage, no one had any illusions about the meaning of the word *virage*. "Those of us in Parizeau's camp," says Jean-François Lisée, "our goal was to achieve sovereignty and we knew that, in order to do so, the two leaders, Mr. Parizeau and Mr. Bouchard, had to come together. So, our task was not to divide them, but to unite them. But one of them did not want to play the game at that point. It was Lucien Bouchard who had put the word *virage* in his text. It was a code word, but *we* knew what he meant by it: he meant a second referendum. And he was emphasizing the need for a radical change of direction in the sovereignty proposal. He wanted the referendum question changed so that it would allow for a second referendum. That is, there would be a first referendum on sovereignty, accompanied by the statement that any agreement with Canada would be ratified in a second referendum. He wanted to reintroduce the notion of association, as in the 1980 referendum."[61]

Nevertheless, until the end of that Friday evening, all went well. At the reception given for the diplomatic corps, immediately after the speech, the two men conversed, and there was nothing to suggest the confrontation that would ensue in the hours ahead. Parizeau's entourage did, however, begin to show their displeasure openly once they realized how Bouchard's people were interpreting the text. "In our jargon, we call that *spin*," says Jean Royer. "(Mr. Bouchard's) entourage began to influence the press in its perception: the *virage* was bigger than it seemed. It was a major change of direction, and it was important that the Parti Québécois, or the sovereigntists generally, agree to expand the offer to be made to the rest of Canada. That started on Friday night and Saturday. In politics, perception quickly becomes reality, then truth. Yes, the Bloc people put the pressure on."[62] Lisée is even more categorical: "On our side, we were playing down (the impact of the speech) on the strength of the text itself, while Bouchard, on the other hand, was cueing his advisors to go and tell reporters the opposite, that it really was a signal, a very strong one."[63]

Saturday morning, the newspaper headlines increased the already mounting tension between the two camps. Bouchard added to it with these words to reporters: "While awaiting Mr. Parizeau's decision, I have to wait, but I am not signing a blank cheque. Mr. Parizeau is the leader, with a majority mandate, which gives him considerable room to manoeuver, but in politics, the room to manoeuver is never absolute. It is evident that Jacques Parizeau works with partners and with public opinion."[64] The Bloc leader even raised the possibility of delaying the referendum beyond 1995. To add weight to his position, he had convention participants adopt a resolution he presented himself, recommending partnership with Canada. "Mr. Parizeau may have been somewhat shocked at finding himself in the position of having to deal with this situation, but he knew Mr. Bouchard's stand on the issue. It was no secret," says Pierre-Paul Roy.[65]

On Sunday, Jacques Parizeau was in Quebec City with his minister Jean Garon to open the education Convention *(les États généraux de l'éducation)*. A reporter asked him if he still considered himself leader of the sovereigntist troops. "I don't know," he replied, "I would hope there are several. However, I do know there is only one premier at a time!"[66] Bouchard shot back at Parizeau immediately that, yes, there was only one premier, but that he had his own responsibilities to see to. "Bouchard was not under orders to Mr. Parizeau," Roy concludes, "Nor was he subject to the Bélanger-Campeau commission, or the Bloc Québécois, or in the referendum campaign. He was a bit piqued (by Parizeau's comment) because he was not questioning the fact that Parizeau was premier of Quebec or that the ball was mainly in Parizeau's court. But he could not let himself be dismissed either, be told, 'If Bouchard doesn't like it here, let him go play somewhere else!'"[67]

On Monday morning, April 10, Lucien Bouchard asked the president of the Bloc's political committee, Daniel Turp, "to put some flesh on the bones of the partnership," before he was to participate in a radio broadcast of *Le Midi Quinze* on *Radio-Canada*.

The exchange between host Michel Lacombe and the leader of the Bloc, at a certain point, went like this:

Lacombe: Why did you decide to speak about a change of direction yourself?

Bouchard: Because we need a change of direction. Clearly a change of direction is necessary, and it seems to me that what the people are demanding is a change of direction. Are we going to hold a referendum if, by the time fall comes, we have changed nothing, and we realize that we are still at 40, 44, 43%? Will we hold a referendum to lose it? If there is one thing I do not want, sir, I'm not the one who will decide it, but, if there is one thing I do not wish, it is to see or participate in a referendum campaign that would surely lead us to defeat. I do not want Quebec to get battered a second time.

Lacombe: See or participate?

Bouchard: I will ask myself all the questions. But I do not want to see that happen. Participate? As I said, we shall see.

Lacombe: You have just told Mr. Parizeau, if I understand correctly: if you hold the referendum, while knowing we would lose, don't count on my partnership.

Bouchard: No, I did not say that.

Lacombe: You didn't?

Bouchard: I did not say that, at least, I have not said it so far. I said that I did not want to see that happen. Mr. Parizeau reminded us yesterday that he is the premier and that there is only one. I think we all more or less knew that already. I myself said it several times during the weekend, that Mr. Parizeau was the premier of Quebec. It is obvious, if you look at the evidence, that he is, furthermore, the sovereigntist leader. He is the great sovereigntist leader; I know that. I also know he can decide everything on his own. But to win, we have to be a team.

At that moment, Jean-François Lisée, listening to the radio in his car, heard Bouchard's words. "I heard him say, I don't have the exact words, that he was not absolutely certain he would participate in the referendum campaign if he was not satisfied with the question or the direction," he recalls "I thought, 'Wow! He has just said that publicly.' Now, our crisis was really escalating. Now, we were in a major crisis. There was a publicly confirmed threat by one of our two leaders that he would withdraw if he was not satisfied. I felt we were really on the brink of disaster."[68]

Was Parizeau aware of Bouchard's remarks? Half an hour after the broadcast, before the Laval Chamber of Commerce, Parizeau spoke as if to take up the gauntlet: "There is someone who has the responsibility of having to decide and that person is me. I will have to decide and no one will decide for me."[69] But Lisée was not in Laval. He hurried over to the office and told Jean Royer what he had just heard. As their leader was in a bad enough mood already, they decided together—"naïvely," says Lisée—not to report Bouchard's remarks to him. They feared his reaction at a meeting, planned several days earlier, but to take place that same afternoon, which would gather around the table the Partners for Sovereignty, the community groups, the unions, and the business people. As well as Parizeau and Bouchard. "All we wanted that day was to survive, and to send a signal of dialogue," says Lisée. "We wanted to say, 'whatever things aren't working, we need to talk about them.' That's all we wanted that day."[70]

The Partners for Sovereignty came to the aid of Parizeau's two advisors. Serge Turgeon, then president of the artists' union, said, "We have the impression that you two are performing a play, but you are never on the same page. We could say about you, they liked each other a lot, but never at the same time!" The representatives of the CSN, the FTQ[71] and the others all gave the same message: "Talk to each other. Listen to each other!" "You could see," recalls Jean-François Lisée, "that Mr. Bouchard was waiting for a sign of openness from Mr. Parizeau, for him to say, 'Listen, I'm not very happy with the way things are going, but it is certain that we are meant to come to an understanding.' There was no sign. And Mr. Parizeau waited for a sign of self-criticism from Mr. Bouchard, if he could have said, for example, 'Listen, sometimes there are loudmouth shouts. We know each other, but the important thing is to get along.' But neither of them gave a signal. They both seemed to dig in their heels."[72]

After the meeting, Bouchard, flanked by his advisors, headed towards the elevator. Lisée followed them. "What I wanted to say to them was that it couldn't be over. But I had nothing to say because I could not report words that I had not heard (from the mouth of my leader)." The elevator doors closed. Lisée watched Bouchard and his advisors leave, saying to himself, "They're going. This doesn't make sense, it can't end like this."[73] They had reached the breaking point.

CHAPTER V

The Partnership

Jean-François Lisée returned home, deeply disturbed. He took it upon himself to do something he had never done before. He picked up the phone and called Lucien Bouchard. He said to him, "Mr. Bouchard, I think we are at the edge of the cliff. No one must move another inch. We want you to know that there are people on the Parizeau team who believe we need to repair the damage that has been done. We cannot achieve sovereignty unless our two leaders unite." "I did not say that I agreed with him," Lisée recalls today. "In fact, I disagreed with this idea of two referendums. It would have been a strategic disaster. And there was another signal I wanted to give him: they had to talk to each other!" Bouchard listened attentively. The call produced its desired effect: nothing was said subsequently to worsen relations between the two camps. "We felt we could begin then to envisage ways out of the crisis," said Lisée.[1]

However, in the days following the Bloc Québécois convention, the communication breakdown persisted. Nothing negative happened, but nothing positive happened either. And the fear among Parizeau's entourage was that everyone would settle into the crisis. Despite Lisée's phone call to Lucien Bouchard, each camp might retreat to its position, until the split became complete. "There was one point when Mr. Parizeau was, psychologically, rather taken aback by what had happened with Mr. Bouchard and Mr. Landry," Lisée recalls. "He sort of instinctively withdrew into his comfort zone, the Parti Québécois and his allies within the Parti Québécois."[2]

Five or six days went by. Then, Lisée decided to send Parizeau a note. What he told him, in essence, was, "that the chances of realizing sovereignty under the current political conditions were zero; it was up to him, as leader of the sovereignty movement and Premier of Quebec, to reopen the dialogue." Lisée remembers telling him "that he had to create a situation that would let him take back the initiative and restate the rules of the game by modifying his personal position, by agreeing to have discussions with others, and by showing a willingness to amend the proposal. But he had to stay in charge of the game." In that same note, Lisée reminded Jacques Parizeau that, during the referendum campaign, it was unimportant what Bouchard's role would be. It was he, Parizeau, who would be Premier and he would continue to be Premier if the YES forces won. "You must use Lucien Bouchard's strength," Lisée advised, "but if people try to make it look as if you're not in the game anymore, our opponents will use that false impression to remind Quebecers that if there's a YES victory, it won't be Bouchard, but Parizeau who will be in power. Politically, we would pay dearly for that. So, even with the 'change in direction,' you need to be the one to get things back on track, by modifying your position. You need to begin the game by setting new parameters that will make others want to join in."[3] Not only did Parizeau's entourage need to convince him to establish new rules to play by, but it also had to convince Bouchard and all the others, who were not in the Parizeau camp, that their leader was actually willing to change.

But Jacques Parizeau would not budge. When Jean Royer, his chief of staff, asked him whether he had read Lisée's note, he said, "I lost it." A copy of it was printed up for him, and then a second one. Parizeau simply did not want to get into a discussion about its content. Finally one day, on a government plane taking the Premier and his entourage from Quebec to Montreal, Jean Royer felt the time was right and went on the offensive. "On our own, we do not have the majority we need to achieve sovereignty," he told Mr. Parizeau. "Quebecers are convinced that you do not want association with Canada. Bouchard and Dumont want association. There's one who doesn't, that's Parizeau."[4] Royer also reminded him that when Quebecers are asked whether they are for sovereignty with an offer of partnership, the majority are in favour. Royer and Lisée attempted to persuade Parizeau that it was not a matter of his turning his back on everything he had already said about association. Indeed, Parizeau conceived of a certain form of association, which he had already described as "unavoidable," with a single currency, the free movement of goods and services, the establishment of a tribunal to resolve disputes, etc. But there was a major perception problem, and Lisée reminded him of it. "People think you are against association, and therefore they are against sovereignty. It has to be explained to them that you are in favour of a form of association and that you are also considering a somewhat expanded form of it, if Canada wants it, but that this does not constitute a condition for sovereignty."[5]

Parizeau looked at them and said, "I would have hoped Quebecers didn't need that in order to take the step." He reminded them that his entire being, and all his past political actions, had no other goal than to convince Quebecers that it was sovereignty in itself that was a good thing, and that it wasn't about "the margin to be shared with one's neighbour." The two advisors then cited the conclusions of the regional commissions: "They told us: give us more!" Finally, Parizeau conceded. He agreed to what he called "window dressing," how the proposal would be packaged and presented. And he said to his two advisors, "Very well, I see that you are right. Let's start talking!" "That meant," Lisée explains, "Let's start planning negotiations to bring about a tripartite agreement."[6]

Having the authorization to open negotiations with the Bloc Québécois and Action démocratique was one thing, but getting results that would satisfy both parties was another. With respect to the Bloc, there was hope: the differences between the parties were not ideological in nature. "It was not a case of Parizeau wanting a sovereign Quebec, and Bouchard wanting a recast federalism," says Jean-François Lisée.[7] The political projects of the two groups were very much alike. They were not distinct. The confrontation was essentially over strategy. Bouchard wanted to maintain major ties with neighbouring Canada, while Parizeau felt that this was not necessary and probably unrealistic.

There was another layer to this problem. Even if, in Parizeau's mind, maintaining close relations with neighbouring Canada was neither realistic nor necessary, Quebecers wanted it. In the Bloc camp, anxiety persisted. "I am not the interpreter of Mr. Parizeau's thinking," says Pierre-Paul Roy, who was in the Bouchard camp, "but we did have strong apprehensions that Mr. Parizeau wanted to hold a referendum at all costs, even if it meant losing. That worried us a great deal. I'm not saying Mr. Parizeau didn't want to win the referendum, I've never doubted that… It's what he has fought for all his life. But as far as his strategy and his approach were concerned, he had a much higher risk tolerance for losing than we did."[8] This was confirmed by Jean-François Lisée: "Mr. Bouchard was far more worried than Mr. Parizeau, about the ability to win a majority with a project that was strictly about independence."[9]

Looking back now, Jean Royer considers, for his part, that this crisis should not be overblown since "there will always be crises in politics and we have to be able to deal with them." He then adds that the main problem was to shift the public's understanding from the perceived differences between the two parties to their actual differences. "Mr. Parizeau and Mr. Bouchard were constantly put in the position where, if they did not use the same words to describe a situation, people called it a state of crisis. Not a week went by without a newspaper article stating that Mr. Bouchard wanted Mr. Parizeau's job! Not a week when you didn't get the impression that there was a crisis between Mr. Parizeau and Mr. Bouchard. It all made for a good news story. We had to deal with it."[10] Despite the guarded optimism of his chief of staff, Parizeau would not have an easy time of it. He would have to make concessions, to the point of considerably modifying his proposal, as it was worded in the draft bill.

As for the Action démocratique du Québec, it had agreed to participate in the consultations of the commissions on the future of Quebec. The Parti Québécois saw this as a step in the right direction, but this participation did not mean that Mario Dumont and his troops were ready to be fully committed, with the current state of affairs, alongside the PQ in the referendum campaign. In fact, Dumont was looking for a niche for his party in the coming confrontation. He knew very well that he could not stay on the sidelines, but, as he had done before when playing the regional commissions game, he would negotiate a certain number of conditions. As the Bloc Québécois' position was clearly closer to the ADQ's than the Parti Québécois,' it was with the Bloc that he would seek an alliance. Two weeks before the crisis between the Bloc Québécois and the Parti Québécois burst out into the open, Dumont threw a line to Lucien Bouchard's camp.

The national commission on the future of Quebec was holding a session at Manoir Montmorency. It received about fifty reports, including one from the ADQ[11]. The day before, that party's executive committee had held a private meeting with its most influential members, including delegates from the electoral ridings and the commissioners who had sat on the various regional commissions. The objective of the meeting had been to redefine the party's constitutional position, in light of public opinion gathered from the commissions' sessions. This new definition would have to fit somewhere in the current political debate. The ADQ's report reflected the discussions and conclusions of this meeting. Jean-François Lisée was at Manoir Montmorency, as was Pierre-Paul Roy. The two of them listened carefully as the report was read, knowing that, if they wanted to recreate the broad coalition of 1992, they had to find in that report the small opening they would need to bring Mario Dumont on board.

The Manoir is built on one of the most beautiful promontories in the Quebec region. From its terrace, one is treated to a magnificent view of the Montmorency Falls, the St. Lawrence River and the Île d'Orléans. March, in Quebec, can offer splendid days and, during this final week, it was lavish with its charms. At a certain point, Pierre-Paul Roy decided to go outside and relax by the railing to contemplate the beautiful scenery. Someone walked up to him: it was André Néron, Mario Dumont's chief of staff[12]. "André Néron told me that Mario Dumont was interested in meeting with Mr. Bouchard," recalls Pierre-Paul Roy. "The ADQ, in its report to the Commission, was still operating with the strategy of the Allaire Report[13]. I told André Néron that if there was ever any question of going further, any question of an agreement of any sort, it could not be on the basis of their report. His reply was that, in any case, it was a position from which to negotiate."[14] Pierre-Paul Roy then advised Lucien Bouchard of this conversation, which took place two weeks before the Bloc Québécois convention.

It was thus that, the day after the convention and in the icy climate of his relations with Jacques Parizeau, Lucien Bouchard asked his chief of staff to contact André Néron. This Roy immediately did. "I said to him, Come with a mandate because I have one," recalls Pierre-Paul Roy. "My mandate is to explore. It's not to negotiate an agreement, it's to see if one would be possible." The two men agreed to meet. "I think it was the 13th of April," Roy adds. "When Néron arrived, I asked him whether he had a mandate. He answered, 'Yes, it was Mario Dumont who just dropped me off here, at the restaurant.' That was my first official meeting with André Néron." What Roy rediscovers today, in the notes where he recorded this private conversation, is a very clear comment that "the notion of partnership was not to be made a condition of sovereignty."[15] The two men parted with a promise to report to their respective leaders and then to meet again.

In the meantime, despite his attempt to project an image of harmony to those around him, Parizeau met with some resistance from his delegation and his cabinet. The opinion polls were working against him. The first poll since Lucien Bouchard had spoken of a "change in direction," conducted by Léger Marketing and published on April 21, 1995 in Le Journal de Montreal and in the Globe and Mail, showed sovereignty losing with 44.3% vs. 55.7%, but showed sovereignty-association winning with 53.1% vs. 46.9%. The Globe and Mail title was "Sovereignty a winner, poll finds, if Quebec gets link to Canada." The voices of Bernard Landry, Richard Le Hir, Serge Ménard, Jean-Pierre Charbonneau, Joseph Facal, André Boisclair and Jacques Brassard grew louder as they demanded a change in strategy, towards greater openness.

It was becoming increasingly evident that the Péquistes (PQ), apart from their Bloc members, most of whom automatically joined the PQ ranks, absolutely had to seek the support of the Adéquistes (ADQ). The day after the collapse of the Meech Lake Accord, many disenchanted Liberals had turned towards sovereignty. Most of them returned to federalism when Robert Bourassa rejected the Allaire Report and accepted the Charlottetown Accord. But a significant number did not. "They had that flirtation with sovereignty," says Jean-François Lisée. "So they were available. But they weren't listening to us. They weren't listening to Mr. Parizeau. They were listening a little more to Mr. Bouchard and a lot more to Mr. Dumont, who was a former Liberal. We were down to a margin of less than one percent; there was no more leeway. I told Mr. Parizeau that we needed the widest possible coalition." One day, Lisée saw a button that said, "I hate Parizeau, but I'm voting YES." "I told myself that this was a great victory," Lisée recalls. "We must unite people sufficiently so that those who disagree with us on all kinds of other questions still vote YES on sovereignty."[16] Parizeau was told of the existence of the button, but he never talked about it.

On April 19, the national commission on the future of Quebec submitted its report. In the large *salon rouge* of the National Assembly, it summarized the results of its consultations, which had been conducted throughout all of Quebec. "Sovereignty," it began, "is the only option capable of responding to the collective aspirations of Quebecers." Next, it recommended strongly that an economic union with Canada be sought, and it went so far as to suggest that "the bill should indicate that a sovereign Quebec could propose and negotiate common and mutually beneficial political structures."

The message was clear: the people were adopting the *virage*. In particular, this enabled the premier, who could now yield to the will of the people, to be open to an economic link with Canada without being seen to give in to pressure from Lucien Bouchard, with whom relations continued to be strained. "We have placed our project in the hands of Quebecers," said Parizeau, as he received the report of the national commission. "We wanted them to improve and transform it and, in so doing, to take ownership of it. They have done so." And Parizeau publicly made the observation that the nature of "the relations that a sovereign Quebec should have with neighbouring Canada constituted a topic that preoccupied Quebecers a great deal."

"You have told us, first of all," he stressed, "that Quebecers must become aware of the extraordinary balance of power they hold, which, whatever happens, would make economic association a necessity the day after sovereignty is achieved." He alluded to passages in the commission's report, which expressed the desire of Quebecers for a clearer definition of the proposals to be made by Quebec to Canada regarding common institutions, "in order to better frame, manage and deepen as needed, this unavoidable association." By using the word "unavoidable," Parizeau was reaching out to the leader of the Bloc Québécois. And just in case the latter hadn't noticed, Parizeau added, "I see here the reflection of my own convictions and my own struggle. I believe it also echoes the proposals made not so long ago by Mr. Lucien Bouchard."

The speech had not been improvised. It had been carefully prepared by the premier's entourage and submitted, prior to its delivery, to representatives of the Bloc, who were in general agreement with its content, and to representatives of the ADQ who, on the contrary, were disappointed by the commission's report because it did not go far enough along the path of a rapprochement with the rest of Canada. "They proposed minor changes, which I immediately incorporated," recalls Jean-François Lisée, who drafted the speech. "In fact, I created a sort of three-level stairway for the Premier. On the first level, which corresponded to his position, there was unavoidable association, the common dollar, etc. Then, on the second level, people who thought association was desirable, an association that went further, like a joint Canada-Quebec cabinet that would meet from time to time. And, finally, on the third level, people who thought that there was another form of association possible: for example, should the legislators have a joint forum?" Lisée interpreted Jacques Parizeau's thought with respect to these various options in the following way: "Mr. Parizeau wants all of these people to be talking to each other and creating the voice for change. He told them, 'Yes, I am on the first level, but, now, I am willing to talk with the people on the other two levels.'"[17]

Jacques Parizeau concluded his speech by declaring, on the basis of the national commission's report, "an openness to the views put forward by Mr. Mario Dumont and Mr. Jean Allaire." He was, in fact, bringing together all the ingredients necessary to establish a broad coalition. He was more or less giving the signal for negotiations to start among the Parti Québécois, the Bloc Québécois and the Action démocratique du Québec with a view to achieving an agreement regarding partnership.

The head of the government was, by all accounts, open to a compromise with Lucien Bouchard. But he also wanted to persuade Mario Dumont, because it seemed to him as well as to Bouchard that, in its attitude to the referendum, the ADQ was acting a bit like a chicken with its head cut off. During a joint press conference given by the two sovereigntist leaders on March 22, Bouchard had this to say to a reporter who asked if they agreed with Mario Dumont's approach: "It is not possible to give you a very clear answer because Dumont is not so clear himself. (…) The process by which he wants to achieve his goal is not clear because it is as if there is a missing link, an essential link, the fundamental motivation, which is sovereignty as the obligatory means, creating our country first. And I have not heard Mr. Dumont say this."

However, when he spoke before the national commission on the future of Quebec, Mario Dumont was crystal clear. In fact, his speech emphasized the fundamental gap separating his position from that of the other two leaders. Alluding to the trend that emerged from the consultations of the regional commissions, he stated, "Are we going to brush aside this possible consensus, because the government hopes a different one will suddenly develop around its option over the next few months? Because some people hope that Quebecers will suddenly see a new light in a debate that has been raging for over twenty years? And in order to do what? (…) Let us come away from this commission with a totally new referendum proposal, which will suggest in one way or another a new partnership, a new union with the rest of Canada, a union based on the principles of the European Union."

At the end of April, the Parti Québécois wanted sovereignty and had no use for real association with the rest of Canada. The Bloc Québécois, on the other hand, did not think sovereignty was possible without such an association. The Action démocratique du Québec demanded a new partnership, but did not specify whether it was ready to go the route of sovereignty. That was where things stood when, a week after the report from the national commission on the future of Quebec had been submitted, the leader of the ADQ, without responding to Parizeau's offer, created an opening towards the sovereigntists. He used the occasion of a discussion in the *Commission permanente des institutions de l'Assemblée nationale* (the National Assembly's standing committee on institutions), which was studying the budget of the *ministère du Conseil exécutif* (department of the Executive council) to say: "The coming year will be, I hope, an opportunity to create a unifying project so that the error of 1982 may be rectified, so that Quebec may once again find its rightful place in North America, so that Quebec may once again enjoy the full powers to which it is entitled." He still did not see in a victorious referendum the panacea for all of Quebec's problems, however. "Economic and financial recovery," he said, "are, in my view, of even greater importance."

But the attitude Mario Dumont was adopting would delight the premier. The ADQ leader especially attacked the position of Daniel Johnson, who had expressed his reservations about transplanting the European federalist model to Canada. "If fifteen States, speaking a dozen languages," Dumont said, "decided, over the years, to share their sovereignty, by not hanging on to the past and not grovelling but, rather, by using an approach based on pride expressed by each State and on economic realism (...), it was because there were people there who had a vision of the future." Then he shot this arrow at Johnson: "The only reason the leader of the opposition is convinced that this is not realizable here is that he has a deep faith in the bad faith of the rest of Canada." Then, Dumont completed his thought: "I think we can assume that, to reach that kind of union, we must begin by stepping outside the current constitutional order and that this can only happen through the people of Quebec expressing, in a referendum, their right to sovereignty or a mandate for sovereignty, call it what you will."

Mario Dumont's remarks were music to the ears of Jacques Parizeau. The government leader thanked him for "the openness he had shown" and then launched forth with: "What the member for Rivière-du-Loup has done is, how shall I put it, to indicate a type of approach, a referendum for, he said, a mandate for sovereignty, followed by proposals to be made to Canada. This is rapprochement! (...) I think we can travel a stretch of the road, a good stretch of the road together."

What sustained Jacques Parizeau's hope of being able to "travel a stretch of the road together" was not so much that Mario Dumont had spontaneously subscribed to the sovereignty project, but that he would, in the end, have to choose between the YES side and the NO side. *The Referendum Act* indeed offered him no other option. It was a heart-rending choice he would have to make. "We had quit the Liberal party the day after Meech. It made no sense to be in the camp of Jean Chrétien and those who favoured the status quo," Mario Dumont acknowledges today. "At the same time, I would never have been capable of voting YES in a referendum on Mr. Parizeau's initial question: Are you for or against the independence of Quebec, YES, or NO? That is why, as the commissions on the future of Quebec carried out their work, we defined this idea of a partnership, a true confederation, the idea of a sovereign Quebec within a partnership with the rest of Canada."[18]

For Dumont, the partnership was not just a lure, some kind of front to get Quebecers to vote YES. It was about remaking confederation and nothing less. In the Parizeau camp, it began to dawn on them that they had to stop equivocating on their notion of association, and offer people serious proposals for a minimum of permanent political and economic structures to be established between Canada and a potentially independent Quebec. This was becoming all the more urgent as, in the Bloc Québécois, they could not always figure out the premier's hesitation waltz. "The partnership idea was not new to him," Pierre-Paul Roy recalls. "When we did the book in June of 1993[19], I remember that before publishing it, we had a meeting at the Le Caveau restaurant. Mr. Parizeau was there, as well as Jacques Brassard and Bernard Landry. Jean Royer and Yves Martin too... I remember Mr. Parizeau's reaction. He said, 'As long as there is no hyphen between sovereignty and partnership, I don't have a problem.'"[20]

The notion of partnership was also raised at meetings between the two political leaders during the weeks leading up to the Bloc Québécois convention in April 1995. "Maybe three weeks before the convention, there was a meeting of the referendum committee," recalls Lucien Bouchard's advisor. "It was at the Delta Hotel, I think. Mr. Bouchard kept making the point to Mr. Parizeau, 'You need to understand that we are right at a strategic crossroads. Maybe we have to adapt our strategy a little. My convention is coming up and I have to say something. So, give me some room to manoeuvre, give me an opening.' And Mr. Parizeau did not react negatively. But he did not react positively either. Everyone knew this was not his cup of tea. But the issue wasn't whether it was Mr. Parizeau's 'cup of tea,' it was, 'what must we do to win the referendum?'" At the end of the meeting, Bouchard said to Parizeau, "Listen, we still have a few weeks, let's stay in touch. Then, nearer the time of the convention, let's see." "Mr. Parizeau did not follow up," says Pierre-Paul Roy.[21]

Thus, among the sovereigntists, there were two conflicting arguments. The first held that the day after a victorious referendum, an attempt would be made to maintain a minimal association with the rest of Canada. Jean Royer explains, "Why minimal? Because the rest of Canada would not be in the right frame of mind to develop very integrated or very complex associations." According to this hypothesis, the negotiator for Quebec would be a non-political figure. "We realized," says Jean Royer, "that if the negotiator were a political figure, a high-profile person like Lucien Bouchard, then clearly the federal government would also appoint a political person to the table. We did not want politicking at the negotiating table." The second argument was based on a wish to see, in the proposal made to the rest of Canada, a great openness towards developing more numerous associations and creating multiple institutions. The advantage of this argument was that it was much more reassuring to Quebecers, but it was not shared by Parizeau. "He said," Royer recalls, "that, on the contrary, 'in the early stages, for the first few years, we should agree on a minimum. And when, by mutual agreement, both parties wish to develop a more integrated degree of association, then, they will do it.'"[22]

If the YES camp wanted at all to present a coherent image, then it was essential that the holders of these two arguments find common ground. "Holding elections when you are bickering does not work well, not well at all," says Bob Dufour, the Bloc Québécois' chief organizer. "Because, in Quebec, people will support the battle but they will not tolerate bickering. When a political party bickers, people lose confidence." Another reason why the PQ and the Bloc were destined to come to an understanding in the end was that, according to Dufour, 65% of the Bloc's members were also PQ. However, "about 35% of its members were not necessarily PQ, but considered Mr. Bouchard a good leader."[23] Parizeau had, therefore, to avoid offending this one third of the Bloc, which, in principle, was already sovereigntist. Furthermore, and this carried significant weight, the Bloc was a young party, which had only been in existence for three years. The spectacular results it obtained in the federal election of October 1993 were due in large part to the popularity of its leader. Despite his election campaign organizing talents, which even Jacques Parizeau recognized, Bob Dufour was aware that when it came to experience and human resources for campaign organization, the Parti Québécois was the place to turn. Bouchard, therefore, had no choice but to rely on their machine.

Some strategists in the Parizeau camp interpreted Bouchard's desire for a second referendum as, basically, an attempt to repeat the 1980 referendum. Jean-François Lisée was one of them. For him, Bouchard's speech at the Bloc Québécois' April convention left no question on two essential elements. He wanted to reintroduce, one way or another, the notion of association and, on this point, Parizeau expressed no objection, as long as there was no hyphen. But he also wanted to change the referendum question so that it would involve a second referendum. "That was the case with the 1980 referendum," says Lisée. "The idea was: a first referendum on sovereignty is held, with a promise to ratify the agreement with Canada in a second one."[24] Parizeau and his entourage did not want at any cost to go down that road.

Pierre-Paul Roy's recollections on the question of the second referendum show the degree of misunderstanding that persisted between the two teams: "Mr. Bouchard had no wish to go back to the 1980 approach," he says. "You need to remember that the 1980 approach was a mandate to negotiate sovereignty. Actually, not sovereignty, but sovereignty-association, with a hyphen. My understanding is that Mr. Bouchard did not want to go back to the 1980 approach. He had the same apprehension: to make sovereignty conditional on partnership was problematic, even from a strategic point of view alone. I never saw him propose that. It came out in discussions here and there, but it was never the subject of a definite position."[25]

Reaching agreement with the Bloc presented a number of problems for the Parti Québécois. But the position of the ADQ, announced a few days earlier, meant that negotiations with Mario Dumont's team would involve rather more challenging problems. André Néron had thrown a line to Pierre-Paul Roy at Manoir Montmorency, a call to dialogue no doubt, but with the Bloc, not the Parti Québécois. The Bloc and the ADQ had agreed to meet. This first private conversation had been followed by a second, in which Bob Dufour had participated, and then by a third. Always without a representative from the Parti Québécois. "And we agreed that there seemed to be, both from Mr. Dumont's and Mr. Bouchard's side, an opening," says Roy.[26]

The people from the ADQ, Néron, Jacques Gauthier, the president of the party Ritha Cossette, and others, were suddenly becoming anxious to meet with the leader of the Bloc Québécois. "Mr. Bouchard felt it was too soon," Pierre-Paul Roy recalls. "He said, 'Now that we think (there is an opening on the part of the ADQ), we are going to contact Mr. Parizeau's office.' So, I met with Jean-François Lisée." Lisée was surprised at the contact already established between the Bloc and the ADQ. "I recall that Jean-François Lisée's reaction was rather lukewarm at first," recalls Roy. "We were in a period when relations with Mr. Parizeau were quite cool. The dynamic they were operating from dictated that they should not rush into anything. I remember at the time, Jean-François Lisée had insisted on saying, 'I don't think this is going to work, I'm not sure we should report back to our two leaders.' I said to him, 'Well, I'll be reporting back to Mr. Bouchard.' And we parted on that note."[27] Lisée did report back and, finally, a tripartite committee was established, made up of Lisée and Jean Royer, from the Parizeau team, Gilbert Charland and Roy, from the Bloc Québécois, and André Néron and Jacques Gauthier, often replaced by Claude Carignan, from the ADQ.

Mario Dumont placed two conditions on his joining the YES camp: The partnership had to be part of the referendum question, and the negotiation with the rest of Canada had to take place before any declaration of sovereignty. "The day I stated that, I, a 24-year-old guy, leader of a party that had got 6.7% of the votes (in the last election), I was just about a laughing stock, because Mr. Parizeau, for his part, had made up his mind!" says Dumont. "But political reality caught up with him."[28]

"It demonstrated our ability to bring everyone together,"[29] Jean-François Lisée says today. At the time, he was not unaware of the fact that Dumont, in a poll done at the end of March, had reached the same level of popularity as Parizeau, and that his party had a following of 11% of the population[30]. Although the ADQ had only one member and only relatively modest popular support, it offered Parizeau and his team the opportunity to prove to the people that they were capable of openness: If they were able to come to an agreement with a non-sovereigntist party, then compromises would also be possible with the federalists in Ottawa in future negotiations.

"Our two conditions were not really negotiable," recalls Mario Dumont. "We could negotiate the wording, we could negotiate a lot of things, but the partnership in the question and the negotiation with Canada before the declaration of sovereignty, that was the starting ground from which discussion could take place." However, he was realistic. "When you (only) have 6.7% of the vote, you take note that you are not the premier," he says. "You're not the one who is going to decide the question, you're not the one who is going to negotiate with Ottawa. So, you have to make gestures that are going to help narrow the gap." Dumont wanted to "break open the padlock," his description of a form of federalism which, ever since the repatriation of the Constitution in 1982, had become a kind of straightjacket. A YES vote could do that, he says. "It would open negotiations, discussions, that was what would give us the best chance for working towards a new partnership." In Mario Dumont's mind, the partnership was nothing other than a new confederate structure, through which Quebec would participate in "a union of States, which have a form of sovereignty and autonomy."[31]

When negotiations began, the ADQ was still caught up in the logic of the Allaire Report. Consequently, they could not accept the notion of partnership being reduced to a sort of corollary to the question, somehow appended to it. "That wouldn't do." says Dumont. The idea of a partnership had to be in the question. And on May 5, as if to guard against any compromise that might make him back down from his initial position, he published a thirty-page document entitled *La nouvelle union Québec-Canada: institutions et principes de fonctionnement* (The New Quebec-Canada Union: Institutions and Operating Principles). The ADQ used it to make their profession of faith: In a new relationship with the rest of Canada, Quebec would keep exclusive jurisdiction over some thirty areas and agree to share another fifteen with Canada, through common institutions that would be governed by a parliament of the Union, invested with legislative powers. In other words, despite the façade of optimism shown by Jacques Parizeau, negotiations would be arduous.

Jean-François Lisée nevertheless prepared a draft agreement, which he submitted first to Louis Bernard, the secretary general of the government. Bernard made some minor changes, added his signature to Lisée's, and submitted it to Parizeau. "Initially, he was fine with it. Every week, I reported on the progress of the negotiations. And sometimes, because it was becoming concrete, Mr. Parizeau resisted. There were times when he was no longer sure he wanted to go that far!"[32] What Parizeau feared above all else, was that the success of the talks with Ottawa, particularly on economic union, would become a necessary condition for declaring sovereignty. So, initially, he concurred with the essential points of the draft agreement, then he resisted and, finally, he gave in.

In reality, the Parizeau team was worried: they feared some kind of Bloc Québécois-Action démocratique du Québec alliance behind their back, which might then propose the creation of an elected common parliament, with legislative powers, as the ADQ had outlined in its May 5 document. "In my view, such a proposal would have been a strategic error," says Lisée. "They talked about a joint legislative assembly. But they said that if Quebec became sovereign, there would be an election. Then, if one day the ADQ were elected and it proposed a common parliament, what would happen then?"[33] And the ADQ proposal was not incorporated into the bill.

"It is quite certain," Lisée adds, "coming back to the two months of negotiations, especially the talks between the sovereigntists, that Jacques Parizeau could never have signed a document that did not make Quebec a sovereign country represented in the United Nations. This was never called into question. What was discussed was the level of importance of the proposal that would be made to English Canada."[34] Consequently, the two teams engaged in vigorous discussion, the dialogue being sustained by the respect they had for each other. "We didn't dramatize things," says Pierre-Paul Roy. "There were tensions, but we had to handle the relations between two men carefully!"[35] To avoid a complete breakdown in talks, the two men were invited to meet only when it seemed common ground had been achieved.

And, finally, there was agreement, thanks in large part to Jean-François Lisée, the "advisor for openness," as he is referred to by Jean Royer, who succeeded in overcoming his initial reticence to get Parizeau to play the diversity card. "Jean-François always managed to widen the corridor a little," he says. "Mr. Parizeau, at a certain point, found himself on less familiar ground. There were things that, at first, we did not expect would be on the table. But it is partially through Jean-François' efforts that we were able to reach an agreement on partnership."[36] Finally, Lisée, Gilbert Charland and André Néron drafted a first version, then several others, of the agreement project. "I saw four consecutive versions," Parizeau remembers. "We went right down to the commas, we changed words…"[37]

In the opposing camp, observers followed the progress of these negotiations with close attention, insofar as that was possible, and weighed their consequences. "The YES camp had reached a milestone at that point," Jean Charest says today. He was leader of the federal Conservative party at the time. "They had managed to win Mario Dumont, more or less my (provincial) equivalent, for the YES team, that is, a third member, who would target, as I did, a group of undecided voters who identified more with him. When I saw that, I said to myself, 'We have an adversary that is now better equipped to carry out its referendum campaign.' The YES camp had managed, in a way, to widen its coalition. And, instinctively, I realized that the battle had just changed!"[38] And then there was Daniel Johnson, who had no choice but to look on, helplessly, as a contingent that, not so long ago, had been part of the Liberal party, moved over to the YES camp. Despite all this, he refrained completely from attempting the slightest reconciliation with Mario Dumont. "He would have used that to his own advantage," Johnson says, "probably to denounce us, as they had been doing for years. He would have used the olive branch we offered him to say, 'Look, the Liberals are chasing after me!'"[39]

Johnson's strategy on this was straightforward. He would show that, "if you say you are on the YES side of a question that wants Quebec to be a sovereign country, then you are a sovereigntist."[40] That was how he would attack the credibility of Mario Dumont and his party. John Parisella, Johnson's chief of staff at the time, speaks in the same vein. "For some people, that confirmed where Mario Dumont stood," he says. "For others, it was perceived as an effort by the Parti Québécois to create a certain ambiguity. Mr. Parizeau still preferred the short and direct question, but his PQ strategists preferred another way in order to coat and sweeten the pill." Parisella was, however, aware that, when the ADQ joined the YES camp, a time bomb had started ticking. "We had looked upon Mario Dumont as the individual who could be the key to a referendum victory or defeat," he comments today. The fact that he chose the YES side forced Johnson and the Quebec Liberals to modify their discourse so as to seek support from Quebecers who, while still federalist, were more nationalist. "There was no point defending Canada to Quebecers," Parisella says. "Johnson needed to defend Quebec within Canada. There's an important nuance."[41]

By signing the June 12 agreement, Jacques Parizeau was not just making concessions regarding the referendum question. He was agreeing to deal with a partner, Lucien Bouchard, who had a personality totally opposite to his own. While Parizeau was a man of reason, analytical, a Cartesian thinker, a planner, Bouchard was the intuitive type. "Great strategies discussed in advance, that was not his bag," says Jean-François Lisée about Bouchard. "He relied heavily on his instincts. He played close to the net, when the ball came, catching it as best he could... And it is true that he made good decisions at the net. Strategic preparation, that was less his forte."[42] Pierre-Paul Roy perceived his leader the same way. "We would have discussions," he says. "When he told us, 'I don't feel that,' the discussion was over. I don't mean to imply that he was all intuition and passion and not a man of reason, but he had a more intuitive approach to politics."[43]

People who spent time with Lucien Bouchard said of him that he would fly off the handle and was easily angered. Georges Arès, from Alberta, observed this when Bouchard was secretary of state for the Mulroney government and responsible for French-speaking Canadians. Arès met with him in his capacity as president of the French-Canadian Association of Alberta, to discuss language law in his province. He asked him, among other things, to initiate a referral of the school question to the Supreme Court, to help with the development of the francophone community in Alberta and to conclude an agreement with the provincial government for the translation of the laws. First, Mr. Bouchard tried to get his interlocutor to lower his expectations a little, but the Albertan representative resisted. "Then, he got angry with me," Arès recounts. "He said to me, 'Mr. Arès, you are intransigent!' I replied, 'Mr. Bouchard, when we are speaking about the rights of the Franco-Albertan community, I shall always be intransigent. Rights are not negotiable. Our rights are not up for discussion!' With that, he got even angrier and left the room. His political assistants looked at us, then they said, 'Mr. Bouchard has left. Why don't you go?' Mr. Bouchard came back fifteen minutes later. He had calmed down. He said, 'OK, let's resume our conversation.' I really liked that. If something larger was at stake, he could come back to the discussion."[44] "Just plain common sense," explains Bob Dufour, the Bloc Québécois' organizer. "Yes, he had a temper. But, afterwards, once the dust had settled, he always came up with an intelligent solution. Down deep, his political philosophy was very much based on just plain common sense."[45]

Lucien Bouchard's opponents feared him: "A very dangerous opponent. He was charismatic and he was prepared to say anything to influence," says Eddie Goldenberg, of Jean Chrétien's entourage. "He always seemed like a storm cloud," observes Reform Party member Deborah Grey, whose seat was next to his in the House of Commons, after he had left the Conservatives to sit as an independent. "Very intense, brooding I think would be a word that would come to mind to describe him." "What made Bouchard dangerous from Canada's standpoint," says Preston Manning, whose position as leader of the opposition was snatched away from him by the leader of the Bloc Québécois, "is that he had a vision and a dream of an independent Quebec, and could communicate it with emotion as well as outline it in rational terms." Conservative Senator Pierre-Claude Nolin knows Bouchard well. He had organized his electoral campaign in the riding of Lac-Saint-Jean in June of 1988. "He was an intellectual at that time, a lawyer, an ambassador, far from being a politician. But between 1988 and 1995, he learned. (He became) a shrewd (politician) who knew how to exploit the mistakes of his adversaries. He succeeded in transposing his talents as a negotiator into the political arena. Was he an innovative politician? I wouldn't think so. He was a guy who knew his potential, was aware of the image he projected and was able to exploit his talents to the max. There is no doubt that (on occasion) he raised his voice with Mr. Parizeau."[46] That was the man the premier of Quebec had to contend with, a man now hardened and little inclined to deviate from his opinions.

Alongside them stood a young man, Mario Dumont, who had just turned 25, and had sat as a member for only a few months, occupying his party's benches by himself in the National Assembly, whose rules he was still trying to master. "In addition to being at the centre of the great debates, I had to learn the ropes of being a Member," says

Mario Dumont. "I was surrounded by this really small team, but we nevertheless had people with experience inside the party, like Mr. Allaire on constitutional matters."[47]

According to Daniel Johnson, who knew Dumont while he was in the Liberal party, the ADQ leader is not a team player. Recalling a convention held by the party's youth committee at La Pocatière in 1991, when Dumont was its president, Johnson remembers being struck by the fact that he was the only MNA who bothered to go to a social event organized as part of the convention. "Mr. Dumont had not established a close relationship with the caucus or with the rest of the party leadership," he says. "I was astonished to see how deserted he was, on the occasion of an event that was generally quite popular with pretty well everyone, older people included."[48] In John Parisella's judgment, "Dumont is quite a reserved man. Some would say he could be rather distant. He's not the emotional type. His temperament is a bit like Robert Bourassa's." Parisella recalls how in 1992, on returning from Charlottetown, where Bourassa had signed the agreement that would be submitted to a referendum, he had called Dumont to explain the procedure the government planned to follow. "Our conversation lasted just under an hour," says Parisella. "He listened very respectfully, unless he put the receiver down on the counter. Then, the conversation ended just like that. I called Bourassa to tell him I had made the call. 'How did he react?' Bourassa asked me. 'Iced water in his veins!' I said."[49] To Parisella, Dumont was a young man who saw political life exclusively through the eyes of Quebec and had no sensitivity towards the rest of Canada.

On June 12, the three leaders solemnly signed an agreement at the Château Frontenac, in Quebec. But in order to rally the troops, there was still a lot of work to be done. They had to integrate the content of the agreement into their strategy and, especially, into their speeches, in accordance with the new orientation the agreement demanded. In addition to stipulating that the three political parties "join forces and coordinate their efforts so that Quebecers can vote for a real change: achieve sovereignty for Quebec and a proposal for a new economic and political partnership within Canada," the text of the agreement, almost five full pages in length, stipulated that this common objective would be integrated into the bill and the referendum question. It stipulated as well, in order to ward off any fear in Canada of a unilateral declaration of independence by Parizeau, that an "orientation and supervision committee" would be created, made up of politically independent figures, whose mandate would be to ensure that the negotiations with Ottawa would be conducted properly and with transparency. It stated finally that negotiations with Ottawa would not last more than a year and that, if they were not fruitful, the National Assembly could declare the sovereignty of Quebec without further delay (see the text of the agreement in Appendix A).

While the federal government may not yet have fully appreciated the significance of the agreement that had just been signed by the three parties, the Americans were taking a keen interest in it. In the days following the signing of the document, the U.S. Consulate in Quebec sent the following message to the secretary of state in Washington: "For months, Ottawa pundits have been heaping ridicule on the Parti Québécois' sovereignty project. They have predicted the referendum on sovereignty will be postponed beyond the end of this year, perhaps indefinitely. All signs from here, on the contrary, indicate that they are seriously mistaken. There is every reason to believe there will be a referendum this year, with at least a fifty-fifty chance of passing. (…) Quebec Premier Parizeau's reluctant decision to postpone the vote from the original spring 1995 (makes it) clear he was also waiting until the ADQ and Mario Dumont came on board. The recent tripartite accord signed by Parizeau, Bouchard and Dumont was a major coup for sovereignty and the fruit of a long courtship. Parizeau has been trying to win Dumont over ever since his fledgling party won 6.5% of the popular vote last September, because those votes, if added to the 44.7% the PQ won, would put sovereignty over the top in a referendum. Parizeau's agreement to seek association with Canada once sovereignty has been achieved is a small price to pay for this added support. (…) Canadians and Quebecers would be well advised to fasten their seat belts. The sovereignty train has left the station and is picking up speed. We are lucky we can stay on the sidelines. It is likely to be a rough ride."[50] The Consul's memo seriously reproaches Daniel Johnson's Liberals, saying they "have flatly refused to outline the constitutional vision they say they have in mind for Quebec, preferring to attack every aspect of the government's project in an unremitting drumbeat of negativity."[51]

In fact, the Quebec Liberal Party could not reveal its constitutional position because it was still defining it. At the end of April 1995, a document, prepared by its committee on the evolution of Canadian federalism, a copy of which had been procured by TVA[52] television reporters, proposed the integration of Quebec into the constitutional family on three conditions. They were: a right of veto over any constitutional change, a more flexible federalism, and federal-provincial agreements that would derive from Quebec being recognized as having a specific character. There was no longer any question of its recognition as a "distinct society." The next day, Daniel Johnson termed the document "a preliminary first draft for discussion purposes, put together by a young researcher," and disowned it outright. "Let us begin by rejecting separation," he said, thus giving credence to the U.S. Consul's reading of his attitude.[53]

The day after the agreement was signed, Jacques Parizeau, accompanied by Jean-François Lisée and the head of protocol, Jacques Joli-Coeur, went to Ottawa, at the invitation of the ambassadors of the European Union. These diplomats meet every two weeks and invite Canadian politicians to come to speak to them on various subjects, in conversations that are to remain strictly confidential. On June 13, 1995, the meeting took place at the residence of the German ambassador, Hans Sulimma. There were about fifteen diplomats. They all wanted to know more about the Quebec government's projects.

The ritual is generally the same at every meeting: aperitif, lunch, introduction of the guest, this time by the French ambassador, then the presentation of about fifteen minutes, followed by a short period of questions and answers. Before the meal, Jacques Parizeau had a drink with four of the ambassadors: Christian Fellens, of Belgium, greatly interested in what was happening in Quebec, because his country, like Canada, was bicultural and bilingual; Alfred Siefer-Gaillardin, of

France, who had taken the initiative of inviting Parizeau, even though he was not particularly open to the sovereignty project; the Austrian ambassador; and Jan Fietelaars, of the Netherlands. The conversation proceeded in French, a language spoken by most diplomats in Ottawa, but in which the Dutch ambassador was not very fluent.

Just what did Parizeau say during that desultory conversation? Not much, except that, the next day, one of the four ambassadors, the one from the Netherlands, went to the Canadian Department of Foreign Affairs. The Dutch government was trying at the time to obtain Canada's vote of support for a position it was seeking on the leadership of an international organization. Fietelaars chose this occasion to report Parizeau's remarks. Three weeks later, those remarks would drop like a bombshell, on the referendum debate.

On Friday, July 7, journalist Chantal Hébert, Ottawa bureau chief for *La Presse*, showed up on a Parliament Hill that was practically deserted: many people were on vacation, including her office secretary. She had nothing to do. To pass the time, she thought she would open the mail, which she rarely did. There was a letter addressed to her, which came from the Department of External Affairs. A few weeks earlier, at the request of that same department, she had accepted an invitation to speak on Canadian politics to the foreign ambassadors newly appointed to Ottawa—something that is frequently done in the capital, without remuneration. The journalist thought the letter must be a word of thanks. Nevertheless, she was somewhat intrigued, because the envelope bore the logo of the "Department of External Affairs," while she knew very well that, ever since the Chrétien government had been in power, it was called the "Department of Foreign Affairs." She opened the envelope. It contained the copy of a memo, drafted by senior civil servants and addressed to other civil servants, reporting on their meeting with Ambassador Fietelaars.

"The ambassador had told them," says Chantal Hébert, "that someone had asked Mr. Parizeau what would happen if, once Quebecers had voted YES, they wanted to change their minds? Mr. Parizeau had replied: 'That can't happen, it's impossible. Once Quebecers have voted YES, they will be like lobsters in a lobster pot.'

That is, in a lobster trap." The memo, of no more than ten lines, had been written in English and was dated June 19. It had been circulated to a number of civil servants by Michel Duval, director of relations with Western Europe, in the Foreign Affairs Department. There was no accompanying memo, cover note or comment that came with it. "It suddenly dawned on me that, because of what had just landed on my desk, I was not going to have a peaceful Friday after all," Chantal Hébert adds.[54]

She verified the identity and title of each civil servant on the list. All were correct. She contacted the embassies and learned that in the diplomatic circle, many people were aware of the incident, especially since the reception given at the American Embassy on July 4, on the occasion of the American national holiday. In Ottawa, "a journalist soon learns that you will find out the details of a cabinet shuffle faster by having reliable sources in the American Embassy than by having them in the Prime Minister's Office," says Chantal Hébert. "So, it's a good place to start (your investigation). The (first) two embassies I phoned, including the American one, replied spontaneously, 'Yes, absolutely!' There was even one diplomat who said, 'It was the tastiest tidbit of the week in the diplomatic community in Ottawa. Very smooth indeed, that statement about lobsters!'"[55]

In handling this story, Chantal Hébert encountered two problems. She had not managed to speak to anyone who had actually heard Parizeau make the remarks and—the principle of fairness demanded this—she had to obtain the reaction of the Quebec government leader. To ensure she would get cooperation from Quebec sources, she decided to tell the story of the memo as a good weekend story to the Bloc Québécois communications director in Ottawa, Alain Leclerc. She ended the story by saying, "Excuse me, I must go and write my article!" She knew she would score with that.

Fifteen minutes later, Jean-François Lisée, Jacques Parizeau's political advisor, phoned her. It was an official, clear, irreversible denial. "It's a diabolical invention!" said Lisée. But, as several people were already discussing the information, this would mean an awful lot of them were in on the same prank. Then Lisée's tone became threatening. "He tried to make me worry about my career," Hébert recalls. "He explained to me that if I published this story on Saturday, then on Sunday my career would be over, they would refute my story publicly, my journalistic credibility would be destroyed."[56]

Chantal Hébert is not the type to let herself be intimidated. Therefore, Lisée changed his strategy. He asked for time: If *La Presse* would agree to delay publication of the story until Monday, then he would find three ambassadors who would deny it publicly. "He asked me, 'If I provide you with three ambassadors who say it isn't true, are you still going to publish (the story)?'" says Hébert. "I answered, 'Certainly, if I publish it, their denial will be part of my article.'"[57] Since it was summertime and a lot of reporters were on vacation, the management of *La Presse* in Montreal was not afraid that a competitor would scoop the story, and they agreed to delay its publication until Monday. But Hébert was worried: if a big executive from her newspaper spoke to Parizeau and allowed himself to be convinced by the Premier that he never made these remarks...? And if he then, in turn, told Hébert to cancel the story, what would she do? The TVA network had also been informed of the incident and Benoît Aubin, head of the news department, had decided not to report it.

On Monday, Marcel Desjardins, head of the news department of *La Presse*, informed Chantal Hébert that he was keen to publish the story, the sooner the better. At 3 p.m., Lisée called the journalist. He had found three ambassadors who would communicate with her. An hour later, the phone rang. It was the Belgian Ambassador. "Mr. Jean-François Lisée asked me to call you," said Christian Fellens, who was clearly embarrassed, both for Parizeau and for the diplomatic community, with what was going on. "It was a private luncheon," he added, "and his words were spoken in a context of confidentiality." Hébert was bowled over: she had been expecting a front of denial from all the diplomats who would take the trouble to call. She advised Fellens: "You understand that I will be quoting you. You also understand that you have confirmed that Mr. Parizeau said what he was alleged to have said." The ambassador confirmed it, but added that it was not very diplomatic to make a story of it in the newspapers. Hébert felt she needed to explain to him that the role of a journalist was considerably different than that of a diplomat. He acknowledged this, nevertheless deploring the fact that a public figure could not express himself in private without it being reported. "My hand was shaking," Hébert remembers. "This was incredible! This ambassador, I would never have found him, he would never have called me and, if he had, he would have told me he was not obliged to answer! And here was Parizeau's office sending me an ambassador, who agreed to be quoted and confirmed to me that Jacques Parizeau had said that Quebecers would be like trapped lobsters! This man never called me back to say I had misquoted him!"[58]

Hébert had barely hung up when Parizeau's head of protocol, Jacques Joli-Coeur, contacted her to claim he had never heard such words spoken by Parizeau. When he heard she had spoken to Fellens, he ended the conversation. Then there was another call. It was Fietelaars, "very agitated, stating that Mr. Parizeau did not say that," the journalist recounts. "When I asked him why he had reported it to Foreign Affairs, the conversation became very, very confused."[59]

Chantal Hébert's first article was published Tuesday morning. She had sufficient confidence in her sources to write, "With the new sovereignty project, Premier Jacques Parizeau hopes to urge a majority of Quebecers to jump into the cooking pot of sovereignty. After that, they will be as irreversibly committed to Quebec's separation from the rest of Canada, as 'lobsters thrown into boiling water.' That was, essentially, the analogy, confirmed by diplomatic sources, but vigorously denied by the Quebec government." The title, on the front page of La Presse, was unambiguous: "'After a YES, Quebecers will be like lobsters': Parizeau's words to a group of European ambassadors in Ottawa."

While she had the memo and the confirmation of its content, the journalist still did not know who had sent it to her. It would not be long before she found out. Alvin Cader was a parliamentary correspondent with CBC Radio. He had attended the July 4 party at the U.S. embassy. This reception, the best attended in Ottawa, offers the opportunity to meet diplomats, ministers, deputy ministers, senior civil servants, some of them, on their third or fourth glass, beginning to speak more freely. "A well placed source in the federal government approached me," Cader recounts, "to speak to me about a memo. He was convinced it would humiliate or even discredit Mr. Parizeau, if it came out. He was determined that it should come out and that it should come out in Quebec first."[60] Cader did not know the content of the memo, except that it was a story that would be extremely damaging to Mr. Parizeau, and his source did not want to speak to him about it because it had to come out in French first.

Cader did not identify his informant, but it is now known that it was Howard Balloch, Cabinet Deputy Secretary for Operation Unity.[61] Cader went over the story and found nothing. Monday evening, he got a call from the Dutch Ambassador. "There are people saying I'm the one who spread the lobster story. Well, that's not true," was basically what Jan Fietelaars said. The journalist was baffled. He knew nothing about this story of crustaceans, and even less, how the Dutch ambassador came into it. The journalist's basket was quite empty: a senior civil servant tells him a story without really telling it and an ambassador is anxious to refute it. In the news on Tuesday morning, unaware of the story *La Presse* would carry the same day, Alvin Cader closed the file, stating that the Operation Unity strategists tried to spread information to humiliate Parizeau with respect to something he had said, but that it was a story that was fizzling out because the people who were supposed to have witnessed it now refuted everything.

Hébert could not believe her ears. She called Cader, whom she knew well. Then, she understood where the leak came from: not from a senior civil servant in the Foreign Affairs Department, but from a member of the Canadian Unity Council. She also understood that the memo came from a former civil servant of that department, who had used an old envelope. Before being appointed to the Privy Council, Balloch had worked in the Department of Foreign Affairs, which was then called External Affairs. She called the Canadian Unity Council and asked to speak to Balloch. He acknowledged right away that he knew the whole story, that he thought it would come out one day and that he had spoken about it with reporters in the gardens of the American Embassy, but he totally denied that he was the one who had sent the communication to the journalists.

With hindsight, Parizeau's entourage gives a different version of the incident: Parizeau did not remember having made such remarks; Jean-François Lisée had heard nothing, and neither had Jacques Joli-Coeur. "Our first reaction was: it's an invention," Lisée says today. "But in good faith, we wanted to check it out. We consulted the others who had been present, people from the European embassies. One of them had taken notes. It was then that we realized that Parizeau probably had said it."[62] Even today, Parizeau squarely refuses to come back on the subject: "Ten years later, listen, it's a joke," he says. "At a certain point, you know, 'Feed my lambs, feed my sheep!'"[63]

We will never know the actual words Parizeau used and, even less, the context in which he spoke them. If we rely on the Belgian ambassador's words, it would appear he used the example, in speaking of Quebecers, of a *casier à homards* (lobster pot), saying, "*Vous entrez là et vous ne sortez plus!*" (Once you go in, you never come out.)[64] The problem is that "pot" translates into French as *marmite* (a cooking pot). We must assume that the limited vocabulary of civil servants, unless it was their lack of familiarity with the French language, did the rest. In the Department of Foreign Affairs or the Canadian Unity Council, the lobster pot became *une marmite d'eau bouillante* (a pot of boiling water).

Jean Chrétien and others in the federal government were very reluctant to exploit the lobster story for referendum campaign purposes. But some federalists could not resist. The group organizing the *Cité libre* lectures, including Senator Jacques Hébert, wanted to stage another "Yvette affair"[65] like in 1980, and launched the "National Order of the Lobster," distributing orange-red badges. The stunt didn't go very far and had no impact whatsoever on the referendum campaign.

Ratified in ink on June 12, the rapprochement between Jacques Parizeau and Lucien Bouchard became imprinted in the minds of the people twelve days later when, side by side, they took part, amidst a sea of fleur-de-lys flags, in a Saint-Jean-Baptiste Day parade in

Montreal. Despite his agonizing pain, which he found hard to hide because the itinerary was long and it had been only six months since his operation, Bouchard walked along Sherbrooke Street all the way to Papineau Street, shoulder to shoulder with the government leader, who beamed in front of the 100,000 people cramming the sidewalks, accompanied by a few ministers, the union presidents and several members of the Bloc Québécois and the PQ. "This is the summer of hope," Parizeau said then. "In the fall, our hopes shall be realized and the next parade could well be a victory march."

Three weeks after the agreement was signed, the polls rated the ADQ and Mario Dumont as receiving the same 10% of public support, i.e., more or less the same level of popularity they had at the end of September 1994. The performance of the Parti Québécois was not much better. But Bouchard's *virage* in April, and the agreement of June 12, had put the YES side ahead of the NO side. To the question, "Are you in favour of the sovereignty of Quebec, accompanied by a formal offer of a new economic and political partnership with the rest of Canada?" 45% of the respondents answered YES and 41% NO, with 14% undecided. The summer was off to an auspicious start for Jacques Parizeau and his troops.

CHAPTER VI

"Do you agree...
YES or NO?"

R oy Romanow,[1] premier of Saskatchewan, met Jacques Parizeau
for the first time at the Premiers' Conference held in St. John's,
Newfoundland on August 23–25, 1995. "He is an extremely engaging
individual," he now relates. "Very charming. He has a very firm set of
beliefs with respect to Quebec. He switched from minister to premier
to being more authoritative and therefore, a little more necessitous of
us to deal with him very carefully."

In 1995, Jacques Parizeau was not well known in English
Canada. Some ministers from other provinces had met him at economic or fiscal conferences during his tenure as Finance Minister, but
the country's new provincial leaders—Roy Romanow, Clyde Wells,
Ralph Klein, Mike Harris, Michael Harcourt, to name a few—so far
had only a superficial impression of him. Romanow now points out,
"We always debated in the 1970s whether his becoming a separatist
was occasioned by virtue of some story that he had been turned down
as a Bank of Canada governor, or whether it was something more substantial. I always felt it was something more substantial."

From 1984 on, Parizeau was no longer part of the political landscape of Quebec. He had been forgotten. Bolstered by the 1980 victory, the rest of Canada took comfort in Pierre-Marc Johnson's
"national affirmation," which was seen as a less radical position than
that of René Lévesque. Consequently, the state of mind that had settled in immediately after the 1980 referendum persisted: "People

didn't take seriously the intentions of René Lévesque," David Collenette now says. "And then, when the (1995) referendum came closer, I think the argument was: Quebecers don't want to form their own country. (People were saying,) 'We don't have to worry, we'll fight against the referendum, we'll beat you.'"

The prevailing sentiment in Ottawa towards the possibility of a referendum swept across the nation. It was in this rather cool, but not downright hostile, climate that Parizeau, flanked by ten or so government officials, went to the Newfoundland conference. The conference was presided over by Clyde Wells, an unrelenting opponent of the Meech Lake Accord and of constitutional recognition of Quebec's distinct character.

The schedule planned for the Newfoundland interprovincial conference included discussions on matters that were, by and large, hardly controversial: domestic trade, regional economic development, transportation and environment. Moreover, to ensure that the meeting would run smoothly and harmoniously, Clyde Wells took pains not to invite national-level Native organizations, breaking with the approach adopted four years earlier at Whistler, British Columbia.

So it was in the framework of a conference with no major issues on the table, in a context of relatively peaceful relations with the federal government, that the premiers were introduced to their Québécois counterpart. They quickly came to a worrisome conclusion: "There's no doubt," Romanow goes on, "that Parizeau's agenda was to demonstrate to the people of Quebec that he could go to an annual Premiers' Conference as a separatist and come up with an agreement. The effect of which would be to say to people in Quebec and outside of Quebec: look, if we break away and become an independent country, the normal day-to-day economic and trading relationships will continue, business as usual. (...) We knew (Parizeau) was much more committed and much more determined to achieve it than Lévesque. Lévesque, one had the feeling, was always at heart a democrat. I'm not saying that Parizeau wouldn't adopt a democratic decision, he did in 1995. (But) if there was a yes vote, one had to contemplate the next step might have been a unilateral declaration of independence." On the afternoon of August 25, speaking on behalf of the nine other premiers, Roy Romanow declared, "We will not negotiate with a sovereign Quebec." Later, referring to this conference, Lucien Bouchard would call Romanow and Wells "spectres from the past—commandos who wish to prevent any change."[2]

While the premiers brought their conference in St. John's to a close, the media were publishing the results of a Léger Marketing poll that showed the two options running neck and neck: 49.5% for YES to 50.5% for NO. Ottawa began to grow nervous. On the way out of a cabinet meeting, André Ouellet, who was at that time the minister of foreign affairs, confided to David Collenette: "we could lose the referendum." To this, Collenette replied, "André, that's my feeling going to Quebec. I am not a Quebecer but I speak French. I understand what's going on there and I just have an uneasy feeling." Still, the Quebec referendum question remained the business of the Prime Minister's Office. While the mandarins surrounding Jean Chrétien were instructed to consider the referendum question as a mere formality, the members of the government were reduced to expressing their concern in whispered hallway conversations.

Although they indicated the possibility of a standoff—something that ought to instill in Jacques Parizeau a sense of confidence— the polls also worried his staff, but for other reasons. Jean Royer opened up to Lisette Lapointe: "'Do you think he could still decide not to go through with the referendum at this stage?' he asked me," recalls Parizeau's wife. "I was dumbstruck by this question. I thought he was joking, but he didn't seem to be. Most likely, among the people he had consulted, there were some who were too scared of losing."[3] The thing that worried "those afraid of losing" was the way the polls were being interpreted by four academics that had been analyzing public opinion surveys for 25 years.[4] Their conclusion was not one that would reassure the sovereigntists: "The polls always gave the nationalists a few more points than they actually ended up getting." The authors recalled that, before the 1980 referendum, polls showed the YES vote at 48% when in fact, it ended up with only 40%. According to them, the error consisted in dividing up the undecided vote proportionally to the

gross results of each side, when in fact, the nationalists would generally garner no more than a third of the undecided vote, often as little as
a quarter and sometimes even less. As an example, they cited a poll
published by *La Presse*, the previous June 25: "The gross breakdown
was 45% for YES, 41% for NO and 14% undecided. Dividing up the
undecided vote proportionally, the YES vote found itself in the lead
with 52% to 48% for NO, but when we opt for a more realistic hypothesis (one-quarter of the undecided allotted to the sovereigntists), the
NO carries the day, with nearly 52%. You've got to be wary."

Among the wary was Lucien Bouchard. Drouilly and the others
"were saying that we would lose the referendum," recalls Bob Dufour.
"How do you think that made (Bouchard) feel? This meant that if he
continued to move forward, he would run the risk of falling on his face;
there was the risk that it wouldn't go through; there was the risk that
he would be digging Quebec's grave. Think about it: if he commits to
a strategy that he's convinced will only lead to defeat, but he goes for it
anyway, where does that put him the day after? Because, the day after,
he's got to go back to Ottawa. He's still the leader of the official opposition. So he's in it to win, that's all there is to it. He wants all possible,
imaginable conditions to be there. This is no time for just testing the
waters—not by any stretch!"[5]

Roy Romanow was not the only one to fear a unilateral declaration of independence. This was one of the arguments advanced by a
Quebec City lawyer, who challenged the legitimacy of the government's tactics in court. Over the summer, Guy Bertrand[6] presented to
the Superior Court a motion for an injunction to cancel the referendum,
on the grounds that it was illegal. On August 31, 1995, the judge,
Robert Lesage, declared the request allowable and authorized Mr.
Bertrand to proceed. The government did not consider it worth the
bother to contest the decision. On the following day, in a relatively unprecedented move, the government's lawyers walked out of court. "We
will not subjugate Quebecers' right to vote to a Court decision—that
would run counter to our democratic system," said Jacques Parizeau.
In the same breath, he announced that the referendum calendar would
not be subject to modification by the whims of legal proceedings. As

the Court could not summon a member of the National Assembly while this body was in session, he moved the opening date of the session up to Thursday, September 6, in order to enjoy parliamentary immunity. On September 8, in a declaratory judgment, judge Lesage ruled that the government's actions were "clearly illegal" and that the process could lead to a unilateral declaration of independence—a prerogative that the Canadian Constitution does not grant to any province. Nonetheless, the judge dismissed Guy Bertrand's request in such a way that no injunction would be issued. Bertrand was bursting with pride, happy that the court was subscribing to his argument. However, Quebec Attorney General Paul Bégin rejected the allegations of illegality, recalling that international law allows for situations that challenge the provisions of a national constitution.

Bertrand's legal proceedings were to produce a boomerang effect. In Ottawa, the ruling left everyone perplexed. If the referendum is in contravention of the Constitution, which is its duty to uphold, can the federal government still participate? If, as judge Lesage contends, the referendum process constitutes a "grave threat to the rights and freedoms" protected by the Charter, can federalists be the accomplices of such a process by getting involved in it? Daniel Johnson saved the day by immediately showing the way: the ruling would not modify the strategy of the federalist camp.

Neither legal obstacles nor surveys would alter the plans laid by the premier. On September 6, he unveiled the preamble of the Sovereignty Bill. The ceremony unfolded on the stage of the Grand Théâtre de Québec. Songwriter-poet Gilles Vigneault and novelist Marie Laberge read the text of the preamble, written by six people based on numerous statements submitted to the regional commissions on Quebec's future. The writers included, in addition to Vigneault and Laberge, Jean-François Lisée, sociologist Fernand Dumont and two constitutional specialists, Andrée Lajoie and Henri Brun. The text[7] began with this high-flown passage: "The time has come to reap the fields of history. The time has come at last to harvest what has been sown for us by four hundred years of men and women of courage, rooted in the soil and now returned to it." And it ended with the following declaration: "We, the people of Québec, through our National Assembly, proclaim: Québec is a sovereign country."

There were a thousand people in attendance in the Grand Théâtre, but Lucien Bouchard and Mario Dumont were not among them. While he recognized the symbolic importance of the ceremony, Dumont explained his absence by declaring: "I neither refused nor agreed to be there," he said, in essence. "I had no business there, since it was a government activity and I had no role to play."[8] Today, however, his tone is somewhat different: "We referred to it as the High Mass," he says. "I try to be respectful of what went on there, but to me, all that business was something from outer space. It was a bombastic event. When I see these things, the leaders are in the front row, they read each other poems, they sing each other songs... I'm always afraid that this will convey the message, 'are we really doing this for the people?' It becomes a ceremony for the elites."[9] Certain commentators criticized the ceremony as backward-looking. On the day after the ceremony, Jacques Parizeau defended himself on the program *Le Midi Quinze*: "Roots are roots," he replied to reporter Michel Lacombe. "Roots are not out of fashion. Quebecers still like to look back at their history."[10]

As for Bouchard, he defended himself for having lacked a spirit of solidarity, emphasizing that it had been agreed that, while Parizeau was in Quebec City, he himself would address another thousand people, namely the students of Édouard-Montpetit CEGEP, in Longueuil. The reality was different, however: The ceremony at the Grand Théâtre "was a strategy that did not really include Mr. Bouchard's staff," recounts Pierre-Paul Roy, his advisor at the time. "Mr. Bouchard did not go in for self-congratulation, and we found that there was a hint of that hanging over this operation. At any rate, Mr. Dumont did not wish to be associated with the event. I don't think we're the first to point out that Mr. Parizeau's rhetoric can tend towards the heavy-handed. And it seemed to us that it was not the right time for such things."[11]

Under the terms of the Sovereignty Bill,[12] the government of Quebec would propose to the government of Canada that the two countries enter into an economic and political partnership treaty "on the basis of the tripartite agreement of June 12" and that "a committee charged with the orientation and supervision of the negotiations relating to the partnership treaty" would be established to keep close watch on the progress of these negotiations. The idea of establishing such a committee was nothing new; it had been around since the three parties that would make up the YES side had managed to reach an agreement at the beginning of June. Where had the idea of making negotiations subject to independent monitoring come from? "This committee was established in response to a request made by the ADQ," states Jacques Gauthier, who in 1995 was chairman of the ADQ political committee.[13] Moreover, at that time, a name was already in the air to take on the chairmanship: Jean Allaire, co-founder of the ADQ and advisor to Mario Dumont. But Jean Allaire's name was also being mentioned to fill the chief negotiator's post: "That was the ADQ's position,"[14] says Pierre-Paul Roy. Nonetheless, today, Jacques Parizeau takes credit for this. "I think it was (my idea)," he says. "A fair number of people, including many journalists, were saying, 'Look, you're about the least credible person who could signal to the kids that recess is over. It's got to be someone who isn't answerable to you and who can report to the National Assembly.' With an oversight committee that was aware of everything that went on in negotiations, we could get a pretty good idea of what everyone was doing. It would be the committee's job to determine if negotiations were going nowhere!"[15]

It was true that the federalists, generally speaking, did not trust Parizeau. Many of them believed that the plan to negotiate was just smoke and mirrors. So Parizeau's intent was to give it as much credibility as possible by entrusting the chairmanship of the steering and oversight committee to a personality who would be above any suspicion of partisanship. His choice: Claude Castonguay, a former Liberal minister in the Bourassa government, whose allegiance was now to the Conservatives.[16] "Mr. Parizeau's office contacted me and told me that the premier wanted to meet with me—that he was inviting me to have dinner with him one evening, but without telling me what it was about," recalls Castonguay. The meeting took place at the Chez Pierre restaurant, on Labelle Street, in Montreal. "It was in the course of the conversation," adds Castonguay, "that Mr. Parizeau invited me to preside over a committee that, should the YES side emerge victorious, was to inform and oversee negotiations. I think the general idea was that things would go forward as positively and as amiably as possible, and that the National Assembly and the people would be kept informed of the progress of negotiations. It was important to have someone who could evaluate the progress of negotiations."[17]

Castonguay had respect for Parizeau. He had known him since the 1960s when they had both acted as advisors to the Lesage government. Moreover, he had had occasion to meet members of Parizeau's family, including his father. And yet, he did not give the premier an answer right away. No names were mentioned during this meal as other possible members of the committee, with the exception of the former justice minister in René Lévesque's government, Marc-André Bédard. "I told myself it would be better to wait and see how things turned out," adds Castonguay, who was not in favour of the YES side. "I would be consulted, in due form and when the time came, on the membership of the committee."[18] Part of the committee's make-up would not be known until October 6. Castonguay's name would not appear, but it was still assumed that he would be its chairman.[19]

Whatever the case, the government of Quebec wished to avoid letting Ottawa drag out discussions, leaving Quebec with the onus of declaring that negotiations were leading nowhere. This is why the bill stipulated, "the negotiations relating to the conclusion of the partnership treaty must not extend beyond October 30, 1996, unless the National Assembly decides otherwise." On receiving the oversight committee's report, the National Assembly would decide to proclaim sovereignty or extend the one-year period established for negotiations.

Starting on September 5, the day before the bill was introduced, 40,000 census takers hit the pavement to travel the length and breadth of the province over a five-day period for the purpose of drawing up the first permanent list of electors in the history of Quebec. Also for the first time, the census takers could, in the case of uncertainty, require that voters show proof-of-identity documents, which gave rise to concern and apprehension among federalists, some of whom feared that members of ethnic groups might be victims of intimidation tactics. The chiefs of the four Native communities of Kahnawake, Obedjiwan, Mingan and Kanesatake, prevented the census takers from entering their territory to add the 7,000 people of voting age who lived there to the list. In contrast, Quebecers living outside Quebec signed up en masse: nearly 15,000 of them did so. On September 12, the list had 4,817,407 registrants, an unprecedented number in the history of Quebec. Once revision was complete, this number was to reach 5,087,000 electors.

The long-awaited referendum question was at last made known on September 7. It was formulated as follows: "Do you agree that Quebec should become sovereign after having made a formal offer to Canada for a new economic and political partnership within the scope of the bill respecting the future of Quebec and of the agreement signed on June 12, 1995? YES or NO?" By presenting the question in this way, the premier meant to avoid any ambiguity: "If you choose Quebec as your country, that means that you don't choose Canada," he declared, thus rejecting any possibility that a second referendum would be required if the YES side won. Daniel Johnson immediately pronounced an anathema on the question, a pronouncement that would follow him throughout the referendum campaign: "It's confusing!" he declared, for it left citizens with the impression that they would be declaring their wishes on something other than "political separation." He regretted the absence of the word "country" in the question, suspecting that the premier wanted to gloss over the real consequences of a victory of the YES side. "As far as we were concerned, the question should have been, *Do you want to secede from Canada?*" says John Parisella. Mr. Parizeau's question "was essentially the same question that had been asked in 1980, even if Mr. Lévesque's question was thirty-six words long, with no reference to sovereignty, secession or creation of a sovereign nation."[20] The 1995 question was four times shorter than the 1980 question and fit onto four lines, as opposed to eighteen lines in 1980, but the strategy of the NO side was already shaping up to be the same as fifteen years earlier:

"In 1980, the question asked of us was 'Do you want to secede, YES or NO?' It was as simple as that," continues Parisella. "59% of people answered NO as opposed to 41% who answered YES, because that was a question they could understand. Obviously, in 1995, this was our strategy once again: to instill—through our spokespeople, our campaign, our advertising—this same question in the minds of voters."[21]

The daily newspaper *La Presse* solicited the opinion of pollsters on the referendum question: it is a bit long, but it is simple, with words that everyone understands—in a word, the best question that the leaders of the YES side could ask, since it evokes sovereignty, but also partnership with Canada. For his part, in an observation that immediately earned him a reprimand from a handful of Liberal MNAs, Quebec Chief Electoral Officer Pierre F. Côté declared the question to be clear, concise and unambiguous.

On the evening when the question was tabled, Louis Rukeyser, host of the prestigious *Wall Street Week Business Show*, was in Montreal. At the stock exchange, he recorded a special program on Canada that would be viewed by millions of Americans. "The referendum does not concern me," he said, aligning himself with the official position of his country, but this did not prevent him from ridiculing the question: "If Quebecers understand what the question is, they all deserve a Ph.D.!"[22] The market thought otherwise. On the same day, the rating agency Dominion Bond Rating Service (DBRS) let it be known that they had no intention of changing Quebec's credit rating, even if the YES side were to win. "The agency would modify the rating if there were changes in the fiscal situation or actual deterioration of the economy," declared their analyst Jeff Moore, who nonetheless pointed out that Quebec's secession would push its deficit up to nine billion dollars.

"The question was not as clear as I would have liked," Jacques Parizeau now acknowledges, "because it alluded to a bill and to an agreement. But we did our utmost to ensure that this agreement and this bill were known by sending them out to all citizens."[23] Three million copies of the bill on Quebec's future, on sovereignty and on the tripartite agreement were printed—plus five hundred thousand in

English and a few thousand in Cree and Inuktitut—and sent to every household in Quebec.

The bill on Quebec's future, which Parizeau submitted on September 7, 1995, was considerably different from the draft bill submitted to the members of the National Assembly in December 1994. A year earlier, the government was committing itself to proclaiming that Quebec was a sovereign nation. Now they were entrusting this proclamation to the National Assembly. Moreover, there were elements in the bill that were not present in the 1994 draft bill: the offer of partnership with the rest of Canada; the time limit on negotiations; the affirmation of the francophone character of Quebec; the approval by the people, in a second referendum, of the new country's constitution.

On the YES side, the troops awaited their signal, even as they suspected that the various political strategists were not all lined up in perfect agreement. "In terms of organization, we were ready," says Alain Lupien, coordinator of the campaign to finance the YES side, "but politically... that was another story. We knew that we had to deal with two personalities: Mr. Bouchard and Mr. Parizeau. We had to resist being distracted by current events. In terms of organization, current events serve to mobilize people, but we avoid current events when they don't suit our purposes." While the news media were projecting onto public opinion the tensions at play between the two leaders, Lupien's job was also to reconcile two head offices: those of the Bloc Québécois and of the Parti Québécois. "There was, well I wouldn't say a rivalry, but a certain competitiveness between the two camps," he says. There were, in fact, struggles in several ridings. Bloc Québécois supporters who two years earlier had been Tories, Liberals, Péquistes and nationalists from all walks, were henceforth obliged to join forces with the Parti Québécois to form a single, unified organization. The operation did not always run smoothly. And it was important to avoid ruffling the feathers of ADQ organizers, but from this quarter, "what they brought was essentially the contribution of their leader, for the promotional value," adds Lupien. "As for organization work, they did nothing to advance the cause anywhere in the field. Or if they did, the effects were subtle enough to go unnoticed!"[24]

Now the only thing missing was the date of the referendum. On September 8, the day after the bill was submitted, Parizeau's intentions became transparent. In the interview that he granted *Le Midi Quinze,* he declared that he wanted to be respectful of the National Assembly's workload, that he had to eliminate November 6 as a possible date, as this was the day after the municipal election, that he was keeping November 13 as a second choice and that, all things considered, the date would be October 30. On September 11, initiating debate on the referendum question, he confirmed, before the members of the National Assembly and a group of French parliamentarians visiting Quebec, that the referendum would indeed take place on October 30. Then, as if he were already in the midst of a referendum campaign, he immediately went on the offensive, attacking Jean Chrétien to denounce his "arrogance towards Quebec," and Daniel Johnson, who, according to Parizeau, shared Chrétien's "unitarian vision."

A robust confrontation on the sovereignty project and the referendum question, in which political statements would be intermingled with *ad hominem* attacks, was thus set in motion. Mario Dumont accused Daniel Johnson of carrying on a discourse of "fear—fear of risk-taking, fear of being afraid, fear of change." He also took Jean Chrétien to task, accusing him of "rejecting the idea of a distinct society for Quebec" with his statement, "We *are* distinct, there's no need to write it into the Constitution." Johnson protested, "There's no shame in voting NO!" Christos Sirros attacked the *indépendantistes* who, according to him, practised a "nationalism of exclusion" by giving more importance to the votes of francophones. Parizeau retorted that it was Daniel Johnson who was practising exclusion by saying, during the electoral campaign, that he would be premier for all Quebecers, except the separatists. Dumont made a motion to request that Jean Chrétien commit to recognizing the results of the referendum. Daniel Johnson strongly opposed this motion, declaring that he was not sure himself of accepting the conclusive rule of a majority of 50% plus one vote. "You don't destroy a country on a judicial recount," he said. Dumont countered that the opposition leader was kowtowing to the federal government. People were taking shots from the inside of the National Assembly out: Liza Frulla accused Marcel Masse, chairman of the *Conseil de la langue française* (French Language Council), of racism because he said "Francophones will realize that they don't have control of their destiny if the NO vote carries the day." The tone was set. Yves Duhaime wondered if Lucienne Robillard had what it took to defend the Québécois "race," being the federal MP representing Saint-Henri–Westmount. And the tone remained unchanged, even after the premier closed debate in the National Assembly on September 20, after thirty-seven hours of squabbling foretelling six weeks of unbridled free-for-all.

The campaign had not officially begun and would not begin officially until the writ of election was issued on October 1. But on the weekend of September 9, two events, which had been planned for some time, gave the NO forces a chance to fire the first salvos. In Orford, Jean Charest called on Québécois voters to mobilize for the NO side. Addressing 150 members of the provincial council of the Conservative party, he announced sweeping reforms of Canadian federalism because "a certain sense of fiscal realism (would) oblige Canada to question the nature of its government... a reform that (would) be in line with Quebec's demands," he said, rejecting the idea that a victory of the NO side would condemn Quebec to keeping the *status quo* in the foreseeable future. Meanwhile, in Montreal, an opponent of Charest in the federal arena who was, however, his ally in the fight against the sovereigntists, described her vision of what Quebec's future would be like if the YES side were to win: "It is our youth who will pay the heaviest price for secession," affirmed Lucienne Robillard, representative of the Chrétien government to the NO coalition, speaking before the *jeunes libéraux fédéraux du Québec* (federal young Liberals of Quebec), assembled for their general council. As for Robert Bourassa, he considered the behaviour of the Québécois government to be "original and highly questionable." According to Bourassa, the proposal that the Quebec government would make to English Canada would be unacceptable to them because it proposed a maximum of economic integration while proposing a minimum of political integration. He was not the only former premier to criticize the path chosen by Parizeau: Pierre-Marc Johnson, former PQ leader, announced that he would not take part in the referendum campaign because he did not agree with the government's strategy.

It was immediately apparent that the federalists would be playing the economy card. On September 13, Jean Chrétien received Singaporean Prime Minister Goh Chok Tong, on an official visit to Canada, in the federal capital. He took the opportunity to "isolate" a sovereign Quebec from Asian markets: "If the YES side emerges triumphant from the referendum," he declared, "the Montreal firm Bombardier, which is preparing a proposal to build the Singapore subway system, as well as other firms, will no longer be able to do business with Asian Pacific-Rim nations."

The alarmism that tinged the discourse of federalists in the opening days of September was based on indicators that could leave no one indifferent, since the Léger Marketing poll that had shown the two options running neck and neck. The dollar fell. The Bank of Canada was obliged to raise its rate by 35 points, faced with a currency that had dropped to 74.13 cents on Asian markets. The dollar lost one cent in two days. On September 13 alone, it lost more than half a cent due to a rumour to the effect that the YES was winning, with 70% of votes. The commentary of the supporters of both sides, and the discordant voices of specialists in monetary matters, also contributed to increasing the volatility of the dollar and Canadian securities. Lucien Bouchard declared that if the NO side were to win, the fight for a sovereign Quebec would continue. "The rise in the bank rate and the decrease in the value of the dollar were brought about by the referendum," said a spokesperson of the Canadian Imperial Bank of Commerce (CIBC). "A drop of 5 to 10% in the exchange rate and increases in interest rates of 100 to 200 percentage points are quite plausible if the YES side wins the referendum," argued Maurice Marchon, professor at the *École des hautes études commerciales* (HEC).[25]

In the first week of September, Canadian investors—especially Torontonians—were selling off their Canadian securities en masse. In the second week, foreign investors followed suit.[26] In Japan, the

Central Bank intervened, and speculators sold Canadian securities, which were immediately snapped up by American investors. Since the financial world had learned the date of the referendum, and with this knowledge acquired the certitude that there would be no turning back, the dollar had lost two cents in three days. "We can start using the word crisis," said an economist from the Desjardins Group.

When on September 9, the data from the poll that placed the two options in a dead heat were published, the president of Léger Marketing declared that voters who said they would vote YES were more likely to change their opinion than those on the federalist side. He didn't know just how close to the truth his words were. The reversal came about on Friday the 15th: a survey, conducted by SOM between September 8 and 12 on behalf of La Presse and Télé-Québec, showed the NO ahead by eight points. Optimism returned to the brokerage houses. The dollar made a slight gain of 13 hundredths of a point and on Saturday, Canadian currency traders went to work in the middle of the night to buy Canadian dollars when the market opened in London. At sunrise on Saturday the 16th, the dollar had made another gain of 25 hundredths. Canadian securities were bolstered. Short-term investments brought more than 2% more than their American counterparts. Flight of capital? It was much less pronounced than it had been in 1980. Border towns—Hawkesbury in particular—profited from this. But in this case, it was a matter of irrational panic: taking one's money out of Quebec to invest it in Ontario or New Brunswick, rather than converting it to American dollars, was completely pointless and senseless. If there was an economic crisis in Quebec, there would also be a deep crisis throughout Canada.

Despite the cause-and-effect relationship that politicians and analysts drew between market jitters and the referendum, what the stock market was experiencing was nothing new: this happens any time a political event of some significance takes place. In 1992, at the time of the Charlottetown referendum, the dollar had undergone a similar collapse in relation to American currency. The situation simply showed that investors wished to reposition their portfolios before the referendum, all the more so given that they were aware of the level of indebtedness of Quebec. Nevertheless, the Quebec finance minister, Jean Campeau, felt the need to reassure the banks: they would have access to the Quebec market insofar as an agreement with the federal government would allow Quebec banks to enjoy the same privileges in English Canada.

Amidst the stormy weather of these early days of the referendum season, a voice emerged in support of a NO vote, but it was the YES side that was subsequently rubbing its hands with glee. Mike Keane, the valiant captain of the Montreal Canadiens, declared that he didn't see why he should learn French. He would find out two months later when he was traded to the Colorado Avalanche.[27] Another event, this one more serious, projected onto the coverage of the pre-referendum media campaign an embarrassment of suspicion and mistrust. On September 13, journalist Jean Bédard, covering the Quebec parliament for the *Réseau de l'Information* (RDI), an all-news network, found a document on his desk. He had no idea where it came from, and the envelope bore no information on the sender. However, it was accompanied by a note stating that the document was being circulated among the leaders of the Quebec Liberal Party (QPL) and that the matter addressed therein was a plan for a constitutional change in Quebec. The document contained, among other things, two proposals: one to make Quebec a bilingual province, the other to reopen the Meech Lake Accord project. Bédard knew that he was the exclusive recipient of this information. He did not seek to verify the authenticity of the document, being fairly sure that the QPL would deny the content. Still, his eleven years of experience in the Quebec parliament, his thorough knowledge of the constitutional background of the Liberal party, the document's form and its technical format—all of these things combined to dispel any doubt in the journalist's mind: this document was authentic. Bédard spread the news, taking care to state that the document was only a working dossier and did not represent the official position of the Liberal party. Daniel Johnson immediately called a press conference to denounce the "fabricated evidence put together by the YES campaign" and, the next day in the National Assembly, he asked, "Who will benefit from the crime?" But it was too late to change anything. The news was taken up by the media, not always with as much care as the RDI correspondent had shown. Bédard would pay for this: he was to be reprimanded by his management, taken off campaign coverage and suspended for two weeks.[28]

When he formed his cabinet, Jacques Parizeau gave Richard Le Hir the task of preparing a series of studies on the consequences of sovereignty. The former president of the *Association des manufacturiers du Québec* (Quebec Manufacturers Association) was a disappointed man, not having been named minister of industry and commerce as he had been promised, he said, when he agreed to be a candidate for the 1994 election.[29] Nevertheless, he set to work on the task at hand and recruited a bevy of academics and specialists who then produced, in the year to come, a good forty studies, which Parizeau hoped would demonstrate the merits of sovereignty. Le Hir submitted the first study—and it was a major one—on the last day of August 1995. It pleased the minister no end. According to two actuaries, Claude Lamonde and Pierre Renaud, "the budget deficit of a sovereign Québec would amount to 7.9 billion dollars in 1996–1997—an improvement of more than 7 billion dollars compared to the position evaluated for 1993–1994,"[30] under the leadership of Daniel Johnson's Liberal government. Which led Jacques Parizeau to say, on September 7, that the Quebec deficit, after secession, would reach a little more than eight billion—"on the high side, but bearable"—provoking an immediate reaction from the C.D. Howe Institute: "It's a very small number," said Bill Robson, the organization's top analyst, "by comparison with estimates made by a variety of outside people, some of whom were even quite sympathetic to the sovereignty cause."[31]

But on September 14, 1995, a new study, this one not officially submitted by Le Hir, set the Year-1 deficit of a sovereign Quebec at three billion dollars higher than the Lamonde and Renaud study. Prepared by Georges Mathews, economist and demographer at the *Institut national de la recherche scientifique* (INRS, Quebec National Institute of Scientific Research), the report was challenged and its publication prevented by the Institute itself. This was enough for the

Liberals to accuse the government of releasing only those studies that suited their purposes, and the INRS of having become a "subsidiary" of the Parti Québécois government.[32] Jean-Claude Thibodeau, the director of INRS-Urbanisation, who oversaw both studies, was then obliged to intervene to confirm that it was indeed the Institute that had blocked publication of the Mathews study because "it (raised) serious questions in regard to research methodology." In fact, the INRS had suggested that Mathews publish the problems raised by his document in an in-house collection in order to submit his methodology to peer review. The economist was humiliated. In a long piece published by *Le Devoir* on September 16, he defended his methods. "As a researcher," he said, "I consider intellectual rigour to be of the utmost importance. And as a sovereigntist, I refuse and will always refuse to work according to labels. There is no such thing as sovereigntist science and federalist science. There are simply analyses that are thorough and those that are not."[33]

Calculating a future deficit is not a simple task. According to the budget presented in May 1995 by Finance Minister Jean Campeau, Quebec's revenues for 1995–1996 would be $38 billion, made up of 19 billion in income tax, 7 billion in consumer taxes, and another 2 billion from permits, licences, fines, and so on: $28 billion in all from Quebec's taxpayers, to which another 2 billion would be added from public companies, Loto-Québec, la Société des Alcools (the provincial liquor distribution board) and Hydro-Québec (the provincial electrical power utility). The remaining 8 billion would come, for the most part, from federal transfer payments. Moreover, expenditures (for health, education, social welfare, public safety, agriculture, culture, etc.) would be in the neighbourhood of $36 billion. On top of this would be added the cost of the debt, for a total of $43 billion.[34] The contradictions among the different studies were explainable by the way the money Québécois taxpayers sent to Ottawa in varying forms and for varying reasons, along with federal spending in Quebec—including federal transfer payments—were added to revenues. They also arose from the difficulty of figuring savings obtained by elimination of overlapping federal and provincial services: "2.8 billion," said

Parizeau; "one billion," said Mathews and two other researchers, Claude Fluet and Pierre Lefebvre.[35] And finally, the contradictions emerged from the fact that it is impossible to predict precisely just how much the economy would slow down—if indeed it was to slow down— in a sovereign Quebec.

It was Daniel Johnson who, on September 18, unveiled the study prepared by Claude Fluet and Pierre Lefebvre, two econo- mists from the *Université du Québec à Montréal* (UQAM), who pro- posed six scenarios for evaluating the Year-1 deficit, which would range from a minimum of $9.5 billion to a maximum of $14.1 billion. "Yet another study stopped in its tracks by the INRS, because it was deemed to be unsatisfactory," railed Parizeau in the National Assembly that same day.

As a matter of fact, four studies were blocked by the INRS, only to be made public later by the *Secrétariat à la Restructuration* (Restructuring secretariat). The blocked studies were two studies prepared by Georges Mathews on public finances and the monetary union, the one by Fluet and Lefebvre and an additional study pro- duced by Ivan Bernier, international economic law expert and pro- fessor at the faculty of law at *Université Laval*. Bernier especially aroused the government's anger because he challenged two of the po- sitions it had been defending for several months: the quasi-automatic inclusion of Quebec in the North American Free Trade Agreement (NAFTA), and the continuation of an extended economic union with Canada. According to Bernier, the matter to be discussed should be a customs union rather than an economic union, because Canada would not allow a small country like Quebec to have a say in its economic policy.[36]

It was the coordinator of the INRS studies, Pierre Lamonde,[37] who unblocked the studies: "The study by Messrs. (Claude) Lamonde and (Pierre) Renaud had the good fortune to be released more quickly than the others, but this does not mean that it has our endorsement more than the others. Those being released today prompted reserva- tions within the government. But for three of these studies, the INRS did not share these reservations and considered that the mandate had been carried out satisfactorily, considering their modest budget." The INRS considered the Fluet-Lefebvre study to be valid while acknowledging that it had remained "temporarily shelved" all summer long.[38]

On the other side of the country, the Fraser Institute, in Vancouver, was not the least bit subtle in its analysis. The Year-1 deficit would be somewhere between $19 and 25.8 billion, according to the estimate of the director of the Institute's International Centre for the Study of Public Debt, Robin Richardson.[39] Quebec's debt would then move it from 28th to 19th place in the list of the most indebted countries, behind Madagascar and just in front of Jamaica. The burden of this debt would be $23.7 billion, compared to $15.3 billion if Quebec remained part of Confederation. And finally, Quebecers would receive fewer than half of the services that they receive if they stay in Confederation![40]

The debate on the deficit and the indebtedness of Quebec-as-a-country was impossible to follow: voters were lost in this piling up of numbers where, in public discourse, political interests took precedence over scientific rigour. The matter of the studies prompted a free-for-all in the National Assembly. Insults and invective flowed freely. A Liberal MP called Mario Dumont a "sell-out" and another called him an "asshole." Daniel Johnson condemned the government for naming itself "the final judge of what is credible and, above all, what may be shown to Quebecers before the referendum in matters of public finances and the deficit."

On September 19, the volume was turned up another notch when the member for Châteauguay, Jean-Marc Fournier, revealed that minister Le Hir had granted nearly half a million dollars worth of contracts to three companies who had a privileged relationship with an advisor from the *Secrétariat à la Restructuration*. This advisor was Claude Lafrance, with whom Le Hir had worked during his time as president of the *Association des manufacturiers du Québec*, and whom he had recruited, in January 1995, to help the secretariat with the management of studies contracted to the private sector. Lafrance was president of the firm Solin, where Pierre Campeau had been vice-president from 1989 to 1994, before Le Hir hired him as a deputy minister. Campeau had acted as associate secretary general of restructuring since October 31, 1994. Lafrance, still president and sole shareholder at Solin, held two-thirds of Comsol's shares and 20% of consulting firm Guay, Montpetit Services Conseils. These were the very same three firms that were pointed out by Fournier, and they all had overlapping shares in the contracts obtained from the Secretariat.

Le Hir counterattacked immediately, qualifying Fournier's statements as "very serious" and "part of a smear campaign." The very next day, he asked Guy Breton, Quebec's auditor general, to conduct an investigation into this affair, in a word, to determine whether there had been a conflict of interest. This camouflage attempt did not work. Daniel Johnson asked for the minister's resignation "because he lied to the people and to the members of parliament." He declared in the National Assembly: "How can the premier keep a straight face and keep the minister responsible for restructuring on staff—the prime contractor of the greatest operation of manipulation and secrecy?"

Richard Le Hir was inconsistent as a parliamentarian. Every time he took the floor of the National Assembly to defend a study, he was called to order... by the researchers themselves who had to correct what he had said. Already, over the summer, he had put the government in an embarrassing position when at a cost of nearly $100,000, he sent abstracts of the specialists' studies—no less than 130,000 copies mailed—to town councils, law offices and school principals' offices, all accompanied by a letter that had an air of propaganda: "We will be most grateful," they read, "if you would do us the kindness of passing out these newsletters in the institution of learning of which you are the principal." Parizeau became defensive whenever the subject of his minister came up. He could not let him go in the middle of a race in which the slightest misstep could cost him thousands of votes—not without doing some damage. So he protected him and would continue protecting him until after the referendum. But not for long. Journalists, who during election campaigns are in the habit of naming the buses in which they follow the leaders around on the campaign trail, named the YES bus the "Hirobus" and the NO bus the "Hiroplane."

The auditor general's report would be submitted to the government at the end of November. It was unambiguous: under the terms of applicable rules and measures on conflicts of interest, "conducting business transactions with oneself is one of the situations that constitutes a conflict of interest. Claude Lafrance, whose duty was to act as advisor to the Secretariat with regard to performance of administrative restructuring studies to be carried out by the private sector, was in a situation of real or potential conflict of interest."[41] The firms with which he was associated obtained contracts amounting to a total of 430,000 dollars.[42]

While in Quebec City, debate was raging on the subject of the "Le Hir studies," a nationwide survey came along whose findings would both encourage and discourage the sovereigntists: Canadians from other provinces, by a margin of 51% to 41, considered that Canada should agree to negotiate with a sovereign Quebec. But the majority was also opposed to Quebecers' using Canadian currency and holding Canadian passports, while 40% of Quebecers were expecting the opposite. And the most troubling thing for the sovereigntists was that 22% of people surveyed still believed that, even if the YES side were to win, Quebec would continue sending MPs to Ottawa.

On Sunday, September 17, a rainy day hinting that autumn was not far off, the coalition of NO forces launched a major offensive at the Saint-Joseph-de-Beauce sports centre. Daniel Johnson made an impassioned speech before a crowd of 2,000 people: "Who are they to tell me that they are more Québécois than the people assembled here today?" Lucienne Robillard, who was with him, was not ruling out the possibility of a commercial agreement between Canada and an independent Quebec, but insisted on the fact that Quebecers would lose their Canadian citizenship. Michel Bélanger, in his remarks, maintained that Canada would have no reason to negotiate, as according to the rules of international commerce, Canada would have access to Quebec markets anyway.

Jean Charest, who was also at the podium, was not in top form. Over the preceding week, he had been to Côte-Nord and while en route from Sept-Îles to Montreal, he stopped off here and there—in particu-

lar in Charlevoix—to take a break from this long car trip. "I couldn't
afford other means of transportation,"[43] recalls the former leader of the
Conservative party, a party that had then lost a good deal of its lustre
and whose coffers were considerably less full than when Mulroney was
reigning in Ottawa. During this trip, Charest came down with the flu,
so that when he arrived in the Beauce region, he was weary and beginning to lose his voice. In the car that drove him to Saint-Joseph, he and
his staff were looking for an idea to draw on. Someone then suggested
they talk about the importance of the Canadian passport. The idea was
a good one and, since he did not intend to speak for very long, Charest
decided to show them one. But he couldn't use his own because in
Canada, the passport of parliamentarians is green, while that of the cit-
izenry at large is blue. He was therefore obliged to borrow one, and in
the end, it was one of the organization's staffers who lent him hers.
"And thus began the famous passport speech, which kept on going
until the referendum," he now recalls. Every time he gave it, he used
someone else's passport. "After that, I never relocated my own," he
adds. "When some time later, a secretary from my office phoned the
passport office to get it replaced, a lady asked, 'Are you sure Mr.
Charest didn't leave it on a podium somewhere?'"[44] Charest encountered some success with his passport story, but it was local industrial
leader, Marcel Dutil, of Canam Manac, who grabbed people's attention
the most forcefully and who sounded the trumpet to rally business
people to the cause. In this industrial region of La Beauce, the message
of Dutil and other industry owners was unequivocal: "Those creating
jobs vote NO," he declaimed from atop the tribune.

And they proclaimed their message loud and clear. Two days
later, Guy Saint-Pierre, president of SNC-Lavalin, expressed his fear
of seeing the kind of instability that reigned in the former Yugoslavia
settling in in Quebec, finding that Quebec was too small and weak to
negotiate with the rest of Canada.[45] Economist Michel Bélanger[46] affirmed that it was a false claim to state that Quebec's industry and commerce would develop better in the framework of NAFTA than in a
union with Canada. It was Bombardier, however, that really lowered
the boom. "There is no way," said CEO Laurent Beaudoin, "that a

country shrunk down to the dimensions of an independent Quebec would be able to provide adequate support to sustain development of a company like Bombardier."[47] And as if the words were not sufficient, Bombardier asked its employees to vote NO and to contribute to the war chest of the NO coalition.[48] The incident sent out shockwaves. The way Gaston Leroux, the MP representing the Bloc Québécois in the Richmond-Wolfe riding, tells it, upper management first convened some fifty executives for the purpose of informing them of the company's federalist position and inviting them to convey the message to employees. "An incredible, underhanded trap and a violation of democratic principles," protested Leroux. Guy Chevrette's reaction was even more violent: "What really bowls me over," he said, "is that those who are able to draw on both levels of government come down firmly on the side of fear."[49] "A revolting attitude" cried in his turn Clément Godbout of the FTQ (Fédération des travailleurs et travailleuses du Québec, Quebec Federation of Labour), one of the major unions. The union reacted through its members: the employees of General Motors, in Boisbriand, and Pratt & Whitney, in Longueuil, all FTQ members, voted unanimously to endorse the YES side. In La Pocatière, where Daniel Johnson was received politely but unenthusiastically, Bombardier employees protested against their president's methods, affirming that they would not be influenced in any way. According to *La Presse*, the only result of the Bombardier initiative was to sensitize employees—the majority of whom turned around and voted YES—to the importance of the referendum. Despite the boomerang effect produced by Laurent Beaudoin's declaration within his own company, the directors of other companies—Benisti Import Export, jeans manufacturers Point Zero, Imprimerie Admiral and Dominion Textile—asked their employees to think hard about the harmful effects of a NO vote. In the case of Benisti, this request was made in the form of a letter written in English only, entitled *Declaration of Patriotism to Canada*. A survey of the *Conseil du Patronat du Québec* (Quebec Employer's Council) confirmed that these occurrences of coming out for one side were not isolated cases: 88% of company presidents would vote NO on the referendum.

On September 18, the House of Commons reconvened, and... the war was on. Jean Chrétien was refusing to say whether he would recognize the outcome of the referendum: "If they had asked the question *Do you want to secede from Canada?*—period—I would say, I'd be the first to recognize the outcome—if they had been frank enough to come out with a question that would be absolutely clear to Quebecers." Lucien Bouchard's retort: "Depending on whether Mr. Chrétien is speaking French to Quebecers or English to Mr. Manning, he changes his position." According to the Bloc Québécois, Chrétien told Manning that he would not recognize the outcome of the referendum on the question as it stood, something he didn't dare come out and say clearly to Quebecois voters.[50] Preston Manning and his spokesman on constitutional matters, Stephen Harper, displayed greater openness and invited Chrétien to show more respect for the intelligence of Quebecers. "Whether the response is YES or NO," said Harper, "it will clearly have significance for Canada's future. The prime minister must acknowledge reality." And it was Manning, rather than Bouchard, who took Chrétien to task, enjoining him to admit that a victory of the YES side—no matter the margin of victory—would mean the secession of Quebec. "It would be irresponsible to acknowledge a sovereigntist victory obtained by a very slim margin," retorted the prime minister, "for the character of the October 30 vote is consultative, nothing more."[51]

The fever paralyzing the House of Commons was taking hold of the public service. Treasury Board secretary Bob Giroux sent a letter to all government workers, reminding them that there were certain rules of conduct to observe should they decide to take part in the referendum campaign. Giroux's memorandum was carefully stated: "Given the nature of this referendum and its importance in Canada," he wrote, "employees should consider their responsibilities and duties in the federal public service carefully when making any decisions about participation in referendum-related activities. They must determine whether their involvement would impair—or be seen to impair—their ability to perform their duties effectively and impartially."[52] "Intimidation tactics!" cried union leaders, recalling that since a ruling made by the Supreme Court in 1991, public servants had the right to participate in political campaigns.

The matter of integrating federal public servants into the Quebec public service, should independence come, would haunt the YES forces throughout the campaign. It was Parizeau who first came up with this idea. "It seemed to me a rather elementary matter of justice," he says today, explaining his initiative. "In many small towns or rural areas around Quebec, a woman would decide to go to work for the federal government—at the post office—and another one in the same family would decide to go to work at the courthouse. So the woman who had chosen the post office would lose her job, and the other one would keep hers. Something about that just isn't right. So my answer was, there's still going to be a post office in that town, so yes, ma'am, of course you can keep your job."[53] But Parizeau was the only person thinking this way.

As early as the end of August, Mario Dumont declared that those who believed that a sovereign Quebec would have the capacity to absorb all of Quebec's federal workers were fooling themselves. "Sure, it's possible, but in the long run, do we really need that many people?" he asked. His stand on this issue had an adverse effect on relations among the three leaders. During one of the meetings they held from time to time, Jacques Parizeau explained his position to Bouchard and Dumont. "I let him know," said the leader of the ADQ, "that if questioned on the matter, while I might not purposely stir up trouble, I would certainly say the opposite." Mario Dumont said that he could not back the project while, at the same time, criticizing redundancies in federal and provincial jurisdictions. "It was a point on which our paths diverged, and I think Mr. Bouchard was more or less of my opinion. This had an impact on the outcome of the referendum," he concludes.[54] "It didn't win me any votes in the Ottawa Valley," acknowledges Jacques Parizeau today, "but it cost me some votes in Quebec City, where government workers said to themselves, 'We're going to lose our jobs over this.' In politics, this is what we call an error. Yes, that's it, an error."[55]

On September 22 and 23, two polls came along to encourage the federalists. According to Créatec, who queried 1,004 people for the NO committee, the spread was still at eight points. This was confirmed the next day by the firm Compas, who emphasized, however, that 24% of respondents were undecided. Only Saguenay–Lac-Saint-Jean went merrily their own way: 56% of voters said they would vote YES on the referendum question.[56] Daniel Johnson was bubbling over with optimism, to the point of minimizing his own expectations, should the NO side win. Before a group of his party's organizers assembled in Montreal, he stated that a victory of the NO side did not constitute a promise for constitutional change, but that he could guarantee Québécois voters that they would remain Canadian, keep the Canadian dollar and enjoy all the advantages of the treaties that had been entered into by Canada.[57] He wanted Jean Chrétien to jump into the fray: "He should be part of this," he said on the program *L'Événement* on TVA television. "He is an MP from Saint-Maurice and prime minister of Canada."

On Sunday evening, an unexpected bombshell with unpredictable consequences came along to shake the enthusiasm of the federalists. Before the members of the general council of the Quebec Liberal Party, assembled at the Sheraton hotel in Montreal, a businessman, Claude Garcia, president of Standard Life, tossed off the following: "It's not enough just to win on October 30. We must crush them..." "An unfortunate turn of phrase,"[58] says Senator Pierre-Claude Nolin, very active at the time in organizing the NO campaign. "It was a statement that had an impact in the media," recalls John Parisella. "I think the population saw that there was a certain arrogance, aggressiveness (in the phrase). And Quebecers, even if they were leaning towards voting NO at that time, (remembered) the failure of Meech Lake, the failure of Charlottetown... (they had) the sensation that Quebec had not gotten the respect it deserved. (Garcia's declaration) gave voters the impression that this lack of respect was again showing up in the NO camp. In a way, it broke the momentum that had been gathered at that time."[59]

That weekend, September 23–24, the YES side's popularity had sunk to its lowest point. "It looked like we'd hit rock bottom," says Jean Royer, Parizeau's chief of staff. "From the moment of Mr. Garcia's famous declaration, I felt a reverse trend taking hold."[60]

Claude Garcia's problems did not stop there. Claude Corbo, president of *Université du Québec à Montréal* (UQAM), where Garcia chaired the board of governors, distanced himself from Garcia's statements. Patricio Salgado, president of the *Association générale étudiante des sciences humaines, arts, lettres et communications* (Associated Students of the Humanities, Arts, Letters and Communications), with more than 14,000 students in its ranks, demanded his resignation: "The vast majority of the UQAM student body is sovereigntist," he said. "We are the people Mr. Garcia wants to crush!" The professors also wanted to see him go. Four days after making his declaration, Garcia apologized, but expected to keep his job. Three weeks later, Corbo suspended Garcia and called a special meeting of the board, in November, at which Garcia's fate would be decided. And—it never rains but it pours—the government refused to automatically renew Standard Life's 11.5 million-dollar contract, under which the company administered insurance and payroll for the 35,000 government workers who were members of the FTQ. Henceforth, this contract would be awarded through competitive bidding, and Parizeau made no secret of the fact that Garcia's declaration had played a role in this decision: "There is no vendetta against Standard Life," he said, "but these rather fanatical political declarations did draw our attention to the company."[61]

Both sides were reaching deep into their cupboards in search of a decisive argument that would, on the NO side, accentuate the trend or, on the YES side, bring about a lasting reversal of fortunes. Foreign Affairs Minister André Ouellet and his colleague, Vaudreuil MP Nick Discepola, took up the arguments of Shaw and Albert[62] and spoke of partition. "If the sovereigntists are ready to divide Canada while wanting an indivisible Quebec, the West Island and the Ottawa Valley could then secede from Quebec if Quebec secedes from Canada," declared Discepola. "And the Cree and the Mohawks could join us." Daniel Johnson had a terrible time trying to keep the discourse of NO supporters within rational limits: "The Quebec Liberal Party's position is quite clear. The borders of Quebec are the borders of Quebec as we know them today."[63]

The federalists had a powerful ally on their side in the person of James Blanchard, US ambassador to Canada, who ran around excitedly as if he were reliving the American Civil War. On September 28, he went to the office of John Rae, brother of Bob Rae, who was vice-president of Power Corporation. "Ever since President Clinton's speech in Ottawa" in February 1995, he wrote in his book, "I had been wondering how the United States could help the cause of Canadian unity in a way that wouldn't backfire against either us or Ottawa, and John felt it would be good for me to sit down with him and their federal pollster, Maurice Pinard, to discuss it."[64] Pinard, for his part, confirmed what the polls of the US embassy were already telling him—that Quebecers had a favourable opinion of President Clinton; indeed he was more popular than Parizeau or Chrétien. This is when Pinard suggested that he bring Clinton back into the picture: "It wouldn't hurt if the president were to say something good about Canada," he told Blanchard.

The next day, taking care to apologize if he appeared to be discussing something that didn't concern him—or his country—the ambassador, speaking to the members of the Canadian Institute of International Affairs, stated that if separatists thought that an independent Quebec would be admitted to NAFTA easily or automatically, they were mistaken. Today, he acknowledges that this was a strategy on his part more than a certainty. "I expected questions about our position and I intended to use them to counter the separatists' claim that an independent Quebec would easily or automatically become a member of NAFTA," he wrote. "That's exactly what happened. Though different newspapers reported my remarks differently, they all got the point and the overall coverage was helpful to the federalists."[65]

The next day, September 30, Blanchard was playing golf with Jean Chrétien. "The Prime Minister was confident at that point that the federalists were going to enjoy a decisive victory a month later," he wrote. "We all were, and the polls supported our confidence."[66] In this, he was not mistaken. But other than the survey by Decima Research, which gave the NO side only a one-point lead, the other polls foretold a decisive defeat of the YES side. Léger Marketing showed the federalist option in the lead by six-and-a-half points, and when Quebecers were given the choice between sovereignty and the *status quo*, 45% of them preferred the *status quo*, while only 39% leaned towards sovereignty.[67] These were, within a few decimal points, the 1980 results. Even the referendum question was in a sorry state: there were 8% more Quebecers who said they would answer NO if it were put to them in these last days of September (20–25).

This latest survey, however, showed a division in opinions that would strongly influence the strategy of both sides in the last month of the campaign: NO was prevailing, hands down, in Montreal, at 61% to 39%, but YES was ahead by two points in the rest of Quebec. Another observation would contribute to a change in the sovereigntists' discourse: YES would carry the day with 53% of the vote if Quebecers were certain that a sovereign Quebec would be associated with the rest of Canada. The federalists therefore doggedly sought to demonstrate that the partnership could not be taken for granted, while the sovereigntists would maintain that Canada had no other choice.

CHAPTER VII

In search of a
Winning Strategy

W ith scarcely a month left before the referendum, the NO forces were still fighting amongst themselves. Despite advances indicated in the polls, Daniel Johnson was not unaware that getting the various spokespeople of his coalition to convey a consistent message would be an uphill battle. "When you're the leader of the NO side," he says today, "first of all, you've got to put forward the arguments that show your fellow citizens why voting YES is not to their advantage. Then, secondly, by definition, by choice, by your conviction, you embody Quebecers' sense of being Canadian." He hoped to show how it was possible to be a federalist without necessarily backing the current government, which was already an indication that he was entertaining doubts about the popularity of the federal Liberal party. "It's not a matter of being for or against the policies that the Canadian government of the day represents," he adds, "but rather of standing up for Quebec's interests with a government program that is federalist." The leader of the NO side acknowledges that this simple way of looking at things complicated the debate within his coalition. At the end of September 1995, with the real referendum campaign just a few days away, the members of the federalist marching band were not all marching to the same cadence. "The other members of the coalition," recalls Johnson, "including the Equality Party, which the law required us to include, came right in with all sorts of other arguments that had nothing whatsoever to do with the vision that we, the Quebec Liberal

Party, had for Quebecers as Canadians. They had their own agendas. That, there, was the real difficulty for the leader of the NO side— being the leader of a coalition of people who were all over the map of the non-sovereigntist community."[1]

Daniel Johnson, for example, had to take into consideration the political formation of Montreal's West Island anglophones, with their uncompromising rhetoric tinged with references to partitioning Quebec and redefining borders. And he had to consider the former nationalist Liberals, while avoiding throwing a lifeline to Mario Dumont, about whom Johnson says "there was no imaginable bridge or gangway that he would have been inclined to extend, much less cross over!" And finally, the leader of the NO coalition had to take the various federalist partners into consideration—including the Liberal Party of Canada, which was one of the major players.

Theoretically, the federal government could stay on the sidelines of the referendum. Ottawa wondered, for a time, whether it would be opportune to take part in the campaign. "The fundamental question was posed in 1980, not in 1995," says Jean Chrétien today. "In 1980, there had been a debate in the Cabinet. Many ministers were saying that Canada was indivisible. (But) we were banking on democracy. If people—clearly, not on ambiguous questions, and at 50% plus one— didn't want to remain in Canada, well then, we would accept it. In 1995, it was too late to say, 'we won't participate!' But we had reservations. If the outcome had been positive for the YES side, this would have provided a considerable amount of ammunition to those who wished to separate—even if they never wrote the word 'separation' into the question."[2]

The Canadian Constitution has no provision for what to do in the case of a referendum on separation. The sovereigntists "were making up their own rules," adds Chrétien. "So I considered that I was entitled to make up my own rules too. I was Prime Minister of Canada, and the country had the right to speak. (For) there would have been consequences for the rest of Canada." Chrétien then evokes the division of colonial India into modern India and Pakistan and the division of Pakistan, which created Bangladesh. "There was this whole notion, that had been debated, of even partitioning Quebec," he adds. "The Quebec of 1763 was quite a bit smaller than the Quebec of today. So there was plenty of room for a good discussion, which would have been interesting. But I'm really glad we never had it!"[3]

There was, in fact, only one minister, Ron Irwin, charged with Indian and Northern Affairs, who opposed the Canadian government's participation in the referendum debate—which was nothing new, considering he had the same reservations in 1980. But there were many who regretted being trapped by the choice Pierre Elliott Trudeau had made, in 1980, to participate in the referendum. Among them was David Collenette, one of the most influential ministers in Chrétien's cabinet. Trudeau "legitimized the fact that a YES vote would lead to separation," he says. "I never accepted that and I believe most people outside Quebec would never accept that. And that is why, when we went to the '95 referendum, we ran into the same problem, we had set the precedent, that is, if the YES side won, then that's the end of the country. And key federal politicians basically said that to be the case. That was wrong."

As the Canadian Constitution was silent on the matter, it was Justice Minister Allan Rock who, beyond the reach of any political analysis that might take place on the matter in the federal Cabinet, became the person responsible for framing, from a legal standpoint, the government's action with respect to a possible division of the country. He was therefore at the centre of the earliest discussions to take place in Ottawa in early 1994—even before the election of the Parti Québécois—on the possibility of Quebec's separation. "That issue came up in the early part of '94. Because it was suggested that we had a choice to declare the country indivisible and to say that no such referendum should be held because the country, Canada, could not be severed," recalls Allan Rock. "But it was quickly decided that there was no future in that position. I think it was the prime minister himself who said at the time, in early '95, we really have crossed the bridge, we can't go back, we can't now say it's indivisible because, in 1980, we recognized that the question could properly be put to the people." As for John Manley, he does not remember that the idea that the federal government might abstain from taking part ever came up in Cabinet discussions: "I don't think we discussed whether or not we should participate. The argument was not going to be over the legitimacy of the referendum process, if it went the wrong way," he says. "Most of us believed that we were better to fight the consultation to the degree we were able to do so from the federal side, rather than waiting until Quebecers had answered the question and the rest of Canada had somehow... failed to even make their views heard." The problem with a position like Manley's was that the organizers of the NO campaign did not wish to see federal politicians meddling in a referendum that was of concern only to Quebecers.

The point that made the federal government's choice—and more specifically, Jean Chrétien's choice—to participate in the referendum easier, was the assurance they held that they would win easily. "At the time, we were pretty certain we would win, we would win big," says Eddy Goldenberg, at that time advisor to Jean Chrétien. "It would be very hard to explain why we were not participating." But the political instincts of certain members of Cabinet, among them Brian Tobin, kept them from sharing the optimism of the Prime Minister's Office. "We were confident but we knew it was going to be a closer race than in 1980, that it wasn't going to be a 60-40 split," remembers Tobin. "We were in far more serious circumstances in 1994–1995 than we were in 1980. Don't forget, in 1980, Mr. Trudeau had 74 of 75 seats in Quebec. In 1994–1995, we were not the majority in Quebec."

The Liberal Party of Canada would therefore join the NO side. But to do what? According to Preston Manning, the government had no plan to counter the sovereignty project. During "my first interview with Mr. Chrétien after the '93 election," he says, "when I brought up, 'and what about Quebec?' I got the sense that there was not a winning federalist strategy. He gave the impression, which he maintained for quite a long time until you couldn't hold it any longer, that everything was OK and everything was under control and Canada was the best country in the world and why would anybody want to leave it and all you have to do is keep saying it." The former leader of the Reform Party likes to recall the time in 1963 when Lester

B. Pearson told his father, then premier of Alberta, about the mandate of the Royal Commission on Bilingualism and Biculturalism. Ernest Manning had declared, "This is not going to solve the unity problem, and we're going to have a full-blown secession crisis down the road," remembers Preston Manning. The Reform leader's fear of Quebec secession reaches back to that time, when he took his father's advice and began studying the political conditions that led the United States to the Civil War.

Haunted by his readings on the American Civil War, Preston Manning was fearful of the consequences of a refusal by the federal government to acknowledge a victory of the YES side. He was wary of Jean Chrétien because, in his view, Chrétien was not a democrat. "The Prime minister is not a democrat. He said in the House, one time, he hates these referendums. He doesn't believe in people having a direct say in public policy. If there'd been a clear democratic mandate for better or for worse and he was just going to trample on that, I don't think we'd have supported him in that because, if he can reject democracy in that case, he'll reject it in other cases."

In fact, Jean Chrétien gives a different, less formalistic meaning to consultation of the people. "What exactly is a referendum?" he asks. "It's like a worker. I was a union lawyer when I started out in public life. In union meetings, when a man votes to go out on strike, it's not that he wants a strike. He wants his union to use the mandate of the strike to get a raise in salary or better working conditions. His deep desire is to have a good contract. Now, people who saw the YES vote as a mandate to negotiate were in a similar frame of mind. They wanted to give the government of Quebec a means of exerting more pressure in order to obtain certain things that were sometimes defined with varying degrees of clarity."[4]

So Daniel Johnson found himself at the head of a rather disparate group when he officially became the leader of the NO side at the end of September 1995. In addition he had to deal with a man—Jean Chrétien—whose intentions were unknown to him, but whose interest in everything that went on in Quebec—a province that might well have become the arena of his political career—was indeed known. This man, who had wanted to be an architect, entered politics to avoid disappointing his father. Willie Chrétien, a machinist in a Shawinigan paper mill, had a dream above all others: to see his son become a politician. At the age of 13, young Jean was already immersed in politics: he distributed pamphlets door to door, pasted up posters and set out chairs in the meeting room of the town hall. At age 15, he was talking politics with his father in the poolroom near their home. When he finished his *collège classique*[5] studies, his father said to him, "You go to the law faculty."

"And in those days," recalls Jean Chrétien, "when mom or dad would say something, we'd listen. So, I listened to my father and I went to the law faculty rather than become an architect. He said, 'You will not be elected in Shawinigan as an architect, you will be elected as a lawyer.'"[6]

Called to the bar in 1958, he practised his profession in the town where he was born, awaiting the opportunity to enter politics. There was no provincial riding available, but there was one in the federal arena: Saint-Maurice–Laflèche. In 1962, the Federal Liberals lost this riding to Réal Caouette's *Créditistes*. As Lester B. Pearson's Liberal government was a minority government, Canadians returned to the polls the following year. The Liberals needed to find themselves a candidate in the Saint-Maurice–Laflèche riding. "I chose Ottawa because there was an opening in my riding at the federal level," says Chrétien. "I liked politics. Federal, provincial, it didn't make much difference to me."[7] He won the election but quickly realized that he had a serious handicap for anyone who wanted to have a career in Ottawa: he scarcely spoke a word of English.

The following year, René Lévesque, the natural resources minister in Jean Lesage's Quebec government, proposed, during a lunch at the George V restaurant, that Chrétien leave federal politics behind and come to serve in Quebec City. The provincial riding of Saint-Maurice was now free; René Hamel, justice minister in the Lesage government, had been appointed a judge. "Jean, you have no future in Ottawa, (Lévesque said,) because in five years Ottawa will not exist for us."[8] Chrétien concluded from this that Lévesque was already a separatist. And, as Lévesque could not guarantee him a minister's post, he went to Jean Lesage himself. Without being too explicit in regard to a Cabinet position, the premier gave him such a warm welcome that Chrétien was left with the difficult choice of coming to fill an important post in the Quebec government or hanging in with Lester B. Pearson's minority government in Ottawa.

Was Chrétien ever, at some point in his life, tempted to join the separatist adventure? "A little bit,"[9] he says. He had been affected by the case of a federal public servant, Marcel Chaput, who was dismissed on the sole grounds that he was a francophone and a staunch nationalist.[10] "I remember, I had a debate with a bunch of lawyers in Trois-Rivières. I was really unhappy about the incident of Chaput and I was dumping on English Canada at the lunchtime. And one of my friends said, 'Jean, you've never been out of Quebec, you don't know what Canada is all about'... It was tough for me. The court was in Trois-Rivières. I had to drive back to Shawinigan, twenty miles. The first five miles, I was mad at him. The next five miles, I started to reflect a bit. In the last five miles, I said, 'He's right, I'm talking about something I don't know.'"[11]

Forty years later, he has nothing but praise for this country that he has come to know. "It is an exemplary country," he says. "Because of our diversity, our tolerance... we don't have problems with religion, we don't really have language quarrels that can't be managed—we've always found the right solutions..." Jean Chrétien loves his country— which he can't imagine without Quebec—with a passion, and he does not love Quebec any less for all that, but in his own way. "When you go to the United Nations, it's very nice to see your flag there, but you have to search hard to find it. There's a lot of flags there. There are countries with a population of 35,000, and they have flags! I remember the photograph that was taken for the 50th anniversary of the United Nations; they were never able to identify everyone in the picture! We were all heads of state... So, well, it's important to put things in their proper perspective. I've always thought that if we're still speaking French, it's because there is Canada. My father spent his youth in Manchester, New Hampshire. If he had stayed there, I'd probably be an anglophone today!"[12]

His discourse towards Quebecers would therefore be a loving discourse, filled with emotion, rather than musings on points of contention between Quebec City and Ottawa that had dragged on for years and on endless disputes between the two levels of government. With a partner such as this, Daniel Johnson, whose discourse was rather one of profitable federalism, knew that he had to leave sufficient room for emotion, but he also knew that this would not in itself suffice. "Of course the emotional side was important, but people who emphasized that side of things, it's because they experienced 1980," says John Parisella, Johnson's political advisor, who then recalls the great gathering of May 14 at the Paul-Sauvé Arena. "Sure, the flag stirred people's emotions... and, at the time, people were even talking about the Rocky Mountains. But you had to be realistic. If there had been a referendum on sovereignty three days or three weeks after the failure of Meech Lake, it would have gone through! We couldn't forget that. With the failure of Charlottetown, Quebecers felt that they had been sidelined. This was 1995 (not 1980), we were coming out of a recession, the second in fifteen years, our dollar was taking a dive, we had two constitutional failures, we nearly flirted with sovereignty... I think that, under the circumstances, if you were looking for emotion, you had to go a long way to find it! It was fine for the unconditional federalist vote but did nothing for the nationalist federalist vote. And then, to get *that* vote, you had to appeal to reason, not just emotional arguments. It's perhaps a bit too easy to say we needed to play on emotions; this loses sight of what went on between 1980 and 1995. There was nothing in federalist reform that could say to young people, who hadn't voted in 1980, 'let's go!' Meech Lake and Charlottetown were too recent."[13] But no need to give lessons on how to talk to Quebecers to a man who was considered by surveys in 1968 to be a legitimate successor to Jean Lesage and who, in the fall of 1976, was approached to become the leader of the Quebec Liberal Party, when Robert Bourassa was leaving politics after the victory of the Parti Québécois. "I almost went!"[14] says Jean Chrétien.

With the referendum a month away, Jean Chrétien considered that he knew Quebec well enough to have no further doubts as to the outcome. "I'm a U.S. ambassador, not a confidential advisor of his," said James Blanchard. "We were good friends, we still are good friends. He was really confident that Quebecers, if they knew what they were voting on, would vote no. And I think most of Canada misunderstood how hard-line he was against the separatists. Because they thought, since he was French-speaking and a francophone, he could manage this event. They didn't realize that because he was such a strong federalist, that brought a lot of anger and hostility in Quebec."

Daniel Johnson did not know Jean Chrétien well. He was wary about trusting him, for he was not far from thinking that the Prime Minister of Canada had manoeuvred, before the September 1994 election, to put the Parti Québécois in a position to win the elections so that they could "fight it out with the sovereigntists, once and for all." During the 1980 referendum campaign, Johnson had indeed given a few speeches, but as he was not yet a member of the National Assembly, he never found himself sharing the platform with Chrétien who, for his part, had been very active as a spokesperson of the federal government then. "We didn't really see much of each other," he says. "He wasn't someone that I knew personally or with whom I'd had any sort of exchange."[15] After the 1994 federal budget, he openly expressed his disgruntlement with Chrétien and his government, so that as the referendum drew near, the two men were not on particularly friendly terms.

Chrétien was part of the problem that Daniel Johnson had to face: how to prevent the federalists, who, since 1980, had consistently turned a deaf ear to Quebec's demands, from providing fodder for the sovereigntists' discourse by virtue of their presence in the referendum campaign. But he was a good sport. On September 24, during an interview on the program *L'Événement*, on the TVA network, he didn't flinch when host Stéphan Bureau reminded him of Chrétien's uncompromising attitude towards Quebec; indeed, he wanted the Canadian Prime Minister to participate in the campaign. But at number 4354 Saint-Denis street, where the NO campaign had its headquarters, the intent was to keep the federal politicians and anyone who was not a

Quebecer on the sidelines. The debate would take place among Quebecers only. "I was transmitting a message from the coalition," recalls Eddy Goldenberg, "whose view had been, it was primarily the provincial Liberals, that the campaign was a Quebec campaign and that bringing people in from outside of Quebec would have been counterproductive. It was a consensus that was reached. And again I go back to the fact that during this whole time we were doing very well, so that the strategy seemed to be working."

So the NO side managed to keep the federal politicians on the sidelines, and Jean Chrétien respected the terms of this strategy, as did all of his ministers. But not without a certain amount of grumbling. "You had Mr. Johnson who said, 'look, we're going to handle this, Ottawa, you guys, stay out!'" recalls David Collenette. "And I think Mr. Chrétien was very sensitive to that. The polls say we're ten points up, Jacques Parizeau is not a René Lévesque, does not have the credibility. And there was a degree of arrogance that we're going to win anyway, so let's not rock the boat."

Jean Chrétien however, made no secret of the fact that the exclusion of politicians from outside Quebec was arousing heated discussions in the backrooms of his government and across the rest of the country. "There were some who were frustrated not to be able to take part (in the campaign) because the NO group had decided that they didn't want people from outside," he says today. "It was their country that was at stake, and they had to stand by and do nothing. I can understand their frustration."[16] Among the frustrated, there was the Minister of Industry, John Manley. "I questioned the wisdom but I was prepared to accept it," he says today. "Very frustrating, very difficult. With all the problems I dealt with over ten years, 9/11, the budget…, it was in the run-up to the referendum that I lost sleep. And the only time I lost sleep." Manley was haunted by visions of people rushing the banks to withdraw their money if the YES side won. "Banks had to be sufficiently liquid," he said. "If everybody wants their money all on the same day, there could be a problem." He also worried about businesses that might move away, both during and after the referendum campaign, especially if the YES were to win. "It was very hard to plan a response to that," he says. "And indeed, if you did and it became known, it might in turn undermine to some extent the campaign before the vote." Manley thought that Jean Chrétien needed to get involved in the campaign, and do so from the very start. "He was from Quebec. He was the Prime Minister of Canada," he says. "If I were the Prime Minister of Canada, I would not remain silent during a debate of this sort."

The frustration affected all the members of the Liberal caucus. If they wanted to get involved, they had no choice but to go through Alfonso Gagliano, secretary of state for parliamentary affairs, who was coordinating interventions. "The caucus colleagues in Quebec, were hearing from constituents, 'This is a big deal, you know, we'll have the passport, we'll have the Canadian dollar, and we'll be Quebec!'" recounts Jane Stewart, the MP from Brant, Ontario, who chaired the caucus.[17] "More and more, the frustration elevated. Because there wasn't a mechanism for us to engage. If people had suggestions or ideas, they could coordinate it through (Gagliano's) office. There was an overwhelming sense that it wasn't our game, that the NO side managed it. There was a huge sense of frustration and, in some cases, (it) turned to anger, just that complete sense of uselessness."

"People started coming up with all sorts of scenarios," says Jean Chrétien, "some of them half-baked, but we set those aside. When you're the leader, you're the one who decides." In spite of it all, no one was suggesting that the military general staff develop closer ties with the government, as is often the case during a period of crisis. Chrétien states that among the "half-baked ideas" that came his way, nobody suggested that he send troops to Quebec: "Send in the—...? Please!" he says. "Some guys just need to hear themselves talk! (The military people) never brought this up with me. I didn't talk about this with the defence minister at the time. I'm sure I didn't. In any case, if it did come up, it didn't stick in my mind."[18]

But Jean Chrétien, who was not a man to back down from a fight, was himself quite annoyed at being confined to a spectator's role, with a few token outings planned by the NO forces: "I was a bit frustrated (at) having accepted the advice to stay behind and not to participate," he says, recalling that in 1980 the NO committee didn't want to see Trudeau up on the platform either, and that he had also been disappointed. "And some said, too, that because I had opposed Meech, that it was making the people unhappy. My view is people are never unhappy when you speak up your mind in politics."[19] Plans were made for the Prime Minister of Canada to make a few speeches during the campaign, and it was with some trepidation that the NO committee watched the date of Chrétien's first speech approaching. And yet, it was in the heart of his fiefdom: Shawinigan. He had Johnson, Jean Charest and Lucienne Robillard at his side. His speech was bland: it was possible to be distinctly Quebecois and Canadian at the same time, was basically what he said, while lambasting the partnership offer as "an insult to our intelligence."

The NO organizers winced: "When Mr. Chrétien got involved—I'm thinking of Shawinigan—we'd lose points in the polls," says one of the organizers, Senator Pierre-Claude Nolin. "He was not our best player." According to Nolin, Jean Charest was more popular than Chrétien by far. Now Charest, though a Quebecer and leader of a federal party, like Chrétien, thought that the NO side's strategy was the right one to use. "I agreed with it for a very simple reason," he says. "It was hard to see, with the way the campaign was being run, what contribution could be made by people brought in from the outside. It had to be an affair that was settled among Quebecers, because it concerned Quebecers. If we'd given the people of Quebec the impression that someone from the outside was trying to tell them how to vote, I think it would have backfired on us."[20]

Why then did Charest take part in the campaign and not Chrétien? Jean Pelletier, Jean Chrétien's chief of staff, offers the following explanation: "The Quebec Liberal Party is distinct from the Liberal Party of Canada. And we mustn't forget that Daniel Johnson comes from a Conservative family. So he could be a Liberal in Quebec, but in Ottawa, he was more of an ally to the Conservatives."[21] Eddy Goldenberg was of the same opinion, but he broadened the scope of Johnson's Conservative affinities to include the entire Quebec Liberal Party: "Between 1984 and 1993," he says, "the provincial Liberal party was very close to Brian Mulroney's Conservatives. And the Johnson family had traditionally been *Union Nationale*. When Daniel Johnson joined the Liberal party provincially, he joined as a federalist; he didn't join as a federal Liberal. And there were views that he might be more comfortable as a Conservative in terms of his federal politics."

The leader of the Quebec Liberal Party and the prime minister of Canada saw eye to eye on one point about the referendum: they both opposed independence for Quebec. But for the rest, they had to come up with a *modus vivendi*, which was no easy task. "I really think Mr. Chrétien and Mr. Johnson had no choice but to find a way to get along, but it certainly did not come naturally to them to work together," says Jean Pelletier. "I always sensed that for the Quebec Liberal Party, it was a Québécois referendum. It would have been hard for them to tell Chrétien, 'you're not a Quebecer at all!' The presence of the federal Liberals was not wanted in the campaign. It had to be as discreet as possible." Under these circumstances, Pelletier had to calm the federal Liberal MPs from Quebec, who had a hard time understanding why they were being kept at bay. "We had to come up with statements and agreements to deal with the particular cases that arose each day," adds Pelletier, "to arrange, in the end, for the federal people to be present on the NO committee. I'm not saying we didn't squabble. We didn't swear at each other, but we felt that our presence around the table was tolerated with a certain reticence. I always felt that."[22]

In Jean Chrétien's office, while observing the strategy set forth by Johnson, people continued to reflect upon the role that the Prime Minister might play. "My view of it was that his role should be very strategic," Eddy Goldenberg, one of Chrétien's principal advisors, says today, "that there is a very grave danger of depreciating the coinage by being out every night on television. If you are talking all the time, when you have something really important to say, nobody notices. That's why I thought a few strategic appearances would be much better, just like in 1980, (when) Mr. Trudeau appeared three times during the campaign."

It was then agreed that Labour Minister Lucienne Robillard's role on the NO committee would be the same role Jean Chrétien had played alongside Claude Ryan in 1980. The choice was not made by chance. Robillard had been a minister in the cabinets of Robert Bourassa and Daniel Johnson. "She worked well with the provincial Liberals," explains Goldenberg, who nonetheless acknowledges that she was somewhat put aside by the NO coalition during the campaign. "She was marginalized a little bit during the campaign," he says, hazarding an explanation. "We were doing so well that some of the provincial Liberal organizers almost lost sight of the objective, which was to win the referendum, and started to look at this as an opportunity to really beat the Parti Québécois. They were looking more in the context at one stage of the next provincial election." Daniel Johnson does not share Goldenberg's opinion of Robillard. "If the Liberal Party of Canada decides that Mrs. X or Mr. Y will be at such and such a gathering, that they'll be speaking on their behalf, under the NO umbrella, as a member of the coalition, let them! I have no reason to believe that Mrs. Robillard did anything but excellent work when she had the opportunity to do so. It was not up to us—the QLP—to decide who would be there for the Liberal Party of Canada. I would even go so far as to say, quite the contrary!"[23] On the other hand, his former chief of staff, who was part of the strategic core of the NO campaign, does not deny that Lucienne Robillard may have felt left out. "Mrs. Robillard's style was not as dynamic as Mr. Chrétien's in 1980," says John Parisella. "In 1980, Chrétien was not unpopular. Therefore, with his fiery, colourful style, he really was a rather significant asset. Mrs. Robillard has a much more reserved style, she was not a rising star on the federal stage, she was a graduate of the school of provincial politics"[24]

Indeed, Lucienne Robillard was eclipsed by Jean Charest. "As a speaker, and in terms of charisma," adds Parisella, "Mr. Charest was among those who had withstood the 1993 wave of Liberalism, in Quebec in particular. He had that freshness of a young politician, who had nearly won the Conservative leadership race against Kim Campbell. And he had a sense of image... of caricature... (remember) the passport story. So, Mrs. Robillard felt a bit stuck. For those of us who attached some importance to the communications side of things, it was obvious that Mrs. Robillard's style was not as much of a draw as Mr. Charest's."[25]

Finally, it is important not to underestimate the consequences of a major dispute between Lucienne Robillard and Daniel Johnson concerning acknowledgment of a YES victory. The federal minister had clearly established her position on September 12, three weeks before the real referendum campaign got underway: Ottawa would have to acknowledge a YES victory, even if the margin were narrow. "We have always respected democracy in this country," she said. "Ottawa will respect the democratic process underway in Quebec."[26] One week later, on September 19, Daniel Johnson sang a much more ambiguous tune: he was no longer sure whether he would accept the decisive rule of a majority of 50% plus one voice. "You don't destroy a country on a judicial recount," he said. Robillard would make amends later in the campaign, but such a marked divergence of opinion—not only from Johnson's position, but also from the position of many federalists—stated so clearly and openly at the beginning of the campaign, was sufficient reason for the NO forces to shelter Robillard from journalists' questions.

Several politicians all across Canada were champing at the bit to get involved in the referendum debate, Preston Manning, to name one. But neither Chrétien's office nor the NO committee wanted to see him hanging around. "I'm not sure that Preston Manning, given the views of the Reform Party, would have been terribly productive in terms of the campaign," quips Eddy Goldenberg. As for Senator Pierre-Claude Nolin, of the NO forces' central committee, his answer was clear: "Manning was not invited. He asked to take part (in the campaign). He was made to understand that this was an affair to be handled by Quebecers and that if he really wanted us to have a successful outcome, it would be better for all involved if he stayed away. That lasted all the way through to the end of the campaign. Was he frustrated by that? Yes, I'm sure he was. But he understood that in Quebec, he was perceived more as part of the problem than of the solution."[27] Even *Alliance Québec* invited Preston Manning to stay out of the campaign. "The YES forces will use him against us from the moment he sets foot in Quebec," says Michael Hamelin, who was then the organization's president. "When he takes the floor in the House to talk about the referendum, or when he backs the Prime Minister into a corner, the Bloc Québécois are the only ones smiling and rubbing their hands with glee."[28] Which prompted Stephen Harper to call *Alliance Québec* a "Liberal lapdog."

This impediment did not prevent the leader of the Reform Party from being active outside Quebec. He held no fewer than seventy public meetings in the West, demanding that a referendum be held if a majority of Quebecers were to vote YES. In the House of Commons, he proposed a resolution on renewed federalism in an attempt to bring the government to a debate on changes to the constitution and on the principle of a majority made up of 50% plus one vote in a referendum—two issues in which Chrétien did not want to get involved, by any means. In fact, he suggested twenty amendments to the Constitution and presented twenty sets of circumstances that Canada would need to face if Quebec were to separate. Today, he is disappointed with the results achieved: "You (would) have a speech with 40 minutes on the new federalism and five minutes on how to handle the consequences of secession. You could count on the media's story being on the negative side because conflict is more newsworthy than cooperation."

Manning was not the only one who, after being deemed to be an undesirable element on the NO committee, chose to work elsewhere in the country. Some provincial premiers, rather than going to Quebec to campaign, sent messages to Quebecers from their region. In Victoria, British Columbia premier, Mike Harcourt, declared that his province would refuse to negotiate an association between Canada and Quebec should the YES side win, and even suggested that contracts that Quebec companies had with B.C. might be terminated. As for Frank McKenna, re-elected to a third term as premier of New Brunswick on September 11, he stated, on the day after the election, that he could get involved in Quebec more credibly now that the Confederation of Regions Party (COR)—that staunchly opposed bilingualism—had been wiped off the face of his province's electoral map: "The message will be one of love and affection and one of conciliation,"[29] he said.

Some politicians from outside Quebec, including the premier of New Brunswick, nonetheless came along with offers to contribute to the work of the NO committee. McKenna knew Daniel Johnson, and John Parisella even better, calling him "a good friend and... a person I respect a great deal." Some of his ministers came to canvass and, McKenna adds, "we were much more active probably than most Canadian Provinces. But there was a bit of fear that people who are not sensitive to the nuances of politics in Quebec could end up entering the debate and stepping into a land mine inadvertently."

So Daniel Johnson was the leader of the NO coalition, but he had no control over outside elements who might, to borrow McKenna's expression, "step into a land mine." Don Boudria, Ontario MP from Glengarry-Prescott-Russell, took part in the campaign in Argenteuil, across the Ottawa River from his own riding. The mayor of Ottawa, Jacqueline Holzman, speaking to the Ottawa Women's Canadian Club, announced her intent to get involved in the referendum. In Gatineau (the former riding of Hull), the federal intergovernmental affairs minister co-chaired the NO committee alongside municipal councillor Claude Lemay and MPP Robert Lesage.

Ontario premier Mike Harris made a splash with his entry. In a highly anticipated speech to the prestigious Toronto Canadian Club, he made the following statement: "Let me be very clear. I said this to Premier Parizeau at the premiers' conference in Newfoundland: internal trade patterns exist amongst provinces within a country, not between countries."[30] He reminded listeners that if Quebec were to become independent, there would be a border to cross to get into Ontario. The speech had been prepared in consultation with two former Ontario premiers, New Democrat Bob Rae and Liberal David Peterson. It was televised on *Newsworld* and reproduced in full in the *Toronto Star*. To bring home the point that all of Ontario thought as he did, Harris brought along Bob Rae and Liberal party leader Lyn McLeod to the Canadian Club. And to make it perfectly clear that he was not in contradiction with the NO committee, he made sure he had Michel Bélanger, one of its leaders, at his side. "If Quebec separates, one thing is certain," he added. "Quebecers would no longer have access to the Canadian advantages, they would no longer be a part of Canada. We would have no special obligations tied to history or common national interest." The Ontario premier also added that a NO victory would usher in an era of decentralization and flexibility within Confederation,[31] words that, later in the campaign, would bring a scathing response from Lucien Bouchard, directed at both him and McKenna: "This reminds me of an old black-and-white film," he said to more than a thousand people in Joliette. "They pulled this on René Lévesque in 1982, which prompted him to lay his cards out on the table. But during the night, they cleared the table. I'll be having none of that, thank you very much! (As for McKenna,) he tells us he wants change. I don't believe it for a minute. Last time, we formed an alliance and we lost our shirts!"[32] he added, recalling that the New Brunswick premier had been the first provincial government leader to reject the original wording of the Meech Lake Accord.

It was these politicians that Daniel Johnson and the NO committee did not wish to see weighing in on the debate. John Parisella explains their sentiment: "Unfortunately, Canadian politicians had not developed a deeper understanding of the reality of Quebec. Mr. Manning denied the existence of a distinct society made up of a francophone majority. What's more, we had enough resources: the federal MPs, the provincial MPs, Conservative leader Charest, Liberal leader Johnson, Mr. Chrétien (in well planned appearances), and Mrs. Robillard. We didn't need Mr. Manning or others who had opposed not only Meech Lake, but Charlottetown as well. That wasn't going to help!"[33] And yet, in spite of efforts by his strategists to curb the threats and exhortations coming in from beyond the borders, the better to channel the actions of the federalists into a common message, how could Daniel Johnson orchestrate such an offensive from his perch at the leadership of the coalition? He entrusted coordination of activities to a professional organizer, Pietro Perrino,[34] who soon realized how difficult it would be to get the federalists to work together—especially when they came from different parties. The budget available to him was a mere $5 million, and already, as of the last day of September, although the campaign had officially not yet begun, he had spent

$100,000 dollars on advertising. Perrino was faced with mission impossible.

Meanwhile, in the North, a brush fire was breaking out. The federalists were deploying their energies on trying to get out the Aboriginal vote. "It's always amazing," observes Matthew Coon Come, "when there's a swing vote, the federal government will always come in and encourage the Aboriginal leaders to tell their people to come out to vote. There were requests and they came in trying to appease us, so that we can encourage our people to vote. Because they knew probably the majority would have said no anyway." But Aboriginal voters would not vote in the Quebec referendum. On the contrary, the Crees announced that they would hold their own referendum on October 24, six days before the one in Quebec. The Inuit followed suit, planning a referendum of their own within their community, two days later. The Parizeau government then attempted to cut off any debate on the matter through the involvement of David Cliche, the premier's parliamentary assistant for Native Affairs. Even while recognizing the right of Aboriginal peoples to self-determination, Cliche reaffirmed the principle of Quebec's territorial integrity and rejected any impulse they might have to separate from Quebec. Moreover, he promised that the government of an independent Quebec would assume Ottawa's obligations, as set forth in the James Bay Agreement. Coon Come retorted, that there would be legal battles on the Aboriginal question. This issue would haunt the YES side throughout the referendum campaign.

The debate had long since spilled over beyond Canadian borders. On September 14, the very same day that Jacques Parizeau was addressing the international community to convince them that the sovereigntist project "showed great openness and generosity, particularly in regard to minorities and First Nations," the federal government was calling its ambassadors to their posts in certain strategically chosen countries, such as France, Mexico and the United States. Their instructions: to put people's minds at ease and invite these countries to align with the Canadian position.

Jacques Parizeau was fully aware that obtaining diplomatic recognition from the United States would not be an easy matter. But he had his own strategy, which his staff referred to as *le grand jeu* (the big production), a strategy that he had previously tried out during a dinner at the Ritz in Washington, on March 4, 1993. There were many guests, among them Reed Scowen, the delegate from Quebec, the Canadian Embassy's second-in-command, friends from Quebec, lobbyists and a member of the National Security Council, Barry Lowenkron.[35] Parizeau then told Americans, in substance, "We understand that it will not be easy for you to inform English Canada that for obvious reasons, it is in your best interest to accept an independent Quebec into NAFTA. Therefore, Quebec will first seek recognition from France. Then it will be easier for you to do so when the time is right for you."

"At some point," recalls Parizeau, "the person from the National Security Council, which is the voice of the White House, banged his fist on the table and said, 'We will never let the Frenchies recognize you, we'll recognize you first.' There was a brief silence. It was the Monroe doctrine coming out."[36] Ambassador James Blanchard issued a more tempered statement: "I don't think the Monroe doctrine is ever a treaty and didn't really matter and I don't know what James Monroe would have said other than the North Americans are bailiwick…"

With regard to France, however, the government of Quebec had a good head start on Ottawa. Jacques Parizeau, who traveled to Paris regularly, had been cultivating relations for some time and had even managed to get into President François Mitterrand's good graces, in spite of Mitterrand's lack of enthusiasm with regard to Quebec's sovereignty plans. At the time of Parizeau's last trip, in January 1995, Mitterrand was still president, but it was former president Valéry Giscard d'Estaing who headed the *Commission des Affaires Étrangères* (Foreign Affairs Committee) of the *Assemblée Nationale* (National Assembly). Parizeau, accompanied by Jean-François Lisée and Jacques Joli-Coeur, among others, paid him a visit. "When we got there, we met with someone who was much more familiar with the issue than I would have imagined," recounts Parizeau. "He started right in with the following question—point blank: 'You want France to recognize you? But you say that we should recognize you as soon as you have won the referendum. A referendum, Mr. Parizeau, is not even an intention. It is, at best, an authorization. You will have to make a gesture that engages the government of Quebec. Once you have made this gesture, France will be able to recognize you. Your project, in its current state, cannot lead to recognition of an independent Quebec by France.'"[37] This encounter was to determine the government's strategy in the days that would immediately follow a victory of the YES side.

The Quebec premier's trip to Paris gave him the opportunity to benefit from the political climate in France at the time and to score points on many counts. Édouard Balladur was prime minister with aspirations to the presidency, which was to become vacant four months later, in May. Jacques Chirac was mayor of Paris and also had ambitions to take François Mitterrand's place at the Élysée palace. Parizeau's trip, it goes without saying, was organized in collaboration with the *ministère des Affaires Étrangères* (Foreign Affairs ministry) led by Alain Juppé who, in private, showed a certain affinity for the sovereigntist cause. Moreover Quebec had a powerful ally in the French capital, namely, Philippe Séguin. A member of parliament for more than fifteen years, former minister and a member of a great many parliamentary committees—including the foreign affairs committee— Séguin was, at the time of Parizeau's trip, president of *l'Assemblée Nationale* (the French National Assembly). Both Chirac and Balladur sought his support in their race for the nomination by the Right.

Parizeau's visit to the National Assembly, then, took on the air of a state visit. The motorcade of black automobiles transporting the Québécois delegation crossed Paris at the height of rush hour and entered the courtyard of the Palais Bourbon through the main gate— which had not been opened for a foreign visitor since President Woodrow Wilson had come to call some three-quarters of a century earlier. Philippe Séguin received the Quebec premier and, flanked by two rows of Republican Guards, the two men climbed the stairs to the Casimir-Périer room. "Your presence here today," said the president of the National Assembly then, speaking to Parizeau in front of more than three hundred gathered guests, "carries with it, for the French people, a promise—a mutual promise made not by cousins, as we are called, but something better: brothers. For we do now and will always recognize you as such." The word "recognize" was music to the ears of Jacques Parizeau.

In 1995, the Canadian ambassador to Paris was Benoît Bouchard,[38] a former Conservative minister that the Chrétien government kept on board. His objective was to "play down," as he put it, the Quebec premier's visit. When the main gate of the Palais Bourbon was opened to Parizeau, the temptation was strong for Bouchard to express his anger with the Quai d'Orsay. But he contained himself. He also opened himself to the possibility of compromise when the time came for him to meet with Jacques Parizeau. Canadian protocol holds that when the premier of a province is on an official visit to the French capital, he or she meets with the Canadian ambassador...at the Canadian embassy. "I avoided demanding that we meet at the embassy," says Bouchard. "To avoid a kerfuffle, I met him at the *Délégation du Québec*." Before the arrival of Jacques Parizeau, he made the first move, explaining to the Parisian press that it was the Canadian embassy's heartfelt desire to expose the French to Québécois culture, and that they would continue to do so. Upon arriving at the *Délégation du Québec*, he was taken aside by Yves Michaud, a former delegate general who was traveling with Parizeau. Benoît Bouchard relates the story: "Mr. Michaud said to me, 'I read your statement in the papers, and I don't agree that Canada puts that much energy into cultural matters.' I replied, 'as long as Quebec is part of Canada, the Canadian Embassy in Paris will continue to concern itself with Québécois artists who come to Paris and with culture in general.' It was Mr. Parizeau who then chimed in with, 'Mr. Ambassador, I came to Paris for that reason!' To which I replied, 'I am delighted, Mr. Premier, I had not raised the question myself.'"[39]

Relations between the Canadian ambassador and Philippe Séguin, the president of the French National Assembly, were abrasive, to say the least. About ten days before the arrival of the Quebec delegation in Paris, a reporter from the *Globe and Mail*, Rhéal Séguin, had asked Benoît Bouchard if Quebec sovereignty had strong support in France. The ambassador answered that in his opinion, "the French people (were) not particularly interested" in the matter. The reporter then went on with, "What about Philippe Séguin? He made a statement for all to hear." "I answered yes, but Mr. Séguin is a 'loose cannon'—which the French press translated as *'électron libre,'*" recalls Benoît Bouchard. "Obviously, I made two mistakes. The first was to use a word from another language, something that is not done in this sort of interview. The second was to have said it at all. The problem was not believing what I said—I still do—but saying it out loud. An ambassador doesn't say that sort of thing. The columnists in Quebec were furious, those from the *Toronto Star* and the *Globe and Mail*, lavish in their praise. The French papers didn't pick it up."[40]

The visit to the National Assembly was followed by an official dinner hosted by the foreign affairs minister in honour of Jacques Parizeau. Benoît Bouchard was among the twenty or so guests. At one point, the minister, Alain Juppé, rose and gave a toast: "We have known each other for so long that, when the time comes, we will recognize one another," he said. Upon these words, everyone rose, with the exception of Benoît Bouchard, who did not bat an eye.[41] It was during this soirée that Philippe Séguin was told by an assistant about the Canadian ambassador's remarks concerning him, printed in the *Globe and Mail*. He did not immediately understand the meaning of the expression "loose cannon," but he would soon find out.

Already responsible for having organized the welcome, worthy of a head of State, that the French National Assembly had extended to the Quebec premier, Philippe Séguin undertook, at the last minute, to arrange an interview with Jacques Chirac at the Paris City Hall. To avoid offending Balladur, who would be Chirac's opponent for the Right's nomination for the presidential race, and in observance of a long tradition of prudence and conservative conduct that characterized this ministry, the officials of the Quai d'Orsay had not planned a visit to the Paris City Hall for Parizeau. But it would take place, organized at the eleventh hour, two days after the Quai d'Orsay incident.

Jacques Parizeau was wary of Chirac, who had been cozy with Jean Chrétien's chief of staff during meetings of the *Association internationale des maires des villes francophones* (International association of mayors of francophone cities), during the tenure of Jean Pelletier as mayor of Quebec City. Moreover, he was not unaware that Chirac had never forgiven the Parti Québécois for asking him to join the Socialist International in 1982.[42] Finally, he may also have known about the things Jacques Chirac had said, scarcely six months earlier, when Jean Chrétien had been in France. It was in June 1994, for the 50th anniversary of the Normandy landing. The two men had never met before. The interview took place in Chirac's offices in City Hall and covered several topics, including the inevitable Quebec City-Paris-Ottawa triangle. Jean Pelletier, Chrétien's chief of staff, attended the meeting. "Mr. Chirac said at that time that since the 1980 referendum, he had thought a great deal about the matter and that he had come to the conclusion that Quebec's Frenchness would be better protected if Quebec continued to be part of Canada than if it were to secede," recalls Pelletier. "This was reassuring for me. I said to myself, Chirac will always be respectful of the decision that Quebecers will take, but never will he take part in the debate underway in support of the sovereigntist side."[43] Whatever the case, Parizeau did go to City Hall in Philippe Séguin's car, in spite of everything, feeling somewhat unsettled about the welcome that he would be given but confident just the same that the president of the National Assembly had seen to everything and that the meeting would go well.

Atop the flagpole at City Hall, two flags flapped in the wind: the French flag and the flag of Quebec. "I was furious," says Benoît Bouchard. "I got in touch with Quai d'Orsay to let them know that I didn't think this was appropriate. They answered me in that way that the French sometimes have: 'Mr. Ambassador, it is not our place to tell the mayor of Paris which flags should fly over City Hall.' In other words, 'we mind our business, you mind yours.'"[44] Inside, the welcome was warm. "If the referendum has a positive outcome," said Jacques Chirac, "a certain number of francophone countries, France included, should quite naturally recognize the reality of the people's decision, which is the expression of the people's sovereignty."

Meanwhile, Jean Chrétien was on the other side of the world, on an official visit to Chile. He was informed of Jacques Chirac's words.

He was not unaware that the mayor of Paris was lagging behind Balladur in the polls. And this was reflected in the tone of his reaction: "Jacques Chirac has as much chance of becoming president as Quebec has of becoming sovereign,"[45] he said. Three months later, Chirac was elected president of the French Republic.

Jacques Parizeau then met, in turn, Prime Minister Balladur, who had words of encouragement for his visitor, and President Mitterrand, who, while considerably weakened by the cancer destroying him, still gave the premier a warm welcome. Parizeau now gives a more rational explanation of Mitterrand's attitude towards him. "For all those years, Mitterrand did not relish the idea of a sovereign Quebec," he says. "But it was as if he were taking out an insurance policy, in case, out of the blue, (as if he was saying to himself) they got the sovereignty they were after! And, very early on, Mitterrand would open his door to me. In France, when you have access to the president, you have access to everybody and everything. I realized, however, that there was still some resistance from Quai d'Orsay. So, at one point, Mitterrand made the following proposal: 'Give me the name of someone who will handle communications between you and me, without going through the whole apparatus.'"[46] Parizeau then gave him two names, two women, whom he refuses to this day to identify, who acted as go-betweens between the premier of Quebec and the president of the French Republic. These two women were Louise Beaudoin, a minister in his government, and the journalist, Denise Bombardier.[47]

"I knew that President Mitterrand would not take a stand," adds former ambassador Bouchard, thus summing up the climate that surrounded Parizeau's trip to Paris. "I was present, I was receiving official invitations right and left—even when Mr. Parizeau addressed the National Assembly. I was not especially comfortable, since this was not a particularly favourable environment. Clearly, there was some tension, and there was some hostility between individuals, but I didn't want this to become the main story for the press. It went well!"[48]

Things did indeed go well, most especially for the government of Quebec, which was also assured that several francophone countries would follow France's example when the time came. "During my trip," said Parizeau, "I had a number of contacts with francophone countries. The important thing is this: when France leads the way, a number of francophone countries need to follow suit in the days that follow."[49]

This was the first part of the "Great Game." The second part, stateside, would be more difficult. "The American Civil War happened not so very long ago, and Americans remember the horrible outcome of this war," says Raymond Chrétien, who was the Canadian ambassador to the United States at the time of the referendum. "It was the bloodiest conflict in the history of the United States, with more than 500,000 killed. For Americans, this situation, which bore some resemblance to the time before their Civil War, was scary, stirring up a lot of emotion and trauma. I experienced this every week. Every time I made a speech in the United States, I always saw anxious faces when this matter was brought up. I could see what they were thinking and the awful memories that this stirred up. Not a fertile field for planting ideas of independence."[50]

Nonetheless, Americans' interest for what was going on in Canada and Quebec in particular was growing day by day during the year of the referendum. "An absolutely amazing interest… that was something that I had never witnessed in the almost seven years I spent in Washington," said Raymond Chrétien. His duties took him all over the country, including to the west coast and, everywhere he went, he had to answer the same question: *what if…?* He observed that Americans had the jitters right up to the highest reaches of the political hierarchy: "I mean President Clinton, Vice-President Gore, State Secretary Christopher, with that issue were always very careful, prudent, worried. And rightly so," he adds.[51]

Jacques Parizeau's game plan did not escape the attention of the ambassador, who maintained excellent relations with his French counterpart, François Bujon de l'Estang,[52] who indeed had been ambassador to Canada before being assigned to Washington. "I could talk to him about anything," says Raymond Chrétien,[53] "including the Quebec question. When you represent Canada in Washington, there are very few things that you are not aware of. You cannot come to

Washington, anybody from Canada or Quebec, totally incognito. Obviously, I was aware. I would go to Congress myself, to the Hill, and I would be told, 'Listen, we just saw the representative of Quebec yesterday and that's what she told us.'"[54]

James Blanchard, the United States ambassador to Canada, attached little importance to the steps taken by Quebec's Washington office. According to him, Canada was a confederation with strong provinces and a weak central government. But Americans viewed the provinces as they viewed their states, and it wouldn't occur to them that a governor from a US state might travel to Ottawa to reach an agreement with the prime minister of Canada. In spite of this conviction, the American ambassador nonetheless felt the need to go to Washington to talk about the referendum. "I didn't want," he says, "some reporter, some Quebecer coming down and saying, 'if we break up, will you still work with us?' and then, you know, he says, 'oh sure, we'll still love you.' The press coverage of what the US people would say in Quebec was outrageously inaccurate, including things I said, outrageously inaccurate. Any janitor in the State Department could have said, 'I like Quebec,' and it would be, 'State Department officials hail new nation.' So I came down to caution all key people in Congress, when somebody asks, 'will you support us if we break up?' to say, 'oh, it's a nice day out!'"

The sovereigntist camp was quite annoyed by the American ambassador's encroachments into Quebecois affairs. As long as Washington was saying "It is up to Canadians to decide," Parizeau and his staff were content. But they were concerned that James Blanchard might push President Clinton or the Secretary of State to adopt a firmer position. "We knew we had a problem with Ambassador Blanchard," says Jean-François Lisée. "He became nearly the only significant advisor on the Canadian and Quebecois question. And we know what he thought—he wrote it in his book[55]— that it was a mistake for British colonists to have allowed Quebecers to continue speaking French.[56] In other words, we were dealing with a dinosaur from the get-go."[57]

However, this was a "dinosaur" who carried some weight. He was convinced that the admission of an independent Quebec into treaties such as the North American Free Trade Agreement would not be automatic, and he was very outspoken about it: "Our kind of passive friendship," he says "'any change in the status of Canada is for Canadians to decide,' that mantra was being used by the hardliners in Quebec as if to say, 'the United States doesn't really care: we'll have NAFTA, we'll have the auto pact, we'll have NORAD, NATO.' That's the kind of stuff I was hearing all over as I moved around. That was nonsense. We would have to renegotiate NAFTA, all those treaties, they were not automatic."

Jacques Parizeau was perfectly aware that Quebec would have to negotiate membership in NAFTA. But his optimism rested on two points: a study that the Quebec government commissioned with a New York law firm, and a clause in the free trade agreement. The study, whose conclusions were made public on March 13, 1995, was prepared by the firm Rogers & Wells, a law firm with some 400 lawyers, headed up by senior partner William Rogers, former Secretary of State under Richard Nixon. His assignment was to analyze the continuity, with Quebec, of five accords in force between the United States and Canada. The general conclusion of the study, based on established practice, was that it was probable that the United States would recognize Quebec "as an heir nation for the purposes of bilateral agreements... although Quebec could probably not claim automatic entitlement... it is extremely probable that the United States would allow Quebec to take part..." stated the study, for which research was conducted, without mentioning Quebec by name, at several American government departments.

The second reason that Parizeau did not doubt that Quebec would be admitted to NAFTA was a clause of this agreement referred to as a *docking clause*. This provision is, in a manner of speaking, an explicit authorization granted to other countries to belong to the agreement, enjoining such countries to comply with the terms and conditions of the treaty. The principle underlying this clause reassured Parizeau. But he was also concerned, for other reasons. "The agreement states that no new country can sign onto NAFTA without meeting the conditions advanced by the founding members," he acknowledges. "But the article in question does not state the conditions for accession to the treaty, and this is a real problem. Obviously, it would be a matter of economic market conditions, legal regulations, trade conflicts... But as it is not clearly defined, what's to prevent one of these docking clauses from being something like, oh, I don't know, protection of anglophones' rights in Quebec. It's a bit of a sticking point, a rather gnarly issue."[58]

And there was yet another problem: before it could be extended to another partner, NAFTA would have to go back through the US congress. "The mere inclusion of a 'docking clause' (an explicit authorization for the accession of additional countries to an agreement) does not mean that new countries can join without action by Congress," stated a document published by Washington Trade Reports, an organization specializing in international market analysis. "NAFTA provides for the accession of other countries, for example, but Congress wrote a provision into the NAFTA implementing legislation specifying that no accessions will be permitted without the express authorization of Congress."[59]

Membership in NAFTA of an independent Quebec, then, would not be automatic, and Bernard Landry was simplifying things when he invoked the rule of succession of states to say that Quebec would not have to negotiate its right to participate. "The avenue open to Quebec is, rather, that of the succession of states," he had declared in February, "in compliance with standard practice and international law, in particular the Vienna Convention on Succession of States in Respect of Treaties." According to Landry, the Vienna Convention could "mark out the path to Quebec's entry into NAFTA."[60] The Vienna Convention in fact states that, provided certain conditions are met, a nation that has acquired independence can become a party to certain multilateral treaties signed by the predecessor nation. The problem with referring to this convention, however, was that Canada did not sign it—nor did the United States or Mexico—and moreover, the convention was irrelevant, not having been ratified by a sufficient number of nations. Ratification by fifteen nations was required for it to become effective, whereas it had attained only thirteen.

Consequently, Quebec would have to negotiate its entry into NAFTA—a negotiation that might well be tense and difficult, according to Professor Joseph Jockel.[61] In a study that he conducted for the Center for Strategic and International Studies, he maintained that negotiations would require the approval not only of the US congress, but also of the governments of Mexico and Canada. "Immediate admission to NAFTA by virtue of the rule of succession of states does not seem to be within the realm of possibility," he wrote. Professor Ivan Bernier, of the law faculty of Université Laval, arrived at the same conclusions and aroused the government's ire by warning against an overly simplistic approach to this problem.

Down in Mexico (the other potential partner in NAFTA), there would be no hope for Quebec's aspirations. "When Mexico was accepted into NAFTA, they had the impression, as the Polish proverb says, that they'd manage to grab onto the feet of baby Jesus," says Jacques Parizeau, "and anything that might cause any discomfort—let alone indignation—to Ottawa was taboo for the Mexicans. And the primary taboo was a sovereign Quebec. So they really were very bad company to keep."[62] According to the former premier, the Mexicans and, in particular, the ambassador at the time, Sandra Fuentès-Berain, were quite uncomfortable with not being able to "pass the Quebec sovereigntists off as scoundrels or people 'carrying knives between their teeth,'" for they all knew that Bernard Landry was quite familiar with Mexico and had important relations there, having taught for several years in Spanish at the University of Mexico City. "They were rather at a loss. They showed a great deal of ill humour in private and said little in public," adds Parizeau.[63]

The government of a sovereign Quebec, then, could look forward to negotiating its entry into NAFTA with three partners who would not make life easy for them. The same held true for Quebec's admission to other international treaties in which Canada was a participant, whether it be GATT or NORAD. Moreover, no membership in major international organizations would be automatic. At the United Nations, for example,[64] a favourable vote by 9 of the 15 members of the Security Council would be required, along with the support of at least two-thirds of the General Assembly before a new nation could be admitted. At the OECD, all member countries would have to agree to admit the new country during a meeting of the Council at the ministerial level. As for Asia-Pacific Economic Cooperation (APEC), at the time of the referendum, there was a moratorium on new memberships in effect until 1997 and, according to the government of Canada, "an independent Quebec would no longer be a Pacific Rim country and would likely be unable to join APEC." Quebec could apply to be a part of the Organization of American States (OAS), but Canada would be a force to be reckoned with, insofar as their budget contribution amounted to 12% of the total. As for the World Trade Organization (WTO), Quebec would have to negotiate, and the contracting parties, in particular the United States and Canada, would be able to ask for trade concessions—in the area of agriculture, for example, or in other important sectors of the Quebecois economy. Finally, regarding the International Monetary Fund (IMF), Quebec would have to meet conditions for membership and, if admitted, might obtain a seat at the World Bank, pending approval by the board of directors of the recommendation of the Bank's administrators. At the time of the referendum, Canada was a signatory of more than 3,000 bilateral and multilateral treaties—as many unknown elements for an independent Quebec.

As September 1995 drew to a close, the opposing camps were at an impasse concerning the possibility of a televised debate. An agreement had been reached between Radio-Canada, TVA and Radio-Québec[65] to present a face-off between Parizeau and Johnson. But the YES side considered Jean Chrétien's presence critical and therefore proposed a four-way debate in which Lucien Bouchard would also take part. The initial response of the NO side was more than lukewarm: "There is only one leader of the YES side and one leader of the NO side," retorted Pierre Anctil, Daniel Johnson's Chief of Staff.[66] In fact, the NO side was not interested in seeing the sort of confrontations that took place on a daily basis at the House of Commons on TV. "Clearly, the opponent was now Lucien Bouchard," says Johnson today. "He wanted to cross swords with Jean Chrétien. His whipping boy was Chrétien. As for us—Quebec Liberals—he dismissed us with a toss of the hand, making all manner of insinuations concerning our Québécois identity. Every time the matter of a debate came up, the response of the YES side was categorically 'no'—unless Lucien Bouchard could debate Jean Chrétien."[67] The latter declined the invitation. The networks grew impatient, and negotiations went forward with little hope of resolution.

CHAPTER VIII

Lucien Bouchard
Takes the Ball

In an unused piece of land in Montreal's Plateau-Mont-Royal neighbourhood, people were catching referendum fever. Ever since
October 2, they had been gathering every noon hour—amidst forty
potted trees, a dozen park benches and about twenty garbage bins—
around bleachers borrowed from a sports park, to hear writers, artists
and poets talk about an independent Quebec.[1] It was artist Gilles
Bissonnette who had invented the "ephemeral park" at the corner of
Mont-Royal Avenue and Hôtel-de-ville Street, which had as its back-
drop a brick wall with lines from a poem by Gilbert Langevin scrawled
across it. And it was former Rhinoceros Party leader François Gourd
who had arranged for the park's collective ownership. "It was a space
without limits, a space where you could say anything, do anything,"
remembers Sophie Bélanger, a sociology student at UQAM at the
time. "Some people came with a 'superintellectual' point of view, while
others were there with philosophical, artistic and cultural concerns...
There was a mike that was almost always on, so everybody could come
and express themselves. It was beautiful to see." In this atmosphere of
a people's gathering place, Sophie Bélanger had a strong sense of being
part of a whole. "A coherent whole," she says, "something with foun-
dations, principles and ideas."[2]

Numerous artists turned up at this park. Their intent was to
provide a kind of response to a report on the Radio-Canada program
Le Point, which had asked earlier on in the campaign why the artists

were absent from the referendum debate. The report was not only a reproach, it also gave rise to disagreements within the artistic community: could one be neutral, or favour federalism, without being condemned to disdain by one's peers? A number of artists together with some intellectuals, took a stand by publishing a collection of testimonials for the YES side, called *Trente lettres pour un oui* (Thirty letters for a yes),[3] an undertaking inspired by Gilles Vigneault and led by Andrée Ferretti, and which had the support of Quebec's French-language writers union (*Union des écrivaines et des écrivains du Québec—UNEQ*). But others refused to join the group of thirty, among them, playwright René-Daniel Dubois. Without mincing his words, he declared he was fed up with Quebec society and loudly proclaimed his right to dissent from the sovereignty project.[4] There were still others, who did not wish to be claimed by either of the two camps. This was the case with Jean-Guy Moreau who came to say as much in the "ephemeral park": "I leave your flags and your idealistic slogans all to you. I remain a caricaturist. I am neither a Péquiste nor a federalist. I don't want to be won over by anyone."

Philosopher Marc Chabot wrote in *Trente lettres pour un oui* that "there is only one way to free oneself from an idea, and that is to realize it." The dimensions of reality, however, were much more complex. The YES camp had one month to the day to "realize its idea," to get it across and have a majority of Quebec's five million voters accept it. The government's order to hold a referendum was issued on October 1. It simply stated: "The order is hereby given, on the recommendation of the premier, to charge the Chief Electoral Officer with holding a referendum on Monday, October 30, 1995, in each of the following electoral ridings." Listed in alphabetical order thereafter, from Abitibi-Est to Westmount–Saint-Louis, were the names of the 125 ridings. That was all. But it was also the starting signal, and the simple fact of establishing a date set off a frenzy of activity in all the organizations. The writs were issued immediately to all the returning officers.

That same day, Premier Jacques Parizeau addressed the people of Quebec on television. "This referendum, this rendezvous," he told them, "may be the last one, the last chance you will have to procure for yourselves a country that is truly yours." Then, in a dramatic tone, he added, "It is not given to all peoples to have a second chance."[5] When Daniel Johnson came back with, "A YES vote will only provoke social, economic and political uncertainty," he was also defining the grounds on which he intended to fight. The referendum campaign had officially begun.

Maybe they were still not clear on what their main themes should be or what strategies to follow, but the YES camp's campaign buses were ready. One of them was specifically outfitted for the three leaders, with computers, fax machine, photocopiers and even a bed and some comfortable chairs, to allow them to get some rest between rallies. Everything had been thought of. The next two buses were for the reporters, with a third on standby, should it be required,[6] because the Quebec referendum aroused curiosity not only in Canada, but also in several countries of the Americas and Europe. No fewer than 70 media had registered with the YES committee. "New teams arrived, teams we had never heard of," said Julie Arcand, who was in charge of the foreign press.[7]

Jacques Parizeau had to be convinced of the importance of organizing a caravan. He didn't believe in that type of campaign. In his view, the bus arrangement was not conducive to the debating of ideas. He felt that a caravan enclosed the premier or the party leader in a kind of "cloister," in a bubble, and that after a few days, the media coverage would degenerate into the recounting of anecdotes. "I had tried to push for something that was probably too radical to be accepted; I tried to get Mr. Bouchard and Mr. Dumont to let go of the bus idea," he says. "I have always considered the atmosphere that results between a leader and the journalists who are holed up with him for days on end extremely unhealthy."[8] Voted down, he went along with the opinion of his strategists.

On the afternoon of October 1, the YES camp's executive committee for the referendum, made up of some 26 people, including Jacques Parizeau, Lucien Bouchard, and Mario Dumont, held an initial meeting in a Quebec hotel. They faced a rather disappointing conclusion: the YES side was lagging behind in the polls, by five points.

However, they were somewhat consoled by a fact that emerged from one of the studies, by SOM-Environics: 61% of Quebecers were convinced that a NO victory would mean keeping the constitutional status quo for several years.[9] The same survey also revealed that 84% of Canadians from the other provinces rejected the idea of granting special powers and the right of veto to the only province in the country with a francophone majority. This was merely grist for the mill to the sovereigntists who had maintained for a long time that Quebec would never be recognized as a distinct society.

Jacques Parizeau used this as the inspiration for his first campaign speech: "I understand that Canadians do not want to accept that we are a people," he addressed the crowd of 150 people, gathered in the square in front of Quebec's City Hall, where he was the guest of Mayor Jean-Paul L'Allier on October 2. "But we are a people, we have always been a people and we must remain a people." His wife, Lisette Lapointe, and Lucien Bouchard accompanied him. Mayor L'Allier assured them of his unconditional support, which came as no surprise, given that he had presided over the capital's regional commission on the future of Quebec.

The caravan then embarked on its first campaign tour, heading for the Beauce region, where no support had been garnered as yet. In Saint-Georges, the two YES leaders met with the local press. Parizeau, aware that he was in an area he could not count on winning, invited the people to choose sovereignty even if they didn't like him or his party. He knew what he was talking about: In the 1993 federal elections, Beauce did not ride the Bloc Québécois wave, but had opted instead to elect an independent member. Nor did they get caught up in the nationalist fervour of the year that followed and, in the September 1994 provincial election, Beauce-Nord and Beauce-Sud had elected Liberal representatives to the National Assembly.

Mario Dumont was not part of the caravan. He was in Laval in the Montreal region where, accompanied by Jean Allaire, he was holding a rally. As if to give weight to the words uttered by Parizeau in Saint-Georges, he stated that his presence in the YES camp was purely circumstantial. "I fought against the Parti Québécois in the last election and will do so again in the next,"[10] he affirmed, thus indicating clearly he did not want to be swallowed up by the Péquiste machine and that he would campaign separately. "We had to save our own skin, too," Mario Dumont reflects today. "The day after the referendum, we would be going right back into the political game and the PQ would become our opponent. We would have another election to prepare for. (During the referendum), of the 2,000 people who might turn out to cheer me on, perhaps 1800 were PQ. In the next election, these same people would be going around saying the ADQ was a ridiculous party and they would be working against us."[11]

The strategy that the ADQ leader would follow throughout the entire referendum campaign was dictated by his, and his party's, need to survive. That's why he demanded, and received from Jacques Parizeau, some measure of freedom to act in the YES camp. If his party were to blend in with the rest of the YES side, it would risk its very existence. Moreover, it is not certain that Jean Allaire would have agreed to be part of a camp that would then be labelled as exclusively sovereigntist, and that would be perceived as such by the voters in general. Dumont had ended up in the YES camp because he did not want to share a platform with the Liberals, from whom he had split three years earlier. And, as he could not sit by and do nothing during a debate as crucial as this one was for Quebec, he had chosen the camp that would do his party the least damage. The ADQ's constitutional position in 1995 was inspired by the Allaire report[12] and corresponded neither to the PQ's radical position nor to the Liberal party's "same-old-same-old" position. Consequently, Dumont had negotiated all the scope he wanted for soft-pedalling the sovereignty issue and developing his speeches around the question of partnership. Furthermore, in 1995, the ADQ was a very young party that did not yet have the financial resources or the personnel to build a solid infrastructure. "He was trying to carve out a niche," says Guy Chevrette. "Imagine, he was the only member of his party in the National Assembly. It was his party that was running his campaign, when you come right down to it. It was the party's director general and a few political associates. There was no campaign organization, or very little anyway."[13]

After Laval, Dumont headed for Hull, where he spoke at the *Palais des congrès* (convention centre) and sensed the time bomb that was ticking away in the federal civil service. "The day after the vote, there is no way we are going to drop the Outaouais region," he said, even forecasting an expansion, "because this region will become the administrative centre of the Quebec-Canada partnership." But he pointed out that over the long term, Quebec would have to reduce its public service. "There will be no layoffs," he said. "It will be done through early retirements."[14] Next, he moved on to the Bas-du-Fleuve (the lower Saint-Lawrence River, east of Quebec City), where he knew he could count on a welcome from his constituents.

On the same evening as Dumont, and also in Laval, Daniel Johnson launched his campaign, but before a group of business people. By choosing this kind of audience, he made it clear what his theme would be during the 28 days remaining till the referendum: the economy. "The power we have as citizens within the Free Trade Agreement," he said, "will disappear with the separation of Quebec. That is why the sovereigntists would have us believe that there is an automatic succession principle, while all the U.S. diplomats have said that no guarantee of this kind exists."[15] Thus, very early on in the campaign, he had pinned the NAFTA theme to the NO camp's flag.

Jean Charest was not there to support Johnson when he launched his campaign. As the only Quebec Conservative in the House of Commons, he was just as wary as Dumont of being swallowed up, in his case by the battalion of federalist Liberals. In two years, he too would have to face an election—against the federal Liberals, many of whose organizers were working on the ground with the provincial Liberals. Moreover, the party he led was less well-off financially than the Liberal party. He therefore kicked off his campaign in Ottawa, with a press conference held in a small room of the parliamentary buildings.

Around this time, people on the other side of the country were experiencing the first practical consequences of a hypothetical YES victory. The municipality of Surrey, B.C., which held 30 million dollars in matured Quebec bonds, announced that it would not be buying any more of them until after October 30, as it was prohibited, under British Columbia law, from buying foreign bonds!

On closer examination, the SOM-Environics survey[16] revealed information that was quite distressing to the YES camp. To a direct question on "the separation of Quebec from the rest of Canada," respondents favoured the NO side in a ratio of 55 to 45, after apportionment of the undecided respondents. To 46% of them, the referendum question was still confusing. The NO side was ahead more or less everywhere in Quebec, except in the suburbs of Montreal and Quebec and in the Saguenay–Lac-Saint-Jean. It was meagre consolation for the YES side that they were ahead by two measly points among the francophones, a fact hard to interpret since two thirds of Quebecers stated they "felt a deep attachment to Canada, while almost all felt an attachment to Quebec."[17] Enough to stump even the brightest strategists!

With this kind of data, the dollar began to gain, going up 25 points to 74.8 cents U.S. on October 2, and another 45 points the next day. Daniel Johnson used the opportunity to cast doubt on the use of the Canadian dollar by an independent Quebec. "Any country that used another country's currency found it could not hold on to it for any length of time," he stated, before the *Association des femmes d'affaires du Québec* (Quebec business women's association). "A country that does not have its own currency does not control its interest rates, its money supply or its exchange rate, the result being a country that cannot take its own major economic decisions."[18]

The results of the polls and the strong performance of the Canadian dollar returned smiles to the faces of investors. "Everyone expected the financial markets to be jittery. And they were, for a week and a half. Then, suddenly, the markets decided that the NO side seemed to be winning," explained Robert Fairholm, chief economist at DRI/McGraw-Hill.[19] Granted, when the IMF (International Monetary Fund) revised its projections for Canada's economic growth downward, due to the political uncertainty created by the situation in Quebec, it did put a bit of a damper on things. And the governor of the Bank of Canada, Gordon Thiessen, did confirm that the markets had been volatile over the previous several months. He maintained, however, that several factors now allowed them to anticipate very positive economic prospects, and this is what the business people retained. As a result, they were optimistic and the president of Power Corporation, Paul Desmarais, asked them to get more involved in the referendum campaign. On October 3, Desmarais introduced Laurent Beaudoin, the guest speaker at a luncheon gathering at the Metropolitan Montreal Chamber of Commerce, with these words: "If we are against the sovereignty project, we must consider it our duty and have the courage to say so, and to assume the consequences of our stance."[20] Beaudoin, who ten days earlier, at a press conference in Quebec, had expressed his doubts that a "shrunken" Quebec would be able to support a giant company like Bombardier, now went even further, suggesting that the company might move away. "I hope Quebecers understand that this is a definite possibility,"[21] he said.

The economic dangers of independence fuelled every speech, even the speeches of those in positions requiring discretion. On October 4, the Canadian ambassador to the U.S. warned a Chamber of Commerce audience in Sainte-Foy, near Quebec City, that a divided Canada-Quebec front in Washington would seriously harm the economic interests of both parties. The American Consulate in Quebec lost no time reporting his speech to the State Department. "(Raymond) Chrétien said the mood, in Washington, has become much more isolationist since last November, and much less enthusiastic about free trade, especially since the Mexican peso crisis.[22] As a result, it seemed highly unlikely that any new members of NAFTA would be admitted until well after presidential elections.[23] Chrétien specifically referred to Chile, but when asked by a questioner later whether he was also talking about Quebec, he said (...) that the same rules and problems would apply to any candidate member." The debate over the admission of a sovereign Quebec to NAFTA, set off by Daniel Johnson on the first day of the campaign, would rage on right up to the day of the referendum itself. "(Chrétien) also said during the Q&A that he was 'confident' that Quebec was not going to separate from Canada."[24] The ambassador's remarks served to bolster the optimism already spreading in the NO camp.

The interventions being made by big business interests, in particular the actions of Laurent Beaudoin, provoked the ire of the YES
leaders. Jacques Parizeau felt certain this had been planned several
months ago. He claimed, when he spoke in Montmagny, that it was a
response to contracts and subsidies paid out as incentives. "Contracts
are being awarded to companies to encourage them to intimidate their
employees," he thundered before a group of sixty militants.[25] In
Charny, near Quebec City, he ridiculed Desmarais. "He left Quebec a
long time ago," he said before an audience of 300. "He sold Domtar
and Montreal Trust and invested everything in Paribas in Europe. All
he has left here are *La Presse*, *Le Nouvelliste* and *La Voix de l'Est* and,
if he's looking to sell the huge *La Presse*, I'm buying,"[26] he said ironi-
cally. Next, he gave Beaudoin a taste of his own medicine.
"Bombardier is here because it's good for Bombardier," he said.
"These scare tactics, he's been using them for twenty-five years:
'Don't move, you look best when you're down on your knees. If you
raise your head, even slightly, I'm leaving.' I don't think so."[27] The interventions from business people and, especially, the threat made by
Beaudoin, gave sovereigntist leaders occasion to recall painful mo-
ments in the history of Quebec's struggle for independence. "Before,
it was Brinks and Sun Life telling Quebecers to stay down, now it's
Standard Life and Laurent Beaudoin," Parizeau went on. But the
harshest words of all came from minister Guy Chevrette: "There is a
Power-state secret currently hanging over Quebec," he said. "Brian
Mulroney was an intimate of Power Corporation, Paul Martin is one
of its right hand men, Jean Chrétien has family ties with Power, Daniel
Johnson comes from Power and John Rae, one of the principal organizers for the NO camp, is vice-president of Power."[28]

On October 5, the NO coalition marched on Montreal and
packed the Metropolis. Daniel Johnson, Lucienne Robillard and
Michel Bélanger took their turns at the podium, but it was Jean
Charest who really stirred up the crowd when he reproached Jacques
Parizeau for refusing to meet with China's prime minister, Li Peng,
during his forthcoming visit to Canada on October 13. "His empty
chair represents the pitfall of the dogma of separation," he said. "Right

now, opportunities for employment and for economic growth are being lost." He urged people to come out of the polling booth on October 30, passport in hand. "Don't leave it to Parizeau!" he shouted. A video presentation followed, starring Laurent Beaudoin, who explained why he planned on remaining Canadian. It won sustained applause.

The referendum was now fuelling the speeches of all politicians in all parts of the country. How could the NO camp limit their presence in Quebec? Speakers outside the province were hopeful their message would reach Quebecers through the media. It was in Ottawa that Jean Chrétien first entered the official campaign. At the inauguration of a new campus for *Cité collégiale*, the first French-language college of applied arts and technology in Ontario, he encouraged those present to try to influence Quebecers. "It is important that each of you in the next three weeks take time to talk to Quebecers you know, to tell them that the French family in this country stretches from the Atlantic to the Pacific."[29] At the same time, Paul Martin declared that Quebec was under an illusion if it believed that economic union between Canada and a sovereign Quebec would be easy to achieve. In his view, Alberta and British Columbia, with only 3% of their exports going to Quebec, would reject union, even if it were in the interests of Ontario to accept it.[30] In Toronto, former premier of Ontario David Peterson was worried that the NO forces had peaked too early: "I don't think we can be too cocky about this. (The polls) still say 4.5 people out of 10 believe in some form of sovereignty. The most consistent ingredient of modern politics is its volatility."[31]

Meanwhile, in his own riding, where he knew support was a given, Mario Dumont soldiered on bravely by himself, but now in the leaders' campaign bus. Parizeau had stayed behind in Quebec City for a Cabinet meeting, so the ADQ leader was accompanied by the journalists who travelled on board the other two buses in the caravan. Dumont discovered how difficult it was to bear the torch in the leader's absence. After visiting a small enterprise in Saint-Pacôme, a plant producing raspberry wine, he decided that, for the trip from there to Saint-Cyprien, he would join the print media journalists in their bus instead of travelling in the leaders' bus. He was quite aware that the latest polls showed the YES to be several points behind the NO. In a casual conversation with some reporters, he attacked what he termed the "loser mentality" he observed within certain elements of the sovereignty camp. His criticism was levelled particularly at sociologist Pierre Drouilly and other like-minded individuals, who thought the undecided vote in the polls should not be apportioned in the same ratio as the rest of the votes, since rarely are more than a quarter of them inclined towards sovereignty. "To be a pessimist at the outset, to display a loser's attitude, that's not something I favour strongly," Dumont said during a press briefing in Rivière-du-Loup. "When I throw myself into a campaign, it's to win." Today, he likes to recall how from that moment on, everywhere in Quebec, militants adopted as their slogan, *"On va gagner!"* (We will win!).

During that same press briefing, someone asked Dumont what would happen if the NO side won. He replied that they could expect "a redeployment of the nationalist forces in Quebec." Even though he had taken the precaution of highlighting Jacques Parizeau's qualities, Dumont's remarks nevertheless threw tour organizers into a cold sweat. They tried to tell reporters not to take the ADQ leader's comments seriously, stressing that this had not been an official conversation.[32] Despite the agreement made between the three leaders on June 12, one could sense that all had not been anticipated: travelling in such close quarters with reporters, day after day, could—as Jacques Parizeau had feared—create an atmosphere of familiarity that made it easy to slip up.

On October 4, a delegation from the YES camp met with the new U.S. Consul General in Quebec, Stephen R. Kelly,[33] who had replaced Marie T. Huhtala during the summer. There were three of them: David Cliche, parliamentary assistant to Jacques Parizeau and his advisor on Native Affairs, Michel Lepage, the YES camp's pollster, and Marcel Landry, the minister of Agriculture. They did not hide their discouragement. Kelly's report to Washington read in part as follows: "Cliche said he is part of a small group that meets every morning to review campaign strategy. He stated bluntly that if the next round of published polls does not show an improvement in the YES position, the sovereignty battle is lost. Cliche noted that the last round of polls showed a 45-55 advantage for the NO side. The YES side needed to show it was closing the gap to develop some badly needed momentum. Cliche said the PQ strategists have decided the only way for them to win is to focus their attention on French-speakers who have told poll-sters they intend to vote NO. Cliche said this is based on an estimate that 95% of the 18% of Quebecers who are non-French speakers will vote NO, and there is nothing the PQ can do about them. Recent polls estimate after apportioning the undecided that 57 percent of francoph-ones will vote YES. But this figure must be nearly 60% to overcome the anglophone deficit. Cliche said the PQ will attack this problem in two ways. First, many of those who say they will vote NO are worried about economic factors. This economic angst is especially prevalent among the 800,000 Quebecers who live on public assistance and among women who stay at home. In the days to come, Cliche said the YES side will try to clarify the message that a sovereign Quebec can be economically viable. The other line of attack, according to Cliche, will be to spark the pride of Quebecers."[34]

In-house polls showed, however, that the gap was narrowing, standing now at only 6 points. On October 5, Michel Lepage returned to the consulate and shared with Kelly all the details of this internal poll, which showed that the YES side had gained a lot of ground on September 28 and 29. These statistics were all the more significant for the YES side considering that, in the process of arriving at them, Lepage had apportioned 70% of the 10% who were undecided to the NO side. "The race isn't won," said Lepage, "but it is still winnable."[35] That same day, Léger Marketing published the results of an opinion survey done between October 1 and 4.[36] They confirmed Lepage's statistics: 52.8% of the votes for the NO vs. 47.2% of the votes for the YES. While the YES camp was buoyed up by these re-sults, one statistic still worried them greatly. Half of Quebecers felt that the NO side was dominating the referendum debate and only a quarter of them believed it was the YES side that was getting its views across successfully.

Despite this very clear signal, which should have prompted him to explore other avenues, Jacques Parizeau did not change his strategy: he continued to do battle with the heads of corporations. At the Matane Chamber of Commerce, he denounced them as "a chorus of 'railers and wailers,' directed by choirmaster Daniel Johnson." "Whether we're talking about SNC, Bombardier or the Royal Bank," he declared, "when one has become a billionaire with the money of Quebecers (with the help of the REA[37] plan), one does not spit on those who did not do as well.[38] It was your taxes that paid the fiscal subsidies of all those who bought half of Bombardier's capital stock. Now they are biting the hand that fed them, but we are the ones who financed that."[39]

While the leaders of the two camps tried, out on the road, to persuade Quebecers of the merits of their respective options, the U.S. ambassador to Canada, James Blanchard, travelled to Washington to try to sensitize American journalists to the importance of keeping Canada united and the need to keep this in mind in their particular media. "My purpose was to get a few ringing endorsements for a united Canada in the press and make sure that nobody in Congress said anything that would inflame the issue back in Quebec," he wrote in his autobiography. "My first appointment was with E.J. Dionne and John Anderson of *The Washington Post* editorial board. I found Dionne particularly interested, because his family was originally from Quebec. (...) I went on: 'The polls look good. It could even be a decisive victory. But we can't be sure, anything could happen. It's a very fuzzy question. It's an emotional issue. Ethnic tribalism is on the rise. Populism is on the rise.'"[40] Ten years later, Dionne recalls his meeting with Blanchard. "He and I spoke of this fairly often (I had known him when he was Governor of Michigan). I always would joke with him that I had a Quebec perspective on the issue. His account sounds broadly right to me."[41]

The campaign was barely underway when endorsements for both camps came rushing in, unexpectedly, from the most unlikely quarters. Victor Tchernomyrdine, the Prime Minister of the Federation of Russia, who was in Ottawa to visit Jean Chrétien, told reporters when he met with them, "We hope to be doing business with a united Canada." Acadians were rallying around the NO side, behind the former president of the *Fédération des communautés francophones et acadienne du Canada* (Canadian Federation of Francophone and Acadian communities), Professor Yvon Fontaine of the University of Moncton. In Saint-Laurent, the students at the anglophone Champlain College expressed their opinion loud and clear in a poll revealing 92% of them to be in favour of the NO side. Endorsements for the YES side were no less surprising. The extreme right-wing group Heritage Front, seen as a Neo-Nazi movement by many observers, expressed a strong desire to see Quebec leave the Canadian Confederation, so that bilingualism could be abolished in this country forever. "Quebec has everything to gain by separating," said its president, Wolfgang Droege. "It would be a small country like many in Europe, easy to administer. Quality of life could only improve for Quebecers in a sovereign Quebec. You know, the same ethnic groups share the same values."[42]

Jean Chrétien showed up in Quebec for the first time on the evening of October 6, in Shawinigan. He was flanked by Daniel Johnson, Jean Charest and Lucienne Robillard, before an audience of a thousand people. He spoke for about forty minutes, making no promises whatsoever for change that could persuade YES supporters to switch. Instead, his speech focused on the advantages for Quebecers of living in "a strong Quebec in a united Canada." He extolled the flexibility of a country that allowed Quebec to have its own policies and its own institutions like the *Caisse de dépôt et placement* (Deposit and investment bank), the *Régie des rentes* (Government pension plan) and *Hydro-Québec*. With *Trente lettres pour un oui* still fresh in his mind and the argument between René-Daniel Dubois and Andrée Ferretti having been broadcast just two days earlier on *Le Point*, he criticized the artists who supported the YES camp. He reminded them that it was two federal institutions—the Canada Council for the Arts and the National Film Board—that were their "bread and butter." His speech was positive. He avoided attacking the sovereigntists too harshly, like someone who, reassured by the results of the polls of the last few days, wished to let sleeping dogs lie. But there was one temptation he was unable to resist: knowing he could rouse his audience with it, he repeated the term that Claude Garcia had used. He congratulated Daniel Johnson and his team on having "crushed" their adversaries during the debate in the National Assembly. Reaction would be swift.

But the adversary was worried, not so much because the fortune-tellers, consulted around a crystal ball or a pack of tarot cards in Montreal's *Salon de l'ésotérisme*, had foretold a crushing victory for the NO side,[43] but because of the brutal fact that their campaign was going nowhere. There were only 24 days left, a little over three weeks, and the gap was still five to seven points wide. It was this realization that prompted an important meeting, held behind closed doors on Friday, October 6, in Montreal. In the presence of Jacques Parizeau, the 16 regional presidents and the PQ representatives of the 125 electoral ridings took stock of the YES strategy. "The people would rather see more of Mr. Bouchard," said the president of Montreal–Ville-Marie, Sylvain Lépine, to journalist Denis Lessard of *La Presse*. "The work he does in the House of Commons is fine, but they want to see him out there, on the road." And it was the same story from the other regional presidents.

Jacques Parizeau listened to them: it was not the first time he had heard the YES "lieutenants" demand more visibility for Bouchard. A few days earlier, in Quebec City, he had met with the ridings' presidents of that region. "I think it was at the Loews," recalls Alain Lupien, campaign-financing coordinator for the YES. "It was a private meeting. Mr. Parizeau listened to the comments from the presidents. They put forward various proposals, one of which was to put Mr. Bouchard out in front. There was discussion and, I felt, when people left the meeting, that something big had been decided."[44]

The window was now open: the second week of October, the House of Commons would adjourn until the 16th. It was unclear just what was planned for Saturday, but it was already determined that the following week, Bouchard would travel in the caravan bus for two or three days. The agreement between Bouchard's entourage and

Parizeau's was that the premier would continue campaigning and that the leader of the Bloc would intervene as much as possible, while at the same time fulfilling his responsibilities as leader of the opposition and leader of the Bloc Québécois in Ottawa. It had also been decided that Bouchard would give the major media interviews. It was a gruelling schedule: during the first week of the referendum campaign, there were three occasions when, after participating in the sessions in the House, he left the capital to take part in a rally in Quebec. But this was the first time he would be at the head of the caravan.

The decision Parizeau was preparing to take would have another positive side effect, one that had not been anticipated and one that was probably not fully appreciated: getting Bouchard out of the House of Commons would be a good thing for the YES side. In one of his columns, journalist Michel Vastel had written, not long before, that they should get him out of there. "Bouchard had not been particularly effective in question period," recalls Eddie Goldenberg. "Prime Minister (Chrétien) was giving a better performance." Chrétien agrees. Ten years after the referendum, he still likes to recall Vastel's column: "Things were going very well. Michel Vastel had written, 'Mr. Bouchard, you really should leave because you are not doing well in the House of Commons.' The polls were good."[45] The truth was that Mr. Bouchard's presence in the federal parliament was allowing Jean Chrétien to score big time with the media.

However, the idea of making Lucien Bouchard the chief negotiator was not new. It even went back several months. "My recollection is that the idea came from Mario Dumont," Jean-François Lisée says today. "But we got the message that Mr. Bouchard did not want to be chief negotiator and so, we more or less abandoned that idea."[46] Especially since, at that time, in the premier's mind, the chief negotiator was to be someone less prominent who was not a political personality but, rather, a kind of technocrat, whose mandate would be to represent Quebec in negotiations that would clearly be difficult and complex.

Although he had already thought of the role of chief negotiator, Lisée continued to look for a role Lucien Bouchard could play, should the YES win the referendum. "In August," he says, "I wrote a note to Mr. Parizeau, who was to meet with Mr. Bouchard, saying 'You could propose to Mr. Bouchard the chairmanship of the steering and oversight committee. In that case, he would not be your negotiator. He would have the role of judge.' But this was not followed up."[47] There was another idea floating around in Jacques Parizeau's entourage. After sovereignty was proclaimed, there would no longer be a lieutenant-governor. Who then would become the head of state? "We could have said we were going to create the role of president," says Lisée, "a president perhaps designated by the National Assembly, with significant powers in matters of international relations, therefore, relations with Canada, our neighbouring nation. I was trying to find a role for Mr. Bouchard. But we also knew that Mr. Parizeau was not too keen to talk to Mr. Bouchard about it, and neither was Mr. Bouchard."[48]

They kept on looking for ideas, but the one of making Mr. Bouchard chief negotiator would not go away. "I would say that at the end of August, beginning of September, it was an idea to which we were not giving a lot of thought,"[49] recalls Jean Royer. The YES camp was however conducting more surveys than ever, in order to get a sense of its strengths and weaknesses and to find a strategy that would increase its support among the people. Jean-François Lisée attended several focus groups held for that purpose. Then one day, unable to meet while one of them was in Montreal and the other in Quebec, he phoned Jean Royer. He told him he was surprised to note that, for a lot of people, a YES victory meant that Mr. Bouchard would no longer be head of the opposition in Ottawa because there would be no more Bloc representatives in the House of Commons and, therefore, very quickly, he would cease to play a significant role as MP. Lisée then suggested to Royer the conclusion he drew from this: "What would you think of proposing in the focus groups a number of possibilities for the role that Mr. Bouchard could play?" Royer thought the idea deserved to be explored, but took no initiative on it before discussing it with his leader and with Lucien Bouchard. Prudence was in order since, as soon as a question about a possible role for Lucien Bouchard

223

after the referendum was put to a poll or a focus group, the media would be sure to grab it for the news. Royer decided to confide to Parizeau the fears that emanate from the focus groups and he phoned Bouchard. "I think it made him smile more than anything else,"[50] he says. Royer did not however raise at that time the proposal to have him head the negotiating team.

In any event, initial surveys showed immediately that the proposal did appeal and—something that was a bonus to the YES camp—that it appealed as well to a large number of Quebecers who were not automatically sympathetic to their cause. Royer met with Parizeau and conveyed these initial results to him. "I told him I believed there was real potential here," Royer recalls. Parizeau was aware that Royer had a special talent for analyzing polls. "He answered, 'Just continue and when you have the final results of all your work, come back and we'll talk again.'"[51]

The leader of the Bloc Québécois and his staff were deliberating too. Bob Dufour, organizer for the Bloc in the 1993 election, had been convinced for a long time that Lucien Bouchard should be given more exposure. "Someone with an aura like his, you don't leave him sitting on the bench, a guy like that, you put him out on the ice," he says. "He was so popular that Mr. Parizeau spoke of him as an icon."[52] But it was up to Parizeau to take the decision, and Bouchard, with the exception of a few local meetings, had so far been limited to a role in the House of Commons, which gave him little chance to impact the campaign.

Royer and Lisée continued their research and came to the conclusion "that there was something there that was likely to create what, in the language of poll analysis, would be called a trend,"[53] as Royer puts it. When he informed his leader that the results of his study were conclusive, Parizeau replied, "Draw up a scenario for me showing what it would mean if we appointed Mr. Bouchard as chief negotiator. And then, we'll see!" He had neither accepted nor rejected the idea. Royer's only mandate was to go and see Lucien Bouchard, to explain the results to him and, unless Bouchard refused categorically, to develop a scenario leading up to the announcement of his appointment. Bouchard listened and then expressed one condition: the plan was to remain absolutely confidential. These exchanges took place in September, before the official opening of the referendum campaign.

It was as late as the first week of October however that Jean Royer presented his scenario to the premier. The campaign was in full swing and the YES side had still not managed to take off. On Friday, the premier would announce the names of the first five members appointed to the oversight committee for negotiations with Canada,[54] but that would not be enough to reverse the trend. Royer went to Jacques Parizeau's residence in Quebec City and, in the second floor living room, told him, "You asked me for a scenario. Well, here it is!" Jacques Parizeau's chief of staff was a meticulous individual. When he submitted a proposal to his leader, he was totally familiar with it and ready to defend it. "I knew I had a good presentation," he says, "but if he had said, at the end of it, that he was not going to go for it—he was the boss—I would have accepted it... We would have carried on, not just me, but all of us."[55] The discussion about the presentation itself was brief. Parizeau faced the evidence: Lucien Bouchard had to be put out in front. In their discussion of barely half an hour, they talked mostly organization. A rally at the University of Montreal had been planned ten days ago. The conversation covered how things would be handled, what should happen and who should be present.

Not a word passed between the two men about what the decision that had just been taken by Jacques Parizeau meant for him personally first of all and, secondly, about what it signified politically. Just as, perhaps, he was about to pick the fruit he had dreamed of for twenty-five years, he was being asked to stand back and allow another to take his place, as the great winner of independence for Quebec. "It was difficult. I understood what this represented," says Royer. "But when you've got to do it, you've got to do it."[56] The two men knew each other well, they had worked together for several years and they had the greatest respect for one another. But Parizeau had never used the familiar *tu* when he addressed Royer, or called him by his first name, a rule he followed with all those close to him. When he felt inclined to use a more familiar tone, he would use the last name by itself. But that day, the matter at hand was too grave for familiar terms. As Royer was about to leave the residence, Parizeau called after him. Royer turned around and saw his leader at the top of the stairway: "Mr. Royer," he said, "Call Mr. Bouchard. Explain my decision to him and tell him I will call him at ten o'clock tomorrow morning to make the proposal."

After leaving Parizeau, Jean Royer immediately phoned Lucien Bouchard and told him, "I have spoken to Mr. Parizeau and he has agreed. I must explain to you the nature of his decision to find out if you are comfortable with everything. He will speak with you directly tomorrow at 10 a.m." Then, he hit the road, getting to Montreal around midnight. He made a detour to the campaign headquarters, where he had a couple of soft drinks with Hubert Thibault, who was always there, and then went home. Thibault would be the only person to know of Parizeau's decision prior to Royer's meeting with Lucien Bouchard, which took place early the next morning around 7:30 or 8. Bouchard had stayed in Montreal. It went well. A few minutes after 10, Royer received a call from Parizeau: "Mr. Bouchard and I have agreed." He went on, "Start the ball rolling..." "That meant," explains Jean Royer, "advise those who need to know. But there weren't a lot of people to tell, because the element of surprise was crucial to the whole thing."[57] The secret remained well guarded for a few days.

On Thursday, Bouchard passed through the riding of Papineau, and then took off for Saguenay–Lac-Saint-Jean. Friday, he visited a group of elderly citizens in Alma and met with reporters in the area. "The fundamental reason to vote YES is to stand up for our identity. That's what it's all about."[58] But not a word about the bombshell that would explode the next day.

The pressure being put on Jacques Parizeau was coming not just from his inner circle. Certain ministers were waking up to the fact that the campaign was not rousing people and that a larger role had somehow to be given to Lucien Bouchard soon. In the mind of those ministers who had had the opportunity to campaign with him, there was no longer any doubt possible. But they had to tell Parizeau. Guy Chevrette, Bernard Landry and Pauline Marois had discussions amongst themselves, unaware that Jean-François Lisée and Jean Royer had come to the same conclusion and had already taken the first step in that direction. They decided someone should talk to their leader about it. On Friday, October 6, the opportunity presented itself when they were in an Italian restaurant in the north of Montreal, having a meal with Parizeau. He wanted to consult them on a particular aspect of the campaign. "It was one of the most difficult moments I have ever experienced in politics," says Guy Chevrette. "I found it a terrible thing to have to say to him. I was nervous, shaking with emotion. He listened without moving a muscle. All he did was twirl his moustache, he didn't say a word, except, if my memory serves me correctly, 'I am taking note.'"[59] None of them knew the decision had already been taken and would be announced in less than 24 hours.

Saturday, October 7. The auditorium of the University of Montreal is packed. Upon arrival, Jean-François Lisée runs into the U.S. Consul General in Montreal, Eleanor Savage, leaving the hall. He shows her the program for the day, pointing out the exact time when Parizeau will speak. "Don't leave," he says to her, "that's when the campaign is going to change. You really should be here at that time!" The consul just replies that she has something else to do and goes off. It was one of the rare events in the referendum campaign of which the Americans had not been apprised. Lisée enters and sits down at the back of the hall to be able to see the reaction of the 1500 people assembled there when Jacques Parizeau announces Lucien Bouchard's appointment.

"The chief negotiator must be," the premier began, "a person who inspires deep confidence, not only in the majority of Quebecers who have voted YES, but also in a great number of Quebecers who will have voted NO.[60] It will take someone who is a good negotiator, who knows English Canada, and who is a sovereigntist."[61] Then he called out, "Lucien Bouchard." "It was as if an electric charge of 100,000 volts had gone through the seats," Lisée remembers. "The audience bolted from their seats to applaud. It was a magic moment."[62] The two men embraced and Bouchard stepped up to the microphone. His speech was passionate. He came back on Jean Chrétien's speech in Shawinigan: "Mr. Chrétien said yesterday that he was pleased because, he thinks, Daniel Johnson crushed the Parizeau government in the National Assembly. Crushed was the word he used. And Mr. Johnson is very happy. He likes that. To see people crushed. That's how they see us." Then he shouted, "With the vote three weeks away, it's not over, it's only just begun!" In the audience, the supporters could hardly contain their joy. They had not had much to be joyful about since the beginning of the referendum campaign. Guy Chevrette had not been let in on the plan, nor had almost any other minister. "To our great surprise, certainly to mine," he says, "he announced that his chief negotiator would be Lucien Bouchard. The crowd was ecstatic. I said to myself, 'is he clever or what!' He had made his point that he would decide what form Lucien Bouchard's role would take. He told the crowd: 'you did your duty, as you told me you would.' He was fantastic."[63]

"It was not a decision I took in the midst of catastrophe," Jacques Parizeau says today. "The House of Commons was adjourning for a week. (Prior to that,) Mr. Bouchard had to fulfil his duties as leader of the opposition. Obviously he had a much better public image than I had. Given these conditions, as I discussed with Jean Royer, it was clear we needed a sort of extra push, clear that Mr. Bouchard should intervene, that he should take the ball and run with it."[64] A decision that was nevertheless not easy for the government leader. "We understood what it meant," says Lisette Lapointe, wife of the premier. "It meant he would be number one; Jacques Parizeau would be second. I am certain that was very, very hard for him. But, at the receptions that were held, on the tours, you could see so clearly that the people were infatuated with Lucien Bouchard. Jacques Parizeau wanted to win. And that is why he did what he did. And he did it gladly. I'm not saying it didn't hurt his pride. But he was ready to make any sacrifice."[65]

That morning of October 7 was also the beginning of the Thanksgiving weekend. Jean Charest was visiting his father in Sherbrooke. The phone rang. He went up to his parents' room to answer. Someone told him the news. "I said to myself: the campaign has just changed," he recalls. The challenge for Charest was particularly difficult because he knew the adversary. He had faced him when he led the special committee on the Meech Lake Accords, the conclusions of which had prompted Bouchard to resign from the Mulroney cabinet. The two men were no longer on speaking terms. "I knew that politically, it was not easy to pit oneself against Lucien Bouchard. He was very popular and much loved. He had a powerful influence over crowds. We immediately felt the difference in the campaign."[66]

As for Daniel Johnson, he was taken totally by surprise. "That was something you could not see coming," he says. "But you can understand it. Let us not forget how Bernard Landry, a former military man, had said publicly, through his light brigade metaphor, that he did not want to move that fast. At that time, you could sense that Lucien Bouchard and Landry were on the same wavelength. They were pressuring Parizeau. So it had already happened a few months earlier, so to speak. And it could happen (again). But to put the squeeze on the premier of Quebec, while it was his project in the first place, took a lot of nerve! It was pretty unprecedented and, therefore, unforeseeable." Johnson admits this manoeuvre changed the game. "Bouchard was much harder to criticize," he continues, "Figures were not important to him, the economic future of Quebec, public finance, they had absolutely no importance. His discourse was nationalistic, emotional and traditional."[67]

Daniel Johnson's Liberals believed, likewise, that what they had just witnessed was a case of mutiny: Lucien Bouchard had pushed Jacques Parizeau overboard. "It was tantamount to a *coup d'état*," says John Parisella. "I would not have thought Mr. Bouchard capable of muscling out Mr. Parizeau. And then, it seems, it turned out to be voluntary. Well, it wasn't obvious! I was somewhat astonished that there weren't more observers, from the media, questioning the wisdom of having a leader in Ottawa come to replace the leader who was the duly elected premier of Quebec."[68]

In Parisella's view, Bouchard's arrival totally changed the dynamic of the campaign, to the point of greatly destabilizing the strategy of the NO side. "It was all very well to have a campaign plan," he adds, "but it was as if something beyond the scope of reason had burst in on the scene and we were stuck with it." He admits that even if the NO camp had anticipated the manoeuvre, it would have been difficult to make a countermove. "The federalists had recorded no successes in the previous few years," he says, "There were only failures. And their leader certainly wasn't as charismatic."[69]

The leader of the NO did not underestimate his new opponent. On the contrary. Today, when Johnson looks back on Bouchard's referendum campaign, his memory is vivid: "He was extremely opportunistic. He did not hesitate as much as Mr. Parizeau to seize upon every little comma, anything... He was a litigation lawyer, don't forget. Secondly, his tone. Mr. Bourassa always said, 'Lucien expresses himself like a tormented soul at all times. He is a powerful orator in that genre.' And, thirdly, he was a street fighter. No-one had ever attacked my personal integrity or my Quebec identity, but he did!"[70] His friend, Bob Rae, former premier of Ontario, explained why Parizeau's decision had been a surprise to the federalists. "We overestimated Mr. Parizeau's ego and his determination to lead the campaign to the finish," he says. "And we underestimated the personal impact Mr. Bouchard would have."

In Jean Chrétien's office they were just as stunned. "We were surprised," says Eddie Goldenberg, the prime minister's advisor. "The initial reaction some of us had was to say the YES campaign must be in great trouble. You don't change leaders mid-campaign." "Who could have thought it?" exclaims Jean Pelletier, Chrétien's chief of staff. "Mr. Parizeau was premier of Quebec, it was a referendum ordered by the National Assembly of Quebec, in accordance with a Quebec Act. And the premier of Quebec is suddenly going to step down for a federal MP who isn't even a member of the National Assembly! Who could have thought of that?" Rapidly, the federal Liberals came to believe that Mr. Bouchard was not just assuming the role of chief negotiator, but the role of chairing the YES committee as well. "We saw Mr. Parizeau being literally eclipsed," adds Pelletier. "It took a few days before Ottawa realized exactly what was going on and what Mr. Bouchard's real role was."[71] As for Jean Chrétien, he repeats today what he said at the time: "It was a sign that the YES camp was in trouble. When Mr. Bouchard effectively became the new bus driver, nah, I figured it was the same bus."[72]

In Ottawa, it was not just Chrétien's office that was taken by surprise. Everyone on the Hill was baffled and confused. "For a while, there was a pause," says Brian Tobin, who was then a minister. "There was that kind of blind thing that happens when you're driving down the road and suddenly your car is out of control. Your first instinct is to simply hold on to the wheel and go for a ride. When really you ought to be trying to do something to steer you away out of that skid. I think the initial reaction of those who were the authors of the strategy, both in cabinet and outside of cabinet, was a degree of paralysis." In Fredericton, the premier of New Brunswick expressed his worry: "I became very concerned," says Frank McKenna. "Mr. Bouchard (was) charismatic, and talented, and pure, in terms of not having baggage. I became extremely apprehensive."

Pierre-Claude Nolin, one of the key strategists in the NO camp, was well aware of the significance of Bouchard's arrival at the head of the YES campaign. "It suited us very well to have Mr. Parizeau take all the attention," he says. "When we saw Bouchard step into his place, it was foreseeable, but we would have wished, we would have liked, for it not to happen. But it did. We were hoping Mr. Parizeau would not agree and would be offended at giving that kind of importance to Mr. Bouchard. But that's not how it went."[73]

It was not just the leadership of the YES campaign that changed when Bouchard was nominated as chief negotiator. It was also the message that would, from then on, emphasize partnership rather than sovereignty. "Mr. Bouchard was more wedded to the idea of partnership than Mr. Parizeau was," Mario Dumont says today. "In any event, people connected his image more with that notion. The Monday morning following (the announcement), four or five days later, in every region of Quebec, every supporter of the YES side had adopted the slogan, *On va gagner!*"[74]

Coming out of the stupor of those first few days, the NO camp tried to adjust. "We had to change our way of anticipating what would happen next," says Senator Nolin. "You heard premiers from the other provinces stating they would never accept a partnership like the one Bouchard was proposing. I'm thinking of Mr. McKenna, among others. And Mr. Harris."[75] Five days after Bouchard's appointment, the premier of Ontario delivered, before the Canadian Club of Toronto, a speech that the entire economic community of Ontario had been waiting for. He warned Quebec: if it became independent, it would be a foreign country and would have to forget about the possibility of economic union with Ontario. "I felt it was important to get a message to Quebecers," he says today, "and to encourage my fellow Ontarians that whatever opportunity they had, through business or social or friends or family, to send a message to Quebecers that we indeed consider them part of Canada. And secondly, that we shared some very legitimate concerns, in Ontario, on constitutional issues."

Harris analyzes Jacques Parizeau's decision this way: "If he wanted to be premier of Quebec and leader of the PQ party, on into the future, it turned out not to be a very smart move. If he saw his future, that if he didn't win this referendum, his future was doomed anyway, then it was a smart move. So, either way, it's history."

Harris then makes a comparison between Bouchard and Pierre Elliott Trudeau. "Mr. Trudeau, I think, just destroyed the country. I hate to say that, because he's passed on. I thought his policies took us to economic ruin. I was a tremendous admirer of Mr. Trudeau, his political ability to convince voters, to gain their trust, don't worry, I'm on your side, you can trust me. Mr. Bouchard, clearly, had that quality. He was very charming, he was persuasive, he was able to gain the confidence like no other Quebec politician was. He clearly had charisma." Jean Chrétien did not mention charisma, but the perfectly tailored speeches. "He succeeded," he says, "in touching a nerve that provoked a rapid change, obliging us to wake up to this new reality. It was unexpected. They themselves had not anticipated it any more than we did."[76] He does not know how true that was.

"For weeks, we hadn't had time to talk about it," Bob Dufour, Lucien Bouchard's close associate in the YES camp, acknowledges. "It happened so quickly, we had no strategy for it."[77] Alain Lupien, from his vantage point, could see the numerous logistical adjustments that would have to be made. "Mr. Bouchard's arrival on the scene was not an obvious development," he says. "For the organization, it was like changing horses in mid-stream. Many of the militants identified more strongly with one leader than the other. So it was essential that, at some point, people would come to accept the change. Not only that. It had to provide a real boost."[78]

Apart from the organizational adjustments required on the campaign tour, and the instructions to respect the sensitivities of each leader's followers, the chief difficulty lay in the need to rearrange the buses. In September and during the first week of October, Lucien Bouchard had hardly been covered by the media, if at all. Everyday, he would leave from Ottawa, where he continued in his role as leader of the opposition, and head directly over to wherever he had to take part in a rally. But he had not been trailed by the press. "So, it was important," says Jean-François Lisée, "to start having him ride in the main bus. Campaign trail coverage would have to be shared by all three leaders, Mr. Bouchard, Mr. Parizeau and, when he was there, Mario Dumont. The Bloc people wanted more coverage. So, that had to be renegotiated. There would be a second bus for Mr. Parizeau. Believe me, that created a few interesting moments!"[79]

To manage those "interesting moments," Jacques Parizeau called on Guy Chevrette. "Jean Royer told me, 'Mr. Parizeau absolutely wants you to be on the national (permanent committee) because it is in a real mess!'" the former minister recalls. "So and so wants to make a speech in the evening, but such and such a leader is insisting on being with a certain minister, or else he won't go. Or, the other way around. A minister says he wants to be with Mr. Bouchard while another wants something else. Everyone was looking for visibility. They were saying, for example that Madame Marois should be with Mr. Dumont, in the Estrie region. Yes, but Mr. Dumont never gets a big crowd. There weren't any full-blown arguments. It's the little everyday hassles that are hard to deal with. That was also how you really got to know people. What I found most trying was the prima donna attitude: 'I have to be with Lucien! I don't want to go with Dumont. I would rather go with Lucien...' I'm telling you, it was quite the mix-up!"[80]

The three parties in the YES coalition each had a representative on the national permanent committee: Bob Dufour for the Bloc,

André Néron for the ADQ and Monique Simard, vice-president of the Parti Québécois. And each of them was assisted by a team standing ready to defend vigorously their leader's rightful due. Jean Royer advised Chevrette of Parizeau's wishes, but the minister of municipal affairs lived in Joliette, in his riding, where he had to ensure a strong win for the YES. This meant that every morning he had to drive into Montreal, where the national permanent committee sat, analyze the arguments and pay a visit to one of the groups to convince them to "put water in their wine."

At the end of the first campaign week, each camp had reasons to be worried. But for very different reasons, depending on whether you were in the YES or the NO camp. The YES was still dragging behind in the polls by six or seven points, and there were some indicators that deeply disturbed its organizers. The latest SOM-Environics poll, even though it had been done a week earlier, showed that of the 740,000 voters in the 19 ridings of the Quebec City region, only 47% favoured the YES side, scarcely 2% more than in the 1980 referendum. It was suspected that the province's civil servants were harbouring a certain amount of resentment against the government. In the daily *Le Soleil*, their union president, Danielle-Maude Gosselin, admitted that the nationalistic fervour of its 35,000 employees remained lukewarm and she attributed this more to the economic gloom pervading the region than to a shift in their political leanings.[81] But, whatever was prompting their ill humour, the YES strategists had three weeks to transform it into patriotic ardour.

What they needed in the Quebec City region was a major breakthrough, and they needed one in the rest of the province as well. Beyond the sovereignty message, which would always have its core of followers, they would rely on two new factors: Lucien Bouchard's arrival, which thrust the element of partnership into the centre of the campaign, and advertising, which had now become authorized. In fact, starting October 8, the YES camp could spend one million dollars on advertising—from which they expected a great deal, because they were giving it a particularly aggressive character: on some of the signs, the first letter of *OUI* was replaced with a coin, the Canadian loonie![82] Billboards took over the highways and the main roads of cities, towns and villages. Only the YES and NO committees had the legal authority to put up advertising, whether on signs, in the newspapers or in the electronic media. And they would milk it for all it was worth.

While the YES camp had to reassess its strategy, under pain of losing the referendum, the NO camp, in order to maintain its lead, had to adapt its strategy to the new threat looming before them. "It's very difficult to change your strategy during a campaign," says Bob Rae who, in addition to having considerable experience as a politician, learned what a change in strategy meant to the NO side from his brother, who was one of its active members. "Having to change strategy created a problem. We could see it. It was an enormous problem." When Parizeau made his announcement at the University of Montreal, Daniel Johnson was in Sept-Îles. The tactics that came to him on the spur of the moment were not to attack Lucien Bouchard, for fear that such remarks would explode right in his face. He recalled that the real leader of the YES camp was still Parizeau. "They are trying to transform a referendum on the future of Quebec into a popularity contest,"[83] he said. Then he drew an amusing conclusion: "By appointing Bouchard chief separator, Parizeau created the only job that could be created by the political separation of Quebec."

On the permanent committee of the NO, they were aware of the danger, and the official word from now on was, "Don't blow it." "Error-free was the only option we had left," says Pierre-Claude Nolin. Some strategists wanted to bring Pierre Elliott Trudeau back out of his retirement. "But that was out of the question," adds Nolin. "Some would have wanted that, yes. We had to play absolutely all our cards, and play them skillfully, put out our highest trumps, not lay ourselves open to attack by an opponent who was very capable and who could have made the most of the tiniest little error."[84]

But if they did not want Trudeau identified with the NO camp, did the same apply to all the federal politicians in Ottawa, champing at the bit to intervene? "This (had) now become more difficult, more dangerous," says Brian Tobin, "this (was) no time for those who (didn't) understand the land, or landscape, to become involved, (they told us,) so leave this to those of us who live in Quebec, who know Quebec, please leave this alone." But those instructions, while they were more or less respected during the next two weeks of the campaign, would be totally ignored during the final one.

CHAPTER IX

The "Walking Miracle"

The first gathering held by the new chief negotiator Lucien Bouchard was held on Sunday evening in Kingsey Falls, a small town in the Bois-Francs region, famous for its native son, Conrad Kirouac, who became botanist Frère Marie-Victorin, and for its principal industry, the Cascades paper mill. Bloc Québécois organizer, Bob Dufour, recalls the surprise that awaited the caravan. "To Mr. Bouchard's great astonishment," he says, "this tiny church had, I think, something like 1,000 or 1,200 people crowded into it. The atmosphere was euphoric. Mr. Bouchard had a hard time making his way into and out of the church. It was a phenomenon we couldn't quite understand."[1]

That evening, in Toronto, federal cabinet minister David Collenette was watching the television news with his wife. He saw the images of Kingsey Falls. First, he tried to understand, and then he switched to RDI, the continuous news channel of the French-language network. "And then, I turned to my wife and I said, you know, we've got trouble," he recalls. "That night, I was just scared. And some of us started to speak about this in the days following."

Was it just the way the tours happened to be organized? Or were we to imagine that, at the very last minute, the strategists caught on to the fact that, henceforth, the future of the YES side was married to the idea of the partnership? Be that as it may, it was with Mario Dumont that the newly appointed chief negotiator for the Quebec government took to the road on Sunday, October 8, for Sherbrooke, Windsor and

Kingsey Falls. Lucien Bouchard's message for those who showed up to welcome him focused on the future: The day after a YES victory, he said in essence, there would be no more sovereigntists in Quebec, there would only be Quebecers. Michel Bélanger, Daniel Johnson and Jean Charest were going to have to support the Quebec project because the people would have decided on it. And, as far as negotiations with Canada were concerned, they would be peaceful and short. This message generated enthusiasm at every stop Lucien Bouchard made.

With the arrival of Bouchard on the scene, the discourse of the YES side quickly changed from tense to optimistic. While the leader of the Bloc made a brief stop in Windsor, Mario Dumont visited the J.-A. Bombardier Museum in Valcourt, some twenty kilometres away. What he said there was almost identical: "Even the president of Bombardier will be among the first to support the Quebec-Ottawa partnership project," he said. He recalled that, no matter how multinational it was today, Bombardier ought to remember that it owed its existence to the Quebec inventor who knew how to struggle to establish it, and that its growth would not have been possible without the help of the taxpayers, notably, the taxpayers of Quebec.

Lucien Bouchard, who, until the day before, had remained rather unobtrusively in the shadow of Jacques Parizeau, now threw himself into the campaign like an army general. The manoeuvre had no equal in Canadian political history. Never before had a provincial premier, leader of a government that was well established, entrusted to a federal MP, who did not have a seat in the National Assembly and therefore did not represent his party, the task of defending his vision in an electoral or referendum campaign. This was a novel, incredible, almost quirky, situation, of the kind that the NO camp would try to turn to their advantage. Some federalists would say it had every appearance of being a coup d'état, an attempted putsch. Others tried to downplay the Bouchard effect, reminding voters that, if the YES side won, it was still Parizeau who would be running the ship. Some would interpret it as proof that discord was beginning to take root inside the YES camp, while others would maintain that the ill-feeling had already spread. The *Globe and Mail*, for example, claimed it was more than discord, it was revolt: "A revolt brewing in sovereigntist ranks led Premier Jacques Parizeau to hand over the reins of the Yes campaign to Bloc Québécois (leader) Lucien Bouchard, sources say," wrote its Quebec correspondent, Rhéal Séguin. According to the journalist, Bouchard's appointment was not part of a strategy planned long in advance. "Sources who asked not to be identified," he added, "confirmed that pressure to put Mr. Bouchard at the head of the campaign erupted last week when it became evident the Yes side was headed for certain defeat."[2]

The *Globe and Mail* article appeared Monday morning. A few hours later, in the "ephemeral park"[3], before a crowd of 300 people, Lucien Bouchard responded: "This is not a one-person campaign. I bring negotiating experience and a 10-year acquaintance with the federal scene. This is not about establishing me as the key figure."

Discourse in the NO camp was ambiguous: It was still Parizeau who would be at the helm after the referendum. Unless he was shoved aside by Bouchard. It was not just a rhetorical question: Had Lucien Bouchard himself wished to push Jacques Parizeau out of his position as head of the YES camp and, ultimately, as leader of the Parti Québécois? Bloc Québécois organizer, Bob Dufour, denies this emphatically: "We never had that in mind," he says. "There was never a strategy (of that kind), we never discussed, or even touched on, the idea of taking Mr. Parizeau's job." And all the testimonies on this point were unanimous: no one could have pushed Parizeau aside unless he pushed himself aside, which he did when he understood it was the only way to win his referendum. Dufour admits, however, that the pressure was great. "I went on the tours, I covered a lot of territory, I talked to the people, got a sense of how they felt, saw how they reacted," he says today. "They were telling us, 'You, Mr. Bouchard, you should be in Mr. Parizeau's place. You would be a much better leader for the PQ.' Yes, that's what they were telling us!"[4]

The whole manoeuvre was so unusual, that even Lisette Lapointe felt compelled to say, in an interview with the *Journal de Montréal*, "there was no competition between Jacques Parizeau and Lucien Bouchard."[5] Bouchard himself had to rush to clarify his position vis-à-vis the leader of the YES camp. He did so on Monday, October 9, on Radio-Canada's *Le Midi Quinze* program, insisting he was not taking Jacques Parizeau's place at the head of the YES forces. "He remains the *primus inter pares*, the first to intervene," he said. "My role is to carry out any mandate given to me." He used the opportunity to dispel any misunderstanding in the minds of the public about a second referendum on negotiations between Quebec and Ottawa.

So far, the YES camp had been giving the impression it was not really ready. It was behind in the polls. It was likewise behind in preparing for its campaign, which had not yet officially begun. While its machinery sat waiting for the government order, the signal to swing into action, Daniel Johnson's tours were getting into their stride in the final week of September in the Bas-du-Fleuve and in Montreal. The NO posters were everywhere and the billboards, prepared far in advance, loudly proclaimed the virtues of federalism. The message was aggressive: the red and blue signs displayed the word "separation" split in two by a huge NO, resulting in "sepa-NO-ration." It was in total violation of the law that the NO camp, during the weekend of September 16, had thousands of signs erected along the expressways and the provincial highways. In Quebec City, Laurier Boulevard and Grande Allée were bedecked with NO posters, which appeared in the newspapers and on television as well. On September 19, the Deputy Minister of Transport, Yvan Demers, sent a letter to the two committee directors, Benoît Savard of the NO and Normand Brouillet of the YES, to remind them of the conditions for erecting signs along the roads. The law forbade any signage "affecting the roads, outside of a formal electoral or referendum campaign"[6] and there was no formal campaign in process as long as the writs had not been issued. The deputy minister ordered the NO camp to remove its posters, failing which, members of his ministry's staff would do so. The NO camp immediately demanded an injunction before the courts, citing that a Ministry of Transport official had given them authorization to put up the posters. The injunction was thrown out. The City of Quebec, too, demanded that the two committees, the YES and the NO, respect the law until the start of the referendum campaign. During this time, the

YES camp was waiting for the necessary funds and the authorization to spend them, which finally came, in accordance with the provisions of the law, on Sunday, October 8.

As of that day, everything changed, and it wasn't just because of the signs. "Before Mr. Bouchard's appointment, it looked as if there was a kind of ceiling on the potential number of votes," says Jacques Parizeau's chief of staff, Jean Royer. "People remained impervious to our arguments. Then, suddenly, they opened up, the same people who, the day before, had been closed."[7] These people would turn everything upside down for the YES campaign organization, right down to the tiniest details. As soon as Bouchard hit the campaign trail, the YES side experienced a new effervescence, "an infatuation with Mr. Bouchard that we had not dared to hope for. But it was working!" says Alain Lupien, coordinator of the financing campaign for the YES. The YES organization had established a standard for the size of rooms where meetings would be held. But "we had to review all that," Lupien adds. "We even had to check, for example, whether we had a hall that could accommodate 2,000 people, and what to do if it became overcrowded. We always had to have equipment on hand to broadcast outside the hall in case of an overflow. We could never tell ahead of time how large the attendance at an event would be. Rather than having to shrink the meeting rooms so they would look fuller, we were now having to figuring out how to expand them, so they could hold as many people as possible."[8]

The NO camp was more shaken up than they let on. "The effect was real," recalls Jean Charest. "This changed the referendum campaign. We felt a difference right away. At first, none of us, including myself, could figure out how to begin to deal with all of this. It reminded me of the 1993 federal campaign. Mr. Bouchard was very popular and, frankly, his opponents did not know how to approach him. You could not attack him personally. The NO camp was simply frustrated and was looking for a way to combat his influence without appearing to attack him personally."[9] Bob Rae saw immediately that the campaign dynamic was going to change. Daniel Johnson had to take a different tack in his speeches. "Mr. Johnson was a very practical man, had a very practical approach," says Rae, who points out that Johnson had thus far managed, to a certain extent, to keep the debate focused around the need for improvement in the relationship with the federal government. But when Bouchard arrived on the scene, "there (wasn't) any question," adds Rae, "that (he would play on) the mythology of Meech, his view that there were a series of betrayals, a series of efforts, being stabbed in the back, the Night of Long Knives, and an English Canada that somehow had turned its back on Quebec." For Rae, Bouchard used this mythology to rouse the resentment lingering in the psyches of Quebecers.

The NO camp felt powerless to attack Lucien Bouchard's political career; it had been too short and he had handled his responsibilities well. Nor could they attack his personal life, as it was not in the political tradition of this country to do so, and in any event, what did they have on him? How, then, was this man to be confronted? The federal strategists decided to organize discussion groups. "We did studies to see how we could counter the Bouchard effect," John Parisella admits today. "Was this effect so strong because our society lacked a critical sense? In the focus groups, we showed participants images of Mr. Bouchard and asked them: Do you find that disturbing? Do you agree with that? When they didn't agree with what Mr. Bouchard was saying, they replied, 'Maybe that isn't what he really meant!'"[10] In Parisella's view, the problem they faced was rooted in the realm of the irrational, in a realm where discourse and dialectic no longer had a place.

"My moment of realization that something had changed," says Daniel Johnson, "was when reporters told us they had seen someone touching his (Lucien Bouchard's) jacket with a rosary, in Sainte-Marie de Beauce or wherever. I had never seen anyone do that; perhaps in other countries, but certainly not in Quebec, in 1995. It was partly due to a mass phenomenon. We were no longer in a referendum debate, we were in an episode that revolved around someone's personality, his story, his way of going about things, his way of expressing himself."[11] Even Jean Chrétien, who had met some rather exceptional characters in the course of his political career, could not get over it: "There were people practically asking him to bless the fleur-de-lys, come on!" he exclaims, even today. "You have to admit, it was just a bit unusual. I've been in politics a long time, but that kind of situation, I had never witnessed that before. It wasn't politics anymore. I don't want to sound like Mr. Ryan, but it was like the hand of God intervening in the minds of a lot of people. We had to (deal) with that reality. People thought that he was the Messiah."[12] A lot of former members of the NO camp use the word Messiah to describe the Bouchard effect. "One night," recalls Pierre-Claude Nolin, "while I was watching the news, I observed what people were like in Mr. Bouchard's presence, how they, in fact, wanted to touch him. I saw people who were looking at him almost as if he were a Messiah who would come and save Quebecers. It was very worrisome."[13]

Even people in the YES camp couldn't get over it. "He was a walking miracle, making his way through Quebec," says Guy Chevrette. The former minister recalls a rally in which Bouchard was taking part. It was Friday, October 13, at Marie-Charlotte School in Joliette. Everyone wanted to touch him. "The walls seemed about to cave in," he says. "He had just suffered the flesh-eating disease, he had struggled, he had come through, it was considered a miracle. This had made an impact on the public. He was charismatic."[14] "He was almost more popular than Brother André at the height of his glory," admits Bob Dufour. "It was like a religious phenomenon."[15] "People wanted to touch him the way they want to touch a holy man, as if he had come close to God," recalls Alain Lupien.[16]

For Pierre-Paul Roy, who had been part of his entourage, the Bouchard effect could be explained by many of the man's personality traits. "There was, first of all, some of the same effect there was with René Lévesque," he says. "And then, Mr. Bouchard was an important man, who came from Ottawa, who had sacrificed a career as a minister and as an ambassador, who had become simply an MP, who took the bus, who formed a party... And he had a reassuring side to him, which Mr. Parizeau did not. He was a man with a lot of charm and, in politics, he used that charm, consciously and appropriately. And, obviously, there had been the illness. We cannot disregard his illness. That is what created the empathy. It was a blend of all those things."[17]

In hindsight, Jacques Parizeau draws a parallel with the Trudeaumania of the seventies. "Pierre Elliott Trudeau was followed by hordes of people who kissed him, kissed his clothing," he says. "Those are important things, and one must learn how to utilize them. It's not something you plan, but it's something you can exploit. It was not a coincidence, for example, that when Pierre Trudeau was speaking before a Montreal Chamber of Commerce, he suddenly found himself surrounded by twenty attractive women who had been waiting for an hour and a half on the lower level of the *Cercle canadien de Montréal* (Canadian Club of Montreal). You know, there's the spontaneous and the less spontaneous!"[18] In the YES camp, had they "exploited" the "Bouchardmania"? Jacques Parizeau was non-committal: "I wouldn't know anything about that," he replies. "You would have to talk to his organizer, a remarkable organizer, the best one I've ever met!"[19] According to organizer Bob Dufour, there was no need to orchestrate "Bouchardmania." "People were holding his hand, they felt as though they were talking to a saint," he says, to indicate no staging had been necessary. "It had nothing to do with logic. There was just something there. I've been in politics for a long time. A phenomenon like that, I have never seen!"[20]

To just what extent did Lucien Bouchard's disability make him the charismatic man he became? During his time in hospital, three quarters of Quebecers stated they had confidence in him, an unprecedented level of popularity in polls on political figures. Did he then seek to take advantage of this during the referendum campaign in order to win greater sympathy from the public? "Mr. Bouchard did not make a display of his disability," says Alain Lupien. "He never allowed it to limit his activities. When we constructed stages for his meetings, there was no question of adapting them to allow him to slip out by a side exit. He wanted to be the politician he was and walk as all the other politicians had to walk. Remember the Saint-Jean parade. He could very easily have done the route by car, and the people would have accepted it. No, he wanted to walk. He never sought to capitalize on his disability. He had charisma. He didn't need any choreography."[21]

Regardless of how Lucien Bouchard's new role was perceived by the people or how important the notion of partnership would henceforth be in the YES campaign, Jacques Parizeau continued to conduct himself as its leader and to maintain the same discourse on the sovereignty of Quebec. He had, in the days just prior, strongly resented the heavyweights of the Quebec economy intervening in the referendum debate. He responded by convening a meeting of some 400 small and medium-sized business leaders, who were not against the march toward sovereignty. "I asked Bernard Landry to gather the business people who were willing to give witness to their Quebec identity and demonstrate that they did not have an inferiority complex towards English Canada,"[22] he says. But it was Pierre Péladeau, the CEO of Quebecor, who dealt the final blow to Beaudoin, Desmarais and Garcia when the president of Quebecor asked Bombardier's CEO to kindly "shut up." While acknowledging that business people had the right to express their preferences in the referendum campaign, he stated in a telephone interview with Le Devoir that for a corporation the size of Bombardier to claim it could be seriously threatened in an independent Quebec was "bullshit." "And it is not the place of a company CEO to circulate a letter to its employees in an attempt to influence their decision,"[23] he added. It was a clarification that carried weight and the sovereigntists applauded.

Meanwhile, the leader of the NO camp stayed on course: he spoke of the economy. In the kingdom of Lucien Bouchard, before about a hundred people gathered in a Chicoutimi hotel, Daniel Johnson warned that Quebec independence posed a threat to some 3,500 jobs, in particular, at the Bagotville airbase. "If Quebec separates," he said, "we will not be stronger, we will not be richer, and there will be fewer jobs for young people."[24] He stressed that Quebec was dependent on equalization payments, "the 3.5 billion dollars that Quebec receives, every year, from British Columbia, Alberta and Ontario."[25]

In the rest of Canada, however, it was not the matter of equalization payments that was worrying Canadians, but rather, the referendum itself. They considered it one of the greatest problems Canada had to deal with. An Angus Reid poll showed that West Coast inhabitants were experiencing greater anxiety over the referendum than Quebecers themselves, an anxiety fuelled by their premier, Michael Harcourt, who conjured up its "terrible consequences."[26]

Harcourt's message got through. In a small bar at Simon Fraser University, students of the Centre for Canadian Studies posted a notice inviting all those interested in what was going on in Quebec to a meeting. Part-time student and professional landscape painter Judith Atkinson was among those who responded. Along with four other students,[27] she decided they had to tell Quebecers just how much importance the rest of the country attached to their being part of Canada. The action plan was to send as many postcards as possible to people in Quebec. As a teacher at the Shadbolt Centre for the Arts in Burnaby, Atkinson was able to recruit the help of her young pupils, aged six to nine. Across from the small bar at the university, she set up easels where anyone who wanted could create their own postcard, using the felt-tipped markers provided. If they were not feeling inspired, they used the ones the children had made, which were prominently displayed, strung across a kind of clothesline. Some had Quebec postal addresses on them, while others did not. No problem: telephone directories were available at a nearby bookstore! "So people really lined up," Atkinson recalls today. "We had two days and people, really, for the time we were there, it was packed." Some received replies to their postcards!

There was another student at Simon Fraser University who was just as passionate about events in Quebec, but for a different reason: Anouk Bélanger, a doctoral student at the School of Communications, was from Quebec. She decided to explain to the campus population, through the university newspaper, that a YES or a NO could have multiple meanings. "I was fed up," she says today to justify her article, "with answering people who only wanted to know if I was going to vote YES or NO. I was also fed up with seeing how the YES and the NO were being understood in the news media over there. It always revolved around economic arguments. There was no reference to cultural or national identity."[28] In her short text, she proceeded to explain how there could be a deeper reason for voting YES, there could be a more nuanced YES, and there could even be a YES expressed out of pure spite. She expected that by writing this article, she would be spared the flood of questions she was being asked every day. But the result was just the opposite. She became the authority and the public relations department of the university gave her name to any reporter in the city who wanted to talk to an expert on the subject.

Anouk Bélanger agreed to take part, with her sister Sophie who was visiting Vancouver, in a phone-in show, hosted by David Abbott, a personality known for his flamboyant language and frequent lapses into demagoguery. Planned for just twenty minutes, the show stretched into two hours and the two sisters emerged rather battle-scarred. "We went on radio with a host who liked to provoke argument," recalls Sophie. "And we knew our political opinions were controversial!"[29] "A lot of times we walked right into the lion's mouth," says her sister Anouk. "I realized that to explain a political position, when you do not really have mastery of the language, is difficult. When you go out on a limb and do it anyway, you end up lending credibility to the stereotypical image of the Quebecer who claims to be a sovereigntist, but can't explain why. The language becomes a bit of a handicap and reinforces the stereotype of the emotional and irrational young person who has a hard time explaining him or herself."[30]

The economy continued to dominate the referendum debate, especially with the rather jittery behaviour of the dollar. On Tuesday, October 10, the Bank of Canada raised its rate by 13 points, to 6.63%, in order to bolster a dollar that was gradually losing ground to its U.S. counterpart. It now stood at 74.89 cents U.S. on the North American interbank market. In Quebec, Jacques Parizeau promised, in a TVA appearance, not to increase the tax burden of Quebecers in the first two years following a YES victory. He used the opportunity to address the remarks Johnson had made in Chicoutimi. He maintained that, far from prompting the closure of the base at Bagotville, independence would allow it to increase its staff, which could translate into 250 additional jobs. Daniel Johnson, with great self-assurance, came back to

Parizeau with a shattering reply: No way would a YES victory create employment, it would bring about the loss of 92,300 jobs! He claimed he was not being alarmist: he was able to produce a whole range of studies by experts, including five that were part of the forty or so commissioned by Minister Le Hir. "Researchers unanimously agree," said the leader of the NO. "No study claiming an improvement in the employment situation in a separated Quebec exists or can be located."[31] False, replied Employment Minister Louise Harel. On the contrary, a sovereign Quebec would generate some 25,000 new jobs, deriving from increased investments in the fields of research and development as well as from the purchase of goods and services.

The federalists did not deviate from their course, hammering home the economy. They scanned the Le Hir studies for elements supporting their option. In Ottawa, Marcel Massé, minister of Intergovernmental Affairs, announced that due to the climate of political uncertainty, the minister of Finance would postpone until after the referendum his speech on the state of the economy, which was normally delivered in mid-October. He added: "Lucien Bouchard's popularity was having a negative impact on the markets."[32] He, too, made use of a Le Hir study, one by Professor Marcel Saint-Germain, to assert that "job losses in the public service (would) be very heavy, perhaps on the order of 15 to 18,000 in the Outaouais region."

That was too much for Lucien Bouchard. Standing in the yard of a plant in Chambly, he shouted at a group of reporters: "I don't want to hear anything about those Le Hir studies. They are not my studies. They are his. They're history as far as I'm concerned. That campaign is over." He admitted he had hardly read a word of those 47 studies, which someone had simply plunked on his desk one day, and which had been prepared at a cost of about 10 million dollars from the public purse. He had no use for them in his speeches. But there was a snag the YES faced in this regard: Jacques Parizeau continued to use most of these studies—which he considered quite valid—to support his economic arguments. Ten years after the fact, when he is asked to recall this episode, the former premier maintains his Olympian reserve: "I saw very clearly the deeply embarrassing situation he would get himself into," he says. "We saw it when he became premier and wanted to resume the fight for sovereignty. He had to commission a new set of studies, saying that the previous ones were irrelevant. The fact of the matter is that he was not acquainted with the content of those studies. Yet, no responsible government could avoid paying attention to them if it wanted to organize a country effectively. He would learn not to make those kinds of statements."[33] Guy Chevrette, who felt the malaise created by Bouchard's statement, explains it this way: "To him, it was not the accumulation of studies that would advance the cause among the people. It might be important for an intellectual class wanting to pave the way for the transition from federalism to sovereignty, but he felt they were receiving too much emphasis. To him, the real issue was one of pride, our ability to achieve…"[34] It was Lucien Bouchard's way of trying to distract people from the economy as the principal campaign issue. And John Parisella drew this conclusion: "There was no one to challenge him on what he said," he notes. "The campaign began to revolve very much around one person."[35]

Former prime minister Brian Mulroney made his first public statement in the *New York Times* a week after his wife Mila announced his intention to a NO gathering at the Metropolis. Published on the op-ed page of the widely read American daily, under the title "Quebec separatists want it both ways," Mulroney mocked the sovereigntists. "How unfair has the Canadian state been to justify the break-up of one of the world's leading nations?" he asked. "Not very, because the principal promise separatists make is that after seceding, Quebecers will be able to retain their Canadian citizenship. And Canadian passports. And Canadian currency. And Canada's economic union. How brazen!" The text was accompanied by a cartoon: the large head of a baby who was bawling its eyes out, its forehead marked with a fleur-de-lys and each tear identified with the letter C.

The reply was instant. "How is it," Lucien Bouchard challenged him, during a press conference in Sorel, "that this man feels the need to escape to the safety of the United States to make this kind of statement? It's because that's where he'll be the least booed!"[36] He was alluding to the way Mulroney had been received by a large crowd of onlookers gathered in front of Notre-Dame Basilica in Montreal, when he and his wife stepped out of their limo to attend the wedding of Céline Dion and René Angelil on December 17, 1994. The weekend prior to the publication of his text in the *New York Times*, Mulroney passed it around, during a summit of former world leaders in Colorado Springs, to Margaret Thatcher, François Mitterrand, Mikhaïl Gorbachev and George Bush Senior. Two of them, Bush and Gorbachev, took the liberty of giving their opinion on the referendum. Bouchard didn't miss a beat: during the same press conference, he delivered these jabs in passing. He recalled that Bush was a friend of Mulroney, which would explain his support of the NO side, and that Gorbachev, having overseen the dissolution of the Soviet Union, had little to teach Quebecers about unity, especially as he had treated its minorities in a "disgraceful" and "inconceivable" manner.

Five days before a televised debate was scheduled to be broadcast, the YES camp hesitated. They demanded equal distribution of airtime for the consequences of a YES vote and the consequences of a NO vote. Their demand was met. Then they presented a series of new conditions and tried to cast doubt on the impartiality of the consortium of television networks. Actually, it was really starting to look as if the YES camp did not want a televised debate. Lucien Bouchard's arrival at the forefront had boosted the sovereigntist campaign, and strategists feared a setback if there was a debate pitting Jacques Parizeau, alone, against Daniel Johnson. The premier was self-assured and knew his material better than Lucien Bouchard, but his pompous tone and his sometimes-caustic humour had the wrong effect when shot close up on the television screen. Lucien Bouchard, in contrast, always found the right word, the right tone and he displayed an empathy that could move two or three million television viewers. Furthermore, Parizeau could not delegate to his partner a debate that the NO camp would turn down and certainly greet with scornful laughter. As a result, already in the second week of the referendum campaign, it appeared that in all likelihood, there would be no debate.

Meanwhile, Radio-Canada was getting into hot water over its refusal to broadcast one of the two YES advertisements. The ad consisted of a series of written statements: "We want a strong Quebec," "We want a French Quebec," "We want full employment for Quebec," punctuated by images of Jean Chrétien, Daniel Johnson, André Ouellet and Lucienne Robillard, shouting a resounding NO. Radio-Canada insisted that they demonstrate that each of the NOs had indeed been expressed in relation to each of the statements. Clearly such a demonstration was not possible. But, as the other broadcasters did not have the same scruples, Radio-Canada had to endure a volley of criticism from the YES camp and was reproached by the Telecaster Committee of Canada as well. "There is nothing here that goes against our guidelines," declared its president, Patricia Beatty. In the opinion of communications specialist Claude Cossette, "It was a case of cold feet."

Daniel Johnson, who, up to this point, had been setting the tone for the NO campaign, felt that he was now on the defensive, now that Lucien Bouchard had arrived on the scene. He needed to get voters to refocus their attention on Jacques Parizeau, who would still be the leader in Quebec the day after the referendum. "Running out of arguments now that he has lost the economic battle, Jacques Parizeau has decided to lie to Quebecers," he declared before the members of the Saint-Jérôme Chamber of Commerce. "He is relying squarely on falsehoods when he estimates the deficit of a sovereign Quebec, when he does not admit the massive losses in employment and when he promises he will not raise taxes for two years."[37]

Despite a Parti Québécois poll, conducted among 1,285 voters two days after Lucien Bouchard's appointment, which placed the two options more or less neck and neck, the federalist camp still denied the evidence. It maintained that its own surveys indicated that the NO side was ahead by six points and that, even if it had lost a point, the federalist option was increasingly taking root in the intentions of the voters. Daniel Johnson claimed that the YES side was in panic, which did not, however, prevent the loonie from losing a little more of its shine, the stock market from becoming more and more jittery, or Bob Rae from speaking of an unnecessary tragedy.

On Tuesday, October 11, the Crees reappeared on the referendum landscape. They published a 500-page work entitled *Sovereign
Injustice*,[38] in which they reaffirmed that the Aboriginal nations
have a right to self-determination, which includes the right to
remain a part of Canada. The work, which reproduced the key portions of the study presented in February 1992 before the United
Nations Human Rights Commission, relied on a wide range of
analyses and studies by Canadian and international specialists. It
maintained, in particular, that international law provided no basis
for a Quebec that wanted to keep its current borders. The document
was published only in English, but the Crees also addressed francophone Quebecers by purchasing a full page of advertising in most
of the French-language dailies. Among other things, it had a map il-
lustrating the size of the Cree territory, before it was annexed to
Quebec in 1898,[39] which the Aboriginal people intended to retain as
their own, should Quebec become independent. "They created
Canada, nobody ever asked us if we want (ed) to be part of Canada,
they didn't. Do you think we're going to miss the boat this time?"
said Matthew Coon Come.

"We were always careful to get into that kind of debate," adds the
Cree chief, "because it would be on the principles of (the) right to self-
determination. Under international law, do the indigenous people
have that same right? And what are the criteria for being recognized as
a people and as a nation? To be recognized as having the right to self-
determination? Those were the arguments that we pushed for." Coon
Come did not hide the fact that his community feared Quebec. "There
were fears that there might be retaliation (for) the position we took,
that they might send in the police force. We said what could be worse,
they trampled on our rights, they keep cutting trees and they keep
flying (over) our lands and we're not going to say boo?" Coon Come
claims that the Aboriginal people would never have talked of secession
from Quebec if the Parti Québécois had not done so. But, once the
thing was made possible, they pressured the federal government to announce its intentions, should Quebec become independent. "We don't
like the Indian Act, we never did," he says. "Why is there an act called

the Indian Act, when there's none for the Jewish, none for the Italian, none for any other immigrants that came to this country?"

The *La Presse* daily, however, cast a bit of a shadow over the claims of the Crees by arguing, two days later, that the Aboriginal people would not have the right to secede.[40] Relying on an internal document of the Privy Council, written back in December 1994, the newspaper asserted that the Aboriginal people could not separate from either an independent Quebec or Canada. The document, which was drafted in legal terms, nevertheless stated—thus offering some consolation to the Aboriginal people—that it was "especially the political factors that would determine what was really going to happen." Political factors included, particularly, the way Quebec would treat its indigenous minority, that is whether, for example, there would be flagrant violation of human rights or attempted genocide. The study went further: Should Quebec become independent, "it (was) impossible to say what Canada's obligations would be towards the Aboriginal peoples of Quebec." It was the courts that would have to decide, and it was not ruled out that Ottawa's obligations would be totally transferred to Quebec.

An unexpected source of support for the NO side came from the Lower North Shore. The president of the fishermen's association maintained that, in an independent Quebec, its members would suffer huge losses because they would lose access to the fishing zones of the Atlantic Provinces. "There are two industries on the Lower North Shore," said Randy Jones, "fishing and unemployment. And both are federal jurisdictions!"[41] Brian Tobin, the federal minister of Fisheries, did not let the opportunity pass him by: "Are Nova Scotians going to accept people from another country fishing just off their coastline? Are the Newfoundlanders going to accept fishermen from another country fishing off their shores?"[42] The YES camp had its answer all ready: "Just plain geography makes it clear that Quebec would own, and have complete sovereignty over, a very large proportion of the Gulf of Saint Lawrence,"[43] said Bernard Landry. Jacques Parizeau reacted more sharply: "Mr. Tobin has got to be totally kidding himself," he said. "By becoming a sovereign country, we will be opening up to Quebec fishermen not only the waters of the Gulf, but also international waters."[44] Despite the confidence displayed by both parties, the issue of fishing rights in the Gulf was so difficult that, were Quebec to have become independent, it could have ended up before the International Court in The Hague. The dispute was reminiscent of, albeit more complex than, the one that existed between Canada and France over fishing rights around the Saint-Pierre-et-Miquelon islands, which did wind up before the International Court.

Three weeks before the referendum, Jacques Parizeau still found himself having to combat the notion of "renewed federalism." It was as prevalent in federalist quarters, anxious to offer an alternative to still undecided voters, as among YES supporters. For example, businessman Jean-Denis Côté of Groupe Masson, who was on the business people's committee for the YES, affirmed that, although he was a federalist, he would be voting YES, in order to "give Lucien Bouchard a strong mandate, more leverage for negotiating a thorough renewal of federalism."[45]

Daniel Johnson was well aware that this was a strong sentiment among people and, on October 12, during a radio phone-in show on CHEF in Granby, he promised that, if the NO side won, he would work with the premiers of the other provinces for changes to Canadian federalism. Lucienne Robillard and Jean Charest followed suit. Touring the Saguenay–Lac-Saint-Jean area, the federal minister declared that Canada had no choice but to open itself up to a decentralization of powers. The Conservative leader, in the meantime, speaking to the *Jeune barreau de Montréal* (Junior Bar Association of Montreal), stated that the constitutional status quo had ceased to exist and that the current state of public finances would oblige Ottawa to transfer more and more power to the provinces. But it was an argument that couldn't be resolved and, throughout the referendum period, the promises of change to the federal system were up against Jean Chrétien's rigid stance and the scepticism of the sovereigntists, who missed no opportunity to recall the Night of the Long Knives and the Meech and Charlottetown failures.

A serious problem for the strategists was the ambivalence shown by Quebecers: two thirds of them remained deeply attached to

Canada; almost all of them felt attached to Quebec;[46] 68% believed the French language in Quebec was threatened and half felt that independence would not change that. On October 11, the *Mouvement Québec français* entered the fray, in defence of the language. The NO camp recognized the attachment that Quebecers have to their language as an incentive to vote YES; so they brought out one of their big guns: Claude Ryan. According to the former director of *Le Devoir* and one-time Liberal party leader, any claims that the language would disappear and that Montreal would become a city with an anglophone majority were false.[47] "The number of people with French as their mother tongue decreased between 1981 and 1991, by 9.1% in the Island of Montreal and 3.1% in the city of Montreal," admitted the former minister responsible for the French Language Charter, before the *Amis de Cité libre* group, gathered at the *Maison du Egg Roll*. He thus refused to speak of galloping anglicization. "But, over the last 50 years, between 1941 and 1991," he said, "the percentage of the population whose mother tongue is French, has risen from 81.6 to 82.5%."

Claude Ryan's presentation to the *Amis de Cité libre* was however overshadowed by an incident that would stoke the YES discourse in the days following. Political analyst Josée Legault was in the audience. She headed a committee set up by the Quebec government to assess the situation of the French language in Quebec since the adoption of the French Language Charter (Bill 101).[48] Minutes before Ryan began his speech, Senator Jacques Hébert turned to the person beside him, while pointing to Josée Legault, and said, "That's her, the *vache séparatiste* (separatist cow) I was telling you about a moment ago." Several people overheard him, and his remark reached the ears of Josée Legault. She would probably not have reacted if Hébert had called her a *maudite séparatiste* (damned separatist), but the word "cow" was going too far: she was insulted and said so publicly. At first, the Senator pleaded extenuating circumstances: it was a private conversation. That was not enough and, five days later, he apologized: "The words used were absolutely unacceptable," he said. But the damage had been done. The YES camp soon had stickers printed displaying a little cow. Jacques Parizeau had fun with it when he spoke to a group of women in a Montreal restaurant, gathered to honour Josée Legault. First he commended her for her tolerance; then he quipped, "We, on the YES side, believe that tolerance is *vachement* (a heck of a lot) better than arrogance." And anyway, once they had independence, he told them, Quebecers wouldn't have to pay the salaries of Ottawa's senators any more.[49]

On Friday, October 13, a political and diplomatic storm broke out in the referendum sky. Jean Chrétien was holding a reception in Montreal to honour the Prime Minister of the People's Republic of China, Li Peng, there on an official visit to Canada. All the provincial premiers had been invited and had received their invitations as far back as November 1994. It was Li Peng who had chosen the year, 1995, to mark the 25th anniversary of the reestablishment of diplomatic relations between the two countries, and it was also he who had chosen the month of his visit. Jean Chrétien did not know, at that time, that the referendum would take place at the end of October, and he had chosen Montreal for the reception because, during the weekend selected by the Chinese prime minister, the NDP would be holding a convention in Ottawa, the one at which Alexa McDonough was elected leader. Although he had received his invitation much earlier, it was only at the beginning of October that Jacques Parizeau wrote the Prime Minister to turn down the invitation, reproaching him for holding a diplomatic meeting in Montreal right in the middle of the referendum campaign. In fact, Parizeau did not like finding himself on a par with the other nine provincial premiers. However, the situation in the YES camp was further complicated when Lucien Bouchard announced, while on tour in the Chambly region, that he, in his capacity as leader of the official opposition in Ottawa, had requested a meeting with the foreign dignitary. The federal government's response did not sound promising: The request had come rather late; they would see whether a visit could still be arranged despite Li Peng's full schedule. The day before the reception in Montreal, China's ambassador to Ottawa wrote Bouchard: The visitor's schedule was such that he would not be able to meet with the leader of the opposition.

On the same day, two polls gave each of the camps something to chew on. The Gallup poll, conducted with 1,013 participants at the beginning of the week and published in *La Presse*, put the distance between the two options at six points with the NO in the lead. The data prior to the pro rata distribution of the undecided vote indicated that the YES was still below 40%, four points behind the NO. But on the same day the *Journal de Montréal* published the results of another survey, this one by Léger Marketing, done using the same number of voters: the NO was ahead by only one and a half points. This survey had a particularly encouraging aspect for the YES camp: the results had been weighted with the help of statistics from the 1991 census and, moreover, prior to the distribution of the undecided vote, the YES was ahead by two and a half points. This did not prevent the NO camp from maintaining publicly that they held an 8% majority. Former finance minister, André Bourbeau, even said that he did not accord much credibility to Léger Marketing. Ottawa projected the same outer calm: Jean Chrétien stated he was not worried; the strategy was working well and should be maintained.

Behind closed doors, however, fear was taking hold in the NO camp: an internal poll produced the same results as Léger Marketing. The strategists continued to search for a way to oppose Lucien Bouchard and refocus their campaign on Jacques Parizeau. They decided to give Jean Charest a more important role. He was a better orator and more populist than Daniel Johnson and Lucienne Robillard. In his riding of Vaudreuil, where a thousand people had crowded into the Île-Perrot community centre, Johnson went on the offensive: What Parizeau has always wanted, he said in essence, is separation, and Bouchard's appointment as chief negotiator is of no consequence because there will be nothing to negotiate. In fact, Johnson's camp was in desperate need of a shot of adrenalin. And help did come, but not from within. It was Lucien Bouchard himself who would provide the service, by getting himself into a predicament.

The YES camp noted, in poll after poll, that women were more lukewarm than men towards the sovereigntist option. Two thirds of undecided voters were women. Therefore, the YES camp decided this was the group to target. Women of all backgrounds—the arts, politics, unions—went door to door, distributed flyers and took over Montreal's subway stations. Lucien Bouchard likewise rolled up his sleeves for the battle to win this segment of the population, which had to be stirred up at all costs, if the referendum was not to be lost. On Saturday, October 14, addressing some 400 women gathered in Anjou, in Northeast Montréal, he began by decrying the cuts to social services that the Harris government had just imposed in Ontario. He then went on to make a remark that would haunt him for a long time afterwards. He asked, "Do you think it makes sense that we have so few children in Quebec? We are one of the white races that have the fewest children. That means something. It means that we have not resolved our family problems."[50]

These words provoked an immediate general protest from the most diverse sources. Jean Charest remembers that Saturday. "I immediately phoned the campaign office to say we had to respond to that."[51] The next morning, he was in Toronto, where his responsibilities as leader of the Conservative party required him to be, and so, it was from the capital of Ontario that he denounced Bouchard's comments. "I can't fathom what he's implying," he declared. "I think it might be that in an independent Quebec, white women would be able to have more babies. It shows a leadership out of control."[52] "Look back at this episode," says Jean Charest today, "and you will see how the media reacted. They forgave Lucien Bouchard immediately. Even Françoise David, of the *Fédération des femmes du Québec* (Quebec women's federation), came to his defence."[53] Furthermore, three days after Bouchard's statement, Daniel Johnson's wife, Suzanne Marcil, wrote to Françoise David to ask her to criticize Bouchard's remarks, which she viewed as "reactionary and humiliating." Françoise David defended her position by saying that "the NO camp was currently trying to convince women that Mr. Bouchard was only interested in their reproductive functions. This is a crass tactic," she said, "and brings to mind the unhappy memory of the Yvette affair."[54] The following day, Françoise David stood by Lucien Bouchard's side as he tried, during a press conference, to calm the storm.

"If I had said that," Jean Chrétien muses today, "I would have been 'hauled over the coals' as they say, big time."[55] Eddy Goldenberg explains why he thinks Quebecers were tolerant of Lucien Bouchard's remarks: "Any other politician who would have said that would probably not have lasted more than five minutes. (But) people forgave him. And a good part of it was the fact that he had miraculously recovered from his illness."

For the first time since being appointed chief negotiator and since running his vigorous campaign, Lucien Bouchard was on the defensive. The day after his statement, he tried to change his focus: "The future of Quebec is now in the hands of women," he said during a trip through the riding of Hochelaga-Maisonneuve. "It is a heavy responsibility but we have confidence in them."[56] There again, he provoked a negative reaction among some, who accused him of wanting women to shoulder the blame for a possible failure of the YES. He was going from bad to worse: "The notion of blaming women for anything whatsoever, regardless of how they vote, would never enter my mind," he said to some reporters bombarding him with questions on the subject.

A communiqué was issued by the organization SOS Racisme denouncing Bouchard's words because they "could be perceived by fascist or white supremacist groups as legitimizing their actions."[57] The leaders of the NO did not let go of this morsel and emulated SOS Racisme, accusing him of racism and sexism. "According to Lucien Bouchard's statement, to be a good Quebecer, you should be white rather than coloured," declared Jean Chrétien. Daniel Johnson in turn claimed, "Lucien Bouchard has found a solution for women who cannot find a job: stay home barefoot and pregnant."[58] They were trying to generate a wave of opposition to Lucien Bouchard's remarks, among women who were sympathetic to the NO side. Some of them accused him of wanting to turn the women of Quebec into "hens-a-laying for the fatherland." "Lucien Bouchard's statements are not acceptable," cried Chantal Corriveau, spokesperson for a group of federalist women. "They are simplistic and condescending with respect to the role of women, which he reduces to that of 'baby-making,' and because he is saying that the choice to be made by a people boils down to a question of race."[59]

Lucien Bouchard, who just wished his comments on the demography of Quebec would quickly fade from memory, tried to dodge the issue another way. He explained that his comments had been made in the context of a speech where he was deploring the fact that Quebecers did not have a real family policy they could count on. During a press briefing he added that the expression "white race" was a "term used by demographers" and that he had never meant to insinuate that women could be "forced" to have children. "I acknowledge that it was clumsy and inappropriate and might lead certain non-white people to feel that they are not part of the people of Quebec," he told journalists. "That was not my intention. I regret that statement and I repudiate it." In a communiqué, issued on the Tuesday, the YES camp wished to counter what they termed the "disinformation" and clarify Bouchard's thought: "He was only reporting a scientific observation made by the demographers: the birthrate in Quebec is down."

For Bouchard, the problem with this defence was that when demographers describe the reproductive state of a collective entity, they rarely refer to the birthrate, which only serves to establish the ratio of the number of births to the average population over a given period. It is possible that there are a smaller number of women of childbearing age and for this to be the reason for a decrease in the number of births. In this scenario, women of childbearing age might be having just as many children, but the number of newborns for the group diminishes. What demographers generally use is the fertility index, which is the ratio of the number of births to the number of women of childbearing age. At the time of Bouchard's statement, the index in Quebec was 1.6 children per woman and it had in fact risen since 1988, when it was as low as 1.37, "the second or third lowest rate in the world," according to demographer Georges Mathews. In 1995, it had a higher index than such countries as Germany, Austria and Spain, but one that was definitely lower than that of the U.S. or the allophone communities of Quebec. Furthermore, it was quite comparable to the index for Canada, which was 1.7.[60] Ten years later, Guy Chevrette tries to downplay the significance of Lucien Bouchard's words: "It wasn't the first time a leader was misinterpreted," he says, "or misquoted... or that a leader didn't explain himself clearly enough for people to grasp what he meant."[61]

The NO camp still felt they had struck a goldmine and did their utmost not to let Bouchard's gaffe fade from view. Daniel Johnson scoffed at his opponent's excuses and, at a meeting he was chairing in Portneuf, became quite virulent: "Lucien Bouchard has been clumsy and insensitive and has demonstrated his ignorance," he charged. "He knows nothing about family policy, nothing about birth policy and nothing about demography. He subscribes to a reactionary vision of the role of women in society."[62]

The more the YES camp sought to get out of this quagmire, the more the blunders piled up. They tried advertising: in the newspapers of Monday, October 16, the YES strategists thought of publishing a page full of job ads with the caption, clearly displayed, "Here's how we picture the future!" There was only one problem: These classified ads, a selection of job offers for women, were not too brilliant. Some of them (for example, "Seeking dynamic, attractive-looking receptionist, etc.") were so sexist that a shamefaced Claude Plante, communications director for the YES committee, had to explain that he had not read these "classifieds" when he approved the advertisement. At a NO rally in Quebec, Jean Charest seized this opportunity and challenged the women supporting the YES side with a resounding "Rise up!" while the member for Sillery, Margaret Delisle, declared, "Quebec women do not walk under the threat of the referendum wand, magic or not."[63] The reference to the "magic wand" was not just random: she wanted to call to mind another remark Lucien Bouchard had let out two days earlier, when, at the head of the YES caravan, he spoke before a thousand people in Hochelaga-Maisonneuve. "Sovereignty," he had said, "has something magical about it. With the wave of a wand, it will transform our entire situation. It will create in us solidarity and unity."

Three unfortunate declarations by Bouchard, two about women and a simplistic one about Quebec's "magical" conversion from a province into a country, did not, however, make any difference.

Despite all the efforts by the NO camp to ridicule them, Lucien Bouchard continued to drum up enthusiasm wherever he went, whether in Hochelaga-Maisonneuve, at CEGEP Ahuntsic or on Île-Perrot. The NO camp couldn't get over it. "The magic wand that was to solve all the problems," recalls Jean Chrétien. "Imagine if me (sic) I had said things like that. Here I see *The Globe and Mail*, *The National Post* and all the gang dumping by the truckload on me. And, in Quebec, nobody picked up the pen and said that makes no sense."[64]

However, bad luck continued to plague the YES camp. A letter written both in French and in English, addressed "to all the cultural minorities in Quebec," was circulating in Brossard, a municipality with a strong multi-ethnic concentration. "I consider my people as being patient, warm and non-violent," the message said. "We have welcomed you with pleasure and warmth on Quebec soil. (...) Your hearts and thoughts are focused on your native country, so you have two homelands. Being a descendent of Quebec land-clearers who died while defending their homeland, I only have one home and I desire no other. (...) If you feel sorrow for having left your native country and still long for it, then go back! If you want to live and prosper as Englishmen and women, I am sure that the Englishmen of other countries will welcome you. An overwhelming 'No' from minorities and immigrants to Quebec's sovereignty will mean for me that you are not interested in showing any kind of respect for me in my own home and country and that you are willing to side with the English people to expropriate me."

The letter, which was simply signed "André Prévost, patriot," had already appeared several days earlier, on the South Shore. People were trying to find the author. The fact that his name did not appear either in the Brossard telephone directory or on the voters list for the electoral riding of La Pinière, where the municipality was located, gave credibility to the theory that it was a hoax. "Who would be interested in doing a thing like that?" wondered the former PQ minister Jocelyne Ouellet, who chaired the YES committee in the riding. "One can only speculate."[65] They suspected it was a plot hatched by the other side. But a local journalist tracked down the author, thus demolishing any theory of deception by the NO camp. André Prévost did indeed exist and he lived in Saint-Constant, a municipality neighbouring Brossard. He announced to journalist Léo Gagnon of the weekly *Brossard Éclair* that he planned to carry out the same action in other localities. Then, he added, "If the NO wins, I do not think I will accept it. My reaction will be very spiteful."

When the major media picked up the news, it sent out a shock wave. During the second week of the campaign, the leading lights of the YES would be using every opportunity to dissociate themselves from the letter and to reaffirm the openness of an independent Quebec to the cultural minorities. "If this letter exists," said Lucien Bouchard at a meeting in Anjou, in northeast Montreal, where the presence of the Italian-Québécois minority was very strong, "I reject this attitude. There is no difference among Quebecers, regardless of their origin." Then, he accompanied Bernard Landry to meet with a group of Muslims at the Radisson Les Gouverneurs hotel in Montreal, where he declared, "Quebecers know that Islam is a great religion, a great culture and a great tradition." Landry added, "You are living proof that you don't have to be a Gagnon or a Tremblay, or have ancestors who tilled the soil on the Île d'Orléans, to be deeply Québécois," he said.

Between the triumphant parade of June 24 and the start of the campaign on October 1, the YES side had travelled a treacherous road. The second week of the campaign had also been tough and it looked as if the remainder might be even tougher. "I was very, very afraid for the referendum campaign," Jean-François Lisée says today. "I was afraid that, in the scrums, the three leaders would start to contradict one another."[66]

For the issue at the heart of the referendum remained ambiguous in the speeches of the spokespersons for the YES. For Jacques Parizeau, it was clear: it was the independence of Quebec. Lucien Bouchard, on the other hand, couldn't conceive of that without a partnership with the rest of Canada, and his campaign had all the more impact with voters because he was riding a wave that threatened to sweep the premier and leader of the YES off the stage entirely. As for Mario Dumont, the YES knew that he was not a sovereigntist and that his membership in the coalition was purely *ad hoc*. The ADQ leader might go four or five days without mentioning the sovereignty declaration. Even more worrisome, he could, at any time, turn his back on it. His necessary alliance with the sovereign-tists was doing his young party harm and the farther they got into the campaign, the more he could feel that when he was out among the people. Ten years later, Mario Dumont acknowledges that signing the agreement was by far the action that cost his party the most, politically. "We lost members," he says. "Our members understood that the ADQ had to be in the YES camp, even if our intent was to have a referendum on partnership. But (when they saw in the media) the image of the three leaders, seated together, signing the agreement of June 12... Of course there were members who left." During the campaign, Dumont therefore had to bend over backwards to explain the significance of that image. "I had to explain that the government's project had recently changed," he adds, "that it was a new project in which Parizeau was one of three play-ers. It was easier for the Bloc and the PQ, but our party represented more moderate nationalists, people who were ready for sovereignty, but in a more moderate form, and others who preferred a major renewal of feder-alism, but were not ready to take the step towards sovereignty..."[67] Jean-François Lisée was therefore afraid Dumont would contradict Jacques Parizeau on the referendum issue, and this concern would haunt the YES strategists throughout the entire campaign.

The second week ended with an unfortunate incident, for which the YES camp could ultimately be held responsible: two incendiary bombs were thrown through the window of a NO committee meeting room in Laval-Ouest. But the week also ended with the hope that there might finally be a televised debate. The most plausible date was Friday, October 20 and it could not be any later. Advance polls would be held October 22 and 23, and it seemed unfair to everyone to push the debate beyond those dates. Negotiations between the two camps and the broadcasters were fiercely pursued. Each side was fully aware that a televised debate would give it the chance to bring the focus of the campaign back to the real issue and to the merits of each of the two op-tions. But before winning the debate itself, each camp first wanted to win the arguments over its structure and content.

CHAPTER X

Panic in the NO Camp

D aniel Johnson believed he had found a way to counter the Bouchard attack: look for examples, throughout the world, of new countries grappling with problems of economic growth. On Sunday, October 15, in his riding of Vaudreuil, he met with some supporters being trained for a door-to-door offensive. He provided them with some ammunition: "There are always huge disappointments after a country separates, even though some think it's going to be easy, as was the case with Czechoslovakia." Then, taking his cue from articles by *Globe and Mail* journalist Jeffrey Simpson, he painted a gloomy picture of the economic situation in Slovakia,[1] which had become independent less than three years earlier: "No-one had anticipated that the standard of living would drop 35%," he said, "that trade would be reduced by 40%, that the common currency would last a mere 39 days and that citizens would not be able to retain dual citizenship."[2]

Johnson's remarks provided a refreshing change in a referendum campaign that was getting bogged down in redundancy and personal attacks. Radio-Canada was spurred to despatch its star journalist, Jean-François Lépine, to Slovakia for a report it planned to broadcast as soon as possible. Without ignoring the dissimilarities between the two situations, the comparison would help to flesh out the theories and hypotheses that had been stoking the debate thus far. Lucien Bouchard immediately categorized Johnson's model as inadmissible. Johnson could forecast the devaluation of Quebec currency to 63 cents if he wanted to, he replied, but the Czech Republic and Slovakia, when they were still Czechoslovakia, had spent sixty years under a Communist regime, whose currency was not internationally recognized. "The Canadian dollar has been around for a long time," he said. "It is quoted on the market. It will work just like before. There will be no change, not even a ripple."[3]

The argument comparing Quebec and Slovakia did indeed have holes in it. In Czechoslovakia, and in Yugoslavia too, for that matter, existing countries were dissolved, thereby losing their legal status. Canada, however, would continue to exist. According to a Privy Council document,[4] a comparison with Pakistan would be more appropriate. It cites a legal opinion from the United Nations Secretariat, which establishes a parallel between the situation that would come about in Canada and the case of India and Pakistan, or, possibly, "the case of the free state of Ireland which separated itself from Great Britain, or that of Belgium which seceded from the Netherlands."

Furthermore, in 1995, Slovakia's economic situation was not as disastrous as the leader of the NO camp was suggesting: while the first year was difficult, mainly because the Slovakian leaders had remained opposed to liberal reforms, the country soon recovered and, in 1995, unemployment declined, the rate of inflation dropped 4 points to an acceptable 10%, and the private sector—still in the developing stages—was already generating 60% of the gross national product. It had a growth rate of 9%, the highest of any European country, its balance of payments was good and the value of its new currency appreciated by 20% during the year.[5] The revival plan devised by Daniel Johnson didn't fly; Slovakia disappeared from the scene of the referendum debate as quickly as it had entered.

The NO camp had excluded Preston Manning from its coalition, but he did not abide by their decision. On that mid-campaign weekend, he showed up in Montreal to present his vision for renewed federalism. The manifesto was entitled *A New Confederation: Building the New Canada with a New Federalism*. Manning's proposal was for a country where the provinces would all be on the same footing and powers decentralized. As Manning did not speak French, it fell to Stephen Harper to explain this project of "federalism and co-operation" to

Quebecers. In an interview that evening, on the program *L'Événement*, which aired on the private network TVA, he outlined the Reform Party's twenty or so proposals—though these were not new. Then, at a press conference, he labelled the notion of distinct society a meaningless expression, stressing the need for deep changes rather than constitutional debates, with which Canadians had been saturated.

The next day, Preston Manning reaffirmed, in an interview with the daily *Le Devoir*, his party's position on the distinct society question. He maintained that the rest of Canada would not grant such recognition. Then, inviting Quebecers to rally to "the great pan-Canadian coalition," he himself rejected the notion of the two founding peoples.[6] Deborah Grey, Reform MP at the time, explains today the rationale for taking that stance: "We are equal partners in Confederation," she says, "and the fact that historically it was the coming together of two founding nations, cool. We're now about a hundred and some years down the road from that and what does that say to people who are as Canadian as you and I, but their mother tongue is neither French or English and their ethnic background is quite different as well. And there are 9 or 10 million Canadians in that (situation). So, the historical part is true but it doesn't fit in this day and age. I don't think Alberta should be enshrined in the constitution to have distinct society status any more than Quebec or anymore that anybody else." The issue of recognition of Quebec as a distinct society would haunt the NO camp right up to the day of the referendum.

Preston Manning was concerned about the fate, in an independent Quebec, of those who would reject separation. He suggested that, in the event of a YES victory, the federal government should help Quebecers to leave the province if they wished: "It would be possible to conclude an agreement to ensure that these rights would be protected by an independent Quebec," he said. "I imagine that it would also be possible to facilitate the move to Canada of those who wished to do so."[7]

The federal political parties gradually tried to define themselves in relation to the reality of a referendum that could result in the breakup of Canada. On the same day that Preston Manning presented what he believed to be the solution to the Quebec-Canada malaise, Alexa McDonough, newly elected to head the New Democratic Party, announced that her party would recognize the results of a referendum, whatever they were: "A decision will be taken by Quebecers on their future," she said. "We totally respect the process and we will respect whatever choice is made." But she was careful not to touch on the partnership question.

The Bouchard effect spread rapidly and dramatically. An opinion poll[8] conducted by SOM one week after the leader of the Bloc Québécois was appointed as chief negotiator, i.e., between October 13 and 16, revealed that the NO was now ahead by only 0.6% and that the two camps were pretty much neck and neck. It confirmed Bouchard's extraordinary popularity: if he were to lead the Parti Québécois in a provincial election, he would obtain almost 55% of the vote while Jacques Parizeau, if he stayed in power, would obtain only 48.7%. As for the ADQ, Mario Dumont's worst fears were being realized: his party was disappearing from Quebec's political map. He obtained only 3.6% of the popular support and the party's members were consumed with anxiety: Dumont's choice to support the YES camp split the membership and some of them went public with their support for the NO.

However, the SOM poll did contain a statistic that pleased Parizeau: half of Quebecers believed that if the YES side won, the absence of a partnership agreement should not prevent Quebec from unilaterally declaring its independence. And there was another statistic, which he preferred not to think about: if the NO side won, 80% of respondents felt that the governments should tackle constitutional changes.

Typically, the value of Quebec shares drops whenever there is an election campaign. This time, however, it rose. A poll conducted among brokers[9] showed that while shares in small Quebec companies were attracting fewer investors, shares in large corporations, like Bombardier and Alcan, had climbed faster than the stock markets as a whole since the beginning of the year. The experts were confused, especially since the markets remained impervious to the progress the

YES side had been making in the last 10 days, and since the dollar was steadying again, staying close to 75 cents U.S. The difference between Canadian and Quebec bonds, when invested for 10 years, was still 55 cents. With this sort of data, the YES camp was inclined to declare that its option was not frightening investors away. But the most plausible explanation, according to the specialists, was that these investors continued to believe that the NO was going to win.

In Fredericton, Frank McKenna read the pulse of Quebecers more accurately than the investors in Toronto or the politicians in Western Canada. He was already worried, and was now beginning to feel truly alarmed. "New Brunswick," he says, "is different from all the other provinces. We live on the edge of the fault line. In the case of Ontario, they're big enough that they don't fall in the hole. In the case of New Brunswick, that's not true." He recalled that a third of the people in his province were francophone and that many of them had close and numerous ties with Quebec. "For us, this is not an academic exercise," he adds. "It's a fight in the family. And it's personal and it's emotional. And around our cabinet table, a huge amount of anxiety was expressed from both francophone and anglophone ministers about the way things were going." Some of these ministers, in particular, those responsible for Culture, Finance and Intergovernmental Affairs, did not hesitate, furthermore, to intervene in Eastern Quebec to make Quebecers aware of the problems that would befall the Acadians if Quebec separated from Canada. Their presence in Rimouski made YES organizers in the region furious, especially PQ member Solange Charest.

Paul Martin, minister of finance in Ottawa, enjoyed strong credibility in all matters concerning the economy. He introduced an alarming statistic into the debate: if Quebec became independent, nearly a million jobs would be lost. Speaking to members of the *Association des professionnels en développement économique du Québec* (Association of economic development professionals of Quebec), he explained that even if the new country was admitted to NAFTA, it could no longer benefit from certain provisions guaranteeing protection because the United States would refuse to apply them. Given the enormous number quoted by Martin, Daniel Johnson reacted immediately, saying Paul Martin's words have been misinterpreted. But Jacques Parizeau, not being one to let an opportunity slide, riposted with, "A week ago, the NO people estimated job losses at under 100,000, today, it's a million. What will it be next week? Ten million? There are only 3,200,000 jobs in Quebec!" He added sarcastically that, at the rate the NO camp was announcing job losses in a sovereign Quebec, the government would have to import unemployed people to meet the sombre predictions "of the horsemen of the Apocalypse."[10] The day after he had made the statement, Paul Martin, while on a visit to Chicoutimi, shifted his position. "I never said these jobs would be lost," he said. "The threat is that Quebec's competitors in the rest of Canada and the United States will be able to harass Quebec exporters."[11]

Thanks to a brochure, which he had ordered to be distributed throughout Quebec, the Chief Electoral Officer unintentionally put Daniel Johnson on the defensive. The purpose of the document was to explain to Quebecers the options being submitted to the vote of the electorate on the day of the referendum. The Referendum Act required him to do so. In the brochure, two long texts, apparently drafted by officials from each camp, presented the advantages of each of the options. The NO text read, in part: "Within the Canadian federation, we form a distinct society. (...) The Quebec government must enjoy full autonomy in the areas within its jurisdiction." Although the NO position was preceded by a word of introduction with his photo, and although it had the tone of his political harangue, Daniel Johnson distanced himself from this text. In an interview with the TVA network, he avoided making any promises that in the event of a NO victory, the Liberal party would recover all Quebec's powers in its areas of jurisdiction. He insisted on the fact that his party had not formulated a constitutional position and that the referendum was only about one thing: the separation of Quebec. But since the document in question was of an official nature, Jacques Parizeau, while in the Ottawa-Hull region, demanded that Jean Chrétien make a statement about its content. He asked the prime minister of Canada if it was true that the federal government would have to withdraw entirely from Quebec's areas of jurisdiction. It was federal Liberal party spokesperson Lucienne Robillard who answered the question on behalf of Chrétien, at the same time remaining vague about the federal government's intentions: a NO victory would open the door to "change" within the Canadian federation.[12]

The lack of cohesiveness among the Liberals, who were firing in all directions, was proof of the fear that gripped them. On Tuesday, October 17, Eddie Goldenberg phoned the U.S. ambassador, James Blanchard. "The polls are now 50-50," he said, "and those are our own numbers." Blanchard asked him, "Counting Pinard's 5 or 6 percent hidden vote?"[13] "Yes," replied Jean Chrétien's advisor. "We're dead even. The other side did very well last week." The American diplomat sensed from his voice that the federalists didn't have a fallback position. "Well," he said, "we're planning to have (Warren) Christopher make a nice statement, certainly repeat and maybe strengthen what the president said in February. But we want to make sure we say it right. We don't want to hurt you with Quebecers." Goldenberg's reply betrayed discouragement: "Don't worry about that," he said. "Nothing is going to hurt us now."[14]

Eddie Goldenberg was not the only one to feel powerless before the Bouchard wave. The official word in the NO camp was still to keep the federal ministers in the role of observer, which weighed more and more heavily on them. The referendum campaign was at the halfway mark now and there was still no mention in Ottawa of a change in strategy. "There was (sic) no general discussions after mid-October about formal contingency planning, not that I'm aware of," said Allan Rock, Canada's minister of justice at the time, who should normally have been informed of any constitutional initiative envisaged by the federal government.

It seemed there was no argument to be found that could revive the NO campaign. A CROP-*La Presse* poll showed that the approaches explored by Daniel Johnson and his associates left the majority of Quebecers unmoved: Johnson's statement on the loss of 92,300 jobs affected only 40% of respondents, the threats made by Bombardier's president left almost 60% indifferent, and fewer than one in four

Quebecers attached any importance to the comments of Mike Harris.[15] The only statistic from this poll liable to boost the morale of the federalists at all was that, when the answers obtained were analyzed using the Drouilly method, the NO was still ahead by five points.[16]

The blunders mounted on both sides and, in the torrent of speeches and press briefings feeding the public debate, the spectre of racism was never far off. On October 17, the sovereigntist MNA for Rimouski-Témiscouata, Suzanne Tremblay, made some remarks that put the YES camp in a serious predicament. First of all, she declared to reporters that the sovereignty of Quebec would allow the new country to better defend the interests of francophones outside Quebec. A Radio-Canada journalist, Joyce Napier, then asked her to explain how this would be possible. Tremblay looked at her and said, "If you knew something of our history... But judging from your accent and your language, maybe you are not originally from Quebec? Have you studied the history of Quebec?"[17] People were appalled. But on the same day, even before the NO camp had a chance to exploit the offending remarks, their effect was neutralized by another gaffe—this one made by federal minister Marcel Massé. Massé made a comment linking several sovereigntists with *L'appel de la race*[18] (Call of the race) by Canon Lionel Groulx. The minister denounced Lucien Bouchard who, in his view, only considered white Quebecers to be "true Quebecers," and he accused several sovereigntists of being "racist," of wanting whites to "dominate society."[19]

But it was not this form of racism that frightened Franco-Ontarians. What they feared was that, if Quebec became independent, it was English Canada that would display a racist attitude towards them. According to the president of the *Association canadienne-française de l'Ontario* (ACFO), André Lalonde, it was the francophone minority outside Quebec that stood to lose the most in this referendum. Recalling a statement along these lines made by the premier of Saskatchewan, Roy Romanow, he expressed the fear that the provinces would end up paying no attention to the constitutional provisions requiring them to take the francophone minority into account in education matters.

On Wednesday, October 18, the Montreal Convention Centre was swarming with business people in favour of the NO. This event had been in the works for a long time. Back in 1994, Daniel Johnson had asked Guylaine Saucier, former president of Groupe Gérard Saucier Ltée, to head a committee responsible for mobilizing Montreal's business community. In the meantime, Saucier was appointed chairperson of the board of directors of Société Radio-Canada, and Philip O'Brien, president of Devencore, took over. The NO committee's wish was to see some 2,000 people in three-piece suits come together at the Convention Centre, in order to show people that the business community was overwhelmingly in favour of the NO. But strategists at federalist headquarters doubted that O'Brien and his organization could rally that number. Consequently, the hall booked turned out to be too small. About 1,500 people were crammed into it, and hundreds more had to remain outside.

The meeting was a success, but Philip O'Brien was not satisfied. "In the Parti Québécois, you could feel there was a real spirit, there was a challenge to rise up to," he says today. "On the NO side, it was more a question of business, it was mechanical; there was no heart in it, there wasn't the same kind of passion as on the YES side. We felt frustrated. We said to ourselves, 'Look, the country is going to break apart, and we are managing the situation as if we were managing a bank.' I felt there was no emotion. The NO people had decided to book a smaller room because they wanted to be sure it would be filled. It's an example of their lack of faith. They were afraid of losing. If you want to win, you have to have the desire to win."[20]

The very next day, O'Brien contacted a few businessmen and, together, they agreed, "Why don't we do something ourselves, forget the NO committee, forget the political parties, forget the Liberal machine, both federal and provincial? Let's do it ourselves. Let's borrow from the Parti Québécois, think of their spirit, their excitement and we can do the same thing." On Friday, October 20, the small group met. "So that's when we decided," O'Brien recalls, "to have a rally. We thought, if you can get 20 or 25,000 people out onto the streets, it will work!"[21] The idea of the great rally at Place du Canada, to take place eight days later, had been born. But how to get 25,000 people in such a short time?

Jonathan Wener, CEO of Canderel Management, was a member of the group. That weekend he would be managing Combined Jewish Appeal's fund-raising campaign. His idea was to bring 25,000 Jews supporting the NO out onto the streets. "Jonathan, I don't need 25,000 Jews!" O'Brien told him. "What I want is to see 25,000 Hungarians, Greeks, Italians, French Canadians, whatever. It has to be a mix..." Over the weekend, hundreds of people made calls for the annual fundraiser for the Jewish community and, at the same time, asked the person on the line whether they wanted to take part in a big rally in support of the NO at Place du Canada. On Sunday night, Wener phoned O'Brien: "I have your 25,000 Jews," he said. O'Brien answered, "OK, let's go!"

Now they needed a demonstration permit. CJAD reporter Rick Leckner, who had contacts in the police force, obtained it. Starting on the Monday, the group, consisting of about a dozen people, met at an exclusive club, the Mont-Royal, located on Sherbrooke Street, in the western part of downtown Montreal. "We treated ourselves quite well," O'Brien says. "One of us was a member of the club; he offered to get us a suitable room." The Club Mont-Royal became the headquarters for the O'Brien group, which met every morning at 7:30, for talks that sometimes went for three hours. Each member of the group took charge of a committee: transportation, safety, printing and distribution of flyers for the schools and in the subway, etc. "It really was passion that drove these people to do this," O'Brien adds. "And also, fear. They wanted to be Montrealers and stay here in Quebec and be part of Canada."[22] The machine was up and running. It would be an exhausting week for the O'Brien group, but they had no inkling yet of the scope and character that the event they had just set in motion was about to take on.

On the same day as the business people's rally at the Convention Centre, a poll threw the NO camp from worry into panic. The gap between the two options, which had been eight points in favour of the NO three weeks earlier, had disappeared, and the YES was now ahead, by one point.[23] Even more than this shattering fact, another now preoccupied the federalist camp totally: greater Montreal favoured the NO in a ratio of 58 to 42, while the rest of the province favoured the YES in the same proportion, a shocking split between the francophone and anglophone vote. The sovereigntist camp, while pleased to be on a par with the adversary, saw a trend emerging in the same poll, a trend that could become the cause of their downfall: the allophone choice was leaning towards the NO, by 95%.

For the first time, Jean Chrétien acknowledged that a NO victory was no longer guaranteed and that Canada, without Quebec, would have to redefine itself in every aspect, as it would no longer be a country. "Nothing leads us to believe," he said in his second major appearance in the campaign, "that the other provinces would be prepared to give the federal government a free hand in establishing the terms of the dissolution of the country. And who can predict whether the other provinces would ever reach a consensus?"[24] The prime minister softened his tone and, before the members of the Quebec City area Chamber of Commerce, stated that Quebecers make up a distinct society and that they should vote NO in order to benefit from the "positive changes" that lay ahead for the country. He made sure to refrain, however, from promising any amendments to the Constitution, speaking merely of "change without breakup" and "evolution of the Federation using a restrained approach," made necessary by the precariousness of the public finance situation.

The reversal of public opinion in favour of the YES did not necessarily reassure Jacques Parizeau's inner circle. The discussion around Quebec's membership in NAFTA did not get much reaction from people and the sovereigntists were happy about that, but the government learned from an American diplomatic source that increasing pressure was being put on the White House to issue a "more operational statement." "What did that mean—a more operational statement?" says Jean-François Lisée. "What we were afraid of was that they would say something about employment, American investment in Quebec, I mean, the economic nerve!"[25]

The anxiety in Parizeau's camp was not unfounded. On October 18, in the morning, James Blanchard left Ottawa for

Washington, accompanied by his wife Janet. He had just read in *The Globe and Mail* that Paul Martin's speech about the loss of a million jobs had provoked a negative reaction among the NO forces. "I was more convinced than ever that it was time for the United States to indicate its support for a united Canada," he writes in his autobiography. Blanchard was certain that the government of an independent Quebec would head straight for Washington, not Paris, given that its trade volume with the U.S. was much higher than with France. Accordingly, he was not afraid the sovereigntists would make a big fuss if the U.S. government took a stronger stand in defence of a united Canada. He was certain as well that President Clinton and Secretary of State Warren Christopher thought the same way as he did. "They just needed someone with political antennae to verify for them how far the United States government could go without insulting Canadians,"[26] he writes in his book.

Upon his arrival in Washington, Blanchard raced over to the secretary of state to meet with Christopher, the undersecretary of state for political affairs, Peter Tarnoff, and the director of the Canada Desk, Lynne Lambert, as well as a few government officials. He offered Christopher a text he could use as a statement in support of Canadian federalism. "Now tell me why we're doing this," the secretary of state asked him. Blanchard then explained that the referendum battle was very tight and that Quebecers attach a very great importance to what Americans think. "I've talked to the prime minister's people, and they agree," he told him. "Everybody agrees." Christopher then replied, "I gather you feel strongly about this, Jim? Well, I just wanted to hear your thinking. But, don't worry, I'm there."[27]

Later on that day, Warren Christopher had a private meeting with the Canadian Minister of Foreign Affairs, André Ouellet, who was in Washington to discuss renewal of the North American Aerospace Defence Command (NORAD).[28] At a press briefing following the meeting, the Secretary of State went beyond Washington's traditional position. "I don't want to intrude on what is rightfully an internal issue in Canada," he told reporters. "But, at the same time, I want to emphasize how much we've benefited here in the United States from the opportunity to have the kind of relationship that we do have at the present time with a strong and united Canada. (...) I think we shouldn't take for granted that a different kind of organization would not obviously have exactly the same kind of ties."[29] Blanchard was jubilant: the remarks and attitude of his boss were exactly as he had hoped. He now had to ensure that what Christopher had said would be accurately reported by the press. The next day, he flew to Boston to speak with the senior editorial staff of the *Boston Globe*. That was when he received a call from the U.S. Consul General in Quebec, Stephen Kelly, who advised him that Christopher's intervention did not sit well with Bernard Landry, that he had a letter to forward to him and that he wanted it delivered to the ambassador in person.

The Quebec government had taken less than 24 hours to react to Christopher's remarks. While Bernard Landry's letter was being sent to Kelly, a copy of it was despatched to the U.S. capital, care of Jacques Parizeau's special advisor in Washington, René Marleau, with instructions to deliver it to the White House. "I don't know why to the White House," Marleau still wonders today, "since the letter was addressed to Warren Christopher."[30] Like a good public servant, Marleau followed orders and asked his political attaché to deliver the letter to the White House. "I was dumbfounded on reading the letter," he said. "Why? Because it went completely counter to one of the principles of our presence in Washington, especially during this period, namely, not to antagonize the Americans."[31] Later, Marleau met with his contact at the Secretary of State, Lynne Lambert, who confirmed that Christopher had indeed received the letter. According to Jean-François Lisée, however, while the letter may have been addressed to Warren Christopher, "the real addressee was the White House."[32]

What was striking about the letter was its firm tone. "That declaration, made less than two weeks before referendum day in Quebec," wrote Landry, "inevitably attracted considerable attention here, and it was presented by opponents to the project of our government as a clear shift in the traditional position of the United States." He recalled the determining role played by Quebec with respect to the Free Trade

Agreement, when Jean Chrétien's Liberal party was opposed to it. "A sovereign Quebec would be, after all, your eighth largest trading partner," he added. Landry stressed that "Should American declarations be publicly perceived as a factor in the decision that Quebecers are to make, they would enter into our collective memory and the history books."

"If the Yes side wins, as is now probable," the letter went on, "Quebec voters and the historians will remember that the sovereignty of Quebec was achieved despite or even against the American will. That will make more difficult our task of developing with the United States the productive and friendly relations we hold dear."

"If victory eludes the Yes side by a slim margin, as is plausible, those who did vote Yes—a clear majority of francophone Quebecers— will be tempted to assign responsibility to the United States for part of their profound disappointment. I do not know how many decades it will take to dispel that feeling." Landry's conclusion read, "In the days to come, should American declarations be more emphatic, or should they come from the higher levels of the Administration, the deeper would be the traces left in our history."

"This guy's crazy," Blanchard reacted to the report he received from Stephen Kelly. "Tell him that you've talked to me and I will call him. It's going to make him look foolish in Washington, you know, to appear to be threatening the secretary of state of the United States. Tell him, if he's got any brains at all, he won't tell anyone he's done this or show it to anybody. Tell him I'll keep confidential, but tell him that I think he's made a big mistake in writing it."[33] Warren Christopher's office had indeed received the letter but had the Secretary of State read it? According to Blanchard, he didn't even know who Bernard Landry was. Had it made any impact on Washington? "They never saw it," the ambassador claims. "I guess our Canada Desk did, and they just thought it was goofy. I didn't want to make him look bad. My job is not to make somebody look bad. And this is a private letter anyway…" For Blanchard, the letter showed that the Parti Québécois was more determined than he had thought, "more fanatical and more problematic." On his instructions, Lynne Lambert,[34] at the Canada Desk of the Secretary of State filed it away, destined never to receive a reply.

Who had taken this initiative in Quebec? "Obviously, the letter had been approved by Mr. Parizeau,"[35] says Jean-François Lisée, who wrote it. But Parizeau says he was not aware of it: "It was Mr. Landry's initiative," he says. "That was his prerogative as deputy premier and minister responsible for international relations."[36] And one is inclined to believe him, for, when Parizeau appointed René Marleau as special advisor to Washington, a few weeks earlier, he had made two recommendations: "To keep him informed of how Americans perceived sovereignty, and not to rock the boat!"[37] Marleau recalls. In any event, the letter was prepared in a hurry, with no consultation of the few lobbyists the Quebec government uses in the U.S. capital. Jean-François Lisée, whose career has given him the opportunity to get to know Americans well, explains the firm tone of the letter: "Either we act like sheep, and the Americans will treat us like sheep, or we tell them: Watch out!"[38]

Contrary to the American ambassador's wishes, the letter or, at least its contents, did not remain confidential. The Quebec government phoned certain governors, especially those in New England, notably, Angus King of Maine, and William Weld of Massachusetts. "To tell them," Lisée explains, "Listen, all we ask is that there be no negative interventions and we invite you to pass this message on to the White House."[39] Did they talk about Landry's letter to Christopher in those calls? Blanchard does not rule it out. Two days later, the U.S. Consul in Quebec came to Parizeau's assistants with a question that they considered proof of the operation's success: Kelly wanted to know how many governors had been contacted. So, the message had made it, then, to the Secretary of State. Lisée considered it proof of something else as well because, the following week, President Clinton, in his declaration of support for Canada, would feel obliged to soften it and to state that it was up to Quebecers and Canadians to decide. But Parizeau's special advisor in Washington, René Marleau, does not share that view: "It is my opinion," he says, "that the statements that were made by the American authorities after they had received the letter would have been made in any event."[40]

While agitation grew at diplomatic headquarters, on the ground, the campaign went forward at a furious pace. In Rivière-du-Loup,

Lucien Bouchard made a faux pas. He affirmed that Quebec would proclaim sovereignty first, and then proceed to negotiations. "The mandate sought by Mr. Parizeau and the sovereigntists," he said, "is for Quebec to achieve sovereignty, and for Quebec, on the strength of that sovereignty, to try subsequently to negotiate a partnership agreement.[41] But he was quick to salvage the situation. In Rimouski, he reversed his statement: "First there will be negotiation, where we will exhaust every peaceful and democratic means," he clarified, asking, however, for a strong mandate so that considerable pressure could be placed on the federal government."[42] And no one took him to task for his blunder, which confirmed the opinion of the NO camp that, no matter what he said, he would always be forgiven.

Henceforth, everything seemed to favour the YES camp. Even a bad joke someone played on them turned out to their advantage when, that same evening, Jacques Parizeau showed up in a triumphant mood at the University of Montreal. Basking in the morning's polls, he decided to mingle with the crowds and had difficulty making his way through the throng of students. He had barely begun his speech when a bomb scare forced the evacuation of the hall. Far from causing disruption, the incident served to enhance the rapport Parizeau wanted to establish with the young people, because it forced him to deliver his speech with a megaphone, outdoors, surrounded by those who had come to hear him.

The question of monetary union continued to create confusion in the minds of the people. Relying on a study by the C.D. Howe institute, Daniel Johnson pronounced it not feasible, and predicted that Quebec would have no choice but to create its own currency, "which would then be immediately devalued in relation to the Canadian dollar, which, itself, would be devalued in relation to the U.S. dollar."[43] A few hours later, Canada's minister of finance stated in turn that he did not believe that kind of monetary union could last very long. "It's not my decision," said Paul Martin in an interview with *Le Devoir*, "it's the decision that thousands of Quebecers, Canadians and businesses that are going to lose confidence will have to make." He did not comment, however, on whether he thought the new country would have to create its own currency as soon as it became independent.

The economic consequences of sovereignty continued to fuel the speeches, negative consequences according to one camp, positive according to the other, but reality hit everyone on Friday, October 20: the dollar plunged to 73.87 cents, losing 72 points on the U.S. dollar. The Bank of Canada intervened through a massive purchase of Canadian currency on the financial markets, which had witnessed a considerable sell-off of Canadian assets. This nervousness could be explained by the publication of two polls, one conducted by Angus Reid for Wood Gundy and the CIBC, which assigned a two-point lead to the YES, and the other by Léger Marketing, which placed the two options at about even. These statistics were not in the least reassuring for the financial world. *The Globe and Mail* claimed it was not just the possibility of a YES victory that upset the market but the prospect of an inconclusive vote. It was basing its statement on the analysis of Ross Preston, CEO of WEFA Canada Inc. WEFA specialized in creating econometric models to be used in analyzing industrial and macroeconomic activities. Preston compared the situation in Canada with the one in Mexico at the beginning of the year.[44] If the referendum result was not decisive, regardless of who won, the dollar would drop below 70 cents U.S. "Fear is mounting in the financial community," said the influential daily, "that a Quebec referendum with no clear winner would plunge Ottawa and the provinces into a financial crisis and even push the country into recession." What did it mean by no clear winner? "Assume, for the sake of scenario building," the article continued, in the voice of journalist Jeffrey Simpson, "that the NO side wins narrowly, say by 53-47 or 52-48. That kind of slim NO victory would arguably be the worst of all conceivable outcomes."[45]

Following the Angus Reid and Léger Marketing polls the anxiety in the NO camp changed to consternation when an internal survey gave the opposing camp a seven-point lead. "It was alarming," says John Parisella. "We began losing the campaign on Thursday, October 19. The survey showed plainly that momentum was not on our side." The NO organizers then held an emergency meeting and

decided that a speech by Jean Chrétien to the nation might produce results. "I went out of my way," Parisella recalls, "asking that this speech
be more conciliatory, more acceptable to Quebecers. We knew it was
coming down basically to a choice of country. We were in a post-
Meech, post-Charlottetown dynamic. The country was either functional or dysfunctional. We had to respond to the hopes of those who
wanted it to be functional."[46] Blanchard, for his part, contacted Angus
Reid to get confirmation of the poll results. He decided to do his
utmost to get President Clinton, who was very popular in Quebec, to
make a statement.

On the ground, Jean Charest could feel the wind change direction. Campaigning in the Bas-du-Fleuve, he stopped at a gas station in
Mont-Joli to make a phone call. The attendant recognized him and
came out to greet him. "A man in his forties," Charest recalls, "more
or less representative of our target group, people who were undecided." The two struck up a conversation and finally, the attendant
said to Charest, "You know that if we vote YES in the referendum, it's
going to be tough, don't you?" Charest did not miss this opportunity:
"Yes, it will be tough," he answered. "And, after a brief silence, the attendant said, 'You know, if we vote NO in the referendum, it's going
to be tough, eh?' I understood then," Charest recalls, "that we had a
serious problem. I was in the Bas-du-Fleuve, where the unemployment rate was high, where the recession of the '90s had been particularly hard and where the YES camp had managed to find supporters by
convincing people they had nothing to lose." The leader of the
Conservative party at the time now concludes, "That was essentially
where the YES campaign was successful, in convincing a number of
Quebecers that they had nothing to lose by voting YES, while, in fact,
they had a lot to lose."[47]

That same day, Lucien Bouchard's political advisor, Pierre-Paul
Roy, sent his leader a note: "We're about 50-50 now. We can win!"
Both camps felt this final phase was their last chance to get it right, but
it seemed the YES was in the lead.

On Friday, October 20, Jean Chrétien arrived in New York. 1995
was the year that marked the 50th anniversary of the United Nations

and there would be a ceremony with almost all the world's heads of state in attendance. The Canadian Prime Minister and his wife Aline went down to Hotel Pierre, where Canada's ambassador to Washington, who was also their nephew, was to meet them, accompanied by his wife, for a family supper.

At noon that day, on Wall Street, in fulfilment of a longstanding promise, Raymond Chrétien had addressed a group of fifty business people with investments in Canada and in Quebec. "I gave them the usual sales pitch on the extraordinary relationship that exists between Canada and the U.S.," says the ambassador, who discovered, however, that these investors were following very closely what was going on over the border and were not ignorant of the fact that a NO victory was far from being a *fait accompli*. "I realized that they were reacting very cautiously to my perhaps somewhat exaggerated optimism with respect to a victory for the Canadian government," Raymond Chrétien admits today. "These people told me in no uncertain terms, 'Listen Mr. Ambassador. You seem to think you're going to win. But the information we have shows that the race is so tight, there's no telling any more what's going to happen.'"[48]

The ambassador came away from the luncheon rather shaken. He could not help thinking about the potential consequences of the dominant perception among these business people, who controlled hundreds of millions of investment dollars in Canada. After passing by the Canadian consulate, he arrived at The Pierre at the end of the day to greet the Prime Minister. It was in a quiet corner of the hotel restaurant, one of the finest in New York, that Raymond Chrétien recounted to the Prime Minister what had happened at the luncheon and shared his concerns with him. "I said, 'Listen, Jean, where we are now is the most important country on the planet. Let me tell you what I have just experienced, and these are not people who just make things up.' The Prime Minister paid close attention to what I said. It was a point of view he had not heard before. He certainly had heard a lot of views expressed by his colleagues or various people in Canada. It was probably the first time he was hearing the view from his man, his ambassador in Washington, about the mood or the perception of

American businessmen to the referendum and the possibility that it could be lost. I felt lucky to have had that chance to tell him, that night: listen, we have to shake up, and fast."[49]

The ambassador also warned Jean Chrétien what to expect the next day. "As soon as you leave this hotel tomorrow morning, as soon as you arrive at the United Nations, you'll be flooded with questions concerning what is going to happen, where do you stand, are you going to win, is it not dangerous that you could lose? I wanted to just warn him that the perception among those with a direct interest in Quebec and Canada, was that it was too close to call."[50]

While the ambassador had aroused anxiety in his prime minister, the prime minister would have a similar effect on him: "For me, it was an opportunity to suddenly realize that we didn't have a Plan B," the diplomat says. "My point was: what do I do in a week, what do I tell President Clinton, his government, if Canada loses? What is our message? Do we accept, do we refuse conditions? My job in Washington was to relate to the American administration what our position was on this."[51]

The idea of an intervention by President Clinton was gaining ground. Obviously, he could not take the initiative on this himself without causing a serious diplomatic incident. Nor could Prime Minister Chrétien formally request the intervention, without sacrificing Canada's sovereignty. Only one solution remained: a "chance" meeting on the Saturday, when the two men would be attending the United Nations' 50th anniversary celebrations. And Ambassador Blanchard had taken the necessary steps to ensure their paths would cross.

How did it happen? "I don't remember," says Jean Chrétien. "Maybe when we were at the UN, he (President Clinton) inquired, 'Jean, how are things?' And I explained to him… Maybe it was at that point that I spoke to him. It was not an (official) undertaking. We were just being neighbourly. He was following it (the referendum story) closely. He adores politics, so, for him, it was a political problem that was bound to interest him. But I never called Clinton to say to him, 'Bill, I would like you to make a statement.' No, it didn't happen like that."[52] But James Blanchard, although not without a fair bit of embarrassment, was more categorical. "He asked him to help," he says. "That was in New York. He asked him to help, he didn't get into this, that, and the other."

On Saturday morning, October 21, the NO camp met, as they did every Saturday morning, still looking for a way to counter the Bouchard effect. The meeting started around 8:30 and lasted more than an hour and a half. Daniel Johnson took part in the discussions. Around 10 a.m., a few people withdrew to a smaller room to work on drafting the speech that Jean Chrétien would deliver the following Tuesday, at the big rally in Verdun. Several ideas sprang from the discussion, including that of a commitment by Ottawa to make changes to the Constitution. "Someone suggested it," Eddie Goldenberg recalls. "Others said we shouldn't talk about it. And some said we should think about it over the weekend. Mr. Johnson left the meeting at that point because he had other appointments."

Daniel Johnson's first appointment took him to Longueuil. He used the opportunity of a reporter's question to send out a call for help to Jean Chrétien. He asked him to make a statement one way or the other, now, on the distinct society question. He pointed out that the members of the federalist coalition had approved the NO manifesto, incorporated into the document sent out by the Chief Electoral Officer to every household in Quebec. The manifesto was clear: "Within the Canadian federation," it read, "we form a distinct society." Johnson recalled that Jean Chrétien had already defended the NO manifesto in the House of Commons. "He could be more specific in his remarks or not wish to be more specific," he said, "but I think that any extent to which he would endorse what we say would of course be desirable." He was not unaware that three hours earlier, the Ottawa federalists had rebuffed the vice-president of the NO committee, Lisa Frulla, for having raised the possibility that the distinct character of Quebec might be enshrined in the Constitution. But, by harping on this point, Daniel Johnson hoped the prime minister would show, at the very least, some openness.

Bob Rae joined him in the morning, to accompany him on this tour that, after Longueuil, would take him to Laval and to Lachute.

"Do you know what the prime minister will say?" he asked Johnson. "I was only expressing a preference," he answered. "I'm sure it won't be a big deal!"[53]

The words had barely escaped his lips when they reached Chrétien in New York and were used in a question by one of the reporters following him. "No," Chrétien answered dryly. "We're not talking about the Constitution, we're talking about the separation of Quebec from the rest of Canada." But he added, "I voted for the Charlottetown Accord while the Péquistes voted against it. The distinct society clause was in Charlottetown. I have already recognized it."

Daniel Johnson returned to Montreal and in the early evening, around 6 p.m., Eddie Goldenberg, Jean Chrétien's political advisor, ran into him on the stairs at the NO headquarters. He remembers that exchange with the federalist camp leader: "He said, 'I think I screwed up this afternoon, I made a mistake and maybe I should call the prime minister and talk to him.'" Chrétien's aide dissuaded him: "I said no, don't, you don't have to do that. It's a tough time for all of us. Just go out and campaign. We understand. We all make mistakes and there's nothing to worry about."

Looking back, Daniel Johnson regrets that he answered the reporter the way he did. "I should have answered that there was no constitutional round on the horizon and that the issue was the sovereignty project. I should simply have dismissed the question," he says today. "The funny part is," he adds, "that in Shawinigan, in his first major speech, Jean Chrétien spoke of the distinct character of Quebec." The NO leader recalls that on that occasion, he stood beside the prime minister of Canada. "We were all standing on the platform and we saw one another's notes," he remembers. "He had added it to his speech by hand. He added it, and he said it." This is why Johnson believes that, on this question, "the federal side has not fully delivered the goods." In his view, the difference of opinion would not have taken on such exaggerated proportions if, in New York on the Saturday, Jean Chrétien had stated right away, "that which we had agreed on, but which he was very hesitant to say," rather than stating it a day later by means of a communiqué.[54]

The disagreement between the two men made the front pages of the big dailies on Sunday. *La Presse* ran the headline, *Chrétien dit non à Johnson* (Chrétien says no to Johnson). Mending the tear in the federalist fabric was urgent. The two men spoke: "I remember the Sunday morning on the phone with Mr. Johnson and I discussed a bit with him and I agreed to do more,"[55] Jean Chrétien recalls. During an unplanned press conference at the Radisson Hotel in Montreal, Daniel Johnson gave journalists a communiqué, which he himself terms "a damage control tool." The text, approved by both leaders, proclaimed that Quebec was a distinct society. "We are convinced that the Canadian federal system is flexible and capable of making changes that will allow it to adapt and better reflect the reality and the diversity of the country, including the distinct character of Quebec," they said. "Messrs. Bouchard and Parizeau are trying to twist our words and claim that we are in contradiction. (…) Today, we speak together and with one voice. We state unequivocally that Quebec is a distinct society. We remind you that we both supported the inclusion of this principle in the Canadian constitution each time Quebec demanded it." The communiqué dismissed, however, any possibility of making it an issue in the referendum debate. "There is only one question," it read, "which Quebecers must answer: Do you want Quebec to separate from Canada or not?"

In New York, Jean Chrétien had a full schedule: he was meeting with the Emir of Kuwait, Jaber al-Ahmad al-Sabbah, President Suharto of Indonesia, Prime Minister Carlsson of Sweden, President Frei of Chile and President Kuchma of the Ukraine. But reporters were interested only in his disagreement with Johnson. Minutes before his meeting with the Prime Minister of Israel, Yitzhak Rabin, the question was put to him again. This time, he did not hide either his annoyance or his surprise. "I don't understand this," he replied. "I voted for a distinct society in Parliament and in the Charlottetown (accord). I'm still for it. There's no ambiguity in my mind. Suddenly, there is this ambiguity and I wanted (to) reconfirm what I meant."[56] But he carefully avoided promising any kind of constitutional changes whatsoever.

Meanwhile, Bob Rae telephoned certain provincial premiers, urging them not to react to the communiqué from the NO camp when it would be made public. "I think I even spoke to Mr. Wells that night," he recalls, "and said: this is something which is being thought about. You might want to think about what your response would be. But Mr. Wells is a very precise man. He does not hold back. If you say: your shirt is blue, it's not just blue. It's got to be a particular shade of blue. He wants to make it clear that he's reserving his right to make clear what his opinion is, if it's asked." Monday morning, he was indeed asked, and he replied, Quebec must not obtain special status at the expense of the other Canadian provinces and Quebecers are in the wrong if they believe that, by voting YES, they are giving themselves the power to negotiate with the rest of Canada.

In John Parisella's view, Jean Chrétien was fuelling the ambiguity himself because he did not want to be drawn into a debate on constitutional changes. "He did not want to be caught in a situation where he would have to interpret a NO vote as it had been interpreted in 1980, and which would usher in an era of constitutional renewal," he said. "Mr. Trudeau was keen on that. It was more or less his legacy that was at stake. Victoria had failed.[57] He had missed another opportunity when he lost the elections in 1979,[58] but then, he had the chance to win the referendum, to act quickly and repatriate the Constitution. Mr. Chrétien did not want to be caught in that scenario. You could sense that. When we started preparing the NO documents, to write the manifesto, you could feel the resistance. We did not want to embark on something that would be interpreted as a commitment to constitutional reform."[59] The Canadian government had all the more reason to resist opening its doors to constitutional concessions since the Parti Québécois was still in the early part of its mandate and, for three of four years to come, it could harass Chrétien and his government to get them to start implementing reforms.

Ten years on, Jean Chrétien explains his reluctance at the time. He considers the expression "distinct society" void of meaning.[60] "That was where Mr. Trudeau and I differed," he says. "He insisted there wasn't a single meaningless word in the Constitution. I remember a debate he and I had in Toronto, with my friend Gérard Pelletier. I said, 'We have the Civil Code in Quebec, which does not apply in the rest of Canada; the majority in Quebec speak French, which is not the case in the other provinces.' Several court rulings recognize these established facts. The expression, *distinct society* creates a problem. This often happens in politics. Take, for example, same-sex unions. If you are talking about a civil contract, no one objects. If you call it a *marriage*, you get a lot of opposition, but it doesn't change anything in reality. The problem is with the word. These are battles that create illusions. When you don't get results, it creates bitterness. That's why, when I became prime minister, I never thought that everyone's problems could be solved by changing the Constitution. It's the easiest solution. When you have a deficit problem or you're short of funds, or you have a problem concerning participation in a war like the Iraq war, it's not the Constitution that's going to decide, it's political power, it's the government."[61] For Jean Chrétien, a country's constitution does not have that much importance. "There is a myth that if you change the Constitution, you know…" he says. "In France, they had twenty new constitutions in two hundreds years. And the Brits don't have yet a constitution. And they have the same population and virtually the same standard of living. Jean Marchand[62] used to say: changing the Constitution will not have potatoes to grow in Labrador in the winter, you know."[63]

By refusing, just ten days prior to the referendum, to commit to enshrining the notion of "distinct society" in the Constitution, Jean Chrétien was going against the position held by most of the country's politicians, who had been made more open towards Quebec by the new and very real danger of a YES victory. Paul Martin stated very clearly that he wanted the notion entrenched. Frank McKenna took the same position. The Ontario parliament's 130 members unanimously adopted a resolution introduced by their premier, Mike Harris who declared that "the Legislative Assembly and the people of Ontario affirm that we have a deep affection for Canada and that we attach great importance to the distinctive character of Quebec within our country." Nova Scotia followed suit and had the Quebec flag raised in the Legislative Assembly. In Winnipeg, Premier Gary Filmon, one of the artisans of the Meech Lake collapse, now asserted he was ready to recognize Quebec as a distinct society in the constitutional round planned for 1997. In Newfoundland, an about-face from Clyde Wells, arriving late in the day, flabbergasted everyone: his parliament unanimously adopted a resolution stating that "the Constitution must be amended to recognize the distinctive character of Quebec for its language, its culture and its legal institutions." Subsequently, however, Clyde Wells would withdraw into complete silence on the referendum question. In British Columbia, on the other hand, and in Alberta, neither Michael Harcourt nor Ralph Klein was willing to "get involved in a constitutional debate on distinct society status."

The Chrétien-Johnson dispute was creating an atmosphere of crisis at the NO headquarters. The tension between the Ottawa federalists and the Quebec federalists was becoming untenable. "That could have led to a major split," says John Parisella. "That weekend I really felt we formed two different groups. And these were not people prepared to make compromises. It could have turned even more sour, but we were able to come together and focus on the final week."[64] Not only did the NO strategists have to manage the tension, which was reaching a critical peak because of the disagreement between the two leaders. They had to handle the shock they had been hit with that morning when the coalition's official pollster, Grégoire Gollin, informed them that their camp was lagging behind by five to seven points. "That Saturday morning," Pierre-Claude Nolin recalls, "just like every Saturday, Mr. Gollin arrived with his data. Let's just say it was like a cold shower! That was the toughest weekend. We had fewer than ten days left to turn things around."[65]

In Ottawa, the poll results only added to the consternation that had begun to permeate the Prime Minister's entourage these last few days. Up to this point, his advisors had been clinging to the hope that the slide backwards was only temporary, but now they realized it was accelerating towards a point where it would be irreversible. A conference call was set up which connected Eddie Goldenberg and Peter

Donolo in Ottawa, John Rae of the NO committee in Montreal, and Jean Pelletier and Patrick Parisot (Jean Chrétien's attaché de presse) in Québec, with the prime minister who was in New York. Eddie Goldenberg said to Chrétien, "We have good news and bad news. The bad news is that we are lagging behind by seven points in the polls. The good news is that we still have a week and we are counting on you to help us out." The prime minister was bewildered. "When I left, the polls were still good," he recalls. "But I was a bit stunned by that news." He chose, nevertheless to stay in New York, because he felt that although it was mainly a protocol event, this gathering of all the heads of state in the world could allow for some interesting exchanges. "I had a pleasant conversation with Fidel Castro," he likes to recall. "It was the first time I had met him and he was delighted to speak Spanish with Aline!"[66]

In the meantime, the Privy Council leaked out some economic data that was enough to make the sovereigntists break out into a cold sweat. According to a document obtained by *The Globe and Mail*, an independent Quebec would become one of the most indebted countries in the world and its annual deficit would increase five-fold to 18 billion dollars. It would therefore lose all influence in its relationships with its principal trading partners. The Privy Council study, prepared under the direction of Howard Balloch, Cabinet Deputy Secretary for Operation Unity, went further: Quebec would encounter major difficulties trying to maintain the viability of its health, textile, tobacco, furniture poultry, dairy and chemical product industries.[67]

The Privy Council's predictions compounded the anxieties sparked by the nervous, capricious and uncontrollable behaviour of the stocks and bonds market. Despite outward self-assurance, the Quebec government had no illusions about the upheaval the new country's economy might be subject to if the YES came out ahead. Financial interests, which were beyond its control and were considerable, could throw its economic system into ruin. Investors might unload a large quantity of Quebec and Hydro-Quebec bonds onto the market, thereby setting off a panic situation. If the bond price fell, yield rates would rise, and the gap between Quebec and Ontario bond prices, for example, would widen. Before the *Caisse de dépôt et placement* was created, the minister of finance would have to try to agree, with a bank or a broker, on some way of stopping the flow of funds. "They had been playing that one on us ever since Honoré Mercier," says Jacques Parizeau. "It's one of the reasons why we founded the *Caisse*. We had to put an end to that little game."[68] But the wind gusts of bygone decades were nothing compared to the tornado threatening to hit a separated Quebec.

Therefore, one morning, shortly before the referendum, Minister of Finance Jean Campeau showed up with his deputy minister at Parizeau's office. They had come up with a plan, later called the O Plan (O for *obligations*, the French word for bonds), which would allow Quebec to have at its disposal a 17 billion dollar reserve in order to foil any attempt to discredit the value of Quebec bonds. The reserve was held in the coffers of the *Caisse de dépôt et placement*. It consisted of amortization funds, Hydro-Quebec funds, *Commission de la santé et de la sécurité du travail* (CSST—Health and unemployment commission) funds, *Régie des rentes* (Quebec pension board) funds, construction industry pension funds, etc. "It was through transactions of that nature that Quebec governments made themselves independent of the financial interests that had dominated them for a century," says Parizeau, who even sees it as an advantage: "The financial institutions sell off their Quebec government securities and absorb the losses," he adds. "Then, you buy back, which sends the rates back up. That's why so many private financial institutions followed our example. All they had to do was to piggyback, simply hop on our back and follow us."[69]

The *Caisse de dépôt et placement* had prepared well by stocking up on U.S. government bonds (Treasury Bonds). "It could sell American bonds, if the need arose, to bolster the Quebec securities market," Campeau explains. "It also had Canadian government bonds it could have sold. If Quebec securities had collapsed, as was claimed would happen, then Canadian securities would have collapsed too."[70]

Only a few initiates knew of the O Plan. "I had never heard of it," says Mario Dumont. "Mr. Parizeau told us, citing his knowledge of the financial markets, that he was in control on that score. We were never given a detailed presentation on what that meant for the various financial institutions. But we never probed him about it either."[71] Lucien Bouchard did not know any more about it than Dumont. "When I raised the subject again with Mr. Bouchard recently," says Pierre-Paul Roy, "he was unaware of it. It was a well-kept secret. However, I think it would have been more appropriate to keep Mr. Bouchard informed."[72]

On Saturday, October 21, in the midst of the "distinct society" turmoil, *The Gazette* tossed yet another cause for concern into the campaign: the flight of capital. "The referendum: Money moving out as polls get closer, financial firms say. As the referendum date gets closer and the polls get tighter, some Quebecers are shifting their Canadian dollar savings and investments out of the province or into foreign currencies," the article stated. Its title was alarming: *Money leaving as polls show tight race: financial institutions.*[73] But the sources cited were more moderate and were confirmed in an article which appeared in *La Presse* a few days later: according to brokers and financial institution spokespersons, "the flow was relatively small and even marginal."[74]

Between August and October 1995, the total worth of personal savings accounts was 50 billion 477 million dollars. Between the February-to-April quarter and the August-to-October quarter, that total decreased by 535 million dollars but, according to the analysts, it is difficult to say whether the difference is attributable to flight of capital. "Some people are transferring their money to Ontario. We have seen an increase in this phenomenon since Friday, but there is no crisis. Far from it," Raymond Chouinard, communications director for the Royal Bank, told *La Presse*. A *Caisse populaire* branch manager pointed out that "people are especially worried about the trend in interest rates."[75] Indeed, between September 12 and October 24, the official market rate of the Bank of Canada climbed almost a whole point, to 7.65%, and the dollar dropped by 1.66 to 73.23 cents U.S.

As the campaign entered its final week, storm clouds gathered in the sky over the NO camp, while the YES camp took wing, held aloft by the "distinct society" debate. Lucien Bouchard even ventured some humour in front of an audience of some five hundred people gathered in Sept-Îles, by inviting Daniel Johnson, "now that you know who it is you are dealing with," to vote YES. At NO headquarters, which the strategists called the *war room*, the sarcasm was painful and added to the panic. "It was tough," said Bob Rae. "There weren't a lot of laughs. It was very tense. People were very worried. People weren't entirely sure of their ground. You just never quite knew what to do." Sunday morning, another meeting: "And, it was then that we finally decided to have the big demonstration at Place du Canada, which had not been planned up to that point,"[76] says Pierre-Claude Nolin. Actually, the decision the NO camp made that day was not a decision to organize a big demonstration, but to take over the project of the O'Brien group, which was already under way, and to transform it into a mega-event.

Jean Chrétien returned to Ottawa on the Monday. "At that point, I had some decisions to make. Sitting down at my desk, I spent several hours reviewing everything. And, afterwards, we decided."[77] "We decided," says Jean Pelletier, "that we would no longer ask anyone for permission and that we just had to jump in. The war was at its crucial stage. Well, in war, you don't ask anyone permission. You risk all for all."[78] The message was clear and the prime minister's administrative staff had to draw up a strategy for the final week. The Ottawa brigade chose, on its own initiative, to go on the offensive, and the strategists in the NO headquarters in Montreal would have to adapt.

CHAPTER XI

In Ottawa, Time to Take the Initiative

W ithout Chrétien's knowledge, and while he was still in New York, a few of his ministers got together at the Café Henri Burger in Hull on Sunday evening to discuss their concerns and seek solutions. The food was great but the mood was sombre. They were all from English-speaking Canada and had gradually become aware, these last few days, of a reality which until now they had thought very remote: it was possible that, in a week's time, their country would break apart, and they had no idea what would happen then.

"We didn't get into a scenario in any kind of detail on what happens if the referendum is lost," recalls Brian Tobin, who was at the supper. "But we acknowledged that that was a real possibility. And if that occurred, it couldn't be business as usual." The group speculated on where things might go from there. "We'd have to ask the hard questions," Tobin continues, "like: can a prime minister from Quebec represent Canada in a negotiation where there's just been a mandate given to break up this country? Can the team from Quebec who, at that point, occupied almost all of the major portfolios in the Cabinet of Canada comprise the negotiation team for Canada if the subject of negotiation was the sovereignty of Quebec? The answer is: they couldn't."

Without trying to define what the changes might be, it seemed to them that if the YES side won, the structure of the government would have to be radically transformed. The government, as it currently existed, could not last very long and new coalitions would have to be formed. They all declared their willingness to assume any responsibilities that might be entrusted to them in the circumstances. "We looked each other in the eye," Tobin adds, "and said: if it is necessary for us to ask these hard questions and to develop the appropriate answers and to seek the collaboration of other parties in Parliament, we'll do our jobs." At least one minister, David Collenette, refused to participate in the meeting. He had just returned from Europe and was rather tired, but he justified his absence with a different reason: "I believed that to have that kind of discussion at that particular point in time was unproductive, unhelpful and almost seditious," he says.

As his ministers readied themselves for defeat, Jean Chrétien, when he returned from New York the next day, immediately set about mobilizing his inner circle for the final week. There was meeting after meeting. "We realized," says Eddie Goldenberg, "that probably the most important event would be the speech that the prime minister would give in Verdun on the Tuesday. (...) Later, the suggestion was made actually by Pierre Anctil, who was the organizer for Mr. Johnson, that perhaps it would be useful for Mr. Chrétien to go on television. And then, they wanted him to make a few more appearances, one on a very popular television show called *Mongrain*, on the private network."

But, for now, it was something happening on another television network—a foreign one, in fact—that was attracting attention. Larry King is an American television institution: his show, *Larry King Live*, is watched by millions of Americans, and by a great many Canadians as well. Not only does the show air the host's interviews with his guests, it also lets viewers have their say and converse with the guests during the phone-in. On Monday, October 23, President Chirac, who had also come to New York for the United Nations 50th anniversary celebrations, was among King's guests. A viewer from Montreal called with a question. The telephone conversation was brief:

The viewer: Mr. President, would the government of France be prepared to recognize a unilateral declaration of independence by Quebec?

Chirac: The French government (does) not want to interfere in Canadian affairs.

King: That was not the question.

Chirac: That was not the question?

King: The question was: will you recognize…

Chirac: Yes, I am coming to that.

King: Okay.

Chirac: You have a referendum…

King: Next week.

Chirac: … and we will see. And we will say what we think just after the referendum, but we don't want to interfere.

King: Well, if Quebec decides to separate…

Chirac: Mm-mm…

King: His question was: will you recognize the new government?

Chirac: If the referendum (is) positive…

King: Yeah.

Chirac: … the government will recognize the fact.

King: So France will recognize the facts?

Chirac: These facts, of course.

King: So, you have no recommendations to the people of Quebec, as to how they should vote?

Chirac: I told you, I don't want to interfere in Quebec affairs.

Jean Chrétien was at his home at 24 Sussex, with Eddie Goldenberg and Patrick Parisot, his press secretary. The three of them were working on the speech the prime minister would give the next evening, in Verdun. The phone rang. It was James Blanchard, the United States ambassador in Ottawa and a great friend of Goldenberg's. "Did you hear Chirac?" asked Blanchard. "No," replied Goldenberg. "What did he say?" In fact, Goldenberg was not very interested in what Chirac might have said on American television. He knew what stand France would take if the YES side came out of the referendum on top, and that this concern would be just one of many. He left the prime minister's residence around 12:30 in the morning. "I was more preoccupied," he says today, "by the fact that if there was a YES win, there were going to be very grave consequences in all sorts of areas. We knew that (France's attitude) would be one of the numerous problems, if the YES had won." A few weeks earlier, Chrétien's advisor had met with the French ambassador, Alfred Siefer-Gaillardin. While a federalist himself, the ambassador had told him, "You must win. Because in France, a simple majority is sufficient. We signed on to the Treaty of Maastricht, which established the European Monetary Union, with a majority of 52%."

Jean Chrétien's chief of staff found the warning offered by Ambassador Siefer-Gaillardin more irritating than worrisome: "He was taking part in the debate," says Jean Pelletier. "It's my view that a French ambassador in Ottawa should not be saying anything without first consulting his prime minister and his president."[1] Pelletier was, however, much more tolerant towards the American ambassador, who was acting like a worked-up orchestra conductor. "I was quite disturbed," recounts James Blanchard, "because I thought he was meddling more than anybody could accuse Bill Clinton of having done." From Albany, New York, he phoned Pelletier to express his criticism of the French president. Chrétien's chief of staff reassured him by telling him he didn't think Chirac would intervene in the debate. The confidence expressed by Pelletier was based on a meeting between the Canadian prime minister and Chirac in June 1994, when Chirac was still mayor of Paris. "At that time, Mr. Chirac said that he had reflected a lot on the subject since the 1980 referendum," Pelletier recalls. "With all due respect to what Quebecers and Canadians would decide, he had come to the conclusion that the French fact and the French language were better protected by Quebec's membership in Canada than they would be by Quebec's separation from Canada. Therefore, when he said, on American television, 'I will respect the decision made by Quebecers,' I was not annoyed by it. I said to myself: what else could he say? It did not mean he was supporting the sovereigntist camp. Not at all." Nor did Pelletier fear the attitude of the other French-speaking countries: "I would have been surprised if the other French-speaking countries had made a statement before France did," he says. "And I think France would have been extremely prudent in this matter."[2]

Nor did the prime minister believe that, during the referendum, France would demonstrate great enthusiasm for the sovereignty option. Moreover, he has his doubts, even today, as to whether France would have recognized the legitimacy of a YES vote and granted the new country diplomatic recognition. He took a very pragmatic view of Jacques Chirac's statement on CNN. "There was some legitimacy to the referendum," Chrétien says. "That was an important seeking of opinion. It's a consultation; it is not a definitive act. I discussed that with him before. I don't remember the words but I would have been very surprised that the day after, he would have done that. Because right away he would have had people in Pays Basque or Corsica and other places saying: good, sir, when are you doing the same thing here. He would have had to reflect on that, I'm sure."[3]

In Paris, however, Canadian ambassador Benoît Bouchard went to the source regarding the French president's statement on CNN. "I was told by officials in France that he wasn't absolutely sure about the question itself," he claims. "But in the preceding months, with the exception of the statement on American television, neither Mr. Chirac nor Prime Minister Juppé had ever, in a concrete or official way, made any declarations whatsoever that went against France's official policy of non-interference and non-indifference. Through the contacts we had at the Élysée with Mr. Védrine,[4] Mr. Juppé's chief of staff, we felt assured France was not interested in putting itself in a position that would invite accusations at home, the next day, of following a double standard: denying independence to Corsica while endorsing it for Quebec."[5]

Benoît Bouchard's interpretation of Chirac's remarks and the way he analyzed his attitude towards the referendum are in keeping with the approach he determined to use during Jacques Parizeau's trip to the French capital in January and for the entire duration of his assignment in Paris: downplay all situations. He avoided drawing attention to the skirmishes with the general delegation from Quebec, led by Claude Roquet at the time. "Roquet was a career diplomat and, even during the most intense or delicate situations, we always kept the lines of communication open," adds Bouchard. In fact, during the summer, Bouchard had sent Jean Chrétien a six-page letter suggesting he not react to what might appear to be a provocation. "I feared," he says, "that Ottawa would start (as in 1980) to send communication memos to Foreign Affairs in France complaining about how they had received Mr. Parizeau and how they had failed to raise the Canadian flag at City Hall, and so forth."[6]

Despite his wish to minimize the tension, the Ambassador got more than his share of it during the final week of the referendum, as Quebec's pressure on the French government did not let up. Jacques-Yvan Morin had come to Paris a few days earlier with a mandate to obtain the French government's recognition as soon as possible after a YES victory.[7] For, if Ottawa had doubts as to what France would do, Quebec was just as uncertain and aimed to keep up the pressure. "We were perfectly aware of the relationship between Jean Pelletier and Jacques Chirac, and there was always some doubt in Mr. Parizeau's mind," says Jean-François Lisée. "Would the French do what they said? We needed to be sure! So, Mr. Parizeau wanted to pin them down." The premier of Quebec, therefore, played all his cards and sent his own representative, first of all, to indicate the importance he attached to France's attitude and, then, to have on site someone who would inform him daily of developments. "I must say," adds Jean-François Lisée, "that Quebec's delegate general in Paris, who was a top calibre individual, was not appointed by Mr. Parizeau!"[8]

Morin's mission was thus to ensure that the National Assembly, presided over by Philippe Séguin, would recognize the political act constituted by the referendum, should the Élysée refuse to do so. "Or at least," Lisée continues, "to ensure that the presidency knew it had to act because, if it didn't, it would be contradicted by the National Assembly." As the French Foreign Office remained very timid in matters concerning Quebec, Philippe Séguin, whom they felt they could count on, "provided a counterbalance and offered direct access to Mr. Chirac," says Lisée.[9]

At first, it was not Jacques-Yvan Morin, but Jean-François Lisée that Parizeau wanted to send to Paris. The political advisor preferred to spend the final days of the campaign in Quebec and, moreover, "in 1995, to have me at the Élysée, I would have looked like a teenager!" he says. "It would have been a casting error to put me there, something

Mr. Parizeau did not seem to realize, while Mr. Morin was an ideal candidate."[10]

A small Franco-Québécois committee was formed in Paris, which included Morin and Roquet. Their mandate was to finalize the text that would constitute France's official statement, in the event of a YES victory on October 30. In Quebec, Jean-François Lisée wrote a first draft, which he proposed, after approval by Parizeau, to this committee. It said: "France duly notes the wish of the people of Quebec, democratically expressed by them today, to attain sovereignty, as is their right. Once the Quebec government has given formal expression to this wish for sovereignty, France will, quite naturally, recognize the new state."[11] Subsequently, different wordings were sent back and forth between Paris and Québec. "There was one point," Lisée recalls, "when it was the French who said, 'We would like to incorporate into the text the fact that there will be negotiation about the partnership.' Of course, we said, 'Very, very good!' and we even said, 'If you want to add a sentence saying France wishes to maintain excellent relations with Canada, please do. Because we too want good relations with Canada.' So, that was fine."[12]

This dance around Philippe Séguin seemed, to the Canadian ambassador in Paris, "to smack of folklore and the irrational." "How could anyone imagine," says Benoît Bouchard, "that Philippe Séguin, who is supposed to be non-partisan because he is president of the National Assembly, would be able to unite five, six different political parties, the communists, the left, the greens... The right itself has at least three different parties... How could anyone believe that, on a foreign policy question, without the French government having declared its position, these people would spontaneously get up and say: We recognize Quebec!"[13] Bouchard felt that the *députés* did not have the power to take such action. He also felt that Séguin and *député* Pierre-André Wiltzer, a strong supporter of Quebec sovereignty,[14] had insufficient authority to bring others, like Lionel Jospin and the Socialists, on board for their endeavour. "Two or three *députés* and the President of the National Assembly took a stand, out of 531," he says by way of conclusion. "It was a strategy of intellectuals."[15]

In Ottawa, events in the French capital seemed unimportant in the eyes of the government and the Prime Minister's entourage, compared to the numerous other concerns they had to deal with. On Tuesday, October 24, at 7:30 in the morning, Eddie Goldenberg took it upon himself to refresh Jean Chrétien's memory: The YES side was still ahead, and the gathering to take place that evening in Verdun was becoming a crucial step in the efforts of the NO side to close the gap. "Everyone is expecting your speech tonight to turn things around," he told him. "That's why they pay me such big bucks," Chrétien replied.

The Prime Minister's Office had chartered a coach to take the staff to Verdun and Jean Chrétien invited some MPs onboard as well, including Liberal caucus president Jane Stewart. At the last minute, she gave up her place, choosing instead to join a group of MPs who had rented a school bus for the trip. Getting into Montreal from the West end of the city is difficult. "It was well after rush hour but still to find ourselves in a jam that just got worse and worse as we neared the auditorium," she recalls. Finally, fearing she would miss the evening, she got off the bus and chose to walk all the way to where the gathering would take place. Other MPs joined her and, as they walked, they conversed with the people in the neighbourhood. When they got there, they saw that the auditorium was full and that the large crowd outside was growing. So, MP Barry Campbell suggested they use the door reserved for reporters. "There was a crunch of people at the inside entrance of the arena," Stewart recounts, "it was the prime minister. He stopped before entering and returned to the closed locked outside glass doors. Folks outside were banging hard to get in. He went right up to the doors. There was a hand contact with glass in-between, it was quite amazing."

Speaking before an audience of 12,500 people, crammed into the auditorium, the prime minister renewed his promise for change. His speech, which for his entourage and for the NO camp was to mark a major turnaround in the campaign, revolved around three ideas: demonstrate that a YES victory would have disastrous consequences for Quebec, talk about Canada with emotion, and repeat that the federal government was disposed to change the status quo in its relations with Quebec. "For us, everything is possible. We are rejecting one thing only: separation," he said. "I have listened to my fellow Quebecers saying that they are deeply attached to Canada. But they have also been saying they want to see this country change and evolve toward their aspirations. They want to see Quebec recognized as a distinct society within Canada by virtue of its language, culture and institutions. I have said it before and I'll say it again: I agree. I have supported that position in the past, I support it today, and I will support it in the future, whatever the circumstances. I know that some people are thinking about voting YES because they think it's the best way to bring about changes within Canada. A NO does not mean giving up any position whatsoever with regard to Canada's Constitution. We will be keeping open all other paths for change, including the administrative and constitutional paths." Nine times, during the course of his speech, the prime minister implored Quebecers to "think it through before you vote."

However, while he promised to keep the constitutional path to change open, Chrétien left it ambiguous—intentionally so—as to how he would use that route to fulfil the aspirations of Quebecers. There would "not necessarily be constitutional changes," explains Eddie Goldenberg, who had spent several hours with Chrétien preparing the speech. "But rather, changes on, maybe, employment and other elements." Chrétien also refrained from making any formal commitment to enshrining the notion of distinct society in the Constitution. "He approached the question of distinct society recognition," Goldenberg continues, "not from a constitutional standpoint, but rather the way he did immediately after the referendum, in a resolution before the House of Commons."[16] Jean Charest was among those who felt the Constitution should be amended. He made a formal commitment before the thousands of supporters gathered there that night: "I signed the (NO) manifesto and put my credibility on the line," he exclaimed. "I know that, in Canada, there is a feeling of impatience for changes. And I will stand with you, therefore, to demand those changes."[17]

The Conservative leader believes that the Verdun gathering was the pivotal event that turned the tide in the campaign. "It was that rallying-together that gave the federalists their break, in the sense that that was the day that turned things around,"[18] Charest says. Daniel Johnson believes that too, but he insists the Verdun gathering was a normal part of the general plan for the NO campaign, as envisaged at the outset. The first stage consisted of demolishing the referendum question, the second, of debating the economic costs of separation, "a debate which we definitely won," says Johnson, and thirdly, "a much more positive, constructive phase, of looking to the future, defining the issues, our vision of the world, of Canada, of Quebec."[19] His political advisor, John Parisella, gives a more pragmatic interpretation of the tone of the speech in Verdun. He recalls that in October 1995, the economic picture in Canada was not "very bright," that Chrétien had not succeeded in eliminating the deficit, which remained high, and that the dollar was depreciating. In his view, therefore, the NO camp would be unable to offer an idyllic vision of Canada with which to counter the YES campaign. "Consequently," he says, "the feeling in the Quebec Liberal Party was to have a speech that would strike more of a sensitive chord with Quebecers, that would satisfy Quebec's demands."[20]

Does this explain, in part, why an invitation extended to Pierre Elliott Trudeau, to participate in the Verdun gathering, was later withdrawn? Several days before the event, while having a coffee, as they did every morning at the permanent committee of the NO camp, John Rae informed Pierre-Claude Nolin that Jean Chrétien had invited the former prime ministers who were of Quebec origin, namely, Trudeau and Brian Mulroney, to take part in the Verdun gathering. Nolin, a Conservative Senator, reacted very negatively. "I said to him, 'I do not agree with having Mr. Trudeau as part of our strategy.' I remembered, as I am sure many Quebecers did, the first referendum campaign in 1980, during which Mr. Trudeau had made promises to Quebecers, which he then failed to keep."[21] Nolin explained clearly to John Rae that there was no way Jean Charest, whom he was advising, would appear at an event in which Trudeau was participating. To avoid embarrassing Chrétien, he promised to phone Mulroney himself, and he did.

Mulroney confirmed that he had received the invitation and had accepted it. "It will be perfect," he told Nolin. "Quebecers need to remember that there were Quebec prime ministers who governed the country, and that that was done in their interests." The Senator then explained to his former boss that he believed it was not a good idea to have Trudeau come up onto the platform "promising Quebecers 'all over again' that they had been heard and that in the future, it was going to be different." Mulroney did not agree and stuck to his position. But it was Nolin's viewpoint that finally prevailed. "It didn't take much to figure out that our opponents would be quick to capitalize on an error like that,"[22] the Conservative Senator concluded. In the meantime, John Rae looked after phoning Pierre Elliott Trudeau to cancel his invitation.

These dealings took place without the leader of the NO camp being informed, but, today, he is not overly offended about that. "I did not think it was necessarily in the order of things" to have them participate, Johnson says, "when you think about the circumstances in which the former federal prime ministers were invited. When you are dealing with people of their stature, who have left their mark, for better or worse, why invite them to take part in a campaign from which they had, after all, been absent? And why at the last minute? What message did that give? It was a federal decision, yes, but there are always people who take initiative without going over the details."[23]

There would be other initiatives during the week that the leader of the NO would not be informed about or on which he would not be consulted. "I decided the last week, now I do it my way," Jean Chrétien says today. "And I did it. I give credit to Mr. Johnson. He came along and he did not complain and he participated in the meeting, made a good speech at the Verdun rally. (...) I went on the air and so on. He agreed with all that. And it was not his fault. He had done a good job until they replaced Parizeau by Bouchard."[24]

The rally in Verdun on Tuesday, October 24, almost completely eclipsed the referendum held by the Crees, on the same day. The 6,380 voters had to answer the following question: "Do you consent, as a people, that the Government of Quebec separate the James Bay Crees and Cree traditional territory from Canada in the event of a Yes vote in the Quebec referendum?" The overwhelming majority of voters, 96.3%, expressed their preference for Canada, where they planned to stay, even if the YES side won. The level of participation, at 77% of the voters, was astonishing insofar as the referendum had been prepared in a short time and took place at the height of the hunting season. Three helicopters were used continuously in order to reach the voters. "The people have spoken and the message is clear," Grand Chief Matthew Coon Come had commented. "We won't go. This is not the 50% plus one that Jacques Parizeau says is democracy. This is a virtually unanimous message from my people. We won't go."[25] Although it went almost unnoticed in Southern Quebec, the referendum nevertheless constituted, for Coon Come, an important step in Cree progress towards self-determination. "It was a sign of (the) era," he says. "You must understand that our people were not allowed to vote until 1960. And here, we were determining a question, asking our people to get involved in a process that we developed, that came from us. And to ask them a question which could determine their place in a future possibly independent of Quebec. It meant a lot to the people."

The government of Quebec, which had no illusions about the results of the Cree referendum, had already riposted: "They are positioning themselves, both nationally and internationally, in preparation for a YES victory," said David Cliche, the premier's parliamentary assistant for Native Affairs. "The odds are that the day after a victorious Quebec referendum, I will find myself on the same flight with Grand Chief Matthew Coon Come, bound for the European Parliament."[26]

Coon Come immediately wrote a letter to Jacques Parizeau, with copies to Jean Chrétien and Lucien Bouchard. There was no reply except for the usual acknowledgement of receipt. "I certainly did not receive a telephone call from anybody congratulating us on what we did," he adds. It was to journalist Gilles Proulx, at the Taverne Magnan, in southwest Montreal, that Lucien Bouchard would express his reaction to the Cree referendum and to Matthew Coon Come's remarks: an independent Quebec would respect the decision of the Crees, but its territory remains indivisible.

One would have expected Jean Chrétien to be buoyed up by the triumph in Verdun as he headed over to the Liberal party caucus meeting the next morning. However, it was a shaken and uncertain prime minister who addressed his members of Parliament, even as they looked to him for the miraculous solution to the pending disaster. Jane Stewart kept a personal journal of those unforgettable days and she agreed to share it publicly. In Verdun, she says, "it seems to me, in the context of the thousands that were there, that the majority seemed to be anglophone and there was some worry in my mind, and certainly in the minds of my colleagues, that francophones were not in attendance. What we felt was a spell that had overtaken this whole question. It felt to us like there was nothing that we could do, those of us who were on the NO side, to break that spell. It was such a frustration for us because there just seemed to be no way to kind of shake the cage and say: Are you paying attention, here? Do you know if you vote yes, that what you are voting for is to separate from Canada?"

The feeling of powerlessness, therefore, that had been haunting the Liberal members for days, and which the Verdun rally had even served to reinforce, did not leave them when Jean Chrétien came in and joined them that Wednesday morning. Never until then had they felt so clearly the consequences of having been—for the first time in the history of the Liberal party—brought to power without significant support from Quebec and, what is more, as a majority government. This almost unconditionally guaranteed base, which Québec had generally provided to the Liberals ever since Wilfrid Laurier, had not been there in October 1993, and seemed to remain absent from the referendum campaign. Jane Stewart presided over the caucus. She remembers the moment Jean Chrétien entered the room. "When I saw him come into the caucus room, my visceral response was dramatic," she says. "I started to shake and feel sick to my stomach. The look I saw was one I know, stress and perhaps panic. I felt like crying."

There were over two hundred MPs and senators in the room. As he entered, they all rose to greet their leader with extended applause. That Wednesday, October 25, marked the second anniversary of the election that brought Jean Chrétien and his team to power. But their minds were not on celebrating. "I noticed he was just short of tears but I didn't think this was visible from the floor," says Stewart. Everyone sat down to hear the first report, coming from Parliamentary Leader Herb Gray, who ended his presentation with something like, "We will have a great victory for the YES!" "Faux pas but ominous. I could sense the prime minister was totally distracted," Stewart recalls. The reports followed, one upon the other. Then Chrétien leaned over to the caucus president to inform her that he might leave the meeting before it was over. Stewart passed him a note: No problem, the caucus is proud and united. "He touched my arm," Stewart continues, "and said, this is terribly difficult, this responsibility. I thought he was referring to Alfonso's job as ground coordinator, as Alfonso (Gagliano) was making his report at the time. But immediately, from his eyes, I understood he meant his own responsibility. I said, it'll be fine, we're all with you."

At that point, Brian Tobin asked to be put on the list of speakers. He would normally have to wait his turn but, as Chrétien indicated he was planning to leave any time after he himself had spoken, the caucus chair gave him the floor right away, after the presentation of reports was over. While Tobin gave an update on the big rally at Place du Canada, to take place on Friday, Stewart leaned towards Chrétien: "This is a terrible thing to say, but if things go bad, you've got my seat in Brent." Chrétien then smiled faintly and said, "I'd never do that."

The prime minister got up to speak to his MPs, who cheered him, standing. "I could feel his pain and his solitude," Stewart recalls. He told them that in 32 years, he had never seen anything like this in Quebec: there was no logic to it at all, lies, trickery, while for the NO side, nothing was working. That is how he justified his wish to address the nation that very evening. After a lengthy reflection on his career and on the confidence voters of Saint-Maurice had always shown in him, he admitted he did not understand why Canada, "the best country in the world," would find itself in this situation. He referred to Israel, Palestine and other countries threatened with breakup. Another ovation. He turned to leave the room, regained his composure, returned and continued speaking. "There were tears everywhere," says

Stewart. "The prime minister finished, everyone stood and clapped." Then Jean Chrétien withdrew to prepare his address to the nation.

"At one point," recounts Brian Tobin, "there was certainly a sense that we were likely to lose it. I mean, nothing manifested that better than the prime minister himself talking to his caucus and really having quite an emotional moment with his caucus. When he shared with them the stakes in this campaign and the possibility of defeat in this campaign." At no point did Chrétien clearly say to his MPs that Canada was in danger, that the NO could lose or that he feared the NO could lose. But "he talked in such an emotional way," Tobin adds, "it was very clear to everybody in the room, that what wasn't being said was present. You know, usually the caucus draws its strengths from the leader. Occasionally, the leader has to draw his from the caucus. That was the day when the caucus was giving back to the leader, in essence, wrapping around him and saying, carry on, this is a crucial moment."

In Washington that morning, journalist Henry Champ attended, as he did on most mornings, a press briefing by a White House spokesperson. Its purpose was essentially to inform reporters who were covering American politics about what issues were shaping up to be important that day. A routine meeting, nothing more. Champ was an old hand at journalism. He had worked fifteen years with the program W5 on the CTV network, he was even in Vietnam just before Saigon fell to Ho Chi Minh's forces, and he had been a foreign correspondent for the American network, NBC, before joining the CBC in 1993. Since he had also worked in Montreal, he took a keen interest in the referendum and had tried, on a number of occasions during those morning press briefings, to get a sense of Washington's interest in what was happening in Quebec, without much success.

Therefore, he could hardly believe his ears when, around 11:30 a.m., he received a call from Dave Johnson of the National Security Office, saying, "The President wants to make a statement on the Quebec referendum this afternoon, and we would like you to be at the press conference. Would you please, at the appropriate moment, ask a question on the subject?" "That was the first time that it ever happened, and it's the last time," the journalist remarks today.

Johnson's call was surprising not only in itself, but also by virtue of the motives behind it. The referendum question was not making headline news in the United States. During the previous two months, apart from an article in the *Washington Post* and one or two in the *New York Times*, Quebec had not appeared in any significant way in the American media. Champ was nevertheless delighted, since his hopes of obtaining an official statement from the American government were being fulfilled. Johnson did not explain the motives for the statement, but Champ drew his own conclusions. "There was no doubt in my mind," he says, "that he was attempting to do a favour for Prime Minister Chrétien and that he had been apprised of the possibility that this referendum wasn't going as well as everybody thought."

The intervention by Bill Clinton had been meticulously prepared. The day before, the United States ambassador to Canada, James Blanchard, was in Albany, New York. He received a call from Washington. "The White House is now finalizing the language to say something about Canada," said Jim Walsh, of the state department. "Maybe today, maybe tomorrow, maybe the next day. They've just called and they're really nervous, really worried. There's a front page *Washington Post* story saying the separatists could win, so they now realize it's for real."[27] Walsh then put Blanchard in touch with State Department staff for a long discussion on the statement being prepared.

On the Canadian side, there was a feeling of uncertainty about Clinton's intentions. "The question was: would the president speak and what would he say?" recalls Canada's ambassador in Washington, Raymond Chrétien. "It is a difficult line to follow. Not only what they would say but also how it would be perceived back home. Would it help the cause of Canadian unity or would it hurt it? It was very difficult to assess."[28]

When the President walked into the room, his glance met Henry Champ's, with the kind of eye contact that says, "I see you are here! I will acknowledge you in a moment." But it was not Champ who asked the question. At a certain point, Carl Hanlon, a correspondent with the Global network, intervened. Dave Johnson had phoned him too, as he had Champ. Since Hanlon was, in Champ's words, "pretty aggressive" on the subject of the referendum, he too had been trying for some time to obtain an official statement from both the White House and the secretary of state. "Mr. President," asked the Canadian journalist, "are you concerned about the possible breakup of Canada and the impact it could have on the North American economy and U.S.-Canadian trade relations?" "Let me give you a careful answer," replied the president. "When I was in Canada last year, I said that I thought that Canada had served as a model to the United States and to the entire world about how people of different cultures could live together in harmony, respecting their differences, but working together. This vote is a Canadian internal issue for the Canadian people to decide. And I will not presume to interfere with that. I can tell you that a strong and united Canada has been a wonderful partner for the United States and an incredibly important and constructive citizen throughout the entire world. Just since I've been president, I have seen how our partnership works, how the leadership of Canada in so many ways around the world works, and what it means to the rest of the world to think that there's a country like Canada, where things basically work. Everybody's got problems, but it looks like a country that's doing the right things, moving in the right direction, has the kind of values that we'll all be proud of. And they have been a strong and powerful ally of ours. And I have to tell you that I hope we'll be able to continue that. I have to say that I hope that will continue. That's been good to the United States. Now the people of Quebec will have to cast their votes as their lights guide them. But Canada has been a great model for the rest of the world and has been a great partner for the United States, and I hope that can continue."[29]

The president's reply lasted, at the very most, a minute and a half, but given the delicate circumstances in which it was made, five days before the referendum, it provided an exceptional boost to the federalist cause. The Canadian ambassador in Washington was very pleased. "One of the key moments in the referendum campaign. He was respectful of the Canadian democratic process, while at the same time emphasizing his support of a sure and loyal ally. He was on slippery terrain, because there could have been a second question. But, fortunately, everything went well."[30]

The sovereigntists, who had feared the worst, were also satisfied to emerge unscathed. Lucien Bouchard, while campaigning in Montreal, was delighted that Clinton had, on balance, stuck to traditional American positions. In fact, it was the Americans themselves who would be upset to note, in the headlines the next day, that the statement made by their president was upstaged by Prime Minister Chrétien's address to the nation and the speech by Lucien Bouchard, Opposition leader, both broadcast that same day, on television.

The idea of a speech by Jean Chrétien to the nation had already been circulating among federal strategists for some days, but it was only on the Tuesday morning that the prime minister took his decision. At an emergency meeting of his inner circle, he announced his decision: things had reached such a critical point that it was time to speak directly to the people and especially to Quebecers, via the television medium. It would be broadcast Wednesday evening, October 25. There was not much time left; once the decision was made, airtime had to be booked and an official order obtained. At the NO headquarters in Montreal, people were nervous. All they knew was that the event would take place Wednesday, the same evening as the great YES rally in Verdun. But no one had been consulted. On the morning of the 25, Pierre-Claude Nolin and Liberal John Rae discussed the federal initiative on their coffee break. Both of them were aware that Chrétien was a double-edged sword in the referendum campaign. "I could not change him," Nolin recalls. "He was, after all, the prime minister, and there was no way you could push him aside for two months and pretend he didn't exist. It was a matter of using him in an environment where it would do us the least damage. The idea of having him go alone on television did not leave us feeling very reassured. We crossed our fingers and thought: whatever happens, let's hope it goes all right."[31]

The speech had been prepared at the last minute, "more or less in a mad rush,"[32] Jean Pelletier recalls. In the process, Jean Chrétien's inner circle faced a number of problems, the main one being how much importance to give to the referendum question, in other words, to the interpretation to be given to a YES victory. "We knew Jacques Parizeau considered a YES victory to mean a vote for separation," says Eddie Goldenberg. "We wanted to reserve to ourselves the ability afterwards to say that the question was so unclear that people really weren't voting for separation. But, at the same time, if we didn't make it very clear to people that there were consequences to a YES vote, they might vote for it. So, the dilemma was in saying: a YES vote is a vote to break up the country, and not wanting to put ourselves in the position that, the day after the referendum, we would not be able to say: a YES vote was not a vote to break up the country." They chose therefore not to reveal anything about what Ottawa's position would be in the event of a YES victory, but to say that Jacques Parizeau would interpret such a victory as a vote for independence.

The speech was to be recorded at 5 p.m. Things got a bit behind schedule, and it was Jean Pelletier's chauffeur who finally delivered the two cassettes, one in French and one in English, to the CBC/Radio-Canada studios in Ottawa, four minutes before the scheduled broadcast time of 7 p.m.

Jean Chrétien had requisitioned the airtime, as he was permitted to do by law,[33] and, in order to justify his decision, he cited, at the very beginning of his speech, the urgent nature of the situation. "For the first time in my mandate as prime minister, I have asked to speak directly to Canadians tonight. I do so because we are in an exceptional situation," he said. The entire first part of his speech was a direct appeal to Quebecers. "Someone in a position of authority, a powerful position of authority, had to make Quebecers reflect about what was at stake, the importance of that, the consequences," Jean Pelletier, his chief of staff, explains today.[34]

"Don't be fooled," the prime minister urged. "And I say to my fellow Quebecers, don't let anyone diminish or take away what we have accomplished. Don't let anyone tell you that you cannot be a proud Quebecer and a proud Canadian. I ask you to remember all that this government has done over the last two years to help create change—positive change." He picked up the themes of his Verdun speech: "We must recognize that Quebec's language, its culture and institutions," he went on, "make it a distinct society. And no constitutional change that affects the powers of Quebec should ever be made without the consent of Quebecers." This was the equivalent of giving Quebecers the right of veto, which had been implicitly recognized until the early 1980s. He then addressed Canadians in the rest of the country: "Continue to tell them (Quebecers) that you hope deeply and profoundly that they choose Canada on Monday," he asked them.

Chrétien's intervention on television did not greatly surprise the sovereigntists, and the leader of the YES camp even less. "It was a normal thing for him to do," Jacques Parizeau says today. "The man was there to defend Canadian unity. It was within the rules of the game. Each of us did our work with the tools we had at our disposal. What I found distressing, at a certain point, was that I did not have all the tools available to me that a prime minister of Canada could have. That was frustrating. During the referendum campaign, we had succeeded in establishing pretty normal conditions with Radio-Québec, but, by God, were the negotiations to get a bit of airtime ever difficult!"[35]

It was agreed that the YES camp would also have the opportunity to address Canadians and Quebecers, immediately after Chrétien's speech. "We didn't want the issue in the last few days of the campaign to be that we were not democrats," says Goldenberg. "We thought it was far better to allow him to speak than to have a new issue in the campaign." But it was not Parizeau who gave the reply to the Canadian prime minister. It was Lucien Bouchard, who chose to give two different speeches, one addressed to the anglophone audience, the other to Quebecers. And why Bouchard instead of Parizeau? The official reason was that they had agreed between them that whenever there was a federal matter and Jean Chrétien was speaking in his capacity as head of the Government, the leader of the Bloc Québécois, who was also leader of the Opposition, would take responsibility. But the popularity of the Bloc leader, beyond any doubt, played an equally large role in the choice to have him, rather than Jacques Parizeau, appear on television.

Bouchard's speech in French constituted a full-blown attack on Chrétien. "This man has stood in the path of Quebecers each time they wanted to act as a people," he said. "How ill-mannered of this man to try to make us believe, this evening, that he plans to recognize the distinct character of Quebec. The man who is asking you for a blank cheque on our future this evening, is the same one who took advantage of our weakness after the NO vote in 1980, tearing up the Constitution of our ancestors and imposing another, which reduced Quebec's powers in the areas of language and education. René Lévesque, and a Quebec weakened and wounded by this debilitating NO of 1980, had signed an agreement with seven provincial premiers from English Canada. We know the rest. Lévesque found himself alone on the Quebec shore of the Ottawa River, abandoned by his allies. Thanks but no thanks to alliances! We have already tasted that and the morning after is too bitter. Mr. Chrétien, you will not do this to us a second time!" Then, in a different tone, he spoke even more directly to Quebecers. "In the days following (the referendum), we will have a first meeting of peoples, of two peoples who have never really met and who do not know each other very well." He then explained how the partnership would function, the harmonization of the various governing bodies that would be created to administer the agreements in the different sectors. And, buoyed up by his popularity, he ended with, "I'm counting on you!"

His speech in English was more rational. He invited English-speaking Canadians to understand the action that Quebecers were about to take and, in a very conciliatory tone, he said he was certain that "Canada is not deprived of resources and expertise, and I firmly believe it can speedily bring together its best minds, men and women of good faith, to sit at a table with Quebec and negotiate what is in its best interest." "I believe strongly in a future partnership between Canada and Quebec and I think I can speak for an overwhelming majority of Quebecers, if not all Quebecers, who will also want this negotiation to succeed after a YES."

For Jean Pelletier, this was not a reply because "Mr. Bouchard had no knowledge of Mr. Chrétien's text before he prepared his own.

They prepared their speeches at the same time without knowing what their counterpart would say." But he severely reproached him for giving two different speeches, "while it was always the sovereigntists who accused the federalists of having two speeches, one for Quebec and another one for the rest of the country."[36] Bouchard's remarks left the prime minister beside himself. "That speech was very unacceptable," Jean Chrétien still maintains today, "attacking me personally, calling me a traitor, when I've always been a very proud Quebecer and a very proud French-Canadian. I thought it was completely uncalled-for, unacceptable and vicious. And I said so. I told him privately and publicly."[37] The sovereigntists defend themselves against these comments: "Did we say anything about his family or personal relationships or even about his business problems?" retorted Jean-François Lisée. "No. We talked about political actions, which he carried out on behalf of the Government of Canada, when he was minister of Justice. It was not personal, it was political. He decided to get involved in the campaign, so it was quite normal for us to say, 'the person asking you to trust him with your future, here is what he has done in the recent past.' I am surprised that it surprised him."[38]

The two speeches were broadcast live on a giant screen in the auditorium in Verdun, where a big YES rally was under way. Jean Chrétien's speech was copiously booed, as was to be expected, while Bouchard's was welcomed, as one can imagine. Right after recording his speeches, the Bloc Québécois leader went to Verdun. "We had a tough time getting him up on the stage," recalls Alain Lupien, one of the YES organizers. "He was not content to enter by a small side door. The people wanted to touch him. They elbowed their way forward to be able to touch him. It was suffocating. At a certain point, we were afraid and wondered, what if we couldn't control the crowd? We were quite nervous."[39]

The Verdun rally held special importance for the YES since, the day before, the NO camp had attracted over 12,000 people in the same auditorium. Jacques Parizeau still has a vivid memory of this gathering, which represented a sort of climax for the YES campaign. "The image that comes back to me the most," he says, "is the young faces.

They were there. There were, I don't know… it seemed 70% of the hall was made up of young people." Why hold a gathering the day after a big NO camp rally and in the same hall? "It was because the auditorium was available," he says. "People should not imagine that we wanted to fire back: if the NO people went to Verdun, then we had to go to Verdun. No, no. This issue of booking halls created a whole problem that had not entered our minds…"[40] But the facts were somewhat different. According to Jean Royer, Parizeau's chief of staff, it was not easy to convince the three YES leaders to agree to take on the challenge. "We were strong in the East while the NO was strong in the West," he recounts. "I remember, we were in the premier's office at Hydro-Québec, and I suggested to Messrs. Parizeau, Bouchard and Dumont the idea of one-upping the NO camp and to hold a rally in Verdun, where there would be a larger number of participants than the Liberals had had. The three of them looked at me, somewhat sceptical, saying, 'why take this chance?' Mr. Parizeau said to me 'Are you sure, Mr. Royer?' Mr. Bouchard said, 'Are you sure?' Mr. Dumont scrutinized me, as if to say, 'Will he be able to deliver…?'"[41] Every resource was mobilized: the Parti Québécois, the unions, and the YES camp partners. The auditorium was packed. Jacques Parizeau received a tremendous ovation, "as a gesture of gratitude for having appointed Lucien Bouchard negotiator," says Royer, who adds, "At the end of the evening, when Mr. Parizeau got into the car, he said to me, 'Mr. Royer, I have enjoyed my evening very much.' I understood that what he meant was: we made the right decision."[42]

The results of a poll, published by *La Presse*[43] on Thursday morning, which gave the YES a two-point lead, no longer had great significance. The poll had been conducted between October 19 and 23, that is, before the two rallies in Verdun and before the televised speeches by Bouchard and Chrétien. But these results still helped to bolster enthusiasm in the YES camp: "Within our own groups," Guy Chevrette recalls, "there were people saying, 'I think we can win it' and 'we're going to win it!'"[44] By contrast, in Ottawa, this was considered such a critical time that the PMO cancelled all the prime minister's engagements for the week: he did not take part in question period in the House of Commons, he would not meet with five heads of government from Central America, whose visits had been planned for Thursday and Friday, and he would not address, as had been planned, the members of the Canadian Association of Broadcasters on Saturday.

In the middle of the week, Ontario Premier Mike Harris asked his deputy minister of Governmental Affairs to go and get a sense of the intentions of Jean Chrétien's office. Richard Discerny met with members of the Privy Council and learned that the federal government might not recognize a YES victory. Mike Harris thinks it was ambiguous that "the government's language went from saying this means the breakup of Canada to it's an irrelevant vote." On hearing the comments of his deputy minister, he thought that in Ottawa, "gee, they think they might lose here."

After the results of the Cree referendum, the results of the one held by the leaders of the Inuit and Montagnais communities on Thursday, October 26, came as no surprise. In the Nouveau-Québec area (the North), of the 4,300 Inuit of voting age, 76% turned out at the polls. To the question: "Do you agree with Quebec becoming sovereign?" 95% answered no. Immediately, Makivik, the firm that administers the Inuit funds proceeding from the signing of the James Bay agreement, cited two legal opinions to declare, "the consent of the Inuit must be obtained before their rights and status may be affected by the sovereignty of Quebec." Among the Montagnais people of the communities of Schefferville, Mingan, Natashquan, La Romaine and Pakuashipi, the results were even more striking: 99% of the 1,050 who voted, that is, 70% of eligible voters, said no to the question, "Do you agree with having the Inuit (Montagnais) people and their traditional territory be associated with Quebec if Quebec becomes an independent state?"

These results did not intimidate Jacques Parizeau. According to him, the Crees, the Naskapis and the Inuit were subject to the James Bay agreement, according to which these nations had given up all territorial claims, in exchange for the benefits they gained from the agreement. This had occasioned a federal law, which recognized the transfer of these territorial rights to Quebec. "Therefore, the referendums that took place among the Inuit and the Crees were a declaration of intent," he says, "in anticipation of discussion with the chiefs of these nations. But the legal framework (of these discussions) was clear and it fully respected the territorial integrity of Quebec." What was of greater worry to the premier was the attitude towards a sovereign Quebec on the part of the Aboriginal nations who lived along the St. Lawrence River: the Micmacs, the Attikameks, the Abénaquis, and the Mohawks. "These people had never renounced their territorial rights," he adds. "Consequently, if Quebec became a sovereign country, it would be forced to enter into negotiations with them. And those negotiations could go on for a very long time."[45]

On Thursday, October 26, the leader of the YES camp was campaigning in the Saguenay region, where the military base in Bagotville remained an important issue, since many people there feared it would close if Quebec became sovereign. "The military base in Bagotville remains a strategic installation for a sovereign Quebec," Parizeau declared. "There's no way it will close! The CF-18s will remain in Québec. That's not hard to grasp. They're ours."

The whole military question was and would remain a thorny issue throughout the referendum campaign. And if Parizeau initiated the topic of the military base in Bagotville while in the Saguenay, it was not because he was anxious to bring up the controversy on the sharing of military assets all over again at this point, but because Daniel Johnson had, on October 9, announced there would be major job losses at the base, if Quebec became sovereign. In fact, it was such a complex matter that the YES camp did not intend to give it more exposure than necessary. It so happened that on the same day that Parizeau touched on this question in the Saguenay, a Bloc Québécois MP launched an appeal to the Quebec military from Ottawa. Jean-Marc Jacob was the House of Commons representative for the riding of Charlesbourg, the location of the military base of Valcartier. He was vice-chairman of the standing committee on defence and official Opposition critic for national defence. Acting in that capacity, and on letterhead from the Office of the Opposition leader, he issued a communiqué in which he stated that a sovereign Quebec "should make the best use of the resources already deployed on its territory in order to allow all military responsibilities, the defence of its territory, participation in strategic alliances, peace missions, to be carried out at the least cost." And he added, "The day after a YES win, Quebec should immediately create a Department of Defence, the beginnings of a military headquarters, and offer all Quebecers serving in the Canadian Forces the chance to integrate into the Quebec Forces, while keeping their rank, seniority, wage and pension, as a means to ensure a better transition."

The press release, in its English-language version, caused a commotion at National Defence. While the French expression *"au lendemain de"* can, metaphorically or figuratively, mean *"dans l'avenir"*[46] (in the future), the English expression "the day after a YES win" could refer only to that day. Minister David Collenette reacted violently: "I thought that that was bordering on sedition," he says. "That an elected Member of Parliament would entreat the military who were in the service of all Canadians to somehow not discharge their legal obligation. (…) I think it was highly irresponsible, inflammatory and just plain dumb."

Should we see a cause-and-effect relationship here? Should we see anything in the fact that certain pilots were Quebecers?[47] Regardless, the fact remains that, starting the next day, there was a lot of activity in the sky over Bagotville, a sky that would become increasingly silent in the days following. Eighteen CF-18 Hornet fighter jets, which formed the wing of the base,[48] flew in small formations towards the United States: some headed for Oceana Naval Air Station in Virginia Beach, Virginia, while others set their course for Marine Corps Station in Beaufort, South Carolina. As of October 24, no trace could be found of eight other fighters, which might just as easily have been in a repair hangar somewhere as on standby for a NORAD mission, ready to fly at any moment, even during the night from October 30 to 31.[49] None of the jets that had gone to the U.S. would reappear in Bagotville again until after the referendum was over.

However, up to the 26th, the month of October had been very active at the base. Analysis of the daily registers[50] shows that there were 217 activities by 26 planes, which, over the course of the month, had been entered in the register. Some of these planes, 745, 769 and 782, made as many as 10 flights, while others had remained grounded, for example, 787 and 788. It was observed, furthermore, that other planes, 716, 768, 785 and 786, had made only one flight, registered after October 17, which might indicate that they were in Bagotville only temporarily or that they had been deployed elsewhere. The last activity before the referendum, a flight by jet 727, was entered on the 26, the only flight that day. Between the 27th and the 30th of October, the register is blank. Another detail, though impossible to verify, remains troubling: while the base normally counts on a fleet of 36 jets, only 26 appeared in the flight register for the month of October, which leads to speculation that the others might have been sent to another base prior to the month of October.

Friday morning started with a new poll by SOM,[51] a much more significant poll, since it took into account the opinions expressed by Quebecers between the previous Sunday and Chrétien's address to the nation. It gave a six-point lead to the YES, with the undivided vote proportionally distributed, and a slight advantage of one point to the NO, with three quarters of the undecided vote going to the federalists. The split between the two linguistic groups was clear: among francophones, without considering the undecided vote, the YES was ahead by 15 points, while the NO had picked up 75% of the non-francophone vote. The poll finally confirmed the Bouchard "effect": 31% of respondents admitted that Lucien Bouchard had influenced them. Angus Reid supported the data from SOM, granting the YES a four-point lead based on a survey conducted with 1,029 people between October 23 and 25. The suspense continued as the NO camp prepared its final salvo: the great rally at Place du Canada.

CHAPTER XII

"Quebecers, We Love You!"

That day, business was good for the flower vendor at the corner of Peel and René-Lévesque in Montreal. Early that week, someone had come up to her and said, "Friday, you won't need to trouble yourself with selling flowers. We'll be renting your stall for the day, and we'll compensate you for the lost sales." And on Friday, October 27, the florist's little booth was transformed into the headquarters for the NO campaign, protected by two rows of anti-riot barricades. Cell phones replaced flowers, and Pierre-Claude Nolin replaced the florist. The Senator threw together a network of informants, including former federal minister Serge Joyal, posted in one of the upper floors of Château Champlain, and, on the ground, an army of police officers and security guards who would attempt to control a crowd, the size of which it was still too early to estimate.

Four days earlier, the gathering, which was to be of a predictable size, organized by and for Montrealers, had gotten out of control for the NO committee. In the offices of Fisheries Canada, in Ottawa, Brian Tobin commandeered the event. And yet, the day had started out like any other. Government workers had all taken up the files left on their desks the previous Friday. As was his habit on Mondays, the Honourable Brian Tobin called a meeting of his deputy minister and a dozen public officials, representing the various branches of the ministry as well as the nation's regions, to assess the state of the fisheries. As one of his assistants painted the portrait of redfish fishing in the

Gulf of St. Lawrence, the minister's mind was elsewhere. "I had just had this dinner the night before with some of my cabinet colleagues who were grim in facing the possibility, at least, of a defeat. And I'm sitting, listening to the state of play of redfish," recalls Tobin, who suddenly came to the realization that, on that morning, in every government department, people were going about their daily routine, buried in their usual work. "This is crazy!" he thought. "We're sleepwalking toward perhaps the end of Canada."

The minister brought the meeting to an abrupt end and immediately summoned his deputy minister, William Rowat, along with a handful of senior officials, including one Quebecer, Françoise Ducros. He said to them, "There may be somebody with a strategy, somewhere in a tower of the Prime Minister's Office, somebody who knows how we're going to get out of this. But in the meantime I don't think we should just be sitting on our hands." Ducros went to find out what was going on, then informed her minister that businesspeople were organizing a rally, the following Friday, in Montreal, for the purpose of sending a clear message to Quebecers, to the effect, "it is important that you remain a part of Canada." "And I just came up with this idea that we should all go," says Tobin, "(that) we should encourage as many people in Canada, all across Canada, to go and to be there, and to negate the message that we didn't care." And at that moment, Tobin sat down and began to make phone calls.

In Montreal, the machine was already in motion, grinding towards Friday's rally. At the Sunday meeting of the NO camp, someone brought up the memory of a large assembly organized by the Conservative Claude Dupras, which had, in 1984, attracted some ten thousand people to the foot of Place Ville-Marie to cheer on Brian Mulroney. "Why not do it again?" people wondered, even as they turned to another Conservative, Pierre-Claude Nolin. The Senator then asked to have a half-hour to think it over, whereupon he withdrew to an adjoining room to confer with Pietro Perrino, the Liberal organizer handling the job of activities coordinator for the NO camp. As Conservative representation in the group was minute, Nolin said to Perrino, "I'll organize this rally, Pietro, if you get on board with me.

Because there's no way I'm going to do this alone. I'll need a staff, and it will probably be your staff that I'll use." Perrino agreed, and Nolin went back to the meeting room. "I'll do it," he told the committee. "And here's how."

At the same time, the NO committee learned, through John Rae, that a group of business people, led by Philip O'Brien, were, on their own initiative, also preparing a march in the streets of the city, from Park Avenue to the city centre, possibly to Dominion Square. This was the same Philip O'Brien who had organized, three days earlier, an assembly of business people at the Palais des congrès.[1] These people would need to be contacted. The organizational method that Nolin came up with was simple, but required a great deal of work. The idea was to find, in every commercial building in the neighbourhood, one person per floor or per prime tenant, whose role would be to notify employees that a rally was being organized on Friday, and that they were invited to take part. Flyers were quickly printed and passed out, on which were indicated the date, time and location of the rally. "And it was a bit like a snowball that builds on its own momentum," says Nolin. "Word of mouth did the rest."[2]

The objective of the NO forces was to muster 15,000 people. Nolin immediately decided on the location—Place du Canada—and the décor: a flatbed trailer and acoustic loudspeakers. On the flatbed trailer, there would be three people: the three leaders, Johnson, Chrétien and Charest. "Some people were telling me that Sheila Copps might want to speak," said Nolin. "I said, 'there's no way. The three leaders—period.'"[3] A discussion ensued, on the matter of who should act as master of ceremonies. In the end, the honour went to Lisa Frulla.

On Monday morning, John Rae, who was the NO campaign's go-between with Ottawa, asked Nolin whether he would accept having people from other provinces take part in the rally and, if so, could they bring their flags along? "My answer was yes to both questions—something that I regret having accepted," says the Conservative Senator today. "The referendum was a matter for Quebecers to settle, an issue to be settled in Quebec by Quebecers."[4] Rae then invited Nolin to get in touch with Brian Tobin.

Daniel Johnson had his notion of what Friday's gathering should be like, and he frowned when he learned that in Ottawa, steps were being taken that fell outside the realm of the established strategy. "It started out as an event involving Montreal and adjoining areas," he recalls. The plan, as conceived by the NO campaign, was to get as many downtown workers as possible out of their offices at noon, to come and eat their lunch together at Place du Canada. "We were sure there'd be 8,000 people," remembers Daniel Johnson, "maybe 10,000 tops... We sounded the call in the 450 (area code) zone."[5]

On Monday evening, Nolin phoned the Fisheries minister through the central switchboard of the prime minister. He told him that John Rae had talked about him that morning and confirmed that he had agreed to let participation in the gathering be extended to Canadians outside Quebec. Tobin again asked him if people could bring along flags. The Conservative Senator repeated his approval. "I didn't want a rally full of maple leaves," says the former Fisheries minister today. "I wanted to make sure that there were flags present, that we would have both the fleur-de-lys and the maple leaf. I also wanted to invite every province to bring their own flag, and I encouraged people to do that."

Nolin looked into the means of transportation that would be used by these people from outside Quebec and how expenses would be defrayed. He was aware that the rest of Canada might not be familiar with Quebec's laws on spending controls during election or referendum campaigns. "So," he says, "I informed him that it was out of the question that transportation be free of charge. At the very least, people would have to pay for the cost of their own travel. Come if you like, I told him, but it's out of the question that you make it a free trip." Tobin listened attentively to what he was hearing from the Conservative organizer, who became emphatic: "...because in the end, it's Mr. Johnson and the election agent who will be held responsible for this breach of Quebec's electoral law," he added.[6]

The very next morning, Nolin informed Pierre Anctil, Daniel Johnson's representative and, in a way, the chairman of the NO headquarters. Anctil then wanted to be sure that Quebec's laws would be observed. He immediately published a memo, which was distributed to a great many people in Ottawa and the different provincial capitals.

Brian Tobin's phone was ringing off the hook. He called on influential Liberals throughout the country, the airlines and railroads and, also, sponsors likely to make financial contributions to the operation. He got in touch with some provincial premiers. "If we decide we're going to have a rally," he asked them, "will you come? Will you bring people? Will you encourage our political organizations to be there?"

On Tuesday morning, Brian Tobin reported to the cabinet. He told his colleagues about his numerous phone calls and informed them that it would be possible to have planes, buses, and Via Rail trains. "People are interested," he told them. "I'm convinced we can have a pretty good turnout from across the country." The ministers discussed the plan, some of them calling for prudence: "Won't a gang of anglophones from other provinces coming to Montreal tend to have the opposite effect? What happens if no one comes? That would be terrible and would reinforce Lucien Bouchard's position that no one cares about what happens in Quebec." This was, in substance, what the ministers said to their colleague from Fisheries. Tobin then turned towards the prime minister, and said, "This is Tuesday. We only have (three) days. The referendum is the following Monday. Either tell me no, and we'll go back to cabinet business, or let me leave this room now—I have a lot of work to do." Jean Chrétien asked him, "How many will come?" Tobin replied, "I guarantee you we'll have 10,000 or 15,000." Chrétien wanted to be sure: "Are you sure?" he asked. "I am sure," replied Tobin. Chrétien then said to him, "Go!" And Brian Tobin left the cabinet meeting.

In fact, the apparatus was already in motion, and if the prime minister had not approved the operation, it would have been hard to stop. Early Wednesday morning, before the meeting of the caucus of Liberal MPs, Brian Tobin did an interview with Valerie Pringle, moderator of the program *Canada AM,* on the CTV network. "I'm not organizing the rally in Montreal," he told her. "There is a rally by the NO campaign being organized in Montreal, in Quebec, by the NO committee chaired by Mr. Johnson. But what we're doing is we're asking people from all across Canada to come and join in that NO rally, that crusade for Canada. You've seen the formation of committees here in Ottawa. There are committees under way in Toronto. There are charter aircraft coming out of Western Canada and out of Atlantic Canada. Canadian Airlines has announced what it calls its Unity Fare: up to 90% discounts for people who want to purchase tickets into Montreal from anywhere in Canada." Two hours after the interview was broadcast, Tobin got a phone call from Canadian Airlines, imploring him to stop talking about the special fare, because the seats were sold out.

Brian Tobin contacted Hollis Harris, chairman of Air Canada. He was looking for planes and told him he would need them in British Columbia, Alberta, Newfoundland and everywhere else. He said to him, "I'm not calling you as a member of the cabinet or of Parliament. I don't have the authority to do so. I'm calling you as a citizen. I need all the planes you have available, and I want them at the best possible rate." Harris answered with his American accent, "Yes, sir. You'll have your planes. And you'll have them at the best possible rate." Tobin felt it necessary to point out that this was not a request from the Canadian government. Harris answered, "I understand, sir. You'll get your planes..." This is how Tobin remembers the conversation today: "It was kind of a chuckle because either he was an extraordinarily dedicated new Canadian and understood the importance of what I was asking as a citizen, or he really didn't believe that I wasn't calling on behalf of the government. But we got our aircraft." And at the same rate as the Canadian Airlines ones at that.

While the Fisheries minister was sending off his staff and deciding to devote his week to the referendum campaign, Andy Scott, the federal MP from Fredericton and former senior policy advisor to Frank McKenna, was in his office in the Confederation Building. When Tobin called and asked him to get himself immediately to a meeting in the conference room of his ministry, he did not know why he was being summoned, but he rushed over, thinking it might be about a problem with the fishery in his region. Several people were present. The atmosphere was one of sadness and anger, but also determination. MP Dennis Mills, for example, was furious at the way the campaign had been run up to that point and came right out and said he had the feeling he'd been manipulated and played for a fool. Criticisms were flying in every direction, primarily aimed at the NO forces and the Quebec Liberal Party. Scott made himself available: "I don't know if I reacted for my country or for myself," he says today. "I didn't know if it would work or not. But it will relieve me of having to feel for the rest of my life that I didn't do anything. I don't know if that's noble or selfish or what it is. But I know that I didn't come to Ottawa as a Member of Parliament to watch my country's disintegration."

Tobin then informed them that on Wednesday morning, he would go on CTV to invite Canadians from all over the country to come to Montreal on Friday. But he admitted that, quite frankly, he was afraid: if the operation were to fail, he did not want to be seen as the person responsible for the failure—not only for his own image, but in regard to the result itself as well. Consequently, he asked the people around the table what they thought of the idea, and he asked them to be very specific about what they could contribute to making the affair a success. Combining their efforts, they attempted to imagine how many people they could bring to Montreal. How many could Scott send from New Brunswick? How many could Ronnie MacDonald send from Nova Scotia? And Sergio Marchi—how many from Toronto? Each one of them made his own calculations. At the end of the meeting, Tobin asked, "Can you guarantee these numbers?" Scott offered to call Frank McKenna during the evening; his reaction would provide a good test.

In Fredericton, Frank McKenna had just turned in for the night. The phone rang once. It was already late… indeed an hour later than the time in Ottawa. It was Scott. "I'm sorry, Andy, but he's sleeping," answered the premier's wife. Scott was insistent. "Please, Julie, wake him up. I think it's important." McKenna picked up the phone, and Scott laid out the plan for him. The idea appealed to him. Soon after, it was Tobin's turn to talk to him. "On the phone that night, I expressed my view that we were at the stage where we had to take a high risk," recalls McKenna, "and that the emotional impact might be very positive. But I was preaching to the converted. They were really calling me to tell me that they had concluded that things were very, very bad and that something had to be done. And as the province that would have the most meaningful relationship with Quebec, could we envision such a rally coming off?"

Brian Tobin's interview on CTV was broadcast nationwide. The MPs' constituency offices were inundated with phone calls from people asking how to get to Montreal. Thus began the search for buses. In Montreal, at NO headquarters, the strategists were suddenly unable to determine how big the event would be. They had to keep going back to the municipal authorities to have their demonstration permit changed. "At first, it was just for Place du Canada," says Pierre-Claude Nolin. "But the bigger it got... at one point, the city authorities said to us, 'Look, we can't give you a permit just for Place du Canada. We'll have to give you a permit for Dominion Square as well. We're going to have to close off some streets.'"[7]

On the previous Saturday, a member of the O'Brien committee, Jonathan Wener from the firm Canderel, joined CJAD radio reporter Rick Leckner at his cottage in the Laurentians to talk about the march that was being prepared. Leckner was a traffic and public safety specialist. Wener said to him, "You know Jacques Duchesneau. You should handle security." Leckner, even though he was a journalist, did not show the slightest hesitation. He spoke to the police chief, who then told him that a march was much more problematic than a gathering that stayed in one place. The O'Brien committee then opted for a stationary demonstration at Dominion Square. As the consolidation of the two committees was now a *fait accompli*, it was Leckner who, having taken a week off to make the event successful, worked in co-operation with Lieutenant Peter McKay of the Guy Street police station, which had jurisdiction over the quadrangle including Place du Canada and Dominion Square. Friday at noon, the journalist would be at the reins of a staff of 125 volunteers whose job would be to handle security during the demonstration.

Andy Scott's and Brian Tobin's phone calls to Frank McKenna set into motion what was probably Canada's most powerful electoral apparatus. On Wednesday, after attending the Liberal caucus, Scott caught a plane to Fredericton, but McKenna's organization had already taken charge. People, in great numbers, were calling the office of the Fredericton MP. Scott put out calls on the radio, inviting people to get themselves to Montreal or, at the very least, to make their vehicles available to the organization. The response from the bus companies was impressive: "Whatever you want, we've got it!" In a matter of hours, there wasn't a single bus left anywhere in the province. The organizers were now looking for school buses, vans and station wagons. Even Tim Hortons contributed their Foundation's minibuses, normally used to carry children to summer camp.

"It was just like a war where logistics were the biggest issue," says Frank McKenna, who now likes to point out that people in his province remember where they were on that day, in the same way people remember where they were on September 11, 2001, or when John F. Kennedy was assassinated. "This became a massive logistical exercise but became a hugely emotional exercise too," he adds. People were designated as "captains" of buses and coaches to ensure that no one got lost in the shuffle and left behind in Montreal for the return trip. The rallying point for all transport vehicles: Edmunston.

On the other side of the country, attorney Celso Boscariol, two-time Liberal candidate defeated by a Reformer in the federal elections of 1993 and 1997, was in his office at the firm Watson Goepel Maledy. It was late in the day on October 23 when the phone rang. It was Brian Tobin calling to explain his plan. Boscariol's immediate reaction was to think, "It's Monday night. This can't be done by Friday." But Tobin wouldn't give up: "No, listen. You have to do it. It's for the country. Say yes, and see what you can do." And then he hung up.

Celso Boscariol, who was president of the Liberal Party of Canada in British Columbia, could count on a wide network of organizers. He set to work right away. After a few calls, he called David Stow, chairman of the party's fundraising committee, and said to him, "We've checked with Air Canada. They tell us that chartering a plane to Montreal represents 14 hours of flying time, which costs something like $10,000 an hour, for a total of $161,000. We're going to divvy up the seats between Edmonton, Calgary, Saskatchewan and Manitoba, and everyone will pay a pro rata share. Our share in British Columbia will come to 60 or 70,000 dollars. Do you think we can come up with it?" The phone cascade was set into motion. "Suddenly," Boscariol recalls today, "the money started pouring in. And then, by that time, news hit the street that we were doing this. And (there was this) outpouring of people wanting to come on the flight. And so, in order to defray some of the costs, we said, 'it will be $250 per person to fly on a flight.'" Staff at Watson Goepel Maledy were put to work making phone calls, fundraising, making bank deposits and whatever else was needed. Boscariol was bowled over by the patriotic response of businesses. "In instances where you'd ask for $1,000, they came in with $5,000, simply because they felt the importance of the event. And it's not like there was any political receipt involved that they'd get a tax rebate for." All signs indicated that the plane would indeed be flying.

In Edmunston, seventy motor coaches, buses of every kind, vans and several personal automobiles, having come in from every direction during the day on Thursday, were now lined up in the huge parking lot of a shopping mall where all of the caravans were to converge. They came not only from New Brunswick, but also from Prince Edward Island, Nova Scotia and even Newfoundland. The atmosphere was feverish and, awaiting the departure, hundreds of people sat down to coffee and doughnuts in the mall, which was open to them. A local radio station gave Andy Scott a megaphone, and he attempted to establish some order among the troops assembled in the parking lot. "It was exciting, it was electric," he says, while acknowledging that, at a certain point, the organizers were no longer in control of events. "We were overwhelmed with both the availability of buses and the interest of people. It became a lot less organized."

Someone pointed out to Frank McKenna, who came in on a plane during the day, that the Edmunston airport was right near the Quebec border and that if nothing was done to prevent the YES side from achieving victory, he would be in proximity to a foreign country. The premier was now going from coach to coach, greeting people and "telling them 'thank you' and how important what they were doing

was, and inviting them to tell Quebecers how much they loved them."
"It was wonderful," recalls McKenna today. "It was the most magical
day." Night had fallen by the time the string of vehicles, which
stretched for miles, got onto the Trans-Canada Highway bound for
Montreal.

The YES forces watched, powerless, as the snowball gathered
girth, and they began to get nervous. "We didn't know what to
expect," says Alain Lupien. "But we knew it was going to be big. We
knew that these people in the buses would be consuming beer. They
weren't coming to tell us they loved us, they were coming to take part
in a party." The thing that the YES strategists feared above all was a
loss of control. "If violence was to break out in the midst of all this,"
adds Lupien, "the image of the referendum would not be very positive. Violence has always been bad for the sovereigntist side."[8]

Pierre-Paul Roy, advisor to Lucien Bouchard, was of the opinion
that holding this rally, with its timing at the end of the campaign, was
somewhat uncouth. And like Lupien, he was getting worried. "It was
rather provocative," he says, "to swoop into downtown Montreal, a
few days before the referendum, utterly ignoring every rule and
throwing money around." Like Lupien, Roy knew that if things got
out of control, it was the YES side that would lose out. "There was a
watchword that was very clear, very to the point," he recalls, "which
was to stay well away from there, to let these people demonstrate
peacefully, hoping that everything would go smoothly."[9]

And at noon on Wednesday, in the course of an interview broadcast on the radio from Taverne Magnan in southwest Montreal, Lucien
Bouchard, speaking to an enthusiastic crowd, let it be known that he did
not approve of the announced demonstration. After referring to Jean
Chrétien's speech the night before, in Verdun, as "dishwater" and dismissing the idea of a distinct society as meaningless, he questioned the
motives of these last-minute declarations of love, coming from those
who had "torn up" the Canadian Constitution in 1982.[10]

All the YES coordinators in the region were summoned to
Montreal "so that," explains Lupien, "we could identify some of the
hotheads—sovereigntists who would feel inclined, with this sort of

event, to go give their new friends a piece of their mind." The YES side had no doubts about the effectiveness of the police forces, nor were they concerned about intelligence, but they wanted to keep the "hotheads" away from Place du Canada. Teams were set up inside the Métro stations. "If we spotted a Joe Troublemaker who was known to us, we'd stop him, reason with him and tell him, 'Look, don't do that, OK? That's really not what we need right now…'"[11]

In the meantime, the rest of the country was getting organized. MPs and ministers were attempting to bring busloads of NO supporters from their ridings into downtown Montreal. Jane Stewart phoned the owner of a bus company, Don Sharp. "Don," she said to him, "I need buses. I don't know how many, but at least one." She got three, free of charge. "He just donated (them). That was his way of making a contribution." In a baseball park in eastern Ottawa, the buses—several hundred of them—and cars were stacking up. John Manley was the minister responsible for eastern Ontario, and he handled the organization needed to get as many people as possible to Montreal. On Thursday, there was not a single bus left in the region, "even in northern New York State," recalls Manley. The fleet of buses and vehicles of every kind that left for Montreal in the early morning hours was considerable.

In Vancouver, people climbed aboard singing *O Canada* to the applause of a crowd that had turned out to see them off. The event was repeated in Edmonton. In Regina, a crowd squeezed into the airport, both to cheer on the travellers and to see the plane. It was the first time a Boeing 747 had landed at the airport in Saskatchewan's capital. When the aircraft took off from Winnipeg for the last leg of its trip, it was full.

The man who took the initiative to transform a Montreal-sized rally into a nationwide expression of love towards Quebecers caught the first flight for Montreal and settled into the 20th floor of a hotel that gave him a bird's-eye view of Place du Canada and the surrounding neighbourhood. Brian Tobin spent the late-morning hours in front of his window. He watched the workers erecting the speakers' platform, others placing security barriers around the perimeter, technicians setting up the sound equipment, and so on. He downed coffee upon coffee, a sense of anguish growing inside him as the morning progressed, seeing that there was little activity around the workers, who were busying themselves with set-up. A half an hour, perhaps a little bit more, before the start of the event, there were a couple of thousand people there, but the park was far from being filled to capacity. "I remember feeling, oh my God, maybe the nay-sayers were right, maybe people aren't coming," he recalls, "and I was sitting there with this absolute chill in my heart, looking down twenty floors below. And all of a sudden, I guess the buses began to arrive, or maybe the train arrived, or the people got in from the airport. All of a sudden, people began to filter in from the side streets and the place began to fill up." Tobin, his wife, his children, and Sheila Copps—who, along with her family, also had a suite on the same floor of the hotel—all applauded every time a wave of supporters joined the crowd.

At noon on Friday, October 27, Place du Canada was full and overflowing onto Dominion Square and down the neighbouring streets. On the speakers' platform, Jean Chrétien proclaimed that this day belonged to the citizens rather than the politicians, and he called on every voter to think of future generations when they went to vote on Monday. The speeches of Daniel Johnson and Jean Charest were no less impassioned, but the crowd attached little importance to their content. The real message was not coming from the rostrum, it was in the atmosphere. "The speeches, in a context like that—it was really complicated," recalls Jean Charest. "We were talking to the people, but you had the feeling that it was so big that we couldn't even be sure that the people could hear what we were saying. But this allowed us to keep a certain momentum going for the campaign. That was how it felt to me."[12]

In the crowd of tens of thousands of people, a man strolled through, incognito, impressed, but also frustrated by the turn of events. Without Philip O'Brien, this great gathering would not have taken place. At noon, he had been invited, along with the members of his committee, to come and shake hands with Jean Chrétien and Daniel Johnson as the leaders came out of Place Ville-Marie. "The humble little organization committee was to meet them at the door," he recalls. But things did not go according to plan. "Everyone was supposed to exit from Place Ville-Marie at the same time," he says. "The team that had put together the gathering was to go out with the first ministers, and everyone was supposed to march in a big parade to Dominion Square and Place du Canada and to meet up with them on the speakers' platform. But they didn't leave us room. RCMP officers surrounded Johnson and Chrétien. They didn't know who we were. So we were ejected, like a cork from a champagne bottle! We never saw a thing!"[13]

O'Brien and some members of his committee then took another route, going through the western entrance of Place Ville-Marie rather than the main door. They thus managed to get to the next street over, Mansfield Street, by way of René-Lévesque Boulevard. They were still a good block away from Place du Canada. "I couldn't go a step further," O'Brien says, "there were so many people. As it turned out, the committee took part in the demonstration just like everyone else. The RCMP didn't know who we were, couldn't care less who we were. But the politicians knew who we were, obviously, because they'd asked us to be very much involved. But it was not our show. It was their show. They decided it was their show and 'goodbye, guys, you're gone!' We never even made it anywhere near the place, anywhere. We were out of there."[14] Subsequently, Philip O'Brien never got a phone call or communication of any kind to express the least bit of recognition to him or his committee.

Mike Harris, who had been premier of his province for only four months,[15] chose to lose himself in the throng. Going nearly incognito, he preferred to take part in the gathering as a family man rather than as a politician and government leader. "I felt that if I went with my son, I could go and represent Ontario families that overwhelmingly, in the mainstream I had heard from, wanted to send this signal to Quebecers that we wanted them to be part of Canada. It was very exciting. There was a lot of emotion; there was a lot of passion. I don't know how many people were there, but we felt the whole world was there. We *were* the world at that moment. It was quite a moving time. A lot of tears at that, some of joy, some of fear, some of concern."

Frank McKenna was also in Montreal, but he never lost sight of the interests of his province, even when the interests of Canada were at stake. "I've a very embarrassing memory. Coincidentally, the day of the Montreal rally, I also had scheduled a business meeting in Montreal with a company that was interested in investing in New Brunswick. I had a reputation for doing that, and I can't honestly tell you it was a good reputation, of trying to get business wherever I could." While New Brunswickers thronged to Montreal to express their affection to Quebecers, in buses that he had helped to fill, Frank McKenna was busy plundering: attempting to attract a Montreal company to set up shop in his province. "I got some criticism for that," he concludes. "It was just bad timing."

Nor did Bob Rae take part in the rally. He doesn't even remember if he was invited. "Frankly," he says, "it was taken over by the Grits and the premiers. And I was not a Grit and I was not a premier. So, I just let it happen." There were other parties absent: several provincial premiers and Preston Manning, who was politely asked not to attend.

October 27 was a typical fall day, sunny but windy. The demonstration went forth beneath the colours of a multitude of flags—from the other provinces and from Quebec—flapping in the wind, but it was an immense Canadian flag that stirred people's emotions most of all. It was a flag of uncommon proportions, and it moved over the heads of the people gathered. "I still get emotional when I think about that," says Mike Harris today. "The symbol that we're Canada here in Quebec. And as you saw this huge flag being passed through the crowd and rippling, it was more powerful than all the words. That had the greatest impact on us all."

Celso Boscariol also cherishes an enduring memory of the flag: "Everybody was seeking to touch the flag, it was almost like, you know, touching the Holy Grail, just trying to have a piece of it…" Georges Arès, an active member of the *Association canadienne-française de l'Alberta*, had come to Verdun for the gathering of the NO forces on Tuesday. He was persuaded by the arguments of a member of the board of directors of the *Association canadienne d'éducation de langue française*, Charlotte Ouellet, that he should stay in Montreal until Friday. He was at the Place du Canada rally and remains marked by the incident of the Maple Leaf. "There were speeches," he recalls, "but the main thing was this great big flag that was moving around, showing everyone that this was a rally for Canada, for the place held by *la Francophonie* in Canada."[16]

When the flag brushed over Philip O'Brien's head, he forgot the moment of bitterness that he had felt when he was pushed aside from the procession of dignitaries. "We were underneath the flag," he recalls, "and the sunlight was shining through it. So, this red colour... you were kind of enveloped in red and the big maple leaf was coming over you and the wind was hitting this thing. We thought we'd just take off in the air, like a parachute sort of thing. This was not meant to be. They were going to put the flag somewhere but it was too big, (so) somebody decided to use it as a... It was an accident. Like the rally itself, we weren't planning 100,000 people. These are the things that are caused by passion..."[17]

A hundred thousand people? Ten years after the event, conversations become passionate when an attempt is made to put a figure on the crowd that amassed on that day at Place du Canada. On the day after the referendum, giving a speech in Toronto, Jean Chrétien estimated the size of the crowd at 150,000 people, 25,000 more than the estimate made by Sheila Copps during the event. As for Pierre-Claude Nolin, he estimated the crowd at 200,000 people.

Roger Laroche, traffic reporter for Radio-Canada, was flying over the rally in a helicopter. Three people were on board: the pilot, a cameraman and the reporter, all three strapped in, because the door of the craft had been left open. The night before, Laroche had had the privilege, in the company of Rick Leckner—another traffic reporter who, for the occasion, had chosen, rather, to work for the O'Brien committee—to go to a meeting attended by representatives of various authorities affected by the event that was taking shape: Quebec department of Transport, the city of Montreal, the Montreal police force, the Royal Canadian Mounted Police, etc. Those present were in unanimous agreement on an important fact: the capacity of Place du Canada and Dominion Square was between 32,000 and 35,000 people.

When he observed the multitude from the air, Laroche remembered this number. As he was equipped with a police scanner, he heard it again in the conversations among the police officers on the ground and the RCMP officers who were also flying over the event in helicopters. Laroche has an image in his mind's eye: "I saw the Olympic Stadium filled to capacity for a Rolling Stones concert," he recalls today. "It can hold around 52 to 53,000 people. I made a mental comparison and chose to play it safe and to inflate the police estimate."[18] He tossed out a figure of 50,000.

Jean Bédard, who was moderating the special broadcast on Radio-Canada, was stationed in a two-story building, such that he did not have the same view as Laroche. However, by his side were commentators Pierre Anctil for the NO side, Jean-François Lisée for the YES side and journalist Michel Vastel. Anctil had a map of the quadrangle with a grid that helped to get a better idea of the size of the crowd, square by square. He made his own evaluations and shared them with Lisée, who found them reasonable. The information that Bédard passed along on the airwaves came to him then, for the most part, from Daniel Johnson's chief of staff, approved by Jacques Parizeau's political advisor and backed up by the information given by Roger Laroche from his helicopter. Just then, someone from the program's control room asked him to stop giving numbers and, from the air, Roger Laroche, who was hearing Sheila Copps talking about 125,000 people, decided to do the same. The estimates put forward by Radio-Canada up to that point were markedly below everything coming from English-language media and politicians.

Senior information programming officers at CBC, in Toronto, quickly got in touch with their counterparts at Radio-Canada to check on the French network's sources, because the estimates were inconsistent. Doubt set in the Montreal newsroom, and Laroche had to explain the nature of his "police source" to his superiors. The Prime Minister's Office, in Ottawa, was shocked: "The reality is that the report on Radio-Canada was at 3 or 4 o'clock in the afternoon and probably nobody was watching," says Eddie Goldenberg. "But it was just unfair. There had been a perception over a long period of time, rightly or wrongly, that Radio-Canada had a separatist bias. So, this seemed to symbolize it. People were very upset and very angry, but we knew there was not very much you could do about it. I think that the press office probably spoke to people at Radio-Canada."

To get things out in the open, and to be in a position to answer all the accusations flying their way, the information programming people at Radio-Canada brought out the big guns. In the days that followed, they tuned to aerial images of the location and solicited the services of a surveyors' firm to assess the maximum capacity of Place du Canada and Dominion Square. Filled to capacity, the space could not have held more than 70,000 people.

Who was there? How many people came from outside Quebec? About fifteen thousand, according to Pierre-Claude Nolin. "It was Montrealers for the most part," confirms Daniel Johnson today. "The NO committee had brought in a great many people from our electoral constituency associations, from greater Montreal, what is now called the 450 zone. It's true that in the street, I met students from Cornwall and young Franco-Ontarians who had come in by car for the day, and people from New Brunswick. It was a bit of a patchwork. It started out that it was supposed to be a demonstration for office-workers in downtown Montreal who would come down on their lunch hour then go back to work. And for the most part, that's the sort of people who were there."[19]

At the end of the afternoon, Place du Canada was nearly empty. Philip O'Brien, whose office was just around the corner, returned to the site. "I went walking through the site. I saw flags on the ground," he recalls with some sadness. "I was on the steps of the Mary Queen of the World Cathedral, on the northwest side. You could see Windsor Station and the whole of the square. The history of our country and the monuments of various prime ministers and wars... When the Irish came to Canada, my ancestors, several were buried under Dominion Square. It's a vary sacred place, that place. What I saw was a vast battlefield. It was as if there were arms strewn about on the ground, only there were no arms, there were flags. I had a sense that something was wrong, a strange feeling. I didn't know if I should be happy or unhappy because, there on the ground, there were Canadian flags and Quebec flags. I didn't feel good, I felt bad. I was not alone. There were about a hundred people moving about. The streets were still closed. I told myself, 'this is all because of me.' It was almost like a modern-day war. Someone came along pushing a bicycle. A young man of about twenty. He was weeping. He was gathering up Quebec flags and putting them in a basket on the handlebars of his bike, one by one. Then he looked right at me and said, 'You've killed my country.' I said to myself, 'That's what I've done all right!' I'm going to remember that day for a long, long time. It gives me the shivers right now just to think of it."[20]

Johnson doesn't believe that the rally had a significant impact on the referendum results. "I've never thought that it helped," he says today. "But to what extent was it harmful? I've never thought that it went our way. What has never been understood, what Brian Tobin never grasped, was that this was not the time to ask ourselves, 'what can we do for Quebec?' He was five years late! Or he was early—he was being presumptuous about the results! The rally gave the impression that we needed help on the NO side. This put static into the system, a spanner in the works... call it what you like, it diminished the impact of the gathering, of what was meant to be a gathering of Montrealers. It didn't help the cause." Johnson is not far from thinking that the demonstration on Place du Canada was, rather, a boost to the YES side, but he condemns the political hay that the sovereigntists made of it. "It gave them the chance to make speeches for half a day, then to scream that we'd spent 4.3 million dollars. Not 4.2 mind you, or 4.4: 4.3 million! That's hogwash!"[21]

Pierre-Claude Nolin comes to the same conclusions as the leader of the NO side. "When we look at the internal polls of Saturday and Sunday—that is, after Friday's event—the federalist numbers started to go back down. The event, according to the way Quebecers perceived it, was damaging to the NO side's cause. I think that Mr. Bouchard managed to convince them by claiming a barbarian invasion. They saw it as a demonstration of foreigners, even if this was not the case."[22]

John Rae, Jean Chrétien's man in the NO camp, was now up-braiding Philip O'Brien: "He told me he'd felt that the rally had a neg-ative impact," says O'Brien, who was shaken by this. "It's no fun when somebody who has got that much power—and I know this guy, he's a friend, we do business together—but when people that close to power kind of tell you that you screwed it up, you know...'OK, thank you very much. Next time, I won't take on the job.'" As for O'Brien himself, without whom this gigantic rally would not have taken place, he has an ambivalent assessment of the event's impact. "I'm glad that people from outside the province came to Montreal,"[23] he says, and speaks of the passion and interest that most Canadians have for Quebec. "I've been told by both sides, more often by the people from Ottawa, the Liberals, that I caused them to lose votes. But yet I was also told by the other side, the YES side, that I shouldn't be surprised to find myself in cement boots at the bottom of the St. Lawrence. You know, I was not exactly popular one side or the other."

Friday at noon, Jacques Parizeau and his wife were in their suite at the Ritz-Carlton, where they preferred to stay for security reasons. The clamour reached them. "The first thing I heard was a din, as if there was a huge parade," recalls Lisette Lapointe. "A sea of human-ity washing into the streets around." They attended the demonstration through the intermediary of television. "So," adds Lapointe, "I said to myself, oops! This could have an impact, a very significant impact on people who are still fearful, a bit undecided, who might let themselves get carried away by their feelings."[24] And yet, the on-the-spot polls that the YES side ran daily would show the opposite. "That evening," says Jean-François Lisée, "the YES side gained a few fractions of a point, or a point or two, and the NO side lost ground. The overall im-mediate effect was rather positive for the YES side."[25] In his assess-ment, the YES side had regained the point or two that they had lost on Wednesday due to the dramatic effect of Chrétien's statement on TV.

Despite the data in the polls, Jacques Parizeau remains sceptical. When he considers the hypothesis that when all was said and done, the rally may have boosted the YES side's standings, he maintains that this was just what the federalists would want people to think. "There are many people who realize, on the federalist side, that they won by a tiny margin by means of an activity that violated every financial law in the books of the Quebec government that applied to referendums," he says. "And with impunity. A situation such as this is a very serious matter. Still today, I can't help thinking that, on that afternoon, a few provincial governments, the federal government, a few state-run companies, a phone company and airline companies spent twice what the YES side and the NO side combined spent on the entire campaign. It was illegal in regard to our laws. And there was nothing we could do about it."[26]

The Chief Electoral Officer, who was unable to enforce Quebec's laws in the context of the demonstration's organization, believes, for his part, that it had an impact. "I don't know if this rally tilted the balance on the vote, but it did influence it. This is very clear. It's true that it's a rare thing for events during a campaign to tilt the balance of votes to one side or the other. But it happens, because a referendum or an election comes down to the undecided voters."[27] The evaluation made by experts concerning the influence of the rally on the results of the referendum is subtler. "The event came too late to get an accurate picture of its effect from the latest polls conducted and made public," say the two political pundits Denis Monière and Jean H. Guay. "But all signs indicate that there was only a slight impact, since the last segment of the trend curve, built from the latest polls (conducted before Friday, October 27), hit the referendum results right on the head: to wit, a few decimal points below the 50% mark for the YES vote."[28]

We'll never know how much the great gathering at Place du Canada really cost. A great deal of the expense of this event was never accounted for in the expenditures of the NO side. This was not the primary preoccupation of the people who contributed to moving thousands of Canadians across the country in buses, planes, trains and cars. Their way of thinking was entirely based on emotions and did not fit well into the wording of a law—all the more so when the law in question was a provincial one. "It never occurred to me that we were against Quebec spending rules," says MP Andy Scott of Fredericton, who organized the bus caravan from New Brunswick to Montreal. "In my mind, we weren't part of the campaign. This was a spontaneous act by Canadians to express themselves on this subject. Clearly, we were on the NO side but we weren't part of the campaign itself. It would be no different, frankly, than a bunch of people coming to a large demonstration in front of my office in the middle of an election campaign. We have every right, in the same way that anybody would have the right to, sort of, express themselves in this way around something like this."

Brian Tobin justifies his take on Quebec's laws in the same way. "When the future of your country is at stake, and when a referendum is, by definition, a citizen mandate being exercised, I found it an extraordinary notion that, as a Canadian, I could not come to Montreal and hold a flag. I found it so extraordinary that I rejected it. I guess that the record is clear that at the end of the day, despite all of the threats of people being prosecuted, those prosecutions never happened. I don't think they could have stood the test of a court of law." In so many words, individuals are free to express themselves as they see fit without having to stand under the umbrella of the NO side or the YES side.

Daniel Johnson reacted sharply to Tobin's words and to federalists who claimed that it was not a matter for Quebecers alone to decide on the future of the country. "They mixed things up a lot, a whole lot," he says. "To begin with, they could have avoided all that by supporting the Meech Lake accord five years earlier. Secondly, it is up to Quebecers to decide on their own future. This is something these people have failed to grasp. Every premier of Quebec, one after another, myself included, has made this statement at least once before the National Assembly. You can't come in from outside and prevent Quebecers from making their wishes known as to how they see their future. And what's more, no one can say, today, that a YES vote with a 1% majority would have put an end to Canada."[29]

The concept of liberty of which Tobin and Scott spoke would be invoked by every person that the Chief Electoral Officer of Quebec sought to question on the matter of improper practices that occurred during the referendum campaign. "There was Mr. Tobin, Mr. Gagliano, a certain number of ministers that we wanted to question," declares Pierre F. Côté. "The person responsible for legal matters in the House of Commons told us, erroneously, in my opinion, that we weren't entitled to question them, we weren't entitled to call on them. We were compelled to bow to this decision."[30]

The Chief Electoral Officer of Quebec came up against the same refusals to answer when he contacted other government authorities. "The argument they gave," he says, "an argument that carries some weight, you have to admit, was this: 'we're in a free country, we are entitled to express ourselves, we have the right to spend money as we like.'" But as the person duly mandated by the government of Quebec to enforce the laws governing elections and referendums, such an attitude was not of a nature to satisfy him in his capacity. "The big problem," he adds, "is that in Canada, we live in a state of law in which there is a division of responsibilities between the two sorts of government. However, as concerns the Referendum Act, I'm tempted to say that we're in a half-state of law, because what is enacted in Quebec cannot be enforced elsewhere, in regard to Canadians who live outside the territory of the province of Quebec. The question to ask ourselves is this: can we violate the provisions of the law and do whatever we want however we want? If I answer 'yes' to this question, it leads us to question whether we live in a state of law or not. Are we free or aren't we, in a free, democratic society, to adopt legislation that affects the carrying out of activities inherently provincial or of an inherently Québécois character?"[31]

The matter of financing remains at the heart of the Chief Electoral Officer's queries. In his view, the people who took part in the great gathering at Place du Canada were undoubtedly entitled to express themselves as they did. But he asks the following question: "Can we agree that, to organize this rally, there were non-regulated expenditures that did not fit into the framework of the umbrella committees? They were entitled to come to Quebec, they were entitled to come and express their opinion. What was prohibited by law was that their expenditures be picked up by other stakeholders."[32] According to Pierre F. Côté, Celso Boscariol, who chartered a plane in Vancouver at a cost of $161,000, would have acted in observance of the law if he had asked the passengers on board the aircraft to reimburse this amount. However, by the attorney's own admission, the passengers paid only $250 apiece for the round trip to Montreal, the rest of the tab being picked up by firms or individuals who did not make the trip.

Brian Tobin has a more simplistic take on things: "I never accepted it in 1980, and I will never accept in the future the notion that the future of Canada is a decision to be made by one province on behalf of ten provinces and three territories. Let one group of electors, defined by a set of provincial boundaries, decide, for all Canadians, the future of the country? I've never accepted it. I don't like the process. I don't believe in the process."

To this day, Jacques Parizeau remains indignant. "I'm part of the generation that was very much marked by the laws on financing political parties and René Lévesque's laws on referendums," he says. "And I believe in these laws. My sense of indignation dates back to that day. They talk to us a lot about the state of law. After a demonstration like that one, one asks oneself, 'state of *what* law?' What is the law that applies? A society can't establish rules to hold votes among its people without having someone else intervene on the basis of different rules, saying, 'pass whatever law you like to govern yourselves; I'll just do whatever I want.' A strange sort of state of law, if you ask me!" The former premier speaks of the last days of the campaign, when the coffers of both sides were nearly empty. "You don't have 5 or 10,000 dollars to spend. Everything is committed. And the NO side is in the same boat: all of their money is spoken for. The NO side, in Quebec, was irreproachable in regard to these laws. When I talk about the federal government, I really mean the federal government."[33]

The rally of October 27, then, gave factions from outside the NO camp the opportunity to spend money without the least regard for the provisions of Quebec's laws, which established that each side could count on a maximum amount of approximately 5 million dollars; but October 27 was not the day on which the balance was tipped. Earlier than that, on September 17, two weeks before the official start of the campaign, the federal government extended a grant of $4.8 million to the Canadian Unity Council's Option Canada program. "If

I'm accused of having spent money to save my country, I plead guilty as charged," declared Sheila Copps, Canadian Heritage minister at the time.[34] From that day, a code of conduct had been established: no Quebec law could prevent anyone from outside Quebec from taking any initiative to defend the federalist cause. After the referendum, the Chief Electoral Officer of Quebec would file no fewer than 91 complaints, 11 of them against businesses. A fruitless effort, as the complaints had to be withdrawn when the Supreme Court of Canada invalidated certain provisions of the Quebec law.

With the Place du Canada celebration over, Brian Tobin decided to campaign in maritime Quebec. He stopped off in Quebec City, where his department had a major office, then went out to win over the fishing communities in the eastern part of the province. His tour would take him to the North Shore and as far as the Magdalen Islands. During the preceding week, the NO side's ban on Ottawa federalists' participation in the campaign was no longer holding sway. It was now a free-for-all, with individuals taking their own initiatives without regard to the strategies of the NO campaign. As for Andy Scott, he went home to Fredericton, wondering how he could devote the remaining three days before the referendum to the cause that was dear to his heart. Then he had an idea: he would call every Scott in the Montreal phone book and say to them, "I'm Andy Scott. I live in Fredericton. I'm a Member of Parliament. I'm respectful of the fact that this decision is Quebec's to make. But I also wouldn't want you to think that I don't have an interest in the outcome, because I do." And so, with the phone book on his lap, he sat down by the phone...

Jacques Parizeau took the phone companies to task. According to him, they had obtained the authorization of the CRTC to give their subscribers five minutes of long-distance calls to Quebec, free of charge. On a visit to the Lanaudière region, he affirmed that the phone companies in New Brunswick, Manitoba and British Columbia had lists of Quebec citizens' names that their subscribers could consult. CRTC chairman, Keith Spicer, denied that such authorization had been given and, the following Sunday, on the advice of the federal watchdog organization, the companies withdrew their discount offer.

If Preston Manning was kept away from the great rally in Montreal, this did not mean that he remained idle. Flanked by a staff of Reformers, he worked on projects for the days following the referendum. While the Place du Canada demonstration was taking place, he was calling the United States embassy. James Blanchard was in Montreal, and it was from a hotel room that he called him. In his book, Blanchard summed up their phone conversation as follows: "Then Preston Manning called. 'It doesn't look good,' he said. 'I'm here with my people working through scenarios in the event of a YES victory, and we'd like to sit down and talk with you about it at some point. We're going to need your help. (...) I think maybe we should have an international panel—the United States, the U.K., Japan, as well as Canada and Quebec—to think about it (...). I'm putting this stuff together and I'll get it over to you at the embassy.'"[35] Manning recalls the conversation. "I do recall having a conversation with him," he says, "that this was one of the challenges: what do you do about national debt, when one chunk of the country decides to remove itself and no longer assume any obligation for it? And, of course, Canada's three biggest creditors were the United States, Britain and Japan. We tried to think through what you could do to reassure those creditors because, if you couldn't reassure them, you'd have a financial crisis like the country had never experienced before. One of the suggestions for resolving this was that you would have a committee of your main creditors that could be negotiated with, that you could give assurances as to how the debt would be stabilized."

In an interview, Blanchard goes further: "He said, 'look, this thing could go the wrong way and it doesn't look very good. I am just thinking about how we put together a plan here for some sort of new federalism or something. And I want, at some point, to talk to you about this.' I thought it was a little unusual that he was preparing for a loss, while we were sitting there, trying every way to be helpful for a win. I think that, later, the prime minister took Manning to task on that. He's a policy wonk, he was thinking about what happens, what's this new federalism going to be, coming out of Calgary. Manning had met with President Clinton. He'd talked about his new federalism briefly with President Clinton in my family room. I did not view it as an act of hostility toward the federalists. I just thought that all of us were worrying about winning, not what happens after."

In the ongoing debates in the House of Commons, Manning expressed concern about Canada's future if the YES vote were to carry the day, but he suggested above all that the Chrétien government propose, not only to Quebec but to the whole country, profound changes to Canadian federalism with a view to developing a "federalism for the 21st century." "I certainly felt that they were being very irresponsible," says John Manley, referring to Reform Party MPs, "that they were trying to use it. They almost seemed at times like they preferred to get a YES vote. They would ask provocative questions in the House of Commons, which seemed to undermine the strategy to try to win the referendum."

On Saturday, the *Journal de Montréal* and the *Globe and Mail* published a Léger Marketing poll stating that, after dividing up the undecided vote, each option got 50% of voting intentions. The suspense was so great that the referendum became a hot subject to cover for the copy rooms of the major international media. Some thirty American TV teams, and even more from countries such as France, Norway, Chile, Great Britain, Portugal, Germany, Japan, Sweden and Turkey, landed in Quebec. More than 450 foreign journalists, some of them representing the biggest dailies on the planet—the *Los Angeles Times*, *El Mundo*, *Libération*, the *Financial Times*, etc.—settled in to cover what promised to be the tightest referendum ever and, even more importantly, the outcome of which might mean the breakup of one of the world's most prosperous nations.

CHAPTER XIII

What if the YES Side Wins?

Justice Minister Allan Rock was no longer ruling out the possibility that the YES side might win. On Sunday, the day before the referendum, he called an emergency meeting in his office. The eventuality of a vote in favour of sovereignty for Quebec, which no one in Ottawa could foresee prior to the week that had just come to an end, had plunged the federal government into a night of terrors full of possible and impossible hypotheses and an infinite range of unknowns. Until then, the party line had always been the same: the NO forces were not to show signs of weakness by seeking backup solutions, *just in case*—for victory was a certainty. But now the threat was present, palpable and imminent. John Manley, who was present at the meeting, now says, "We felt that it was necessary at that point to be developing a plan of action, so that people didn't think that the government seemed adrift and unknowing of what to do."

At this meeting, which was completely unofficial, there was only one question on the agenda, but it covered a lot of ground: what advice would the Justice minister give to the prime minister and the cabinet if, the next day, the YES side were to win? Rock was surrounded, in the conference room of his department, by a handful of ministers—among them Manley and Anne McLellan—who were his friends, attorneys whose opinion he valued and, most importantly, an expert in constitutional law, Peter Hogg, to whom he regularly turned for advice.[1] If there was a common denominator among those present, it was their legal background and the fact that they happened to be in Ottawa that day. At some point, there was a phone discussion underway with Paul Martin, Finance minister, whose task it would be to reassure the markets, but who was also in a position in his capacity as an MP representing a Montreal riding to provide a clearer picture of what was going on in Quebec. The atmosphere was sullen, fraught with pessimism and exceptionally grave. All present were imbued with a sense of responsibility, faced with the urgency of advice to be given and decisions to be made. Questions were raised that had never before been addressed by a Canadian government.

All shared the minister's fear that Jacques Parizeau would make a unilateral declaration of independence, even if a YES victory were to be obtained only by a very narrow margin. "Our concern," says Allan Rock, "was that it might be a unilateral declaration of independence based on even the narrowest of margins for the YES. My concern was a unilateral declaration of independence, which some countries might theoretically have recognized or acknowledged, pitching us into real uncertainty. I wasn't concerned about civil unrest, it was the uncertainty that was the major concern." Today, John Manley is no longer in doubt: "What we didn't know at the time, which subsequently became apparent," he says, "was that Mr. Parizeau considered the vote to have legal effect and was prepared to declare some kind of unilateral independence the following day, no matter how close the vote was. That should have been not only illegal but also a breach of faith with what had been said to Quebecers."

To a certain extent, Parizeau's attitude on this matter justified the apprehension that Allan Rock's guests felt, even if a closer look at the facts—in particular the provisions of the Sovereignty Bill and Parizeau's speeches on partnership—would have shown this apprehension to be relatively groundless. It was his silence on this subject and his determination to proclaim independence, if the federal government refused to negotiate or dragged out negotiations interminably, that contributed to keeping this doubt alive. Known in Ottawa as a man of action, at no time did he formally repudiate the idea of a unilateral declaration of independence. Moreover, he was to confirm this in a book published in 1997: "One may observe that my speeches, when they address the matter of negotiations with Canada, are written so as to allow for just such a declaration of sovereignty," he writes. "And I have never promised, in public or in private, not to make a unilateral declaration of sovereignty. Everything that has been written in the papers on this subject demonstrates yet again that in these matters, those who speak do not know, and those who know do not speak."[2]

The concern in this area, however, was greater in Ottawa than in the YES camp. Mario Dumont was among those who were not fearful that Jacques Parizeau might stray from the agreed-upon path. "Let's suppose," he says, "that one of the players in the YES camp comes along after the vote and says, 'Mr. Parizeau is going to usurp his mandate; the referendum question was this, but he's going to do this other thing.' It's sad to say, but the only power that would then remain would be a political crisis. Suppose Lucien Bouchard, the chief negotiator, has been pushed aside, and he no longer has a mandate to negotiate... I've never feared that this might happen. From the moment when Mr. Parizeau signed the June 12 agreement and accepted the negotiation committee—the oversight committee—he had committed to a particular path; there was no turning back."[3] Parizeau's political advisor, Jean-François Lisée, had a similar discourse: "He was working within a political reality: we had built the YES camp in a coalition; we would have had to make the transition in a coalition."[4] Lisée nonetheless acknowledged that the commitments that connected Parizeau to the two other leaders of the YES side were a burden to him. "It's quite understandable," he adds, "that in the last days before the referendum, he expressed, shall we say, a desire to free himself from all of these ties that he'd established. But the fact remains that, afterwards, these ties would have been just as real as before—perhaps even more so."[5] Parizeau's hands were tied, in a manner of speaking, by a certain logic regarding things to be put into place, and he had no qualms about acknowledging this. "That's what all the studies done on restructuring the government of Quebec were for," he says. "We wouldn't be able, for example, to merge the Revenue departments of both governments. Transfer millions of tax forms in two weeks? There's a whole series of things that would have to be put into place. You've got to be responsible."[6]

In Ottawa, Allan Rock's guests did not attach as much importance to the June 12 agreement, if indeed they were aware of it, and
they nourished a tremendous mistrust of Jacques Parizeau.
Consequently, they were unanimous on a certain number of points,
each point meant to prevent the success of both sovereignty for
Quebec and a unilateral proclamation of independence by Parizeau.
For example, the Canadian prime minister would have to issue a call
for calm and immediately declare that a referendum is the political
expression of a desire, but has no effect as a legal order. It would be
necessary to state very clearly that the Canadian Constitution contained no provision foreseeing the separation of a province. But
above all, it would be necessary—very quickly, so that Canadians
would understand the importance of the legal and constitutional implications of the political event that had just taken place—to stipulate
that a number of questions would be referred to the Supreme Court.
Does the vote in a referendum have legal value? If it has none, how to
confront the legal implications? What constitutes a clear question in
a referendum? At what percentage may we say that a victory becomes
significant?

"These were questions that we did not need to ask until mid-
October 1995, but to which, on October 30, we still had no answers,"
says Allan Rock. The minister saw another advantage to going to the
highest court in the land with all of these questions. "We thought, as
well, that the option of going to the court would provide a period of
time within which we could encourage the population, both in Quebec
and in the rest of the country, to remain calm and to await an orderly
outcome of just where we go from here."

One of the meeting's participants wondered about the clarity of
the referendum question. "If the YES wins tomorrow night," he said,
"Quebecers will have spoken, but what will they have said? What is
the meaning of a response to a question that was not clear? We don't
know what people had in mind when they voted YES." Another
brought up the possibility of a Canada-wide referendum, "because of
the implications of Quebec sovereignty for the rest of the country" and
the importance, for the Canadian government, of having a mandate to

negotiate with an independent Quebec. All of these unanswered questions could begin to be clarified by a decision of the Supreme Court.

The meeting at the Justice minister's office did not yield any formal recommendation, but its conclusions were sure to fuel discussion when the cabinet met on Tuesday, if the YES side had emerged victorious the night before. On Monday, the day of the referendum, Allan Rock filed, with the Clerk of Privy Council, a simple report that, for the moment, would serve no purpose, but that would resurface in 1996 when the government decided on a referral to the Supreme Court and debated the Referendum Clarity Act in the House of Commons. "The result of the meeting, really, was that no matter what the outcome was on Monday night, whether it was the YES or the NO that prevailed, we could never again allow Canada to face this uncertainty."

Only a few days before, the Canadian government, including the Justice minister, still hadn't thought it necessary to clear up all of these questions, so obvious did it seem to them that 1995 would be a repeat performance of 1980. It was the polls of the past week, indicating the possibility of a YES victory, which had plunged them into their current state of consternation. However, among the NO strategists, who had an up-close relationship with the realities of Quebec politics, even if confidence reigned, they were taking nothing for granted, and if, perchance, the YES were to prevail, the interpretation to be made of this majority had been at the heart of their concerns for some time. Their leader, Daniel Johnson had serious misgivings concerning the principle of a simple majority (50% plus one vote). "We recognize the (democratic) institution," he says. "We are taking part in it. We hope that we will win. But if it is the YES that carries the day by a narrow margin, there's a whole series of unknowns that follows. We could ask, 'If there were another referendum, one month later, when people had had a chance to see how Jacques Parizeau, Bernard Landry and other sovereigntist ministers had conducted themselves, would not Quebecers, quite surprised to see how a YES victory had been interpreted, now vote NO?' The question remains."[7]

Jean Charest was haunted by the same prospect. "The day after a referendum," he said, "the result is measured on the basis of the question. You have a result, now what does it mean? And considering the question, there would have been a great deal of confusion—what, during the campaign, I was calling the *black hole*."[8] For the federalists, a NO victory by a very slight majority would pose no problems, as it would not bring any deep changes to the federal framework and would, after a fashion, maintain the *status quo*—even if this meant modifying said framework through negotiations, which those involved would take the time to prepare properly, and which might last a long time. A YES victory on the other hand, according to them, must be decisive and indisputable, because of the major transformations that it would imply, in the immediate future, for the nation as a whole.

For the sovereigntists, on the other hand, there was no doubt that a victory by a single vote would remain a victory nonetheless. "That's what a democratic election is: 50% plus one," says Bob Dufour, the organizer of Lucien Bouchard's campaign, invoking adoption of the Maastricht Treaty following a victory obtained by a few decimal points. "We have seen," he adds, "Members of Parliament elected by a margin of three or five votes." He recalls the 1993 federal election in which the Bloc Québécois, with fewer votes, had more MPs than the Reform Party. "The Reformers wanted to be the official opposition," he says. "Senator Beaudoin,[9] our constitutional oracle, settled matters once and for all, saying it was not the percentage that mattered, but the number of MPs. So if the YES wins at, say, 50.5%, we're not going to say, start over because that's not enough votes. Winning with a 50.5% vote, I would have been comfortable with that."[10] Minister Guy Chevrette, while he would have accepted such a victory, would have been less comfortable with a victory of 50.5%: "No one would have been unhappy if we'd got 50.5%," he says, "but it may have been more difficult than 53%. In a democracy, too bad, it's not the minority that leads. At 49.5%, *we* accepted the results of the vote on the evening of the referendum."[11] Jacques Parizeau expresses it in even clearer terms: "49.5% is not a moral victory, it's a defeat," he says. "You have two choices: if I'm the one with 49.5%, there's nothing I can do, so that's what I do: nothing. If I'm the one with 50.5%, then I do what I said

I would do. I have no hesitation in this area. I'll go looking for a mandate and, if it's there, I'm off and running."[12]

In Jacques Parizeau's mind, a result of 50.1% would mean a victory for the YES and "the referendum was a binding referendum." Consequently, the very next day, he would spring into action. "I've always maintained that immediately after a YES victory, the first phone call we'd get would be from the governor of the Bank of Canada," he says, "saying, 'We're not going to do anything rash, now, are we?' And we would answer, 'No, we're not doing anything rash!' Obviously, maintaining the stability of the Canadian dollar implies that we keep our heads. It is primarily the responsibility of the Bank of Canada to ensure this stability."[13] There was no doubt in anyone's mind that in the event of a YES victory, the dollar would fall. "Drastically," says Jean-François Lisée. "And the stocks of English-Canadian businesses listed on the Toronto or New York Stock Exchange would have dropped dramatically as well. But the concern of the English-Canadian financial and industrial elite would be to re-stabilize the situation as quickly as possible. The calls that would have been made to the Prime Minister's Office would have been, 'Stabilize, fast!'"[14]

Mike Harris, whose government was already working on a strategy aimed at assuring investors that the referendum vote "meant nothing other than business as usual," had no long-term apprehensions whatsoever. "There was a concern with what the short-term would be," he says. "(But) I, personally, was not concerned for the long term, and I've indicated throughout that we'd work our way through this." During the referendum campaign, some provincial premiers communicated with one another and agreed that they did not recognize the federal government's power to speak on their behalf in negotiations with Quebec. Roy Romanow went to New York to speak to a few people who managed billions of dollars in loans, in particular to Canada, to explain to them the intricacies of the Canadian federal system, "...the sub-nationality called Quebec, called Saskatchewan, but there's an over-arching nationality called Canada." Jacques Parizeau was therefore not mistaken in thinking that politicians would have undertaken to reassure the business world to stabilize the dollar and investments as quickly as possible.

Jacques Parizeau's first move, should the YES vote prevail, would be to appoint a transition committee, which would gather around him the ministers responsible for Public Safety, Intergovernmental Affairs, the Treasury Board and Justice. Provisions would immediately be made to convene the National Assembly as soon as possible. As regulations require 48 hours' notice, members of the National Assembly would be called to sit on Thursday, November 2, to adopt a motion to bring a proclamation of sovereignty within the year. Finally, the premier would prepare a major cabinet shuffle, to take place soon after the end-of-the-year holidays. "Because there were clearly ministers for whom sovereignty would still have been something of a discovery,"[15] he says.

Why a motion? Parizeau wanted to act quickly, and a motion could be introduced to the National Assembly without advance notice—which was not the case for a bill. Moreover, since September 7, the government already had a bill authorizing a proclamation of sovereignty following negotiations with Canada, within the year, in the event of a favourable referendum result. The objective of the motion would be to confirm that the government was taking cognizance of the referendum results and intended to act upon them.

In Parizeau's mind, a motion would be required for at least two reasons. First of all, as a referendum is nothing more than a consultation of the populace, the people would need to be told clearly that the government was not going to change its mind. Then, measures would need to be taken to ensure that the French government, knowing the intentions of the government of Quebec, would be able to say, "as soon as Quebecers are ready to decree sovereignty, we will recognize them." The motion would be the bearer of those two messages. "It was Valéry Giscard d'Estaing who showed us that there was a step missing," says Parizeau. "He made us understand that a referendum is not even an intention—at the very most, it's an authorization—and that we would not have been able to turn to France for support as long as this link in the chain, the motion, had not been put in place."[16]

The motion would comprise only one article, to avoid unending debate. According to the rules of the National Assembly, each member can speak for twenty minutes on each article of a motion. The more articles a bill has, the longer the debate will be. In this case, Parizeau wanted the motion to be adopted within 24 hours.

With this way of proceeding, it became important for the government to know how the Liberal opposition, generally speaking, viewed ensuing events. Over the weekend that preceded the vote, Jacques Parizeau's chief of staff, Jean Royer, contacted John Parisella, influential advisor to Daniel Johnson. He did not want to talk to his counterpart, Pierre Anctil, to avoid giving his action an official air. And considering that his relations with Parisella were good, the choice of a contact person was easy to make. "For this sort of discussion, I had to talk to someone who didn't have an official title and who wasn't afraid that I was leading him into a bear trap," says Royer, "but someone, on the other hand, who was extremely well connected and who had access to all the important people in the Liberal camp."[17]

On Sunday morning, the two men met in a restaurant in Montreal's InterContinental hotel. "I knew that he was going to start by telling me that the NO was going to win," recalls Royer. "So I said to him, 'Try to set aside your certainty and play along with me for a minute; just suppose that the YES is going to win.'"[18] He then asked how the leaders of the NO camp, especially Daniel Johnson and his party, would act in the following days and how they would react to a YES victory. He was well aware that Parisella had undoubtedly informed his boss that they were meeting, but he put his cards on the table, and the two men shared their ideas on the moves that the government was getting ready to make.

Royer brought up the matter of the motion in the National Assembly and asked Parisella if the opposition was ready to back it. Ten years later, Parisella recalls this meeting. "He asked me if I could commit to talking to Mr. Johnson," he says. "I told him that I couldn't promise to do this, and I told him that at that time, I was even having a hard time interpreting Mr. Johnson's way of thinking, which was so federalist, and that I didn't see him recognizing the results. I couldn't see myself making a commitment on his behalf."[19] Johnson's advisor then said to Royer, "His convictions are deep, and you expect him to back sovereignty?" Royer corrected him: "Just acknowledge the results of the referendum." In the government, the belief was that Johnson might oppose the motion, but that Liberal MNAs with more nationalist leanings would be inclined to back it. On this point as well, Parisella was careful not to give the slightest hint that it might be possible.

From their conversation, which lasted about two hours, Parizeau's chief of staff remembers, in essence, that Daniel Johnson would accept the verdict of the people but that in Ottawa, "there would be some resistance and that it wouldn't be as easy." Parisella avoided talking to Daniel Johnson about his conversation with Royer, but he discussed it with Johnson's chief of staff, Pierre Anctil, who did not take this initiative by Jacques Parizeau's chief of staff very seriously. In retrospect, Johnson sees this as a "form of psychological intimidation." "In the preceding days," he recalls, "I was called every name in the book. My identity as a Quebecer was called into question, and here they were expecting me to rally to their cause. I found this rather amazing. It was a huge joke that Mr. Parizeau wanted to play on me. They wanted to undermine our confidence for the day of the vote."[20]

Quebec's premier knew where he was going. He had been plotting out this path since March 18, 1987, the day he became president of the Parti Québécois. This man, who never wanted to be premier of a province unless it was to lead Quebec to independence, was 24 hours from seeing the dream that he had been nurturing since the day he joined the party in 1969, 26 years earlier, become a reality. And yet, in spite of the time that had gone by, many matters, the solutions to which were not entirely in his hands, remained unsettled.

If the YES were to win, what would happen to Lucien Bouchard and the Bloc Québécois? The leader's future would be at once simple and complex. Simple because he would have a mandate to negotiate, on Quebec's behalf, the adjustments that would now be required to Quebec's relationship with Canada. But complex because he was the Leader of Her Majesty's Opposition. Would he be able to continue filling both roles? "I don't have an answer to that," says his political advisor, Pierre-Paul Roy. "I don't know that there was such a great contradiction between the two jobs. I don't think that was really part of the problem."[21]

And if we ask about Bouchard's future, the question of the future of the Bloc Québécois is implicit. Without a doubt, during negotiations, Bloc MPs would have continued to be very much a part of proceedings in the House of Commons, participating in committees and contributing to debates. But then what? "In the event of a partnership agreement," says Roy, "if there had been joint institutions, the Bloc could have been considered to be the parliamentary wing. But here again, there would have been a problem: we no longer wanted to have elected officials. Would these people have needed to be temporarily delegated? I don't see how it could have worked, because the Bloc's term was not finished. Ultimately, if I look at the texts as they were written, the Bloc would have had to go."[22]

Once negotiations between Canada and Quebec were completed or broken off—if indeed they were held—and the Bloc had disappeared, what would have remained for Lucien Bouchard? As the position of lieutenant-governor would disappear along with the province of Quebec, one can imagine, according to a hypothesis advanced by Jean-François Lisée, that Bouchard might have taken on the duties of president of the Republic of Quebec, with precisely defined responsibilities in the international arena. However, for the position of president of the Republic to exist, there would first need to be a Quebec Constitution defining this position. Now, under the terms of the Quebec Sovereignty Bill, introduced before the National Assembly on September 7, this Constitution would first have to be drafted by a commission made up of members and non-members of parliament and be approved by the National Assembly before being submitted to the people in another referendum. In other words, for Lucien Bouchard, the transition from negotiator to president of the Republic would take some time.

What would become of Mario Dumont? He would once again become what he had been before the referendum, leader of a third party—and he had no intention of accepting any role that the government might offer him. He had already established what he thought to be his responsibility and the responsibility of his party. "If the YES had won 52% to 48%," he says, "48% is a lot of people. These people could react in two ways: either they would accept the result, roll up their sleeves and set to work building Quebec on a new foundation or, as is sometimes said in French in the world of farming, they could 'set their behinds down in the feeding trough.' People like this are everywhere in society: in the business world, in banks, in the cultural communities obviously, in the anglophone community... if everyone were to get in the way, things could get very difficult. So the role that we gave ourselves in the ADQ was to be a buffer and to oil the machinery. In a word, to be a moderate voice. Most ADQ people had a Liberal background, so we would play a role in reuniting Quebec."[23]

What would become of Daniel Johnson? At the time of the meeting between Jean Royer and John Parisella, Parizeau and his staff already knew how Johnson planned to behave if he lost the referendum. Two weeks earlier, in an interview on RDI, he had stated that he was prepared to work with the Parizeau government on "damage control" and, generally speaking, to ensure that Quebec did not lose strength economically. "I would have called on my experience and my convictions to do the job that, in our institutions, the opposition leader is expected to do," he says today. "Because the next morning, I would still have been the opposition leader at the National Assembly, with a duty to ensure the orderly development of Quebec."[24]

And Jean Chrétien? What would happen to him if Quebec became sovereign? He would still be a Quebecer, representing a Quebec riding in the parliament of a country which had became a foreign land—a country that he led in spite of his Quebec roots and allegiance. Should he quit? The situation in which he would find himself was without precedent in the history of Canada, such that politicians and analysts could see no source of inspiration and no lessons to be drawn from Canadian history. Opinion was divided.

"The prime minister (could) continue," says Allan Rock. "He (was) the prime minister of the country. He was a prime minister who had fought for the unity of the country in 1980 and in 1995. He is a champion of Canada. I do expect that Canadians would have had confidence in him to carry on. And I think the issue was not so much his legitimacy, the issue was 'what do we do now?'" However, the Justice minister considered that Chrétien would have nonetheless had to go and drum up a popular mandate before undertaking negotiations with a sovereign Quebec.

John Manley believed that there was at least one legitimacy that could not be called into question, and this was the legitimacy of the Liberal party. It would necessarily continue to form the government, as it still held the majority in the House of Commons, even without the Quebec MPs. And he wonders who could have taken on the prime minister's job if Jean Chrétien had left his post. "He was, to my view, a wise leader when it came to some of these issues," he says. But still he wondered, most of all, about how Canadians would react to Jean Chrétien still acting as prime minister: "How tolerant would the rest of Canada be to the Canadian side in that negotiation being somehow led by a Quebecer? Can he continue as prime minister but somehow be apart from the discussion that would necessarily follow between Canada and Quebec? I thought that if it came to a negotiation over the independence of Quebec from the rest of Canada, that Canadians would believe that necessarily Quebecers were on one side of that issue and non-Quebecers were on the other side of the issue. It was going to be a complicated issue."

Brian Tobin, on the other hand, did not see how the government could have hung onto power. "The government," he says, "as it was currently constituted and functioning, would not last many days, then some new structure would have to emerge and some new coalition would have to emerge. We talked about that in the most general terms, no detail, but just an understanding that if this thing went wrong, if there were a majority of 55-45 for sovereignty, it would not be 'business as usual' on the morning after."

David Collenette felt it was of little importance whether Jean Chrétien remained as prime minister or not. On this point, his view lines up with Tobin's. A government of national unity would be required in order to confront the situation. "There would have been an outcry from across the country for some government of national unity—whoever would lead, Jean Chrétien or someone else—to really deal with the fundamental challenge. You had to involve everybody in Parliament. It went beyond politics. And, in that scenario, Jean Chrétien would have been obliged to bring in people from the Reform Party, from the NDP, maybe from outside, like Bill Davis or Peter Lougheed."

The idea of forming a government of national unity had been entertained by some ministers, but it had never been considered officially, or even unofficially, before the referendum, even when the YES had a substantial lead, in the final week. If it had been, Jean Charest, who was the leader of the Conservative party, would have got wind of it. "It never became an issue," he says. "There were people who talked about it, perhaps out loud, but it never got very far. It was never taken very seriously. For us, in any case, neither I nor anyone else in my party was ever approached on the matter."[25] Of course, if the Conservative party had indeed been called upon, it would have been more because of their prestige than the weight they carried in Parliament, because they had only two MPs.

Jean Chrétien's political adversaries were much less indulgent towards him. Preston Manning's disappointment at having been obliged, in 1993, to give his job as official opposition leader over to Lucien Bouchard, surfaces in his evaluation of the situation. He considers that the government would have lost all of its credibility in the eyes of the people because, for months, it had been assuring people that it was in control of the situation. "I think the government would have been obliged to resign... Perhaps the middle course would have been the prime minister and some of the main people responsible for that campaign resigning and someone else from the government side trying to form a government for the rest of Canada. Perhaps the thing to do would have been to move a measure of non-confidence in the prime minister, not the government." And yet, the latter hypothesis is the one that Manning favoured. Stephen Harper did not go quite as far: "Mr. Chrétien, a Quebecer, would have been in a poor position to speak on behalf of Canada," was his succinct assessment a few days before the referendum. But he did not explicitly call for his resignation. Deborah Grey, deputy leader of the Reform party in Parliament, did not entertain any doubts: "He would have had to step down from office the next day," she says. Finally, ten years later, others, including Jean Charest and Mike Harris, still do not know what the Prime Minister would have had to do. "He would have needed help," says the former Ontario premier, nonetheless, "as, towards the end, he needed help from a lot of people in the second half of the referendum. It would have had to have been a team effort."

If we are to believe John Manley's assessment of the situation, Jean Chrétien himself did not have a very clear idea of what he would have done if the YES had prevailed. "After the referendum," says the former Trade minister, "he had commented to me, 'I really don't know what would have been the appropriate thing for me to do if we had lost the referendum.'" Today, Chrétien affirms that he would have stayed in office. "I was the prime minister of the government and I would have remained prime minister as long as I had the confidence of the House. And I'm sure that in a crisis like that I would have kept the confidence of the House. People love to speculate on all sorts of scenarios. It might be that some of my ministers thought that perhaps Chrétien will resign and I'll have a chance to become prime minister. Normal human beings want to go to the top."[26]

His attitude in this area was distinct from the attitude held by Pierre Elliott Trudeau who, in 1980, would have resigned along with his entire cabinet if the YES had prevailed—even if some ministers, Chrétien among them—disagreed. Chrétien draws a parallel between the two situations: "In 1980, Trudeau said, 'We will resign, we're laying our seats on the line.' I did not refuse. If he had resigned, I would have resigned as well. In retrospect, I think that must have had an effect on people. But what if we had lost? I think that it would have been more reasonable not to say this and to approach the problem differently. And this is why I didn't repeat this statement for the 1995 referendum."[27] Jean Chrétien bases his confidence on the conviction that replacing the prime minister in such circumstances would only add to the country's uncertainty, but also on a poll taken very early in October, which confirmed that at the very least, he had the confidence of the Canadian people: 81% of Canadians then considered that he could stay in office if Quebec voted YES in the majority.[28]

So Jean Chrétien would stay as prime minister, but what would he do? Did he have a backup plan, a sort of overall strategy of governance in the event of a YES victory? His nephew, Raymond Chrétien, who was the Canadian ambassador in Washington at the time, and who dined with him about ten days before the referendum, says, without any trace of hesitation, that he had none. Had there been a backup plan, Jean Chrétien would have been able to turn to this plan for answers to three questions that now demanded his attention. First and foremost, must he recognize the results of the referendum? Secondly, if he did not recognize the results and if the government of Quebec began to conduct itself like an independent nation, that is, deciding that it has the "exclusive jurisdiction to make laws and levy taxes in its territory and act on the international scene for the making of agreements and treaties,"[29] must he send in the army? And thirdly, must he dissolve the House of Commons and call a general election?

Jean Chrétien had fought the YES forces during the referendum campaign by brandishing the dangers of sovereignty, but it seems that we can now take for granted that he would not have interpreted a YES victory as an expression of Quebecers' desire to separate from Canada. On the day of the referendum, in collaboration with Eddie Goldenberg, he had prepared a speech to this effect, to be delivered if the YES vote had prevailed. "A two- or three-page speech," recalls Goldenberg, his political advisor. "The main elements of this speech were the following: the question was ambiguous and did not bear on Quebec's separation from Canada; we would not accept it and we were not ready to break up the country; we understood that Quebecers were not satisfied with the *status quo*, and we were ready to work together to make the necessary changes."

John Manley was on the same wavelength. "When we talked about what our strategy might be (in the event of a YES victory), nobody considered that that vote would mean Quebec ceased to be part of Canada," he says. "We would not recognize that consequence of the vote without further steps having to be taken. We would have been engaged in a political war where we would have tried to use every resource to impugn the question, that it does not mean the end of Canada. So we would not accept that the question meant separation."

David Collenette was even more unequivocal. "No prime minister—Jean Chrétien or anyone—could recognize a YES victory as the dismemberment of Canada. I didn't, and none of the ministers have really thought that way. And, certainly, the prime minister didn't think that way." Even Roy Romanow, his friend and ally from the November 1981 constitutional conference, who continued to be in touch with him during the referendum campaign, advised him not to recognize a YES victory. "He never quite told me, 'look, I'm not going to recognize the results,' but I sensed that he was on that side of the fence."

Today, Chrétien comes back to this question with more transparency than he showed at the time: "Look, say we had lost the referendum. What would we have done? Quebec would have wanted to be recognized abroad, but I'm not sure there were tons of countries that would have recognized Quebec. What we would have said is this: 'the question was ambiguous. Winning a referendum by one vote… you don't break up a country because someone forgot their reading glasses when they went to vote. It requires a qualified majority.'" In Chrétien's mind, what exactly is a qualified majority? "To void the charter of a hunting and fishing club, you need a second vote," he adds. "In the constitution of the CSN,[30] to get rid of the president, you need more than 50 plus one, if memory serves. So, what can I say?"[31]

He recounts what the day after a YES victory would have looked like for him. "I would not have got up at 11 o'clock in the morning," he says. "I would have been starting to work. But it was not complicated. We would have had to inform people that there had been a vote and that the question was ambiguous and that it didn't mean that Canada would split. You advise all the leaders of all the governments of the world. And after that, probably, the Quebec government would have called them asking them to recognize it. How many (would have done so)? Not many. Some countries recognize Taiwan. They cannot recognize mainland China. But Taiwan is not at the UN, China is. The diplomats having their different cocktails, it's a bit different, it's not my main preoccupation. (What concerns me is) what happens on the ground."[32]

It is well known that the strategy of the Quebec government would have been to pressure France so that the French government, once the motion had been adopted by the National Assembly, would immediately commit to recognizing a sovereign Quebec as soon as a proclamation of independence had been made, thus triggering a domino effect heading towards the United States and francophone countries. The parallel drawn by Chrétien between a newly sovereign Quebec and Taiwan leaves several questions hanging for which there will never be answers. But it gives us a glimpse of the kind of diplomatic war that Canada would have waged against Quebec in the international arena.

Jean Chrétien, then, did not plan to recognize the validity of a YES victory, first of all, because of the question, and secondly, because he rejected the idea that the nation could be broken up by the slimmest of margins. There were, however, a few people on the federalist side who thought differently than Jean Chrétien and his ministers. Jean Charest believed that if the results of a referendum were to yield a victory by a one-vote margin, "you must indeed accept the decision." "The next day, we would have had to face that reality," he says. "Then what would we have done? We would have had to interpret things once again. The most difficult scenario is what to do when victory is by a very slim margin." Charest believed, in contrast to Chrétien's strategists, that Quebecers had understood the question. "They knew what they were voting on," he adds. "I think they knew that if they voted YES, there was going to be a breakup or the risk of a breakup."[33]

In addition to having to fight for keeping a modicum of unity of thinking and action in his cabinet, Chrétien would have had to face a rebellion from the Reform Party, who had always maintained that a YES vote had to be recognized as meaning the sovereignty of Quebec. "They almost seemed at times like they preferred to get a YES vote," says John Manley, "and they would ask provocative questions in the House of Commons which seemed to undermine the strategy to try to win the referendum. This was a complete break with parliamentary tradition. Preston Manning and Reform were actually throwing gasoline on the fire." Even if it did not constitute a significant opposition, with its nine MPs, the NDP would also have opposed Chrétien's position. We remember that the day after she was elected to the party leadership, Alexa McDonough had declared that the NDP would recognize the result of the referendum, whatever this result might be. Before sitting down around a negotiation table with Quebec, then, if indeed it agreed to do so, the federal government would have had to endure long and lively debates in the House of Commons involving the Reform Party, the NDP and the Bloc Québécois. Not to mention the fact that talks would have had to be undertaken right away with the governments of the anglophone provinces, which would have expected to have their voices heard as events unfolded.

The Prime Minister would have to answer another question that, like all of the others, was not addressed in the Constitution. Are Quebecers the only ones who have a say in the matter of Canada's being torn asunder? "Having gone through the experiences of '81, '82, the notion that this country could be broken up by one segment, as important as it is historically, and as good as its grievances may or may not be," says Roy Romanow, "is anathema to me. This'll involve all of us." Former Ontario Premier Bob Rae's comments are essentially similar: "We're not bound by it. It's an important expression of opinion in Quebec but it's not definitive for the future of the country. It can't be." Preston Manning, who had given a great deal of thought to the matter, maintains that Quebec could not separate from Canada without an amendment to the Constitution. "That's the legal way to separate a country and it was important, in international law, that you do it legally. We had argued, since Charlottetown, that you're not going to ever have a big constitutional amendment in Canada without a referendum for people to say: do we go along with this?"

Daniel Johnson, on the other hand, never wavered on the matter: "It is up to Quebecers to decide on their future,"[34] he states without hesitation. But John Parisella, his policy advisor during the referendum, is not so sure. "That would be the ideal," he says. "But here, we're living in another world. Quebec is part of Canada. We are geographically located in a country in such a way that, in the hypothetical event of complete sovereignty for Quebec, Canada would be split in two by another country. The United States cannot be indifferent to this, nor can the rest of Canada. We're not talking about a little piece of land, here. Quebec is in the country's heartland. We have a federal system because of Quebec. Without Quebec, we would be headed for more of a unitary government. If you think that this is a matter that concerns only Quebecers, to be settled among Quebecers, you're dreaming in Technicolor. You've got to be living in your own world if you think that the rest of America can't take an interest when a new nation emerges."[35]

If Chrétien refuses to recognize the results of a YES vote while the Parizeau government conducts itself as if Quebec had become a sovereign nation, enjoining the people to stop paying federal income tax, for example, what can Chrétien do? The question preoccupied the prime minister for a long time. Not long after the referendum, in mid-January of 1996, accompanied by a group of business people and provincial premiers, he was in Pakistan to sign six new bilateral accords between the two countries. Benazir Bhutto, the Pakistani prime minister, was asking questions about the seismic event that had just rocked Canada. All of a sudden, recalls Frank McKenna, who was part of the Team Canada delegation, "our prime minister, speaking on behalf of all of us, just asked, 'what would you have done, Mrs. Bhutto, in such a situation?' She said, 'Well, I would have sent the army in, of course.' Just as if to say, 'What a stupid question... you can't just allow anybody who wants to separate, to separate.'"

According to Deborah Grey, the government had not completely ruled out the possibility of sending in the army. "There were some documents that came forward out of the department (of Defence) that said they were prepared to use military force." David Collenette, the Defence minister at the time, has a discourse that clearly indicates that intervention by the armed forces had not been ruled out. When journalist Lawrence Martin interviewed him in preparation for writing his book, *Iron Man*, Collenette limited such an intervention to protecting federal facilities and outbreak of civil war in Quebec. Journalist Martin backs the credibility of the latter hypothesis, writing, "Few could imagine a civil war playing out in a country like Canada. But this alarming mix of circumstances suddenly made it seem possible. It was perhaps even likely."[36]

Looking back at this period today, the former Defence minister paints a singularly broader picture of the circumstances that might have motivated an intervention by the army. "My biggest concern was the whole issue of public order," he says. "If the YES side had won and precipitous actions had been taken by the Quebec government, as Jacques Parizeau has declared, I think the public would have expected the government of Canada to ensure that there was order in the country, pending a political resolution of the difficulties." Collenette had a precise idea of what was meant by public order: "You have to make sure that life can go on in a normal fashion," he adds. "If the Quebec government said, 'we're independent, you don't have to pay your taxes (to Ottawa), you don't have to obey the Criminal Code of Canada,' I think that it was totally illegal to say that."

When asked if the government would have sent in troops, the former minister does not answer the question directly. "The fact is that there are troops in Quebec, there are troops in every part of the country. And under the National Defence Act, the only way troops can be deployed in the country for public order is to ensure that certain conditions of the National Defence Act are met. And one of these is that the attorney general of a province requests that the minister of Defence and the chief of defence staff respond. In the case of Quebec, there were two very notable examples, in 1970 (for the October Crisis) and in 1990, the Oka crisis. And where in effect, the Canadian military reported to the attorney general. That's when you're looking at a normal situation. That's daily life. When I say order, I mean the normalcy of daily life. And the institutions, the Constitution, the laws, the courts, everyone would be able to deal with whatever situation came forward. It became clear very quickly, and it's been expounded upon by

Mr. Parizeau, that he would have moved the country, certainly in Quebec but, by extension, the country to something that could be characterized as disorder."

It is unknown to this day to what extent Jean Chrétien was aware of his Defence minister's assessment of the situation, the concept he had of disorder and the way in which he intended to carry out his duties. In the days that followed publication of *Iron Man*, in October 2003, Jean Chrétien, on tour in Asia, declared, in reply to a question from a reporter, "I don't know how you say this in French, but that's bullshit. I never thought any such thing."[37] Today, he maintains the same position. "I've never been informed of anything. They move people all the time in the army. Some people might have been moved in Quebec or out of Quebec at that time, I don't know. I don't know if they've done something there. I read some articles about it that surprised me. Because, if it had been a dramatic move, they would have come to me. I wasn't meeting with the army every day, you know."[38] But Chrétien was indeed holding meetings with his ministers and, at the Tuesday cabinet meeting in the week before the referendum, the Quebec file took up a lot of floor time. In fact, Collenette never spoke of moving troops, but rather of measures that he was thinking of taking if ever the situation in Quebec were to become "disorderly." In Jean Chrétien's and David Collenette's own words, until that day, the two men had not discussed these measures.

The solution, for Jean Chrétien, in the hypothetical event that he would have wanted to make sure his legitimacy was unequivocal, might have been found in a call for a general election. But this solution was not completely worry-free either. "Either he resigns, acknowledging the people's decision," comments political analyst Duncan Cameron of the University of Ottawa, "or, considering that the results are not conclusive, he calls a general election. Mr. Parizeau would then have to decide whether he accepted that a federal election be held in Quebec. This could precipitate a declaration of sovereignty and create a major crisis." With, moreover, according to professor Desmond Morton of McGill University, secondary effects for the government of Quebec if they were to prevent this election from being held in their territory: "This is not the wisest way of winning over everyone's re-spect, especially Americans, with their love of elections,"[39] he says. The possibility of calling a general election would likely have been set aside, if only due to the general mood among the Canadian people: a Gallup poll conducted in mid-October indicated that a majority of Canadians did not want an election.[40] Other political experts, such as Philip Resnik of Vancouver, considered that Jean Chrétien must either contest the legitimacy of the Quebec vote through a Canada-wide ref-erendum or go to court to plead for the inviolability of the Canadian Constitution. In a word, he must block the path to sovereignty either by a popular vote or by legal means.[41]

And, a touchy subject for Jean Chrétien if ever there was one: what happens to the Maritimes—four provinces henceforth geograph-ically cut off from the country to which they belong? There was a joke going around during the referendum in the Maritime provinces, which Frank McKenna likes to retell: "If Quebec is no longer in Canada, we'll be able to get to Toronto faster." The reality, however, did not lend itself to humour, and the isolation of the Maritimes from the rest of the country would have created situations that were extremely complex, both politically and economically. "We sure didn't know what Plan B was," says McKenna. "So, what happens the next day? What do we do? Do we just go on about our business and say, 'we'll use passports to get through Quebec but we'd still get to Toronto'?" Preston Manning speaks very seriously about negotiating a corridor through Quebec, which would have connected the Maritime provinces to the rest of Canada. Jacques Parizeau wasn't talking about a corridor, but rather an accord, entered into very quickly. "The government of Quebec goes to see the Canadian government and says to them, 'as quickly as possible, we need an accord for the free movement of vehicles and people, by land, sea and air, between Ontario and the Maritime provinces.' Do you think the Canadian federal government would have said no?"[42]

And what about francophones outside Quebec? With Quebec no longer a part of Confederation, could the Canadian government fail to take an interest in these people? "The anglophone provinces would have then wanted to rewrite the Constitution," thinks Albertan

Georges Arès. "The rights of francophones that are found in the Constitution would have been casualties of this process. I think the first people who would have wanted to deny us those rights would have been the very people who had been sympathetic to our cause, who had placed their children in immersion schools, who had made gestures of trust in the future, ensuring that their children learn French. They would have felt betrayed. Schools, school administration and the things that make Canada a bilingual country, recognizing linguistic duality as a fundamental characteristic, these things were in danger of disappearing. Being a French-Canadian outside Quebec is an ongoing battle."[43]

And how about Quebec's Native population? This was one of the most difficult issues that the Canadian government would have had to resolve. Would the Government still have duties towards them? Matthew Coon Come wonders about the will of the federal government to enforce the constitutional provisions on Aboriginal rights. "We wanted them to be able to get our consent, should that referendum of Quebec be a YES vote, so we're not just transferred like cattle to a new independent Quebec." It is however not certain, once Quebec had separated from Canada, that the Aboriginals living there would have continued to fall under federal jurisdiction. A Privy Council document, prepared one year before the referendum, suggests that the Canadian government might cease to be the trustee of Aboriginal rights, and that Aboriginal people should abandon any ideas they might have of seceding from Quebec. According to this document, their future would be dependent upon factors of a strictly political nature.[44] Moreover, the position of the government of Quebec was firm: negotiations, yes, but respecting the territorial integrity of Quebec. Long discussions, including with Quebec, inevitably awaited the Canadian government.

Whatever the areas addressed, the issues called forth, the problems raised, Jean Chrétien maintained an air of mystery right up to the end over what his government would do if the YES side were to obtain a majority on Monday. Did he not go so far as to refuse, in a program aired on TVA on Thursday, October 26, to say whether the unemployed, retirees and veterans would still be receiving their cheques on the day following the referendum? "If you vote NO, you will keep everything, there will be no problem," he answered moderator Jean-Luc Mongrain. "If the YES side wins, there will be major problems. After that, everything is up in the air."[45] The referendum debate had lasted for more than a year and the official campaign a good, long month. And yet, so many questions remained unresolved. Jean Chrétien, the other federal politicians, the leaders of the YES and NO camps and, to a certain extent, the provincial premiers of Canada who got involved, either could not find answers to these questions or did not wish to answer them. They would be there on their desks, in big, bold letters, the morning after a YES vote.

In the meantime, the campaign pressed forward toward the finishing tape, in last-ditch speeches clinging to themes and slogans that the strategists still believed to be effective. Jean Chrétien, speaking to 10,000 people packed into and spilling out of the Canadian Museum of Civilization in Hull, reaffirmed his confidence that Quebecers would understand that "their homeland is still Quebec and their country, Canada." Jacques Parizeau, in a symbolic gesture, chose the Taillon riding, which René Lévesque had represented in the National Assembly for nine years, to finish off his campaign and to issue a final appeal to undecided voters. At his side were Lucien Bouchard and Mario Dumont, surrounded by a group of artists come to present their end-of-campaign show to a crowd of 5,000 people. Daniel Johnson was in Saint-Leonard, in northwest Montreal, where, speaking to 800 members of the Italian community, he said that he was persuaded that Quebecers had understood what the cost of separation would be.

In Ottawa, just before turning in for the night, Eddie Goldenberg phoned the pollsters of the NO camp. One of them said to him, "Tomorrow, we're going to get between 54 and 56% of the vote." Goldenberg insisted: "Give me the real numbers. I don't need numbers that will let me sleep soundly. I need the real numbers so I can give the prime minister of Canada good advice, because he will have some very important decisions to make tomorrow morning." And the polltaker repeated his numbers: between 54 and 56% for the NO.

CHAPTER XIV
"Not by Much"

When Monique Simard walked in, on Monday morning, to the central committee of the YES camp at 1200 Papineau Street, she was in low spirits: "Maybe this is going to be tougher than we imagined," she announced to the group. She had just returned from a one-on-one debate with John Parisella, on an English-language radio station, and Daniel Johnson's advisor had been extremely convincing: the NO would carry the day with 53 or 54% of the votes. Monique Simard's pessimism was contagious and the YES camp's enthusiasm dwindled rapidly.

Jean Royer decided he had to do something. He called the staff together into a meeting room, and a speakerphone was placed on the table. He called Parisella at the NO committee. Everyone could hear the conversation. "I understand that you saw Monique Simard this morning," said Royer. "She told us you are sure you are going to win. If you are so sure, I will bet you $25,000 that we are the ones who are going to win." "I could hear the silence at the other end," Royer recalls today. "Then John answered, 'No, no, I never gamble.' Everyone present in the room interpreted his silence as proof that he wasn't all that sure of winning, after all." And Jean Royer sent everyone back to their work, saying, "It's the YES that's going to win." "Deep down," says Royer, "I knew very well that it was not in John's nature to gamble, I knew he would say no. I took the chance. I don't know what I would have done if he had said yes, because I didn't have the $25,000."[1] Today, Parisella reflects back on the incident with humour: "I think they were taking us for a bit of a ride that day,"[2] he says.

Jean Royer was confident. "The polls showed a trend that increased our side to 52%," he points out. "The method that Michel Lepage, the YES camp pollster, and I used for distributing the undecided vote, led us to conclude we would win."[3] Lucien Bouchard's organizer, Bob Dufour, was more cautious: "Yes, the polls put us at 52 or 53%," he says. "But the sovereigntist movement has always had, even in provincial elections, a problem referred to as 'the ballot box tax.' We are always 2 or 3% short. We have never been able to understand why. What it meant was that, with the ballot box tax, we were left with only 49 or 50%."[4]

One of the organizers' primary concerns was to 'get the vote out.' "We knew," recalls Jean-François Lisée, "that if the voter turnout was below 80%, it wasn't good for us. It meant that the young people were voting less than at election time, and our majority depended on the young people." The YES camp knew that the proportion of non-francophones who intended to vote was very high. "If the number of voters was below 80%, it would mean that within any given group, there was a higher proportion of non-francophones than francophones who voted," Lisée adds.[5]

Alain Lupien was responsible for coordinating the operation throughout Quebec and he was in continuous contact with each riding "to see where our weaknesses lay." Every hour, at fifteen minutes to the hour, helpers went to the polling divisions—more than 3,000 in all—to pick up the information that would give some idea of the direction the vote was taking. And, every hour, this data was entered into a computer to allow the strategists to analyze the trends and adjust them, as required. Lupien and two other individuals shared Quebec among them, "about forty constituencies each." "We each had a set of goals," he recalls. "We watched to see if we were ahead or behind in voter turnout. We turned up the pressure wherever things were not going so well." From around 4 p.m., the reports came in not every hour but every half-hour. "We had to report back," Lupien adds. "Mr. Bouchard and Mr. Parizeau, they wanted to know."[6]

While Michel Carpentier, the recent replacement for Louis Bernard as secretary general of the government's executive committee, was finalizing a rapid action plan for a YES win scenario, Jean-François Lisée withdrew to draft two letters: one for Jacques Chirac, the other for Bill Clinton. He also jotted down some notes that could be useful to the various spokespersons of the YES camp, should they be interviewed at the end of the day, regardless of the outcome of the referendum. He also prepared an interview he would be giving, any minute, to a *Business Week* reporter, because the YES victory, if it materialized, would be the magazine's cover story the following week.

In the NO camp, the effervescence had spilled over into the ridings. The organization was more decentralized than in the YES camp, and each riding had its own structure. "We had done all that we could," says Pierre-Claude Nolin. "As far as we were concerned, our work was finished; around the table, there were no big decisions to be made that day: we touched wood, crossed our fingers, then we would await the results. The waiting was dreadful."[7] Daniel Johnson says the same thing: "I was in wait mode," he recalls. "Everything was done. There was nothing else we could do. It was up to millions of Quebecers then to act, while we sat and waited…" But Johnson was definite: "I never believed that the YES could win," he says.[8]

Jean Charest returned to Sherbrooke. By far the best orator in the NO camp, he felt he had run a good campaign. After stopping by to thank the organizers of the local committee, he would go to his father's place for lunch, with his wife, Michèle—a custom he had maintained ever since starting to participate in election campaigns. "We were very, very, very nervous all day long," he says. In the afternoon, with his family, he joined some friends and supporters in a hotel room in Montreal to watch the initial results of the vote on television, before moving on to the Metropolis where the NO supporters were to gather.

In Ottawa, the atmosphere on Parliament Hill felt oppressive, as just before a storm; the anxious hours that had to be endured before the final *dénouement* seemed interminable. Everyone was holding their breath. "People were not talking to each other," recalls Jane Stewart, president of the Liberal caucus. Eddie Goldenberg couldn't stay still any longer. "There had been numerous polls, polls that went up, polls that went down; we were nervous, obviously," he says. "But I had a job to do: prepare the speech, as at every election, the speech acknowledging defeat. It was extremely emotional because we were talking about the possible breakup of our country. Clearly, our plan was to say that this was not a vote for separation, that we were not prepared to let the country be broken up, that we intended to make changes… but it was not easy to write that text." Even before knowing the result of the vote, in Jean Chrétien's office, they had decided they would not accept a YES victory. In the late afternoon, Goldenberg went over to 24 Sussex Drive, where he would spend the evening in the company of the prime minister's family, some friends and advisors.

Jean Chrétien, who is known for remaining calm in the worst of circumstances, was restless. Would he be the prime minister to preside over the splitting up of this 128-year-old country? "I became somewhat nervous when, the Saturday night or the Sunday," he recalls, "Eddie (Goldenberg) called me and a couple of others and told me that we had suddenly dropped in the polls. We were realistic, we could lose. If there was not a win, we had to be ready." That afternoon, he phoned Roy Romanow, who "was a long-standing friend." The premier of Saskatchewan was in a hotel room in Montreal; he was slated to do television commentary in the evening. "Roy," he told him, "we have a serious situation on our hands. We could lose by three or four percentage points. I felt I had to tell you. I'm going to call one or two other premiers as well. Prepare a response just in case, will you… Had you thought about it?" Romanow had already considered the possibility of a YES victory, and Chrétien knew that. He told the prime minister of Canada how he would respond: "I told him," Romanow recounts today, "that this was a question which was so porous that you could not give legitimacy to the YES vote and, in any event, we were not going to preside over the dissolution of the union."

For Jacques Parizeau, the campaign had been a tough one but, looking back over it, he felt satisfied. For the first time in a long time, the day's schedule looked light: first, go and vote, then go to the riding of L'Assomption, which was the constituency he represented in the National Assembly, and meet as many supporters as possible. When he got up in the morning, though, he was seized by a wild panic. "I was afraid," he admits. "I said to myself, 'What if it doesn't work out!' Can you imagine the responsibility that represents? Towards thousands, tens of thousands of people I had led on this adventure for years, people who in amounts of $20 and $50 had raised 32 million dollars. Driven by what faith? Faith in a goal, in an ideal, in a man whom they thought made a certain amount of sense… Well, that morning, I said: 'My God, I hope it's going to work!'"[9] He remained confident, but tense, and very nervous.

His first activity of the day was to do his civic duty. When he showed up at the polling station, in Outremont, where he lived, his nervousness was apparent: he walked directly over to the booth, forgetting to take a ballot. "I was so emotional," he said, in an interview on the show *L'Événement*, broadcast on TVA. "They directed me back to the table to pick up a ballot. And then, in the booth, I just wanted to make sure of one thing: to put the X beside the YES, not beside the NO! I had kind of a flash: don't go getting it wrong, now! I came out of the booth, not knowing to whom I should give my ballot. I was completely out of it that morning."[10]

After voting, Parizeau went, with his wife and some close associates, to his constituency of L'Assomption. There he met supporters and had a meal, in Repentigny, with some of the organizers. Then, he headed for his constituency office, where he granted the interview to the TVA network. This interview had been planned for some time. Parizeau had a lot of confidence in Stéphan Bureau, with whom he had met on a number of occasions in the past and who had always respected the agreements they made between them. He attached a great deal of importance to this conversation, which would be kept under embargo, that is to say, which could not be broadcast, until after the referendum. The purpose was to inform Quebecers what the period following a YES victory would look like. But at the same time, what he was preparing to say would, in a way, serve as a political testament and he weighed each word carefully.

Bureau asked him: Have you said to yourself: this is a case of 'make or break'? It has to happen now, or it's no longer I who will be able...

Parizeau: Ah, but of course, it's quite obvious, that goes without saying. (...) If I fail, I must be capable of telling myself: it's my fault, I was not clever enough, enough of a unifier. And, clearly, I would draw conclusions. One must never impose oneself in these kinds of circumstances. The independence of a country is not just a passing thing. If I have not managed to achieve it, well then, I will have to remove myself from the scene pretty quickly and let someone else try their hand at it.

Bureau: What you are saying is that tonight, if perchance you learn that Quebec has decided to say NO, you will very soon be changing hats as you just mentioned.

Parizeau: Oh, absolutely. There has never been a shadow of a doubt in my mind, as far as that goes. Let's understand each other. We are just a few hours from the referendum results. I am telling you clearly: there is no doubt in my mind that, if it's a NO, my useful phase in this area has come to an end.

Bureau: You would nevertheless remain premier and stay in office for a period of time?

Parizeau: Yes, but not for long.

Bureau: You have opted, then, to say goodbye to the position you hold?

Parizeau: I am in politics to achieve sovereignty for Quebec, not necessarily to run things. I was financial and economic advisor to Jean Lesage and to Daniel Johnson Senior. I have relished the taste of power. Listen, to cling to power at my age is completely ridiculous. You don't hang on. That would be ridiculous.[11]

Even though most people in his entourage knew that he was not going to hang on to power if there was a NO victory, they were all in shock. "There were a few of us, a very small group, his press attaché, crouched down in the corridor during the interview," Lisette Lapointe recalls. "There was a little monitor on the floor. We had our faces right up close to it. And he said: 'If it's NO, I leave!' Something like that..." Yet she had known for a long time that he would leave politics if he lost the referendum. "As soon as our relationship became serious, in 1992," she says, "he said to me: 'Listen, it's not for twenty years that I'm going to be in politics. If we make our life together, I see myself in politics for three or four more years. I would like to be elected premier of Quebec, then, eight or ten months later, to hold a referendum. If it's YES, I'll stay eight or ten months to get the train on the right track. If it's NO, I'll leave.' I've known it from the beginning and he had repeated it on other occasions." But she had been trying, for several days, to prevent him from leaving on impulse. "If ever it's NO," she told him, "don't make a snap decision. Wait and see what happens after. Maybe you should wait a while and let the dust settle."[12] So, to hear him repeat it, on a television monitor, on the day of the referendum itself, without having warned her... She did not agree, because she believed the YES would win. "It would, however, be rather special," she explained, "to see a television program a week later, with the premier, who had just won his referendum, saying that."

Marie-Josée Gagnon, Parizeau's press attaché, immediately advised Jean Royer. "This was a gal who did not get worked up over small things," says Royer. "I could sense the commotion at the other end right away. It didn't surprise me. Mr. Parizeau had told me twenty or thirty times, and not only during the referendum campaign. When he returned to politics, he told me, 'The reason I've come back is to achieve sovereignty. If I fail, I don't like politics enough to stay after that.'"[13]

Jacques Parizeau left his constituency in his official vehicle, accompanied by Marie-Josée Gagnon, to go to Radio-Québec, where he would record a speech, in both languages, to be aired the same evening, if the YES side won. Radio-Québec, acting as producer for Parizeau's speech, was negotiating with other networks, who were hesitant to rebroadcast the speech, unsure whether it was a partisan speech or an address by a head of state. These other networks did finally make a commitment, which they would never have to keep, as the speech would never be aired.

The recording process was much more arduous than anticipated. Parizeau was exhausted. He stumbled over his words. They had to start over several times, as there was only one camera, which ruled out any possibility of editing. "It took a whole eighteen or twenty minutes," recalls Jean-François Lisée. "He had to do it in a single take and it had to be perfect. He started over two or three times, in French. Then, it had to be done in English. And his fatigue level was already high. It was laboured. It took us quite some time."[14] But when, finally, he succeeded, the words he addressed to the population that had just shown its confidence in him were serene and forward-looking. "A simple and strong decision has been taken tonight: Quebec will become sovereign," he said. "It has taken great courage for the men and women of Quebec to overcome the formidable obstacles placed in their path, from the very beginning right up to this day. Today, you have outdone yourselves. You have inscribed your name on the face of the earth. Each of you should know, tonight, that the Government of Quebec will proceed in the coming days with the same clarity, the same serene determination, the same courage and the same openness that you, the citizens of Quebec, have shown today."[15] And, as if in anticipation of the federal government's reaction to a YES victory, he added, "On October 18, Jean Chrétien declared that the referendum, and I quote, 'was the definitive, irreversible choice of a country.' Last week, in his address to the nation, he indicated that the decision that would be made today was 'serious and irreversible.' We agree with him."

The recording completed, Jacques Parizeau moved on to his premier's office, located in the Hydro-Québec building. On arrival, he would chat with his chief of staff. As soon as Royer saw him, he said, with a half-smile, "You couldn't resist, you had to say it!" Parizeau answered, "Yes, I said it. Does that surprise you?" "No," answered Royer, "it doesn't."[16]

Royer and Jean-François Lisée were part of a select group who knew that the premier did not intend to hold on to his position if he lost the referendum. But what they retained from the interview their leader had given to the TVA network was that he would remain premier "not for long." This meant that they would have to deal with the situation much sooner than anticipated. "Royer and I, we took him aside to discuss what his attitude would be in the case of a NO victory," recalls Lisée. "We convinced him not to announce his resignation (immediately) because, already, the shock of having lost the referendum would be hard enough for the sovereigntists to absorb. If they had to lose their leader at the same time, it would be too much, it would be too much to ask of Quebecers in a single evening, to lose both at once." Lisée then told him, "We would need your unifying talents. It's a grandfather figure we would need tonight, someone who could see beyond this particular defeat." According to Lisée, Parizeau seemed to agree with that vision of how to approach the coming events. The sense the political advisor was left with after that exchange was that "they could discuss resignation the next day or the day after."[17]

At that point, everyone, including his inner circle, felt that there would be time to let things take their course and that they could, for now, devote their energies to more urgent matters. Their leader had just stated to Stéphan Bureau that, if the NO side won, he would remain premier for a certain period of time. This confirmed remarks he had made two months earlier, in an interview on Radio-Canada's radio program *Le Midi Quinze*. It may have been in order to avoid de-mobilizing the YES forces, but he did not let on in any way at that time that there could be a premature departure. In fact, he had said clearly to host Michel Lacombe that he planned to continue administering the affairs of the government.

Lacombe asked him: Will you stay in office after the referendum, then, regardless of the outcome?

Parizeau: I do not have the reputation of being a quitter. I'm not a quitter.

Lacombe: And if Quebec says NO?

Parizeau: I am working to have them say YES. And the PQ will be in power for a few more years. People can hypothesize all they want, but we have no reason not to be clear about our present intentions regarding the referendum and, on the other hand, to offer our assurance of a government that will remain in power for a few more years, a government that still has quite a lot on its plate.

So, the strategists had nothing to worry about: Jacques Parizeau would still be at the helm after the referendum, no matter what. Looking back on these events today, Jacques Parizeau justifies his attitude and the remarks he made to Bureau: "I wanted to protect myself," he says. "I could not see myself starting over or trying to start over. When that interview was recorded, at noon, the results were still not known. I did not want to give the impression that I was waiting for the results before deciding. I indicated what I was going to do in the case of each of the possible outcomes: if we win, here's what we're going to do. If we fail, I'm going to leave." And, ten years later, he adds, "Looking at the question more seriously, perhaps I would not have resigned if I had known what was going to happen afterwards. But it took me several years to understand that. At the time, it was clear I had to leave. But a few years later, it's another matter."[18]

Parizeau's two allies knew nothing of the interview with TVA. Lucien Bouchard was in Lac-Saint-Jean, where he voted in his riding of Alma. Mario Dumont had already gone to Rivière-du-Loup the evening before, to cast his ballot and to meet with his supporters. For security reasons, the ADQ leader spent the night at a hotel. On getting up in the morning, he turned on the television and, as is often the case in hotels, it was tuned to an American channel, the ABC network. "The first three news bulletin items were about Quebec," he recalls. The first report was on the referendum, the second was on the diplomatic consequences with the U.S., and the third was on the economic consequences. Sitting up in bed, leaning back on the pillows, I said to myself: 'Yeah, it's a pretty big deal, this thing we've undertaken!'"[19]

The plane that would take Lucien Bouchard back to Montreal made a detour to Rivière-du-Loup to pick up Mario Dumont, so as to save him the four-hour drive. Flying several thousand feet up in the air over Quebec, which they had spent a month criss-crossing in every direction, the two men reflected on their campaign, shared notes on their speeches for that evening, and discussed the latest polls—which had the two options tied. "The polling companies were removing the decimal points and rounding off the figures, in order to play it safe,"[20] recalls Mario Dumont.

Jacques Parizeau and his chief of staff, still in the premier's office, were staying closely tuned to the day's events and to the determining factor for the outcome: voter participation. The data they were receiving indicated a particularly high rate of participation, which became increasingly impressive as the day wore on. Royer explained to his leader that, the greater the voter turnout, the better the chances of a YES win, because a higher rate of participation would approach more closely the model used for the polls. Parizeau then looked his chief of staff straight in the eyes. "I felt he was probing the depths of my soul," recalls Royer, "and asking 'Are you sure?' So, I reviewed my explanations with him."[21]

Parizeau and Bouchard each had a suite at the *Palais des congrès de Montréal* (Montreal Convention Centre) while Mario Dumont had one at the Delta Hotel on Sherbrooke Street. Around 3 o'clock in the afternoon, Bouchard was in his suite with his team, which included Pierre-Paul Roy, Gilbert Charland, François Leblanc and Bob Dufour. They were awaiting the initial results, following closely how the vote was progressing in the province as a whole. Around 4 p.m., Bouchard began to write his two speeches, one for victory and one for defeat. His entourage tried to contact Jacques Parizeau. Without success. "It wasn't for lack of trying," says Roy. "But Mr. Parizeau had made himself incommunicado. We were to understand it was a decision he had made."[22] No one was too worried about it, though, because the leaders were scheduled to meet at 5 p.m.

It was now 4:45 p.m. Bouchard turned to his political advisor. "Pierre-Paul," he said, "call and get in touch." Roy managed to contact Éric Bédard, a member of the Parizeau team. "And Mr. Bédard gave me to understand," Pierre-Paul Roy recounts today, "that there would be no meeting and that, at that particular moment, no contact was planned. And none, in fact, occurred."[23] Thus, throughout the entire day of the referendum, Jacques Parizeau and Lucien Bouchard did not speak to one another other, an omen suggesting that the evening would require a fair amount of improvisation.

After meeting with his principal advisors, Jacques Parizeau left the Hydro-Québec building and returned to the hotel, where he and his wife had been living during most of the campaign. He felt extremely tired after the hellish month that had just come to an end and after a day whose stress he had just barely managed to withstand. He was played out and aching all over. At the time of the scheduled appointment with the other two YES leaders, he was stretched out, submitting to a treatment by the expert hands of the Ritz Carlton masseur, whom Lisette Lapointe had summoned to their room. "It was an amazing experience," he says with some amusement today. "It's a strange thing to say, but I had never had a massage before and it did me a lot of good."[24] The couple then had a light meal delivered to their room and watched the suspense build on television before going over to the *Palais des congrès*.

Dramatic intensity reached its zenith at 8 p.m., once the polling stations had closed, and the radio and television stations reread the wording of the referendum question and began to announce the initial results. On the second floor of the *Palais des congrès*, in a room that could hold about 20 people, Jacques Parizeau's inner circle—of about half a dozen people—was riveted to the television screen. The premier's chief of staff had just asked numerous people to leave, all but the five or six closest assistants of the leader of the YES camp.

The atmosphere was tense, but calm. Jacques Parizeau set the tone: he said nothing, moving from one television screen to another. People said little to one another, exchanging only brief comments, each person trying to give an explanation of the results as they started trickling in. The first results were from the Magdalen Islands, where the stations always close an hour earlier because of their time zone. They were better than anticipated, but the atmosphere did not change. "I think we're going to win it," Royer said simply. They knew that the YES had to pick up as much as 58% in certain ridings in order to make up for the 40% they would have to accept in others. For a few moments, Jacques Parizeau and those who were with him saw before their eyes the image of a country of their own. Within thirty minutes of the polling stations closing, the YES reached the 56% mark. Everyone relied on Royer's analysis to guide them. But the number of votes expressed was still very small: 1%. All of a sudden, shortly after 8:30,

numbers started rolling in, without, however, suggesting any particular trend—until the results for the Quebec region appeared on the
screen, lower than what the YES camp had hoped.

An hour and a half after the polling stations had closed, by which
time 62% of the results were known, the YES was ahead by 8,000 votes;
they had 50.14% of the vote, out of a total of about 3 million. Parizeau
approached Jean Royer: "What do you think?" he asked him. Royer
told him that the majorities obtained were not at the levels they had
counted on. While on the screen, the YES still had about 54%, the projections by Royer and Michel Lepage, the YES camp's pollster, relied
on data that was too strong to allow them to remain optimistic. "The
atmosphere didn't change," Jean Royer recounts today. "It was part of
our job not to get excited. We knew that, if we did, it could affect the
boss. So, the tone stayed calm, no one expressed disappointment."[25]

Four minutes later, the YES lead was only 1,000 votes and, by
8:36 p.m., there was a tie: 50% and 50%.[26] "In Beauce, where we didn't
expect much," Jean-François Lisée recalls, "the result was even lower
than we expected."[27] And this was the case in other ridings around
Quebec City as well. "Five or six ridings must have come in, one after
the other, from which I could deduce a kind of trend," Jean Royer recalls today. "Lepage and I had developed a model which allowed us to
make projections using a minimum of data. That's how I was able to
tell pretty quickly that we were not going to get 52%. And when the
first results from Montreal came in, we could see that we were not
going to win."[28]

Although the YES strategists knew that, in most districts of
Montreal, the YES had little support, they hoped to pick up maybe
15% here, 20% there. But the NO tide was sweeping through all of
Montreal. That's when Jean Royer said, "We don't stand a chance
now." Those present in the room heard the explanations Royer was
giving his leader, and they understood, from what he was saying, that
the results still to come would have no further influence on the trend.
Parizeau remained standing beside him—without flinching. Had he
grasped at that moment that defeat was certain, or was he still hanging
on to some last flicker of hope? "I don't know at what point the fact

that we would not win registered with Mr. Parizeau,"[29] his chief of staff says casually, although he was familiar with his moods. Lisette Lapointe was at her husband's side. "It was a dreadful moment, sending shivers down your spine," she says today. "It was not just a disappointment. It was a major blow. His entire dream went up in smoke. It had been the struggle of a lifetime."[30]

Jean Royer then turned towards Jean-François Lisée: "We're going to be short," he confirmed, adding that their job was now to help Jacques Parizeau come to terms with the defeat and conduct himself as a premier who accepts the verdict of his people. Lisée was sitting at his laptop, ready to draft the speech acknowledging defeat. "History will judge you on what you are going to say tonight," he told Jacques Parizeau. But Parizeau wasn't listening. He was now seething with anger, anger he tried to shake by pacing furiously from one side of the room to the other. Then suddenly, the conversation took a totally different turn. Parizeau did not wish to discuss what the defeat meant for him personally. "It really was very personal," Lisée recalls. "From what I observed, it was as if he had never prepared himself for the eventuality of a NO victory. Even though there were times during the campaign that we thought we might lose, even though we had talked about it in the afternoon, it was as if, for him, this was a new situation."[31]

Parizeau lashed out at everyone, the English-language press, the daily *La Presse,* editorial writer Alain Dubuc. "It was the wounded person speaking that night when he said, 'All of it would have been worth it, if I had won. But now that I have lost, it wasn't worth it,'" adds his political advisor. He and Jean Royer let the storm pass, telling themselves they would rather see his frustration expressed now than later. "But the storm lasted a long time," Lisée adds. "We had a hard time getting him calmed down. We told him, 'It's a major gain over 1980, you need to look at the positive side. And we know that a majority of francophones voted YES. And besides, it's not over...' But we couldn't really tell to what extent we had managed to break through to his state of mind with our efforts." Lisée then asked Parizeau, "Do you want me to draft some notes for you?"[32] Finally, Parizeau listened and accepted.

Others now entered the room, some to congratulate Parizeau on raising the sovereignty vote from the 40%, where it stood in 1980, to 50%, others to deplore the 'failure' in the Quebec region. Parizeau regained his composure, thanking some, congratulating others "for the marvellous campaign that you ran in your area."

On the next floor up, the initial results from the Magdalen Islands had also generated a lot of hope. About fifteen people, his principal collaborators, some of the organizers and members of his family, surrounded Lucien Bouchard, who was following the results very calmly. But the atmosphere was feverish. Large windows looked out onto the huge auditorium of the *Palais des congrès* where the crowd reacted enthusiastically to each new result that came in. "But," says Bob Dufour, "we knew very well, from having done it for years, that we were better to wait till 11 p.m. than to start celebrating at 8:30."[33] The further the evening progressed, the more the YES fell behind. Bouchard kept his eyes focused on the screen: he was in deep concentration and not very talkative.

The Bloc Québécois leader had established what he called "a comfort zone" which he had set at roughly 52%. Not that he would question a YES victory at 50% plus one vote, but he saw, in a tighter outcome, the promise of enormous difficulties. "The comfort zone," Roy explains, "meant a level above which one is more and more comfortable, and below which one is less and less comfortable, in that the margin of difficulty would be increasingly large." Therefore, the results, which were making a NO victory practically inevitable, did not throw Bouchard's entourage into consternation. "I do not remember people feeling crushed," says Pierre-Paul Roy, the political advisor, who had been seated on a sofa, beside his leader. "We shared the feeling, expressed by some, that 'with a number like that, we may be better off losing than winning.' But there were others who said, 'winning is winning.' The general sentiment was, however, that, having come that close to winning, there was no way we were now going to throw in the towel."[34] Once he had absorbed the shock of defeat, Bouchard turned his mind to what he would say to the crowd filling the auditorium three storeys below.

Amidst the highly charged atmosphere in the Metropolis, Daniel Johnson remained calm. He felt certain of his victory. "I never felt that the YES could win," he says today. As the percentages of the vote for each region appeared on television, his entourage incorporated them into the results anticipated by the NO camp, thus making it easier to project the final result. "I saw the results coming in, and I was never worried," Johnson adds. "When you know Quebec and you see the trend of the vote in one region, and then in another region, experience allows you to project. I never believed we would lose. That's experience for you."[35] The earliest results, out of Saguenay–Lac-Saint-Jean, had quickly reassured him. "I expected percentages of around 72 or 75% for the YES in that region," says Pierre-Claude Nolin, "but they were not that high." The highest percentage obtained by the YES in that part of Quebec, 73.33%, was in the riding of Saguenay, while only 71% of the riding of Jonquière voted YES and 68.9% of Chicoutimi. "And when Quebec City began to come in," Nolin adds, "the percentages were not 60% for the YES, as we had anticipated, but around 50%."[36] While the sovereignty vote in the riding of Taschereau was 58%, most of the ridings in the region immediately surrounding Quebec recorded percentages below 55%, and in Jean-Talon, the percentage was below 50%.

As soon as the first results came in from Quebec City, and were flashed onto the screen, Nolin turned to a Radio-Canada journalist and said, "It's going to be a long evening, but I think we are going to win." John Parisella shared his optimism. He was deferring to other analysts, including former premier Robert Bourassa, who predicted a NO victory of 53%, and Bob Rae, whose projections reduced the gap to 2%. Parisella took part in a round table discussion in the evening on Radio-Canada. At the same time, he stayed connected to the organizers and NO camp pollster Grégoire Gollin, with a cellphone. "I was the calmest at the table because I had put the idea into my head that we would win,"[37] he says. What also reassured him was that sovereigntist Josée Legault, another participant in the round table, did not hide her disappointment with the initial results coming out of the Quebec region.

At 24 Sussex Drive, in Ottawa, Prime Minister Jean Chrétien was surrounded by his family and his chief collaborators. Jean Pelletier, his chief of staff, was at his side, in the prime minister's personal lounge. "There was a certain amount of tension," he recalls, but the prime minister, as usual on these occasions, was very calm, very preoccupied, very conscious of the gravity of the moment."[38] The polling stations had not yet closed when he said to his son-in-law, André Desmarais, "Watch Les Îles-de-la-Madeleine. Because that is one of the ridings that always comes in early and switches often. But the margins are not huge on one side or the other."[39] When these results did start coming in, the YES was ahead, while Chrétien had predicted that the NO would win in that riding, which had voted Liberal in the federal election of 1993. So, he said to those beside him, "Oops! It's going to be a long evening." Then he started analyzing the YES lead and the gap between the YES and the NO in a few other ridings. Then he turned to Desmarais and said, "the gap is going to be less than 2% or thereabouts, between 1 and 2% of the vote."

Chrétien's prediction was not reassuring to those around him. Eddie Goldenberg, who had arrived at the prime minister's residence earlier on, in the late afternoon, was antsy and hovered over the bowls of chips and hors d'oeuvres while waiting for further, more substantial results to come in. He finally settled down, with some other people, on the second floor of the residence. "We were very nervous," he recalls. "We were sitting on pins and needles throughout most of the evening." At a certain point, he couldn't stand it anymore. He went downstairs again, looking for a spot where he could be by himself in front of a television. Shortly afterwards, he was joined by others. "Not to follow me," he says, "but they just wanted to get away, and there weren't that many television sets in the house. That's human nature."

The president of the Liberal caucus, Jane Stewart, made arrangements for her party's MPs to be able to see and hear the results in a room reserved especially for that purpose in the West Block of the Parliament Buildings. However, not too many people showed up. Most people had chosen to follow the evening in the intimacy of their own home, apartment or office. But this was not the case for Reform

Party MPs. As most of them came from Western Canada, they were farther away from their ridings and about forty of them gathered in another room in the Parliament Buildings, in order to spend the evening together. Not being very familiar with Quebec's sociological realities, the arrival of the initial results filled them with great anxiety, as they thought for a while that this sovereigntist wave was going to sweep through all of Quebec.

The tension had begun to die down, however, when the results from Montreal West were announced: nine ridings from that part of the island would place more than 80% of their votes behind the NO, and fourteen of them, more than 70%, just as in Hull and Gatineau. The trend, in these ridings, became clear very quickly and, from 9 p.m. onwards, the anxiety generated by the results from the Magdalen Islands gradually gave way to hope.

At 234 Wellington Street, in Ottawa, the evening of October 30 was marked by exceptional bustle and excitement, not a typical atmosphere for upper-echelon bankers. All the Bank of Canada's top-level management, including Governor Gordon Thiessen and Senior Deputy Governor Bernard Bonin, were gathered on the fourth floor of the main building, along with a team of financial market analysts. This was only the second time, since he had joined the Bank seven years earlier, that Bonin had deviated from his normal work schedule. The purpose of the meeting was to prepare to intervene, should the dollar drop below the acceptable limit. The Bank's role, in such circumstances, was to help stabilize the economy by ensuring sufficient liquidity in the banking system. In a way, the Bank trailed behind the behaviour of the markets. But the markets had no compass to guide them in a climate of political uncertainty. There was a total absence, therefore, of projections that were sufficiently valid to allow the Bank of Canada to come up with any sort of corrective plan whatsoever. The commercial banks always maintained settlement balances through the Canadian Payments Association,[40] but, if there were a run on the banks, they could need lines of credit, which the Bank of Canada would make available to them rather than have them rely on external financing. The central Bank was, therefore, preparing to intervene in the markets, if necessary.

Throughout the day, bankers and professional investors had remained cautious. As at the Bank of Canada, money market staff was
putting in overtime, and the Canadian Dow Jones news service stayed
open until after 9 p.m. The dollar was jittery all day. At 8 a.m., it was
listed at 73.3 cents U.S. It picked up a little around 10 a.m. and held
steady between 73.36 and 73.47 cents, which was its value when
polling stations closed at 8 p.m. But, between 8 and 8:30 p.m., it gradually declined: at 8:31, its value was down to 72.5 cents. Then it began
a slow climb back up, reaching more than 73.5 cents by 9 p.m. It made
another sudden gain when, at 9:30 p.m., fifty minutes before the NO
victory was confirmed, CBC's anchorman Peter Mansbridge took it
upon himself to say on the air that he expected the NO, which had just
overtaken the YES, to maintain its lead. At 9:33 p.m., the Canadian
dollar was worth 74.85 cents U.S.

At the end of the evening, the Bank of Canada did not consider it
necessary to increase the lines of credit extended to the commercial
banks and, around 11 p.m., everyone went home. Moreover, the
Finance minister himself had not, at any time, given in to panic, since
he had not thought it wise, prior to the referendum, to increase the
Bank of Canada's reserves, which were then in the order of 16 billion
dollars U.S. According to Bank of Canada analysts, if the coffers had
not held the reserves and liquidity necessary to prevent the dollar from
plummeting dramatically, Jean Campeau's "O" plan would have been
powerless to stem the disaster. In their view, the objective of the
Campeau plan was not so much to support the Canadian dollar as to
prevent Quebec from having to go onto the international markets.[41]

Mario Dumont's supporters were not at the *Palais des congrès*,
but at the Delta Hotel, and it was there that shortly after 10 p.m., their
leader addressed them. "This evening," he told them, "Canada exists
only on paper. The whole world can see that one of Canada's two
founding peoples is not part of it. Quebec is not really part of Canada
when one in two Quebecers says YES to a mandate for sovereignty and
when the YES carries the day in the great majority of our regions. If I
were in the other camp, I would, in all prudence, hesitate to celebrate
the outcome." He then left for the *Palais des congrès*, where he went

directly to Lucien Bouchard's suite with some of his collaborators, including his chief of staff, André Néron, who was lamenting the results.

The NO victory was now a known fact and the hall was still jam-packed with YES supporters. Mario Dumont, who, according to Jean-François Lisée, was supposed to speak only at the Delta Hotel, also wanted to address the YES supporters gathered at the *Palais des congrès*. Since the meeting scheduled for five o'clock had not taken place, each of the leaders was waiting for a signal from the other, in a climate of improvisation, which the entourages were trying to manage. There had been some telephone communication over the course of the evening but, from the moment the NO victory was confirmed, everyone waited for Jacques Parizeau's reaction.

Tired of waiting, Lucien Bouchard finally said to his assistants, "Listen, I'm going down there. You can't just let the people wait like that in the auditorium. We have to go and meet them, we have to talk to them." He boarded the elevator, which, three storeys below, would take him directly backstage. Mario Dumont was with him, as were their entourages. Someone, possibly a bodyguard, then approached Bouchard, saying, "Mr. Parizeau wants to see you upstairs." Bouchard replied, "Listen, the people are waiting for us. I came down here to speak to them," and he kept right on walking towards the stage. Someone else came along with a cellphone. Just seconds before Bouchard moved past the curtain, the two men finally spoke. Bouchard gave Parizeau the general gist of what he would say. Parizeau answered, "Yes, that's very good. I will go further!" (A bit further, according to Royer; much further, according to Lisée.) It was almost 11 o'clock.

But Parizeau was still in his suite. Because of the media coverage, especially by television, he wanted to speak after Daniel Johnson, who was at the Metropolis. The discussion continued and time went by. Finally, Jean Royer interrupted: "If you want to be heard," he said to Parizeau, "you must speak now, after Mr. Bouchard and Mr. Dumont."

Jean-François Lisée had been trying for a while to put some ideas together into a draft for a unifying speech. But when he heard his leader tell Lucien Bouchard that he would go on "further," he was puzzled.

What he thought then was that Parizeau would denounce the media, as he had done to his entourage during the referendum campaign. But, for Lisée, that would be a manageable issue. Parizeau finally took the elevator while Lisée finished drafting the speech, which he would hand to him a few minutes later, backstage, while Dumont and Bouchard made their concluding remarks.

Their speeches had focused on appeasement and solidarity. Both had evoked the memory of René Lévesque. "It is not I who will say to you tonight: 'Till next time,'" said Mario Dumont. "The author of those words, whom I sense to be very present tonight, is far too great a man for us to borrow his language." "Democracy is the foundation of everything and, right from the start, René Lévesque's struggle was founded on respect for democratic values and democratic rule," declared Lucien Bouchard. "Don't give up hope, because the next time will be the right time."

Once he had ended his speech, Bouchard, on the advice of his chief organizer, left the stage immediately. "We saw Mr. Parizeau arrive," Bob Dufour explains today. "We knew what kind of politician he was. He used to say it himself: he was 'politically incorrect,' and he would say what he thought all the time. We had no idea what he was going to say."[42] As Bouchard's managers did not know what Parizeau would say, there was no question of their letting him remain on stage beside him. Bouchard met Parizeau behind the stage curtain and exchanged a word or two with him. Then, the two men shook hands. "There was a sadness that passed between them," recalls Lisée. "There was a certain complicity in the failure."[43] Bouchard went back up to his suite, together with Dumont.

During Mario Dumont's speech, Jean-François Lisée had tried to brighten things up: "Mr. Dumont is still talking about sovereignty tonight. That's a good thing," he said. Parizeau didn't react. The victory speech, which had been prepared long in advance, opened with "Quebec has stood up!" But, before tonight, nothing had been planned for the scenario of defeat. Lisée had written the speech in haste, based on conversations he had had with his leader on previous days, "a positive speech of two or three pages," his political advisor recalls. He handed it to the Premier. "Mr. Parizeau took my sheets," he recalls, "unfolded them, read them, re-folded them, put them in his pocket and said nothing. Well, with that, I really wasn't sure that he was going to use them!"[44] As Parizeau walked out onto the stage, Lisée went to join a group of advisors in the auditorium.

It was 11:15 when Parizeau finally approached the microphone. The speech Lisée had prepared remained in his pocket. He spoke without a text. "We have lost, but not by much," he said, in his opening remarks. "And, on a certain level, we have succeeded. If you like, we will stop talking about the francophones of Quebec if you don't mind. We will talk about us, 60% of us voted YES. We fought the good fight and we, we did succeed in showing clearly what we want. We lost, by a small margin, some tens of thousands of votes. Fine, what do you do in a case like that? You spit in your hands and roll up your sleeves, and you start over. It's true that we have been beaten. In essence, by what? By money, by the ethnic vote, essentially. And so, what this means is that the next time round, instead of 60 or 61% voting YES, there will be 63 or 64%, and that will suffice."

At that moment, Jean-François Lisée was in conversation with some people in the area at the front of the hall that was reserved for collaborators of the YES leaders. "And suddenly, I heard Mr. Parizeau say things I hadn't written, two horrible sentences," recalls Lisée. "For the last year and a half, our discourse had been one of unity, and there, he was setting us years back, just with a single sentence."[45] Marie-Josée Gagnon, Parizeau's press attaché, looked at Lisée. They were both aghast: what had he just said? Just then, David Payne came over to Lisée. Payne was the only anglophone Parti Québécois member in the National Assembly.[46] "I am so sorry," he said to him. Then a reporter shouted at Lisée: "Did you write that speech?" she asked. "Are you crazy?" he answered her, as Isabelle, Jacques Parizeau's daughter, asked him, "What did you think of it?" "He has just committed suicide," answered the political advisor.

Parizeau finished his speech and left. Lisée decided not to follow him, disappointed that his leader had, with one fell swoop, demolished all the pride and enthusiasm that the speeches of Dumont and

Bouchard had rebuilt in the auditorium that night. He went to get his coat and was preparing to leave, but he found himself face to face with Parizeau, who said, "Well, Mr. Lisée, too bold?" "If you were afraid people might insult you," answered his political advisor, "now, you can be sure they will! You have ruined your exit." Parizeau said nothing and turned to leave. Each went their separate way.

Jean Royer had already left the *Palais des congrès*. He decided to visit lawyer Yvon Martineau, friend and legal advisor to Jacques Parizeau, appointed by the Premier to the presidency of Hydro-Québec. He had promised to be there and it was a commitment he intended to keep, with his wife. "Victory or defeat, it wouldn't have changed the end of my evening," Royer says. "Win or lose, we had to be at the office the next day, and I knew it would be demanding." He was, however, overcome with regret for not having taken a moment, when Parizeau arrived at the *Palais des congrès*, to draw up with him the general outline of his speech, regardless of the outcome of the evening. "Would it have changed anything, I can't say," he concludes today, "but I should have done it." What did he think of his leader at that moment? Royer had been, from the start, an indefatigable assistant to Jacques Parizeau. And he is not about to back down from that loyalty now. "My role was to advise Mr. Parizeau," he says. "I am not going to judge him today. It is not for me to start saying, now that the situation is behind me, whether it was a good or a bad speech. I will keep my impressions to myself."[47] But, the next day, he would tell his leader quite clearly what his impression was.

In his suite, Lucien Bouchard was in conversation with someone, during Parizeau's speech. They stood, coat in hand, ready to leave. "I felt my knees buckle," says Bob Dufour, who turned to Bouchard. "What did he say?" his leader asked. Dufour repeated Parizeau's remarks. Bouchard was stunned. "Did he really say that?" he asked. "Yes," his chief organizer replied. "You could hear a murmur in the auditorium," Dufour recalls today. "What we said to each other was: We have a problem on our hands for tomorrow. How is he going to explain that?"[48] At first, Mario Dumont, who was standing beside Bouchard, did not fully grasp the import of what Jacques Parizeau had just said. "You're aware there's been a wrong note in there somewhere, that something is off," he says. "Then, you realize it's going to be reported by the international press and you see the consequences. A terrible speech for the people who could have benefited from an exercise that would generate profits in terms of changes to the Canadian system. That opportunity was wasted!"[49] Lucien Bouchard slowly got into his coat, left the *Palais des congrès* and climbed into his car. He drove straight to Ottawa, where he would have to be in the House of Commons the next morning, and he also had a Wednesday evening caucus meeting to prepare for. At that moment, he could hardly have guessed what Parizeau was planning for the next day.

Ten years later, reflecting back on his speech the night after the referendum, Jacques Parizeau admits he was furious. "Probably with the whole world and with myself," he says. And, given a second chance, would he do it again? "Basically, I would make the same kind of statement, but not in the same words. I would also talk about the Quebec City region... And then, something I've never seen in politics, polling stations, like in d'Arcy McGee, where there were 0 YES votes! Has anyone else ever seen that in a ballot count: 0 YES? When, in cultural communities that everyone knows, you have 234 votes for the NO and 0 for the YES, can we not speak of a polarized vote? Can we not say: listen, there's something abnormal about this situation?"[50]

Jacques Parizeau had barely finished his speech, when Liza Frulla condemned it from the stage of the Metropolis. It was 11:25 p.m. and Daniel Johnson went up to join her, along with his wife, Suzanne Marcil. When the leader of the NO camp finally spoke, only a few hundred people remained of the thousand who had gathered there. It was a unifying speech. Addressing "all Quebecers," he declared that "with an outcome as close as the one we have witnessed tonight, it is important that we rapidly ensure the reconciliation of all our fellow citizens with this democratic and legitimate result." He affirmed that the vote was a vote for change. "Further changes in the months and years to come," he said. "Constitutional and administrative changes, changes to our institutions and to the way power is exercised in Canada." He did not, however, raise the words Jacques

Parizeau had spoken half an hour earlier. "I was finalizing my speech notes," he says today. "But when I really understood what he had said, I was a little upset, to say the least. He missed a good opportunity to say things differently."[51]

Jean Chrétien had left 24 Sussex a few minutes before 11 o'clock, for his parliamentary office, from which he would address the nation. He was at his office when he heard Jacques Parizeau's words. He would not mention them in his speech, but this was neither out of indulgence nor respect for the defeated adversary. "We didn't have time to adjust," says Eddie Goldenberg. "In hindsight, I wish we'd had, but we didn't have time to adjust."

Nevertheless, the prime minister of Canada extended his hand to Jacques Parizeau. "Tonight," he said, "I ask the premier of Quebec and his government to work with the government of Canada to respond together to the real and pressing needs of Quebecers. It is up to those of us in Ottawa and Quebec City to respond to these expectations. Mr. Premier, I extend my hand to you. Let us now work together to make the appropriate changes to bring our country together. In particular, this includes the recognition of the distinct character of Quebec society."

During his political career, Jean Chrétien had always prepared two speeches for election day: one to celebrate victory, the other to acknowledge defeat. "I have seen politicians react poorly in defeat, who could therefore never return," he says. "When you are sure of winning, you can afford to be very generous in the speech for a defeat. But that day, it was a more serious matter. It was much tougher."[52]

As he left the Parliament Buildings, some young muscular types lifted him up in their arms. "I got a kick out of that. It was fun,"[53] he says. When Goldenberg drove him back to his residence, Jean Chrétien said to his advisor: "I preferred delivering that speech over the other one you prepared for me!"

Jean Charest's speech was crowded out by Jean Chrétien's. While Charest had been a partner in the NO camp, he was an opponent in the House of Commons. It was five minutes before midnight when the leader of the Conservative party went up to the microphone at the Metropolis to speak to an almost empty auditorium, but to a still significant television audience. One minute and twenty seconds later, he disappeared from the television screen, to make room for the prime minister of Canada. "Mr. Charest and I have asked ourselves the question many times: was it a deliberate act on his part?" Senator Pierre-Claude Nolin recounts today. "I, personally, think it was a deliberate move. Chrétien had a TV screen in front of him. He saw Mr. Charest, who had just begun to speak. All of Canada was glued to their television screens. I do not think it was a producer, in Ottawa, who decided that Mr. Chrétien would speak just at that moment. I think it was Mr. Chrétien who decided."[54] As soon as the NO coalition was dissolved, party politics took over once again.

One might have expected that the emotional character of the referendum campaign would lead to excesses on voting day itself. But the day progressed in relative calm. The Montreal police had been geared up since morning and felt prepared to prevent a repetition of the events of 1980. During the first referendum, once the NO victory had been announced, a small crowd had gathered at the Paul-Sauvé Arena, and started heading west. Along the way, the group just snowballed, reaching several thousand by the time it got to Crescent and Stanley, in the western part of downtown Montreal. Inevitably, there had been brawls with anglophones who were coming out of the bars. Windows had been smashed. And, finally, the police had managed to chase the demonstrators up into Mont-Royal where they calmed down, exhausted. In 1995, police headquarters remembered their lesson.

Furthermore, as soon as the referendum writs had been issued, on October 2, the Chief Electoral Officer had sent a notice to the head of the emergency measures department of the *Sûreté du Québec* (Quebec provincial police force) and to all the municipal police force chiefs in the province, reminding them, particularly, of the most important provisions of the special version of the Election Act for the holding of a referendum, and urging them to seriously respect the lines of communication established by his office with the emergency measures department of the *Sûreté du Québec*. Thus, on the morning of voting day, the Montreal Urban Community police force deployed between 400 and 500 special police officers, some of them undercover, throughout the area, ready to lend a hand to the officers of the 23 police stations, whose orders were to give priority to any incident related to the vote. There was only one incident that required rapid intervention by the anti-riot squad: starting at about 9:45 p.m., some YES supporters came and taunted the NO supporters in front of the Metropolis. The two groups threatened each other a number of times, requiring the police to intervene each time, but the situation did not deteriorate into a major incident.

It was almost midnight when Jacques Parizeau and his wife left the *Palais des congrès* and returned to their hotel, with a heavy heart, but no regret. In front of the Ritz-Carlton, a few sovereigntists waved Quebec flags, but Parizeau didn't see them. Inside, anglophones were celebrating. The couple went up to their room, talked a little about what the prime minister had said, about the vote in the cultural communities and about the *"nous"* ("us"), for which he would be bitterly reproached by his deputy premier, Bernard Landry, who deemed it too exclusivist.

Talking about the *"nous"* today, Parizeau has not changed his thinking. "83% of Quebecers are francophone and it is not acceptable to say 'nous'?" he says. "From all extractions, not just of Quebec origin. We have to say: francophone Quebecers, anglophone Quebecers, allophone Quebecers… It's ridiculous. Do you know the proportion of people in Ontario who speak English at home? The same proportion: 83%. And yet, when you talk about an Ontarian, you are not expected to add: francophone, allophone… you are just Ontarian. But in Quebec, when you talk about this population, whose great majority is francophone and you say 'we,' everyone, in certain circles, says: you are excluding us because we are anglophone."[55] Alone with his wife, in his hotel room, Jacques Parizeau regretted nothing and he prepared to announce a decision that would radically change his life and that of all of Quebec. He would resign the next day. He could have done it that night, but Lisette Lapointe advised him against it. "'Wait until tomorrow,' she told me, 'think of the situation in the streets,'" recalls Parizeau. "And she was right. It was wiser to wait."[56]

In the meantime, that night, there was a car on its way to Ottawa. Suddenly, while still on the Quebec side of the border, it pulled over to the shoulder and stopped. Brian Tobin and members of his staff stepped out. "Look up," Tobin said to them. "It is a beautiful night. You can see every star in the constellation. Look at this. We're still in Canada, the stars are still aligned as they always were, we're still one country. And nobody will remember, a few years from now, whether we won by 1% or by 20%. All they'll remember is there was a referendum, and that Canada is still together."

There were 5,087,009 people who were eligible to vote; 4,757,509 of them, i.e. 93.52%, exercised their right to vote. The NO harvested 50.58% of those votes, while 49.42% went to the YES. Its majority, then, was less than 1.2%. Only 27,145 more votes in favour of the YES would have been required, and all that followed would have been very different. Of the 14,800 Quebecers living outside of Quebec at the time of the referendum and registered on the voters list, 9,000 voted. Just barely making it in certain cases, for, the Friday preceding the referendum, the mailbags had accumulated at Canada Post. The offices were closed. In order to be able to count these ballots, the Chief Electoral Officer, Pierre-F. Côté, had to absorb the cost of the overtime hours worked by Canada Post employees. "It was not important to me to imagine who they would be voting for," says Côté. "It was the exercise of their right to vote that was at stake."[57] Nobody doubts that these votes from Quebecers outside Quebec went to the NO. As did the votes of the new Canadian citizens, welcomed in short order during the weeks preceding the referendum.[58] Throughout the course of the referendum campaign, the YES camp denounced what it considered to be blatant irregularities by the opposing party, and the massive distribution of citizenship certificates constituted one of its major grievances.[59] The Chief Electoral Officer believes that "Immigration Canada brought in citizenship judges from other provinces to accelerate the process." "There were certainly several thousand people who became Canadian citizens and were therefore likely to vote," adds Côté.[60]

The politicians, tried, through the prism of their particular allegiance, to identify the determining factor that would explain the voting results: "The final week, especially the great gathering at Place du Canada," say certain NO supporters, like John Parisella; "The federal civil servants," according to others, who found it significant that 70% in the ridings of Hull and Gatineau had voted NO. Most of the YES strategists pointed to the Quebec City region as the factor really responsible for the failure of the sovereignist option. Jacques Parizeau acknowledged that his plan to integrate federal civil servants into the Quebec public service was not a brilliant idea and that it may have generated a certain amount of fear among employees of the Quebec government. But he adds another reason, perhaps not unrelated to the first. He recalls a thematic poll conducted by Léger Marketing after the referendum. "They divided Quebec into fourteen regions," he says. "The word 'change' evoked a favourable reaction in all regions, except Quebec City. In Quebec, the word 'change' had an unfavourable connotation. Quebec is a very, very, very conservative city."[61]

There was a consensus among certain academics who had analyzed the results: the referendum vote had essentially been a linguistic vote. "Most analysts estimated that fewer than 5% of the anglophones and allophones supported the YES," political experts Denis Monière and Jean-H. Guay write, in their volume on the referendum. "Among the francophones, this support was in the order of 60%, which means that about one and a half million francophones voted NO. But there can be no doubt: linguistic polarization proved to be the strongest and most decisive factor."[62] This thesis was confirmed by Professor Pierre Drouilly of Université du Québec à Montréal. According to him, there were 80 ridings where the majority voted YES and only 45 that voted NO: this imbalance reflects the imbalance of the geographic distribution of voters according to their mother tongue. "While almost all regions of the province of Quebec supported the YES," he writes, "in the Montreal region, the trend of the vote matched linguistic boundaries very closely. The YES won in 62 of the 69 ridings that were over 90% francophone, in 14 of the 21 ridings that were between 80 and 90% francophone, and in only 4 of the 35 that were less than 80% francophone. The YES lost in all 30 ridings, but one (Mercier), that were less than 75% francophone."[63]

The evening had now drawn to a close. Several YES camp leaders had gathered at the home of Yvon Martineau. The discussion was not about how to explain the results. It was about Parizeau's statement. Bernard Landry, who was also among the guests, was still simmering. He asked Jean Royer whether the meeting of the priorities committee, scheduled for the next day, was still on. There had been talk of postponing it but, as the deputy premier was insistent, Royer phoned Michel Carpentier, the secretary general of the executive committee, and, between them, they decided on 9 a.m., a time that Parizeau considered a bit too early. "The priorities committee was convened by Mr. Landry, who was worked up," he says. "He found it all alarming, dreadful. Frankly, I could have used a few more hours of sleep. Especially as the decision had been made, there was no point in getting all upset."[64]

Lisette Lapointe made one last effort to convince her husband not to resign immediately: "Give yourself time to think it over, wait a few days before announcing your plans." "During that night," she says, "I was spouse, advisor, political supporter, I was the wife who tried to convince her leader not to resign, given the results."[65]

It was a short night, scarcely a few hours. At 7:30 the next morning, the phone rang. It was Bernard Landry. "A very, very, very arrogant call," says Lapointe. "His tone was harsh. You could sense the day was going to be tough."[66] "Are you going to announce your resignation?" Landry asked his premier. "If you don't, I will request it." "It was a really painful, terrible moment," adds Lapointe. "Because Jacques Parizeau was already low. He had already confirmed to Mr. Landry at an earlier meeting, a strategy committee meeting, that he would resign if he lost. So, that morning, that it had to be that brutal, that really affected my husband."[67]

When Parizeau arrived at his office in the Hydro-Québec building, his closest collaborators were already there: Jean Royer, Jean-François Lisée, Michel Carpentier, Marie-Josée Gagnon, Éric Bédard and Serge Guérin. Royer had arrived around 7, followed by Carpentier and, shortly afterwards, Lisée. "The three of us didn't even feel the need to discuss it, we were in agreement that the best thing for Mr. Parizeau, for the government, for the party, was for him to announce that he would resign,"[68] recalls Royer. Not long afterwards, Parizeau's secretary came in to tell them he had arrived. Royer spoke a few moments with Guérin, then entered the premier's office. "What do you think?" Jacques Parizeau asked the man who, for years, had been his most loyal and faithful advisor. "I think you should resign," Royer answered. Parizeau acquiesced: "I am in perfect agreement with you. And here is what I think will be the best way to proceed." The two men agreed quickly on how to proceed with things and then, just before stepping into the priorities committee meeting, Parizeau said to Royer: "I do not wish to tell them, at this moment, that I have taken my decision. I would like, first, to hear their views on the matter. Perhaps they will point things out to me that we had not thought of."

While Parizeau was conversing with his chief of staff, Guy Chevrette, who was on the priorities committee, ran into Lisette Lapointe. She said to him, "He has to resign because it's what he told Stéphan Bureau in an interview." "So, the rest of us didn't know what was going to happen,"[69] says Chevrette, who, in his capacity as parliamentary leader, was not very comfortable in this climate of uncertainty, but did understand that, if what Lapointe had told him was true, he would have some decisions to make very soon.

When Parizeau entered the room, the six committee members were there: Louise Beaudoin, Jean Campeau, Guy Chevrette, Louise Harel, Bernard Landry and Pauline Marois. He summarized the situation briefly and said to them, "I would like to have your opinion on the matter." Bernard Landry was virulent: "It's terrible," he said. "The whole world will look at us and say this is ethnic nationalism. We will have to hide our faces in shame! You know this will be a millstone around our necks. What have you done?"[70] Guy Chevrette spoke much more calmly, but also asked for his leader's resignation. The reason he invoked, however, was not so much the remarks about money and the ethnic vote, but the fact that he had announced it in the TVA interview that was going to be broadcast and could not back out any more. "We saw that there was no other alternative," he says today.

"He had announced it. What is more, he had lost his credibility. When he would have stood up in the Assembly, when he would have delivered a speech as premier, it would have been unbearable. And, in my role as parliamentary leader, I was convinced he could no longer go back on the announcement he had made."[71] The third man on the committee, Jean Campeau, knew nothing of his leader's intentions. In his estimation, Parizeau should stay on in his post, because of the confidence he inspired in the financial sector.

The other three members of the committee were women (Jacques Parizeau had insisted that there be equal representation on the committee, which was, around the premier, the heart of the management of public affairs). Two of them, Pauline Marois and Louise Harel, felt he should not leave. Louise Beaudoin, who knew nothing of her leader's plans, remained undecided, listening to the arguments from all sides.

Parizeau said nothing. He listened. Then, he dropped the bombshell: "I shall announce my resignation today, this afternoon!" They all understood at that moment that his decision had been taken and that he had only listened to them to know their feelings towards him. Some were furious. Others turned their thoughts immediately to what lay ahead. "It was common knowledge that Mr. Landry had aspired to the party leadership for years and years," says Guy Chevrette, "and Madame Marois had entertained vague ambitions in that direction as well. So, I said to myself, 'If he is leaving this afternoon, what is going to happen to us tomorrow?'"[72]

At the very same time, Jean Chrétien had gathered his cabinet around him. He wanted their opinion on where to go from there. The following day, it was a determined man who addressed the many supporters present at the Liberal party fundraising dinner in Toronto. He told them that Parliament was going to recognize the notion of distinct society for Quebec and make a commitment that the Constitution would never be changed without the consent of the Quebec government. But he warned the "leaders of the separatist movement that it's not an exercise in which you can play and play over again until you win." "This country has the right to political stability," he said. "And, as prime minister of Canada, I will make sure that we have political stability in this land. That is my duty, that is my constitutional responsibility." He also made the commitment to "do what is needed to keep this country together."

We already know he would not have recognized a victory of the YES as Quebec's first step towards independence. He quite simply would not accept the separation of his province of origin: "The problem," he says, "is having people of different origins in one country, but you have that everywhere. In Great Britain, they have the Scots, they have the Welsh, they have Northern Ireland. And the French, they have the Basques, they have the Bretons. Germany used to be divided between religions and now they are united with the language. You have the Nordic nations; for times they were together, after that, they were no longer together. You know the problem of Spain. Every nation has some of that. Boutros Boutros-Ghali said: if we let all these things happen around the world, (in) how many countries will India (be divided), between language and religions and regions. There would be 700, 800 countries in the world."[73]

It was after 5 p.m. when Jacques Parizeau appeared in the *Salon rouge* of the National Assembly, accompanied by his wife. Standing in front of some forty Quebec flags, he spoke of the "wild gamble" he had taken seven years earlier and which he had just lost. He did not apologize for the remarks he had made the day before, but said simply that he could have expressed his disappointment "in words much more carefully chosen." Then he let it drop: "I am announcing today that at the end of the fall parliamentary session, I will be relinquishing the posts of Premier, President of the Parti Québécois and Member of the National Assembly for L'Assomption, which the men and women of Quebec have done me the honour of entrusting to me." He had made the right decision. Quebecers agreed with it: in the first public poll conducted after the referendum, 67% believed he had done the right thing by giving up his duties.[74]

In the evening, Guy Chevrette assumed his full responsibilities as parliamentary leader. He caught a plane to Ottawa. "If you're interested in coming, you'll need to come soon," he told Lucien Bouchard.[75]

We are in government. We can't afford to be squabbling among ourselves for months, when we are responsible for the state. If you want to make a move, you must announce it soon, so that the party doesn't engage in a leadership race unnecessarily." "I'll think about it," the Bloc leader replied, "and I'll give you my decision very shortly." He was not taken totally by surprise: During the day, even before Parizeau officially announced his resignation, some ministers, anxious to keep their post in the event of a Bouchard government, had already contacted him. His departure from Ottawa would mean that the Bloc, minus one MP, could lose its title of Her Majesty's Loyal Opposition. But what did it matter? Lucien Bouchard was ready and Quebecers were waiting for him. Jacques Parizeau, the 26th Premier of Quebec, would continue to occupy his position until his successor was sworn in, on January 29, 1996.

CHAPTER 1

1. Quote attributed to king Henry IV of France, who had to change religion in order to ascend the throne. For him, it was more important to convert to Catholicism and therefore to attend mass, in order to become king of France, than to remain a protestant.

2. "Mais l'argument commercial était pour moi tellement important, tellement crucial, que si Paris valait bien une messe, l'association, j'étais prêt à lui donner un sens tout à fait élastique."

3. "On a décidé, en 1974, que cela se ferait par référendum. On vous donnera un bon gouvernement, mais on ne bougera pas tant que le référendum n'aura pas lieu. Cela ne facilite pas le travail de réflexion, de construction et de développement de l'idée de la souveraineté."

4. "Des études qui ont eu assez peu de répercussions et qui sont restées à un niveau un peu abstrait. Et on continuait de vendre la Souveraineté-Association avec de plus en plus de ferveur. On va même mettre un trait d'union pour montrer à quel point les deux sont liées."

5. "Il ne reste que quatre ou cinq ministres autour de la table, se rappelle Jacques Parizeau. Je suis fatigué. Je vais me coucher. Le lendemain matin, à 10 heures, René Lévesque se lève à l'Assemblée nationale pour faire connaître le texte de la question. Ce n'est pas celle sur laquelle on s'est entendu à 11 heures, la veille. Je suis en tab…! Je vois Lévesque. Je lui dis que ça n'a pas de bon sens de procéder comme ça. Il me dit: 'Excusez-moi, j'ai oublié de vous avertir.'"

6. René LÉVESQUE, Memoirs. Toronto: McClelland and Stewart, 1986, p. 300-301.

7. See Jean CHRÉTIEN, Straight From the Heart. Toronto: Key Porter, 1985, p. 124-125.

8. "Je devins le franc-tireur de Pierre Trudeau,. J'étais dans le champ, sur la route tous les soirs. Michelle Tisseyre était maître de cérémonie et Camil Samson, que je connais bien parce qu'il vient de la même paroisse que moi, représentait les créditistes. Il était drôle. Il disait: 'M. Lévesque nous propose de sauter d'un édifice de quatre-vingts étages, mais si vous n'aimez pas ça, rendus au trentième, on va passer une loi pour changer la loi de la gravité…' Puis il disait: 'Je devrais être pour le OUI parce que ma belle-mère vient de l'Ontario, elle aurait besoin d'un passeport pour venir me voir à Rouyn-Noranda.'"

9. "What René Lévesque had said was that one could not truly consider Pierre Elliott Trudeau to be a Québécois since he had (both) a francophone side, his father's, and an anglophone side, his mother's, and had more readily adopted his mother's side." Lise BISSONNETTE, "Le pacte des coups bas" (The low-blows pact), Le Devoir, May 14, 1980. "'Mr. Trudeau's middle name, Elliott, is significant because it shows he is partly anglophone. He decided to follow the Anglo-Saxon part of his heritage,' Mr. Lévesque said, implying that Mr. Trudeau is not a true Quebecer." The Globe and Mail, May 12, 1980.

10. "J'allais déjeuner chez Trudeau (pour discuter de son discours), puis j'apprends la nouvelle. M. Lévesque avait dit: 'Trudeau, ce n'est pas un vrai francophone, ce n'est pas un vrai Québécois parce que son sang écossais est plus épais que son sang français.' J'arrive chez Trudeau, puis je dis: 'Pierre, t'es pas un pur, moi, je suis un pur…' Et là, mon Trudeau, qui aurait pu choisir d'être un anglophone, qui aurait pu aller avec les gens de Westmount au lieu de s'en venir avec Marchand et Pelletier, dit: 'On va mettre nos sièges en jeu.' (J'ai dit:) 'Pierre, tu es à l'âge de la retraite, pas moi. Ça ne sera pas drôle de mettre nos sièges en jeu.' Il a dit: 'Envoie, on n'a pas le choix. On y va!'"

11. "Ici, je m'adresse solennellement à tous les Canadiens des autres provinces, nous mettons nos têtes en jeu, nous, députés québécois, parce que nous disons aux Québécois de voter NON, et nous vous disons à vous des autres provinces que nous n'accepterons pas ensuite que ce NON soit interprété par vous comme une indication que tout va bien, puis que tout peut rester comme c'était auparavant. Nous voulons du change-ment, nous mettons nos sièges en jeu pour avoir du changement."

12. Letter from Roy Romanow to Claude Morin, minister of Intergovernmental Affairs for Quebec at the time of the November conference, dated March 9, 1982.

13. Letter from René Lévesque to Peter Lougheed, dated May 5, 1982.

14. Interview with journalist Terence McKenna, broadcast on CBC's The Journal on November 17, 1991.

15. LÉVESQUE, op. cit., p. 335.

16. "Il est clair qu'il veut s'entendre avec le Québec. Ça le [Mulroney] trouble profondément comme beaucoup de gens comme lui, les fédéralistes, que Québec n'ait pas ratifié la Constitution de 1982, qu'il reste complètement en dehors du processus constitutionnel. Il cherche une solution…"

17. "Je vais démissionner, en fin de compte, sur l'expression du beau risque. Je ne vois pas d'avenir làdedans. La seule raison pour laquelle je fais de la politique, moi, c'est pour faire l'indépendance du Québec. Et là, je ne la vois pas du tout. Pierre-Marc Johnson va tirer les conclusions de ce même cul-desac: l'affirmation nationale, c'est une position d'attente. On ne sait pas très bien ce qui va se passer. L'affirmation nationale découle de l'échec de 1980, au même titre que la 'nuit des longs couteaux,' que l'acceptation du beau risque, en se disant: je ne peux pas faire autrement!"

18. *Le Soleil*, October 30, 1987.

19. *Le Devoir*, October 31, 1987.

20. The main details surrounding Gérald Godin's charge and Lévesque's death were inspired by Pierre DUCHESNE, *Jacques Parizeau. Le Régent.* Montreal: Quebec/Amérique, 2004, p. 57-67.

21. "Il l'a fait de façon très correcte. Je lui en suis reconnaissant, encore aujourd'hui. Ça ne correspondait pas du tout aux orientations que je voulais, mais, quand même, c'était correct."

22. "Je ne suis pas convaincu que tout le monde dans ce parti est gagné à la vision que j'ai, moi, de la souveraineté, qui n'est pas du tout une demi-mesure. Et c'est pour ça que je vais demander dix mille nouveaux membres. Montrez-moi que vous êtes d'accord, qu'un bon nombre de gens sont d'accord avec l'idée que je me fais de la souveraineté du Québec, et, là, j'embarquerai. (Pour devenir premier ministre du Québec?) Non, non, non, non! Mais il faut que je sois premier ministre du Québec pour faire un référendum. Pour moi, la politique, c'est un instrument."

23. "Mon premier geste, quand j'ai été élu président, a été d'appeler Michel Bélanger, le président de la Banque Nationale, créée en 1979, qui nous menaçait de tirer la *plug*. Je lui ai dit: 'S'il vous plaît, donnezmoi quelques mois.' Le parti devait 500 000 dollars à la Banque Nationale. Je ne savais pas où les prendre. Cela a été mon premier geste!"

24. "(Nous étions) deux hommes avec des tempéraments et des caractères diamétralement opposés. Lui, un intellectuel, moi un populiste; moi, un très grand pragmatique, et lui, un grand concepteur, d'un esprit très structuré. On ne s'est jamais chicanés. Il me laissait les rênes de la Chambre et lui s'occupait du parti."

25. "On s'en allait vers une situation absurde. On avait enlevé à Ottawa assez de pouvoirs pour vraiment l'empêcher d'opérer comme un véritable gouvernement, et on n'en avait pas suffisamment de notre côté pour être un véritable gouvernement. On s'en allait tout droit vers un cul-de-sac. Puisque c'est comme ça, puisqu'il n'y a pas de véritable gouvernement à Ottawa, mettons un véritable gouvernement à Québec. Et j'aboutissais à la souveraineté, pas par émotion, pas parce que je me sentais particulièrement souverainiste, mais simplement parce que ça me paraissait une conséquence logique."

26. "Les premières assemblées publiques, où je me rends compte de cette espèce de vague très profonde de nationalisme québécois, m'impressionnent énormément. Moi qui n'ai jamais été en contact avec le vrai monde québécois, je trouve ça beau!"

27. "L'avenir est aux états souverains, pas aux provinces. Être premier ministre d'une province, ça m'a intéressé, il y a trente ans, quand j'étais plus jeune. Le libre-échange, pour les souverainistes, c'est majeur, c'est très, très important."

28. "Quand on dit que ce sont les Québécois qui ont permis au Canada de signer l'accord de libre-échange avec les États-Unis, c'est parfaitement exact. Nous avons fourni à M. Mulroney le poids politique qu'il lui fallait. (…) Si vous décidez de devenir indépendants, nous n'achèterons plus vos textiles, nous n'achèterons plus vos chaussures, nous ne vous vendrons plus notre bœuf!"

29. *La Presse* and the *Toronto Star*, May 27, 1987.

30. Lucien BOUCHARD, *On the Record*. Toronto: Stoddart, 1994, p. 243.

31. "Je reçois, le premier soir du conseil national, un de ses émissaires qui me remet la lettre, la fameuse lettre, qui va avoir une telle importance par la suite. J'ai de la difficulté à croire que cette lettre-là est authen-

tique. Ça me paraît tellement énorme que je dis à l'émissaire: 'Écoutez, vous allez parler à votre patron. Si je reçois officiellement cette lettre, je vais en faire état en public.' Il revient au bout d'une heure, une heure et demie et me dit: 'Il n'a pas d'objection à ce que vous rendiez la lettre publique demain.' Bon, dans ces conditions, tout bien réfléchi, d'accord, très bien. J'ai pris la lettre et je l'ai lu devant le conseil national."

32. BOUCHARD, *op. cit.*, p. 236.

33. The others were Louis Plamondon, Gilbert Chartrand, Benoît Tremblay, Nic Leblanc and Liberal Gilles Rocheleau.

34. "Il a cru jusqu'au mardi que c'était possible. Puis, à partir du mardi, il a commencé à croire que ça ne se ferait pas. Je pense que ce fut très décevant pour lui, surtout en ce qui concerne le verdict de l'Histoire..."

35. "Pour M. Bourassa, c'était une défaite terrible, effrayante. Politiquement, le Québec était par terre, on n'avait plus rien dans les mains. C'est ce soir-là que je lui ai tendu la main, à 'mon premier ministre,' comme je l'ai appelé."

36. "Non. Personne ne pouvait l'envoyer dans une direction où il ne voulait pas aller. Il a été sensible au geste de M. Parizeau, qui était un geste magnanime. Mais, pour M. Bourassa, cela l'aidait parce qu'il fallait qu'il mobilise le monde. Donc, si son discours a réussi à rallier le chef du Parti québécois, le jour même, il était capable de passer la fête de la Saint-Jean bien en selle."

37. "Il était trop prudent. Au cas où (la souveraineté) deviendrait très populaire, il fallait peut-être manœuvrer dans cette direction pendant quelque temps. Mais il était vraiment trop prudent pour s'engager dans une voie comme celle-là. Cependant, il a été profondément impressionné par l'espèce de vague qui a déferlé après l'échec du lac Meech."

38. The Bélanger-Campeau Commission on the constitutional future of Quebec comprised 36 members: 9 Liberals, 6 PQ members, 1 member from the Equality Party and representatives from various areas, employee associations, unions, the municipalities union, etc. The Commission's secretariat was led by an economist respected by all, Henri-Paul Rousseau, today president of the *Caisse de dépôt et placement du Québec*. One of the Commission's co-chairs, Jean Campeau, had a business degree. He had been a stockbroker, assistant deputy minister to Quebec's minister of Finance, CEO of the *Caisse de dépôt et placement du Québec*, chair of Domtar's board of directors and a member of numerous other boards of directors. He was also minister of Finance and Transportation in the Parizeau government. The other cochair was Michel Bélanger, whose first career had been in the federal public service, before becoming economic advisor to René Lévesque in the early 60s, when Lévesque held the Hydraulic Resources portfolio within Quebec's newly created Ministry of Natural Resources. He was a central figure in the Quiet Revolution and is considered one of the key people responsible for the modernization of the Quebec economy. He became the first president of the National Bank when it was created in 1979. He took an active part in favour of the NO side during the 1995 referendum.

39. "Il y avait non seulement les libéraux et les gens du Parti québécois autour de la table. Il fallait aller chercher des fédéralistes, et, dans ce sens, Bouchard va se révéler sans prix. Comme ancien ministre conservateur, très apprécié au Québec par les 'vieux bleus' de l'Union nationale, il va aller chercher des gens chez qui la mouvance péquiste tapait sur les nerfs!"

40. "Il y avait deux choix. Ou on rapatrie nos pouvoirs, on dit au fédéral: 'Arrête d'empiéter chez nous, la clôture est mise. Arrête de venir chercher de l'argent et de dépenser n'importe comment sur notre terrain, dans nos compétences.' Ou, si ça ne marche pas, on fait un référendum sur la souveraineté."

41. Bob Rae has a law degree and was a Rhodes scholar. He was premier of Ontario from 1990 to 1995. He represented his province at the Charlottetown Conference.

42. The Allaire Report had been submitted to the executive committee of the Liberal party at the end of January 1991. It was adopted at their March convention, and then rejected at the convention of the following year, prompting Jean Allaire and Mario Dumont to quit the Liberal party.

43. DUCHESNE, *op. cit.*, p. 195.

44. "Moi, ça me paraissait important qu'il y en ait un. (…) C'est de là qu'est venue la création du Bloc. Ça ne s'est pas fait tout seul. Il a fallu les appeler, un à un, ces anciens conservateurs à Ottawa. Ils voulaient siéger comme indépendants. Il fallait organiser un cadre. Puis avoir de longues discussions avec Bouchard. Parce que Bouchard n'était pas du tout persuadé qu'il devait être chef de parti. Cela a quand même pris quelque temps pour qu'il accepte l'idée. C'est M. Landry qui a été chargé, par nous, d'aider à la constitution de ce qu'est devenu le Bloc québécois. C'est lui qui s'est assuré que le Jell-O prenne et que monsieur Bouchard en accepte la direction!"

45. "Ils n'étaient pas des hommes qui avaient des atomes crochus. Ne serait-ce que sur le plan des personnalités, au sens amical, il n'y avait pas de complicité entre eux. Les échanges entre les deux étaient corrects et se limitaient à leurs responsabilités respectives. On s'en tenait à la politique. Il n'y avait pas d'autres relations, d'autres rapports entre les deux."

46. The Bloc won 54 seats, all in Quebec, with 49.5% of the vote. The Reform Party had two seats less. The Liberals won 177 seats. The Conservatives not only lost power; they lost all but two of their MPs, one of which was Jean Charest. As for the NDP, they had to be satisfied with just nine seats.

47. "M. Johnson avait un passé, du moins son père avait un passé qu'on identifie comme 'bleu.' Mais il avait ses racines dans le Parti libéral qui dataient de 1977 ou de 1978. Il y était entré du temps de Claude Ryan. Ceux qui connaissaient bien M. Johnson savaient que c'était un homme très pragmatique. Puis M. Bourassa voyait le choix de M. Johnson dans une continuité."

48. "Après le référendum de Charlottetown, on avait un peu tous tourné la page sur les grandes manœuvres constitutionnelles. C'est pour ça qu'on avait choisi, en 1993 et 1994, de faire le point sur l'économie du Québec, la création d'emplois, l'allégement de l'État et le service aux citoyens. Moi, j'ai toujours réitéré essentiellement les conditions de Meech comme étant, je dirais, le substrat de notre programme politique en matière constitutionnelle. Il n'y avait pas d'utilité à réinventer un programme constitutionnel. À la conférence des premiers ministres des provinces, à Toronto, à l'été 1994, on s'était entendu sur un texte qui visait à assurer une meilleure coopération afin de décentraliser davantage la fédération canadienne en cherchant un consensus parmi les provinces quant à l'exercice de leurs compétences dans le giron canadien."

CHAPTER 2

1. "On n'était pas satisfaits du résultat. On s'attendait à plus."

2. Jean-François Lisée has been a journalist, and is the author of several books on politics. He was advisor to premiers Jacques Parizeau and Lucien Bouchard. At the time of the interview, he was a researcher on social policy and a member of the *Centre d'études sur les politiques et le développement social* (Centre for the study of social policy and development) at the University of Montreal.

3. "J'arrive au bureau de l'Assemblée nationale. Je vois Bernard Landry, Jacques Parizeau, Jean Royer, Guy Chevrette; des gens qui ont des visages longs, ce ne sont pas des visages de vainqueurs. (…) Certains s'étaient laissés aller à espérer un 50%, le jour de l'élection, ce qui donnait un élan vers le référendum. Il y avait déjà un début de *post-mortem* de la campagne: qu'est-ce qui n'avait pas fonctionné…"

4. "Qu'est-ce qu'on n'a pas fait? À quelle place on s'est trompés?"

5. "Les gens veulent savoir ce qu'on va faire avec la souveraineté. Il y a sept kilomètres de distance entre le sud-ouest et l'est de Montréal. Or, la différence entre les années d'espérance de vie dans un quartier par rapport à l'autre est plus élevé que le nombre de kilomètres qui les séparent! Il était important qu'on n'aille pas seulement dans la souveraineté. La souveraineté, ça ne donne rien, les gens veulent savoir ce qu'on va faire avec."

6. "Dès le printemps, j'avais dit dans une analyse publique: si le Parti québécois veut gagner le référendum, il devrait, dès la campagne électorale, faire une entente avec l'ADQ, qui va lui apporter des votes supplémentaires. La réaction des gens que je connaissais au parti était: tu n'y penses pas? Ça n'a pas de sens? C'est difficile, puis on n'en a pas besoin! Il y avait une mauvaise lecture de la situation électorale dès le depart"

7. "Ce n'était pas énorme à l'époque. Mais, dans le contexte du résultat électoral, c'était un pourcentage qui devenait important, qui devenait crucial et qui obligeait le Parti québécois à se placer en mode d'écoute. Je pense que c'est un peu de là (qu'est née l'idée) des commissions sur l'avenir du Québec. C'était pour essayer de se donner un élan que le résultat électoral n'avait pas donné au PQ."

8. "M. Bouchard a été très déçu. Le résultat était d'autant plus décevant que des facteurs autres que le propre programme du Parti québécois jouaient en faveur d'un changement de gouvernement. Le parti libéral demandait un troisième mandat. Daniel Johnson n'était pas particulièrement charismatique. On était dans la foulée de la victoire du Bloc et il y avait encore cette ambiance d'après Meech, où on sentait qu'il y aurait un choix important qui pouvait se présenter aux Québécois."

9. "La fin de la campagne avait été un peu erratique. Le vendredi, (trois jours avant l'élection), M. Parizeau félicitait tout le monde, puis il disait quasiment que c'était fait, que c'était gagné. Cette attitude triomphaliste n'aide pas, dans une campagne électorale. Tu es triomphaliste, le soir, quand tu as le résultat; tu attends même à onze heures pour avoir les vrais chiffres. Tu ne dis jamais des choses comme ça avant (la fin de) la campagne électorale. Au contraire, tu fouettes le monde... Avec le résultat qu'on avait obtenu, on ne pouvait pas espérer, dans un très court laps de temps, huit, dix mois ou un an, être en mesure de faire un référendum, puis être sûrs de le gagner."

10. "(Malgré la défaite) il était très important que M. Johnson se comporte comme un premier ministre éventuel, pas comme un premier ministre défait. On lui a dit (d'oublier l'élection) que, ça, c'était le début de la prochaine campagne. Une première campagne référendaire puis, la deuxième, ce serait éventuellement celle de (la prochaine) élection. Cela aurait été une erreur de penser que M. Parizeau allait hésiter..."

11. "Dès l'élection de M. Chrétien, on a exprimé nos objectifs d'exercer davantage de maîtrise sur la formation de la main-d'œuvre et d'autres éléments de cette nature. Ce que j'ai rapidement compris, dans la mesure où on peut le faire à la lumière des gestes de l'autre, c'est qu'au fur et à mesure que les mois passaient, le Parti libéral du Canada avait cette particularité d'essayer de prouver aux Québécois, quand le Parti québécois était au pouvoir, que le gouvernement fédéral était capable de faire quelque chose et de livrer la marchandise pour contrer le discours souverainiste... On dirait presque qu'on se sentait plus à l'aise, au fédéral, de traiter avec le Québec quand ce n'était pas des fédéralistes qui étaient au pouvoir. Je ne saisissais pas l'idée du gouvernement de M. Chrétien de refuser de faire des gestes sur la formation de la main-d'œuvre, d'attendre peut-être que le PQ soit au pouvoir, de nous nuire activement en fermant le collège militaire de Saint-Jean, qui était là depuis quarante ans. C'était inexplicable."

12. *Le Devoir*, February 25, 1994.

13. "Était-ce de la grosse négligence (de la part du fédéral) ou est-ce que ça faisait partie d'un grand plan d'ensemble? On peut le décrire comme on veut, ça ne nous a pas aidés!"

14. Bob RAE, *From Protest to Power: Personal Reflections on a Life in Politics.* Toronto: Viking, 1996, p. 256.

15. "Cela ne me surprendrait pas, dans le sens où le gouvernement fédéral, à ce moment-là, voulait peut-être en découdre avec les souverainistes, souhaiter le combat, souhaiter le référendum, puis classer ça une fois pour toutes. (…) Cela nous mettait clairement dans l'embarras; certaines décisions n'étaient pas les bonnes décisions. Et ça n'a rien changé! On demandait au Parti libéral du Canada, au gouvernement fédéral, de ne pas nous nuire, de ne pas faire des gestes nuisibles à la cause fédéraliste. On le demandait, mais ils ne l'ont pas fait."

16. "Personne ne connaît les milieux financiers comme Jean Campeau. Personne n'a son expérience des emprunts internationaux. Pour une province qui veut devenir un pays indépendant, c'est l'homme indispensable, absolument incontournable."

17. "Mme Marois va être au Conseil du trésor spécifiquement pour arranger ça. Et elle va faire des négociations superbes, qui ne vont pas coûter très cher et qui vont être solidement établies pour trois ans, sans un jour de grève."

18. DUCHESNE, *op. cit.*, p. 299.

19. "Mon plus jeune ministre, Daniel Paillé, avait 44 ans. Je m'en allais vers le plus vieux cabinet que le Québec ait connu et ça commençait à se savoir. Les deux psychiatres, (Denis) Lazure et (Camille) Laurin, avaient passé les 70 ans. Ça commençait à être lourd à porter. Peut-être que j'ai eu tort. Je lui ai fait de la peine (à Camille Laurin). Cela a été effrayant d'avoir fait ça. C'était un ami, un complice..."

20. "Dans le bureau (de Parizeau), je lui ai dit: 'Attendez-vous à ce que je vous dise tous les jours qu'il faut élargir la coalition, que vous ne pouvez pas gagner seul,' se souvient Jean-François Lisée. Et là, M. Parizeau m'a regardé, puis il m'a dit: 'M. Lisée, vous allez vous rendre compte que je n'ai pas l'habitude de m'entourer de nouilles!'"

21. "On se comprend. C'est le seul qui sait exactement ce que je veux, où je m'en vais, ce que je cherche à faire. Je tiens pour acquis qu'il sait tout ce qui se passe dans mon bureau. Le chef de cabinet, c'est une sorte de conseiller du possible."

22. "Connaissant M. Parizeau depuis de nombreuses années, je n'avais pas à aller chercher mes instructions toutes les quinze minutes. Je pouvais faire avancer les choses. Conseiller du possible? Je lui rappelais ce que le cardinal de Richelieu disait à Louis XIII: ce qui est possible a été fait, ce qui est impossible se fera!"

23. "Jean-François, c'est une force inimaginable pour trouver des idées et la plupart sont bonnes."

24. "L'appui de Jean Royer sur plusieurs de mes stratégies était fondamental, parce que M. Parizeau avait une énorme confiance en lui, en Michel Carpentier. [...] Souvent, on se concertait, il voyait qu'on était d'accord ensemble et ça donnait beaucoup plus de poids."

25. "Le soir de la mort de Pierre Laporte, René Lévesque convoque, à 2 heures du matin, à la permanence du parti, rue Christophe-Colomb, une réunion d'un certain nombre de gens. Dont moi. Je me présente. Il y a un jeune homme qui fait les cent pas devant la permanence. Il m'arrête et me dit: 'Bonsoir, M. Parizeau.' Je lui dis: 'Bonsoir. Je peux entrer? M. Lévesque m'a demandé d'être là.' (Il me répond:) 'Je n'ai pas votre nom sur la liste, vous ne rentrez pas.' 'Ah! Je dis: comment ça, je n'entrerai pas?' Il me dit: 'Écoutez, je suis peut-être pas mal plus jeune que vous, mais je suis pas mal plus fort aussi. Si vous voulez vous battre, on va se battre, mais vous n'entrerez pas.' (Je lui dis:) 'Allez voir M. Lévesque pour lui demander s'il n'y aurait pas une erreur.' Il dit: 'D'accord, mais reculez.' Alors, je recule. Il revient et dit: 'Oui, c'est une erreur. Vous pouvez entrer.' J'ai dit: 'C'est quoi, votre nom?' (Il répond:) 'Serge Guérin.' (Je lui dis:) 'Bon, à compter de demain matin, vous travaillez pour moi!'"

26. The other members of Parizeau's "bodyguard" were Hubert Thibault, a technocrat well versed in government politics who was his principal advisor; Marie-Josée Gagnon, his press attaché; Bernard Lauzon, a former student of Parizeau's and his advisor in public finance and fiscal matters; lawyer Eric Bédard, whose father was a former PQ minister and who would be Royer's right-hand man; and Yvon Martineau, a close associate of Parizeau, who served as his legal advisor.

27. Alice Poznanska, Jacques Parizeau's first wife, died of cancer on September 30, 1990. The leader of the Parti Québécois remarried on December 12, 1992 at Sainte-Agathe's town hall.

28. "Dans d'autres pays, cela pouvait se faire, pour un premier ministre, de donner à sa femme un certain nombre de dossiers très précis. Mais ici, cela ne s'était jamais fait; donc, c'était impossible à faire. On le comprenait à l'égard d'Hillary Clinton (qui s'est occupée du dossier de l'assurance-maladie aux Etats-Unis, pendant que son mari occupait la présidence); alors moi, j'ai fait ça avec la mienne."

29. "Elle était après tout une employée du cabinet. Il n'y avait pas de raisons pour qu'elle ne siège pas à toute une série de comités de stratégie à l'intérieur du cabinet."

30. "Dans des réunions, on dit parfois des choses qui ne sont pas tout à fait très gentilles pour le patron. Mais, si sa femme est là, on a peut-être peur que, le soir, il y ait des petites choses qui glissent. Cela prend un certain temps avant que la confiance s'établisse."

31. "Comme c'est ma femme, je n'allais pas nier que, le soir, quand on mangeait ensemble, on discutait certainement de ces dossiers. Elle m'a donné des conseils que j'appréciais beaucoup. Je n'allais tout de même pas, pour satisfaire ceux qui étaient jaloux, divorcer de ma femme sous prétexte que je devenais premier ministre. (...) Chaque quinzaine, je recevais mon chèque; j'en gardais un, puis, le suivant, je l'endossais au nom de ma femme."

32. The *Réseau des Carrefours jeunesse-emploi* snowballed in time to the point there are 106 of them in Quebec today.

33. The residence was situated at 1080, des Braves Avenue, in the Upper Town. The property belonged to a subsidiary of the Chamber of Commerce.

34. "Vous savez, cela n'avait rien d'un Élysée, même petit: il y avait une ruelle en arrière avec des cordes à linge! Mais c'était une résidence très bien, très belle... (…) C'était la première fois, pour bien des citoyens, qu'ils pouvaient côtoyer pendant deux heures leur premier ministre."

35. "La mission de la Caisse, c'est la rentabilité, faire de l'argent pour les citoyens et citoyennes du Québec et supporter l'économie du Québec. Alors, le président de la Caisse, dans un temps comme (celui de) la souveraineté, aurait fait attention au portefeuille des obligations du Québec, à ses portefeuilles d'obligations et d'actions. Alors, est-ce que cela aidait d'avoir un souverainiste? Peut-être, mais d'abord, il fallait que l'individu soit compétent."

36. "Hydro-Québec, c'est le vaisseau amiral des sociétés d'État. Ses rapports financiers sont presque aussi importants que ceux du gouvernement du Québec. Il vaut mieux avoir, de ce côté-là, quelqu'un qui, sur le plan de l'orientation fondamentale, ait les mêmes vues."

37. "Québec ne va pas être absolument sans armée. Même si on la limite au minimum, même si cette armée sert à assurer des missions de paix, même s'il ne s'agit que d'avoir un certain nombre de gens qui ne se mettent pas en grève quand tout le monde l'est, il faut un minimum. (…) Notre part des douze frégates canadiennes, c'est trois. Qu'est-ce que vous voulez qu'on fasse avec trois frégates? Puis, vous voyez le genre d'installations portuaires qu'il faudrait installer pour trois frégates? Il vaut mieux les vendre et acheter des petites vedettes suédoises. On a besoin d'une garde côtière, nous, c'est tout! (…) Les Américains ne nous permettront jamais de laisser un grand morceau géographique comme le Québec non patrouillé. Si on ne le patrouille pas nous-mêmes, ils vont le patrouiller pour nous, c'est clair! (…) C'est une opération comptable, d'abord et avant tout."

38. Unclassified. O 131555Z Sep. 94. Fm Amconsul to Secstate WashDC Immediate 9441.

39. Brian Tobin, interview with CBC in Montreal, December 1, 2003.

40. The Canadian Unity Council was not created with a view to the 1995 referendum. It was originally called *Comité Canada*; this was in 1964, in the era when the *Maîtres chez nous* (masters in our own house) slogan of the Jean Lesage government was accompanied by a desire for constitutional reform. The *Rassemblement pour l'indépendance nationale* (RIN) became increasingly active and Quebec became increasingly vocal in expressing its demands. Despite being joined by Pierre Elliott Trudeau, Gérard Pelletier and Jean Marchand, Lester B. Pearson was running a weak minority government in Ottawa. He feared the rise of separatism in Quebec and established the Royal Commission of inquiry on bilingualism and biculturalism (Laurendeau-Dunton). *Comité Canada* would become the Canadian Unity Council in 1975, to project the image of a permanent organization and have a name that corresponded better to its mission. Its activities would take on a more dynamic character with the election of a separatist government in 1976 and would intensify as the 1980 referendum approached. Its position was that the future of Quebec was not a matter to be settled by Quebecers alone. It was a matter that concerned all Canadians. The Council would be one of the major players in the pre-referendum campaign of 1995. For 30 years, the Canadian Unity Council had operated as a "charitable organization," but in 1995, the federal and Quebec ministers of Revenue withdrew the privileges that accompanied this designation in the case of the activities of Option Canada, which had spent, it appears from certain sources (*Le Devoir*, September 15, 2004), 4.8 million dollars in support of Canadian unity during the pre-referendum campaign. Jocelyn Beaudoin, its general director from 1969 to 1995, was appointed as Quebec representative in Toronto by the Charest government.

41. "Dès la fin de l'automne 1994, M. Parizeau a publiquement parlé des fameuses tournées régionales. C'est à ce moment-là que le Conseil pour l'unité canadienne a convoqué sa première réunion. On a commencé à travailler ensemble. L'objectif était de faire le suivi de ces réunions régionales qui étaient, en pratique, des réunions mises en scène par les forces indépendantistes."

42. "On lui a fait comprendre que c'était une affaire de Québécois, et que, s'il avait à cœur la réussite de notre objectif, ce serait mieux pour tout le monde qu'il ne s'en mêle pas."

43. *Le Devoir*, September 21, 1995.

44. "Tout le monde est d'accord sauf qu'à la dernière minute, M. Parizeau a une hésitation: 'Finalement, je vais y aller *ad lib.,*' (dit-il). Je vois Jean Royer, Marie-Josée Gagnon, Éric Bédard, catastrophés. Ils réussissent, surtout Royer, à convaincre le premier ministre d'y aller avec le texte tel que prévu."

45. *La Presse*, November 6, 1994.

46. "Il a été applaudi à tout rompre. M. Parizeau sort, de ce premier test de l'idée d'élargissement, rassuré de sa capacité d'avoir son parti derrière lui."

47. "Dès l'assermentation des ministres, il nous avait donné, à la présidente du Conseil du trésor, Pauline Marois, et à moi-même comme ministre des Finances, la mission de réduire le déficit à zéro, de mettre de l'ordre dans les dépenses et les revenus."

48. "Un déficit de six milliards, c'est extrêmement dangereux. Si on veut faire le référendum, on se trouve constamment menacés par des cotes de crédit, des crisettes sur les marchés financiers, six milliards, c'est trop. (…) Le déficit est tombé de six milliards à quatre, l'année du référendum."

49. *La Presse*, September 14, 1994 (election day was September 12).

50. *Le Devoir*, December 8, 1994.

51. *La Presse*, December 8, 1994.

52. *A Frank Talk between Neighbours about the Present and the Future.* Speech by Jacques Parizeau at the Canadian Club of Toronto, November 22, 1994.

53. *La Presse*, October 13, 1994.

54. CBRS (Canadian Bond Rating Service) is a large company specializing in analyzing and rating companies, governments and their agencies.

55. *Le Devoir*, December 22, 1994.

56. The North American Free Trade Agreement (NAFTA) replaced the Free Trade Agreement between Canada and the United States on January 1, 1994; the new trading bloc includes Mexico.

57. "Les Américains ne peuvent pas imaginer un instant qu'on aurait une zone de libre-échange (ZLÉA) du pôle Nord à la Terre de Feu sans le Québec et Cuba. Le commerce du Québec avec les États-Unis est trop gros pour qu'il puisse être exclu d'un projet comme celui-là. Ça ne tient pas debout, ni sur le plan juridique ni sur le plan politique."

58. "Puis Murphy les regarde et dit: 'Pourquoi pas?' Ça s'est passé à trente pieds de moi! Les journalistes étaient interloqués. Ils ont fait des titres énormes le lendemain…"

59. Matthew Coon Come was born near Mistassini in Quebec. He studied law and political science at Trent and McGill universities. He was chief of the Mistassini Nation before he became grand chief of the Grand Council of the Crees, a position he held from 1987 to 2000, after which he became chief of the Assembly of First Nations. He was defeated in 2003 when he tried to win a second mandate.

60. *Speaking Notes for Matthew Coon Come.* See www.gcc.ca.

61. The Great Whale project was part of the giant northern Quebec hydroelectric development project. After harnessing the La Grande River, Hydro-Quebec intended to build dams on the Great Whale River and to draw as much as possible from the other rivers: the Nottaway, the Broadback and the Rupert. The reduced demand for electricity, the protest campaigns by ecologists and the unceasing battle waged by the Aboriginal Peoples brought this huge project to an end.

CHAPTER 3

1. "À partir de l'échec du lac Meech, nous avions développé une thèse, un corridor qui faisait en sorte qu'à partir du libre-échange, à partir du moment où il y avait une certaine force de l'économie, à partir du moment où le reste du Canada avait dit vraiment non à une position minimaliste, nous arrivions avec un projet, qu'on voulait moderne, où l'ensemble des gens seraient associés."

2. Quebec National Assembly, *Journal des débats* (Record of the debates), Tuesday, December 6, 1994.

3. *La Presse*, December 16, 1994.

4. *Le Soleil*, December 7, 1994.
5. Chrétien, *op. cit.*, p. 150.
6. PBS is not the largest television network in the U.S., but its viewers include intellectuals and those who shape American public opinion.
7. *La Presse*, December 22, 1994.
8. "… il fixait quasiment la date du 25 juin, il ne manquait que l'heure (...). Tu sais, le 25, à midi! Une stratégie ouverte comme ça, ce n'est pas toujours évident. (…) C'était sa grande peur. Se lancer tête baissée dans un défi comme celui-là sans que les affaires (notamment le déficit du Québec) aient été analysées sous tous leurs aspects, c'était très hasardeux. M. Bouchard est quelqu'un qui prend le temps de regarder les affaires à tête reposée. M. Parizeau disait que, quand on a un programme, il faut qu'on le réalise et, si on est pour entrer dans le mur, on va enlever le mur!"
9. "M. Parizeau disait: 'C'est sûr que les Québécois préféreraient ne pas avoir à trancher cette question douloureuse. Si on ne leur donne pas une date butoir, ils ne prendront pas leur décision. On ne peut pas mobiliser sans date butoir.' M. Bouchard, lui, disait, comme il le répétera plus tard: 'Tant qu'on n'a pas la conviction de gagner, il ne faut pas fixer de date butoir.' M. Parizeau ne voulait pas dire publiquement: on n'ira pas si on n'est pas sûrs de gagner, parce que c'est le contraire de la mobilisation. M. Bouchard et d'autres, comme M. Landry, voulaient le lui faire dire. Il y a eu cette danse entre M. Bouchard et M. Parizeau pendant plusieurs mois. Ça nous mettait en porte-à-faux un peu avec les gens du Bloc."
10. *Le Soleil*, February 18, 1995.
11. "Tout devait être fait pour que le premier ministre soit en mesure de déclencher le référendum dans la première année du mandat. On n'était pas à une ou deux semaines près, mais on savait que ça devait se tenir en 1995. On a monté la structure du gouvernement pour que ce soit un gouvernement qui fonctionne, qui opère en sachant qu'il a à respecter une échéance. (…) Il y avait des gens qui nous disaient. 'Avons-nous ce qu'il faut pour tenir un référendum et le gagner?' C'est normal. Des gens doutaient: est-ce qu'on devait y aller maintenant, le reporter, attendre?"
12. "Au cours d'une brève conversation, à quelques semaines du déclenchement de la campagne référendaire, Jean me disait: 'Est-ce que vous pensez qu'il pourrait encore renoncer à le faire maintenant?' Enfin, à peu près dans ces termes-là... J'avais été complètement saisie par cette phrase. J'ai pensé un moment que c'était une boutade, mais ça ne semblait pas l'être. Probablement que, dans les personnes qu'il avait consultées, il y en avait qui avait trop peur de perdre."
13. "Au printemps, c'était tentant, mais je ne nous trouvais pas prêts. Les sondages n'étaient pas particulièrement spectaculaires et, surtout, il ne fallait pas brusquer les commissions sur l'avenir du Québec. Il y a des limites à aller vite! Il fallait leur donner le temps de fournir leurs conclusions, de les absorber, puis de traiter ça avec l'attention que ça méritait."
14. "… mais il était hors de question qu'on donne l'impression qu'on évacuait le printemps, pour faire en sorte que ceux qui ont des échéanciers à rencontrer se disent: on a une saison de plus. Alors, jamais la pression n'a été relâchée, mais, moi, j'ai toujours eu l'impression que c'était l'automne."
15. "La vie politique québécoise est sous un déluge de sondages depuis 40 ans, et on sait qu'il n'y a pas de majorité pour l'indépendance du Québec et qu'il n'y a pas de majorité pour le fédéralisme actuel. Il n'y a que deux majorités possibles: le fédéralisme renouvelé et la souveraineté du Québec avec une association, quelle qu'en soit la forme, avec le reste du Canada. Essayer de réduire les Québécois au fédéralisme actuel ou à la sécession sans volonté d'entente, c'est refuser leur réalité politique et leur volonté politique."
16. "Ça fait partie du jeu politique. Quand vous voulez amener les gens à votre position, de temps à autre vous menacez de vous retirer. J'ai trop fait ça, moi, pendant trente ans pour commencer à reprocher aux autres de le faire. Plus vous vous rapprochez d'une échéance, plus vous tenez à ce que ça aboutisse. Dans ce sens, vous pouvez utiliser des choses comme la menace à certains moments pour obtenir ce que vous voulez. La politique n'est pas un métier d'enfant de chœur."
17. *Le Devoir*, October 7, 1994.
18. *Le Devoir*, November 5, 1994.

19. Marie Malavoy was born in Berlin in 1948. She came to Quebec as a child, completed her studies there, graduating from the University of Montreal, and made her career teaching at the University of Sherbrooke. She was waiting for Quebec to become independent before applying for citizenship, so she could become a naturalized Quebec citizen. In Parizeau's words, "She got caught!"

20. "Le dimanche, quand il est monté dans sa limousine, il avait mal à une jambe. Le lundi, on ne l'a pas vu, puis Gaston Clermont, qui était en quelque sorte sa nounou et un peu son chauffeur, nous a dit qu'il était à l'hôpital, qu'il avait une phlébite." Phlebitis is the inflammation of a vein, accompanied by the formation of a clot at the site. In straightforward cases, doctors usually recommend that the patient rest, keeping the legs raised as much as possible, and apply compresses to the affected area.

21. Every year in Canada, there are between 100 and 200 cases of this illness, which is caused by the flesh-eating bacteria, and which is also called streptococcal gangrene. This illness develops very rapidly and can cause death in 12 to 24 hours. Between 20 and 30 deaths per year in Canada are attributable to this illness. Treatment is radical: the infected tissues must be removed before the bacteria, which can spread throughout the entire body, reach a vital organ.

22. "Mme Bouchard avait gardé cela privé. Elle ne voulait pas que cela soit rendu public à ce moment-là. C'est seulement le mercredi, à ma connaissance, qu'on l'a appris."

23. "Le soir, les médecins nous avaient dit, je pense, qu'il avait comme 75 ou 80% de possibilités de ne pas passer à travers. S'il passe la nuit, on va le savoir demain matin."

24. "Les heures habituelles pour les points de presse ou les conférences de presse étaient passées. J'ai été dans l'immeuble de la tribune parlementaire. J'ai ramassé les journalistes que je pouvais trouver à ce moment-là. C'était le soir, il était autour de 19 heures, quelque chose comme ça. C'est là que j'ai offert mes vœux à Bouchard. J'étais complètement bouleversé. Tout ce que je pouvais dire, c'est: 'Tenez bon, mon vieux!' Cela a été pour moi une sorte de choc psychologique, très, très profond... On ne peut pas concevoir quelque chose d'aussi abominable que ça. Je n'avais jamais entendu parler de ce genre de maladie, et je m'imaginais ce que ça pouvait être. C'était effrayant!"

25. "Mon sentiment immédiat, c'était de me dire que son décès confirmerait, dans l'esprit de beaucoup de Québécois, que le projet souverainiste était victime d'une malédiction. Qu'il était voué à l'échec. Au moment où on voulait essayer, on le perdait, il y avait quelque chose de maudit dans l'affaire. Cela aurait été très grave parce que cela aurait alimenté un sentiment presque atavique chez les Québécois de la défaite des grandes volontés politiques. (...) On sait que, politiquement, dans nos grandes décisions, dans la question nationale, l'histoire du Québec est l'histoire d'une série d'échecs, donc cela aurait frappé un courant existant et l'aurait creusé."

26. "Ce soir-là, on avait une réception, comme tous les jeudis, à la résidence. Comme on a appris la nouvelle à la dernière minute, c'était impossible d'annuler. (…) La réception a été triste, tout le monde était sous le choc."

27. The information concerning the head of protocol's role, on the night from Thursday to Friday, is taken from DUCHESNE, op. cit., p. 334-335.

28. Lucien Bouchard's wife, Audrey Best, is an American, born in California. In December 1994, at the time of Bouchard's illness, the couple had two children, Alexandre, 5, and Simon, 3. Audrey Best had the reputation in political circles of being a very discreet person. At the time, she was studying law at McGill University. She remains little known to Quebecers.

29. "Line et moi étions assez proches d'Audrey, Line encore plus que moi. On a tenté de la joindre à la maison. La gardienne, dans tous ses états, nous répétait qu'elle était dans la douche et qu'elle n'en sortait pas. Alors, Line et moi, on a décidé d'aller à Montréal pour voir si Audrey n'avait pas besoin d'aide."

30. "Je suis porteur d'une lettre. Je ne suis que le messager."

31. Michel VASTEL, Lucien Bouchard: En attendant la suite. Montreal: Lanctôt, 1996, p. 193.

32. "Audrey était très bouleversée. Et je ne sais pas, à ce moment-là, il y a eu un malentendu terrible qui dure encore aujourd'hui. Je ne sais pas si elle a pensé que j'étais un peu l'émissaire du premier ministre pour aller voir ce qui se passait. Ce n'était tellement pas ça! (...) On se parlait d'une façon polie et très officielle, mais on n'a jamais pu reparler de ça. (...) C'est un épisode de femmes."

33. "M. Bernard a demandé une minute ou deux de silence. On attendait des nouvelles. J'avais mon cellulaire. J'ai dit à Louis Bernard que Gilbert (Charland) avait peut-être déjà appris des médecins ce qu'il en était et qu'il m'appellerait. Effectivement, vers 8 h 15, 8 h 30, Gilbert m'a appelé pour nous annoncer: 'Les médecins disent qu'il est sauvé; il va passer à travers.'"

34. "Pour des raisons non politiques, pour des raisons personnelles. On sentait qu'au-delà des divergences et de leur incapacité à vraiment connecter, un lien s'était créé, une complicité entre les deux."

35. "Pour eux, M. Bouchard, c'était quelqu'un avec qui ils pouvaient parler. C'étaient les commentaires qu'on avait des premiers ministres ou des gens de la classe politique des autres provinces, pas nécessairement d'Ottawa. Les gens avaient beaucoup de respect pour M. Bouchard. Ils trouvaient que cet homme-là était plus 'parlable' que M. Parizeau chez qui on sentait plus de rigidité et beaucoup moins d'ouverture à la discussion."

36. *La Presse*, November 4, 1994, and *Le Devoir*, November 10, 1994.

37. *Le Devoir*, November 7, 1994.

38. *La Presse*, November 9, 1994.

39. "Cela a toujours été un peu le péché mignon du Parti québécois de considérer que le projet de souveraineté, c'est à lui. L'indépendance du Québec n'est pas l'affaire d'un seul parti. Le Parti québécois peut en être le fer de lance, il peut assurer les ressources nécessaires, mais ce n'est pas son projet. (...) C'est dommage que les libéraux n'aient pas voulu embarquer dans cette opération-là, parce qu'à peu près tout le monde dans notre société, sauf eux, est embarqué."

40. *La Presse*, December 16, 1994.

41. "Il posait des questions intelligentes. Dans un langage un peu nouveau, pas du tout langue de bois, qui avait souvent beaucoup de sens. C'était agréable de pouvoir lui dire: 'Écoutez, oui, on va regarder ça...' J'ai eu de très bons rapports avec lui à l'Assemblée nationale."

42. Poll by *La Presse*, December 9, 1994.

43. *Le Devoir*, December 20, 1994.

44. *The Toronto Star*, December 20, 1994.

45. "Ça me surprendrait que des gens (du parti) aient fait cet effort. Ils ont convenu que M. Dumont avait fait son lit et qu'il n'était pas question pour lui de s'associer avec le Parti libéral du Québec pour défendre le fédéralisme."

46. *Le Soleil*, December 31, 1994.

47. *Aujourd'hui dimanche, Radio-Canada*, January 8, 1995.

48. "... mais, malgré tout, les gens nous parlent constamment du danger d'un nouvel échec. La hantise de l'échec existe et on est en train d'en sortir. Et on est certain que la présence de Lucien Bouchard, son charisme, fait partie de la combinaison."

49. "À la période de questions, une des premières est: que fera M. Bouchard après le référendum si le OUI gagne? Ma seule réponse était: c'est une excellente question, il faudra y réfléchir! (...) C'était une question extrêmement délicate, compte tenu des rapports Parizeau-Bouchard. Alors, j'écris à M. Parizeau: il faut, assez tôt avant le référendum, établir quel sera le rôle de M. Bouchard qui est déjà le politicien le plus aimé, le plus respecté de l'histoire du Québec. (...) Si on ne dit pas, pendant la campagne référendaire, ce qu'il va faire après le OUI, nos adversaires vont dire: voter OUI, c'est perdre Bouchard, c'est se retrouver seulement avec Parizeau."

50. "On ne savait pas trop, de part et d'autre, quelle était la façon de positionner M. Bouchard dans la campagne référendaire. Mais sa ligne de conduite à ce moment-là, et jusqu'au 7 octobre, a été de dire: 'Moi, je vais jouer le rôle qu'on va m'assigner dans la campagne.' Il était conscient que c'était M. Parizeau qui en était le maître d'œuvre. Je n'ai jamais entendu M. Bouchard dire: 'Ça va être ça, ou bien je n'embarque pas!'"

51. DUCHESNE, *op. cit.*, p. 337.

52. *Le Soleil*, February 20, 1995.

53. "Après sa maladie, il m'avait dit: 'Il y a autre chose dans la vie que la politique. Retiens ça: les autres choses sont plus importantes.' Pour M. Bouchard, être en politique, ce n'était pas naturel. Il ne se voyait pas comme un politicien de carrière. Il était un avocat, c'était ce qu'il aimait. Sa famille est arrivée tard. Pour lui, sa famille, c'est une valeur fondamentale. C'est sûr qu'il était en contradiction par rapport à son engagement politique."

54. "Il (Lucien Bouchard) n'était pas tout à fait rétabli, avec sa prothèse et tout ça. Mais il avait décidé d'aller rencontrer M. Clinton. Car, évidemment, comme chef de l'opposition, il avait droit d'avoir une rencontre avec M. Clinton."

55. *Debates of the House of Commons of Canada (Hansard)*, February 23, 1995.

56. *La Presse*, February 25, 1995.

57. Excerpt from the autobiography of James BLANCHARD, *Behind the Embassy Door: Canada, Clinton and Quebec*. Toronto: McClelland & Stewart, 1998, p. 118.

58. *Ibid.*, p. 199.

59. Raymond Chrétien is the nephew of Jean Chrétien. Admitted to the Bar in Quebec in 1966, he immediately joined the Department of External Affairs. His first diplomatic mission took him to Zaïre (Democratic Republic of Congo). Later, he was ambassador to Mexico, before becoming Under-Secretary of State for External Affairs. He was appointed ambassador to Belgium and Luxembourg in 1991 and, as of January 1994, to the U.S. and, finally, to France, from 2000 to 2003.

60. "Jusqu'à deux heures de l'après-midi, la rencontre aurait pu ne pas avoir lieu. Mais si elle n'avait pas eu lieu, nous aurions eu une autre sorte de problème, un problème médiatique peut-être difficile à régler. (…) J'avais parlé à James Blanchard, à André Ouellet, au premier ministre. Il me restait à parler à Lucien Bouchard. Nous pouvions jouer la candeur l'un avec l'autre, raconte Chrétien, et nous dire: 'Lucien, ça ne marchera pas, nous ne pouvons faire ça;' 'Raymond, vous allez trop loin!' Qui était pour? Qui était contre? On était sept ou huit dans le petit groupe qui décidait de ces choses."

61. "Évidemment, il se devait d'être d'accord. Il a dit: 'Raymond, parfait!' On a réglé ça entre la poire et le fromage, chez le gouverneur général. Et nous avons terminé notre café dans la bonne humeur, car la rencontre aurait lieu."

62. "Je me rappellerai toujours. Il faisait froid. Il faisait mauvais. Je n'avais pas de parapluie. Il grêlait. Il pleuvait. Pour moi, c'était une occasion de causer, plus longuement, plus facilement avec lui que lors du déjeuner. Alors, il m'a dit un petit peu comment il avait l'intention de procéder. Je lui ai répondu que, d'après moi, c'était la meilleure façon de faire les choses… Nous sommes arrivés. Je me rappellerai toujours, la voiture glissait, tellement la glace était dangereuse. J'avais vraiment peur que nous tombions en pleine face. On a marché tous les deux, je ne sais plus si c'était bras dessus bras dessous ou main dans la main, mais essayant de ne pas tomber, pour nous rendre au haut des marches du balcon, tellement c'était glissant. Tous les gardes du corps, au lieu de nous regarder, regardaient vers les montagnes, vers les arbres, comme si une menace allait venir du ciel. Alors, totalement isolés, montant les marches… c'était quand même extraordinaire comme scène!"

63. BLANCHARD, *op. cit.*, p. 214-215.

64. *Ibid.*, p. 215.

65. *Ibid.*, p. 215.

66. "Il l'a fait de façon très structurée, très organisée. Tout le monde l'a écouté. Il l'a fait de façon sereine, non passionnée, très correcte, et, bien sûr, en anglais."

67. BLANCHARD, *op. cit.*, p. 215-216.

CHAPTER 4

1. *Le Devoir*, December 20, 1994.

2. *The Gazette*, December 16, 1994.

3. Excerpt from CHRÉTIEN, *op. cit.*, p. 150: "At a town meeting in Alma, Quebec, in the early 1970s, a very intelligent Liberal got up and said, 'Chrétien, when will you tell the separatists that there will never be independence, that the federal government will never allow it to happen? If the people of Texas were to propose independence from the United States, the Marines would be there within hours and that would be that.' (…) But I didn't agree. 'We'll put our faith in democracy,' I said, 'We'll convince the people that they should stay in Canada and we'll win. If we don't win, I'll respect the wishes of Quebeckers (sic | and let them separate.'"

4. *Le Soleil*, December 21, 1994.

5. *The Gazette*, December 17, 1994.

6. *The Ottawa Citizen*, December 17, 1994.

7. Today, Michel Robert is the Chief Justice of the Quebec Court of Appeal. He has been President of the Quebec Bar Association, member of the Royal Commission on the Economic Union and Development Prospects for Canada (the Macdonald Commission), President of the Young Liberals and President of the Liberal Party of Canada.

8. "M. Parizeau n'avait pas de compromis dans sa formule à 50 plus un. Il serait allé de l'avant. Cela aurait été un chaos épouvantable sur le plan politique au Canada s'il avait fallu que ce soit 50 plus un, mais pour le OUI. (…) J'ai toujours pensé que M. Lévesque ne voulait pas briser le Canada. Il voulait un autre *deal*. Ce n'était pas nécessairement la séparation pure et dure qu'il recherchait."

9. "Le référendum de 1995 n'était pas purement consultatif, dans la mesure où le gouvernement du Québec, une fois l'offre de partenariat déposée, sans préciser combien de temps l'autre partie avait pour répondre, pouvait déclarer la souveraineté du Québec à l'Assemblée nationale. Donc, une déclaration unilatérale de l'indépendance, finalement, après une offre de partenariat, discutée ou pas, c'était ça, la démarche de Parizeau, et il ne s'en serait pas privé!"

10. "Tout ça ne se fait pas en un jour. C'est pour cela que le délai d'un an, dont on parlait, était nécessaire. Il fallait le plus tôt possible avoir un certain nombre d'idées assez précises sur ce qu'on avait l'intention de faire."

11. "On boude pendant un bout, puis, après, il y a une couple de sujets qui nous forcent à nous asseoir à la table. Au début, on ne s'entend pas, mais alors, quand on entend le tic tac du cadran, le temps, puis les événements, puis la pression populaire font à un moment donné que le gros bon sens prend le dessus."

12. "Ce n'est pas sérieux! (…) On a droit au quart, un peu moins que le quart, des actifs du gouvernement fédéral. Cela dépend du critère: est-ce que vous utilisez la population, est-ce que vous utilisez le produit national brut? Et il est évident que, le pourcentage en question, vous allez l'appliquer à la dette fédérale."

13. According to this study, Canada's debt, in 1994, was 414 billion dollars, an increase of 90 billion over the debt of 1991, and it had grown five times larger in the thirteen years since 1981. The two actuaries estimated that the value of the Canadian government's assets was at least 163 billion dollars. Taking into account the fact that these assets "were constituted over a period of more that one hundred years, when the proportion of the federal government's fiscal revenue drawn from Quebec was much greater than it is today," they assessed the share of these assets that should come back to Quebec to be 28.7%, or 46 billion dollars. Starting from the principle that the contribution of Quebecers to the repayment of the debt should remain the same after secession, they estimated that the share of the federal government's debt owing to third parties, that the government of Quebec should assume, was about 98 billion, or 23%. Claude LAMONDE and Jacques BOLDUC, *Le partage des actifs et des passifs du gouvernement du Canada* (The Sharing of the Assets and Liabilities of the Government of Canada). Québec: Publications du Québec, 1995.

14. See, on this subject, Jacques PARIZEAU, *Pour un Quebec souverain*. Montreal: VLB, 1997, p. 195.

15. *La Presse*, January 16, 1995.

16. After the referendum, Howard Balloch returned to the Department of External Affairs, to which he had been attached since 1976. A specialist in Asian questions, he was appointed Ambassador to China in 1996, accredited to Mongolia and to the Democratic Republic of Korea. On his retirement, in July 2001, he pursued his career in the private sector, putting to good use his familiarity with China, where he opened a consulting office.

17. "Le plan de match n'est pas fait, il faut le faire vite. À Ottawa, une certaine partie de la fonction publique, qui détenait l'Évangile et la vérité, disait que ce n'était pas nécessaire de faire quoi que ce soit, que ça n'arriverait pas... Quand le référendum a été déclenché, l'appareil fédéral a réalisé qu'il était un peu démuni et il a été obligé de réagir en vitesse et de mettre sur pied une équipe pour créer une boîte responsable du référendum. Elle a été confiée à un haut fonctionnaire, Howard Balloch, qui est entré au Conseil privé à titre de sous-secrétaire du Conseil des ministres pour l'Opération unité. Cette équipe a patiné plus vite, elle a couru plus vite pour rattraper le temps perdu. On n'était pas prêt parce qu'on n'avait pas envisagé qu'il aurait pu y avoir un OUI comme ultime réponse. On avait toujours été persuadé que le NON l'emporterait."

18. *Le Devoir*, March 17, 1995.

19. *L'Acadie nouvelle*, October 27, 1995.

20. Preston Manning was elected to the House of Commons for the first time in 1993. Son of a former premier who had led Alberta for 25 years, a graduate in economics from the University of Alberta, he founded, in 1987, the Reform Party, whose program found its inspiration in the Conservative and fundamentalist roots of his father's party, Social Credit. The Reform Party's aim was to decentralize power in Canada so as to free the West from the influence of the central provinces. Manning was the official Opposition leader in the House of Commons from 1997-2000. But, to get into power, the party needed to shed its image of a Prairie party and gain support in Eastern Canada. Consequently, in March 2000, Manning founded the Canadian Conservative Reform Alliance, which absorbed the Reform Party and was intended to supplant the Conservative party as the principal alternative to the Liberal party. Unable to maintain the leadership of his party, he relinquished his seat in 2001.

21. The document was obtained by The Canadian Press, which had to invoke the *Access to Information Act* to be allowed access to its content. Cited in *La Presse*, June 26, 1995.

22. *Le Devoir*, March 14, 1995. Well-known economist Bernard Bonin enjoys strong credibility in Quebec. He was professor at the *École des hautes études commerciales* (School of advanced business studies) before becoming assistant deputy minister in the *ministère de l'Immigration* and in the *ministère des Affaires intergouvernementales du Québec*. As professor at the *École nationale d'administration publique*, he prepared several studies on behalf of the government of René Lévesque on the economic aspects of sovereignty. Jacques Parizeau would often cite these studies. Bernard Bonin was appointed deputy governor of the Bank of Canada in 1988. He became its senior deputy governor six years later and held this post until 1999.

23. *Le Devoir*, March 17, 1994.

24. In Canadian French, *piastre* refers to a Canadian dollar.

25. A parallel stock market that speculates, not on the stocks, but on the derivatives of these stocks: rights issued by banks, access to foreign currencies to settle transactions, exchange risks, interest rates, etc. Enormous amounts of capital flow through this market, which is not highly regulated.

26. Zebedee Nungak is a journalist and author. He lives in Nunavik, in arctic Quebec. Born in Saputiligait, in an encampment of nomadic Inuit hunters, he studied at Puvirnituq, then at Ottawa, before working for the Department of Indian Affairs. He performed various roles in Inuit movements and was for a time the President of Makivik, a company dedicated to the social, political and economic development of the 8,300 Inuit living in the 16 communities settled along the Ungava Coast, the Hudson Strait and Hudson Bay.

27. In 1898, in accordance with the British North America Act, the Canadian Government decreed that the borders of the province of Quebec would be extended northward as far as James Bay, and eastward as far as the Hamilton River, in Labrador. In 1912, it further expanded the territory of Quebec, establishing the new borders as far North as the northern tip of Ungava, and as far East as the northern Hamilton River. All of Labrador would therefore be part of Quebec, until the Privy Council of London annexed it to Newfoundland. (Source: Frédéric DORION, "Le Labrador québécois," *L'Action nationale*, vol. LXX, n° 8, p. 645-656.) The law approving the James Bay-Northern Quebec Agreement, adopted after two years of negotiations with the Crees and the Inuit, and signed in November 1975, would expand this territory even further.

28. René BOUDREAULT, "Autonomie et territoire," *Relations*, March 1995, p. 37-38. René Boudreault has been acting as advisor for the Aboriginal people for almost twenty years. He has assumed, in various capacities, mandates to negotiate, consult and do research in a great variety of fields.

29. *James Bay and Northern Québec Agreement and Complementary Agreements.* Sainte-Foy: Publications du Québec, 1997, p. 5. This agreement recognized the rights of Aboriginals to occupy and use a part of the immense James Bay territory in exchange for sums of money. It was in 1971 that Premier Robert Bourassa announced the giant hydroelectric development project at James Bay, but it had taken some years of negotiation before an agreement was reached. The agreement stipulated that the Grand Council of the Crees would obtain exclusive rights over 5,544 square kilometres of territory and the Inuit over 8,151. Additionally, the Crees and the Inuit received 225 million dollars over a period of 20 years. But, in return, the Crees and Inuit agreed to give up their ancestral rights over a territory of about a million square kilometres, which allowed Hydro-Quebec to flood enormous spaces by creating lakes upstream from its dams.

30. "Nous, il y a un principe à l'égard duquel on n'a jamais changé. On reconnaît onze nations autochtones au Québec, on leur reconnaît le droit à l'autodétermination, on leur reconnaît le droit de participer activement à leur développement, dans le maintien de l'intégrité du territoire québécois. Jusqu'à ce que tout le monde soit prêt à discuter dans un cadre comme celui-ci, moi, le *statu quo* ne me dérange pas."

31. *Le Soleil*, September 29, 1994.

32. This part of the interview was conducted in English.

33. William F. SHAW and Lionel ALBERT, *Partition: The Price of Quebec's Independence*. Montreal: Thornhill, 1980. William F. Shaw was a dental surgeon from Kirkland, on the West Island. He was a *Union nationale* member in the National Assembly from 1976 to 1981. Lionel Albert has a B.A. in Political Science from McGill University and is a computer analyst. They were both losing candidates on behalf of the Equality Party in the general election of 2003, Shaw in D'Arcy McGee, Albert in Brome-Missisquoi.

34. "The Rupert's Land territory would be retained by Canada without discussion. It is historically British and, by an act of the British Parliament, Canadian. It does not have any valid French historical character." *Ibid.*, p. 23.

35. "The St. Lawrence Seaway and its seaward access and the land corridor south of the St. Lawrence River containing the principal road, rail and telecommunications routes between Ontario and the Maritimes." *Ibid.*, p. 25.

36. *Ibid.*, p. 25.

37. The text of Section 43 of the Constitution Act, 1982: "An amendment to the Constitution of Canada in relation to any provision that applies to one or more, but not all, provinces, including (…) any alteration to boundaries between provinces, (…) may be made by proclamation issued by the Governor General (…) only where so authorized by resolutions of the Senate and House of Commons and of the legislative assembly of each province to which the amendment applies."

38. "Tant que le Québec est dans la Confédération, le gouvernement fédéral ne peut pas changer les frontières du Québec. Et quand le Québec n'est plus dans la Confédération, si le Canada veut changer les frontières du Québec, qu'est-ce que c'est? C'est de l'agression sur le plan du droit international. Avant, il ne peut pas. Après, il est trop tard!"

39. *Le Devoir*, March 17, 1995.

40. *Le Devoir*, March 6, 1995.

41. Source: *An Evening with a "Commission on the Future of Quebec,"* P281924Z FEB 1995, FM AMCONSUL QUEBEC TO SECSTATE WASHDC PRIORITY 9643.

42. "Vous savez ce que vous aviez comme auditoire, hier? J'ai dit: non. Il a dit: 400 000! Pour une commission sur l'avenir du Québec!"

43. "J'ai de la misère à dire que, les commissions, c'est ce qui a fait cheminer M. Parizeau. Je pense que, ce qui l'a fait davantage cheminer, c'est quelque chose de fort simple, qu'on pourrait appeler la réalité politique. Il avait en main les sondages, il regardait l'opinion publique. Une fois les commissions finies, la réalité fondamentale demeurait: poser aux Québécois une question et lancer l'idée d'indépendance du Québec, sans partenariat, sans rien. Les gens n'étaient pas prêts à ça."

44. On October 25, 1854, British troops, based in the small port of Balaklava, in the shelter of its cliffs, were preparing an attack on Sebastopol, a Russian fortress situated a few kilometers away, at the southwestern tip of the Crimean peninsula, on the Black Sea. In the morning, the Russians seized the Turkish gun installations at the foot of the cliffs. But they were halted by a Scottish regiment. The commander-in-chief of the Anglo-Turkish troops, Lord Raglan, took his chances and sent Lord Cardigan and his Light Brigade against the Russians, whom he wanted to dislodge from the hills. The commander of the brigade, who only had 673 lancers, saw clearly the futility of the operation, but was afraid to oppose his superior. After 20 minutes of combat, the Light Brigade had suffered 113 dead, 247 wounded and 475 fallen horses on the battlefield. Remaining for posterity are the cardigan (a knitted jacket) and the raglan (an overcoat without shoulder seams)...and one of Lord Alfred Tennyson's beautiful poems, *The Charge of the Light Brigade*.

45. "C'est sûr qu'on avait pris la décision bien avant, probablement en mars, qu'il n'y aurait pas de référendum au printemps. On attendait simplement le moment de l'annoncer. Et on s'est dit: on va en faire l'annonce avant le congrès du Bloc québécois pour lever cette hypothèque, pour que le Bloc ait plus d'espace. C'est le lendemain que Bernard Landry a fait son point de presse sur le fait qu'il ne voulait pas être comme la Brigade légère et se faire décimer sans raison. Mais, la veille, l'ordre d'attaque avait été suspendu. En fait, Landry est un peu entré dans une porte ouverte. Évidemment, il voulait se positionner publiquement entre M. Parizeau et M. Bouchard (...). Il voulait apparaître comme un modéré dans ce débat. (...) Il y avait des discussions entre M. Landry et M. Parizeau, un peu de la même nature qu'entre M. Bouchard et M. Parizeau. M. Landry voulait avoir l'assurance qu'il n'y aurait pas de référendum sans une certaine probabilité de victoire et M. Parizeau refusait de le dire publiquement. Pour des raisons de mobilisation. Alors, il y avait un peu de tension."

46. "J'aime mieux ne pas faire de commentaires, parce que je pourrais devenir grossier. Et je n'aime pas être grossier. Mais ça fait partie des épisodes de l'existence."

47. *Le Soleil*, April 1, 1995.

48. *La Presse*, April 25, 1995.

49. Alain Lupien, an electrotechnician and computer expert, had been a militant member of the Parti Québécois since the age of 16. Already, during the 1980 referendum, he was first in line among the students for the YES side at the Maisonneuve *Cégep*. Under his leadership, the PQ financing campaign exceeded its objectives in 1995, reaching 3.3 million dollars. The pre-referendum campaign that followed raised 2.7 million, and also served to identify the strengths and weaknesses of each electoral riding. This data made it possible to "link up" the weakest organizations with the strongest ones and, sometimes, to restore good relations between MNAs and their leadership committee.

50. "On aurait voulu un balayage plus imposant (à l'élection générale de septembre 1994) de façon à se situer pour un référendum plus rapproché. Mais, comme les résultats ont été inférieurs à notre attente, on savait très bien, à l'organisation, que ça allait peut-être faire en sorte de retarder le référendum pour reconstruire un *momentum*. (...) dégager des fenêtres d'opportunité, peut-être pour le printemps, au pis aller, pour l'automne qui va suivre. En matière d'organisation, il fallait laisser la fenêtre du printemps ouverte parce qu'il aurait pu se passer un moment magique, il aurait fallu être prêt. Mais la fenêtre d'opportunité pour l'organisation était plus intéressante à l'automne. Pour deux raisons. Premièrement, la question du *momentum* politique et, deuxièmement, comme il y avait eu restructuration à l'intérieur du parti, ça nous laissait davantage de temps pour faire une série de formations qu'on souhaitait faire. Pour préparer les troupes, on prévoyait quatre tournées de formation sur les plans du contenu et de l'organisation. Il fallait prendre le temps de faire ça!"

51. The literal meaning of *virage* is "a turn, curve, bend or corner"; the figurative meaning, common in politics, is "a change in policy or direction."

52. "Nous avons été désagréablement surpris. Car, lorsqu'il (Bouchard) revient, on n'est plus en montée (dans les sondages), on est dans un petit ressac. (…) Notre vision des choses, c'est qu'il y aura une phase d'écoute, puis un moment où on se remet en phase de proposition. Pendant la phase d'écoute, c'est sûr qu'on ne sera pas en remontée. Notre stratégie, à ce moment-là, c'était: remettons-nous en phase de proposition, avec les améliorations à apporter, compte tenu de ce qu'on a entendu, dans le sens de: je vous ai compris, on a modifié notre projet, voici notre nouvelle proposition. Et là, on se remet en mode vente. Mais lorsque M. Bouchard fait ses interventions, il dit que ça ne va pas, qu'il faut changer de stratégie. Donc, c'est le début du virage. Ce qu'il dit n'est pas très opérationnel. Il ne dit pas qu'il faut changer de stratégie et par quoi la remplacer. C'est plutôt un signe de mauvaise humeur, une critique. Et notre réaction, c'est: qu'est-ce qu'il propose? On le saura dans les semaines qui suivent, mais pas le premier jour."

53. "Il y avait un soupçon, qui était toujours là, que M. Bouchard n'était pas un vrai souverainiste. (…) il y avait un soupçon plus ou moins de traîtrise qui traînait dans l'air."

54. Gilbert Charland has been in active politics for almost 20 years, as press attaché, political advisor and cabinet leader. His training is in history and political science. In 2000 and 2001, he was assistant deputy minister, then deputy minister for the Environment department. From 2001 to 2003, he was Secretary General attached to the Secretariat for Canadian Intergovernmental Affairs. He has been a member of the Transition committee for the Urban Community of Montreal and is currently visiting administrator at ÉNAP *(École nationale d'administration publique)*.

55. "Une des grandes questions de M. Bouchard était: est-ce que j'utilise le terme 'virage' ou non? Il était conscient que la perception qu'on en aurait pouvait être un peu plus forte que ce qu'il voulait. Il cherchait le mot juste, mais, en même temps, il souhaitait que le message soit compris, qu'il soit clair. Il nous a demandé de lui trouver des synonymes du mot 'virage.' On a sorti les dictionnaires… (…) Le texte avançait, mais cette phrase-là n'était toujours pas 'canée,' comme on dit. Et, à la fin de l'après-midi, quelqu'un a dit à M. Bouchard: 'Écoutez, on a fait le tour de la question et ça s'appelle un virage.' M. Bouchard a encore hésité, puis il a dit: '*Ok*, finalement, on y va!'"

56. "M. Bouchard demande à me voir. Il me fait lire les modifications qui ont été apportées au texte. On y trouve le mot 'virage.' Et les illustrations du virage, qui apparaissent dans le texte, sont des exemples qui viennent directement du programme du Parti québécois. Moi, ça ne me pose pas de problème. Mais, même si ça m'en posait, le problème, ce n'est pas moi. Alors, j'en parle à M. Parizeau."

57. "Il s'est fermé les yeux. Il a écouté ça comme quelqu'un qui écoute de la musique ou qui écoute attentivement ce qui se dit; il n'a eu aucune réaction. Des fois, tu peux sentir que quelque chose passe ou ne passe pas, que ça crée une émotion. Là, non. Je n'ai pas senti ça."

58. "La preuve, c'est qu'il est assis dans la première rangée et qu'il applaudit."

59. "La position de M. Bouchard, M. Parizeau la connaissait. Mais si je vous disais que M. Parizeau était d'accord avec cette position-là, je pense que je vous conterais une grosse menterie. Quand un des partenaires importants, comme M. Bouchard, arrive avec une stratégie qui peut être différente, c'est sûr que ça vient un petit peu heurter M. Parizeau. Mais la position de M. Bouchard était partagée par des ministres importants du cabinet de M. Parizeau."

60. "Ce sont des moments plus difficiles, parce que Jacques Parizeau avait une façon de voir les choses. Mais, par contre, il tenait tellement à ce que ça fonctionne…"

61. "Nous, c'était de faire la souveraineté et on savait que, pour la faire, il fallait que les deux chefs, M. Parizeau et M. Bouchard, soient convergents. Donc, notre tâche, ce n'était pas de les diviser, mais de les réunir. Mais l'un des deux ne voulait pas jouer le jeu à ce moment-là. C'était Lucien Bouchard, qui avait mis le mot 'virage' dans son texte. C'est un mot de code, mais, nous, on savait ce qu'il voulait dire: il voulait dire un deuxième référendum. Et il soulignait la nécessité d'un changement radical d'orientation de la proposition souverainiste. Il souhaitait une modification de la question référendaire pour qu'il y ait un second référendum. Donc, on faisait un premier référendum sur la souveraineté, en disant qu'on ratifierait l'entente avec le Canada dans un second référendum. Il voulait réintroduire la notion d'association, comme c'était le cas au référendum de 1980."

62. "Dans notre langage, on appelle ça *spiner*. L'entourage (de M. Bouchard) s'est mis à influencer la presse dans sa perception: le virage était plus important qu'il en avait l'air, c'était un virage majeur, et il était important que le Parti québécois, ou les souverainistes de façon générale, acceptent d'élargir l'offre qui devait être faite au reste du Canada. Cela a commencé le vendredi soir et le samedi. En politique, la perception devient vite la réalité, la vérité. Oui, les gens du Bloc ont mis de la pression."

63. "Nous, on minimisait (l'impact du discours) sur la foi du texte lui-même. Lui, il donnait le signal à ses conseillers d'aller dire le contraire aux journalistes, que c'était un vrai signal, très fort."

64. Quoted in *Le Soleil* on April 9, 1995: Michel VASTEL, "Bouchard pose ses conditions à Parizeau" (Bouchard lays out his conditions for Parizeau). This article is reproduced in DUCHESNE, *op. cit.*, p. 392.

65. "M. Parizeau a peut-être été un peu choqué par le fait d'être placé devant cette situation, mais il connaissait la position de M. Bouchard là-dessus, ce n'était pas un secret."

66. Denis LESSARD, "Parizeau réaffirme son autorité" (Parizeau reaffirms his authority), *La Presse*, April 10, 1995.

67. "M. Bouchard n'était pas aux ordres de M. Parizeau. Ni à la commission Bélanger-Campeau ni au Bloc québécois, ni dans la campagne référendaire. (La déclaration de Parizeau) l'a un peu piqué parce qu'il ne remettait pas en question le fait que M. Parizeau soit premier ministre du Québec et le principal porteur de ballon. Mais il ne pouvait pas se faire envoyer sur les fleurs non plus, en se faisant dire: Bouchard, si ça ne fait pas son affaire, qu'il aille jouer ailleurs!"

68. "Je l'entends dire, je n'ai pas les mots exacts, qu'il n'est pas absolument certain qu'il participera à la campagne référendaire s'il n'est pas satisfait de la question ou de l'orientation. J'ai pensé: Wow! Il vient de dire ça publiquement. Alors là, on vient de monter de trois étages dans la crise. Là, on est vraiment en crise majeure. Il y a une menace publique, confirmée par un de nos deux chefs, de ne pas participer s'il n'est pas satisfait. Je trouvais qu'on était vraiment au bord du gouffre."

69. Remarks reported by Jean Royer to Pierre Duchesne and reproduced in the book cited, p. 396.

70. "Tout ce qu'on voulait, ce jour-là, c'était de survivre et d'envoyer un signal de dialogue. On voulait dire: les choses qui ne fonctionnent pas, il faut en discuter. C'est tout ce qu'on voulait, ce jour-là."

71. *CSN* (Confédération des syndicats nationaux – Confederation of National Unions) and *FTQ* (Fédération des travailleurs et travailleuses du Québec – Quebec Workers' Federation) are two of Quebec's main unions.

72. "On voyait que M. Bouchard attendait de M. Parizeau un signe d'ouverture, qu'il dise: Écoutez, je ne suis pas très content de la façon dont c'est en train de se passer, mais il est certain qu'on est destinés à s'entendre. Ce signe n'est pas venu. Et M. Parizeau attendait de M. Bouchard un signe d'autocritique, qu'il dise par exemple: Écoutez, il y a des coups de gueule, on se connaît, mais l'important, c'est de s'entendre. Ni l'un ni l'autre n'a envoyé de signal, les deux étaient très fermés."

73. "Ma volonté, c'est de leur dire que ça ne se peut pas que ce soit fini. Mais je n'ai rien à dire parce que je ne peux pas porter de paroles que je n'ai pas entendues (de la bouche de mon chef). (...) Ils s'en vont. Ça n'a pas de sens, ça ne peut pas se terminer comme ça."

CHAPTER 5

1. "Je ne disais pas que j'étais d'accord avec lui. En fait, j'étais en désaccord avec cette idée de deux référendums, cela aurait été, stratégiquement, un désastre. Je voulais aussi lui envoyer un autre signal: il fallait se parler! (...) On a pu alors commencer à envisager des scénarios de sortie de crise."

2. "Il y a eu un moment où M. Parizeau, psychologiquement, était un peu sonné par ce qui s'était passé avec M. Bouchard et M. Landry. Il a alors eu un peu le réflexe de se replier sur ce dont il était certain, le Parti québécois et ses alliés au sein du Parti québécois."

3. "... que les chances de réaliser la souveraineté dans les conditions politiques actuelles sont nulles; qu'il lui incombe, en tant que chef du mouvement souverainiste et premier ministre du Québec, de renouer le di-

alogue. (…) Je lui disais qu'il fallait créer une situation où il allait reprendre l'initiative, redonner les règles du jeu en modifiant sa position personnelle, en acceptant la discussion avec les autres, en signalant sa volonté de modifier la proposition, mais qu'il devait être le maître du jeu. (…) Il faut utiliser la force de Lucien Bouchard, lui conseille Lisée, mais, si on essaie de donner l'impression que vous n'êtes plus dans le jeu, nos adversaires utiliseront cette fausse impression pour rappeler aux Québécois qu'advenant une victoire du OUI, ce n'est pas Bouchard, mais Parizeau qui sera toujours là. On le paierait cher politiquement. Donc, même dans le 'virage,' il faut que vous soyez celui qui ramène les choses, en modifiant votre position, en ouvrant le jeu, en donnant de nouveaux paramètres dans lesquels les autres voudront jouer."

4. "Seuls, on n'a pas de majorité pour faire la souveraineté. Les Québécois sont convaincus que vous ne voulez pas d'association avec le Canada. Bouchard et Dumont veulent l'association. Il y en a un qui n'en veut pas, c'est Parizeau."

5. "Les gens pensent que vous êtes contre l'association, donc ils sont contre la souveraineté. Il faut leur expliquer que vous êtes pour une forme d'association et que vous en envisagez aussi une forme un peu plus grande, si le Canada le veut, mais que ce n'est pas là une condition à la souveraineté."

6. "Cela voulait dire: commençons à envisager la négociation qui mènera à l'accord tripartite."

7. "Nous n'étions pas en présence d'un Parizeau, qui veut un Québec souverain, et d'un Bouchard, qui veut une refonte du fédéralisme."

8. "Je ne suis pas l'exégète de la pensée de M. Parizeau, mais, ce que je prétends, c'est qu'il y avait une appréhension forte que M. Parizeau voulait tenir un référendum coûte que coûte, quitte à le perdre. Ça, ça nous inquiétait beaucoup. Je ne dis pas que M. Parizeau ne voulait pas gagner le référendum, je n'en ai jamais douté… C'était le combat de sa vie. Mais, sur le plan de la stratégie et de l'approche, sa tolérance devant le risque de le perdre était beaucoup plus grande qu'elle ne l'était chez nous."

9. "M. Bouchard était beaucoup plus inquiet de la capacité de rassembler une majorité avec un projet strictement indépendantiste que ne l'était M. Parizeau."

10. "… des crises en politique, il y en a et il faut avoir la capacité de les régler. (…) M. Parizeau et M. Bouchard étaient constamment mis dans une situation où, s'ils n'employaient pas les mêmes mots pour décrire une même situation, on parlait d'état de crise. Il n'y avait pas une semaine où l'on ne retrouvait pas, dans un article de journal: M. Bouchard veut le job de M. Parizeau! Pas une semaine où l'on n'avait pas l'impression qu'il y avait une crise entre M. Parizeau et M. Bouchard. Tout cela faisait une bonne nouvelle. Nous devions composer avec ça!"

11. The report from the ADQ was presented March 27, by a close colleague of Dumont, Jacques Gauthier. It was entitled, *Un référendum pour progresser* (A referendum for progress). Gauthier is a lawyer. He was a militant within the Liberal party, which he left at the same time as Mario Dumont and Jean Allaire, in 1992. He played an active role, first in the reflection group that Allaire set up after he left the LPQ, and later, in the founding of the Action démocratique du Québec. He held various posts within the party, including the chairmanship of the legal committee and of two constitutional committees. He specializes in medical law.

12. André Néron had worked in the Parti Québécois organization, then left that party to join the ADQ. He became Mario Dumont's advisor and director general of the ADQ. Shortly after the referendum he became chief of staff to the leader of the Bloc Québécois in Ottawa, Michel Gauthier, when the latter replaced Lucien Bouchard, called to succeed Jacques Parizeau. In 1998, he published a book entitled *Le temps des hypocrites* (The era of the hypocrites), in which he settles accounts with Mario Dumont.

13. The Allaire Report was the fruit of an analysis by the Constitutional Committee of the Quebec Liberal Party, when the Bourassa government still thought it was possible to have the Meech Lake Accord ratified by all the provincial legislatures in Canada. Created in February 1990 and chaired by lawyer Jean Allaire, the Committee's mandate was to prepare a second round of negotiations with Ottawa if the Accord was ratified, and to propose an alternative if it failed. The Committee's report, entitled *A Quebec Free to Choose*, was submitted to the Executive Committee of the party on January 28, 1991 and adopted at its convention the following March 10. It drew up three lists of jurisdictions, those that were exclusive

to the federal government, and those that were exclusive to Quebec and of which it recommended full repatriation and, finally, those jurisdictions shared between the two levels of government. The federal jurisdictions were reduced to defense, territorial security, currency, debt, customs and equalization of taxes. Quebec had twenty-three exclusive areas of jurisdiction and shared eight with Ottawa. In the case of failed negotiations, the report stipulated that Quebec should take the necessary steps to accede to sovereignty and offer Canada economic union, under the governance of a certain number of confederate institutions. Adopted in 1991, the report was rejected by Liberal militants the following year, which provoked the departure of Jean Allaire, Mario Dumont, Jacques Gauthier and several other members of the party.

14. "André Néron me fait part que M. Dumont est intéressé à rencontrer M. Bouchard. Eux, (l'ADQ dans son mémoire à la commission), ils étaient toujours dans la stratégie du rapport Allaire. Je dis à André Néron que, si jamais il est question d'aller plus loin, s'il est question d'une entente quelle qu'elle soit, cela ne peut pas être sur la base de leur mémoire. Il me répond que, de toute façon, c'est une position de négociation."

15. "Je lui ai dit: 'Viens avec un mandat parce que, moi, j'en ai un.' Mon mandat, c'est d'explorer. Il ne s'agit pas de négocier une entente… Il s'agit de voir si elle est possible. (…) Il me semble que c'était le 13 avril. Quand Néron est arrivé, je lui ai demandé s'il avait un mandat. Il m'a répondu: 'Oui, c'est Mario Dumont qui vient de me laisser ici, au restaurant.' Ce fut ma première rencontre officielle avec André Néron. (…) il ne fallait pas que la notion de partenariat rende la souveraineté conditionnelle."

16. "Ils avaient fait ce flirt avec la souveraineté. Donc, ils étaient disponibles. Mais ils ne nous écoutaient pas, ils n'écoutaient pas M. Parizeau. Ils écoutaient un peu plus M. Bouchard, et beaucoup plus M. Dumont, qui est un ancien libéral. On était à un pour cent près, alors il n'y avait pas d'économie à faire. Je disais à M. Parizeau qu'il fallait une coalition la plus large possible. (…) Je me suis dit que c'était une très grande victoire. Il faut rassembler suffisamment pour que des gens qui sont en désaccord avec nous sur toutes sortes de questions, votent OUI sur la question de la souveraineté."

17. "Ils ont proposé des modifications mineures que j'ai tout de suite intégrées. (En fait) j'ai créé un genre d'escalier à trois marches (pour le premier ministre). Sur la première marche où il se trouvait, il y avait l'association incontournable, le dollar commun, etc. Puis, (sur la deuxième marche), des gens qui pensaient qu'une association était souhaitable, une association qui allait plus loin, comme un conseil conjoint de ministres Canada-Québec qui se réunirait de temps en temps. Et, enfin, sur la troisième marche, des gens qui pensaient qu'il y avait une autre forme d'association envisageable: (par exemple), est-ce que les législateurs devraient avoir un forum conjoint? (…) M. Parizeau veut que tous ces gens-là se parlent et créent le camp du changement. 'Moi, leur dit-il, je suis sur la première marche, mais, maintenant, j'accepte de parler avec ceux qui sont sur les deux autres marches.'"

18. "Nous avions démissionné du Parti libéral au lendemain de Meech. Être dans le camp de Jean Chrétien et de ceux qui voulaient le *statu quo* n'avait pas de bon sens. En même temps, je n'aurais jamais été capable de voter OUI à un référendum sur la question initiale de M. Parizeau: Êtes-vous pour ou contre l'indépendance du Québec, OUI ou NON? C'est ainsi qu'au cours des travaux des commissions sur l'avenir du Québec, on a défini cette idée d'un partenariat, d'une véritable confédération, l'idée d'un Québec souverain à l'intérieur d'un partenariat avec le reste du Canada."

19. In 1993, the Bloc Québécois published a small book entitled *Un nouveau parti pour l'étape décisive* (A new party for the decisive stage). The word "partnership" does not occur in it, but the entire document is slanted towards the creation of an association between Quebec and Canada. "The institutional modalities overseeing any association can only reflect the facts of history, demography and geography," it says. "Even if North-South trade flow ends up superseding East-West flow, this in no way lessens the interests of the community uniting the Canadian and Quebec peoples. (…) This common market would be one of the most integrated in the world because it would be accompanied by monetary union (…). In short, Quebec accepts the existing economic integration." (Pages 41-47.)

20. "La question du partenariat n'est pas une surprise. Quand on a fait le livre en juin 1993, je me souviens qu'avant de le publier, il y a eu une rencontre au restaurant Le Caveau. M. Parizeau était présent, ainsi que Jacques Brassard et Bernard Landry. Jean Royer et Yves Martin aussi… Je me souviens que la réaction de M. Parizeau a été de dire: 'Tant qu'il n'y a pas de trait d'union entre souveraineté et partenariat, je n'ai pas de problème.'"

21. "Peut-être trois semaines avant le congrès, il y a eu une rencontre du comité référendaire. C'était à l'hôtel Delta, je pense. M. Bouchard est revenu à la charge en disant à M. Parizeau: 'Comprenez qu'on est en plein cœur d'un moment stratégique. Il faut peut-être adapter un peu notre stratégie. J'ai mon congrès, comprenez bien que je dois dire quelque chose. Alors, donnez-moi un peu de marge de manœuvre, faites-moi une ouverture.' Et M. Parizeau n'a pas réagi négativement, mais pas positivement non plus. Tout le monde savait que ce n'était pas *sa tasse de thé*. Mais la question n'était pas de savoir si c'était la *tasse de thé* de M. Parizeau ou pas, la question était de savoir: qu'est-ce qu'on fait pour gagner le référendum? (…) M. Parizeau n'a pas donné suite."

22. "Pourquoi minimale? Parce que l'état d'esprit du côté du reste du Canada ne sera pas au développement d'associations très intégrées et très complexes. (…) On se disait que si le négociateur était un politique assimilable à quelqu'un qui a le profil de M. Bouchard, c'était clair que les fédéraux nommeraient également à la table un politique. Or, on ne souhaitait pas qu'à la table de négociations, il y ait de la politique. (…) dans un premier temps, pour les premières années, entendons-nous sur un minimum. Et quand, d'un commun accord, les deux parties voudront développer un degré d'association plus intégré, on le fera."

23. "Faire des élections quand il y a de la chicane, ça va mal, ça va mal… Parce que les gens, au Québec, aiment la bataille, mais ils n'aiment pas la chicane. Et quand un parti politique se chicane, la population ne lui fait pas confiance. (…) il y avait environ 35% des militants qui n'étaient pas nécessairement péquistes, mais qui trouvaient que M. Bouchard faisait un bon chef."

24. "Ça, c'était le cas au référendum de 80. Donc, on fait un premier référendum sur la souveraineté en promettant de faire ratifier l'entente avec le Canada dans un second référendum."

25. "M. Bouchard ne voulait pas revenir à la démarche de 1980. Il faut se rappeler que la démarche de 1980, c'était un mandat de négocier la souveraineté. Ce n'était pas la souveraineté, c'était la souveraineté-association avec un trait d'union. Ma compréhension, c'est que M. Bouchard ne voulait pas revenir à la démarche de 1980. Il avait la même appréhension: rendre la souveraineté conditionnelle au partenariat, c'était problématique, ne serait-ce que sur le plan de la stratégie. Je ne l'ai jamais vu proposer ça. Cela a été évoqué dans des discussions ici et là, mais cela n'a jamais vraiment fait l'objet d'une position arrêtée."

26. "Et on a convenu qu'il y avait, semble-t-il, tant du côté de M. Dumont que du côté de M. Bouchard, une ouverture."

27. "M. Bouchard trouvait ça trop rapide. Il a dit: 'Maintenant qu'on pense (qu'il y a une ouverture du côté de l'ADQ), on va contacter le bureau de M. Parizeau.' J'ai alors rencontré Jean-François Lisée. (…) Je me souviens que la réaction de Jean-François n'était pas très chaude au point de départ. On était dans une période où les rapports avec M. Parizeau étaient assez froids. Eux, ils (étaient) dans une dynamique qu'il fallait y aller plutôt tranquillement. Je me souviens qu'à ce moment-là, Jean-François avait insisté pour dire: 'Je ne pense pas que ça va marcher, je ne suis pas sûr que c'est bon de faire rapport à nos deux chefs.' Je lui ai dit: 'Moi, c'est le rapport que je vais faire à M. Bouchard.' On s'est quittés là-dessus."

28. "La journée où j'ai sorti ça, moi, le gars de 24 ans, chef d'un parti qui a eu 6,7% des votes (à la dernière élection), j'étais quasiment la risée parce que M. Parizeau, lui, son idée était faite! Mais la réalité politique l'a rattrapé."

29. "C'était la démonstration de notre capacité de rassemblement."

30. *Le Soleil*, April 1, 1995.

31. "Nos deux conditions n'étaient vraiment pas négociables. On pouvait négocier le choix des mots, on pouvait négocier bien des choses, mais le partenariat dans la question et la négociation avec le Canada avant la déclaration de souveraineté, c'était le solage à partir duquel on pouvait discuter. (…) Quand tu as 6,7% du vote, tu prends acte que tu n'es pas le premier ministre. Ce n'est pas toi qui vas décider de la question, ce n'est pas toi qui vas aller négocier avec Ottawa. Alors, il faut que tu fasses des gestes qui vont te rapprocher. (…) Un vote pour le OUI, ça cassait le 'cadenas.' Ça amorçait la négociation, des discussions, c'était ça qui avait le plus de chances de nous conduire vers un nouveau partenariat. (…) une union d'États, qui ont une forme de souveraineté ou d'autonomie."

32. "Dans un premier temps, ça lui allait. Toutes les semaines, je faisais rapport des progrès des négociations. Et parfois, parce que ça devenait concret, M. Parizeau résistait. Il y avait des moments où il n'était plus certain de vouloir aller jusque-là!"

33. "D'après moi, une telle proposition aurait été une erreur stratégique. On a parlé d'une assemblée législative conjointe. Mais on a dit: si le Québec devient souverain, il y aura des élections. Puis, si un jour le parti de l'ADQ est élu et qu'il propose ce parlement commun, on verra."

34. "Il est certain que Jacques Parizeau n'aurait jamais pu signer un document qui ne fasse pas du Québec un pays souverain représenté aux Nations unies. Ceci n'a jamais été mis en cause. Ce qui a été discuté, c'est le niveau d'importance de la proposition qu'on ferait au Canada anglais."

35. "Ça ne se vivait pas dans le drame. Il y a eu des tensions, mais il fallait gérer les relations entre deux hommes!"

36. "Jean-François réussissait toujours à élargir un peu le corridor. M. Parizeau s'est retrouvé, à un moment donné, dans des sentiers qui lui étaient moins familiers. Il y a des choses qu'au début, nous ne pensions pas avoir sur la table. Mais c'est en partie par les efforts de Jean-François qu'on est arrivés à l'entente sur le partenariat."

37. "J'ai vu quatre versions successives. On allait jusqu'aux virgules, on changeait des mots…"

38. "Le camp du OUI a franchi une étape à ce moment-là. Il avait réussi à aller chercher Mario Dumont, qui était un peu mon équivalent dans l'équipe du OUI, c'est-à-dire un troisième participant qui s'adresse, comme moi, à un groupe d'indécis qui s'identifient davantage à lui. Moi, quand j'ai vu ça, je me suis dit: on a un adversaire qui est maintenant mieux outillé pour faire sa campagne référendaire. Le camp du OUI avait réussi à élargir, en quelque sorte, sa coalition. Et ça, d'instinct, je me disais: la bataille vient de changer!"

39. "Il aurait utilisé ça à son avantage, probablement pour nous dénoncer, comme il l'avait fait pendant des années. Il utiliserait le rameau d'olivier (qu'on lui tendrait, pour dire): 'Regardez, les libéraux courent après moi!'"

40. "… quand on s'affiche pour le OUI sur une question qui veut faire du Québec un pays souverain, c'est qu'on est souverainiste."

41. "Pour certains, cela a confirmé où Mario Dumont logeait. Pour d'autres, cela a été perçu comme un effort du Parti québécois pour créer une certaine ambiguïté. M. Parizeau préfère toujours la question courte, directe, mais les stratèges péquistes préfèrent toujours une autre façon pour colorer, dorer la pilule. (…) On avait vu Mario Dumont comme l'individu qui pouvait être la clé d'une victoire ou d'une défaite référendaire. (…) Il ne fallait pas défendre le Canada au Québec. Il fallait que Johnson défende le Québec dans le Canada. C'est une nuance importante."

42. "Les grandes stratégies discutées d'avance, ce n'est pas tout à fait son *bag*. Il se fie beaucoup à son instinct. Il joue au filet, la balle arrive, on la prend du mieux qu'on peut… Et il est vrai que les bonnes décisions se prennent au filet. La question de la préparation stratégique, c'était moins son fort."

43. "On avait des discussions. Quand il nous disait: 'Je ne le sens pas,' la discussion était finie. Je ne veux pas dire que c'est simplement un être d'intuition et de passion sans être un homme de raison, mais il avait une approche plus intuitive de la politique."

44. "Alors, il s'est fâché contre moi. Il m'a dit: 'M. Arès, vous êtes intransigeant!' J'ai répondu: 'M. Bouchard, lorsqu'on parle des droits de la communauté franco-albertaine, je vais toujours être intransigeant. On ne négocie pas les droits. Nos droits, ce n'est pas discutable!' Là, il s'est fâché encore plus et il est sorti de la salle. Ses adjoints politiques nous regardaient, puis ils ont dit: 'M. Bouchard est parti. Pourquoi ne vous en allez-vous pas?' M. Bouchard est revenu quinze minutes plus tard. Il s'était calmé. Il a dit: 'Bon, on reprend les discussions.' Il était cette sorte d'homme. Il se fâchait, mais il pouvait se calmer assez vite. Moi, j'avais beaucoup aimé ça. Quand il y avait un intérêt plus grand, il pouvait reprendre la discussion."

45. "Le gros bon sens. Oui, il a du tempérament. Mais après, la poussière descendait, puis on arrivait toujours avec une solution intelligente. Pour lui, dans le fond, sa philosophie politique était beaucoup basée sur le gros bon sens."

46. "Il était, à l'époque, un intellectuel, un avocat, un ambassadeur, loin d'être un politicien. Mais il a appris entre 1988 et 1995. (Il est devenu un politicien) habile, qui sait exploiter les erreurs de ses adversaires. Ses talents de négociateur, il a réussi à les transposer dans l'arène politique. Est-ce que c'est un politicien innovateur? Je ne le croirais pas. C'est un gars qui est conscient de son potentiel, de son image et il sait exploiter au maximum ses talents. Il n'y a pas de doute qu'il a levé le ton auprès de M. Parizeau."

47. "En plus d'être au cœur des grands débats, il fallait que j'apprenne l'abc de 'c'est quoi être député.' J'avais autour de moi une toute petite équipe, mais, à l'intérieur du parti, il y avait quand même des gens d'expérience, comme M. Allaire pour les affaires constitutionnelles."

48. "M. Dumont n'avait pas établi de complicité avec le caucus, avec les autres instances du parti. Ça m'avait étonné de voir à quel point il était esseulé, à l'occasion d'un événement qui était en général assez couru par un peu tout le monde, y compris les plus vieux."

49. "Dumont est un homme assez réservé. Certains diraient qu'il pourrait être assez froid. Ce n'est pas un émotif. Il a un peu le tempérament de Robert Bourassa. (…) Notre conversation a duré pas loin d'une heure. Il a écouté très respectueusement, à moins qu'il n'ait déposé le téléphone sur le comptoir. Puis, la conversation s'est arrêtée là. J'ai appelé Bourassa pour lui dire que j'avais fait la démarche. 'Comment a-t-il réagi?' m'a demandé Bourassa. J'ai alors employé une expression anglaise pour décrire la réaction de Dumont: '*Iced water in his veins!*' C'était une autre façon de dire que la conversation avait été polie mais glaciale."

50. Source: p 191332Z JUN 95 FM AM CONSUL QUEBEC TO SESTATE WASHDC.

51. *Ibid.*

52. One of the main television networks in Quebec.

53. *La Presse*, April 26, 1995.

54. "(L'ambassadeur) leur avait raconté qu'on avait demandé à M. Parizeau ce qui se passerait si, une fois que les Québécois auraient voté OUI, ils voulaient changer d'idée? M. Parizeau avait répondu: 'Cela ne peut pas arriver, c'est impossible. Une fois que les Québécois auront voté OUI, ils vont être comme des homards.' La note est en anglais: *in a lobster pot*, dans une trappe à homards. (…)Il devient tout à coup très clair que vient de tomber sur mon bureau quelque chose qui va rendre mon vendredi un peu moins tranquille."

55. "… un journaliste apprend rapidement qu'on peut savoir plus vite comment un cabinet va être remanié, en ayant de bonnes sources à l'ambassade des États-Unis plus qu'en ayant de bonnes sources au bureau du premier ministre. Donc, c'est un bon endroit pour commencer (une enquête). Les deux (premières) ambassades où j'ai téléphoné, y compris celle des États-Unis, m'ont répondu spontanément: 'Oui, absolument!' Il y a même un diplomate qui m'a dit: 'C'est la bouchée la plus délicieuse de la semaine dans la communauté diplomatique à Ottawa. Tout à fait suave, cette déclaration de homards!'"

56. "'C'est une invention du diable!' (…) Il a commencé à s'inquiéter de ma carrière. Il m'a expliqué que, si je publiais cette histoire le samedi, le dimanche, ma carrière serait terminée, qu'on allait me démentir sur la place publique, que ma crédibilité de journaliste était détruite."

57. "Il m'a demandé: 'Si je te fournis trois ambassadeurs qui disent que ce n'est pas vrai, vas-tu publier (l'histoire)?' dit Hébert. Je lui ai répondu: 'C'est sûr que, si je publie, leur démenti va faire partie de mon papier.'"

58. "Ma main tremblait. C'était incroyable! Cet ambassadeur, je ne l'aurais jamais trouvé, il ne m'aurait jamais rappelée et, s'il l'avait fait, il m'aurait dit qu'il n'avait pas à me répondre! Et voilà que le bureau de Parizeau m'envoie un ambassadeur, qui accepte d'être cité et me confirme que Jacques Parizeau a dit que les Québécois seraient comme des homards! Ce monsieur ne m'a jamais rappelée pour me dire que je l'avais mal cité!"

59. "… très agité, pour affirmer que M. Parizeau n'a pas dit cela. Quand je lui ai demandé pourquoi il l'avait raconté aux Affaires étrangères, la conversation est devenue très, très confuse."

60. Interview with Alvin Cader, *Le Téléjournal*, Radio-Canada, July 11, 1995.

61. For more on Balloch, see chapter 4, note 11.

62. "Notre première réaction a été: c'est une invention. On a voulu confirmer de bonne foi. On a consulté d'autres personnes présentes, des gens des ambassades européennes. L'une d'elles avait pris des notes. Alors, on s'est rendu compte que Parizeau l'avait probablement dit."

63. "Dix ans après, écoutez, ce n'est pas sérieux. À un moment donné, tu sais, pais mes agneaux, pais mes brebis!"

64. Chantal Hébert, "Parizeau, dans l'eau bouillante" (Parizeau in hot water), *La Presse*, July 12, 1995.

65. In 1980, then PQ member Lise Payette had labelled federalist women as "Yvettes," referring to the docile subject of a Quebec school reader. In an ironic backlash, it set off a movement of women who proudly called themselves "Yvettes."

CHAPTER 6

1. Roy Romanow is a politician from Saskatchewan, a native of Saskatoon. He was a lawyer, elected to the Legislature for the first time as a New Democrat in 1967. At the November 1981 federal-provincial conference, which Quebec political historiography would remember as the conference of "The Night of the Long Knives," he was minister of intergovernmental affairs in Allan Blakeney's government. It was in this capacity that together with Roy McMurtry, Ontario's justice minister, and Jean Chrétien, justice minister for the Trudeau government, he orchestrated the agreement by the nine provinces other than Quebec on the repatriation of the Constitution. Romanow replaced Blakeney as party leader in November 1987 and became premier of Saskatchewan on November 1, 1991. He was re-elected in June 1995. After his retirement, in 2001, the Chrétien government entrusted him with the chairmanship of the Commission on the Future of Health Care in Canada, which submitted its report in November 2002.

2. *Le Soleil*, September 9, 1995.

3. "'Est-ce que vous pensez qu'il pourrait encore renoncer à faire le référendum maintenant?' m'a-t-il demandé. J'ai été complètement saisie par cette phrase. J'ai pensé que c'était une boutade, mais ce ne semblait pas l'être. Probablement que, dans les personnes qu'il avait consultées, il y en avait qui avaient trop peur de perdre."

4. Jean-Herman GUAY, Pierre DROUILLY, Pierre-Alain COTNOIR, Pierre NOREAU, "Référendum: les souverainistes risquent de rencontrer une dure défaite" (Referendum: sovereigntists may be in for a rude awakening), *La Presse*, August 26, 1995.

5. "(Drouilly et les autres) disent qu'on va perdre le référendum. Comment voulez-vous qu'il (Bouchard) se sente? Ça veut dire que, s'il continue d'aller de l'avant, il y a encore un risque de 'planter,' il y a des risques que ça ne se réalise pas, il y a des risques qu'il (Bouchard) devienne le fossoyeur du Québec. Imaginez, s'il embarque dans une stratégie où il est convaincu de perdre, et qu'il y va quand même, comment il se retrouve le lendemain. Parce que, le lendemain, il faut qu'il retourne à Ottawa. Il est encore chef de l'opposition officielle. Alors, il veut absolument gagner. Il veut que toutes les conditions possibles et imaginables soient là. Il n'est pas question, mais alors pas du tout, de juste faire un essai…!"

6. In the 1960s and 1970s, Guy Bertrand was an activist for the *indépendantistes*. In 1969, he published a little 60-page manifesto entitled *Québec souverain. Avons-nous les moyens? 106 questions et réponses sur la souveraineté politique et le Parti québécois* (Can we afford a sovereign Quebec? 106 questions and answers on political sovereignty and the Parti Québécois), in which he said, notably, "No one can prevent Quebec from achieving independence" and "We can become independent without asking anyone's permission. Liberty is something to be taken, not grovelled after." Since that time, he has gone over to the other side and often found himself, in his duties as a prosecutor, working side by side with the anti-sovereigntists.

7. The complete text of the preamble can be found in Appendix B.

8. *La Presse*, September 7, 1995.

9. "On appelait ça la grand-messe, nous autres, dit-il. J'essaie d'être respectueux de ce qu'il s'y est fait, mais, pour moi, c'était un événement extraterrestre que toute cette affaire. C'était un événement pompeux. Quand je vois ces événements, les *leaders* sont aux premières loges, ils se lisent des poèmes, ils se font des chansons… J'ai toujours peur que cela traduise comme message: est-ce qu'on fait vraiment cela pour le peuple? Cela devient un cérémonial pour les élites."

10. Parizeau granted a live thirty-minute interview to the host of *Le Midi Quinze* on September 8, 1995.

11. "C'est une stratégie (la cérémonie du Grand Théâtre) qui n'a pas vraiment été partagée avec l'entourage de M. Bouchard. M. Bouchard ne voulait aucun triomphalisme et on trouvait qu'il y en avait un soupçon autour de cette opération. De toute façon, M. Dumont ne voulait pas s'y associer. Je pense que nous ne sommes pas les premiers à constater que, parfois, M. Parizeau donnait un peu dans l'emphase. Et cela ne nous semblait pas être le moment de faire cela."

12. The text of the bill is provided in Appendix C.

13. *Le Devoir*, June 10, 1995. Four months later, journalist Michel David confirmed this: "The idea of a supervisory committee was Mario Dumont's," *Le Soleil*, October 7, 1995.

14. "Cela a été la position de l'ADQ."

15. "Je pense que c'est moi (qui ai eu l'idée). Un certain nombre de gens, et pas mal de journalistes, disaient: 'Écoutez, vous êtes à peu près la personne la moins crédible pour siffler la fin de la récréation. Il faut qu'il y ait quelqu'un qui ne relève pas de vous et qui puisse faire rapport à l'Assemblée nationale.' Avec un comité de surveillance qui est au courant de tout ce qui se passe dans les négociations, on pourrait avoir une idée correcte de ce que chacun fait. C'est lui, le comité, qui avait à déterminer si les négociations n'allaient nulle part!"

16. Claude Castonguay is an actuary. A professor at Université Laval, he was elected to parliament in 1970 as part of the Liberal wave that carried Robert Bourassa to power. Bourassa appointed him to Health and Social Services. History would consider Claude Castonguay as the father of health insurance in Quebec. He returned to the private sector during the November 1973 general election. In the course of his career, he took part in the work of numerous committees and commissions, among them *La Commission royale d'enquête sur la santé et le bien-être social* (Royal Commission of Inquiry on Health and Social Welfare), from 1966 to 1970.

17. "Le bureau de M. Parizeau m'a contacté et m'a dit que le premier ministre voulait me rencontrer, qu'il m'invitait à dîner un soir, sans que je sache à l'avance de quoi il s'agissait. (…) C'est au cours de la conversation que M. Parizeau m'a transmis l'invitation de présider un comité qui serait, advenant la victoire du OUI, un comité d'information et de surveillance des négociations. Je pense que l'idée générale était que les choses se déroulent de la façon la plus positive et la plus correcte possible et que l'Assemblée nationale et la population soient informées du déroulement des négociations. Il était important qu'il y ait quelqu'un qui puisse porter un jugement sur le déroulement des négociations."

18. "Je me suis dit qu'il valait mieux attendre de voir quels seraient les résultats. On me consulterait en bonne et due forme au moment opportun sur les membres du comité."

19. The committee was to have eleven members. The first five names were revealed during the first week of the referendum campaign. These were Arthur Tremblay, former deputy minister of education under Paul Gérin-Lajoie and a Conservative Senator; Jean Allaire; Serge Racine, president of the firm Shermag; Denise Verreault, of Groupe Maritime Verreault; and Jacinthe Simard, president of the *Union des municipalités régionales et de comté du Québec* (Union of regional municipalities and counties of Quebec) and former Parti Québécois candidate in Charlevoix.

20. "Pour nous, *voulez-vous vous séparer du Canada?* c'était cela, la question. (La question de M. Parizeau) était essentiellement la même qu'on avait posée en 1980, même si la question de M. Lévesque avait trente-six mots, sans aucune référence à la souveraineté, à la séparation ou à la création d'un pays souverain."

21. "Nous, on avait dit, en 1980: Voulez-vous vous séparer, oui ou non? C'était aussi simple que ça. Le monde a répondu non à 59% contre 41% parce qu'ils avaient compris cette question-là. Il est évident qu'en 1995, c'était encore notre stratégie: créer, par le biais de nos porte-parole, de notre campagne, de notre publicité, cette même question dans l'esprit de l'électeur."

22. *The Gazette*, September 8, 1995.

23. "La question n'était pas aussi claire que je l'aurais voulu, parce qu'elle faisait allusion à un projet de loi et à une entente. Mais nous nous sommes assurés au maximum de la connaissance de cette entente et de ce projet de loi en les envoyant à tous les citoyens."

24. "On était prêts sur le plan de l'organisation, mais, sur le plan politique, c'était autre chose. On savait qu'on avait affaire à deux personnalités, M. Bouchard et M. Parizeau. Il fallait se laisser distraire le moins possible par l'actualité. Sur le plan de l'organisation, l'actualité sert à mobiliser les gens, mais on évite l'actualité quand ça ne fait pas notre affaire. (…) Il y avait, je ne dirais pas une rivalité, mais une certaine compétition entre elles. (…) l'apport a été essentiellement celui de son chef, pour l'aspect de la promotion. Sur le plan de l'organisation, cela n'a pas apporté d'eau au moulin, nulle part sur le terrain. En tout cas, on ne l'a pas senti!"

25. *La Presse*, September 14, 1995.

26. *La Presse*, September 15, 1995.

27. Mike Keane, born in Winnipeg, learned to play hockey in Moose Jaw before signing a contract with the Canadiens in 1985. A middling scorer, but a feisty, courageous player, he was traded along with Patrick Roy for Jocelyn Thibault, Martin Rucinsky and Andrei Kovalenko.

28. Despite Daniel Johnson's denials, the document indeed came from his party. It was the QLP's constitutional affairs committee, headed by MP Maurice Richard, that was behind the document. This committee, made up of about fifteen people, examined every possible avenue to bring Quebec to sign the 1982 Constitution. The committee was in the midst of a period of reflection when Jean Bédard received the document, which was in fact a progress report. His secretary was a young man from the youth commission who later left the party's ranks. "To have written the document that was given to Jean Bédard," declared Maurice Richard eight years later, "the author would absolutely have had to have been present at our meetings. There was nothing official about this document, and it did not represent the committee's unanimous opinion, but it was a remarkable rendering of the leanings that had been expressed by those present. It was certainly not fabricated evidence put together by the YES campaign!" Source: Mario CARDINAL, *Il ne faut pas toujours croire les journalistes* (You can't believe everything reporters say), Montreal: Bayard Canada, 2005, p.87.

29. Richard LE HIR, *La prochaine étape, le défi de la légitimité. Solutions uniques pour une société plus qu'unique* (The next step: the challenge of legitimacy. Unique solutions for a society that is more than unique). Montreal: Les Éditions Stanké, 1997, p.107.

30. Claude LAMONDE, Pierre RENAUD, *L'état des finances publiques du Québec dans l'hypothèse de son accession à la souveraineté. Étude préparée par INRS-Urbanisation* (The state of government finance in Quebec in the event the province should attain sovereignty. A Study undertaken by *INRS-Urbanisation*), August 1995, p. 66.

31. "Deficit? 8 billion PQ says," *The Gazette*, September 8, 1995.

32. The INRS, dedicated to advanced education and research, is connected to the *Université du Québec*. In 2003, the INRS budget was $90 million, their research fund, more than $50 million. The institute counts four research centres: Environment, Energy and Telecommunications, Health and Urban Development, Culture and Society. Its academic personnel are made up of approximately 150 professors and researchers and some 500 students.

33. Georges MATHEWS, "Le mur des finances publiques. Un référendum en fin de mandat aurait été infiniment préférable." (The wall of government finance. An end-of-term referendum would have been so much better), *Le Devoir*, September 16, 1995.

34. Claude PICHER, "Les finances publiques d'un Québec indépendant" (Government finance in an independent Quebec), *La Presse*, October 21, 1995.

35. Alain DUBUC, "Le menteur" (The liar), *La Presse*, October 7, 1995.

36. Michel VENNE, "Québec a refusé trois études de l'INRS" (Quebec City rejected three *INRS* studies), *Le Devoir*, September 20, 1995.

37. Pierre Lamonde is unrelated to Claude Lamonde, the actuary who prepared the study in collaboration with Pierre Renaud.

38. Philippe CANTIN, "Québec avait des réserves. Les objections du gouvernement ont retardé la publication de trois études, dit l'INRS" (Quebec City had reservations. Government objections delayed publication of three studies, says INRS), *La Presse*, September 20, 1995.

39. FRASER INSTITUTE, *The Public Debt of an Independent Quebec*, October 5, 1995.

40. This was the same organization, known for its conservatism that, on the very day that Jean Campeau submitted his first budget, on 9 May 1995, showed Quebec's share of the national debt at $143 billion. The study, entitled *The Public Debt of an Independent Quebec*, thus came up with a figure that exceeded by $40 billion the estimates of the Bélanger-Campeau Commission in 1991, but was $20 billion less than the estimates of Claude Lamonde and Jacques Bolduc in their study *Le partage des actifs et des passifs du gouvernement du Canada* (Sharing the assets and liabilities of the Canadian government). But this did not prevent Jacques Parizeau from raising his arms to the sky and crying out: "People have been spilling ink on The Four Horsemen of the Apocalypse for 2000 years. I imagine The Horseman of the Apocalypse from the Fraser Institute will not last as long. This is fast becoming a display of utter madness. No more, please, the yard is full!"

41. Annual Report of the Quebec Auditor General for the Fiscal Year 1995–1996, Appendix A: *Rapport d'enquête (Secrétariat à la restructuration)* (Investigation report: Restructuring secretariat), November 29, 1995.

42. Le Hir would pay the price soon after the referendum. He was forced to resign from the caucus of the Parti Québécois in December and had to sit as an independent MP. In 1998, Richard Le Hir affirmed his federalist faith and, four years later, was appointed to head the Shipping Federation of Canada. As for Claude Lafrance, found guilty in 1999 of breach of trust and defrauding the government to the tune of $337,600, he was sentenced to a year-and-a-half of prison, but the Court of Appeal allowed him to serve his sentence through community service. As for Pierre Campeau, he left public service a few months after the referendum was held. Source: DUCHESNE, *op. cit.*, p. 456, note 46.

43. "Je n'avais pas les moyens de voyager autrement."

44. "Et là a commencé le fameux discours du passeport, qui a duré jusqu'au référendum. Après, je n'ai jamais retrouvé le mien. Quand, plus tard, une secrétaire de mon bureau a appelé Passeport Canada (pour le remplacer), une dame a dit: ' tes-vous sûre que M. Charest ne l'a pas laissé sur un podium?'"

45. Since the death of Marshall Tito in 1980, Yugoslavia had been breaking up into smaller pieces, marked, starting in January 1991, by unilateral proclamations of independence, first by Macedonia, then, successively, Croatia, Slovenia and Bosnia-Herzegovina. Whereupon followed a period of instability punctuated by serious military engagements that necessitated bringing in the United Nations peacekeeping forces. As the referendum campaign was becoming a reality in Quebec, the presidents of Bosnia, Serbia and Croatia were negotiating with difficulty towards, finally, after three weeks, signing an accord known as the Dayton Accord.

46. Michel Bélanger was one of the technocrats who contributed to making Quebec a modern nation during the Quiet Revolution, in particular as deputy minister of Natural Resources. The first francophone to preside over the Montreal Stock Exchange, in 1973, he organized the merger of the Provincial Bank and the National Bank of Canada, to create the National Bank in 1979, of which he would be the first president. By request from Robert Bourassa, he co-presided over the Bélanger-Campeau Commission set up following the failure of the Lake Meech accord, to make recommendations on the future of Quebec. He died in 1997.

47. *Le Devoir*, September 22, 1995.

48. *Journal de Montréal*, September 22, 1995.

49. *Journal de Montréal*, September 23, 1995.

50. *Le Devoir*, September 19, 1995.

51. *Le Devoir*, September 20, 1995.

52. *The Ottawa Citizen*, September 22, 1995.

53. "Cela me paraissait une question de justice un peu élémentaire. Dans beaucoup de petites villes ou de régions rurales du Québec, une fille a décidé d'aller travailler pour le fédéral, au bureau de poste, et une autre, de la même famille, a décidé d'aller travailler au palais de justice. Celle qui travaille au bureau de poste perdrait son emploi et l'autre le garderait. Il y a quelque chose de pas correct là-dedans. Alors, je disais: il va y avoir de toute façon un bureau de poste dans la ville en question. Alors, bien sûr, Madame, vous pouvez garder votre emploi…"

54. "Je lui ai annoncé séance tenante que, si j'étais questionné là-dessus, je ne ferais peut-être pas exprès pour mettre le trouble, mais que je dirais le contraire! (…) Cela a été un point de divergence entre nous et je pense que M. Bouchard était assez de mon avis. Cela a eu un impact sur le résultat du référendum."

55. "Cela ne m'a pas fait gagner une voix dans l'Outaouais, mais cela m'en a fait perdre dans la ville de Québec, où les fonctionnaires se sont dit qu'ils allaient perdre leur emploi à cause de ça. Cela s'appelle une erreur, en politique. Oui, une erreur."

56. The Créatec survey was commissioned by the NO committee, the Compas survey by the Financial Post, and the Saguenay–Lac-Saint-Jean survey was performed by Pécus for *Progrès-Dimanche*.

57. *The Gazette*, September 24, 1995.

58. "Une phrase malheureuse."

59. "Une déclaration qui a eu un impact dans les médias. Je pense que la population reconnaissait qu'il y avait une certaine arrogance, une agressivité. Et les Québécois, même s'ils penchaient du côté du NON à ce moment-là, (se sont souvenus) de l'échec de Meech, de l'échec de Charlottetown, (ils avaient) le sentiment que le Québec n'avait pas été respecté. (La déclaration de Garcia) a donné l'impression que cette absence de respect se reflétait à nouveau dans le camp du NON. Elle a en quelque sorte stoppé le *momentum* qu'on avait à cette période-là."

60. "On a, je dirais, atteint notre plancher. À partir du moment de la fameuse déclaration de M. Garcia, je sens que s'installe une tendance inverse."

61. *La Presse*, September 30, 1995.

62. William F. SHAW, Lionel ALBERT, *Partition: The Price of Quebec Independence*. Montreal: Thornhill Publishing, 1980.

63. *The Gazette*, September 29, 1995.

64. BLANCHARD, *op. cit.*, p. 224.

65. *Ibid.*, p. 226.

66. *Ibid.*, p. 229.

67. Survey by CROP-TVA-*La Presse-Toronto Star*, the results of which were published on Saturday, September 30.

CHAPTER 7

1. "Quand on est le chef du NON, on a, premièrement, à mettre de l'avant les arguments qui démontrent à nos concitoyens pourquoi voter OUI n'est pas avantageux, puis, deuxièmement, on incarne par définition, par choix, par notre conviction, l'appartenance canadienne des Québécois. (…) Il ne s'agit pas d'être pour ou contre les politiques que le gouvernement canadien du jour peut représenter, mais d'exprimer la défense des intérêts du Québec avec un programme de gouvernement qui est fédéraliste. (…) Les autres membres de la coalition, y compris le Parti Égalité que la loi nous forçait à prendre avec nous, arrivent carrément avec toutes sortes d'autres arguments qui n'ont rien à voir avec la vision que nous, du Parti libéral du Québec, avions des Québécois en tant que Canadiens. Ça n'avait rien à voir. C'est ça, la vraie difficulté pour le chef du NON, d'être le chef d'une coalition de gens qui sont à peu près partout, dans le portrait non souverainiste."

2. "La question fondamentale, c'est en 1980 que c'est arrivé, pas en 1995. En 1980, il y avait eu un débat au Cabinet. Beaucoup de ministres disaient que le Canada était indivisible. (Mais) on va miser sur la démocratie. Si les gens, clairement, pas sur des questions ambiguës, puis à 50% plus un, ne veulent pas rester au Canada, alors, on acceptera. En 1995, il était trop tard pour dire: on ne participe pas! Mais on avait des réserves. S'il y avait eu un vote positif, ça aurait donné une arme considérable à ceux qui voulaient faire la séparation, même s'ils n'ont jamais écrit le mot 'séparation' dans la question."

3. "Eux (les souverainistes), ils faisaient leurs règles. Moi, je dis que j'avais le droit de faire mes propres règles. J'étais premier ministre du Canada, le pays avait le droit de parler. (Car) ça aurait eu des conséquences pour le reste du Canada. (…) Il y avait toute cette notion, qui avait été débattue, de la partition même du Québec. Le Québec de 1763, c'était pas mal plus petit que le Québec d'aujourd'hui. Alors, il y avait beaucoup d'espace pour une bonne discussion, qui aurait été intéressante. Mais je suis bien content de ne pas l'avoir eue!"

4. "Ça veut dire quoi, un référendum? C'est comme un ouvrier. J'étais avocat de syndicat quand j'ai commencé dans la vie publique. Dans des assemblées de syndicats, quand le gars vote pour la grève, ce n'est pas qu'il veut la grève. Il veut qu'on se serve du mandat de grève pour avoir une augmentation de salaire ou de meilleures conditions de travail. Le désir profond, c'est d'avoir un bon contrat. Alors, les gens, qui voyaient le vote pour le OUI comme un mandat de négocier, étaient un peu dans cet esprit-là. Ils voulaient donner un instrument au gouvernement du Québec pour faire plus de pression afin d'obtenir un certain nombre de choses qui, parfois, étaient plus ou moins définies."

5. In Quebec, before the education reform of the 1960s, a school offering a four-year secondary education and a four-year post-secondary program leading to a BA with the curriculum emphasizing classics, literature, philosophy and religion.

6. Jean Chrétien granted an interview to Radio-Canada in both French and English. It was in English that he spoke of his father's interest in politics.

7. "J'ai choisi Ottawa parce que mon comté est devenu ouvert au fédéral. J'aimais la politique. Que ce soit au fédéral ou au provincial, ça ne me dérangeait pas beaucoup."

8. CHRÉTIEN, *op. cit.*, p. 32. The information in this paragraph, for the most part, comes from the same source.

9. This is Chrétiens's answer in the English interview. However, when interviewed in French, his answer was slightly different: "*Ça ne veut pas dire que j'étais pour la séparation. Je n'ai jamais été dans cet esprit-là. Mais j'étais assez fier d'être Français pour que, quand on est collectivement malhereux, je l'étais moi aussi.*" ("That doesn't mean that I was for separation. I was never in that frame of mind. But I was proud enough of being French that, when we were collectively unhappy, so was I.")

10. Marcel Chaput was a chemist employed by the federal government. After being fired in 1961, he published *Pourquoi je suis un séparatiste* (published in translation as *Why I am a Separatist*. Toronto: Ryerson Press, 1962). The same year, he, André d'Allemagne and some other *indépendantistes* founded the *Rassemblement pour l'indépendance nationale* (*RIN*, Coalition for national independence) and became the organization's vice-president. The following year, he left the RIN to found his own political party, the *Parti républicain du Québec* (Quebec republican party). Despite his efforts and a hunger strike lasting several days, in 1963, he was unable to rally the sovereignists to his cause, and his party was dissolved in 1964.

11. This part of the interview was conducted in English.

12. "C'est un pays exemplaire. À cause de sa diversité, de sa tolérance, on n'a pas de problèmes de religion, on n'a pas vraiment de querelles linguistiques ingérables, on a toujours trouvé les bonnes solutions… (…) Quand vous allez aux Nations unies, c'est très plaisant de voir votre drapeau, là, mais il faut fouiller pour le trouver. Il y en a beaucoup. Il y a des pays qui ont 35 000 habitants et qui ont des drapeaux! Je me rappelle la photo du 50e anniversaire des Nations unies; ils n'ont jamais été capables de reconnaître tout le monde! On était tous des chefs d'État… Alors, il faut placer ça en perspective. J'ai toujours pensé que, si nous sommes encore francophones, c'est parce que le Canada existe. Mon père a passé sa jeunesse à Manchester, au New Hampshire. S'il était resté là, je serais probablement un anglophone aujourd'hui!"

13. "Bien sûr que le côté émotif était important, mais, ceux qui disent ça, c'est parce qu'ils ont vécu 1980. C'est sûr que c'était émotif: le drapeau... Et, même à l'époque, on parlait des Rocheuses. Mais il fallait être réaliste. S'il y avait eu un référendum sur la souveraineté trois jours ou trois semaines après l'échec du lac Meech, ça passait! Il ne fallait pas oublier ça. L'échec de Charlottetown, les Québécois ont senti qu'ils y avaient été marginalisés. On est en 1995 (pas en 1980), on sort d'une récession, la deuxième en quinze ans, notre dollar plonge, on a deux échecs constitutionnels, on a failli flirter avec la souveraineté... Je pense que l'émotion, là, il faut aller la chercher loin! C'est bon pour le vote fédéraliste inconditionnel, mais ça ne fait rien pour le vote fédéraliste nationaliste. Puis ce vote-là, il faut faire appel à la raison (pour aller le chercher), pas juste à l'émotivité. C'est peut-être un peu trop facile de dire qu'il fallait amener de l'émotivité, c'est perdre de vue ce qui s'est passé entre 1980 et 1995. Il n'y avait rien dans la réforme du fédéralisme qui pouvait dire à des jeunes, qui n'avaient pas voté en 1980: Allons-y! Meech et Charlottetown étaient trop récents."

14. "J'ai failli venir!"

15. "Je ne l'ai pas vraiment côtoyé. Ce n'est pas quelqu'un que je connaissais personnellement et avec qui j'avais échangé de quelque façon."

16. "Il y avait des gens qui étaient frustrés de ne pouvoir participer (à la campagne) parce que le groupe du NON avait décidé qu'il ne voulait pas avoir de gens de l'extérieur. C'était leur pays qui était en jeu et ils ne pouvaient rien faire. Je les comprends."

17. Jane Stewart, a human resources consultant, was elected for the first time in 1993. At the time of the referendum, she was caucus chair. Three months later, she would become minister of national revenue. Re-elected in 1997, she was appointed to the Department of Indian and Northern Affairs. In August 1999, Jean Chrétien assigned her the Human Resources Development portfolio. She was elected again in October 2000 and kept the same duties in the Cabinet, despite a job grants scandal that implicated her department.

18. "Il y en a qui se sont mis à penser à toutes sortes de scénarios. Il y en avait qui en proposaient des vertes et des pas mûres, mais on les laissait de côté. Quand vous êtes le chef, c'est vous qui décidez. (...) Envoyer...? Voyons donc! Il y a des gars qui ont besoin de noircir du papier. Ils (les militaires) n'ont jamais parlé de ça avec moi. Je n'ai pas parlé de ça avec le ministre de la Défense de l'époque. Je suis sûr que non. Si, en tout cas, on m'en a parlé, ça ne m'a pas frappé."

19. This part of the interview was conducted in English.

20. "Lorsque M. Chrétien a fait des grandes manifestations, je pense à Shawinigan, on perdait des points dans les sondages. Il n'était pas notre meilleur joueur. (...) J'étais d'accord pour une raison fort simple. C'était difficile de voir dans la configuration de la campagne quelle pouvait être la contribution de gens qui arrivaient de l'extérieur. Il fallait que ce soit une affaire entre Québécois parce que ça concernait les Québécois. Si on avait donné l'impression aux Québécois qu'il y avait quelqu'un de l'extérieur qui tentait de diriger leur choix, je pense que ça aurait eu l'effet inverse."

21. "Le Parti libéral du Québec est distinct du Parti libéral du Canada. Et il faut se rappeler que Daniel Johnson est d'une famille conservatrice. Alors, il pouvait être libéral à Québec, mais, à Ottawa, il était plus l'allié des conservateurs."

22. "Je pense bien que M. Chrétien et M. Johnson étaient condamnés à s'entendre, mais cela ne leur était pas absolument naturel de collaborer. J'ai toujours senti que, pour le Parti libéral du Québec, c'était un référendum québécois. C'était difficile pour eux de dire à Chrétien: 'Vous, vous n'êtes pas un Québécois du tout!' On ne voulait pas la présence des libéraux fédéraux dans la campagne. On la voulait la plus discrète possible. (...) Il a fallu trouver des formules et des ententes ad hoc de jour en jour pour finalement bien assurer la présence des fédéraux dans le comité du NON. Je ne dis pas qu'on ne s'est pas chicanés. On ne s'est pas dit de gros mots, mais on sentait que nous étions reçus à la table avec une certaine réticence. Je l'ai toujours sentie."

23. "Si le Parti libéral du Canada décide que c'est madame X ou monsieur Y qui va être à tel rassemblement, qui va parler en leur nom comme membre de la coalition, sous le parapluie du NON, qu'il le fasse! Je n'ai

pas de raisons de croire que Mme Robillard n'a pas fait un excellent travail quand elle a eu l'occasion de le faire. Ce n'était pas à nous, du PLQ, de décider qui était là pour le PLC. Je dirais même, bien au contraire!"

24. "Le style de Mme Robillard n'était pas aussi percutant que le style de M. Chrétien en 1980. En 1980, Chrétien n'était pas impopulaire. Donc, avec son style fougueux, coloré, il était vraiment un atout assez important. Mme Robillard a un style beaucoup plus réservé, elle n'avait pas une ascendance sur la scène fédérale, elle était une personne qui avait *gradué* du côté provincial."

25. "Comme orateur, sur le plan de son charisme, M. Charest était un de ceux qui avaient résisté à la vague libérale de 1993, au Québec en particulier. Il avait cette fraîcheur du politicien jeune, qui avait quasiment gagné la course au leadership conservateur contre Kim Campbell. Et il avait le sens de l'image, de la caricature, (souvenez-vous du) fameux passeport. Donc, Mme Robillard s'est sentie un petit peu coincée. Pour nous qui attachions de l'importance au volet des communications, c'était clair que le style de Mme Robillard n'attirait pas autant que celui de M. Charest."

26. *La Presse*, September 13, 1995.

27. "Manning n'a pas été invité. Il a demandé de participer (à la campagne). On lui a fait comprendre que c'était une affaire de Québécois et que, s'il avait à cœur la réussite de notre objectif, ce serait mieux pour tout le monde qu'il ne s'en mêle pas. Cela a tenu jusqu'au bout. Est-ce qu'il en a été frustré? Oui, sûrement. Mais il a compris qu'au Québec, il faisait un peu plus partie du problème que de la solution."

28. *Le Devoir*, September 29, 1995.

29. *The Gazette*, September 13, 1995.

30. *Toronto Star*, October 13, 1995.

31. *Le Devoir*, October 13, 1995.

32. *Ibid.*

33. "La classe politique canadienne, malheureusement, n'avait pas évolué vers une plus grande compréhension de la réalité du Québec. M. Manning niait l'existence d'une société distincte, majoritaire et francophone. Par ailleurs, on avait suffisamment de ressources: les députés du fédéral, les députés du provincial, le chef conservateur Charest, le chef libéral Johnson, M. Chrétien dans des interventions bien planifiées et Mme Robillard. On n'avait pas besoin de M. Manning et d'autres qui se sont opposés non seulement à Meech, mais à Charlottetown. Ça n'aidait pas, ça!"

34. Pietro Perrino had been moving in Liberal government circles in both Ottawa and Quebec for some time. As early as 1987, he was political advisor to Robert Bourassa on youth issues. He subsequently acted as chief of staff and special advisor to the staff of the Liberal opposition leader until 1999. We find him at the head of Paul Martin's team in Quebec, alongside federal and provincial Liberals, but this did not prevent him from earning an MBA in 2001. When Jean Charest's government asked Louis Roquet to leave in 2004, Pietro Perrino was appointed to the board of directors of the *Société des Alcools du Québec* (SAQ—Quebec Liquor Board).

35. From 1993 to 2002, Barry Lowenkron worked in various capacities for US intelligence services, including a stint at the CIA as special assistant to the director. At the time of Parizeau's visit to Washington, he was director of European Security Affairs on the National Security Council. A specialist in national security and intelligence, he teaches at Johns Hopkins University.

36. "À un moment donné, la personne du National Security Council, qui est l'expression de la Maison Blanche, tape sur la table et dit: 'Jamais on ne permettra aux *Frenchies* de vous reconnaître, on vous reconnaîtra d'abord.' Il y a eu comme un silence. C'était la doctrine Monroe." Until the early 19th century, the United States and Europe maintained tense economic and military relations. Spain had colonies in the Americas, had lost them one by one in Republican revolutions, but hoped to get them back. The United States cast an approving eye on these nascent republics and extended diplomatic recognition in 1822. France, Russia, Austria and Prussia formed the Holy Alliance, leading to fears in the US government that all of Europe would back Catholic Spain in its plans to reconquer its former colonies. Russia, which already had trading posts in California, also had colonization designs on the Oregon Territory, which it

wished to annex to Alaska, still a Russian territory. England wanted to come to the aid of the United States, but Secretary of State John Quincy Adams considered that this dispute was a matter for the United States and the United States only. On December 2, 1823, then President James Monroe laid out the foreign policy of the United States, inspired by Quincy Adams. He denounced any European intervention on North American soil. This also meant that Washington would henceforth consider the Americas—from the North Pole to Tierra del Fuego—as its back yard. "We owe it, therefore, to candor and to the amicable relations existing between the United States and (European) powers to declare that we should consider any attempt on their part to extend their system to any portion of this hemisphere as dangerous to our peace and safety," said Monroe (http://www.theglitteringeye.com/archives/000981.html). In exchange, the United States promised not to intervene in Europe. This isolationist policy was to persist until 1917, when the United States decided to take part in World War I. But they would continue to concern themselves with everything that went on in the three Americas, and it was on this sense of "ownership" that Jacques Parizeau meant to draw.

37. "Là, on tombe sur quelqu'un qui connaît le dossier bien mieux que je l'aurais imaginé. Il aborde tout de suite, de front, la question suivante: vous voulez que la France vous reconnaisse? Mais vous indiquez qu'on devrait vous reconnaître dès que vous aurez gagné le référendum. Un référendum, M. Parizeau, ce n'est même pas une intention. C'est, au mieux, une autorisation. Il faut que vous fassiez un geste qui engage le gouvernement du Québec. Une fois que vous aurez fait ce geste, la France peut vous reconnaître. Votre projet, dans l'état où il est, ne peut pas amener une reconnaissance par la France d'un Québec indépendant."

38. Benoît Bouchard is an education professional and a school administrator. He was a Conservative MP for the Roberval riding in 1984 and filled a variety of posts in Brian Mulroney's government; he served as secretary of state, then minister of employment and immigration, transport, industry, and health, before being appointed ambassador to Paris in 1993, just before the Liberal party came to power. Subsequently, he served as chairman of the Transportation Safety Board.

39. "J'ai évité d'exiger que nous nous voyions à l'ambassade. Pour ne pas faire d'histoire, nous sommes allés à la Délégation du Québec. (…) M. Michaud me dit: 'J'ai lu votre déclaration dans les journaux et je ne suis pas d'accord avec vous que le Canada développe autant d'énergie sur la question de la culture.' J'ai répondu: 'Aussi longtemps que le Québec fera partie du Canada, l'ambassade du Canada à Paris va continuer de s'occuper des artistes québécois qui viennent à Paris, et de la culture en général.' À ce moment, c'est M. Parizeau qui a répliqué en disant: 'Monsieur l'Ambassadeur, je suis venu à Paris pour ça!' J'ai répondu: 'J'en suis très heureux, Monsieur le Premier ministre, je n'ai pas soulevé la question moi-même.'"

40. "J'ai répondu oui, mais M. Séguin est un *loose canon*, qu'on a traduit en France par 'électron libre.' Évidemment, j'ai fait deux erreurs. La première étant d'utiliser un mot d'une autre langue, ce qui ne se fait pas dans ce genre d'interview. La seconde étant de l'avoir dit. Le problème n'était pas de le croire, je le crois toujours, mais de le dire. Un ambassadeur ne dit pas ces choses-là. Les éditorialistes du Québec étaient furieux, ceux du *Toronto Star* et du *Globe and Mail*, dithyrambiques. Il n'en a pas été question dans les journaux français."

41. Incident related in DUCHESNE, *op. cit.*, p. 343.

42. DUCHESNE, *op. cit*, p. 344.

43. "M. Chirac a dit, à ce moment-là, que, depuis le référendum de 1980, il avait beaucoup réfléchi et qu'il en était venu à la conclusion que le fait français était mieux protégé par l'appartenance du Québec au Canada que par la séparation du Québec. Ça m'a rassuré. Je me suis dit: 'Chirac sera toujours respectueux de la décision que les Québécois prendront, mais jamais il n'interviendra dans le débat en cours pour soutenir le camp souverainiste.'"

44. "J'étais furieux. J'ai communiqué avec le Quai d'Orsay pour leur faire observer que je ne trouvais pas ça normal. On m'a répondu, de cette façon que les Français vous répondent parfois: 'Monsieur l'Ambassadeur, nous n'avons pas à dire au maire de Paris quels sont les drapeaux qui doivent flotter au-dessus de l'hôtel de ville.' In other words, 'we mind our business, mind your own business.'" The last sentence is in English in the interview granted to CBC.

45. Heard on the program *Téléjournal* on Radio-Canada, on January 26, 1995, related in DUCHESNE, *op. cit.*, p. 345.

46. 'Pendant toutes ces années, Mitterrand n'aimait pas l'idée de la souveraineté du Québec. Mais c'est comme s'il prenait une police d'assurance: tout à coup qu'ils y arriveraient! (se dit-il). Et, très tôt, Mitterrand va m'ouvrir sa porte. En France, quand vous avez accès au président, vous avez accès à tout le reste. Je me rends compte cependant qu'il y a un certain blocage du côté du Quai d'Orsay. Alors, à un moment donné, Mitterrand me propose: 'Désignez-moi quelqu'un qui servira aux contacts entre nous deux, sans passer par la machine.'"

47. Denise Bombardier, telephone conversation, March 22, 2005.

48. "Je savais que le président Mitterrand ne prendrait pas position. J'étais présent, j'étais invité partout officiellement, même lorsque M. Parizeau s'est adressé à l'Assemblée nationale. J'étais plus ou moins mal à l'aise parce que je n'étais pas dans un environnement tellement favorable. Évidemment, il y avait de la tension, il y avait, entre les individus, une certaine hostilité, mais je ne voulais pas que ça devienne, pour la presse, l'élément important. Ça s'est bien passé!"

49. "Pendant mon voyage, j'ai eu plusieurs contacts avec les pays de la francophonie. L'important, c'est que, quand les Français se manifestent, il faut que plusieurs pays de la francophonie puissent se manifester dans son sillage dans les jours qui suivent."

50. "La guerre civile américaine n'est pas si ancienne et les Américains se souviennent de l'horrible résultat de cette guerre. C'est le conflit le plus sanglant de leur histoire. Plus de 500 000 morts. Pour eux, toute situation, qui ressemble un peu à ce qu'ils ont vécu avant la guerre civile, leur fait peur, crée beaucoup d'émotions et de traumatismes. Je le vivais chaque semaine. Chaque fois que je faisais un discours aux États-Unis, je voyais toujours des visages angoissés quand cette question était abordée. Je pouvais voir leur cheminement intellectuel et les souvenirs horribles que cela leur rappelait. Donc, au départ, une terre infertile pour les thèses d'indépendance."

51. Interview conducted in English.

52. François Bujon de l'Estang cut his foreign policy teeth as a diplomatic advisor to General de Gaulle, when de Gaulle was President of the Republic. In 1969, he was sent to Washington as First Secretary. When there was a government change in France, he became an industrialist specializing in uranium production and the development of nuclear fuel. He returned to the diplomatic world in 1986 and, after three years as ambassador to Mexico, he performed the same duties in Ottawa from 1989 until 1991. He had considerable influence at the French foreign affairs ministry on all matters Canadian. "Anything coming out of Quai (d'Orsay) these days, highly influenced by Ambassador Bujon de l'Estang, is pro-federalist," wrote Louise Beaudoin, Quebec minister of intergovernmental affairs at the time (excerpted from a memo from Louise Beaudoin to Jacques Parizeau, entitled *Séjour à Paris, janvier 91* (Stay in Paris, January '91). Archives of Jacques Parizeau. Cited in DUCHESNE, *op. cit.*, p. 258).

53. This part of the interview was conducted in English.

54. When the Parti Québécois came to power, Quebec had 430 representatives in foreign lands, about a hundred of these in the United States—in New York City, where the General Delegation is located, and in Atlanta, Boston, Chicago, Los Angeles and Washington. But the Washington office had only three people—and it was a tourism bureau. In principle, the advisor on American national affairs reports to the General Delegation and would therefore be in New York City. But because of the strategic importance of Washington, it was Anne Legaré, advisor on American national affairs, who acted as head of mission; in a word, she was in charge of the bureau. Anne Legaré, who assumed leadership of a committee on international relations established in 1991 by Jacques Parizeau, specializes in political sociology and teaches at the department of political science at UQAM.

55. JAMES BLANCHARD, *Behind the Embassy Door, Canada, Clinton and Quebec*. Toronto: McClelland & Stewart, 1998.

56. "(M)any Americans believe that English-speaking Canadians only caused trouble by letting the French-speaking Canadians get more and more militant about their language. They would argue it was probably a mistake two hundred years ago to encourage the French colonists to stick to their language in North America after the British Conquest. It created a division that probably needn't have occurred." *Ibid.*, p. 75.

57. "On sait qu'on a un problème avec l'ambassadeur Blanchard. Il est devenu presque le seul conseiller de poids sur la question canadienne et québécoise. Et on sait ce qu'il pense—il l'a écrit dans son livre—que c'était une erreur pour les colons britanniques d'avoir laissé les Québécois parler français. Donc, on part avec un dinosaure."

58. "Il est entendu qu'aucun nouveau pays ne pourra devenir membre de l'ALÉNA sans que les membres fondateurs puissent poser des conditions. Mais l'article en question du traité n'indique pas de quelles conditions il s'agit, et, ça, c'est très embêtant. On comprend très bien qu'il s'agit de conditions quant à l'économie de marché, les règlements juridiques des conflits commerciaux... Mais, comme ce n'est pas très bien défini, il n'y a rien qui pourrait empêcher qu'une de ces *docking clauses* soit, je ne sais pas, la protection des anglophones au Québec. On a là comme un os, on a comme un problème."

59. *Treaties, Executive Agreements, and the Fast Track*, World Trade Reports, 1999, http://www.washingtontradereports.com/treaty.html.

60. *La Presse*, February 2, 1995.

61. Professor Joseph Jockel is head of Canadian Studies at St. Lawrence University in Canton, New York, and Senior Fellow of the Americas Program at the Center for Strategic and International Studies. Excerpts of the Jockel report were taken from: Sylviane TRAMIER, *"L'adhésion aux organismes internationaux? Rien d'automatique, rien d'insurmontable"* (Membership in international organizations? Not a given, not unheard of), *Le Devoir*, February 10, 1995.

62. "Le Mexique, en étant accepté dans l'ALÉNA, avait l'impression, comme dit le proverbe polonais, d'avoir attrapé le petit Jésus par les pieds. Et tout ce qui pouvait provoquer un peu de gêne et, à plus forte raison, d'indignation à Ottawa, était, pour les Mexicains, tabou. Et le principal tabou, c'était un Québec souverain. Alors, ils étaient vraiment de très mauvaise compagnie."

63. "... faire passer les souverainistes québécois comme des affreux ou pour des gens qui ont le couteau entre les dents (...). Ils étaient un peu embêtés, ils manifestaient beaucoup de mauvaise humeur en privé, disaient peu de chose en public."

64. This information and the information that follows are drawn from a document drawn up by the Privy Council, in May 1995, and obtained through the Canadian Access to Information Act. This document is entitled *Fiches d'information: la séparation du Québec sur la scène internationale* (Information Files: The Effect of Quebec's Separation in the International Arena).

65. *An Act respecting the Société de radio-télévision du Québec* founded Radio-Québec in 1969. It was another law, *An Act respecting the Société de télédiffusion du Québec*, adopted in December 1996, that is, after the referendum, that founded Télé-Québec, superseding Radio-Québec.

66. *La Presse*, September 29, 1995.

67. "Clairement, l'adversaire était devenu Lucien Bouchard. Il voulait en découdre avec Jean Chrétien. Sa tête de Turc, c'était Chrétien. Nous, les libéraux du Québec, il nous rejetait du revers de la main avec toutes sortes d'insinuations sur notre identité québécoise. Chaque fois qu'on parlait de débat, c'était un non catégorique du côté du OUI, sauf si Lucien Bouchard pouvait débattre avec Jean Chrétien."

CHAPTER 8

1. Singer Pauline Julien, poet Gaston Miron, sculptor Armand Vaillancourt, actors like Hélène Loiselle and Jean-Claude Germain, comic Jean-Guy Moreau, journalist Ariane Émond, novelist Yves Beauchemin and many others, some 200 in all, came one after the other to rally the crowd of 150 to 200 people who gathered daily at noontime: *La Presse*, October 13, 1995.

2. "C'était un espace qui n'avait pas de limite, un espace où tout pouvait se dire, tout pouvait se faire. Il y avait des gens qui venaient là, qui avaient un point de vue superintellectuel, puis il y avait des gens qui étaient là pour des préoccupations philosophiques, artistiques ou culturelles… Il y avait un micro, ouvert presque en permanence, pour que tout le monde puisse venir s'exprimer. C'était beau à voir. (…) D'un ensemble qui était cohérent, dit-elle, qui avait des bases, des fondements, des idées."

3. Published by Les Éditions Stanké, Montreal in 1995. Gilles Vigneault, Victor Lévy-Beaulieu, Michel Garneau, Pierre Falardeau, Andrée Ferretti, Raôul Duguay, Louis Caron, Yolande Villemaire, Claude Beausoleil, Paul Chamberland, Jean-Claude Germain, Pierre Vadeboncoeur, Marc Chabot. Francine Allard, Denyse Boucher, Hélène Pedneault, Hélène Pelletier-Baillargeon and Marie-Andrée Beaudet were among the authors of these letters, which, for some, were a vibrant call to solidarity and a testimony to an open spirit towards all Quebecers in their diverse cultural communities. "Listen to our story, and it will be yours," wrote poet Beausoleil.

4. Program *Le Point*, Radio-Canada, October 4, 1995.

5. Denis MONIÈRE, Jean H. GUAY, *La bataille du Québec, Troisième épisode: Trente jours qui ébranlent le Canada* (The battle of Quebec, third episode: thirty days that shook Canada). Montreal: Fides, 1996, p. 40.

6. "Les autobus du OUI, prêts à partir" (The YES buses, ready to go), The Canadian Press.

7. *Le Devoir*, September 25, 1995.

8. "J'avais essayé de provoquer quelque chose qui était probablement trop radical pour passer, de faire accepter par M. Bouchard et M. Dumont qu'il n'y ait pas d'autobus. J'ai toujours considéré que c'est extraordinairement malsain, l'atmosphère qui se dégage entre celui qui mène les opérations et les journalistes qui sont enfermés avec lui pendant des jours et des jours."

9. SOM-Environics survey done on behalf of *Le Devoir*, Radio-Canada, *Le Soleil*, *Le Droit* and *The Gazette*, published October 1, 1995.

10. *Le Journal de Montréal*, October 3, 1995.

11. "On vivait aussi pour notre peau. Le lendemain du référendum, on allait revenir dans le jeu de la politique et le PQ allait être notre adversaire. On aurait à préparer une prochaine élection. (Pendant le référendum), il pouvait y avoir 2 000 personnes venues m'applaudir, il y en avait peut-être 1 800 qui étaient péquistes. Ceux-là, à la prochaine élection, ils vont dire que l'ADQ, c'est un parti de malades, puis ils vont travailler contre nous."

12. See chapter V, note 3.

13. "Il essayait de se tailler une place. Imaginez, il était seul de son parti à l'Assemblée nationale. Sa campagne, c'était son parti, dans le fond, qui la faisait, son 'DG' et quelques attachés politiques qui l'encadraient. Il n'avait pas d'organisation, ou très peu."

14. *Le Droit*, October 4, 1995.

15. *La Presse*, October 3, 1995.

16. See note 7 of this chapter.

17. *Le Devoir*, October 3, 1995.

18. *La Presse*, October 5, 1995.

19. *Le Devoir*, October 15, 1995. DRI/McGraw-Hill is a well-known consulting firm specializing in economic growth projections.

20. *La Presse*, October 4, 1995.

21. *Ibid.*

22. When Mexico signed the North American Free Trade Agreement, in January 1994, it had a tall order to fill: restructure its external debt, reduce its protectionist trade barriers, privatize several public corporations, lower the rate of inflation (interest rates had reached almost 15% in May) and, above all, reduce its deficit which had soared from 6 billion in 1989 to 15 billion in 1991 and more than 20 billion in 1993.

This deficit led observers to consider the peso overvalued, which discouraged exports and stimulated imports. In addition to the economic situation, Mexico was experiencing a climate of political instability. In Mexico, 1994 was a presidential election year. On March 23, the most popular election candidate, Luis Donaldo Colosio, was assassinated. One thing happened after another. There was a second political assassination: José Francisco Ruiz Massieu was killed in September, business people were kidnapped, there was rebellion in Chiapas. Less that one year after its entry into NAFTA, Mexico was in economic shambles. On December 20, the government resigned itself to devaluing the peso, but the Mexican currency fell 60% in relation to the U.S. dollar.

23. The next presidential election in the U.S. would take place in November 1996.

24. Source: P04024Z Oct. 95. AMCONSUL QUEBEC TO SECSTATE WASHDC PRIORITY 9853.

25. *Le Soleil*, October 4, 1995.

26. *Ibid.*

27. *Ibid.*

28. *La Presse*, October 8, 1995.

29. *The Globe and Mail*, October 6, 1995.

30. *The Vancouver Sun*, October 6, 1995.

31. *The Toronto Star*, October 6, 1995.

32. *Le Devoir*, October 5, 1995.

33. Stephen R. Kelly began his career as a journalist. After seven years in that field, he served in Zaire in the early '70s as a volunteer with the Peace Corps. He then became a civil servant and, from 1986 to 1991, occupied various posts in Washington's State Department. Earlier, he had worked in Mali, Brussels and Djakarta in Indonesia. He speaks French and Dutch, besides English. Parizeau's entourage considered him more open than his predecessor to the political realities of Quebec.

34. Source: FR AMCONSUL QUEBEC TO SECSTATE WASHDC PRIORITY 9854. SUBJECT: FLAT POLLS WORRY PQ STRATEGISTS.

35. *Ibid.*

36. Survey conducted on behalf of *Journal de Montreal* and *The Globe and Mail*.

37. The *REA* (*Régime d'épargne-action*, investment-savings plan) was created by the Lévesque government in 1979 when Jacques Parizeau was Finance minister. Its purpose was to give Quebecers an incentive to invest in those companies, which, if they met certain conditions, could issue common shares eligible for this program. In return, the investors benefited from a tax rebate up to as much as 100% and, in some cases, more.

38. *Le Soleil*, October 6, 1995.

39. *La Presse*, October 6, 1995.

40 BLANCHARD, *op. cit.*, p. 229-230.

41. E-mail correspondence with the author on September 16, 2004. E.J. Dionne, who spent fourteen years with the *New York Times*, joined *The Washington Post* in 1990 as a columnist. His ancestors are indeed from Quebec, in the Beloeil region. His maternal grandmother, Madame Patenaude, née Galipeau, migrated to the United States in 1898. On his father's side, the Dionnes and the Vincents, originally from Rivière-du-Loup, crossed the border during the great wave of emigrants headed for the cotton mills during the 1850s and '60s.

42. *Le Droit*, October 6, 1995.

43. "Les voyantes prédisent un NON massif: les predictions varient entre 67 et 80%" (Fortune-tellers predict a massive NO win, ranging from 67 to 80%), *La Presse*, October 8, 1995.

44. "Je crois que c'était au Lœws. Cela s'était fait à huis clos. M. Parizeau recevait les commentaires de ses présidents et présidentes. Ceux-ci avançaient des hypothèses, dont celle de mettre M. Bouchard en avant. Il y a eu discussion et j'ai senti, quand les gens sont sortis de la réunion, qu'on venait de régler une grosse affaire!"

45. "Ça allait très bien. Michel Vastel avait écrit: 'M. Bouchard, vous devriez sortir de là parce que vous ne réussissez pas à la Chambre des communes.' Les sondages étaient bons."

46. "Mon souvenir, c'est que l'idée est venue de Mario Dumont. Mais on a eu un signal que M. Bouchard ne voulait pas être négociateur en chef, donc on a abandonné un peu cette idée."

47. "En août, j'ai écrit une note à M. Parizeau, qui devait rencontrer M. Bouchard, en lui disant: 'Vous pourriez proposer à M. Bouchard de présider le comité d'orientation. Dans ce cas-là, il ne serait pas votre négociateur, il serait dans un rôle de juge.' Mais cela n'a pas eu de suite."

48. "On aurait pu dire qu'on allait créer le poste de président, un président peut-être désigné par l'Assemblée nationale, avec des pouvoirs importants en matière de relations internationales, donc avec le Canada, notre nation voisine. J'essayais de trouver un rôle pour M. Bouchard. Mais on savait aussi que M. Parizeau n'était pas très chaud à l'idée de lui en parler et que M. Bouchard n'était pas très chaud d'en parler non plus."

49. "Je vous dirais que, fin août, début septembre, ce n'était pas une idée sur laquelle on travaillait beaucoup."

50. "Je pense que cela l'a fait sourire plus qu'autre chose."

51. "Je lui ai dit que je croyais qu'il y avait là un potentiel. Il m'a répondu: 'Vous continuez et, quand vous aurez parachevé vos travaux, on s'en reparle.'"

52. "Quelqu'un qui a une aura comme la sienne, tu ne le fais pas jouer sur le banc, un gars comme lui, tu le mets sur la glace. Il était tellement populaire que M. Parizeau parlait d'une icône."

53. "qu'il y a là quelque chose qui est susceptible de créer ce qu'on appelle, dans le langage des sondages, une tendance."

54. See chapter VI, note 11.

55. "Je savais que mon dossier était bon, dit-il. Mais s'il m'avait dit, au terme de ma présentation, qu'il n'embarquait pas—c'était lui, le patron—j'aurais assumé… On aurait continué, pas juste moi, mais tout le monde."

56. "C'était difficile, je savais ce que ça représentait. Mais quand il faut le faire, il faut le faire!"

57. "Ce qui voulait dire: informer ceux qui doivent l'être, mais il n'y en avait pas beaucoup. Tout était basé sur l'effet de surprise."

58. *Journal de Montréal*, October 7, 1995.

59. "Ce fut un des moments les plus difficiles que j'ai vécus en politique. J'ai trouvé ça terrible de lui dire. J'en tremblais, j'étais ému. Il a écouté sans broncher. Il ne faisait que se rouler la moustache, il n'a pas dit un mot, sauf, si ma mémoire est fidèle: 'Je prends acte.'"

60. *La Presse*, October 8, 1995.

61. According to the recollections of Jean-François Lisée.

62. "C'est comme s'il y avait eu 100 000 volts dans les sièges. Les gens ont bondi pour applaudir. C'était un moment magique."

63. "À notre grande surprise, en tout cas à la mienne, il annonce que son chef négociateur sera Lucien Bouchard. Ça a été l'euphorie. Je me suis dit: 'Est-il habile! Il a réussi à dire: c'est moi qui vais décider de la forme que va prendre le rôle de Lucien Bouchard. Vous avez fait votre devoir, vous me l'avez dit.' Il est formidable!"

64. "Cela n'a pas été une décision prise en catastrophe. La Chambre des communes ajournait ses travaux pour une semaine. Il fallait que (jusque-là) M. Bouchard joue son rôle de chef de l'opposition. Il est évident qu'il avait une image publique bien meilleure que la mienne. Dans ces conditions, j'en avais discuté avec Jean Royer, c'était clair qu'il fallait une sorte de poussée additionnelle, que M. Bouchard intervienne, qu'il devienne le porteur de ballon."

65. "On comprend ce que cela veut dire. Cela veut dire être numéro un; Jacques Parizeau devient second. Je suis certaine que ce fut très, très dur pour lui. Mais, dans les réceptions qu'on faisait, dans les tournées, on voyait bien l'engouement autour de Lucien Bouchard. Jacques Parizeau voulait gagner. Alors, c'était la chose à faire. Puis il l'a fait de bon cœur. Je ne vous dis pas que cela s'est fait sans pincement à son orgueil, c'est certain. Mais il était prêt à tous les sacrifices."

66. "Je me suis dit: la campagne vient de changer. (…) Je savais que, politiquement, ce n'était pas facile de se mesurer à Lucien Bouchard. Il était très populaire, très aimé. Il avait un ascendant sur les foules. On a senti une différence immédiate dans la campagne."

67. "On ne peut pas voir venir cela. Mais on peut comprendre. Souvenons-nous comment Bernard Landry, ancien militaire, avait fait savoir, avec sa brigade légère, qu'il ne voulait pas aller aussi vite. À l'époque, on pouvait sentir que Lucien Bouchard et Landry étaient du même avis. Ils avaient tassé Parizeau. C'était donc déjà arrivé, entre guillemets, quelques mois plus tôt. Cela pouvait (encore) arriver. Mais tasser le premier ministre du Québec, alors que c'est son projet, il faut le faire! C'était assez inusité, donc imprévisible. (…) Bouchard était plus difficile à critiquer. Les chiffres n'avaient pas d'importance pour lui, l'avenir économique du Québec, les finances publiques, cela n'avait absolument aucune importance. Son discours était un discours nationaliste, émotif, traditionnel."

68. "Cela représentait quasiment un coup d'État. Je n'aurais pas pensé que M. Bouchard aurait pu tasser M. Parizeau. Et là, on voyait que ça semblait être volontaire. Ce n'était pas évident! J'étais un peu étonné qu'il n'y ait pas eu plus d'observateurs, dans les médias, pour questionner le bien-fondé d'avoir un chef à Ottawa qui venait remplacer le chef qui était premier ministre dûment élu au Québec."

69. "On avait beau avoir un plan de campagne, on était pris avec une espèce de coup de vent qui dépassait toute rationalité possible. (…) Les fédéralistes n'avaient pas de réussites derrière eux au cours des dernières années. Ils avaient juste des échecs. Puis, ils n'avaient pas de chef aussi charismatique."

70. "Il était très opportuniste. Il n'hésitait pas autant que M. Parizeau à sauter sur n'importe quelle virgule, n'importe quoi… C'était un avocat de litige, il ne faut pas l'oublier. Deuxièmement, son ton. M. Bourassa disait toujours: 'Lucien s'exprime comme un écorché vif à temps plein. C'est un tribun de cette nature.' Et, troisièmement, c'était un bagarreur. Je n'avais pas eu l'occasion de me faire attaquer personnellement, dans mon intégrité, dans mon identité québécoise. Et cela, il l'a fait!"

71. "Qui aurait pu penser cela? M. Parizeau était premier ministre du Québec, c'était un référendum décrété par l'Assemblée nationale du Québec, suivant une loi du Québec. Et le premier ministre du Québec qui va tout à coup s'effacer devant un député fédéral, qui n'est même pas membre de l'Assemblée nationale! Qui aurait pu penser à cela? (…) On a vu M. Parizeau être littéralement éclipsé. Cela a pris quelques jours avant qu'Ottawa réalise exactement ce qui se produisait, quel était vraiment le rôle de M. Bouchard."

72. "C'était un signe que ça allait mal dans le camp du OUI. Quand M. Bouchard est devenu effectivement le nouveau conducteur de l'autobus, bah, je pensais que c'était le même autobus."

73. "Cela faisait notre affaire de voir M. Parizeau prendre toute la place. Lorsqu'on a vu M. Bouchard arriver, c'était prévisible, mais on aurait rêvé, on aurait aimé que cela ne se produise pas. Mais cela s'est produit. On espérait que M. Parizeau n'accepte pas et prenne ombrage de l'importance à accorder à M. Bouchard. Mais cela ne s'est pas produit."

74. "M. Bouchard était plus marié que M. Parizeau à la notion de partenariat. En tout cas, son image collait plus à cette notion-là. Le lundi matin suivant (l'annonce), quatre ou cinq jours après, dans toutes les régions du Québec, tous les militants du OUI ont adopté le slogan 'On va gagner!'"

75. "Il a fallu changer notre façon d'entrevoir la suite des choses. Vous avez vu des premiers ministres des autres provinces affirmer que jamais ils n'accepteraient un partenariat comme celui que proposait M. Bouchard. Je pense à M. McKenna, entre autres. Et à M. Harris."

76. "Il a réussi à toucher des notes qui ont provoqué un changement rapide qui nous a obligés à nous réveiller à cette nouvelle réalité. Qui n'était pas prévue. Eux-mêmes n'avaient pas prévu cela, pas plus que nous."

77. "On n'a pas eu le temps d'en discuter pendant des semaines. Cela s'est fait tellement vite On n'avait pas de stratégie par rapport à ça."

78. "L'arrivée de M. Bouchard, ce n'était pas évident. Parce que, pour l'organisation, c'est comme si on changeait de lieutenant en plein milieu. Chez les militants, il y a toujours ceux qui s'identifient plus à l'un qu'à l'autre. Il faut que, quelque part, les gens l'acceptent et qu'en même temps, cela ait un effet porteur."

79. "Donc, il fallait désormais le mettre dans l'autobus principal. Il fallait partager les jours de M. Parizeau, ceux de M. Bouchard et ceux de Mario Dumont, lorsque ce dernier serait présent. Les gens du Bloc en voulaient plus. Donc, il y avait une renégociation des autobus à faire. On aurait un deuxième autobus pour M. Parizeau. Cela a créé un certain nombre de moments intéressants!"

80. "Jean Royer m'a dit: 'M. Parizeau te veut absolument au (comité permanent) national parce que ça brasse!' Untel voulait faire un discours le soir, mais, tel chef, il fallait qu'il soit avec tel ministre, sinon il n'y allait pas. Ou l'inverse. Un ministre disait qu'il voulait être avec M. Bouchard, un autre voulait autre chose. Chacun cherchait à avoir de la visibilité. On disait, par exemple que Mme Marois devrait être avec M. Dumont, en Estrie. Oui, mais M. Dumont n'avait jamais de grosses assemblées! Il n'y a pas eu de grosses chicanes. Ce sont les petites chicanes quotidiennes qui sont dures à gérer. C'est là aussi qu'on découvre les personnes. Ce qui me fatiguait le plus, c'était les *prima donna*: 'Il faut que je sois avec Lucien! Je ne veux pas aller avec Dumont. J'aime mieux aller avec Lucien…' Je dois vous dire que ça brassait!"

81. *Le Soleil*, October 8, 1995.

82. Until then, The Referendum Act, which stipulates a period of seven days between the issue of the writs and the publication of the first paid advertisements in the media, prevented the two camps from making use of advertising. Section 429 of the special version of the Election Act for the holding of a referendum reads as follows: "In the seven days following the day on which the order is issued, no person, except the Chief Electoral Officer, may broadcast or cause to be broadcast by a radio or television station or by a cable distribution enterprise, publish or cause to be published in a newspaper or other periodical, or post or cause to be posted in a space leased for that purpose, publicity relating to the election." (www.canlii.org/qc/laws/sta/e-3.3)

83. *La Presse*, October 10, 1995.

84. "Comme on dit en anglais, *error free* était la seule option qui nous restait. (…) Il n'en était pas question. Certains l'auraient voulu. Il fallait absolument jouer toutes nos cartes, et les jouer adéquatement, sortir nos meilleurs atouts, ne pas prêter le flanc à un adversaire fort efficace qui aurait pu maximiser de petites erreurs."

CHAPTER 9

1. "Au grand étonnement de M. Bouchard, il était venu, dans une petite église, je pense, quelque chose comme 1 000 ou 1 200 personnes. C'était l'euphorie. M. Bouchard a eu de la difficulté à entrer dans l'église et à en sortir. On ne comprenait pas trop le phénomène."

2. *The Globe and Mail*, October 9, 1995.

3. See chapter VIII.

4. "On n'a jamais pensé à cela. Il n'y a jamais eu de stratégie, on n'a jamais discuté, on n'a jamais abordé l'idée de prendre *la job* de M. Parizeau. (…) J'en ai fait des tournées, j'en ai fait du terrain, je parlais au monde, j'avais le *feeling* du terrain, je savais comment les gens réagissaient. On se faisait dire: 'Vous, M. Bouchard, vous devriez être à la place de M. Parizeau. Vous seriez un bien meilleur chef pour le PQ.' Bien oui, on se faisait dire ça!"

5. *Journal de Montréal*, October 15, 1995.

6. See Section 304 of the *Code de sécurité routière* (Highway Safety Code), an act adopted in December 1986 under the Robert Bourassa government, when Marc-Yvan Côté was Minister of Transport: Canadian Press text, published in *La Presse* on September 21, 1995.

7. "Avant la nomination de M. Bouchard, cela paraissait qu'il y avait comme une limite dans notre potentiel de votes. Des gens demeuraient hermétiques à notre argumentaire. Et, soudainement, des gens se sont dégagés, eux qui, la veille, étaient fermés."

8. "… un engouement pour M. Bouchard qu'on n'espérait pas tant. Mais ça marchait! (…) Il a fallu tout revoir. Il fallait même prévoir, par exemple, si nous avions une salle capable de recevoir 2 000 personnes, et ce que nous devions faire si ça débordait. Nous devions toujours avoir un équipement de son additionnel pour porter le message hors des salles. On n'arrivait pas à prévoir l'ampleur de chaque événement. Nous n'étions plus dans une dynamique où il fallait rapetisser les salles pour qu'elles aient l'air pleines, mais comment pouvait-on agrandir les salles pour faire entrer le maximum de personnes?"

9. "L'effet était réel. Cela a changé la campagne référendaire. On a senti une différence immédiate. Au début, et moi inclus, on ne savait pas par quel bout prendre tout ça. Cela m'a rappelé la campagne fédérale de 1993. M. Bouchard était très populaire et, franchement, ses adversaires ne savaient pas comment l'aborder. On ne pouvait pas l'attaquer personnellement. Le camp du NON était simplement embêté et cherchait une façon de contrecarrer son effet sans avoir l'air de l'attaquer personnellement."

10. "On a fait des études pour voir comment contrer l'effet Bouchard. Est-ce que cet effet était si fort parce qu'il n'y avait pas de sens critique dans notre société? Dans les *focus groups*, nous avons présenté des images de M. Bouchard aux participants, puis on leur a demandé: Est-ce que ça vous dérange? Êtes-vous d'accord avec ça? Quand ils n'étaient pas d'accord avec ce que M. Bouchard disait, ils répondaient: 'Ce n'est peut-être pas ce qu'il a vraiment voulu dire!'"

11. "Moi, j'ai compris qu'il y avait quelque chose de changé quand des journalistes nous ont dit avoir vu quelqu'un toucher son veston [de Lucien Bouchard] avec un chapelet, à Sainte-Marie de Beauce ou je ne sais pas où. Je n'avais jamais vu ça. Peut-être dans d'autres pays, mais certainement pas au Québec, en 1995. Cela relevait en partie du phénomène de masse. On n'était plus dans un débat référendaire, on était dans un épisode qui tenait à la personnalité de quelqu'un, à son histoire, à son cheminement, à sa façon de s'exprimer."

12. "Il y avait des gens qui lui demandaient quasiment de bénir le drapeau du Québec, voyons donc! Alors, c'était un peu inusité. J'ai fait beaucoup de politique, mais des situations comme celle-là, je n'en avais jamais vues. Ce n'était plus de la politique. Je ne veux pas faire allusion à M. Ryan, mais c'était comme la main de Dieu qui intervenait dans l'esprit de bien des gens." The last two sentences of this passage are not a translation, but Chrétien's own words in the interview.

13. "Un soir, en regardant les nouvelles, je voyais les gens devant M. Bouchard, des gens qui, finalement, voulaient le toucher. Je voyais des gens qui le regardaient un peu comme le Messie qui allait sauver les Québécois. C'était très préoccupant."

14. "C'était un miraculé, qui se promenait au Québec. (…) Les murs en craquaient. Il venait de vivre la maladie de la bactérie mangeuse de chair, il avait lutté, il en était sorti, c'était quasi un miracle. Cela a eu un effet dans le public. Il était charismatique."

15. "Il était quasiment plus populaire que le frère André au sommet de sa gloire. C'était presque religieux."

16. "Les gens voulaient lui toucher comme on veut toucher à un saint homme, comme s'il s'était rapproché de Dieu."

17. "Il y avait d'abord une partie du même effet qu'avec René Lévesque. Et puis, M. Bouchard, c'était un grand homme, débarqué d'Ottawa, qui sacrifiait une carrière de ministre et d'ambassadeur, qui devenait simple député, qui prenait l'autobus, qui formait un parti… Et il avait un côté rassurant, que M. Parizeau n'avait pas. C'était un homme qui avait beaucoup de charme et, en politique, il en usait consciemment et correctement. Et, évidemment, il y a eu la maladie. On ne peut pas faire abstraction de sa maladie. Cela a créé cette empathie-là. Ce fut un mélange de tout cela."

18. "Pierre Elliott Trudeau était suivi par des hordes de gens qui l'embrassaient, embrassaient ses vêtements. Ce sont là des choses importantes. Il faut apprendre à s'en servir. Ce n'est pas quelque chose qu'on planifie, mais on peut l'aménager. Ce n'est pas par hasard si, parlant par exemple devant une chambre de commerce de Montréal, Pierre Trudeau était tout à coup entouré de vingt jolies femmes qui attendaient depuis une heure et demie à l'étage inférieur du Cercle canadien de Montréal. Vous savez, il y a du spontané et il y a du moins spontané!"

19. "Je n'en sais rien. Parlez-en à son organisateur, un organisateur remarquable, le meilleur que je n'ai jamais rencontré!"

20. "Le monde lui donnait la main, ils avaient l'impression de parler à un saint. Cela n'avait aucun bon sens. Il y avait quelque chose là-dedans. J'ai fait beaucoup de politique. Un phénomène comme ça, je n'ai jamais vu ça!"

21. "M. Bouchard ne mettait pas son handicap en évidence. Il n'a jamais accepté qu'il le limite dans ses activités. Dans les scènes qu'on avait à construire pour ses assemblées, il n'était pas question de faire des aménagements pour qu'il puisse se dérober par une porte de côté. Il voulait être l'homme politique qu'il était et marcher comme tous les autres hommes politiques doivent marcher. Souvenez-vous du défilé de la Saint-Jean. Il aurait très bien pu monter dans une auto, et la population l'aurait accepté. Non, il voulait marcher. Il n'a jamais cherché à mettre son handicap à profit. Il avait du charisme. Il n'avait pas besoin de mise en scène."

22. *La Presse*, October 10, 1995. The group included Pierre Laurin, of the Merril Lynch brokerage firm, André Dion, president and principal shareholder of Unibroue brewery, Jacques Girard, director general of Quebecor, Pierre Parent, of Promexpro, Réal Laporte of the Soprin engineering firm, and numerous other owners and managers of SMEs.

23. *Le Devoir*, October 13, 1995.

24. *La Presse*, October 10, 1995.

25. *The Vancouver Sun*, October 10, 1995.

26. *Ibid.*

27. According to the university's student newspaper, they were Val Neaves-Nelson, Michelle Shepherd, Bryce Dalke and Michelle Lang: *The Peak*, vol. 91, n° 9.

28. "J'étais tannée de répondre aux gens qui voulaient juste savoir si j'allais voter OUI ou NON. J'étais tannée aussi de voir comment le OUI et le NON étaient compris là-bas dans les nouvelles des médias. Ça tournait toujours autour d'une logique économique. Il n'était pas question d'identité culturelle, d'identité nationale."

29. "On allait à la radio avec un animateur qui aimait soulever la polémique. Et on savait que nos opinions politiques étaient loin de faire l'unanimité!"

30. "On s'est beaucoup lancées dans la gueule du loup. Je me suis rendu compte qu'expliquer une position politique, quand tu ne possèdes pas bien la langue, c'est difficile. Celui ou celle qui ose le faire accrédite le stéréotype du Québécois qui se veut souverainiste, mais qui est incapable de dire pourquoi. La langue devient un peu un handicap et renforce le stéréotype d'une jeune émotive et irrationnelle qui a de la misère à s'expliquer." Six months later, Sophie Bélanger would return to Vancouver to the same radio station, with the same host, but this time at the request of Gilles Blais of the NFB who was making *Le Grand silence*, in which he tries to explain to his son the work of those who built Quebec.

31. *La Presse*, October 11, 1995.

32. *Le Soleil*, October 11, 1995.

33. "Je sais très bien à quel point lui-même allait se mettre dans une situation extrêmement embarrassante. On l'a vu, quand il est devenu premier ministre et qu'il a voulu recommencer le combat pour la souveraineté. Il fallait qu'il fasse refaire une série d'études, dont il disait qu'elles n'étaient pas pertinentes. En fait, il n'était pas au courant de ce qu'il y avait dans ces études. Des études qu'aucun gouvernement responsable ne peut éviter s'il veut structurer un pays. Il apprendra à ne pas faire des déclarations comme ça!"

34. "Pour lui, dit-il, ce n'était pas l'accumulation d'études qui faisait avancer le débat dans le peuple. Cela pouvait être important pour une classe intellectuelle afin de préparer le passage du fédéralisme à la souveraineté mais il trouvait qu'on ciblait trop là-dessus. Pour lui, c'était plutôt la fierté, notre capacité de faire…"

35. "Il n'y a personne pour lui poser des questions sur ce qu'il a dit. La campagne est devenue très axée sur la personne."

36. *La Presse*, October 11, 1995.

37. *La Presse*, October 12, 1995.

38. GRAND COUNCIL OF THE CREES (of Quebec), *Sovereign Injustice: Forcible Inclusion of the James Bay Crees and Cree Territory into a Sovereign Quebec*. Nemaska: Grand Council of the Crees, 1995.

39. When Canada bought Rupert's Land from the Hudson Bay Company, in 1870, this territory was home to the Inuit, the Crees, the Montagnais, the Naskapis, the Attikameks and the Algonquins. It was annexed to Quebec in various stages thereafter. In 1898, Quebec's Northern border was pushed as far as the Eastern coastline of James Bay, to the mouth of the Eastmain River, which it followed, to the East as far as the Hamilton River, coming down again towards the Western border of Labrador.

40. Denis LESSARD, *"Les Indiens n'auraient pas droit de sécession, selon un document fédéral"* (The native people would not have the right of secession, according to a federal document), *La Presse*, October 13, 1995.

41. *The Globe and Mail*, October 10, 1995.

42. *The Gazette*, October 13, 1995.

43. *La Presse*, October 13, 1995.

44. *Le Devoir*, October 13, 1995.

45. *La Presse*, October 13, 1995.

46. SOM-Environics poll, conducted for *Le Devoir*, Radio-Canada, *Le Soleil*, *Le Droit* and *The Gazette*, published October 3, 1995.

47. *La Presse*, October 13, 1995.

48. Josée Legault is a militant for Quebec independence. She was an instructor at UQAM and columnist for *Le Devoir* and *The Gazette*. The committee's report, known as the Plourde-Legault Report, concluded that the French language was vulnerable in certain regions of Quebec. Josée Legault published *L'invention d'une minorité* (Montreal: Éditions du Boréal, 1992) and *Les nouveaux démons* (Montreal: VLB, 1996). She worked for a time in the cabinet of Bernard Landry before she was dismissed by Brigitte Pelletier when the latter replaced Claude-H. Roy as chief of staff, in December 2002. She did not have any further luck in politics, having been beaten by Robert Perreault at the Parti Québécois nomination for Mercier, in 1998.

49. *Le Devoir*, October 17, 1995.

50. *La Presse*, October 16, 1995. The quote in *La Presse* was substantially the same as that published in *Le Devoir* on October 17: "Quebec society is one of the white races having the fewest children. That doesn't make any sense. That means that we have not resolved our family problems or (the issue of a) family incentives policy."

51. "J'ai tout de suite téléphoné au bureau de la campagne pour dire qu'il fallait répliquer à cela."

52. *The Globe and Mail*, October 16, 1995.

53. "Revoyez cet épisode, et vous verrez comment les médias ont réagi. Ils ont immédiatement pardonné à Lucien Bouchard. Même Françoise David, de la Fédération des femmes du Québec, est venue à sa défense."

54. *La Presse*, October 17, 1995. On March 9, 1980, six weeks before the first Quebec referendum, the day after International Women's Day, 700 women crowded into the Salle du Plateau to listen to sovereigntist speakers. Lise Payette, minister for *la Condition féminine* (Status of women), went up to the microphone: she ridiculed the character of Yvette, found in a school text book, as a model for housewives: she washes dishes, slices bread and sweeps the floor while her little brother practises boxing and swimming. And she added: "Claude Ryan is the kind of man I hate, because he is the type who would love there to be lots of Yvettes in Quebec. He is married to one!" En 1980, Claude Ryan was leader of the NO camp and his wife, Madeleine, was the very opposite of an Yvette. It was a perfect opportunity: a few days later, the NO camp would fill the Forum with women who were outraged by Lise Payette's remarks. Source: Pierre GODIN, *René Lévesque, Tome III, L'espoir et le chagrin* (Hope and despair). Montreal: Les Éditions du Boréal, 2001, p. 520.

55. "Si j'avais dit ça, j'aurais été 'passé au batte' comme on dit, d'une façon radicale."

56. *Le Devoir*, October 16, 1995.

57. MONIÈRE, GUAY, *op. cit.*, p. 53.

58. *La Presse*, October 17, 1995.

59. *La Presse*, October 16, 1995.

60. Source: Yves BOISVERT, "Dénatalité: le Québec, loin du record" (Low birthrates: Quebec far from the lowest), *La Presse*, October 17, 1995.

61. "Ce n'est pas la première fois qu'un chef est mal interprété ou mal cité... ou qu'il n'explique pas assez bien pour que les gens le comprennent."

62. *Le Devoir*, October 17, 1995.

63. *Le Devoir*, October 17, 1995.

64. This part of the interview was conducted in English.

65. *La Presse*, October 6, 1995.

66. "J'avais très, très peur de la campagne référendaire, en ce sens que, avec les *scrums*, les trois chefs se mettent à se contredire.

67. "On a perdu des membres. Nos membres étaient conscients qu'il fallait que l'ADQ soit dans le camp du OUI, même si notre plan était d'avoir un référendum sur le partenariat. Mais (en voyant dans les médias) l'image des trois chefs, assis, à signer l'entente du 12 juin... C'est clair qu'il y a des membres qui ont quitté. (...) Il fallait dire que le projet du gouvernement venait de changer, que c'était un nouveau projet dans lequel M. Parizeau était un joueur sur trois. C'était plus facile pour le Bloc et le PQ, mais nous, on représentait des nationalistes plus modérés, des gens qui étaient prêts pour la souveraineté, mais plus modérés, d'autres qui préféraient un grand renouvellement du fédéralisme, mais qui n'étaient pas prêts à faire le pas de la souveraineté..."

CHAPTER 10

1. After the breakup of Czechoslovakia, it became clear that no form of federation would satisfy both the Czechs and the Slovaks. In July 1992, the Slovakian parliament voted in favour of sovereignty. Throughout the fall, Czechs and Slovaks negotiated the modalities of separation. In November, the federal parliament voted to dissolve the government and on January 1, 1993, the Czech Republic and Slovakia became independent states. On February 15 of the same year, the Slovakian parliament elected Michal Kovac as the first President of the Republic. The new country had about 5,400,000 inhabitants.

2. *Le Journal de Montréal*, October 16, 1995.

3. *Le Journal de Québec*, October 21, 1995.

4. Information sheets: *The separation of Quebec on the international scene*, prepared by the Privy Council, May 15, 1995, obtained by virtue of Canada's Access to Information Act.

5. Data taken from a text entitled *Can Slovakia sustain its rate of growth?*, published in the monthly research services bulletin by Morgan Stanley of London after the referendum and cited by Jacques Parizeau during a meeting that preceded the interviews given to Radio-Canada for the current book.

6. *Le Devoir*, October 18, 1995.

7. *La Presse*, October 17, 1995.

8. SOM survey on behalf of Quebec City's *Le Soleil*

9. Electronic poll by analyst Skot Kortje of Stocktrends Publications, published in *The Globe and Mail*, October 17, 1995.

10. *La Presse* and *Le Devoir*, October 18, 1995.

11. *The Globe and Mail*, October 19, 1995.

12. *Le Devoir*, October 18, 1995.

13. Maurice Pinard, professor at McGill University, was one of the pollsters for the NO camp.

14. See BLANCHARD, *op. cit.*, p. 235.

15. *La Presse*, October 18, 1995.

16. According to pollster Pierre Drouilly, distributing the undecided vote according to the percentages obtained for each of the options is erroneous. He maintains that rarely does more than a quarter of the undecided favour sovereignty.

17. *La Presse*, October 18, 1995.

18. *L'appel de la race* is a novel published in 1922 by Lionel Groulx, priest and author, under the pseudonym Alonié de Lestres. In this novel, the historian recounts the life of a Franco-Ontarian lawyer, Jules Lantagnac, torn by the crisis in Ontario's French-language schools. It is a short book, but one that has caused much controversy, because of its author's reputation, the use of the word "race" in the title and because it constitutes a denunciation of Ontario's policy vis-à-vis the francophones in that province. The novel was published five years after Toronto adopted Regulation 17, a measure aimed at restricting the use of French and making English the principal teaching language in the French-language primary schools of the province. The publication of *L'appel de la race* thus coincided with the bitter fight led by Franco-Ontarians against the application of this regulation.

19. *Le Devoir*, October 18, 1995.

20. "Dans le Parti québécois, tu sentais qu'il y avait vraiment une âme, il y avait un défi à relever. Du côté du NON, c'était davantage *business*, c'était mécanique; il n'y avait pas de cœur là-dedans, il n'y avait pas le même genre de passion que du côté du OUI. On se sentait frustrés. On disait: 'Écoutez, le pays va se défaire et on est en train de gérer ça comme on gère une banque.' Je sentais qu'il n'y avait pas d'émotion. Les gens du NON avaient décidé de réserver une salle plus petite parce qu'ils voulaient s'assurer qu'elle soit pleine. C'était un exemple de leur manque de foi. Ils avaient peur de perdre. Il faut que tu aies le goût de gagner pour pouvoir gagner."

21. This part of the interview was conducted in English.

22. "On se traitait assez bien. L'un de nous était membre du club; il a offert de nous obtenir une salle qui soit convenable. (…) C'est vraiment la passion qui a poussé ces gens à faire ça. Et aussi, la peur. Ils voulaient être Montréalais, rester ici au Québec et faire partie du Canada."

23. CROP poll, for *La Presse*, TVA and the *Toronto Star*: 44.5% for the YES and 42.2% for the NO with 13.2% discretionary.

24. *Le Devoir*, October 19, 1995.

25. "Qu'est-ce que ça veut dire: une déclaration plus opérationnelle? Ce qui nous inquiétait, c'était qu'ils disent quelque chose sur les emplois, l'investissement américain au Québec, le nerf économique quoi!"

26. BLANCHARD, *op. cit.*, p. 235.

27. *Ibid.*, p. 237.

28. NORAD is a Canadian-American Command whose mission is surveillance of the airspace over the North American continent. It was created in 1958 and underwent several modifications over the years. It is periodically renewed, every four or five years. Minister Ouellet and the American Secretary of State were preparing the eight renewal, which was signed in March 1996.

29. *Ibid.*, p. 237.

30. "Je ne sais pas pourquoi à la Maison-Blanche, puisque la lettre était adressée à Warren Christopher."

31. "J'ai été sidéré à la lecture de cette lettre. Pourquoi? Parce qu'elle allait complètement à l'encontre d'un des principes de notre présence à Washington, surtout pendant cette période, c'est-à-dire de ne pas 'antagoniser' les Américains."

32. "… le destinataire réel, c'est la Maison-Blanche."

33. *Ibid.*, p. 241. Landry's letter is reproduced p. 239–241.

34. Lynne Lambert was the first and only contact that representatives of Quebec in Washington had with the Secretary of State. "It was no doubt her responsibility to have me believe that everything was going well, that we were good friends," says Anne Legaré, the Quebec government's advisor on U.S. national affairs, posted in Washington. "I thought we were among good friends, but, afterwards, one could wonder whether we were among good friends and among allies, considering the behaviour of a whole slew of people and the obstacles that were put in our path."

35. "Évidemment, la lettre a été approuvée par M. Parizeau."

36. "C'était une initiative de M. Landry. Cela faisait partie de ses attributions comme vice-premier ministre et chargé des relations internationales."

37. "Le tenir informé de la perception des Américains vis-à-vis de la souveraineté et ne pas faire de vagues!"

38. "Ou on se comporte en mouton, et les Américains vont nous traiter comme des moutons, ou on leur dit: Attention!"

39. "Pour leur dire: écoutez, tout ce qu'on demande, c'est qu'il n'y ait pas d'interventions négatives et on vous invite à appeler à la Maison-Blanche pour 'passer le message.'"

40. "Pour moi, les déclarations qui ont été faites par les autorités américaines après la réception de la lettre auraient été faites de toute façon."

41. *La Presse*, October 20, 1995.

42. *Ibid.*

43. *La Presse*, October 20, 1995.

44. See chapter VIII, note 18.

45. *The Globe and Mail*, October 20, 1995.

46. "C'était alarmant. On a commencé à perdre cette campagne le jeudi (le 19). Il était évident, dans l'enquête, que le *momentum* ne nous favorisait pas. (…) J'ai fait une sortie pour demander que ce discours soit plus convenable et plus acceptable aux Québécois. On sentait qu'on était fondamentalement dans un choix de pays. On était dans une dynamique post Meech, post Charlottetown. Est-ce qu'il fonctionne, ce pays, ou est-ce qu'il ne fonctionne pas? Il fallait qu'on donne un espoir à ceux qui voulaient qu'il fonctionne."

47. "Un homme dans la quarantaine qui représentait un peu nos clientèles, des gens qui étaient indécis. (…) J'ai alors compris qu'on avait un grave problème. J'étais dans le Bas-du-fleuve, où le taux de chômage était élevé, où la récession des années 1990 avait été particulièrement dure et où le camp du OUI avait réussi à aller chercher les gens et à leur faire croire qu'ils n'avaient rien à perdre. (…) Cela a été, dans le fond, le succès de la campagne du OUI, de convaincre un certain nombre de Québécois qu'en votant OUI, il n'avaient rien à perdre alors qu'ils avaient beaucoup à perdre."

48. "Je leur ai fait le boniment habituel sur la relation extraordinaire qui existe entre le Canada et les Etats-Unis. (…) Je me suis rendu compte qu'il y avait beaucoup de prudence à l'égard de mon optimisme, peut-être exagéré, concernant une victoire du gouvernement canadien. Ces gens-là me disaient en termes très clairs: 'Écoutez, monsieur l'ambassadeur. Vous semblez croire que vous allez gagner. Mais nous, nos informations indiquent que c'est tellement serré qu'on ne peut plus prédire ce qui va se passer.'"

49. This part of the interview was conducted in English.

50. This part of the interview was conducted in English.

51. This part of the interview was conducted in English.

52. "Je ne me rappelle pas. Peut-être, alors que nous étions aux Nations unies, qu'il (le président Clinton) s'est informé: 'Jean, comment ça marche?' Et que je lui ai expliqué… C'est peut-être à ce moment-là que je lui ai parlé. Ce n'était pas une démarche (officielle). On était entre voisins. Il suivait cela (la question du référendum) avec attention. Il adore la politique, alors, pour lui, c'était un problème politique qui devait l'intéresser. Mais je n'ai jamais appelé Clinton pour lui dire: 'Bill, j'aimerais que tu fasses une déclaration.' Ce n'est pas comme cela que ça s'est passé."

53. RAE, *op. cit.*, p. 266.

54. "J'aurais dû répondre qu'il n'y avait pas de ronde constitutionnelle à l'horizon et que c'était le projet de souveraineté qui était en cause. J'aurais dû simplement écarter la question. Le plus drôle, c'est qu'à Shawinigan, à son premier discours important, Jean Chrétien a parlé du caractère distinct du Québec. (…) On était tous debout sur l'estrade et on voyait les notes les uns des autres. Or, il l'avait ajouté à la main dans son discours. Il l'avait ajouté, puis il l'avait dit. (…) le côté fédéral n'a pas totalement livré la marchandise (…) ce dont nous avions convenus, mais qu'il hésitait beaucoup à mentionner…"

55. This part of the interview was conducted in English.

56. *The Toronto Star*, October 23, 1995.

57. The constitutional conference in Victoria was held from June 14 to 16, 1971. Its purpose was to adopt an amending formula for the Constitution, which was still only an act of the British Parliament, in such a way that it could be repatriated so that it would become a Canadian document. The "Victoria formula," proposed by Pierre Elliott Trudeau, the then Prime Minister, stipulated in essence that the Canadian government agreed to restrict its power in the appointment of judges and to limit the Governor General's power to repudiate a provincial law. It granted likewise a right of veto to Ontario, Quebec and certain other provinces against any constitutional change. The provinces had eleven days in which to have the formula adopted by their respective parliaments. On June 23, Robert Bourassa, the premier of Québec, rejected the formula, demanding more power in matters of health, social services, revenue and employment. It was a stalemate. Trudeau had failed in his first attempt to repatriate the Constitution and have a Canadian charter of rights and freedoms entrenched in it. His heart had been set on this idea ever since his days as Justice minister in Lester B. Pearson's government.

58. On May 22, 1979, Canadians elected a Conservative government, led by Joe Clark. But the new government was in a minority position and was toppled on December 13 of the same year, following the presentation of the budget. Trudeau was returned to power in February 1980.

59. "Il ne voulait pas être pris dans une interprétation d'un vote pour le NON semblable à 1980, qui amènerait une dynamique en faveur d'une révision constitutionnelle. M. Trudeau, lui, tenait à cela. C'était plus ou moins son héritage qui était en jeu. Victoria avait été un échec. Il avait de nouveau raté l'occasion en perdant les élections en 1979, mais là, il avait l'occasion de gagner le référendum, d'agir rapidement et de rapatrier la Constitution. M. Chrétien ne voulait pas se faire prendre dans cette dynamique. Cela, on l'a ressenti. Quand on a commencé à préparer les documents du NON, à rédiger le manifeste, on sentait le tiraillement. On ne voulait pas s'embarquer dans quelque chose qui serait interprété comme un engagement pour faire une réforme constitutionnelle."

60. According to political expert Denis Monière, it was André Laurendeau, former editor-in-chief of *Le Devoir*, co-chair of the 1963 Commission of Inquiry on Bilingualism and Biculturalism, who was the first to use the expression "distinct society." It can be found in the Commission's preliminary report: Denis MONIÈRE, "La 'société distincte' d'André Laurendeau," *Le Devoir*, March 17, 1989.

61. "C'était le débat que j'avais avec M. Trudeau. Lui, il disait qu'il n'y avait pas de mot dans la Constitution qui ne voulait rien dire. Je me souviens d'un débat que nous avions eu à Toronto, lui, moi et mon ami Gérard Pelletier. Je disais: 'On a le Code civil au Québec, alors qu'il ne s'applique pas dans le reste du Canada; la majorité au Québec parle français, ce n'est pas le cas dans les autres provinces.' Plusieurs décisions de Cour reconnaissent cet état de fait. L'expression *société distincte* crée un problème. Cela arrive souvent en politique. Par exemple, l'union de gens de même sexe. Si c'est un contrat civil, personne ne s'objecte. Si vous appelez ça un *mariage*, vous avez beaucoup d'opposition, mais cela ne change rien dans la réalité. Le problème, c'est le mot. Ce sont des batailles qui créent des illusions. Quand les résultats ne sont pas là, cela crée de l'amertume. C'est pourquoi, quand je suis devenu premier ministre, je n'ai jamais pensé qu'on pouvait régler les problèmes de tout le monde en changeant la Constitution. C'est la solution la plus facile. Quand on a un problème de déficit ou de manque d'argent ou de participation à une guerre comme celle en Irak, ce n'est pas la Constitution qui décide, c'est le pouvoir politique, c'est le gouvernement."

62. Jean Marchand (1918-1988) was an influential member of the Pierre Elliott Trudeau government. A social sciences graduate of Université Laval, he was general secretary of the Confederation of Catholic workers of Canada (*Confédération des travailleurs catholiques du Canada*—CTCC), and then became president of the Confederation of National Trade Unions—CNTU (*Confédération des syndicats nationaux*—CSN), before entering federal politics with Trudeau and Gérard Pelletier, in 1965. He then obtained a Senate seat before being appointed chair of the Transport Commission.

63. This part of the interview was conducted in English.

64. "Cela aurait pu mener à une scission importante. Ce week-end, j'ai vraiment senti qu'il y avait deux formations différentes. Et puis, ce n'était pas des gens prêts à faire des compromis. Cela aurait pu tourner encore plus au vinaigre, mais on a pu se rallier et se concentrer sur la dernière semaine."

65. "Ce samedi matin, comme les autres samedis, M. Gollin est arrivé avec ses données. Disons que cela a été comme une douche d'eau froide! Ce fut la fin de semaine la plus difficile. Il ne nous restait pas dix jours pour renverser la vapeur."

66. "Quand je suis parti, les sondages étaient encore bons, se souvient-il. Mais là, cela m'a un peu assommé. (...) J'ai eu une bonne conversation avec Fidel Castro. C'était la première fois que je le voyais et il était bien content de parler en espagnol avec Aline!"

⁶7. *Globe and Mail*, October 21, 1995.

68. "On nous a fait le coup depuis Honoré Mercier. C'est une des raisons pour lesquelles nous avons constitué la Caisse. Il fallait empêcher ce petit jeu-là."

69. "C'est par des opérations comme celle-là que les gouvernements du Québec se sont rendus indépendants des intérêts financiers qui les avaient dominés pendant un siècle. Les institutions financières se débarrassent des titres du gouvernement du Québec et prennent des pertes. Vous rachetez, ce qui fait monter les cours. C'est pour ça que tellement d'institutions financières privées ont joué dans le même sens que nous. Tout ce qu'elles avaient à faire, c'était, en anglais on dit *piggy-back*, c'était simplement de se mettre sur notre dos et de nous suivre."

70. "Elle pouvait vendre des titres américains, si le besoin se faisait sentir pour supporter le marché des titres du Québec. Elle avait aussi des obligations du gouvernement du Canada qu'elle aurait pu vendre. S'il y avait eu une catastrophe sur les titres du Québec, comme on le prétendait, il y aurait eu aussi une catastrophe sur les titres du Canada."

71. "Je n'avais jamais entendu parler de cela. M. Parizeau nous a dit, invoquant sa connaissance des marchés financiers, qu'il était aux affaires là-dessus. On n'a jamais eu de présentation détaillée sur ce que cela représentait pour les différentes institutions. Mais on ne l'a jamais torturé de questions là-dessus non plus."

72. "Pour en avoir reparlé avec M. Bouchard récemment, il n'était pas au courant. Le secret a été bien gardé. Je pense cependant que cela aurait été plus normal que M. Bouchard soit mis au courant."

73. *The Gazette*, October 21, 1995.

74. *La Presse*, October 25, 1995.

75. *Ibid.*

76. "Et, c'est là qu'on a finalement décidé de faire la grande manifestation à la Place du Canada, ce qui n'avait pas été prévu jusque-là."

77. "Là, il a fallu que je prenne des décisions. Assis à mon bureau, j'ai passé plusieurs heures à tout revoir. Et ensuite, on a pris des décisions."

78. "On a décidé qu'on ne demanderait plus de permission à personne et qu'il fallait sauter. La guerre était entrée dans sa période cruciale. Alors, en guerre, on ne demande de permission à personne. On joue le tout pour le tout."

CHAPTER 11

1. "Il prenait parti dans le débatà. J'imagine qu'un ambassadeur de France à Ottawa n'aurait pas dû ouvrir la bouche sans consulter son premier ministre et son président."

2. "M. Chirac a dit à ce moment-là que, depuis le référendum de 1980, il avait beaucoup réfléchi. Tout en étant respectueux de ce que les Québécois et les Canadiens décideraient, il en était venu à la conclusion que le fait français, que la langue française étaient mieux protégés par l'appartenance du Québec au Canada que par la séparation du Québec du Canada. Aussi, quand il a dit à la télévision américaine: 'Je respecterai la décision des Québécois,' cela ne m'a pas énervé. Je me suis dit: que pouvait-il dire d'autre? Cela ne voulait pas dire qu'il appuyait le camp souverainiste. Pas du tout. (…) Cela m'aurait surpris que les pays de la francophonie se prononcent avant la France. Et je pense que la France aurait été extrêmement prudente dans ce dossier."

3. This part of the interview was conducted in English.

4. Hubert Védrine later became minister of Foreign Affairs, a post he would hold until 2002. He popularized the "hyperpower" concept to describe the U.S., a country he denounced for its "imperialism" and its lack of will to settle the conflict in the Middle East.

5. "Mais, dans les mois qui ont précédé, à l'exception de la déclaration au réseau américain, M. Chirac, comme le premier ministre Juppé, n'avait jamais, de façon concrète et officielle, déclaré quoi que ce soit qui pouvait aller en dehors de la politique officielle de la France de non-ingérence et de non-indifférence. Nous, les contacts que nous avions avec l'Élysée, auprès de M. Védrine, le chef de cabinet de M. Juppé, nous donnaient l'assurance que la France n'était pas intéressée à se placer dans une situation où, dans son propre pays, on lui reprocherait, le jour après, de refuser l'indépendance à la Corse, alors qu'on accepterait celle du Québec." The first sentence was the original English.

6. "… un homme de carrière en diplomatie et, dans les moments les plus intenses et les plus délicats, on s'est toujours parlé (…). Je craignais qu'Ottawa commence (comme en 1980) à envoyer des notes de service aux Affaires étrangères de France, à se plaindre de la façon dont on avait reçu M. Parizeau et de ce qu'on avait oublié de mettre le drapeau du Canada à l'hôtel de ville, etc."

7. Jacques-Yvan Morin was a minister in the René Lévesque government. He taught international and constitutional law at Université de Montréal for fifteen years before being elected MNA for the Montreal constituency of Sauvé, in 1976. He has headed the ministries of Education, of Cultural and Scientific Development, and of Intergovernmental Affairs. He left politics in 1984 to return to teaching.

8. "Nous étions parfaitement conscients des liens entre Jean Pelletier et Jacques Chirac, et il y avait toujours un doute chez M. Parizeau. Est-ce que les Français allaient faire ce qu'ils disaient? Il fallait s'en assurer! Alors, M. Parizeau voulait les encadrer. (…) Il faut dire que le délégué général du Québec à Paris, qui était un homme de très grande qualité, n'avait pas été nommé par M. Parizeau!"

9. "Ou, du moins, que la présidence sache qu'elle devait agir parce que, si elle n'agissait pas, elle serait contredite par l'Assemblée nationale. (…) (Philippe Séguin) faisait contrepoids au Quai d'Orsay et constituait une porte d'entrée directe auprès de M. Chirac."

10. "… en 1995, moi à l'Élysée, j'aurais eu l'air d'un adolescent! Il y avait une erreur de *casting* avec moi, que M. Parizeau ne semblait pas réaliser, alors, que M. Morin était un candidat idéal."

11. Source for the draft communiqué: DUCHESNE, *op. cit.*, p. 517.

12. "Il y a un moment où ce sont les Français qui disaient: on voudrait intégrer dans le texte le fait qu'il y aura négociation sur le partenariat. Alors nous, on disait: très, très bien, et même: si vous voulez ajouter une phrase disant que la France veut conserver d'excellentes relations avec le Canada, ajoutez-la. Parce que, nous aussi, nous voulons de bonnes relations avec le Canada. Donc, ça allait."

13. "Comment peut-on imaginer que Philippe Séguin, qui est supposé être non partisan parce qu'il est président de l'Assemblée nationale, va pouvoir rallier quatre, cinq, six partis politiques différents, les communistes, la gauche, les verts… La droite compte déjà trois partis différents… Comment peut-on croire que, sur une question de politique étrangère, sans que le gouvernement français se soit prononcé, que ces gens-là vont spontanément se lever et dire: On reconnaît le Québec!"

14. Pierre-André Wiltzer was minister of Cooperation and *la Francophonie* in the government of Jean-Pierre Raffarin, until the end of May 2005. He was replaced in this post by Brigitte Girardin in the new government of Dominique de Villepin.

15. "Deux ou trois députés et le président de l'Assemblée nationale se sont prononcés, sur 531. C'était une stratégie d'intellectuels."

16. On December 11, 1995, the federal government had the House of Commons adopt a resolution, recognizing that "Quebec is a distinct society within Canada" and that this distinct society "includes its French-speaking majority, unique culture, and civil law tradition." The formulation was based on what was contained in the Charlottetown agreement, which Quebecers had, however, rejected in the 1992 referendum. The resolution specified that all components of the legislative and executive branches of government were to take note of this recognition and be guided in their conduct accordingly. The government of Quebec would have occasion to single out numerous cases, in the months and years that followed, where the various federal organizations did not take the resolution into account, notably, with regard to the Millennium Scholarship Foundation and the Social Union Framework Agreement in February 1999.

17. *La Presse*, October 25, 1995.

18. "C'est le ralliement qui a été la cassure de la campagne pour les fédéralistes, dans le sens où l'on a renversé la vapeur, cette journée-là."

19. "… un débat qu'on a gagné carrément, (…) une phase beaucoup plus positive, plus constructive, à regarder l'avenir, à définir les enjeux, notre vision du monde, du Canada, du Québec."

20. "Donc, le sentiment, au Parti libéral du Québec, était d'avoir un discours qui touchait plus les cordes sensibles des Québécois, qui répondaient aux revendications du Québec."

21. "Je lui ai dit: 'Je n'accepte pas que M. Trudeau fasse partie de notre stratégie.' J'avais en tête, et je suis sûr que plusieurs Québécois l'avaient aussi en tête, le premier référendum de 1980 lorsque M. Trudeau avait fait des promesses aux Québécois, promesses qu'il n'a pas tenues."

22. "Ça ne prenait pas une grande réflexion pour comprendre que nos adversaires étaient pour utiliser cette erreur-là."

23. "Je ne trouvais pas que c'était nécessairement dans l'ordre des choses. Quand on a affaire à des gens de leur profil, qui ont laissé leurs marques, bonnes comme moins bonnes, pourquoi les inviter dans une campagne où ils ont été, par ailleurs, absents? Pourquoi à la dernière minute? De quoi est-ce que cela avait l'air? C'était une décision du fédéral, mais il y a toujours des gens qui prennent des initiatives sans vérifier les détails."

24. This part of the interview was conducted in English.

25. *Canada News Wire*, October 25, 1995.

26. *Le Devoir*, October 23, 1995.

27. BLANCHARD, *op. cit.*, p. 245.

28. This part of the interview was conducted in English.

29. BLANCHARD, *op. cit.*, p. 247-248.

30. "Un des moments clés de la campagne référendaire. Il l'a fait, respectueux du processus démocratique canadien, tout en soulignant son appui à un allié sûr et fidèle. C'était un terrain glissant, car il aurait pu y avoir une deuxième question. Heureusement, tout s'est bien passé."

31. "Je ne le changerai pas. Le premier ministre, c'était lui, et il n'était pas question qu'on le mette dans le placard pour deux mois en faisant semblant qu'il n'existait pas. Sauf qu'il s'agissait de l'utiliser dans un environnement le moins dommageable possible. Et l'envoyer à la télé, seul, ce n'était pas de nature à nous rassurer. On s'est croisé les doigts, puis on s'est dit: advienne que pourra, espérons que ça passera."

32. "… pratiquement en catastrophe."

33. The Broadcasting Act stipulates in Section 26 (2) that "where the Governor in Council deems the broadcast of any program to be of urgent importance to Canadians (generally or to persons resident in any area of Canada), the Governor in Council may, by order, direct the Commission to issue a notice to licensees

throughout Canada or throughout any area of Canada, of any class specified in the order, requiring the licensees to broadcast the program in accordance with the order, and licensees to whom any such order is addressed shall comply with the notice."

34. "Il fallait que quelqu'un en autorité, et en autorité puissante, fasse réfléchir les Québécois sur l'enjeu, son importance, ses consequences."

35. "C'était normal. Cet homme était là pour défendre l'unité canadienne. Cela faisait partie des règles du jeu. Chacun faisait son travail avec les instruments dont il disposait. Ce que je trouvais désolant, à un certain moment, c'était que je n'avais pas tous les instruments disponibles qu'un premier ministre du Canada pouvait avoir. C'était embêtant. Pendant la campagne référendaire, on avait réussi à établir des conditions à peu près normales avec Radio-Québec, mais, mon Dieu, que les négociations pour avoir un peu de temps d'antenne étaient compliquées!"

36. "M. Bouchard n'a pas eu connaissance du texte de M. Chrétien avant de préparer le sien, chacun préparant son discours en même temps, sans connaître le texte de son vis-à-vis. (…) alors que c'est toujours les souverainistes qui ont accusé les fédéralistes d'avoir deux discours, un pour le Québec, un autre pour le reste du pays."

37. This part of the interwiew was conducted in English.

38. "Est-ce qu'on a parlé de ses relations familiales, intimes ou même de ses problèmes d'affaires? Non. On a parlé de gestes politiques qu'il a faits pour le gouvernement du Canada, lorsqu'il était ministre de la Justice. Ce n'était pas personnel, c'était politique. Il a décidé de s'introduire dans la campagne, alors il était tout à fait normal qu'on dise: la personne qui vous demande de lui faire confiance pour l'avenir, voilà ce qu'elle a fait dans le passé récent. Je m'étonne qu'il s'en étonne."

39. "On a eu assez de misère à le faire atterrir sur scène. Il ne s'est pas contenté de rentrer par une petite porte de côté. Les gens voulaient lui toucher. Les gens se 'garrochaient' pour le toucher. C'était étouffant. À un moment donné, on avait peur: allions-nous être capables de contrôler cette foule? Cela n'a pas été de tout repos!"

40. "L'image qui me revient le plus, ce sont ces têtes de jeunes. Ils étaient là. Il y avait, je ne sais pas… 70% de la salle donnait l'impression d'être composée de jeunes. (…) C'était parce que l'auditorium était disponible. Il ne faut pas s'imaginer qu'on a fait des contre-feux: si les gens du NON sont allés à Verdun, donc il faut aller à Verdun. Non, non. La question de la réservation des salles posait tout un problème dont on ne se rend pas compte…"

41. "Notre force, c'était dans l'est, le NON, sa force, c'était dans l'ouest. Je me rappelle: on se retrouve au bureau du premier ministre à Hydro-Québec, et là, je propose à MM. Parizeau, Bouchard et Dumont d''accoter' le camp du NON et de faire, à Verdun, un rassemblement, où il y aurait un plus grand nombre de participants que les libéraux. Les trois m'ont regardé, un peu sceptiques, en disant: pourquoi prendre ce risque? M. Parizeau m'a dit: ' tes-vous sûr, M. Royer?' M. Bouchard m'a dit: ' tes-vous sûr?' M. Dumont m'a examiné, l'air de se dire: 'Est-ce qu'il va être en mesure de livrer…?'"

42. "… comme dans un geste de reconnaissance pour avoir nommé Lucien Bouchard négociateur. Après la soirée, quand M. Parizeau est monté dans la voiture, il m'a dit: 'M. Royer, j'ai bien aimé ma soirée.' J'ai compris qu'il voulait dire: on a pris la bonne décision."

43. CROP survey for *La Presse*, the TVA network and the *Toronto Star*.

44. "À l'intérieur de nos structures, il y avait des gens, qui disaient: 'Je pense qu'on peut l'avoir, puis on va l'avoir!'"

45. "Alors, les référendums qui ont eu lieu chez les Inuits et chez les Cris, c'était une déclaration d'intention, dit-il, en anticipant la poursuite des discussions avec les chefs de ces nations. Mais le cadre juridique (de ces discussions) était clair et il respectait parfaitement l'intégrité territoriale du Québec. (…) Ces gens-là n'ont jamais renoncé à leurs droits territoriaux. Alors, le Québec, quand il devient un pays souverain, sera forcé d'ouvrir des négociations avec eux. Et celles-ci pourraient durer très longtemps."

46. The *Grand Robert de la langue française* dictionary.

47. The list of pilots includes the names of Captains Larouche, Brosseau, Hébert, Lepage, Roy and others.

48. The Canadian National Defence Department has thirteen airbases, spread throughout the country, from Comox, on Vancouver Island, to Gander, in Newfoundland. Of these thirteen bases, only Bagotville and Cold Lake are bases that have fighter jets. The 3rd wing of Bagotville constitutes a rapid air reinforcement force, at the disposal of NORAD and NATO. In this capacity, it participates in defending the territory of the North American continent and intervenes abroad as a detachment integrated into the multinational NATO forces, as it did in Bosnia-Herzegovina. The 3rd wing comprises more than CF-18 pilots; it also includes Griffon helicopter crews, support and maintenance staff, and a radar squadron.

49. The jets in question are 716, 730, 768, 783, 785, 786, 906 and 915.

50. This analysis was conducted on behalf of Radio-Canada by Colonel Michel W. Drapeau, a legal consultant with Barrick Poulsen of Ottawa.

51. SOM survey, *Le Soleil*, Radio-Québec and *The Gazette*.

CHAPTER 12

1. See chapter X.

2. "Et c'est un peu une boule de neige qui se nourrit d'elle-même. Le bouche à oreille fait le reste."

3. "Il y en a qui me disaient que Mme Copps voudrait peut-être parler. J'ai dit: 'Il n'en est pas question. Les trois chefs, point à la ligne!'"

4. "Ma réponse a été oui aux deux questions, un événement que je regrette d'avoir accepté. Le référendum demeurait une question québécoise, un enjeu qui devait être réglé au Québec par des Québécois."

5. "Au départ, c'était un événement montréalais et de la périphérie. (...) On était sûr qu'il y aurait 8 000 personnes, peut-être 10 000... On a ameuté la zone (de l'indicatif régional) 450."

6. "Alors, je l'ai informé qu'il n'était pas question que ce soit du transport gratuit. Les gens doivent absolument en payer au moins le coût. Venez si vous voulez, lui ai-je dit, mais il n'est pas question que ce soit un voyage gratuit. (...) Car c'est finalement M. Johnson et l'agent électoral qui vont être tenus responsables de cet accroc à la loi électorale du Québec."

7. "Au départ, ce n'était que pour la Place du Canada. Mais plus ça augmentait... À un moment donné, les autorités de la Ville nous ont dit: 'On ne peut pas vous donner un permis juste pour la Place du Canada. On va devoir vous donner aussi un permis pour le Carré Dominion, on va devoir fermer des rues.'"

8. "On ne savait pas ce que ce serait. Mais on savait que ça allait être gros. On savait que ces gens-là, dans des autobus, prenaient de la bière. Ils ne venaient pas nous dire qu'ils nous aimaient, ils venaient pour participer à un party. (...) S'il fallait que la violence éclate là-dedans, l'image du référendum ne serait pas très bonne. La violence a toujours nui au camp souverainiste."

9. "C'était assez provocateur de débarquer dans le centre-ville de Montréal, à quelques jours du référendum, en ne respectant absolument aucune règle et en dépensant de l'argent à flots. (...) Il y avait un mot d'ordre très clair, très net, de se tenir loin de cela, de laisser ces gens-là manifester pacifiquement, en souhaitant que tout se passe bien."

10. Story by Christine Saint-Pierre on Radio-Canada, October 25; *La Presse*, October 26.

11. "... de façon à pouvoir identifier un peu les têtes chaudes, les souverainistes qui, dans ce genre d'événement, vont être tentés d'aller dire leur façon de penser à leurs nouveaux amoureux (...). Si on voyait un Jos clinclin qu'on connaissait, on l'arrêtait, on le raisonnait, on lui disait: 'Écoute, évite de faire ça. Ce n'est pas de ça qu'on a besoin...'"

12. "Les discours, dans un contexte comme celui-là, c'était vraiment compliqué. On s'adressait à la foule, mais on avait le sentiment que c'était tellement gros qu'on n'était pas sûr que les gens entendaient même ce qu'on disait. Mais ça permettait de maintenir un certain *momentum* pour la campagne, c'est ce que j'ai senti."

13. "L'humble petit comité d'organisation devait les rencontrer à la porte. Tout le monde devait sortir de la Place Ville-Marie en même temps. L'équipe qui avait monté le rassemblement devait sortir avec les premiers ministres et tout le monde devait faire la grande parade vers le Carré Dominion, vers la Place du Canada et se retrouver sur l'estrade avec eux. Mais ils ne nous ont pas laissé de place. Les agents de la GRC ont entouré Johnson et Chrétien. Ils ignoraient qui nous étions. Alors, on a sauté comme des bouchons! On n'a jamais rien vu!"

14. "Je ne pouvais pas marcher. Il y avait tellement de monde. En fait, on (le comité) a participé à la manifestation comme tout le monde." The rest of this interview was given in English.

15. Mike Harris was elected MP representing Nipissing in 1981, as a Conservative. He became leader of his party in May 1990, then Ontario's 22nd premier on June 8, 1995, ousting New Democrat Bob Rae.

16. "Il y a eu des discours, mais c'est plutôt ce grand drapeau qui circulait, qui faisait voir à tout le monde que c'était un rallye pour le Canada, pour la place de la francophonie au Canada."

17. This part of the interview was conducted in English.

18. "J'ai vu le stade olympique rempli pendant un spectacle des Rolling Stones. Il peut contenir autour de 52 à 53 000 personnes. J'ai fait la comparaison et j'ai choisi de jouer de prudence et de gonfler l'estimation de la police."

19. "C'était essentiellement des Montréalais. Le comité du NON avait fait venir beaucoup de gens de nos associations de circonscriptions électorales, de la grande périphérie de Montréal, ce qu'on appelle aujourd'hui la zone 450. J'ai rencontré dans la rue, c'est vrai, des étudiants de Cornwall et de jeunes Franco-Ontariens qui étaient venus en auto pour la journée, et des gens du Nouveau-Brunswick. C'était un peu bigarré. Ça devait être, au départ, des travailleurs du centre-ville de Montréal, qui, en prenant leur heure de dîner, descendraient, puis retourneraient ensuite au bureau. Et c'est essentiellement cela qu'il y avait là."

20. Parts of the interview conducted in French: "Je me promenais, je voyais des drapeaux par terre. J'étais sur les marches de la cathédrale Marie-Reine-du-Monde, du côté nord-ouest. (…) Lorsque les Irlandais sont venus au Canada, mes ancêtres, plusieurs ont été enterrés sous le Carré Dominion. (…) Ce que je voyais, c'était un immense champ de bataille, comme s'il y avait eu des armes sur le sol, mais ce n'était pas des armes, c'était des drapeaux. J'avais un drôle de *feeling*, un sentiment étrange. Je ne savais plus si je devais être heureux ou malheureux parce qu'il y avait, par terre, des drapeaux canadiens et des drapeaux québécois. Je ne me sentais pas bien, je me sentais mal. Je n'étais pas seul. Il y avait une centaine de personnes qui circulaient. Les rues étaient encore fermées. Je me disais: c'est moi qui ai causé ça. C'est presque une guerre moderne. Quelqu'un est arrivé en poussant une bicyclette. Un garçon dans la vingtaine. Il pleurait. Il ramassait les drapeaux du Québec et les mettait un à un dans un panier accroché aux guidons de son vélo. Puis, il m'a regardé et m'a dit: 'Vous avez tué mon pays.' Je me suis dit: qu'est-ce que j'ai fait! Je vais m'en souvenir longtemps, longtemps. J'ai même le frisson en ce moment, juste en y pensant."

21. "Je n'ai jamais pensé que cela avait aidé. Mais jusqu'à quel point cela a-t-il nui? Je n'ai jamais pensé que cela avait été de notre côté. Ce qu'on n'a jamais compris, ce que Brian Tobin n'a jamais saisi, c'est que ce n'était pas le moment de dire: qu'est-ce qu'on peut faire pour le Québec? Il était en retard de cinq ans! Ou il était en avance, il présumait du résultat! Le ralliement a donné l'impression que nous avions besoin d'aide, nous du NON. Cela a mis de la *statique* dans le système, de l'eau dans le *gaz*, appelez ça comme vous voudrez. Cela a diminué l'impact du rassemblement de ce qui devait être un rassemblement de Montréalais. Cela n'a pas aidé la cause. (…) Cela leur a permis de faire des discours pendant une demi-journée, puis de hurler qu'on avait dépensé 4,3 millions. Pas 4,2, pas 4,4… 4,3 millions! De la foutaise!"

22. "Lorsqu'on regarde les sondages internes du samedi et du dimanche, donc après l'événement du vendredi, l'option fédéraliste a recommencé à descendre. L'événement, selon la façon dont les Québécois l'ont perçu, a nui à la cause du NON. Je pense que M. Bouchard a réussi à les convaincre en prétendant qu'il s'agissait d'une invasion barbare. Ils l'ont vu comme une manifestation d'étrangers, même si ce n'était pas le cas."

23. "Je suis heureux que des gens de l'extérieur de la province soient venus à Montréal." The rest of the interview was conducted in English.

24. "La première chose que j'ai entendue, c'est un bruit, comme s'il y avait un immense défilé. Une mer humaine qui rentrait dans les rues autour. (…) Alors, je me suis dit: Oups! Ça peut avoir un impact, un impact très important sur les personnes qui sont encore craintives, un peu indécises, qui se laisseront prendre par les sentiments."

25. "Ce soir-là, le OUI a pris quelques fractions de point, ou un point ou deux, et le NON en a perdu. L'effet global, sur le coup, a plutôt été positif pour le OUI."

26. "Il y a pas mal de gens qui se rendent compte, chez les fédéralistes, qu'ils ont gagné, par une toute petite marge, par un geste qui violait toutes les lois financières du gouvernement du Québec, applicables aux consultations populaires. Et impunément. C'est très sérieux, une situation comme celle-là. Encore aujourd'hui, je ne puis m'empêcher de penser que, cet après-midi-là, quelques gouvernements de province, le gouvernement fédéral, quelques sociétés d'État, une compagnie de téléphone et des compagnies aériennes ont dépensé deux fois ce que le camp du OUI et le camp du NON ont dépensé, ensemble, pour toute la campagne. C'était illégal d'après nos lois. Et on n'y pouvait rien."

27. "Je ne sais pas si ce rallye a fait basculer le vote, mais il l'a influencé. C'est très clair. C'est vrai qu'il est rare qu'il y ait des événements, pendant une campagne électorale, qui font basculer les gens d'un côté ou de l'autre. Mais cela arrive parce qu'un référendum ou une élection se joue sur les indécis."

28. MONIÈRE, GUAY, *op. cit.*, p. 202.

29. "Ils mêlaient les choses beaucoup, beaucoup. D'abord, ils auraient pu éviter cela en appuyant l'Accord du lac Meech, cinq ans plus tôt. Ensuite, c'est aux Québécois de décider de leur avenir. Cela, ils ne l'ont pas saisi. Tous les premiers ministres du Québec, les uns après les autres, y compris moi, avons déclaré cela au moins une fois à l'Assemblée nationale. Tu peux pas, de l'extérieur, empêcher les Québécois de se prononcer sur comment ils envisagent leur avenir. Et d'ailleurs, personne ne peut dire aujourd'hui qu'un vote pour le OUI à 1% de majorité aurait mis fin au Canada."

30. "Il y avait M. Tobin, M. Gagliano, un certain nombre de ministres qu'on a voulu interroger. La personne responsable des questions juridiques de la Chambre des communes nous a dit, erronément à mon avis, qu'on n'avait pas le droit de les interroger, on n'avait pas le droit de faire appel à eux. On a été obligés de se plier à cela."

31. "L'argument qu'ils avaient, un argument qui a un certain poids, il faut l'admettre, c'était: on est dans un pays libre, on a le droit de s'exprimer, on a le droit de faire les dépenses qu'on veut. (…) Le grand problème, c'est qu'au Canada, on vit dans un État de droit, où il y a un partage des responsabilités entre les deux sortes de gouvernements. Mais, en ce qui concerne la Loi sur la consultation populaire, j'ai envie de dire qu'on est dans un demi-État de droit parce que, ce qui est édicté au Québec, on ne peut pas l'appliquer ailleurs, aux Canadiens qui demeurent en dehors du territoire de la province de Québec. La question à se poser, c'est: est-ce qu'on peut aller à l'encontre des exigences de la loi et faire ce qu'on veut et comme on veut? Si je réponds oui à cette question, c'est à se demander si on vit dans un État de droit ou pas. Est-ce qu'on est libre ou pas, dans une société libre et démocratique, d'adopter des législations qui concernent le déroulement d'activités proprement provinciales ou à caractère proprement québécois?"

32. "Est-ce que, pour organiser ce rallye, on pouvait être d'accord sur le fait qu'il y avait des dépenses non réglementées qui n'étaient pas dans le cadre des comités-parapluies? Ils avaient le droit de venir au Québec, ils avaient le droit de venir exprimer leur opinion. Ce qui était défendu, c'était que leurs dépenses soient assumées par d'autres intervenants."

33. "Je fais partie de la génération qui a été très marquée par les lois sur le financement des partis politiques et les lois sur les consultations populaires de René Lévesque. Moi, je crois dans ces lois. Mon indignation date de ce jour. On nous parle beaucoup de l'État de droit. Après une manifestation comme celle-là, on dit: l'État de quel droit? Quel est le droit qui s'applique? Une société ne peut pas établir de règles pour tenir des votes dans sa population sans que quelqu'un d'autre puisse intervenir à partir de règles différentes en disant: passez n'importe quelle loi que vous voulez qui s'applique à vous, moi, je ferai ce que je veux. Drôle d'État de droit! (…) Vous n'avez pas 5 000 $ ou 10 000 $ disponibles. Tout est engagé. Et le camp du NON aussi, tout son argent est engagé. Le camp du NON, au Québec, a été absolument correct par rapport à ces lois. Quand je parle du gouvernement fédéral, je veux dire vraiment le gouvernement fédéral."

34. Freely translated excerpt from Jean-François LISÉE, *Sortie de secours: comment échapper au déclin du Québec* (Emergency exit: how to avoid the decline of Quebec). Montréal, Le Boréal, 2000, p. 295.

35. BLANCHARD, *op. cit.*, p. 252.

CHAPTER 13

1. Peter Wardell Hogg is a Toronto lawyer, professor of Law and former dean of Osgoode Hall Law School, a position that he held until June 2003. His written works, in particular the two volumes, *Constitutional Law of Canada* and *Liability of the Crown*, are frequently cited by the Supreme Court of Canada and judicial bodies throughout the British Commonwealth. He earned his LL.B. from the University of New Zealand, his LL.M. from Harvard University and his Ph.D. from Monash University in Melbourne, Australia. In the autumn of 1995, he was in continuous contact with Allan Rock.

2. Freely translated excerpt from PARIZEAU, *op. cit.*, p. 286.

3. "Imaginons qu'un des joueurs du camp du OUI arrive après coup en disant: 'M. Parizeau usurpe son mandat, la question référendaire, c'était ça, mais il fait autre chose.' C'est triste à dire, mais, le seul pouvoir qui restait alors, c'était une crise politique. Imaginons que Lucien Bouchard, le négociateur en chef, ait été tassé et qu'il n'ait plus le mandat de négocier… Je n'ai jamais craint cela. À partir du moment où M. Parizeau a signé l'entente du 12 juin, qu'il a accepté le comité de négociation, le comité de surveillance, il s'est enfermé dans un carcan. Il ne pouvait plus revenir en arrière."

4. "Il était encadré par une réalité politique: nous avions fait le OUI dans un rassemblement; il aurait fallu faire la transition dans un rassemblement."

5. "Je comprends très bien, que, dans les derniers jours avant le référendum, il exprimait un peu la volonté de se libérer de tous ces liens qui avaient été créés. Mais le fait est que, après, ces liens-là auraient été tout aussi existants qu'avant, sinon plus."

6. "C'est ça, le rôle de toutes les études qui ont été faites quant à la restructuration du gouvernement de Québec. On n'est pas capable, par exemple, de monter une fusion du ministère des Revenus des deux gouvernements. Faire en quinze jours le déplacement de millions de formulaires d'impôt? Il y a toute une série de choses qui doivent être mises en place. Il faut être responsable là-dedans!"

7. "On reconnaît l'institution (démocratique). On y participe. On espère qu'on va gagner. Mais si c'est le OUI qui l'emporte dans une courte victoire, il y a tout un enchaînement d'inconnus. On pourrait dire: s'il y avait un autre référendum, un mois plus tard, compte tenu du comportement appréhendé de Jacques Parizeau, de Bernard Landry et d'autres ministres souverainistes, les Québécois, très surpris de voir comment on interprétait la victoire du OUI, n'auraient-ils pas voté NON? La question reste posée."

8. "Le lendemain d'un référendum, le résultat est mesuré à partir de la question. On cherche à connaître la signification du résultat. Et, compte tenu de la question, il y aurait eu beaucoup de confusion. Ce que, pendant la campagne, j'appelais le *trou noir*."

9. Senator Gérald-A. Beaudoin, with degrees from the Université de Montréal and the University of Ottawa, has been a professor, dean of Civil Law and associate director of the University of Ottawa's Human Rights Research and Education Centre. He is the author of many books on the Canadian Constitution, the Charter of Rights, and human rights, both in Canada and abroad. As a Senator, he chaired the Standing Senate Committee on Legal and Constitutional Affairs.

10. "Une élection démocratique, c'est cela: 50% plus un. On a vu des députés être élus par trois, par cinq votes de majorité. (…) Les réformistes voulaient être l'opposition officielle. Le sénateur Beaudoin, qui est notre oracle constitutionnel, a tranché: ce n'est pas le pourcentage qui compte, c'est le nombre de députés. Alors, si le OUI gagne, disons à 50,5%, on ne va pas dire: on va recommencer parce qu'on en a pas assez. Gagner à 50,5%, moi, j'aurais été à l'aise avec cela."

11. "Personne n'aurait été malheureux si on avait eu 50,5%, mais cela aurait été peut-être plus difficile que 53%. En démocratie, c'est bien de valeur, mais ce n'est pas la minorité qui mène. À 49,5%, nous, on a accepté le résultat du vote, le soir du référendum."

12. "49,5%, ce n'est pas une victoire morale, c'est une défaite. De deux choses l'une: si c'est moi qui ai 49,5%, je ne peux rien faire, donc je ne fais rien. Si c'est moi qui ai 50,5%, alors je fais ce que j'ai dit que je ferais. Je n'ai pas d'état d'âme, moi, à cet égard. Je vais chercher un mandat; si je l'ai, je marche."

13. "J'ai toujours soutenu que, toute de suite après une victoire du OUI, le premier coup de téléphone qu'on recevrait serait celui du gouverneur de la Banque du Canada. Et qui dirait: 'On fait pas les fous, hein?' Et nous, on répondrait: 'On fait pas les fous!' Il est évident que maintenir la stabilité du dollar canadien implique qu'on ne s'excite pas. C'est la Banque du Canada qui est essentiellement responsable d'assurer cette stabilité."

14. "Gravement. Et les valeurs des entreprises canadiennes-anglaises, cotées en Bourse à Toronto ou à New York, auraient chuté gravement aussi. Mais l'intérêt de l'élite financière et industrielle canadienne-anglaise était de restabiliser la situation le plus rapidement possible. Les appels qui se seraient faits au bureau du premier ministre fédéral, auraient été: 'Stabilisez, et vite!'"

15. "Parce qu'il y avait manifestement des ministres pour qui la souveraineté aurait encore été une sorte de découverte."

16. "C'est à cause de Valéry Giscard d'Estaing qu'on s'est rendu compte qu'il y avait une étape qui manquait. Il nous a fait comprendre qu'un référendum, ce n'est même pas une intention, c'est tout au plus une autorisation, et que nous n'aurions pu nous appuyer sur la France tant que ce maillon manquant — la motion — n'aurait pas été mis en place."

17. "Ce genre de discussion, je devais l'avoir avec une personne qui n'avait pas de titre officiel et qui ne craignait pas que je l'amène dans un piège à ours. Quelqu'un, par contre, qui était extrêmement bien branché et qui avait accès à tous les intervenants importants du côté des libéraux."

18. "Je sais qu'au début, il va me dire que le NON va gagner. Je lui dis: 'Essaie de faire abstraction de ta certitude et embarque dans la mienne, que c'est le OUI qui va gagner.'"

19. "Il m'a demandé si je pouvais m'engager à en parler à M. Johnson. Je ne pouvais pas m'engager à le faire et je lui ai dit qu'à ce moment, je trouvais même difficile d'interpréter la mentalité de M. Johnson, qui était tellement fédéraliste, et que je ne le verrais pas reconnaître les résultats. Je ne me voyais pas m'engager pour lui."

20. "Dans les jours précédents, j'étais affublé de tous les quolibets. On remettait mon identité québécoise en doute et, là, ils voulaient que je me rallie. J'ai trouvé ça assez extraordinaire. C'était une blague monumentale que M. Parizeau et les autres voulaient me faire. Ils voulaient miner notre confiance pour le jour du vote."

21. "Je n'ai pas de réponse à cela. Je ne sais pas s'il y avait une si grande contradiction entre les deux. Je ne crois pas que cela faisait vraiment partie de la problématique."

22. "Advenant une entente de partenariat, s'il y avait des instances communes, le Bloc aurait pu être considéré comme l'aile parlementaire. Mais, encore là, il y avait un problème: nous ne voulions plus qu'il y ait d'instances élues. Aurait-il fallu que ces gens-là soient délégués temporairement? Je ne vois pas comment cela aurait pu passer parce que le mandat du Bloc n'était pas terminé. Ultimement, si je regarde les textes tels qu'ils sont écrits, le Bloc aurait dû disparaître."

23. "Si le OUI l'emportait par 52% à 48%, 48%, c'est beaucoup de monde. Ces gens-là peuvent réagir de deux façons: ou ils acceptent le résultat, se retroussent les manches et travaillent à construire le Québec sur de nouvelles bases, ou, comme on dit dans le domaine de l'agriculture, ils se 'mettent le derrière de travers dans la crèche.' Il y en a partout dans la société, dans le monde des affaires, des banques, des communautés culturelles évidemment, de la communauté anglophone… Si tout ce monde se met de travers, ça peut devenir pénible. Alors, le rôle qu'on se donnait, à l'ADQ, c'était d'être le tampon et de mettre de l'huile dans les engrenages. En somme, d'être des gens modérés. La plupart des gens à l'ADQ avaient un passé libéral, donc on pensait jouer un rôle pour 'ressouder' le Québec."

24. "J'aurais utilisé mon expérience, mes convictions, pour jouer le rôle que, dans nos institutions, le chef de l'opposition doit jouer. Parce que j'étais toujours, le lendemain matin, chef de l'opposition à l'Assemblée nationale avec la responsabilité d'assurer le développement ordonné du Québec."

25. "Il n'en a jamais été question. Il y a des gens qui en ont parlé, peut-être à voix haute, mais ça n'a jamais été très loin. Ça n'a jamais été pris très au sérieux. Pour nous, en tout cas, ni moi ni quiconque dans mon parti n'avons été approchés là-dessus."

26. This part of the interview was conducted in English.

27. "En 1980, Trudeau a dit: 'On va démissionner, on met nos sièges en jeu.' Je n'ai pas dit non. S'il avait démissionné, j'aurais démissionné aussi. Rétrospectivement, je pense que cela a dû avoir un effet sur les gens. Mais si on avait perdu? Je pense que cela aurait été plus raisonnable de ne pas le dire et de régler le problème d'une façon différente. Et c'est pour cela que je n'ai pas répété cette phrase-là au référendum de 1995."

28. SOM-Environics poll commissioned by *Le Devoir*, Radio-Canada, *Le Soleil*, *Le Droit* and *The Gazette*.

29. As specified in the draft sovereignty bill.

30. *Confédération des syndicats nationaux*—Confederation of National Trade Unions (CNTU).

31. "Écoutez, on a perdu le référendum. Qu'est-ce qu'on fait? Le Québec aurait voulu se faire reconnaître à l'étranger, mais je ne suis pas sûr qu'il y ait des tonnes de pays qui l'auraient reconnu. Nous, on aurait dit: la question était ambiguë. Gagner un référendum par un vote… On ne brise pas un pays parce que quelqu'un a oublié ses lunettes pour aller voter. Ça prend une majorité qualifiée. (…) Pour annuler une charte de club de chasse et pêche, ça prend un deuxième vote. Dans la constitution de la CSN, pour se débarrasser du président, ça prend plus que 50 plus un, si je me rappelle bien. Alors, que voulez-vous…"

32. This part of the interview was conducted in English.

33. "Le lendemain, on aurait été confronté à cette réalité-là. Après, on aurait fait quoi? Il aurait fallu interpréter à nouveau. Le scénario le plus difficile, c'est celui où il y a des victoires qui sont très minces. (…) Ils savaient sur quoi ils votaient. Je pense qu'ils savaient que, s'ils votaient OUI, il allait y avoir une brisure ou le risque d'une brisure."

34. "C'est aux Québécois de décider de leur avenir."

35. "L'idéal, ce serait cela. Mais là, on vit dans un autre monde. Le Québec fait partie du Canada. On est, géographiquement, localisé dans un pays de sorte que, dans l'hypothèse d'une souveraineté intégrale du Québec, le Canada serait séparé en deux par un autre pays. Les États-Unis ne peuvent pas être indifférents à cela, et le reste du Canada non plus. On ne parle pas ici d'un petit bout de territoire. Le Québec est dans le cœur du pays. On a un système fédéral à cause du Québec. Sans le Québec, on s'en irait vers un gouvernement plutôt unitaire. C'est vraiment rêver en couleurs que de penser que ça va se régler entre Québécois, pour les Québécois seulement. Il faut vivre dans un autre monde pour penser que le reste de l'Amérique ne peut pas se sentir intéressé, si un nouveau pays émerge.

36. Lawrence MARTIN, *Iron Man. The Defiant Reign of Jean Chrétien*. Toronto: Viking Canada, 2003, p. 135. When Martin's book was published, Ottawa's reaction was emphatic, and Jean Chrétien, as well as other ministers, attempted to spread confusion about what Collenette had said, but Collenette confirmed that this is indeed what he said.

37. *La Presse*, October 22, 2003.

38. This part of the interview was conducted in English.

39. *La Presse*, October 19, 1995.

40. *La Presse*, October 19, 1995.

41. *Le Devoir*, October 20, 1995.

42. "Le gouvernement de Québec voit le gouvernement canadien et lui dit: 'Le plus vite possible, il faut un accord de libre circulation des véhicules, des personnes, terrestre, maritime, aérienne entre l'Ontario et les provinces maritimes.' Vous pensez que le gouvernement fédéral canadien aurait dit non?"

43. "Les provinces anglophones auraient alors voulu refaire la Constitution. Les droits des francophones, qu'il y a dans la Constitution, y auraient passé. Je pense que ceux qui auraient été les premiers à vouloir nous enlever ces droits-là auraient été les gens qui nous avaient été sympathiques, qui avaient placé leurs enfants dans les écoles d'immersion, qui avaient fait comme un acte de confiance dans l'avenir, assurant que leurs enfants apprennent le français. Ils se seraient sentis trahis. Les écoles, la gestion scolaire et les

choses qui font que le Canada est un pays bilingue, reconnaissant la dualité linguistique comme caractéristique fondamentale, ça risquait de disparaître. Être Canadien français hors du Québec, c'est une bataille de tous les jours."

44. "Les Indiens n'auraient pas droit à la sécession, selon un document fédéral" (Indians would not be entitled to secede, according to a federal document), *La Presse*, October 13, 1995.

45. *La Presse*, October 27, 1995.

CHAPTER 14

1. "'Je sais que tu as vu Monique Simard ce matin. Elle nous a dit que tu étais sûr de gagner. Si tu es si sûr, je te parie 25 000 $ que c'est nous qui allons gagner.' J'ai senti un silence au bout du fil. Puis, John m'a dit: 'Non, non, je ne gage jamais.' Tous ceux qui étaient dans la salle ont interprété son silence comme la preuve qu'il était pas mal moins sûr de gagner. (…) Dans le fond, je savais très bien que ce n'était pas dans la nature de John de parier, je savais qu'il me dirait non. J'ai pris le risque. J'aurais été bien embêté s'il m'avait dit oui parce que je n'avais pas les 25 000 $."

2. "Je pense qu'il s'est payé un petit peu notre gueule cette journée-là."

3. "Je voyais dans les sondages une tendance qui nous menait à 52%. La façon que j'avais, avec le sondeur du camp du OUI, Michel Lepage, de répartir les indécis nous amenait à un résultat gagnant."

4. "Oui, les sondages nous mettaient à 52, 53%. Mais le mouvement souverainiste a toujours eu, même dans les élections provinciales, un problème qu'on appelle 'la prime à l'urne.' Il y a toujours 2%, 3% qui nous manquent. On n'est jamais capable de comprendre pourquoi. Ce qui signifie qu'avec la prime à l'urne, ça nous laissait à 49%, 50%."

5. "On savait que, s'il y avait moins de 80% des électeurs qui votaient, ce n'était pas bon pour nous. Cela voulait dire que les jeunes votaient moins que lors des élections et, notre majorité, elle était plus forte chez les jeunes. (…) Si le nombre d'électeurs était inférieur à 80%, cela signifiait qu'à l'intérieur des groupes, il y avait une proportion plus forte de non-francophones que de francophones qui votaient."

6. "On avait donné des objectifs à chacun. On surveillait pour voir si on était en avance ou en arrière dans la sortie du vote. On mettait la pression là où ça marchait moins bien. (…) On avait des comptes à rendre. M. Bouchard, M. Parizeau voulaient savoir."

7. "Nous avions fait ce que nous pouvions faire. Quant à nous, tout était fini, autour de la table, nous n'avons pas eu de grandes décisions à prendre ce jour-là: on touche du bois, on se croise les doigts, puis on va attendre les résultats. Attendre, c'était épouvantable."

8. "J'étais dans un état d'esprit d'attente. Tout était fait. On ne pouvait plus rien faire. Ça appartenait à des millions de Québécois de faire un geste et, nous, on attendait… Je n'ai jamais pensé que le OUI pouvait gagner."

9. Excerpt from the interview granted during the day to Stéphan Bureau of TVA.

10. *Ibid.*

11. *Ibid.*

12. Excerpt from the interview granted by Lisette Lapointe to Stéphan Bureau, October 30, 1995.

13. "C'est une fille qui ne s'énerve pas pour rien. J'ai tout de suite senti, au bout du fil, qu'il y avait une certaine fébrilité. Cela ne m'a pas surpris. M. Parizeau me l'avait dit vingt fois, trente fois, et pas seulement au moment de la campagne référendaire. Quand il est revenu à la politique, il m'a dit: 'Moi, je reviens pour faire la souveraineté. Si ça ne marche pas, je n'aime pas assez la politique pour faire cela.'"

14. "Ça durait quand même dix-huit minutes. Il fallait qu'il fasse une seule prise et qu'elle soit parfaite. Il a recommencé deux ou trois fois, en français. Puis, il fallait le faire en anglais. Là, son niveau de fatigue était déjà élevé. Ce fut laborieux. Ça nous a pris pas mal de temps."

15. DUCHESNE, *op. cit.*, p. 535.

16. "'Vous ne vous êtes pas retenu, il fallait que vous le disiez!' Parizeau lui répond: 'Oui, je l'ai dit. Ça ne vous surprend pas?' 'Non.'"

17. "Royer et moi, nous l'avons pris à part pour discuter de ce que serait son attitude en cas de victoire du NON. On l'a convaincu de ne pas annoncer (immédiatement) sa démission parce que, déjà, le choc serait dur pour les souverainistes d'avoir perdu le référendum. S'il fallait en plus qu'ils perdent leur leader, ce serait trop, ce serait trop demander aux Québécois, en un seul soir, de perdre les deux en même temps. 'On va avoir besoin de votre talent de rassembleur. C'est d'un grand-père qu'on aura besoin, ce soir, c'est de quelqu'un qui voit plus loin que la défaite ponctuelle.' (…) on pourra discuter de démission demain ou après-demain."

18. "Je voulais me protéger moi-même. Je ne me voyais pas recommencer ou essayer de recommencer. En enregistrant cette interview, le midi, les résultats n'étaient pas connus. Je ne voulais pas donner l'impression que j'attendais le résultat pour me décider. J'indiquais ce que j'allais faire dans chacune des deux branches de l'alternative: si ça passe, voici ce qu'on fait. Si ça ne passe pas, je m'en vais. (…) Sur le fond de la question, peut-être que je n'aurais pas démissionné si j'avais su ce qui allait venir après. Mais ça m'a pris plusieurs années pour comprendre cela. Sur le coup, c'était clair qu'il fallait que je m'en aille. Mais quelques années plus tard, c'est autre chose."

19. "Les trois premiers reportages du bulletin de nouvelles étaient sur le Québec. Le premier, sur le référendum, le deuxième, sur les conséquences diplomatiques avec les États-Unis et, le troisième, sur les conséquences au plan économique. Assis dans le lit, appuyé sur les oreillers, je me suis dit: 'Ouais, c'est une assez grosse affaire dans laquelle on s'est engagés!'"

20. "Les firmes de sondages enlevaient les virgules et arrondissaient les chiffres, de peur de se mouiller."

21. "J'ai senti dans son regard qu'il me sondait l'âme en me disant: 'Vous êtes sûr?' J'ai repris mes explications."

22. "Ce n'est pas faute d'avoir essayé. Mais M. Parizeau avait fait en sorte qu'on ne puisse pas communiquer avec lui. Il faut comprendre que c'était un choix qu'il avait fait."

23. "Et M. Bédard m'a fait comprendre qu'il n'y aurait pas de rencontre, et qu'au moment où on se parlait, il n'y avait pas de contact prévu. Et il n'y en a pas eu."

24. "J'ai trouvé cela étonnant comme expérience. C'est bête à dire, mais cela ne m'était jamais arrivé. Ça m'a fait du bien."

25. "L'atmosphère n'a pas changé. Nous, on était payés pour ne pas nous énerver. On savait que, si on s'énervait, cela pouvait avoir un effet sur le patron. Alors, le ton ne levait pas, il n'y avait pas de déception apparente."

26. Monière, Guay, *op. cit.*, p. 205.

27. "La Beauce, dont on attendait peu, offrait encore moins que ce qu'on attendait."

28. "Cela a dû être l'arrivée d'une séquence de cinq ou six circonscriptions où j'ai vu qu'il y avait une sorte de tendance. Avec Lepage, nous avions développé un modèle qui nous permettait, à partir d'indications minimales, de faire une projection. Alors, je savais assez rapidement que ce ne serait pas 52%. Et, quand sont arrivés les premiers résultats de Montréal, on a vu qu'on ne gagnerait pas."

29. "Je ne sais pas à quel moment M. Parizeau a assimilé le fait qu'on ne gagnerait pas."

30. "Cela a été un moment d'épouvante, de froid dans le dos. Ce n'était pas juste une déception. C'était un coup de masse. Tout son rêve s'envolait. C'était le combat de sa vie."

31. "C'était vraiment personnel. J'ai constaté que c'était comme s'il n'avait jamais été préparé à l'éventualité d'une victoire du NON. Même si nous avions pensé perdre, durant la campagne, même si on en avait discuté dans l'après-midi, c'était comme si, pour lui, c'était une situation nouvelle."

32. "C'est l'homme blessé, qui, ce soir-là, dit: 'Tout cela en valait la peine, si je gagnais. Mais, maintenant que j'ai perdu, ça n'en valait pas la peine.' (…) Mais c'est sorti longtemps. On a eu de la difficulté à le ramener. Et on lui disait: 'C'est un gain important depuis 1980, il faut le voir de façon positive. Et on a l'assurance qu'une majorité de francophones a voté OUI. Et puis, ce n'est pas fini…' Mais nous n'étions pas sûrs dans quelle mesure nous avions réussi à percer son état d'esprit avec cela. (…) 'Voulez-vous que je vous rédige quelques notes?'"

33. "Mais, on sait très bien, pour avoir fait cela pendant des années, qu'on est bien mieux d'attendre à 11 heures, le soir, que de commencer à fêter à 8 h 30."

NOTES

34. "La zone de confort, cela veut dire qu'au-dessus d'elle, on est de plus en plus confortable et, au-dessous, de moins en moins confortable, dans le sens où il y a un coefficient de difficulté qui est de plus en plus important. (…) Je n'ai pas le souvenir que les gens aient été assommés. Les sentiments étaient partagés. Certains disaient: 'Avec un chiffre comme celui-là, on est peut-être mieux d'avoir perdu que d'avoir gagné.' D'autres disaient plutôt que 'gagner, c'est gagner.' Mais le sentiment général était qu'on était passés tellement près que ce n'était pas vrai qu'on allait laisser tomber."

35. "Je n'ai jamais pensé que le OUI pouvait gagner. (…) Je voyais entrer les résultats, et je n'ai jamais été inquiet. Quand on connaît le Québec et qu'on voit la tendance du vote dans telle région, dans telle autre région, l'expérience permet de projeter. Je n'ai jamais cru qu'on perdrait. C'est ça, l'expérience."

36. "Je m'attendais à des pourcentages de 72%, 75% pour le OUI dans cette région-là. Ce n'était pas ça. (…) Et quand la ville de Québec a commencé à entrer, les pourcentages n'étaient pas de 60% pour le OUI, comme nous avions prévu, mais autour de 50%."

37. "J'étais le plus calme à la table parce que je m'étais mis dans la tête qu'on gagnerait."

38. "Il y avait une certaine tension, mais le premier ministre, comme à l'habitude dans ces moments-là, était très calme, très préoccupé, très conscient de la gravité du moment."

39. This part of the interview was conducted in English.

40. The Canadian Payments Association is a non-profit organization established by the federal government in 1980. Its mandate is to maintain clearing and settlement systems that facilitate the exchange of payments between the financial institutions that are members.

41. The "O" plan, developed by Quebec's Finance minister, guaranteed a 17 billion dollar reserve to support Quebec's bonds, if it became sovereign. See chapter X.

42. "Nous avons vu arriver M. Parizeau. On sait quelle sorte d'homme politique il est. Il le dit lui-même: il est *politically uncorrect* (sic), et il dit tout le temps ce qu'il pense. Nous n'avions aucune idée de ce qu'il allait dire."

43. "Il y a de la tristesse entre les deux. Il y a un peu de complicité dans l'échec."

44. "M. Parizeau prend mes feuilles, les déplie, les lit, les replie, les met dans sa poche, et ne dit rien. Alors là, je ne suis pas certain qu'il va lire ça!"

45. "Et, là, j'entends M. Parizeau dire des choses que je n'ai pas écrites, deux phrases terribles. Ça faisait un an et demi qu'on tenait un discours rassembleur, et, là, il nous fait revenir des années en arrière en une seule phrase."

46. David Payne is of British origin. He was the representative for the riding of Vachon from 1981 to 1985 and was defeated in two subsequent elections. Re-elected in 1994 and 1998, he was president of the Commission on culture and parliamentary assistant to the Premier. Payne has degrees in theology, philosophy and sociology, and worked in the public service before entering politics.

47. "Victoire ou défaite, cela n'aurait pas changé ma fin de soirée. Gagne ou perd, le lendemain, nous avions une journée au bureau et je la savais chargée. (…) Est-ce que cela aurait changé quelque chose, je ne peux pas le dire, mais j'aurais dû le faire. (…) M. Parizeau, moi, je l'ai conseillé. Aujourd'hui, je ne suis pas son juge. Ce n'est pas moi qui vais commencer à dire, maintenant que j'en suis sorti, si c'était un bon discours ou un mauvais discours. Mes impressions, je les garde pour moi."

48. "Les deux genoux m'ont plié. (…) On a senti un murmure dans la salle. Nous, on s'est dit: on a un problème pour demain. Comment va-t-il expliquer ça?"

49. "Tu comprends qu'il y a une fausse note, qu'il y a quelque chose qui ne marche pas. Puis, tu te rends compte que ça va être rapporté par la presse internationale et tu vois les conséquences. Un discours horrible pour le peuple qui aurait pu bénéficier d'un exercice capable de générer des bénéfices en termes de changements dans le système canadien. On a gaspillé ça!"

50. "Probablement contre le monde entier et contre moi-même. Si c'était à refaire? Je ferais fondamentalement le même genre de déclaration, mais pas dans les mêmes mots. Je parlerais aussi de la région de Québec… Et puis, je n'ai jamais vu cela en politique, des bureaux de scrutin, comme dans d'Arcy McGee, où il y a 0 OUI! Est-ce que quelqu'un d'autre a déjà vu cela dans un scrutin: 0 OUI? Quand,

dans des communautés culturelles tout à fait connues, vous avez 234 votes NON, 0 OUI, on ne peut pas parler de polarisation des votes? On ne peut pas dire: écoutez, c'est pas normal comme situation?"

51. "Je fignolais mes notes de discours. Mais, quand j'ai vraiment pris connaissance de ce qu'il a dit, j'étais un peu renversé, c'est le moins qu'on puisse dire. Il a manqué une bonne occasion de dire les choses autrement."

52. "J'ai vu des politiciens qui n'avaient pas bien réagi dans la défaite et qui n'ont jamais pu revenir. Quand vous êtes sûr de gagner, vous êtes extrêmement généreux dans votre discours de la défaite. Mais, ce jour-là, c'était plus sérieux, c'était plus corsé."

53. "C'était agréable. C'était le *fun*."

54. "M. Charest et moi, nous nous sommes posé la question plusieurs fois: était-ce un geste délibéré de sa part? Je crois, personnellement, qu'il s'agissait d'un geste délibéré. Chrétien a devant lui un écran de télévision. Il voit M. Charest qui vient de commencer à parler. Le Canada entier était rivé aux écrans de télévision. Je ne pense pas que c'est un réalisateur, à Ottawa, qui a décidé que c'est à ce moment-là que M. Chrétien parlerait. Je pense que c'est M. Chrétien qui a décidé…"

55. "Il y a 83% de francophones au Québec et on ne peut pas dire 'nous'? De toutes origines, pas seulement de souche. Il faut ajouter: Québécois francophones, anglophones, allophones… C'est ridicule. Savez-vous quelle est la proportion de gens, en Ontario, qui parlent anglais à la maison? La même proportion: 83%. Pourtant, quand on parle d'un Ontarien, on n'a jamais besoin de dire: francophone, allophone… On est Ontarien. Mais, au Québec, quand on parle de cette population immensément majoritaire francophone et qu'on dit 'nous,' tout le monde, dans certains milieux, dit: vous nous excluez parce que nous sommes anglophones."

56. "Attends à demain, m'a-t-elle dit, à cause de la situation dans la rue. Et elle a eu raison. C'était sage."

57. "Cela m'importait peu d'imaginer pour qui ils pouvaient voter. C'était l'exercice du droit de vote qui était en cause."

58. In 1995, Canada welcomed 55,705 new citizens, an increase of 12% over the preceding year. In Quebec, the increase was 19.4%, the highest in Canada: 7,882 citizenship certificates were issued in Quebec in 1995, 2,478 of which were issued during the third quarter, a 24% increase over the previous quarter. In October alone, there were 79 oath-taking ceremonies at the Guy-Favreau courthouse in Montreal, and 38 at the Saint-Laurent courthouse.

59. Accusations of irregularities were fired off by both camps to the Chief Electoral Officer, after the referendum. They concerned the financing of operations in each camp, voter registration, and rejected ballots. The daily The Gazette sided with the NO camp, now dissolved, to denounce the rejection of ballots in a number of ridings. The case of Chomedey was exceptional: 11.6% of the ballots were rejected, while the percentages of 5.5% in Marguerite-Bourgeoys and 3.6% in Laurier-Dorion were above the average, which was somewhere between the 0.8 in Roberval and the 2.9 in Marie-Victorin. From the YES side, accusations were made when non-Québécois students from McGill and Bishop universities were registered on the voters list, which forced the Chief Electoral Officer to clarify the distinctions Quebec law makes between the notion of domicile and the notion of residence. Minister Guy Chevrette, who was in charge of electoral reform, lodged a series of complaints with the Chief Electoral Officer concerning the thousands of dollars spent by Canadians who participated in the great demonstration at Place du Canada, asking him to condemn Daniel Johnson for associating himself with it. On October 9, 1997, the Supreme Court of Canada invalidated Section 413 of the special version of the Election Act for the holding of a referendum, which stipulated that during a "referendum period, only an official agent of a national committee, or one of his or her representatives, may incur or authorize regulated expenses." Consequently, the Chief Electoral Officer withdrew, one week later, all the lawsuits that had been initiated following the rally at Place du Canada, and halted the inquiry that he was leading, into Option Canada.

60. "… le ministère de l'Immigration a fait venir des juges de la citoyenneté des autres provinces pour accélérer le processus. (…) Il y a sûrement plusieurs milliers de personnes qui sont devenues citoyennes canadiennes, donc aptes à voter."

470

61. "Ils avaient divisé le Québec en quatorze régions. Le mot 'changement' évoquait quelque chose de favorable dans toutes les régions, sauf à Québec. À Québec, le mot 'changement' était péjoratif. Québec, c'est une ville très, très, très conservatrice."

62. MONIÈRE, GUAY, *op. cit.*, p. 236.

63. Source: http://www.pum.umontreal.ca/apqc/95_96/drouilly/drouilly.htm.

64. "Le comité des priorités est convoqué par M. Landry qui s'excite. Il trouve cela effrayant, épouvantable. Franchement, on aurait pu dormir une couple d'heures de plus. D'autant que la décision était prise, cela ne servait à rien de s'énerver."

65. "Pendant cette nuit-là, c'est l'épouse, c'est la conseillère, c'est la militante, c'est la femme qui essayait de convaincre son chef de ne pas démissionner, compte tenu des résultats."

66. "Un appel très, très, très arrogant. Le ton était dur. On sentait que la journée allait être bien pénible."

67. "C'est un moment vraiment pénible, terrible. Parce que Jacques Parizeau est déjà par terre. Il a déjà confirmé à M. Landry dans une réunion précédente, une réunion d'un comité de stratégie, qu'il démissionnerait s'il perdait. Alors, ce matin-là, que ce soit aussi brutal, cela a beaucoup affecté mon mari."

68. "Les trois, on n'a même pas à discuter, on est d'accord que, la meilleure chose pour M. Parizeau, pour le gouvernement, pour le parti, c'est d'annoncer qu'il va démissionner."

69. "Alors, nous, on ne sait pas ce qui va arriver."

70. Remarks from anonymous sources reported in DUCHESNE, *op. cit.*, p. 561.

71. "On reconnaissait qu'il n'y avait pas d'autres possibilités. Il l'avait annoncée. De plus, il avait perdu sa crédibilité. Quand il se serait levé en Chambre, quand il aurait prononcé un discours comme premier ministre, cela aurait été invivable. Et, moi, comme leader parlementaire, j'étais convaincu qu'il ne pourrait plus revenir sur l'annonce qu'il avait faite, une annonce prématurée, de mon point de vue."

72. "C'était un secret de Polichinelle que M. Landry aspirait à être chef depuis des années et des années, et Mme Marois avait des velléités. Alors, moi, je me suis dit: 'S'il part cet après-midi, qu'est-ce qui nous arrive demain?'"

73. This part of the interview was conducted in English.

74. Sondagem survey, on behalf of *Le Devoir*, directed by political analysts Guy Lachapelle and Pierre Noreau and sociologist Jean Noiseux. The survey was carried out between November 2 and 6, using 934 respondents.

75. The two men had known each other for at least 20 years. In 1974 and 1975, Guy Chevrette had been a member of the Commission of inquiry, chaired by Robert Cliche, into the exercise of union freedom in the construction industry, and Lucien Bouchard had been the chief counsel.

APPENDIX A

Text of the agreement of June 12 1995, between the Parti Québécois, the Bloc Québécois and the Action démocratique du Québec.[1]

A common project

As the representatives of the Parti Québécois, the Bloc Québécois and the Action démocratique du Québec, we have reached agreement on a common project to be submitted in the referendum, a project that responds in a modern, decisive and open way to the long quest of the people of Québec to become masters of their destiny.

We have agreed to join forces and to coordinate our efforts so that in the Fall 1995 referendum, Quebecers can vote for a real change: to achieve sovereignty for Québec and a formal proposal for a new economic and political partnership with Canada, aimed among other things at consolidating the existing economic space.

The elements of this common project will be integrated in the bill that will be tabled in the Fall and on which Quebecers will vote on referendum day.

We believe that this common project respects the wishes of a majority of Quebecers, reflects the historical aspirations of Québec, and embodies, in a concrete way, the concerns expressed before the Commissions on the future of Québec.

Thus, our common project departs from the Canadian status quo, rejected by an immense majority of Quebecers. It is true to the aspirations of Quebecers for autonomy and would allow Québec to achieve sovereignty: to levy all of its taxes, pass all of its laws, sign all of its treaties. Our project also reflects the wish of Quebecers to maintain equitable and flexible ties with our Canadian neighbours, so that we can manage our common economic space together, particularly by means of joint institutions, including institutions of a political nature. We are convinced that this proposal is in the interests of both Québec and Canada, though we cannot of course presume to know what Canadians will decide in this regard.

Finally, our project responds to the wish so often expressed in recent months that the referendum unite as many Quebecers as possible on a clear, modern and open proposal.

The referendum mandate

Following a Yes victory in the referendum, the National Assembly, on the one hand, will be empowered to proclaim the sovereignty of Québec, and the government, on the other hand, will be bound to propose to Canada a treaty on a new economic and political Partnership, so as to, among other things, consolidate the existing economic space. The referendum question will contain these two elements.

Accession to sovereignty

Insofar as the negotiations unfold in a positive fashion, the National Assembly will declare the sovereignty of Québec after an agreement is reached on the Partnership treaty. One of the first acts of a sovereign Québec will be ratification of the Partnership treaty.

The negotiations will not exceed one year, unless the National Assembly decides otherwise.

If the negotiations prove to be fruitless, the National Assembly will be empowered to declare the sovereignty of Québec without further delay.

The treaty

The new rules and the reality of international trade will allow a sovereign Québec, even without a formal Partnership with Canada, continued access to external markets, including the Canadian economic space. Moreover, a sovereign Québec could, on its own initiative, keep the Canadian dollar as its currency.

However, given the volume of trade between Québec and Canada and the extent of their economic integration, it will be to the evident advantage of both States to sign a formal treaty of economic and political Partnership.

The treaty will be binding on the parties and will specify appropriate measures for maintaining and improving the existing economic space. It will establish rules for the division of federal assets and management of the common debt. It will create the joint political institutions required to administer the new Economic and Political Partnership, and lay down their governing rules. It will provide for the establishment of a Council, a Secretariat, an Assembly and a Tribunal for the resolution of disputes.

As a priority, the treaty will ensure that the Partnership has the authority to act in the following areas:

- Customs union;
- Free movement of goods;
- Free movement of individuals;
- Free movement of services;
- Free movement of capital;
- Monetary policy;
- Labour mobility;
- Citizenship.

In accordance with the dynamics of the joint institutions and in step with their aspirations, the two member States will be free to make agreements in any other area of common interest, such as:

- Trade within the Partnership, so as to adapt and strengthen the provisions of the Agreement on Internal Trade;

- International trade (for example, to establish a common position on the exemption with respect to culture contained in the WTO Agreement and NAFTA);
- International representation (for example, the Council could decide, where useful or necessary, that the Partnership will speak with one voice within international organizations);
- Transportation (to facilitate, for example, access to the airports of the two countries or to harmonize highway, rail or inland navigation policies);
- Defence policy (for example, joint participation in peacekeeping operations or a coordinated participation in NATO and NORAD);
- Financial institutions (for example, to define regulations for chartered banks, security rules and sound financial practices);
- Fiscal and budgetary policies (to maintain a dialogue to foster the compatibility of respective actions);
- Environmental protection (in order to set objectives in such areas as cross-border pollution and the transportation and storage of hazardous materials);
- The fight against arms and drug trafficking;
- Postal services;
- Any other matters considered of common interest to the parties.

Joint Institutions

1– The Council

The Partnership Council, made up of an equal number of Ministers from the two States, will have decision-making power with regard to the implementation of the treaty.

The decisions of the Partnership Council will require a unanimous vote, thus each member will have a veto.

The Council will be assisted by a permanent secretariat. The Secretariat will provide operational liaison between the Council and the governments and follow up on the implementation of the Council's decisions. At the request of the Council or the Parliamentary Assembly, the Secretariat will produce reports on any matter relating to the application of the treaty.

2– The Parliamentary Assembly

A Partnership Parliamentary Assembly, made up of Québec and Canadian Members appointed by their respective Legislative Assemblies, will be created.

It will examine the draft text of Partnership Council decisions, and forward its recommendations. It will also have the power to pass resolutions on any aspect of its implementation, particularly after receiving the periodical reports on the state of the Partnership addressed to it by the Secretariat. It will hear, in public sessions, the heads of the bipartite administrative commissions responsible for the application of specific treaty provisions.

The composition of the Assembly will reflect the population distribution within the Partnership. Québec will hold 25% of the seats. Funding for Partnership institutions will be shared equally, except for parliamentarians' expenses, which will be borne by each State.

3– The Tribunal

A tribunal will be set up to resolve disputes relating to the treaty, its implementation and the interpretation of its provisions. Its decisions will be binding upon the parties.

The working procedures of the Tribunal could be modeled on existing mechanisms, such as the panels set up under NAFTA, the Agreement on Internal Trade or the World Trade Organization Agreement.

The Committee

An orientation and supervision committee will be set up for the purposes of the negotiations. It will be made up of independent personalities agreed upon by the three parties (PQ, BQ, ADQ). Its composition will be made public at the appropriate time. The Committee will:

1) Take part in the selection of the chief negotiator;
2) Be allowed an observer at the negotiation table;
3) Advise the government on the progress of the negotiations;
4) Inform the public on the procedures and on the outcome of the negotiations.

The democratically appointed authorities of our three parties, having examined and ratified the present agreement yesterday, Sunday, June 12, 1995—the Action démocratique du Québec having met in Sherbrooke, the Bloc Québécois in Montréal, and the Parti Québécois in Québec—we hereby ratify this common project and we call upon all Quebecers to endorse it.

In witness whereof, we the undersigned

Jacques Parizeau, Chairman of the Parti Québécois
Lucien Bouchard, Leader of the Bloc Québécois
Mario Dumont, Leader of the Action Démocratique du Québec

1. © Gouvernement du Québec, 1997; English text © 1984-2002 Ottawa Researchers & Northern Blue Publishing.

APPENDIX B

The preamble

Below is the complete (translated) text of the declaration of sovereignty, as read on September 6, 1995 at the Grand Théâtre by poet Gilles Vigneault and playwright Marie Laberge.[1]

The time has come to reap the fields of history. The time has come at last to harvest what has been sown for us by four hundred years of men and women of courage, rooted in the soil and now returned to it.

The time has come for us, tomorrow's ancestors, to make ready for our descendents harvests that are worthy of the labours of the past.

May our toil be worthy of them, may they gather us together at last.

At the dawn of the 17th century, the pioneers of what would become a nation and then a people rooted themselves in the soil of Québec. Having come from a great civilization, they were enriched by that of the First Nations, they forged new alliances, and maintained the heritage of France.

The conquest of 1760 did not break the determination of their descendants to remain faithful to a destiny unique in North America. Already in 1774, through the Quebec Act, the conqueror recognized the distinct nature of their institutions. Neither attempts at assimilation nor the Act of Union of 1840 could break their endurance.

The English community that grew up at their side, the immigrants who have joined them, all have contributed to forming this people which became in 1867 one of the two founders of the Canadian federation.

We, the men and women of this place,

- Because we inhabit the territories delimited by our ancestors, from Abitibi to the Îles-de-la-Madeleine, from Ungava to the American border, because for four hundred years we have cleared, ploughed, paced, surveyed, dug, fished, built, started anew, discussed, protected, and loved this land that is cut across and watered by the St. Lawrence River;

- Because the heart of this land beats in French and because that heartbeat is as meaningful as the seasons that hold sway over it, as the winds that bend it, as the men and women who shape it;

- Because we have created here a way of being, of believing, of working that is unique;

- Because as long ago as 1791 we established here one of the first parliamentary democracies in the world, one we have never ceased to improve;

- Because the legacy of the struggles and courage of the past compels us irrevocably to take charge of our own destiny;
- Because it is this land alone that represents our pride and the source of our strength, our sole opportunity to express ourselves in the entirety of our individual natures and of our collective heart;
- Because this land will be all those men and women who inhabit it, who defend it and define it, and because we are all those people;

We, the people of Québec, declare that we are free to choose our future.

We know the winter in our souls. We know its blustery days, its solitude, its false eternity and its apparent deaths. We know what it is to be bitten by the winter cold.

We entered the federation on the faith of a promise of equality in a shared undertaking and of respect for our authority in certain matters that to us are vital.

But what was to follow did not live up to those early hopes. The Canadian State contravened the federative pact, by invading in a thousand ways areas in which we are autonomous, and by serving notice that our secular belief in the equality of the partners was an illusion.

We were hoodwinked in 1982 when the governments of Canada and the English-speaking provinces made changes to the Constitution, in depth and to our detriment, in defiance of the categorical opposition of our National Assembly.

Twice since then attempts were made to right that wrong. The failure of the Meech Lake Accord in 1990 confirmed a refusal to recognize even our distinct character. And in 1992 the rejection of the Charlottetown Accord by both Canadians and Quebecers confirmed the conclusion that no redress was possible.

- Because we have persisted despite the haggling of which we have been the object;
- Because Canada, far from taking pride in and proclaiming to the world the alliance between its two founding peoples, has instead consistently trivialized it and decreed the spurious principle of equality between the provinces;
- Because starting with the Quiet Revolution we reached a decision never again to restrict ourselves to mere survival but from this time on to build upon our difference;
- Because we have the deep-seated conviction that continuing within Canada would be tantamount to condemning ourselves to languish and to debasing our very identity;
- Because the respect we owe ourselves must guide our deeds;

We, the people of Québec, declare it is our will to be in full possession of all the powers of a State: to vote all our laws, to levy all our taxes, to sign all our treaties and to exercise the highest power of all, conceiving, and controlling, by ourselves, our fundamental law.

For the men and women of this country who are the warp and weft of it and its erosion (sic), for those of tomorrow whose growth we are now witnessing, to be comes before to have. And this principle lies at the very heart of our endeavour.

Our language celebrates our love, our beliefs and our dreams for this land and for this country. In order that the profound sense of belonging to a distinct people be now and for all time the very bastion of our identity, we proclaim our will to live in a French-language society.

Our culture relates our identity, it writes of us, it sings us to the world. And through varied and new contributions, our culture takes on fresh colour and amplitude. It is essential that we welcome them in such a way that never will these differences be seen as threats or as reasons for intolerance.

Together we shall celebrate the joys, together we shall suffer the sorrows that life will set upon our road. Above all we shall assume not only our successes but our failures too, for in abundance as in adversity the choices we make will have been our own.

We know what determination has gone into achieving the successes of this land. Those men and women who have forged the dynamism of Québec are eager to pass down their efforts to the determined men and women of tomorrow. Our capacity for mutual support and our appetite for new undertakings are among our greatest strengths. We commit ourselves to recognize and encourage the urge to put our hearts into our work (, which is what) makes us builders.

Along with other countries of like size, we share the virtue of adapting quickly and well to the shifting challenges of work and trade. Our capacity for consensus and our spirit of invention will enable us to take a good and rightful place at the table of nations.

We intend to uphold the imaginative powers and the abilities of local and regional communities in their activities of economic, social and cultural development.

As guardians of the land, the air, the water, we shall act in such a way as to be respectful of the world to come.

We, the men and women of this new country, acknowledge our moral duties of respect, of tolerance, of solidarity towards one another.

Averse to authoritarianism and violence, honouring the will of the people, we commit ourselves to guarantee democracy and the rule of law.

Respect for the dignity of women, men, and children and the recognition of their rights and freedoms constitute the very foundation of our society. We commit ourselves to guarantee the civil and political rights of individuals, notably the right to justice, the right to equality, and the right to freedom.

To battle against misery and poverty, to support the young and the elderly, are essential features of the society we would build. The destitute among us can count upon our compassion and our sense of responsibility. With the equitable sharing of wealth as our objective, we commit ourselves to promote full employment and to guarantee social and economic rights, notably the right to education and the right to health care and other social services.

Our shared future is in the hands of all those for whom Québec is a homeland. Because we take to heart the need to reinforce established alliances and friendships, we shall safeguard the rights of the First Nations and we intend to define with them a new alliance. Likewise, the English-speaking community historically established in Québec enjoys rights that will be maintained.

Independent and hence fully present in the world, we intend to work for cooperation, humanitarian action, tolerance and peace. We shall subscribe to the Universal Declaration of Human Rights and to other international instruments for the protection of rights.

While never repudiating our values, we shall devote ourselves to forging, through treaties and agreements, mutually beneficial links with the peoples of the earth. In particular, we wish to formulate along with the people of Canada, our historic partner, new relations that will allow us to maintain our economic ties and to redefine our political exchanges. And we shall marshal a particular effort to strengthen our ties with the peoples of the United States and France and with those of other countries both in the Americas and in the Francophonie.

To accomplish this design, to maintain the fervour that fills us and impels us, for the time has now come to set in motion this country's vast endeavour;

We, the people of Québec, through our National Assembly, proclaim: Québec is a sovereign country.

---

1. The source for appendices B and C, and for quotes within chapter VI taken from the appendices, is http://www.sfu.ca/~aheard/bill1.html (Simon Fraser University).

APPENDIX C

THE QUEBEC SOVEREIGNTY BILL

Complete (translated) text of the bill submitted on September 7, 1995 to the Quebec National Assembly by the premier, Jacques Parizeau. This bill was to be adopted in the event of a majority vote in favour of the YES side in the referendum.

The Parliament of Québec enacts as follows:

Self-Determination

1. The National Assembly is authorized, within the scope of this Act, to proclaim the sovereignty of Québec.

    The proclamation must be preceded by a formal offer of economic and political partnership with Canada.

Sovereignty

2. On the date fixed in the proclamation of the National Assembly, the Declaration of sovereignty appearing in the Preamble shall take effect and Québec shall become a sovereign country; it shall acquire the exclusive power to pass all its laws, levy all its taxes and conclude all its treaties.

Partnership Treaty

3. The Government is bound to propose to the Government of Canada the conclusion of a treaty of economic and political partnership on the basis of the tripartite agreement of June 12, 1995 reproduced in the schedule.

    The treaty must be approved by the National Assembly before being ratified.

4. A committee charged with the orientation and supervision of the negotiations relating to the partnership treaty, composed of independent personalities appointed by the Government in accordance with the tripartite agreement, shall be established.

5. The Government shall favour the establishment in the Outaouais region of the seat of the institutions created under the partnership treaty.

New Constitution

6. A draft of a new constitution shall be drawn up by a constituent commission established in accordance with the prescriptions of the National Assembly. The commission, consisting of an equal number of

men and women, shall be composed of a majority of non-parliamentarians, and shall include Quebecers of various origins and from various backgrounds.

The proceedings of the commission must be organized so as to ensure the fullest possible participation of citizens in all regions of Québec, notably through the creation of regional sub-commissions, if necessary.

The commission shall table the draft constitution before the National Assembly, which shall approve the final text. The draft constitution shall be submitted to a referendum and shall, once approved, become the fundamental law of Québec.

7. The new constitution shall state that Québec is a French-speaking country and shall impose upon the Government the obligation of protecting Québec culture and ensuring its development.

8. The new constitution shall affirm the rule of law, and shall include a charter of human rights and freedoms. It shall also affirm that citizens have responsibilities towards their fellow citizens.

   The new constitution shall guarantee the English-speaking community that its identity and institutions will be preserved. It shall also recognize the right of the aboriginal nations to self-government on lands over which they have full ownership and their right to participate in the development of Québec; in addition, the existing constitutional rights of the aboriginal nations shall be recognized in the constitution. Such guarantee and such recognition shall be exercised in a manner consistent with the territorial integrity of Québec.

   Representatives of the English-speaking community and of each of the aboriginal nations must be invited by the constituent commission to take part in the proceedings devoted to defining their rights. Such rights shall not be modified otherwise than in accordance with a specific procedure.

9. The new constitution shall affirm the principle of decentralization. Specific powers and corresponding fiscal and financial resources shall be attributed by law to local and regional authorities.

Territory
10. Québec shall retain its boundaries as they exist within the Canadian federation on the date on which Québec becomes a sovereign country. It shall exercise its jurisdiction over the land, air and water forming its territory and over the areas adjacent to its coast, in accordance with the rules of international law.

Citizenship

11. Every person who, on the date on which Québec becomes a sovereign country, holds Canadian citizenship and is domiciled in Québec acquires Québec citizenship.

    Every person born in Québec who, on the date on which Québec becomes a sovereign country, is domiciled outside Québec and who claims Québec citizenship also acquires Québec citizenship.

    In the two years following the date on which Québec becomes a sovereign country, any person holding Canadian citizenship who settles in Québec or who has established a substantial connection with Québec without being domiciled in Québec may claim Québec citizenship.

12. Québec citizenship may be obtained, once Québec has become a sovereign country, in the cases and on the conditions determined by law. The law must provide, in particular, that Québec citizenship shall be granted to every person born in Québec, or born outside Québec to a father or mother holding Québec citizenship.

13. Québec citizenship may be held concurrently with Canadian citizenship or that of any other country.

Currency

14. The currency having legal tender in Québec shall remain the Canadian dollar.

Treaties and International Organizations and Alliances

15. In accordance with the rules of international law, Québec shall assume the obligations and enjoy the rights set forth in the relevant treaties and international conventions and agreements to which Canada or Québec is a party on the date on which Québec becomes a sovereign country, in particular in the North American Free Trade Agreement.

16. The Government is authorized to apply for the admission of Québec to the United Nations Organization and its specialized agencies. It shall take the necessary steps to ensure the participation of Québec in the World Trade Organization, the Organization of American States, the Organization for Economic Cooperation and Development, the Organization for Security and Co-operation in Europe, the Francophonie, the Commonwealth and other international organizations and conferences.

17. The Government shall take the necessary steps to ensure the continuing participation of Québec in the defence alliances of which Canada is a member. Such participation must, however, be compatible with Quebec's desire to give priority to the maintenance of world peace under the leadership of the United Nations Organization.

Continuity of Laws, Pensions, Benefits, Licences and Permits, Contracts and Courts of Justice

18. The Acts of the Parliament of Canada and the regulations thereunder that apply in Québec on the date on which Québec becomes a sovereign country shall be deemed to be laws and regulations of Québec. Such legislative and regulatory provisions shall be maintained in force until they are amended, replaced or repealed.

19. The Government shall ensure the continuity of the unemployment insurance and child tax benefit programs and the payment of the other benefits paid by the Government of Canada to individuals domiciled in Québec on the date on which Québec becomes a sovereign country. Pensions and supplements payable to the elderly and to veterans shall continue to be paid by the Government of Québec according to the same terms and conditions.

20. Permits, licences and other authorizations issued before October 30, 1995 under an Act of the Parliament of Canada that are in force in Québec on the date on which Québec becomes a sovereign country shall be maintained. Those issued or renewed on or after October 30, 1995 shall also be maintained unless they are denounced by the Government within one month following the date on which Québec becomes a sovereign country.

    Permits, licences and other authorizations that are so maintained will be renewable according to law.

21. Agreements and contracts entered into before October 30, 1995 by the Government of Canada or its agencies or organizations that are in force in Québec on the date on which Québec becomes a sovereign country shall be maintained, with the Government of Québec substituted, where required, for the Canadian party. Those entered into on or after October 30, 1995 shall also be maintained, with the Government of Québec substituted, where required, for the Canadian party, unless they are denounced by the Government within one month following the date on which Québec becomes a sovereign country.

22. The courts of justice shall continue to exist after the date on which Québec becomes a sovereign country. Cases pending may be continued until judgment. However, the law may provide that cases pending before the Federal Court or before the Supreme Court shall be transferred to the Québec jurisdiction it determines.

    The Court of Appeal shall become the court of highest jurisdiction until a Supreme Court is established under the new constitution, unless otherwise provided for by law.

Judges appointed by the Government of Canada before October 30, 1995 who are in office on the date on which Québec becomes a sovereign country shall be confirmed in their functions and shall retain their jurisdiction. The judges of the Federal Court and of the Supreme Court of Canada who were members of the Québec Bar shall become, if they so wish, judges of the Superior Court and of the Court of Appeal, respectively.

Federal Public Servants and Employees

23. The Government may, in accordance with the conditions prescribed by law, appoint the necessary personnel and take appropriate steps to facilitate the application of the Canadian laws that continue to apply in Québec pursuant to section 18. The sums required for the application of such laws shall be taken out of the consolidated revenue fund.

The Government shall ensure that the public servants and other employees of the Government of Canada and of its agencies and organizations, appointed before October 30, 1995 and domiciled in Québec on the date on which Québec becomes a sovereign country, shall become, if they so wish, public servants or employees of the Government of Québec. The Government may, for that purpose, conclude agreements with any association of employees or any other person in order to facilitate such transfers. The Government may also set up a program of voluntary retirement; it shall honour any retirement or voluntary departure arrangement made with a transferred person.

Interim Constitution

24. The Parliament of Québec may adopt the text of an interim constitution which will be in force from the date on which Québec becomes a sovereign country until the coming into force of the new constitution of Québec. The interim constitution must ensure the continuity of the democratic institutions of Québec and of the constitutional rights existing on the date on which Québec becomes a sovereign country, in particular those relating to human rights and freedoms, the English-speaking community, access to English-language schools, and the aboriginal nations.

Until the coming into force of the interim constitution, the laws, rules and conventions governing the internal constitution of Québec shall remain in force.

Other Agreements

25. In addition to the partnership treaty, the Government is authorized to conclude with the Government of Canada any other agreement to facilitate the application of this Act, in particular with respect to the equitable apportionment of the assets and liabilities of the Government of Canada.

Coming into Force

26. The negotiations relating to the conclusion of the partnership treaty must not extend beyond October 30, 1996, unless the National Assembly decides otherwise.

   The proclamation of sovereignty may be made as soon as the partnership treaty has been approved by the National Assembly or as soon as the latter, after requesting the opinion of the orientation and supervision committee, has concluded that the negotiations have proved fruitless.

27. This Act comes into force on the day on which it is assented to.